M000275195

The Seminole Freedmen

Race and Culture in the American West
Quintard Taylor, Series Editor

The Seminole Freedmen

A History

Kevin Mulroy

University of Oklahoma Press : Norman

Also by Kevin Mulroy

Freedom on the Border: The Seminole Maroons in Florida, the Indian Territory, Coahuila, and Texas (Lubbock, Tex., 1993)

(ed.) *Western Amerykański: Polish Poster Art and the Western* (Los Angeles and Seattle, 1999)

(ed. with Lawrence B. de Graaf and Quintard Taylor) *Seeking El Dorado: African Americans in California* (Los Angeles and Seattle, 2001)

Library of Congress Cataloging-in-Publication Data

Mulroy, Kevin.
   The Seminole freedmen : a history / Kevin Mulroy.
      p. cm. — (Race and culture in the American West series ; v. 2)
   Includes bibliographical references and index.
   ISBN 978-0-8061-3865-7 (hardcover : alk. paper) 1. Black Seminoles—History. 2. Black Seminoles—Relocation—Oklahoma.
3. Black Seminoles—Government relations. 4. African Americans—Relations with Indians. 5. Slavery—Florida—History. 6. Slavery—Oklahoma—History.
7. Slaveholders—Florida—History. 8. Slaveholders—Oklahoma—History.
I. Title.
E99.S28M85 2007
978.6'00496073—dc22   2007006698

The Seminole Freedmen is Volume 2 in the Race and Culture in the American West series.

1 2 3 4 5 6 7 8 9 10

For my family

In memory of my father, James Mulroy, who loved books

[Most] of the descendants of the pioneers who fled from South Carolina and Georgia maintained their identity of character, living by themselves and maintaining the purity of the African race. [They] settled in separate villages, and the Seminole Indians appeared generally to coincide with the Exiles in the propriety of each maintaining their distinctive character.

—Joshua Giddings, *The Exiles of Florida,* 1858

Contents

List of Illustrations   ix
Preface   xi
Acknowledgments   xvii
Introduction   xxi

 1. Beginnings in Florida   3
 2. Removal to Indian Territory   22
 3. Post-Removal Upheavals   53
 4. Seminole Slave Owners   84
 5. "Only Slaves in Name"   117
 6. The Civil War   155
 7. Reconstruction   194
 8. Intermarriage   224
 9. Language, Society, and Culture   267
10. Relations with Seminoles in Oklahoma   294

Notes   327
Bibliography   394
Index   433

List of Illustrations

FIGURES

Sketch map of Seminole and maroon towns on the Suwannee	18
Sketch map of Boggy Island	27
Asin Yahola	37
Heniha Emathla	41
Pilaklikaha	46
Thomas S. Jesup	47
Mikkoanapa	55
Sketch map of maroon settlements in Indian Territory	66
Talomas Mikko	145
Holata Mikko	156
Ben Bruner	158
Hopothli Yahola	166
Sketch map of the Loyalists' retreat	168
Caesar Bowlegs	208
Seminole lighthorsemen	212
Dennis Cyrus	215
Last execution in the Seminole Nation	216
Bass Reeves	218
Seminole Council members and lighthorsemen	222
Asin Yahola's "wife"	234
Scipio Noble	241

Isaac Bottley and Jim Carter   242
John Chupco   249
Heniha Mikko   250
John F. Brown   255
Caesar Bruner   272
Caesar Bruner's log home   275
Mrs. Constant's integrated school   286
James Coody Johnson, Hulbutta Mikko, and Okchar Harjo   302
George Jones   313
Lance and Lawrence Cudjo   317
Sylvia Davis and her family   319
Bud Crockett   325

MAPS

Florida, the Bahamas, and Cuba   4
Lands of the Five Tribes in the Indian Territory, 1838–61   63
Civil War sites in the Indian Territory and neighboring states   173
Freedman townships in the Seminole Nation around 1885   202

CHARTS

1. Landholdings of Seminole freedmen and mixed-race
   Seminole maroons at the time of allotment   239
2. Indian and freedman populations in the Seminole Nation,
   1870–1905   265
3. Seminole freedman band distribution at the time of allotment   270

Preface

In the cold, late evening of New Year's Eve 1984, I drove my old Ford at high speed down damp country lanes to Keele University in rural England. The goal was to submit before midnight my just-completed Ph.D. thesis, "Relations between Blacks and Seminoles after Removal." I had used every last minute I could. For the past several weeks, my typist and I had worked around the clock, and the Christmas holidays were shot. All possible extensions had been exhausted, and only a little time remained. By the time I arrived at the university, the buildings were dark and deserted, and I had to leave the work with a lone security officer. Acceding to my insistence, the officer agreed to sign and date a note that I had beaten the deadline by less than an hour. Seven years in the making and 777 pages in length, the project that had obsessed me finally had come to an end—or so I thought.

My interest in African Americans in the West had begun in graduate seminars taught by the remarkable Mary Ellison at Keele in 1976 and 1977. In that unlikely academic outpost in the English Midlands, and years before the subject became fashionable, Dr. Ellison taught a course in American Studies on Indian-black relations. Becoming intrigued, I combed the published literature and wrote a graduate paper on relations between Seminoles and runaways from the Carolinas and Georgia in Florida. As Mary explained, however, the literature on African Americans associated with the so-called Five Civilized Tribes dried up after Removal, and that ground was fertile for new Ph.D. theses.

Beginning in the early 1930s, historian Kenneth Porter had published a series of fascinating and important articles on the "Seminole Negroes" in Florida, Coahuila, and Texas. But Porter left the history of Seminole-black relations in the Indian Territory and Oklahoma for others to write. As early as 1946, he was encouraging "some young Oklahoma historian" to spend time in Seminole County researching the later life of the Florida maroon leader Abraham. In 1970, late in his career, Porter advised: "Interested scholars have almost a clear field before them so far as the history of the Negro in the Indian Territory—and indeed, in the territory and state of Oklahoma—is concerned."[1] I determined to help fill that gap.

Commencing my work in January 1978, I sought to discover what happened to relations between Seminoles and Africans once the former allies left their homelands in Florida and resettled in the Indian Territory. During the next three years, I took lengthy trips to Oklahoma, Texas, and Washington, D.C., to conduct research and interviews. Realizing that I needed to be based in Oklahoma for a more extended period to complete my work, in February 1981 I moved to Norman and took up residence there for the next three years.

While living in Oklahoma, I determined to unearth every nugget of information I could find on the Indian Territory experience of Africans associated with the least known and understood of the Five Civilized Tribes. I spent countless hours mining the manuscript resources and rare books in the Western History Collections at the University of Oklahoma, the Indian Archives and Library Resources of the Oklahoma Historical Society, and other archival repositories within the state. I viewed miles of microfilm published by the National Archives. And I steeped myself in the voluminous data compiled by the Dawes Commission for the purposes of enrollment and allotment, creating genealogies, tables, and charts that helped provide clues to the Seminoles' and blacks' otherwise hidden relationship.

Being Caucasian and British, I came to appreciate that I never could understand what it meant to be Seminole or freedman. But my race and nationality facilitated a critical appreciation of the perspective of those producing most of the documentation on the Indians and maroons. It was usually white travelers, army officers, Indian and other government agents, missionaries, and schoolteachers who wrote the reports. Few understood what they sought to describe. The Seminoles and maroons resided beyond the pale of white civilization. Yet observers sought to explain the inexplicable—both to themselves and to their readers—by placing it within a more familiar context. Indigenous American Indians and immigrant Africans and their descendants thus became European-ized. To understand their relationship better, one must cut through that veneer and seek to enter Seminole Indian and freedman civilization. That entails becoming more open to other forms of source material and alternative explanations and interpretations.

During the course of my research, Daniel F. Littlefield, Jr., published a series of books on Indian-black relations among the Seminoles, Creeks, Cherokees, and Chickasaws. Although his study of Africans among the Seminoles ended with emancipation, Littlefield's work influenced mine a great deal. His interpretation often ran counter to the "natural allies" thesis expounded by Porter and his followers. Littlefield's findings supported my own conclusion that Seminole-black relations were considerably more complicated than that, and that they defied simple explanation. Independence, separation, difference, and continuity were key concepts in their relationship, but social and cultural integration were not. It seemed for a while as though Littlefield, or one of his collaborators or graduate students, would beat me to the punch by publishing a history of the Seminole freedmen. Yet only now, some thirty years after the publication of his pioneering *Africans and Seminoles: From Removal to Emancipation* and twenty-three years after I submitted "Relations between Blacks and Seminoles after Removal," is that history finally coming into print.

In 1993, I completed *Freedom on the Border: The Seminole Maroons in Florida, the Indian Territory, Coahuila, and Texas.* Drawing upon several chapters from my thesis, recent interviews with descendants, and some new research, that book concentrated on the band of maroons associated with John Horse that emigrated to Texas and Mexico in the mid-nineteenth century. Like Porter's work, however, *Freedom on the Border* did not include coverage of the group that remained behind in the Indian Territory after 1850. That history still needed to be published. This book also revises and updates my previous work by providing new material on the Seminole maroons in Florida prior to Removal and in the Indian Territory before the migrations to Mexico.

I had kept up with the scholarly literature, but four years ago I re-engaged fully with the Indian Territory and Oklahoma aspects of this story. In 2002 and 2003, wrangling over whether the freedmen should enjoy citizenship rights and be allowed to participate in federal monetary awards as members of the Seminole Nation of Oklahoma received extensive coverage in the American press and popular media. Oversimplified interpretations of their history hit the pages of major national newspapers and our television screens at prime time. They went against what I had discovered in my research, yet my thesis was gathering dust on the library shelves at Keele. "Relations" remained obscure, unpublished, and relatively inaccessible, even to scholars. I determined then to publish a history of the Seminole freedmen that would provide new information and interpretation for others to use, and that could serve as a foundation for future scholarship.

In 2002 the Gilder Lehrman Center at Yale University invited me to deliver a paper on Seminole-black relations at its fifth annual conference, "Unshackled Spaces: Fugitives from Slavery and Maroon Communities in the Americas." That offered me the opportunity to revisit some of the documentation and arguments in my thesis and to review the current scholarly and popular literature. The resulting paper, "Marronage among the Seminoles," extended the scope of *Freedom on the Border* to include all of the former African communities associated with the Seminoles. Adopting an interpretive model suggested by Richard Price and William Sturtevant, it argued that each—including for the first time the Seminole freedmen settlements in the Indian Territory and Oklahoma—should be considered a maroon community and studied within that rubric.

I elaborated upon one important aspect of that argument in "Seminole Maroon Diplomacy," a paper delivered at the conference "Passages to Freedom: The Underground Railroad in American History and Legend," sponsored by the National Underground Railroad Freedom Center and the Smithsonian Institution's National Museum of American History in February 2003. By then, Sturtevant also had enlisted me to write the entry on "Seminole Maroons" for the Smithsonian Institution's *Handbook of North American Indians: Southeast* (2004). That essay took information and interpretation from the thesis, included new research and coverage of recent scholarship, synthesized the arguments presented at the Yale and Smithsonian conferences, and completed the groundwork for this book.

Shortly after receiving my doctorate in 1985, I submitted the thesis to the University of Oklahoma Press for possible publication. John Drayton, then an acquisitions editor for Western History, saw merit in the work but realized that it could not be published without substantial revision. Written in a British passive voice in chapters of sometimes a hundred pages or more, it would not have translated to an American university press book. But John has great patience and never gave up on the project. Upon becoming director of the press, he encouraged me to revise, update, and resubmit the manuscript for consideration. I am delighted that, in the year of the Sooner State's centennial, that great Western press finally has brought this Oklahoma tribal history into print.

Los Angeles
December 16, 2006

Acknowledgments

The British government Department of Education and Science provided part of the financial support for my Ph.D. research in the form of a Major State Studentship and two travel grants. More recently, the Office of the Dean at the University of Southern California (USC) Libraries provided subvention funding toward the costs of publishing the book. I am grateful to Dr. Lynn O'Leary-Archer for facilitating that support. An award from the USC Libraries' Bardin Endowment helped fund the production of the maps and charts, illustrations, and index.

My thanks go first to Dr. Mary Ellison of the Department of American Studies at Keele University, whose graduate classes inspired me to pursue Ph.D. research in this field. Mary patiently supervised my thesis and provided guidance, encouragement, support, and creative criticism throughout its completion. Professor David Adams, also at Keele, greatly improved my analytical skills and critical thinking.

The following individuals facilitated the process of gathering and organizing research materials between 1978 and 1984: Martha Blaine, Indian Archives, Oklahoma Historical Society; Kent Carter, National Archives, Southwest Region, Fort Worth, Texas; Pat Edwards, Gilcrease Museum, Tulsa; Larry Joachim, Kansas State Historical Society; Robert Kvasnicka, National Archives, Washington, D.C.; George Miles, Western Americana Collection, Beinecke Rare Book and Manuscript Library, Yale University; and Daryl Morrison, Western History Collections,

University of Oklahoma Libraries. Lindsay Willoughby helped create what have become charts 1 and 3.

I owe a huge debt to Jack Haley, longtime president of the Oklahoma Historical Society. In the winter of 1978–79 and from 1981 to 1984, when I was based in Norman, Jack was the associate curator at the Western History Collections of the University of Oklahoma. He not only facilitated my use of those marvelous collections but also assumed the role of mentor, colleague, and friend. Without Jack's help, none of this would have been possible. Jack's niece, Sheryl Ellis, and her husband, John, of Dallas, Texas, also provided support while I conducted research at the National Archives, Southwest Region, in Fort Worth.

I first met Rebecca Bateman, Susan Miller, and Richard Sattler in Norman in the early 1980s while we were graduate students conducting research in the Western History Collections. We have maintained close contact ever since, and their research and ideas have influenced and guided my own. I consider their work to be the best in the field, and I am fortunate to be able to call them my closest colleagues. All three took time out of their busy schedules to read earlier versions of this manuscript and offer constructive criticism and advice. Dick Sattler also provided invaluable guidance on Seminole indigenous names. Along the way, Richard Elwanger, Arrell Gibson, Ian Hancock, William Loren Katz, Matthew Kelly, Daniel F. Littlefield, Jr., Theda Perdue, Ron Tyler, and Angela Walton-Raji also provided me with information leads, challenging arguments, and insights.

I am deeply grateful to the following individuals for giving me the benefit of their time, knowledge, and perspectives during interviews and personal communications: Thomas Coker, former long-serving member on the Seminole Council; William Dawson, former Oklahoma state senator for Seminole and attorney for the Seminole freedmen; "Pompey" Bruner Fixico, Seminole maroon descendant, Los Angeles; Mark Goldey, attorney for the Seminole freedmen, Washington, D.C.; Charles Grounds, attorney-at-law, Seminole, Oklahoma; Robert Lee Miller and William Wantland, former secretaries to the Seminole Council and Seminole Nation of Oklahoma administrators; T. B. Miller, former curator of the Seminole Nation Museum, Wewoka; Richmond Tiger, former principal chief, Seminole Nation of Oklahoma; Ben Warrior, former Dosar Barkus bandleader; William "Dub" Warrior, president, Seminole Indian Scouts Cemetery Association, Del Rio, Texas; and Miss Charles Emily Wilson,

Seminole maroon descendant, Brackettville, Texas. Louise Welch, former professor of history at the University of Oklahoma and longtime resident of Seminole, helped organize my interviews in Seminole County in the winter of 1978–79.

David Brion Davis and Robert Forbes of the Gilder Lehrman Center at Yale University inspired my full reengagement with the Seminole freedmen by inviting me to give a paper at the center's annual conference in December 2002. Niani Kilkenny of the National Museum of American History and Orloff Miller of the National Underground Railroad Freedom Center nurtured my revived interest by asking me to present at the "Passages to Freedom" conference at the Smithsonian Institution the following February.

As a graduate student, I first met the eminent William Sturtevant, curator of ethnology at the National Museum of Natural History, in 1979 while conducting research in Washington, D.C. Bill was most generous with his time and ideas, directing me to archival resources and providing introductions to leaders in the field. Most significantly, though, he encouraged me to think of the Seminole blacks as maroons. Since then, Bill has continued to guide and support my work in countless important ways. Most recently, he provided contacts, leads, analysis, and criticism for my "Seminole Maroons" entry in the Smithsonian's *Handbook of North American Indians: Southeast* volume. Dr. Sturtevant's wealth of insights has proven a source of inspiration for this book.

The creative and dedicated Sarah Atlee prepared all of the illustrations for the book, including the maps and charts. Sherry Smith created the index. It has been a pleasure to work again with my friend and collaborator, Quintard Taylor, Jr., the editor of the series in which this book appears. At the University of Oklahoma Press, John Drayton and Charles Rankin remained constant in their support of this project. Emmy Ezzell oversaw the design and publication of the illustrations, Steven Baker managed the editing, and freelancer Rosemary Wetherold copyedited the manuscript. My deepest appreciation is extended to my acquisitions editor, Matthew Bokovoy, who provided me with encouragement and outstanding support and who skillfully and tirelessly steered the book through to successful publication.

Last but not least, I would like to thank my family. My mother, Joan, and my late father, Jim, provided much needed moral and financial support during my Ph.D. research. Laurel Jaworsky, my mother-in-law, has

proven an invaluable supplier of Oklahoma press coverage of the Seminoles' and freedmen's lawsuits. Most important of all, my wife, Sara, and
my son, Kieran, have shown remarkable patience with my commitment
to completing this book. I extend to them my heartfelt gratitude for the
love and encouragement that have sustained me in this endeavor.

Introduction

A CBS *60 Minutes II* show in July 2002 included a story on the Seminoles entitled "A Nation Divided." The segment supported the claim of the Seminole freedmen to be included as members of the Seminole Nation of Oklahoma and to be allowed to participate in a monetary award the Seminoles had received for loss of lands in Florida during the early nineteenth century. It announced to a national prime-time television audience: "What makes the Seminoles unique is that this tribe, unlike any other, has existed for nearly three centuries as a mixture of Indians and blacks, runaway slaves who joined the Indians as warriors in Florida. [Over] the years, some tribe members have intermarried, blurring the color lines even further." The story featured Africanist Joseph Opala, who argued that the Seminoles should not be considered an Indian tribe at all but a "multi-ethnic coalition." With regard to the freedmen, "It makes no sense now, to say they're not Indians," stated Opala; "100 years ago, or 150 years ago, the Seminole Indians would not have been talking about whether or not this black person has Indian blood. It simply wouldn't have mattered. They were Seminoles."[1]

The television show fanned the flames of a fire started by a *New York Times* op-ed piece on April 21, 2002, by columnist Brent Staples entitled "The Seminole Tribe, Running from History." Criticizing the Seminoles for establishing new blood quantum requirements that effectively denied membership in the Seminole Nation to the freedmen, Staples wrote: "The case has a deeper significance for historians, who see yet another example of how the American multicultural past is papered over by the myth of racial and ethnic purity." He spoke with the same Joseph Opala featured in the *60 Minutes II* story. Here Opala argued that the Seminoles "are not a Native American tribe at all, but 'an Afro-Indian tribe.' " Staples stated that the 1907 Oklahoma State Constitution had mandated segregation in the "previously integrated Seminole society." That represented "a clear violation of history for the Seminoles, who were multi-racial from the beginning." The editorial concluded: "The prejudice against black Seminoles can be partly explained by tribal self-hatred and ignorance of history. [Federal] courts will decide whether the Seminoles' treatment of their black brethren is legal. But the court of public opinion will find it mean-spirited and immoral."[2]

The CBS television and *New York Times* editorials are representative of a long, unfortunate, and continuing history of misunderstanding that has dominated discussion of relations between Seminole Indians and people of African descent. Supporters of the freedmen, including documentary filmmakers, reporters, lawyers, academics, and civil rights advocates, have charged the Seminoles with denying their history. The freedmen's attorneys have gone so far as to describe the Seminoles as engaging in "ethnic cleansing, revisionist history."[3] The problem rests mostly with the documentation and interpretation of a partially shared past.

A vital factor missing from this equation is the maroon context within which relations between Africans and Seminoles developed. This book argues that the Seminole freedmen of Oklahoma are descendants of Africans who became associated with Seminole Indians in the eighteenth and early nineteenth centuries and formed maroon communities in Florida. To avoid reenslavement, some chose to quit Florida for the Bahamas, where they again established a maroon society. Most of the remainder removed west with the Seminoles, where they formed new settlements in the Indian Territory. As had the emigrants to the Bahamas, some elected to avoid white encroachment by leaving. Around 1850, a large contingent of maroons rode out of the Indian Territory and sought freedom across the border in Mexico, returning to west Texas only after slavery had been abolished. The Bahamian, Mexican, and Texan maroon communities have survived to the early twenty-first century. Scholars and writers have published studies of their history, with at least four books appearing in print since 1993.[4] With one notable exception, however, the same cannot be said for the group that came to reside in the Indian Territory and Oklahoma.

That exception is Daniel Littlefield's groundbreaking study, *Africans and Seminoles: From Removal to Emancipation* (1977). In the preface to the 2001 paperback edition, Littlefield reviewed the historiography of the field since his book had first appeared in print a quarter of a century before.[5] Although noting the contributions of a number of important unpublished dissertations, Littlefield lamented that his work remained the only book-length study of Seminole-black relations in the Indian Territory. He also noted that it covered just the twenty-eight-year period from 1838 to 1866. Historian Claudio Saunt reinforced the point in an article published in 2004: "Remarkably, not a single monograph explores the history of the Seminole ex-slaves in Indian Territory after 1866."[6] This study attempts to help fill that historical void and suggests that, like their kinsmen in the Bahamas, Mexico, and Texas, the Seminole freedmen of Indian Territory and Oklahoma should be considered maroons.

European and U.S. military officers, Indian agents and other government officials, slave owners, and travelers usually referred to runaways in Florida as simply "Negroes" or "slaves." By the time of the outbreak of the Second Seminole War in 1835, however, the group had come to be known collectively to white Americans as "Seminole Negroes." That became the preferred term of early scholars of the group, such as Kenneth Porter, Laurence Foster, and John Goggin.[7] When "Negroes" became an unacceptable term, scholars used other names, such as "Seminole Blacks," "Afro-Seminoles," "Black Seminole," and "Black Muscogulges" to identify the group.[8] After 1865, whites mostly referred to the Indian Territory group as "Seminole Freedmen," and scholars have adopted that term widely. But group members in Oklahoma identify themselves, and also refer to Seminole maroons in Texas and Mexico, as "freedmans."

Both before and after Removal, and especially during treaty negotiations, Seminole Indians differentiated between themselves and people of African descent when dealing with others—Europeans, white Americans, other Indians, and Mexicans. Africans associated with Seminoles also negotiated separately with U.S. Army officers during the Second Seminole War and with Mexican government agents during their immigration to that country in the early 1850s. The Creek *isti-lásti* apparently dates back to at least the early nineteenth century as a generic term for black people, not just Africans associated with Seminoles.[9] In a 1937 interview, Lucinda Davis, a former Creek slave, recalled, "Dey call all de slaves Istilusti. Dat mean 'black man.' "[10] It is possible, and even likely, that Seminoles generally referred to groups of Africans by their town designations, as in "Opilaklikahi"—"people of Opilaklikaha" (Pilaklikaha), Abraham's town in Alachua during the 1820s and early 1830s.[11]

Since the early twentieth century, "Estelusti" (and variants) has been used on occasion to refer to descendants of Africans associated with Seminoles, mostly by well-meaning whites.[12] But Littlefield's *Africans and Seminoles* brought the term into vogue.[13] There is no evidence to suggest that Africans associated with Seminoles used the term to refer to themselves. At the end of the twentieth and the beginning of the twenty-first century, documentary filmmakers, lawyers, and advocates for the freedmen often used "Estelusti" when suggesting that Africans had become Seminole Indian. In trying to confirm their Indian history and identity, the freedmen also have adopted the name in various suits against the Seminoles and the federal government. Ironically, in those legal disputes, Seminole Indians also have utilized "Estelusti" to identify the freedmen in order to differentiate themselves from that group.

The term "maroons" most accurately describes the group of Africans and their descendants that became associated with Seminole Indians. Although often identified as "Black Indians" nowadays, Africans associated with Seminoles in Florida, the Bahamas, Coahuila, Texas, the Indian Territory, and Oklahoma had most in common with other maroon societies throughout the Americas. They shared many similarities with such groups as the Jamaican Maroons, the Ndjuka and Saramaka "Bush Negroes" of Suriname, and the Border Maroons of Haiti.

Those similarities included building settlements in remote areas for concealment and defense; skills in guerrilla warfare; impressive adaptation to new environments; substantial interaction with American Indians; existence in a state of almost continuous war, which strongly influenced their political and social organization; the emergence of leaders skilled at understanding whites; and the retention of African systems.[14] Africans associated with Seminoles displayed traits typically associated with maroons, such as "heroic resistance, perseverance, an indomitability of spirit, persistence and affirmation of the African ways, [and] a prideful and unbowed blackness."[15] Most importantly, they shared with other maroon societies the internal dynamism that characterized Central and West African cultural systems. The Seminole maroons incorporated adaptations of the most useful elements of their past and present experiences into a unique and complex cultural whole.

Prior to Removal, whites sometimes identified individual and small groups of runaways in Florida as maroons. The Ohio abolitionist and congressman Joshua Giddings referred to the corporate group that way as early as 1858, but he preferred the term "exiles."[16] In 1939, Herbert Aptheker included the group in his brief survey of maroons within the United States,[17] but it was not until 1979 that the name "Seminole maroons" first appeared in print. In a review of Littlefield's *Africans and Seminoles*, ethnologist William Sturtevant made reference to a personal communication from anthropologist Richard Price suggesting that Seminole blacks in the Bahamas and Mexico might appropriately be called Seminole maroons. Sturtevant expanded Price's argument to suggest that the group located in the Indian Territory justifiably could be included in "the history, ethnohistory, and ethnography that should be investigated under that rubric."[18] This is the first book to employ Sturtevant's proposed model.

The premise of this study is that, with only a few notable exceptions, the history of the Seminole freedmen has been misunderstood, misinterpreted, and misrepresented. The primary frame of reference and historical context for studying their past needs to be expanded beyond Native and African North America to encompass maroon communities throughout the Americas. The Seminole freedmen are not today and never were Seminole Indian; they are maroon descendants. From the group's earliest beginnings in Florida, intrigued white observers and panic-stricken U.S. Army officers suggested that Africans were amalgamating with Seminoles and somehow becoming "Black Indians." The reasons behind that suggestion were many and various, and they are explored at length throughout this book. As witnessed most startlingly by the CBS television and *New York Times* coverage, that myth has continued to be the interpretation of choice in the press and popular media into the early twenty-first century. Only within the last twenty years have scholars begun to challenge that interpretation and offer alternatives more closely tied to the evidence.[19]

But if they did not assume a new identity as Black Indians,[20] what then happened to Africans who became associated with Seminoles? In Florida, some Seminole leaders acquired African slaves by capture from neighboring plantations or by purchase. Runaways to the Indians also typically sought the protection of a Seminole leader and became his tributary allies. Most blacks apparently began their relationship with Seminoles by living in an Indian town, as either a slave or a free person. But once their numbers had grown sufficiently to support a community, the great majority moved off and formed separate maroon societies under African leadership. Those maroon communities confused whites by including all three classifications of blacks associated with Seminoles: enslaved Africans, tributary allies, and a smaller number of free nontributary blacks.

Although they differentiated between slaves and free blacks, whites did not distinguish between the enslaved and tributaries. They had no frame of reference for self-emancipated Africans who provided tributes to American Indians, and the lot of tributaries and slaves of Seminoles was similar. Whites also referred to tributaries simply as "free," without recognizing their obligations. Though retaining a close relationship with Seminoles, all three classes of maroons became highly independent and autonomous, pursuing their own political and diplomatic agendas and their own economic, social, and cultural arrangements, attaining in the process a high level of cultural distinctiveness from the Indians.

Although their exploits in Florida have received broad coverage in the scholarly literature, the maroons' subsequent history in the Indian Territory and Oklahoma has not. What happened to the maroons who remained behind in the Indian Territory after the migrations to Mexico at mid-century has remained relatively unknown, yet it is a rich and important history. Littlefield is the only historian to have published a book-length study of that group's experiences in the 1850s and 1860s. He provides comprehensive coverage of the various slave controversies affecting the Seminoles and maroons after Removal and concludes that they caused extensive damage to relations between the two groups.

Adopting a slightly different approach, this study pursues two closely related lines of inquiry: Who were Seminole slave owners, and what did slaveholding mean to Seminoles? And how did slaves of Seminoles fare in the Indian Territory after 1850? In an important letter written in the summer of 1856, Southern Superintendent of Indian Affairs Charles Dean described the system of slavery operating among the Seminoles in the Indian Territory as being almost identical to the one they had employed in Florida prior to Removal. The maroons were "only slaves in name."[21] Littlefield suggests that "the system as he described it was no longer widespread,"[22] but Dean's observations were mostly accurate. Until the outbreak of the Civil War, Seminoles and maroons in the Indian Territory continued to practice the indigenous form of slavery they had developed in Florida.

In *Africans and Seminoles,* Littlefield sees the difficulties of the post-Removal antebellum period as something of an aberration, caused by the traumas of war and relocation and the innumerable slave controversies that resulted. He characterizes that period as sandwiched between times of stronger Indian-black relations in pre-Removal Florida and the post-bellum Indian Territory.[23] But I propose that consistency and continuity were the distinguishing features in post-Removal relations between Seminoles and maroons. The most dramatic manifestation of their relationship—independent communities of armed and mounted maroons under African leadership—survived Removal and flourished in the Indian Territory both before and after the Civil War.

An appreciation of that consistency and continuity is vital to an understanding of Seminole-maroon relations after Removal. The Seminoles' indigenous world transcended the emigrants' journey from Tampa to Fort Gibson, and southeastern Native philosophy and institutions took root in the Indian Territory. They were nurtured by a strong aversion to white acculturation. In 1823 the Apalachee leader Heniha Emathla (Neamathla) had argued that his people would cease to be Indians if whites taught them their ways.[24] In 1847, after reporting that the Seminoles neither had nor wanted a school, subagent Marcellus Duval observed, "They feel themselves, and desire to be considered, as decidedly beyond the pale of civilization, perfectly satisfied to walk in the 'footsteps of their predecessors.' "[25] Duval and his like were unable to comprehend the civilization the Indians and maroons inhabited, and so could not fathom the nature or complexities of their relationship.

Although typically referred to as one of the so-called Five Civilized Tribes, the Seminoles differed fundamentally from the other four in their history and institutions. Among the Cherokees, Creeks, Choctaws, and Chickasaws, intermarried whites and their mixed-race offspring came to assume positions of economic, social, political, and cultural leadership and hastened a program of rapid and massive acculturation. Those elites also came to direct tribal policy regarding Indian-black relations, both before and after the Civil War. That highly acculturated plantocracy instigated the adoption of most of the essential elements of southern white civilization into the four tribes. During the antebellum period, they furthered the cause of institutionalized slavery within the tribes by instigating the incorporation of severe black codes. In the Civil War, they supported the Confederacy, and during Reconstruction, to varying degrees, they opposed the incorporation of the freedmen, denied them equal rights, and stunted their opportunities for advancement.

In contrast, the Seminoles experienced few of those sea changes affecting the other slaveholding tribes. They either displayed a lack of interest in or actively opposed the efforts of white agents of acculturation. The Seminoles never instigated institutionalized black slavery or black codes. Only a small minority of hereditary leaders and their descendants owned any slaves or exercised tributary rights over the maroons. During the Civil War, at least half of the tribe supported the Union and actively opposed the more "civilized" South. From Reconstruction until Oklahoma statehood, Seminoles living in the Indian Territory could be described best as a nation of subsistence farmers who maintained a traditional southeastern aboriginal culture governed by hereditary chiefs. Without question, they were by far the least acculturated of the Five Tribes.

Relations between Seminoles and maroons in the Indian Territory thus developed mostly within a transplanted and largely intact indigenous world and not within a context of rapidly accelerating acculturation. During the Reconstruction period and beyond, observers noted the way the Seminoles treated the maroons. The freedmen acquired equal rights in the Seminole Nation and received political representation on the council. Maroons also attained influential and powerful positions as freedman bandleaders, council members, interpreters and advisers to Seminole leaders, and law enforcement officers.

White observers suggested that massive Indian-black intermarriage best explained why freedmen fared so much better within the Seminole Nation than among the other Civilized Tribes. But evidence does not support the argument that miscegenation was rampant in the Seminole Nation or that freedmen and Indians assimilated. The Seminoles' retention of Native customs and practices, their lack of white intermarriage and acculturation, and the Indians' and maroons' ability to get along while living mostly separate lives provide a more satisfactory explanation.

Amazing though it might seem to producers and consumers of popular media and to contemporary Oklahomans, the freedman townships within the Seminole Nation constituted maroon communities. Those towns were populated and led by people of African descent. They were located in remote areas of the Indian Territory, at a distance from Seminole towns. Whites especially, but also Indians and other African Americans, viewed the Seminole freedman settlements as inhospitable, lawless, dangerous places, to be avoided at all cost. The maroons enjoyed the isolation their reputation brought. A unique culture, drawn from their ancestors' experiences in Africa and on European and American plantations, and from the group's relations with Seminole Indians, developed within their communities. That vibrant maroon culture featured linguistic, religious, and other systemic social and cultural elements that defined the freedmen as unique and quite distinct from either Seminole Indians or other African Americans.

The period from the end of the Civil War to Oklahoma statehood proved to be something of a golden age for the Seminole freedmen in the Indian Territory. Slavery had been abolished, the threat of sale or kidnapping had disappeared, and violence became unusual. The freedman population rose rapidly and dramatically. The maroons had good reason to be grateful for their association with the Seminoles. None of the freedmen affiliated with the other Civilized Tribes received the same benefits as the maroons, and for many, this became a bleak period in their history. But the Seminoles and maroons coexisted peacefully, and under such favorable conditions, the Seminole freedmen thrived and flourished for forty years. Enrollment and land allotment under the Dawes Commission at the turn of the century would mark the beginning of the end of the maroons' splendid isolation. The coming of Jim Crow Oklahoma severely strained relations between Seminoles and maroons, as the forty-sixth state classified Indians as white and freedmen as black.

The maroons tried to withdraw within their isolated communities, but a huge influx of white land grafters, oil speculators, and other immigrants stimulated allotment thefts, fraud, and other forms of corruption, adding pressure to race relations in what had become Seminole County, Oklahoma. Other agents of acculturation invaded the still mostly indigenous Seminole and maroon civilization, demanding integration or exclusion. As white Oklahomans relegated Indians and African Americans to the bottom rungs of the economic and social ladder, status issues took on added importance.

The freedmen took pride in their former relationship with Seminole Indians and saw themselves as better than so-called "state-raised Negroes." They proclaimed that they never had been slaves, and they pointed to their "Indianness." The historical and cultural "otherness" the freedmen perceived resulted not from their having become Seminole Indian but from their maroon heritage. But their historical association with Seminole Indians was foundational to that heritage and to their identity as an ethnic group.

The Seminoles suffered under the taint that they were "the blackest of all the Indian tribes."[26] Some began to deny the benevolence of their forebears, stating that the maroons had been their slaves, that they had been forced to incorporate the freedmen into their nation, and that the U.S. government had given Indian land to blacks. During the course of the twentieth century, Seminoles also made several attempts to deny the freedmen of membership in the Seminole Nation and deprive them of its benefits.

More than halfway through the first decade of the twenty-first century, those issues remain unresolved. Seminoles argue that their relationship with Africans has been misrepresented; they know that the freedmen are not Black Indians. The freedmen feel that their unique history and identity are not being recognized. They know that their ancestors enjoyed a close association with Seminole Indians. The two talk past each other; both are right, and both feel cheated. Seminoles and freedmen now are adversaries in a fierce battle over their heritage and rights. Divided and ruled, both continue to reap the whirlwind of American racial injustice.

The Seminole Freedmen: A History attempts to trace and explain the historical roots of the current difficulties between Seminoles and freedmen. It argues that relations between the two have been central to the experience of both groups. Chapters 1 and 2 discuss the maroons' ethnogenesis in Florida, and the development of their relationship with Seminoles during the period of the first two Seminole Wars. They cover the different classifications of Africans that existed within pre-Removal Seminole society; the similarities and differences between slaves, tributary allies, and free nontributary blacks; and the creation of maroon societies in Florida and the Bahamas.

Chapter 3 looks at how relations between Seminoles and maroons deteriorated during the decade following their Removal to the Indian Territory, causing some to emigrate to Mexico. Chapters 4 and 5 concentrate on those usually overlooked Seminoles and maroons who remained behind in the Indian Territory after the exodus to Mexico at mid-century. Contrary to what might have been expected, the maroons did fairly well during the 1850s. Those chapters explain why, by describing who owned Seminole slaves, why slavery among the Seminoles differed so dramatically from the system practiced by most slave owners within the other Civilized Tribes, and what it meant to be a slave, a tributary ally, and a free nontributary black in the Seminole country during the antebellum period. The continuing strength of indigenous practices among the Seminoles and their resistance to white acculturation provided the maroons with a constant advantage over most Africans associated with the other slaveholding tribes.

Seminole and maroon participation in the American Civil War is covered in Chapter 6. Chapter 7 describes how the Seminoles abided by the terms of the 1866 treaty and accommodated freedmen within their newly established nation at a time when the other Civilized Tribes experienced such difficulty in coming to terms with emancipation and Reconstruction. Chapter 8 provides a new explanation of why the lot of the Seminole maroons was so superior to that of most other freedmen in the Indian Territory during the postbellum period. This interpretation challenges the prevailing myth that intermarriage between Seminoles and maroons was primarily responsible. Chapter 9 continues the argument by proposing that their relations were defined not by integration but by independence, separation, and cultural difference, and that the freedman towns came to constitute easily recognizable maroon communities within the Seminole Nation.

The concluding chapter discusses enrollment and allotment of the Seminole Nation under the Dawes Commission and traces the history of relations between Seminole Indians and freedmen during the century following Oklahoma statehood in 1907. Special attention is paid to the complexities inherent in their relationship, to notions of races, nations, rights, entitlement, and inclusion, and to the roles played by ancestry, history, and pride. To see a more complete picture of the current conflict between Seminoles and freedmen, one must spend time in the past.

This book seeks to increase understanding of the Seminoles' and freedmen's differences, as well as their commonalties. A more informed dialogue on the nature, complexities, and significance of their relationship, and a keener appreciation of both viewpoints, will be the measure of its success. Then, perhaps, the two could look to the future. Were the Seminole freedmen to embrace their maroon ancestry and heritage, Seminole Indians more likely would recognize and celebrate the history they share with this proud and indomitable people, and together these former allies might find new and rewarding ways to fight for what rightfully should be theirs.

The Seminole Freedmen

CHAPTER ONE

Beginnings in Florida

Africans and Seminoles first became acquainted in Florida in the eighteenth century. Beginning in the early 1700s, American Indians who later became known as Seminoles migrated there. The southeastern frontier provided Indians and Africans with unusual opportunities to use international rivalries and contested space to advantage. Florida became a place where immigrant Old World Europeans, New World Americans, Africans, and indigenous Indian peoples interacted substantially in negotiating territory, power, identity, and status.

During the early eighteenth century, towns from the Creek Confederacy moved south into largely depopulated areas of northern Florida.[1] Almost all of the aboriginal inhabitants of the region, Timucuas and Apalachees, had died from European diseases or had been killed or enslaved by British-supported Creeks and Yamasees. As a result of the Yamasee War of 1715, and also because of Indian dissatisfaction with the British trade, Lower Creeks began to withdraw from the British frontier and migrate into Spanish Florida. There they established new towns, based upon established Creek organizational principles, and developed connections with other Indian towns nearby.

Several Lower Creek towns, mostly along the Lower Chattahoochee and the Flint rivers in present-day southwestern Georgia, moved south into the former Apalachee area. Most spoke Hitchiti, a Muskogee language known as Mikasuki among the modern Florida Seminole and Mikasuki people. Further east, Cowkeeper and his band of Okonis estab-

3

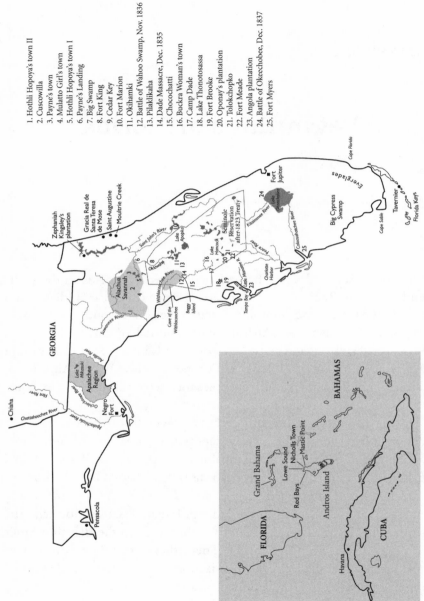

Florida, the Bahamas, and Cuba

lished the town of Cuskowilla on the Alachua Savannah, near present-day Gainesville. Other Hitchiti-speakers from the towns of Chiaha, Apalachicola, and Sawokli also settled in Alachua. By mid-century, a confederacy of Hitchiti-speaking peoples began to emerge in north central Florida and the panhandle. Cowkeeper and his band attained primacy, and his descendants—Payne, the Bowlegses, Mikkoanapa (Micco Nuppa; Micanopy), and the Jumpers—would dominate the principal chieftainship of the Seminoles in Florida and the Indian Territory until 1885.

Other Lower Creeks settled in west Florida, doubling the emerging Seminole population to around two thousand by 1790. Apart from Creeks, a few Apalachee and Yamasee survivors and some Yuchi, Kanchati, and Tawasa immigrants, also settled in Florida. By the time Spain regained control over Florida from the British in 1783, there were Creek-Seminole settlements scattered from the Apalachicola River in the west to the Saint John's River in the east, and from the Georgia line in the north to the Caloosahatchee River, just north of Fort Myers, in the south. The last of the major migrations took place after the Creek War of 1813–14. Creek-speaking Upper Creek Red Sticks, defeated by Andrew Jackson at the Battle of Horseshoe Bend, moved south into Florida after 1814. They more than doubled the Indian population to around five thousand by 1822, and Creek became the dominant language within the Seminole Confederacy.

During the British period in Florida, 1763–83, immigrants gradually separated from the Creek Confederacy and established new bands. The Creeks gave them a new name: *simaló-ni,* later *simanó-li,* which in Creek means "wild" or "undomesticated" in relation to plants and animals. The earliest manifestations of the name given to describe this new Florida group suggest that Lower Creeks considered Seminoles beyond the pale of their more acculturated civilization. The new name for those Creeks who had settled in Florida was borrowed into English. "Seminoles" is first documented in 1765 as the name for the inhabitants of the Alachua area, but it soon expanded to include the settlers in the Apalachee region to the west. Until the end of the Third Seminole War in 1858, English-language sources used "Seminoles" as a general term for all Florida Indians, but descendants of some Creek bands and survivors, such as the Apalachicolas and Apalachees, also retained their individual corporate names.

The Seminoles were mostly exiles from their ancestral homelands—

refugees from war, political intrigue, and oppression. They also were recent immigrants to Florida. The constituent bands of the emerging Seminole Confederacy were fervent in resisting European influences. Both the Spanish and the British tended to leave them to their own devices, and their indigenous economic, social, political, and cultural arrangements remained largely intact or developed independently. The Seminoles' retention of Native practices and institutions would facilitate the incorporation of large numbers of Africans into their society, and would largely determine the nature and course of relations between the two groups.

The emergent Seminole Confederacy could accommodate Africans. It represented a decentralized grouping of bands enjoying a large amount of local autonomy and displaying a great deal of cultural diversity. Indeed, it was to retain or achieve such independence that the majority had settled in Florida. The group that became known as Seminoles came from various geographic areas and spoke different languages. Some of the bands *(italwa)* included more than one town *(talofa)*. Some towns held primacy, while others had a subordinate tributary status. The criteria for inclusion appear to have been quite flexible.

Seminoles were subsistence farmers and hunters. In the 1770s, naturalist William Bartram documented nine Seminole towns and several smaller settlements in northern Florida, southwest of Saint Augustine on the Saint John's River, and west through Alachua to the Suwannee River. Each town consisted of between eight and thirty hamlets (households or compounds). Every hamlet grew a garden of maize, beans, watermelons, and tobacco. At a distance from the town, the men cleared larger fields by burning for planting with fruits, cereals, and vegetables. The women cultivated the crops, and the men hunted game and fished. Seminoles also kept cattle and horses.[2] Little information on social organization has survived from that period, but Sturtevant and anthropologist Jessica Cattelino conclude, "[There] must have been matrilineal clans and matrilocal residence."[3]

By that time, Seminoles employed a communal land system in which the *mikko* (bandleader) levied taxes from residents in the form of agricultural surpluses. This had indigenous Creek roots, but it also had featured in the earlier *sabana* system, a form of vassalage under which Florida Indians cleared land and planted fields for their leaders and for Spanish authorities. Bartram described the system operating among the Creeks.

Every member of the town could enjoy the fruits of his labor, but each deposited a quantity of corn in a large crib as "a tribute or revenue to the mico." The bandleader retained the surplus for the public good, but tributary rights also allowed mikkos to accumulate personal wealth.[4] Payments of tribute and displays of deference were established customs among the Creeks and Seminoles. This would bear heavily upon the positions Africans would assume within the confederacy.

Seminoles had enslaved other Indians before they encountered Africans, but they associated servitude with capture in warfare rather than an organized system of labor. They viewed captives as replacements for tribal members lost during wars, and usually adopted them later. Bartram observed some enslaved Yamasees among the Seminoles in the 1770s. The enslaved dressed better than the Indians they served, both men and women could marry their captors, and their children were "free, and considered in every respect equal" to other members of the community.[5]

When Africans replaced Indians as the enslaved, Seminole slavery changed. Seminoles typically did not adopt black slaves, enter into marriages with Africans, or consider the children of black slaves free and equal to Indians—especially if the child had an African mother. Instead, slaveholding became associated with prestige, property ownership, and, increasingly, profit; a small number of Indian mikkos, their relatives, and their clan heirs came to own or control almost all of the Seminoles' African slaves. Black slavery among the Seminoles never assumed the characteristics of the "Peculiar Institution" operating in the South, or the system adopted by intermarried whites and their mixed-race offspring among the other Civilized Tribes. Nevertheless, some Seminole Indians purchased, derived material benefit from owning, and sold African slaves.[6]

As the Seminoles began to emerge as a new people and acquire a new name, Africans entered their world. It seems likely that Spaniards first introduced blacks to the Seminoles. Enslaved Africans in the British colony of South Carolina had quickly learned that Spanish Florida offered a haven for runaways. The Spanish employed less rigorous slave codes than the British and afforded blacks a greater degree of freedom. Slaves in the British colonies gladly exchanged masters by escaping across the border to Florida. Runaways from South Carolina began arriving in Saint Augustine as early as 1687.[7] The Spanish welcomed the new immigrants and encouraged others to flee by promising them asylum.[8]

In November 1693, the Spanish king issued an edict freeing the runaways to Saint Augustine in the hope of attracting others.[9] In 1704, Governor José de Zuniga y Cerda extended that privilege. In his orders for Apalachee Province, the area in which the Seminoles would settle, he proclaimed: "Any negro of Carolina, Christian or not, free or slave, who wishes to come fugitive, will be [given] complete liberty, so that those who do not want to stay here may pass to other places as they see fit, with their freedom papers which I hereby grant them by way of the king."[10] The Spanish literally offered a passport to freedom to slaves fleeing the Carolinas, and Florida rapidly attained a reputation as a haven for runaways.

On February 16, 1739, Governor Manuel de Montiano set aside for those fugitive Africans an armed garrison near Saint Augustine called Gracia Real de Santa Teresa de Mose, which became the first known free black community in North America. The Spaniards swiftly put to advantage the newly freed blacks in resisting the British invasion of 1740. Facing a return to chattel slavery, none would oppose the invaders with more determination than the runaways. The Spanish fortified Mose and organized its residents and the inhabitants of allied Indian towns into military companies. Of the 965 troops in Saint Augustine, 200 were armed blacks who received the same pay and rations as regular Spanish soldiers and served under officers drawn from their own ranks. Montiano employed free blacks extensively as scouts, and Africans were reported killed and captured in actions outside Saint Augustine.[11] When the Spanish counterattacked Georgia in June 1742, their forces included "a regiment of Negroes" whose black commanders "were clothed in lace, bore the same rank as the white officers, and with equal freedom and familiarity walked and conversed with their commanders and chief."[12]

At the very time Seminole bands were establishing a separate political identity in northern Florida, therefore, their European neighbors were treating Africans favorably. The Spaniards welcomed runaways from southern plantations, granted them freedom, and asked for little in return, save for their cooperation in opposing elements hostile to both parties. The way those Europeans treated their African associates likely made an impression upon their Seminole neighbors, who became aware of their relationship. Allied Indians served in military companies with the residents of Mose, and several of the Mose men had wives in the Indian towns nearby.[13] The Spaniards allowed Africans to live apart, own arms and property, travel at will, choose their own leaders, organize in military companies under black officers, and generally control most aspects of their daily lives. A similar arrangement soon emerged within the nascent Seminole Confederacy.

Under the terms of the 1763 Treaty of Paris, Spain ceded Florida to Britain and transferred the inhabitants of Fort Mose to Cuba. Nevertheless, attracted by the semitropical climate, the inaccessible and inhospitable terrain, sparse white settlement, and the chronic political instability of the area, runaways continued to migrate to Florida in ever-increasing numbers. With the Spaniards gone, those runaways sought an alternative haven. In 1771, Governor John Moultrie reported, "It has been a practice for a good while past, for negroes to run away from their Masters, and get into the Indian towns, from whence it proved very difficult to get them back."[14] Some began to live in Seminole communities, while others founded maroon societies and sought military and trading alliances with the neighboring Indian towns. Most of those runaways assumed tributary ally status and gave a portion of the crop or livestock they raised each year to the Seminole mikko in exchange for his protection against reenslavement. But a few of the self-emancipated runaways remained free and nontributary.

Africans also became associated with Seminoles in two other ways: by capture from plantations nearby and by purchase from whites or other American Indians. Africans purchased by Seminoles became slaves, while captives apparently assumed either tributary ally or slave status, perhaps depending on their Indian band association. Maroon communities came to include all three classes of blacks associated with Seminoles—slaves, tributary allies, and free nontributary blacks—confounding white observers.

During the American Revolution, Seminoles engaged in attacks on colonists' plantations as allies of British loyalists and carried off many Africans. Those actions deeply perturbed white planters in bordering Georgia and the Carolinas, who suddenly faced the nightmare of collusion between Indians and blacks. Petitions poured into Congress and the executive departments for the return of fugitive Africans thought to be residing in the Indian Country. Wartime chaos also provided cover for Africans to escape from British owners. In 1783, when the British evacuated, 4,745 blacks, or 42 percent of the total African population in British East Florida, went missing.[15] To placate Georgians and Carolinians, the U.S. government concluded the treaties of New York (1790) and Colerain

(1796) with the Creeks in an attempt to secure the return of runaways. Both the Americans and the Creeks considered the Seminoles to be part of the Creek Confederacy. But Seminoles considered themselves independent, and they repudiated Creek authority to interfere in their internal affairs and decide the disposition of runaways living among them.[16]

Florida's new Spanish government recognized the presence of Africans in the Indian Country. During the 1781 peace talks in Pensacola, the Spanish had requested Creeks and Seminoles to return fugitive slaves. In 1789, Spaniards asked "that all negroes, horses, goods and American citizens, taken by the Indians, should be restored." And in 1802, at the conclusion of hostilities with Indian forces led by William Augustus Bowles, the Spanish tried to require Mikasukis and Seminoles to return blacks captured from Spanish owners during the conflict. Toward that end, in September, Payne and the Hitchiti leader Jack Kanard even met with a Spanish official at Mikasuki.[17]

It was probably during the British period in Florida that some Seminole mikkos first adopted a form of black slavery. Kenneth Porter has suggested that British officials presented Creek and Seminole leaders with "king's gifts" of enslaved Africans in exchange for service to the crown. Noting that Britons and Spaniards attached prestige to owning Africans, some Seminole mikkos also purchased slaves at that time.[18] Nothing definite is known about black slavery among the Seminoles in its formative years, detailed descriptions coming only much later. It seems likely, however, that it adhered to indigenous principles, with slaves offering individual tributes and deference to their Seminole owners, who typically were mikkos or their heirs. Equally likely, most black slaves remained outside of Seminole Indian society. The accompanying growth of largely independent communities of armed maroons under African leadership probably was a borrowing from the Spanish.

References to blacks living among the Seminoles first appeared soon after Spanish rule was restored in Florida in 1784. During the late 1780s and the 1790s, a population of Africans and African Americans became associated with Lower Creek and emerging Seminole settlements on the Chattahoochee River and Lake Mikasuki and in Alachua. Many had arrived there as captives following Seminole and black slave raids on local plantations in southern Georgia and northern Florida. Others were runaways from plantations in Florida, Georgia, and the Carolinas. According to Saunt, because the mostly marginal pine barrens land they occupied discouraged the development of plantation slavery, "African American residents in the Seminole and outlying Lower Creek towns enjoyed far more autonomy than their counterparts elsewhere in the Deep South Interior."[19]

By the end of 1790, a significant black community had emerged close to Chiaha, a Creek-Seminole town on the Chattahoochee, some thirteen miles below the site of present-day Columbus, Georgia. Julian Carballo, an interpreter for the Spanish, described the residents as "free and maroon Negroes, from the Americans and a few from Pensacola," who numbered "more than 110." Those maroons were "forming a type of palisade" for defense.[20] Leaders of the black community near Chiaha included Philatouche, of African descent, and Cudgomicco, derived from the West African day name "Cudjo" (Monday) and the Creek-Seminole title *mikko*. Throughout the 1790s, the maroons engaged in slave raids with Indian residents of the neighboring towns of Hitchiti and Usiche, and by the end of the decade, according to Saunt, Chiaha "had become the hub of African and Indian relations in the Deep South Interior."[21]

Black Factor was one who engaged in slave raids on local plantations. Factor, a trader among the Lower Creeks, was described as a "half breed negro" but identified himself as Creek Indian and went by the name of Ninnywageechee. He also owned a plantation run by African Americans.[22] Later, Factor was identified as a member of Waka Puchasi's (Mulatto King's) band on the Apalachicola River. He acquired Rose, an Indian-black woman he gave to his son, Sam Factor, for a wife. Upon the death of Black Factor in or prior to 1827, a dispute arose over the ownership of Rose Sena Factor and her children that would play out in both Florida and the Indian Territory.[23]

Kapichee Mikko (Kinhijah; King Heijah), the Mikasuki head of the Apalachee bands, and Payne, leader of the Alachua bands, became early prominent slave owners among the Seminoles. Sometime during the British period, Kapichee Mikko purchased Melinda and Dolly, two African or African American women, from two different men near Saint Augustine. Both became wives of Pompey, also an African or African American. They gave him many children and grandchildren, whom Kapichee Mikko's heirs eventually inherited. By the mid-1830s, that one extended family comprised seventy-four of the maroons associated with the Mikasukis.[24]

By 1793, Payne had accumulated 20 slaves, in addition to 1,500 head of cattle, 400 horses, and many head of sheep and goats.[25] Those Africans represented the beginnings of the Alachua maroons. In 1821, nine years after his death, a report still listed some three hundred residents of "Payne's negro settlements in Alachua," as well as a separate associated maroon community at Pilaklikaha. When Payne died in 1812, his brother Hothli Hopoya (Bowlegs) succeeded him as leader of the Alachua group. Hothli Hopoya inherited or served as guardian for Payne's property and also accumulated slaves of his own. After Hothli Hopoya died in or around 1818, his and Payne's nephew Mikkoanapa succeeded him and inherited most of the Alachua maroons. Sitarkey, another nephew of Payne and Hothli Hopoya, also inherited a large number of blacks. Still other Africans associated with the Alachua group passed down the Bowlegs line. Hothli Hopoya's descendants—Harriet Bowlegs, Eliza Bowlegs, and Holata Mikko (Billy Bowlegs)—also became owners of large numbers of slaves in Florida and the Indian Territory.[26]

Both the Alachuas and the Mikasukis raised livestock, and their leaders purchased slaves with cattle. By about 1810, Indians valued a black slave at forty head of beef cattle, the size and value of the cattle corresponding to the size, age, sex, and value of the slave. At that time, the largest beef cattle fetched $20 per head.[27] Slaves, therefore, were expensive, the most sought-after costing Seminole mikkos the equivalent of $800 in cattle.

Saunt has suggested that Payne and Kapichee Mikko probably used slaves as cowboys. By helping to raise more cattle, those black cowboys would have added to the Seminole mikkos' ability to purchase more slaves. Significantly, even at that early date, Kapichee Mikko's slaves lived in an emerging maroon community about a mile and a half away from the Indian town at Mikasuki. In early 1795, a Spanish officer complained that two blacks accompanying a party of Indians were attempting to persuade slaves in East Florida to flee there. They painted a rosy picture of their lives among the Seminoles and Lower Creeks, praising "to the residents' slaves the good life that people of their color enjoy in the nation where they eat the same as their masters and work only when they wish without fear of punishment."[28]

In a 2000 study, historian Jane Landers suggested that "[Florida's] colonial economy was much more diversified and integrated into the wider Atlantic commerce than previously had been understood."[29] The abundance of European artifacts unearthed at both Seminole Indian and maroon sites in Florida dating to the British period and to the second

Spanish period (1784–1821) attests to both groups' inclusion in such commercial activities. At Pilaklikaha (Abraham's town), for example, archaeologist Terrance Weik uncovered European ceramics, glass beads, trade pipe fragments, bottle glass, brick, cut nails, and other metal fragments, suggesting substantial maroon involvement in trade networks. The maroons might have traded directly with European or American settlers, travelers, or itinerant traders, or European goods could have made their way to the community through trade with American Indians, free blacks, or plantation slaves. Pilaklikaha's strategic location at the hub of a network of Indian trails leading from northern Florida to the cape certainly would have facilitated maroon engagement in trade with Indians riding to hunting grounds in the south.[30]

During the second Spanish period, through free black and Indian-black intermediaries, Seminoles also traded cattle to Spaniards for cash. In 1804, for example, Buckra (Bucker) Woman, a relative of Payne's, sold cattle worth $1,700 to Philip Yonge's Company and received a third in cash at that time.[31] A decade earlier, Payne's Alachua maroons also had sold horses to white traders.[32] As producing items to trade for cash and accumulate wealth became more important to some Seminoles, so did owning Africans. Slaves provided their Indian owners with the means of producing crop and livestock surpluses for sale. Africans provided labor and represented assets, and owning slaves itself became associated with status. By accumulating resources derived from slave ownership, a number of Seminoles and their heirs became quite wealthy.[33]

Spaniards began employing freed Africans, such as Felipe Edinboro and John Gray, to trade with Seminoles. In 1808, the royal treasury in Saint Augustine commissioned Juan Bautista Collins, a free mulatto, to travel to Alachua to purchase cattle from the Indians. After 1812, Collins made several trips to establish relations with Hothli Hopoya, taking gifts to him, and managed to purchase a herd of 125 head of cattle for the Spaniards. Collins acquired considerable knowledge of Indian customs and gained the respect of Seminoles, Hothli Hopoya's "sister" Simency even traveling to Saint Augustine to testify on his behalf during a lawsuit.[34]

African servitude among the Seminoles came to be based on tribute and deference. Slaves of Seminoles rarely were supervised and had little obligation to their owner, except for the annual tribute. In 1836, Myer Cohen, an officer in the U.S. Army, noted that Emathla's (King Phillip's) slaves at Tohopikalika worked for him under armed guard.[35] But that seems to have been an exception, probably presaged by the onset of the Second Seminole War.

Slaves and tributary allies kept most of what they produced; and free nontributary blacks, all. The ability to access land, retain most of the fruits of their labor, and establish separate communities contributed to the Seminole maroons' ethnogenesis. Anthropologist Kenneth Bilby has suggested that contemporary Jamaican Maroons view "their communally held lands not only as a sacred inheritance from their ancestors, but also as a key to their survival as distinct peoples." Owning land and making homes in distinct communities based on interrelated families also has remained foundational to the identity of Seminole maroon groups in Oklahoma, Mexico, Texas, and the Bahamas to the early twenty-first century.[36]

The emergence of the Seminole maroons as an identifiable group can be attributed to three determining factors: the international intrigue, frontier diplomacy, and European and American territorial expansion that characterized the Southeast when the group began to form; the emergence of the Seminole Indians as a "new people" in their own right around that same time; and the roles played by the constituent maroon members themselves in the group's formation.[37] Whether runaways, captives, or slaves purchased by Seminoles, those displaced Africans preferred to live along borders and ally with Spaniards, Britons, or American Indians rather than remain enslaved on southern plantations. The maroons' early and close association with Seminoles contributed strongly to the development of their identity as an ethnic group, yet they forged a history and culture entirely their own.

The maroons shared similar backgrounds of African origins and plantation slavery experience, yet, like the Seminoles, there must have been tremendous diversity within the group. In one slave raid, during July 1812, Seminoles abducted forty-one African men, women, and children from Zephaniah Kingsley's Laurel Grove plantation on the western side of the Saint John's River, near present-day Jacksonville. Most of the adults had been born within various ethnic groups in Central Africa and were recent arrivals. As historian Daniel Schafer has suggested: "Diversity must have been the key feature of the slave quarters, with a proliferation of languages being spoken and great variety in food preparations, clothing and hairstyles, songs and musical instruments, and facial markings a daily staple of life."[38] When it began its association with Seminoles, this group

was composed mostly of families living in household units; it under-
mined the stereotype of the single male runaway who looked to intermarry with Indians. People such as those helped found the emergent
maroon settlements among the Seminoles.

Like other such groups, the Seminole maroons formed communities
primarily for survival, and then to pursue common goals. Ethnicity
would have acted as a structural principle long before their society clearly
emerged as an ethnic group.[39] During their ethnogenesis, it would have
been natural for the Seminole maroons to look to Africa for guidance.
Africa could provide the group with precedents, commonality, and organizational, religious, cultural, and political principles.[40] As with other
emerging maroon communities, negotiation and treaty making became
foundational to Seminole maroon society because they helped foster
independence, leadership, and the identification and articulation of
group interests. The pursuit of recognition, rights, and privileges through
diplomatic channels became a recurring theme in the group's history.
Proclamations of freedom, land grants, and treaties abolishing slavery,
granting rights of citizenship, or recognizing land ownership documented hard-won gains and provided group members with a semblance
of stability and security in an otherwise complex and ever-changing
world. The Seminole maroons pursued independent initiatives and common goals, and in so doing defined themselves, and were defined by
others, as a separate and distinct people.

The Seminole maroons formed communities and created alliances
with Britons, Spaniards, and Native Americans to survive and to avoid
reenslavement on southern plantations. They adapted to a new and harsh
environment by preserving elements from their African past and borrowing from American Indians, Europeans, and Americans. Their ethnogenesis and ethnohistory were similar to those of other maroon societies
throughout the Americas.

References to Africans living among the Seminoles increased in 1812,
when American settlers in Spanish East Florida attempted to seize the
territory for the United States. The perceived need to remove the Seminole and black threat to southern slaveholding interests, however, was at
least as important a consideration to those patriots. State officials mobilized the Georgia militia and planned reprisals should the Seminoles
attack, General John Floyd stating: "Should they take up the cudgels it
will afford a desirable pretext for the Georgians to penetrate their coun-

try, and Breake up a Negroe Town: an important Evil growing under their patronage."[41]

The ensuing campaigns revealed the extent of the Seminole-maroon military alliance in Florida for the first time. Southerners feared that more runaways would join them. On July 30, Colonel Thomas Smith reported that the Seminoles had "several hundred fugative [sic] slaves from the Carolinas & Georgia at present in their Towns & unless they are checked soon they will be so strengthened by desertions from Georgia & Florida [it] will be found troublesome to reduce them."[42] The intervention of Seminole maroons subsequently helped prevent the fall of Saint Augustine. Then an African and Indian force effectively put an end to a scheme to annex East Florida by thwarting Colonel Daniel Newnan's attempt to destroy the Alachua Seminole and maroon settlements. Afterward, reports circulated that the bravest warriors had been those of the black towns. The allies succeeded in delaying the action long enough for Congress to demand a halt to the campaign in Florida.[43]

The southerners, nevertheless, determined upon further action to remove the African and Indian menace. In early February 1813, a substantial force of regular and volunteer troops set out to destroy the Alachua towns. Realizing they were outnumbered, the Seminoles and maroons fled into the swamp. The southern force then destroyed two of their settlements, one being a substantial maroon community near Hothli Hopoya's town. In his report on the action, the American commander provided the first known description of a Seminole maroon community: "Tuesday, Febr. 11 was employed in destroying the Negro town shown us by the [Indian] Prisoners. We burnt three hundred and eighty six houses; consumed and destroyed from fifteen hundred to two thousand bushels of corn; three hundred horses and about four hundred cattle. Two hundred deerskins were found."[44]

During the second Anglo-American war, the British recruited an army of more than three hundred blacks, fugitive Red Stick Creeks, and Choctaws. In 1814, Colonel Edward Nicholls housed that African and Indian force in a fort built in Spanish territory on a cliff atop Prospect Bluff, at the mouth of the Apalachicola River, just sixty miles from the U.S. border. The following year, the British sailed home after learning of the ratification of the Treaty of Ghent, leaving the fort well stocked with arms and ammunition and under the leadership of a maroon named Garçon. Southern slaveholders feared that beacon for runaways, and in

1816, American gunboats dispatched from New Orleans blew up the "Negro Fort," killing most of the residents.[45]

The destruction of the Negro Fort signaled an end to the African power base on the Apalachicola, but almost all of the members of the garrison who were killed or captured were blacks from Pensacola. The runaways from Georgia and South Carolina who had settled along the river outside the fort managed to escape. They fled eastward toward the Suwannee, where Hothli Hopoya and his Indian followers and maroons led by Nero had settled after being forced to flee from the Alachua Savannah in 1813. Other dislodged maroons from Alachua made new communities along the Withlacoochee River or made their way even farther south to Tampa Bay, Charlotte Harbor, and Pease Creek (now Peace River).[46]

In 1815, Captain George Woodbine, who had served with Nicholls, had sailed from the Negro Fort to Tampa Bay with around eighty runaway Africans. There, they established a thriving plantation community with the evocative and intriguing name "Angola," close to the Oyster River at Sarasota Bay, near present-day Sarasota. The settlers became self-supporting and eventually prospered. As the American invasion of northern Florida caused more African and Indian refugees to head southward, Angola's population swelled to around seven hundred.[47]

Farther north, residents of Florida maroon and Indian communities engaged Andrew Jackson in the First Seminole War, 1817–18. Jackson led his Creek and American troops into Florida and advanced from the west on the Suwannee. Three hundred or more maroons under the leadership of Nero had built settlements that extended for three miles along the west banks of the river, a mile or so east of Hothli Hopoya's town. Despite their spirited resistance, the American commander inflicted heavy casualties on the maroons and laid waste to the allies' towns. Jackson later described those campaigns as a "Savage and Negro War."[48]

During the campaigns of 1812–18, Africans and Seminoles had sided with Spaniards and the British in opposing efforts by Americans to seize Florida for the United States. Maroons bore arms and organized in separate companies under their own leaders, but they clearly enjoyed an excellent understanding with Seminoles. The many references to "Negro towns" in the Alachua, Apalachee, Suwannee, and Withlacoochee regions suggest that they typically had settled apart from the Indians. The maroons had established communities based on farming, stock raising,

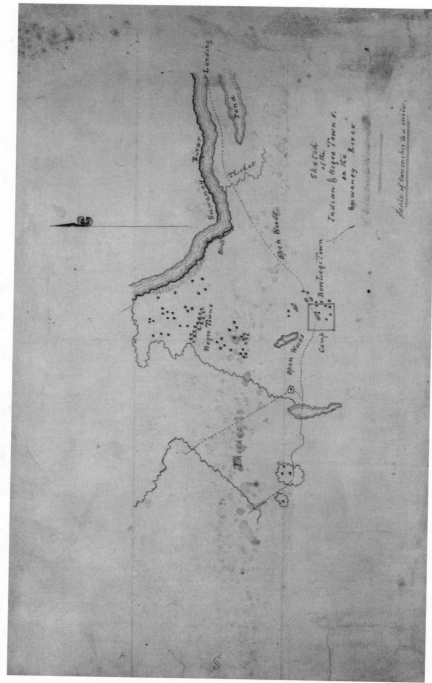

"Sketch of the Indian and Negro Towns on the Suwaney River." Circa 1818. (National Archives)

and hunting. They grew corn, rice, and peanuts; kept large herds of horses and cattle; and hunted deer for their meat and skins. Their communities had become substantial and successful.

The First Seminole War also caused more Indians and maroons to head south to the Pease Creek region. Among them was Oponay, an Okmulgee Upper Creek who had allied with the Red Stick leader Peter McQueen. Oponay established a large plantation near Lake Hancock, north of present-day Barstow in Polk County. His twenty slaves lived about two miles from his residence on the other side of the lake and to the east of Saddle Creek in a village called Minatti (Manatee). In Oponay's fields around the southern borders of Lake Hancock, his blacks worked an extensive peach orchard and produced corn, potatoes, rice, and other crops. McQueen also settled along Pease Creek, to the south of Oponay's plantation.

Jackson's invasion during the First Seminole War exposed Spain's inability to resist any serious demand from the United States for the annexation of Florida. On February 19, 1819, a treaty provided for its transfer for a fee of $5 million, and the United States formally annexed the province in July 1821. Jackson quickly recognized the danger the Angola plantation and Pease Creek settlements posed to southern slaveholding interests and to the new U.S. territory of Florida. He worked with influential Georgians to persuade William McIntosh, leader of the Lower Creek Kawitas, to attack the Red Stick and maroon communities south of Tampa. Their plan called for resettling the fugitive Red Sticks in Georgia and returning the runaways to slavery. In June 1821, McIntosh's force attacked Angola. The Kawitas torched the houses, destroyed the plantation, and captured around three hundred of its residents. They then continued to attack settlements along Pease Creek, sending Africans and Indians into headlong flight. On the journey home, the Kawitas attacked the flourishing town of Chocochatti to the north, capturing around sixty Africans as well as large numbers of cattle and horses.[49]

Nevertheless, many of the Angola and Pease Creek maroons managed to escape the Kawita onslaught. Trader Horatio Dexter visited Oponay's plantation in 1823 and noted that it was thriving. Some of the Angola maroons apparently joined the Minatti village residents. When he died, in May 1823, Oponay left his estate to Pulepucka, said to be the father of Sitarkey. Dexter listed forty Indians and seventy blacks in Pulepucka's town of Apilchapcoche. He also listed "about 80 refugee Negroes belonging to Indians and citizens of this territory who are established on the sea coast near Tampa where they are employed by the Havanna fishery smacks and pass to Cuba frequently," adding that "the crews of these smacks bring goods to trade with the Indians." Those maroons were living in "several settlements" on the inner chain of islands that stretched from Tampa Bay to Charlotte Harbor, "all completely armed with Spanish musquets, Bayonets and Cartouche boxes."[50]

A decade later, slave hunter John Winslett reported "a band of desperadoes, runaways, murderers, and thieves (negroes and Indians, a majority runaway slaves)" to be living on an island south of Charlotte Harbor. The island maroons cut timber, fished, and traded goods with Cuban fishermen for rum and firearms. Winslett also noted "another settlement of lawless persons (Indians and absconded slaves) on a creek between Manatia [Little Manatee] River and Charlotte's Harbor, some miles west of the latter."[51]

Other African residents of Angola and Pease Creek made their way by canoe around Cape Sable and regrouped at Cape Florida on the east coast. A number chose to quit the peninsula to avoid slave hunters and American encroachment. Some sailed with fishermen to Cuba, where Spaniards had taken the Fort Mose families in 1763 and Africans from Saint Augustine after leaving Florida in 1821.[52] Others bargained with captains of English and Bahamian wreckers at Tavernier for a passage to New Providence (Bahamas), the nearest substantial territory of their former ally, Great Britain. They settled mostly on Saint Andrews (Andros) Island. In 1823, around ninety Africans were reported to be living there, with thirty more on the Grand Bahama and neighboring islands.[53]

During the next twenty years, other maroons made the crossing to Andros in Seminole dugout canoes fitted with paddles and sails. That group continued the tradition of *marronage* by establishing communities in remote and inaccessible parts of the island. Their first settlement was on the northwestern tip of the island at Red Bays. Scipio Bowlegs was one of the community's early leaders. Some of the maroons later moved to Lowe Sound, Nicholls Town—named after the British officer who built the Negro Fort at Prospect Bluff—and Mastic Point in the east of the island, where their descendants still resided in the late 1990s.[54]

The emigrants to Cuba and the Bahamas left behind several hundred Africans living mostly in maroon communities in northern Florida. The peninsula recently had become a U.S. territory. Florida no longer offered an international border that runaways could cross to attain freedom or that maroons could ply to advantage. Instead, Africans strengthened their alliance with another foreign power, the Seminoles. With the anticipated rapid immigration of white Americans into Florida after 1821, that re-markable alliance suddenly came under intense scrutiny.

CHAPTER TWO

Removal to Indian Territory

Soon after the United States annexed Florida, American travelers and government officials began to provide reports on Seminole-black relations. In 1821, the Florida Indian agent referred to "the maroon negroes, who live among the Indians," as "lawless freebooters, among whom runaway negroes will always find a refuge."[1] According to other white observers, Africans who were associated with Seminoles went unsupervised and generally had no obligation, save for the giving of an annual tribute. In 1822, William Hayne Simmons, a South Carolinian settler in East Florida, penned the first description of the system operating among the Seminole mikkos. The blacks "never furnished the Indians with any surplus produce, for the purpose of trade; but barely made them sufficient provisions for necessary consumption."[2]

The following year, Horatio Dexter provided the first estimate of the fraction of a maroon community's crop that was contributed to a Seminole mikko: "The Negroes possessed by the Indians live apart from them and they give the master half what the lands produce; he provides them nothing and they are at liberty to employ themselves as they please."[3] Dexter's were firsthand observations based on his personal interactions with Seminoles and maroons. He had visited Pilaklikaha for several days, and his observation referred specifically to that community.

In 1827, Florida Indian agent Gad Humphreys noted: "The negroes of the Seminole Indians are wholly independent, or at least regardless of the authority of their masters; and are Slaves but in name; they work only when it suits their inclination."[4] Yet according to U.S. Army officer Woodburne Potter, Seminole leaders relied heavily on the tribute provided by Africans. The Indians were "poor agriculturists and husbandmen and withal too indolent to till the ground, and without the negroes would literally starve."[5]

In 1835, Seminole agent Wiley Thompson described the typical individual African contribution: "[The] slave supplies his owner annually, from the product of his little field, with corn in proportion to the amount of the crop; and in no instance that has come to my knowledge, exceeding ten bushels; the residue is considered the property of the slave."[6] Like Dexter, Major General George McCall addressed the amount that one maroon community contributed to its associated Seminole mikko in this description: "They are chiefly runaway slaves from Georgia, who have put themselves under the protection of Micanopy, or some other chief, whom they call master; and to whom, for this consideration, they render a tribute of one-third of the produce of the land, and one-third of the horses, cattle and fowls they may raise. Otherwise they are free to go and come at pleasure."[7] Again, McCall's comments referred specifically to Pilaklikaha.

The observations of Dexter, Thompson, and McCall regarding the size of the typical annual tribute that individual slaves and maroon communities provided Seminole mikkos demand further attention. Anthropologist Richard Sattler rightly cautions against underestimating the economic significance of slaves to their Seminole owners:

> These people also provided labor to till the fields and tend the cattle of their masters (both of which were episodic endeavors, rather than continuous) along with corvee from within the town. This allowed the owners, primarily chiefs and their families, to produce far more than others. The 10 bushels of corn is also generally sufficient to support one person for a year. Multiply that by a few hundred slaves and tributaries and you have a significant source of wealth for the chiefly families.[8]

According to Sattler, between 1700 and 1783, in the two primary Seminole settlement areas of Apalachee and Alachua, Native cultivation could produce between twenty and forty bushels of corn per acre.[9] To raise the ten bushels of corn Thompson suggested, therefore, individual slaves would have needed to cultivate between one-fourth and one-half acre to fulfill their annual tribute to a Seminole owner. In 1774, Bartram indicated that Seminoles planted as much as twenty acres per household in their town fields.[10] Documentation from the period 1812–18 on the maroon communities in Alachua and on the Suwannee suggests that they planted acreages of similar size. Even if only half the land were planted with corn, that could result in a harvest of two hundred to four hundred bushels of corn per household, representing a sizable surplus in normal years. At least until the disruptions and relocations caused by the patriots' scheme to annex East Florida, the destruction of the Negro Fort, the First Seminole War, Spain's transfer of Florida to the United States, and the Kawita raid, an obligation of ten bushels per year usually would not have caused maroons hardship. Meanwhile, farther east, at his Saint John's River plantations, Zephaniah Kingsley noted that many of his slaves were able to produce surpluses of twenty bushels of corn each year for sale.[11]

From the documentation available, it emerges that maroon communities in Florida proved more than capable of producing large agricultural surpluses for Seminole mikkos, and for themselves as well. In 1823, despite the recent upheavals, Pilaklikaha's population of 160 had 120 acres planted with corn, rice, and peanuts. According to Dexter, corn planted there would yield forty bushels to the acre, and "the Rice, indeed everything planted here, is equal to any I have seen in Florida."[12] If the maroons planted two-thirds of their acreage with corn, the yield would be 3,200 bushels. Half of that would be needed to feed the community, leaving a surplus of 1,600 bushels per annum. Based on McCall's estimated 33 percent obligation, such a harvest would equate to an annual tribute to Mikkoanapa of more than 1,000 bushels, leaving 600 as surplus for the maroons. According to McCall, the maroons also would contribute one-third of their other crops and a further third of their extensive herds of cattle and horses and flocks of chickens to Mikkoanapa. Using Dexter's 50 percent tribute, the Pilaklikaha maroons would contribute 1,600 bushels of corn that year to the mikko, leaving them with no surplus. Even after some distribution for the public good, Mikkoanapa still would have had huge crop surpluses in his granary for trade or sale.

In a compelling essay, archaeologist Brent Weisman supports this argument by proposing that "the incorporation of the so-called Black Seminoles into the Seminole agricultural system after the 1790s underpinned the Seminole contribution to the colonial economy through the creation of an agricultural surplus." By increasing the amount of tribute they received from growing numbers of runaways, captives, and slaves, Seminole slave owners were able to produce substantial and diversified agricultural surpluses for trade or sale. As evidence, Weisman points to the large number of European trade goods archaeologists have discovered in Florida Indian towns "that attest to the relative wealth of the former Seminole occupants." Moreover, consumer goods, such as an imported European tea set found at Payne's town, were not strictly utilitarian but luxury items meant to indicate the mikko's wealth and prestige. Ceramics such as those would have been acquired through purchase rather than barter, suggesting a nascent cash economy among the Seminole slave-owning elite. That became possible only through "the development of a new set of obligatory relationships with the Black Seminoles, who lived apart in their own villages but were bound to individual Seminoles through tribute."[13] This helps explain why Seminole mikkos became so concerned with acquiring and retaining African slaves and tributaries.

General Edmund Gaines described the maroons as the Seminoles' "vassals and allies."[14] Porter took that a step further when he described the relationship as "primitive democratic feudalism."[15] The system the Seminoles employed indeed appears to have included borrowings from Spain and to have resembled European vassalage, yet so did the earlier system of tributary status relationships operating among the Indians themselves. The obligation of the maroon communities was not much different from that of Indian towns having a tributary status. Relations between Seminoles and maroons also had Indian and African roots, and they developed largely in response to European and American chattel slavery. What emerged was a Native American institution, practiced by Indians and affecting immigrant Africans. The primary context for their relationship was not European vassalage but indigenous economic and social systems and circum-Caribbean marronage on North American soil.

Although some slaves resided in Indian towns, Seminoles also allowed Africans to live apart in settlements headed by their own principal men and to enjoy most of the products of their labor. Simmons wrote: "The Negroes dwell in towns apart from the Indians, and they are the finest looking people I have ever seen," while Thompson stated, "They live in villages separate, and, in many cases, remote from their owners, [enjoying] equal liberty with their owners." And the noted Florida author John Lee Williams wrote in 1837, "The Seminole negroes, for the most part, live separately from their masters, and manage their stocks and crops as they please, giving such a share of the produce to their masters as they like."[16] The term "Seminole Negroes" became prominent in the writings of white observers during the mid- to late 1830s and contributed to outside perceptions that the maroons constituted a group separate from the Seminole Indians or from other blacks.[17] Clearly, and for a long time before that, the maroons also perceived of themselves as an independent group.

Simmons reported that, like the Indians, the maroons practiced a system of communal agriculture.[18] If, as sources suggest, maroons engaged in agricultural practices similar to those of Seminoles in Florida, they cultivated both small individual garden plots near their cabins and large communal "town fields" at a distance from their settlements. In the gardens, the women and children grew fruit and vegetables for the household's consumption, but the bulk of the maroons' crops were raised in their large town fields, which were separate from those of the Indians. Unlike individual gardens, the entire settlement cultivated town fields in common. Within the larger field, every family would have a plot marked off and at harvest time would gather its own crops. Each then would contribute a portion of its harvest to the large communal granary in the center of the town field. From that, the community would provide its annual tribute to the mikko. Like the Seminoles, the maroons divided work by gender. At Pilaklikaha, Dexter observed, "most of the labor is performed by the Women, the men are indulged, in following the habits of their owners, and pass most of their time in idleness, occasionally hunting."[19]

On April 25, 1837, Ensel, a black guide and interpreter, led American forces to a communal town field of maroons associated with Sitarkey. The field was situated at the center of Boggy Island, on the southeast banks of the Withlacoochee River. Asin Yahola's (Osceola's; Powel's) abandoned town was north of the river about a mile away. The maroons had chosen that location carefully. The Boggy Island interior was accessible only by crossing a muddy expanse by way of a narrow trail, and reaching the trailhead required a difficult canoe ride up shallow Withlacoochee creeks. The maroons marked the landing place with a "blazed Cypress tree." Diarist Lieutenant Henry Prince observed: "This island is accessible only by its northern extremity. It is a hiding place but little known even among the Indians. There is a field in the interior—here is where the negroes

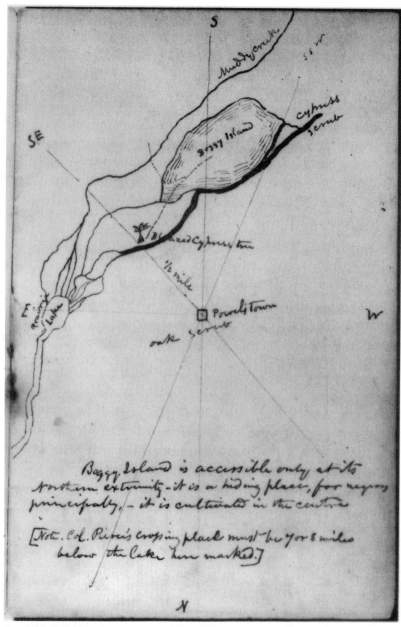

Asin Yahola's (Powel's) town and Boggy Island—"a hiding place for Negroes" with "blazed Cypress tree" entry. Sketch map by Lieutenant Henry Prince, April 1837. (P. K. Yonge Library of Florida History, University of Florida)

mostly concealed themselves in time of war." Prince also noted that the field was "cultivated."[20] Communal landholding had African as well as Indian precedents, and similar practices have been found among Gullahs in the Sea Islands of Georgia and South Carolina.

Under such favorable conditions, the maroons prospered, as witnessed by the amount of crops and livestock found at the community at Alachua in 1813. A number of the Seminole maroons became quite wealthy. Thompson stated, "Many of these slaves had stocks of horses, cows and hogs with which the Indian owner never assumes the right to intermeddle." McCall completed the picture. At Pilaklikaha, he wrote, "we found these negroes in possession of large fields of the finest land, producing large crops of corn, beans, melons, pumpkins, and other esculent vegetables. [I] saw, while riding along the borders of the ponds, fine rice growing, and in the village large corn-cribs were filled, while the houses were larger and more comfortable than those of the Indians themselves." They also owned guns for defense and for hunting, and could travel at will.[21] There can be little doubt that the Seminole maroons were able to control most aspects of their daily lives.

Africans also proved to be of great value to Seminoles in both military and diplomatic matters. Independent and formidable warriors, if need be, they would defend their liberty to the last. Army surgeon Jacob Motte noted, "They had none of the servility of our northern blacks."[22] They also were familiar with the ways and the languages of whites and were useful to the Indians in formulating military tactics and during negotiations. As Florida came under the American flag, Seminoles used maroons more and more as interpreters and intermediaries. By 1822, for example, Whan (Juan), a Spanish black, had emerged as a leading interpreter. He had served Payne in that capacity, and Simmons stated that the Indians placed "the utmost confidence in him, when making use of his services, in their dealings with the whites."[23] Dexter noted that the maroons could "speak English as well as Indian," leading them to "possess considerable influence with their masters."[24] In such ways, some of the maroons obtained positions of considerable power and authority among the Seminoles.

White observers focused on the Seminoles' typical unwillingness to sell their slaves to whites or other Indians, attributing this as resulting from affection. Simmons observed, "Though hunger and want be stronger than even the *sacra funes auri,* the greatest pressure of these evils, never occasions them to impose onerous labours on the Negroes, or to dispose of them, though tempted by high offers, if the latter are unwilling to be sold." Again, others supported that notion, Thompson adding, "[An] Indian would almost as soon sell his child as his slave, except when under the influence of intoxicating liquors. The almost affection of the Indian for his slave, the slave's fear of being placed in a worse condition, and the influence which the negroes have over the Indians, have all been made to subserve the views of the government." Potter wrote in 1836:

> [These] Indians have always evinced great reluctance to parting with slaves: Indeed, the Indian loves his negro as much as one of his own children, and the sternest necessity alone would drive him to the parting. [The] negro is also much more provident and ambitious than his master, and the peculiar localities of the country eminently facilitate him in furnishing the Indian with rum and tobacco, which give him a controlling influence over the latter.

Williams went even further, suggesting, "There exists a law among the Seminoles, forbidding individuals from selling their negroes to white people; and any attempt to evade that law, has always raised great commotion among them."[25]

Those last observations of Thompson, Potter, and Williams should be read with caution. They probably related to individual instances of kinship slavery rather than general practice. Whites, shocked when they observed the situation of some of the maroons, became prone to speculation and exaggeration. Dexter was familiar with Simmons's *Notices of East Florida*. As the Seminole agent, Wiley Thompson also likely had read Simmons, and Potter's language suggests that he was familiar with Thompson's observations. Through repetition, the notion that "affection" was a determinant in the development of Seminole-black relations became the conventional wisdom. But evidence suggests that only a small number of Seminole leaders and their descendants owned, acted as guardians toward, or exercised tributary rights over most of the maroons, and that most wanted to retain that relationship to maintain their status and growing wealth.

It was not so much a "law," as Williams suggested, but indigenous practice that worked against Seminole owners selling slaves to outsiders. And while mikkos could bequeath tributary rights, tributary allies also should not be sold. That would become much more apparent after Removal. Moreover, after the First Seminole War, some Indian owners became more aware of the value of their property, and the risky nature of their investment, and became more amenable to parting with their slaves. Again, some Seminoles' willingness to sell slaves would become more pronounced and better documented in the Indian Territory.

The maroons certainly adopted elements of Seminole culture. They resided in cabins of split logs lashed to upright cypress posts and thatched with palm leaves, as did the Indians. They also borrowed from Seminole foodways and dressed in Southeastern Indian fashion. Either the maroons made pottery similar to Seminole ceramics, or they might have traded for it.[26] Being able to own firearms and horses, work the land as a group, and keep most of the crops they grew and the livestock they raised differentiated the Seminole maroons from other Africans and African Americans in the South and Southeast and contributed greatly to their emerging identity as a people.

Africans also might have influenced Seminole cultural expressions in Florida. Art historian Thomas Larose argues, "The Seminoles could have adopted and adapted African culture as easily as the former slaves had adopted theirs."[27] Scholars have suggested, for example, that Seminole beaded shoulder bags, or bandoleers, from the pre-Removal period sometimes bore irregular patterns, asymmetrical compositions, and filled-in designs more typical of African than American Indian or European beadwork.[28] The diamond motifs in Seminole beadwork are similar to those in Kongo culture. But African art historian Babatunde Lawal has suggested that "the Yoruba constituted a sizeable part of the slave population in Florida [and] a good majority of the symbols, colors, styles, and techniques associated with the changes in Seminole beadwork can easily be matched with Yoruba beadwork."[29] Musicologist Frances Densmore, while conducting fieldwork among the Florida Seminoles in the 1930s, noted several African influences in Seminole music, including use of the "labial m" and improvisation of "changes of a melody in its repetitions." Densmore also recorded Seminole songs about blacks, notably "My Old Slaves," which she believed predated the Second Seminole War.[30]

Yet most Africans associated with Seminoles never became members of Indian society. Only a few maroon leaders seem to have been adopted into Indian clans or bands, the mainstays of Seminole civilization. Those two institutions determined most facets of a Seminole's existence, including family relations, marital partners, political allegiance, leadership prospects, inheritance rights, and social activities. To be excluded from clans and bands meant not being included in Indian society. George Stiggins, the son of a Virginia trader and a Natchez woman, wrote of the Creeks in the 1830s: "The strongest link in their political and social standing as a nation is in their clanship or families." All Creeks were "linked, harmonized, and consolidated as one large connected family."[31] The same could be said for the Seminoles. As Saunt has argued, for Southeastern Indians, generally, "these kin relations formed a significant part of a person's identity. Deer people identified themselves not as Creeks, but as Deer people."[32] To Deer people, Africans were not Deer people. In the early twenty-first century, Florida Seminole Betty Mae Tiger Jumper and Oklahoma Seminole Susan Miller restated the significance of blacks' not being included in Indian clans.[33] Exclusion meant that the maroons were considered outsiders, and not a part of the Seminole cosmos.

Relatively little is known about maroon society prior to Removal, but Africanisms appear to have been prevalent. Africanist Tolagbe Ogunleye has looked for clues in Simmons's *Notices of East Florida* and other contemporary accounts. Although he clearly saw that cultural practices differentiated the maroons from Seminoles, Simmons, like other white observers both before and after Removal, was not an expert on Africa and did not recognize or understand many of the customs he reported. Interpreting Simmons's and others' observations, Ogunleye discerns among the maroons Africanisms such as shrines and altars built to African gods and ancestors, call and response forms of worship, ring shouts, counterclockwise dancing and singing, child-naming ceremonies, personal and place naming practices, Ebonics as a first language, methods of preparing foods like cassava, and pictorial writing systems. Ogunleye suggests that the maroons created a *dobale,* a society that combined and synthesized aspects of the many African cultures represented among their constituents.[34] To their rich *dobale,* however, the maroons also added borrowings from Europeans, white Americans, and American Indians.

Scholarship covering the post-Removal period helps cast light on pre-Removal maroon society. Likely, their kinship system was not based on the matrilineal clan, and thus it differed fundamentally from that of the Seminoles. After Removal, maroon society was organized around intragroup marriages, the consanguineal household, and endogamous residential patterns. Those social arrangements probably originated in Florida. The

maroons did share with the Seminoles another significant domestic organizational pattern. Some prominent leaders were polygynous, fathering
children by different women they maintained in separate households.
That practice became pronounced among the Seminole freedmen in the
Indian Territory after the Civil War, but again likely originated in Florida.
Those patterns led to complex kinship ties linking a series of large extended families within the maroon community. Moreover, the maroons'
first language was not Hitchiti or Creek but an English-based Creole.
Their religious and naming practices, deriving from Africa and their
experience on southern plantations, also differed completely from those
of the Seminoles. The maroons' unique language, society, and culture gave
rise to a sense of ethnic and cultural distinctiveness and sustained the
growth of a strong group identity. While certain aspects of the maroons'
and Seminoles' daily lives were similar, many others were not. The differences formed the bases of the maroons' ethnicity and defined them as a
people.[35]

Some intermarriage between maroons and Seminoles took place in
Florida. Mixed marriages tended to include Indians or maroons with
high profiles.[36] A few others came to light during the Second Seminole
War, causing comment from curious whites. But Seminole-black intermarriage never was widespread, either before or after Removal. Because
of the Seminoles' matrilineal descent system, offspring of Indian men and
maroon women would be born outside of Seminole society. Nor did
adoption into Seminole clans and bands always accompany intermarriage, especially if the maroon participant was female. The Seminoles did
adopt a small number of leading African males into their clans and bands.
In 1837, for example, Abraham, leader of the Alachua maroons and the
interpreter and adviser of Principal Chief Mikkoanapa, signed a letter
with his Seminole busk name "Souanaffe Tustenuggee" (Tastanaki).[37]
John Kibbetts, who later became a maroon leader in Mexico and Texas,
also used the busk name "Sittertastonacky" (Chitto Tastanaki; Snake
Warrior) on occasion. However, those appear to have been the exceptions that proved the rule that adoption was uncommon.

White travelers and government agents tended to note the similarities
between maroons and Seminoles and draw comparisons with the situation of slaves in the South, with which they were more familiar. Those
observers either overlooked or minimized the differences between the
two groups. When left to their own devices, Indians and maroons pre-

ferred separation to integration. They interacted substantially only during military campaigns, and then they fought in separate companies under their own leaders.

Although he was referring to the immediate post-Removal period and his language embodies Victorian sensibilities, Giddings came closest among contemporary white observers to capturing the underlying dynamic shaping the relationship:

> [Most] of the descendants of the pioneers who fled from South Carolina and Georgia maintained their identity of character, living by themselves and maintaining the purity of the African race. [They] settled in separate villages, and the Seminole Indians appeared generally to coincide with the Exiles in the propriety of each maintaining their distinctive character.[38]

Despite the proximity of their settlements, many facets of the lifestyles of residents of maroon and Seminole communities were quite different. When not facing external threats, Africans and Seminoles chose to live apart and maintain their own economic, social, and political arrangements. The maroon townships were accommodated fairly easily within the Seminole Confederacy, but Seminoles did not consider Africans to be Indian. Nor did the maroons consider themselves Seminole.

In 1821, Captain John Bell produced a list of thirty-five towns in the Seminole Confederacy that included four maroon communities: Mulatto Girl's town, south of Cuskowilla Lake; Buckra Woman's town, near Long Swamp east of Big Hammock; "Payne's negro settlements in Alachua" ("these are slaves belonging to the Seminoles, in all about three hundred"); and a town of Mikkoanapa's blacks at Pilaklikaha, about six miles south of the mikko's Alachua Indian settlement at Okihamki.[39] The year after Bell produced his list, an African named Cudjo (Cudjoe) headed the most prominent of the deceased Payne's remaining black settlements in Alachua, at Big Swamp.[40]

There were no female mikkos at that time, and Seminoles did not name Indian bands or towns after women. As Sattler explains, "Women were expressly excluded from participation in political affairs. They held no exclusive offices and were eligible for none of those held by males."[41] Mulatto Girl's town, south of Alachua, and Buckra Woman's town, on the southern Withlacoochee River, were named after the individuals to whom the inhabitants paid tribute. It did not mean that the named individuals lived in the settlements. Through matrilineal descent of property and tributary rights, Seminole women such as Buckra Woman and Mulatto Girl came to own, or serve as guardians over, many slaves and obligations of tributary allies. That would become even more important to Seminole-black relations after Removal.

"Buckra" clearly derived from the Ibo expression meaning "master," or a person of predominantly white rather than African descent, typically used by southern blacks in a disparaging way. Historian Canter Brown has suggested that Buckra Woman was a sister of Payne and Hothli Hopoya and the mother of Holata Mikko.[42] But more likely, Holata Mikko was the grandnephew, not the nephew, of Hothli Hopoya and Payne. If Buckra Woman was Holata Mikko's mother, she likely was a sister of Mikkoanapa and Sitarkey.[43] Brown and historian Larry Rivers have suggested that, by 1823, Buckra Woman had transferred her extensive cattle operations and her black town farther south to a new location on a stream that flowed westward into Pease Creek, about three miles south of Fort Meade. That stream retains the name "Bowlegs Creek." Buckra Woman called the town Tobasa or Wahoo.[44]

The maroons would have had their own names for their settlements. A community would have had a Seminole place-name, like Pilaklikaha (Opilaklikaha; Scattered Swamps or Ponds), but they also might have referred to it by a leader's name, as in Abraham's town. Maroons also might have identified their communities by English place-names, such as Big Swamp or Boggy Island. After Removal, during the antebellum period, Seminole maroon towns in the Indian Territory were known both by place—such as on the Deep Fork and at Wewoka—and by their leader, as in settlements named after Ben, Charles, Cudjo, Juan, Noblio (Noble), and Tom.[45] From the end of the Civil War to Oklahoma statehood, the Seminole maroon communities in the Indian Territory retained their association with place—Little River and Turkey Creek, for example—but mostly they came to be known by the leading male in the community, as in Bruner Town, Noble Town, Scipio, and Thomas Town. Seminole freedman bands also came to be named after their male leaders.

At least three other Florida maroon communities should be added to the four Bell listed. By 1820, and probably before then, Africans associated with Sitarkey established a black town within the isolated but fertile

Cove of the Withlacoochee River at Boggy (now Kettle) Island. Prince documented the access to the communal field of that settlement in April 1837. There the maroons cultivated corn, rice, beans, squash, and other crops and raised horses, cattle, hogs, and other livestock. They also grew a substantial stand of sugarcane.[46] In 1822, Simmons also visited a town of Kapichee Mikko's blacks situated thirty miles to the west of Cudjo's town in the Big Swamp.[47] Pompey probably headed the community. Bell likely mistook that Mikasuki town for one of Payne's former tributaries. Another settlement of 200 to 300 maroons was associated with Emathla, the father of Kowakochi (Coacoochee; Wild Cat). In 1823, Emathla's town was situated on the west side of the Saint John's River, thirty-five miles from Volusia. Sensing that hostilities were imminent in 1835, Emathla moved his band and its maroon associates to a more strategic location at Tohopikalika, the largest island in Lake Apopka. That, apparently, was an older settlement site. In 1823, Dexter reported 120 Indians and 8 blacks to be living there under the leadership of a "half breed" named Bradley. By the time Emathla and his supporters moved to the island, John Caesar led the Tohopikalika maroons.[48]

Besides the inhabitants of maroon communities, other Africans associated with Seminoles resided in Indian towns. In 1826, for example, John Horse was living in the town of his owner, Charles Cavallo, on Lake Thonotosassa twelve miles from Fort Brooke, near Tampa Bay. Three years earlier, Dexter had listed Cavallo's town as having 70 Indian and 10 black residents. Horse's father is believed to have been of American Indian and Spanish admixture, and his mother of African and American Indian descent. Charles Cavallo also might have owned Horse's mother and might have been his father. John Horse would have been around fifteen years of age in the mid-1820s and likely lived with his mother. Within a few years, however, Horse would head a maroon community on the Oklawaha River.[49]

In his 1823 *Observations on the Seminole Indians,* Dexter listed eighteen Seminole towns and one maroon town, together with their leaders and populations. He listed 300 "scattered Indians" and 80 "refugee Negroes" separately. Dexter's list contained a total of 430 "Negroes." Of the nineteen towns, only Pilaklikaha's population of 160 did not include any Indians, while eight Indian towns contained no blacks. The other ten included both Seminoles and blacks. In seven of those ten, the black population totaled 10 or fewer. According to Dexter, 150 other blacks were associated with the communities of Apilchopko, Apilchapcoche, and Tolokchopco. The Indian populations of those three communities totaled only 165; indeed, at Apilchapcoche, blacks outnumbered Seminoles by 70 to 40.[50] Their numbers suggest that, as at Pilaklikaha, the blacks in those three towns were living apart from the Indians in separate settlements.

Sattler has identified "at least three" maroon communities and their leaders during the early stages of the Second Seminole War. Pompey headed a settlement at Panosufkee Swamp, near the Wahoo Swamp on the Withlacoochee River that was associated with the Mikasuki; Abraham was the leader of the Alachua maroons at Pilaklikaha; and John Horse led the Oklawaha maroon settlements near the headwaters of the Oklawaha River.[51] Besides Abraham, July and August also were leaders at Pilaklikaha.[52] Even after its destruction, the town's residents remained associated with Mikkoanapa, both before and after Removal. Also during the Second Seminole War, John Horse and the Oklawaha maroons became associated with Kowakochi and his emergent Oklawaha band, a relationship that grew in importance after Removal.[53]

To Sattler's list should be added two other communities: the Tohopikalika maroons at Lake Apopka, led by John Caesar and associated with Emathla; and the Boggy Island maroons on the Withlacoochee, associated with Sitarkey. Asin Yahola apparently developed ties to the Boggy Island maroons, as "Powel's town" was situated just a mile from their communal field. His support among the maroons was strong. Fifty-two of Asin Yahola's fifty-five followers taken prisoner by the American forces after a skirmish in January 1837 were black.[54] Besides the two other isolated Indian and black settlements near Charlotte Harbor that Winslett reported in 1833, those constitute the only documented maroon communities remaining at the onset of the Second Seminole War. The Charlotte Harbor and Pease Creek groups might have fled to the Bahamas or to Cuba. Likely, most of the remaining maroons in Florida consolidated into larger groups as conflict threatened and then war broke out.

Sattler also suggests: "In addition to these Maroons, two other groups of blacks lived among the Seminoles. These consisted of free black members of Indian bands and slaves belonging to the Indians. The latter group, acquired through purchase or capture, lived either in the communities of their owners or with the Maroons. The free blacks lived among the Indians as regular members of the Indian bands."[55]

Asseola, a Seminole leader (Asin Yahola). Lithograph after Charles Bird King, published ca. 1836–44. (From McKenney and Hall, *The Indian Tribes of North America*)

It seems likely that, in the late eighteenth and early nineteenth centuries, many runaways, captives, and newly acquired African slaves would have begun their association with Seminoles by residing in an Indian town. Once their society had grown sufficiently large in relation to that of the neighboring Seminoles, Africans would form a separate settlement. Later, when maroon communities had become established, runaways, captives, and most newly acquired slaves probably would have made their way directly to those locations. Africans who continued to live in Seminole towns likely did so because they were too few to form a separate community, were too far removed from an existing maroon settlement, or had Indian family members. As Sattler succinctly concludes, despite the complexities surrounding their various statuses, between 1818 and 1843, "the situation of the Seminole Negroes remained stable. All enjoyed considerable freedom and most had complete autonomy."[56]

The maroon communities, and even some families within them, included individuals occupying slave, tributary ally, and free nontributary status. A slave living in a maroon community might also retain an individual obligation to an Indian owner.[57] Africans living in Indian towns appear to have enjoyed no less independence than the maroons, but free blacks living as members of Seminole bands seem to have been few and far between.

Since it appeared, Sattler has elaborated upon some of the points he made in his groundbreaking 1987 dissertation. On how it was decided whether Africans lived in Indian towns or maroon communities, he suggests that practice among the Seminoles might have differed, with Mikasukis and Alachuas favoring settlement apart and Apalachicolas preferring that slaves lived in Indian settlements. Sattler also suggests that much of the confusion arising over the various classifications of Africans associated with Seminoles derives from contemporary American observers' insistence that most or all "Seminole Negroes" were slaves. Indeed, given that most of their obligations were similar, the difference between a slave and a tributary ally in Seminole society was more quantitative than qualitative. Whites did not appreciate the difference, yet references from the 1820s and 1830s indicate that Seminoles distinguished between the two, referring to some of their African associates as slaves and others as free (but probably tributary):

[The] difference between the categories is in the nature of the rights owned in them. For allies these were tributary rights, which appear to be partible and alienable (mikkos transferred them to close relatives). In the case of slaves, these were property rights of ownership and individuals could be bought or sold, given away, or otherwise disposed of. We have references to such transfers in the early 19th century. This is similar to the patterns in a number of non-Western slave systems in Asia and Africa.

In other words, Seminoles could inherit and bequeath slaves as individuals but only the rights to obligations of tributary allies. Seminole owners could sell slaves but not tributaries. This was an important distinction that whites missed but the maroons clearly understood. It would assume great importance during and after Removal.

Sattler suggests that indigenous Seminole and Creek servitude most closely resembled West African forms of slavery, in particular that practiced by the Hausa: "[Slaves] often owned property, maintained separate villages, held offices in the chiefly bureaucracy, and owed only stipulated forms of tribute to their masters." Again, the European-American experience that informed most of the surviving contemporary documentation is found inadequate. Sattler now argues that the comparative context for analyzing Seminole-maroon relations must be expanded even beyond indigenous North America and the circum-Caribbean to include Africa and Asia.[58]

After the American annexation, relations between Seminoles and the maroons remaining in Florida became strained. The Indians might have blamed the presence of blacks among them for the First Seminole War. After all, Jackson's incursions into Florida proved to be a thinly disguised slave-hunting expedition. Florida's becoming an American territory led to an immediate infusion of white settlers demanding Seminole territory. The Kawita raid also damaged Seminole-maroon relations. Seeing the risks involved in owning blacks, some Seminoles became more inclined to sell Africans, as Indians disposed of thirty of the sixty-six slaves whose sales were recorded in Saint Augustine in 1821.[59] Then, under the terms of the Treaty of Moultrie Creek, September 18, 1823, the Seminoles agreed to prevent more runaways from entering their settlements and to return those already living among them. By agreeing to return runaways, the Seminoles likely appeared to the maroons to be in cahoots with speculators and kidnappers.

After Moultrie Creek, Tacosa Emathla (John Hicks), who had replaced the deceased Kapichee Mikko as the Mikasuki mikko, sounded willing to abide by the treaty stipulations that the Indians not harbor runaways. During an 1826 delegation to Washington, Tacosa Emathla suggested, "The laws of our nation are strong and oblige a man having the property of another in his possession to give it up to the right owner."[60] Evidence suggests that such statements were mere rhetoric aimed at appeasing whites and that Mikasuki and other Seminole mikkos never intended to return runaways to their former owners. Nevertheless, such talk of blacks constituting "property" and Indians abiding by rights of ownership surely only added to the suspicions and distrust felt by the maroons.

Under the terms of the Treaty of Moultrie Creek, the Seminoles agreed to remove from their fertile lands in northern Florida to a large interior reservation farther south. Their new lands stretched from the north shore of Lake Okeechobee nearly as far north as present-day Gainesville. The reservation was situated entirely inland with no access to the coasts, because the Americans feared Seminole and maroon dealings with the Bahamas and Cuba. Although a few Seminole towns were already situated within these new lands, most of their settlements were outside it in areas they ceded to the United States. Much of this prospective five-million-acre reservation was swampland, inundated and impossible to cultivate. Six influential leaders signed the unfavorable treaty because of bribes and promises that they could remain on their lands to the north of the new reservation. The signatories included the Apalachicolas Yawohli (John Blount), Ikonchatta Mikko, and Waka Puchasi and the Apalachee Speaker of the Seminole Council, Heniha Emathla. An Indian agent at that time described Waka Puchasi—better known to whites as Mulatto King—as "half negro and Indian."[61]

Although the influential Heniha Emathla signed the treaty, he rejected the schools it provided for the Seminoles: "We wish our children to remain as the Great Spirit made them, and as our fathers are, Indians. [If] you establish a school, and teach our people the knowledge of the white people, they will cease to be Indians." Heniha Emathla explained his reasoning. After making the world, the Maker of Life made three attempts at creating humans, resulting in a white man, a red (Indian) man, and a black man. The Maker of Life found the white man pale and weak, and only tolerated him. The Indian was the favorite, but the black was told, "I do not like you. You may stand aside." The black was provided

Nea-Math-La, a Seminole chief (Heniha Emathla). Lithograph after Charles Bird King, published ca. 1836–44. (From McKenney and Hall, *The Indian Tribes of North America*)

with "axes and hoes, with buckets to carry water in, and long whips for driving oxen, which meant that the negro must work for both the red and the white man, and it has been so ever since."[62]

Such aversion to white acculturation became a strong and recurring theme in Seminole Indian history. Historian Theda Perdue has suggested that "other Southeastern peoples had similar explanations for the three races: they had separate origins and purposes. These accounts originated after Europeans and Africans arrived in the Americas and reflected colonial race relations. Nevertheless, they expressed how many nineteenth-century Native southerners viewed their role in the world and explained why they were reluctant to jeopardize their place as the Great Spirit's favorite."[63] Saunt suggests that there were African precedents for Heniha Emathla's story that date back to 1698, and that some folklorists believe that cultural convergence between Africans and Indians in the Southeast gave rise to accounts of separate origins.[64] Miller concludes that this story illustrates that at least some Seminoles believed in a racial hierarchy.[65] Within that hierarchy, Indians were on top, whites were in the middle, and blacks were on the bottom.

The terms of the Treaty of Moultrie Creek were not implemented effectively. Many Seminoles did not consider themselves obligated to the treaty and stayed where they were. Local American settlers also coveted some of the Seminoles' new lands and their slaves, whom they considered runaways. The American government was not able to demarcate the reservation and was unable to protect Seminoles living within its confines from local settlers. By 1826, however, most of the Seminoles and maroons were living within their new reservation, although they continued to search for food outside its boundaries. Over the next few years, many maroons and Seminoles became semi-transient, surviving by stealing cattle from settlers to the north.[66] Given that most Seminoles lacked sufficient resources to support themselves during the remainder of the 1820s, the tributes of slaves and maroon communities likely became more important to the mikkos. The activities of slave catchers in the area also increased, and they captured a number of blacks. The 1820s proved to be a difficult decade for both the Seminoles and the maroons, and their relationship suffered accordingly.

Africans and Indians soon became involved in a massive conflict with the United States over the proposed Removal of the Seminoles to the Indian Territory. On May 28, 1830, Congress passed the Indian Removal Act. Anxious to appease Florida settlers, who complained of Indian and maroon depredations, and southern planters concerned over the loss of runaways, the Jackson administration sought an immediate Removal treaty with the Seminoles. Disenchanted with their new reservation, and suffering considerable hardships following the drought of 1831, Seminoles seemed ready to listen to offers of a tract of their own in the West, far away from white encroachment.

Seminole leaders signed a provisional Removal treaty at Payne's Landing on May 9, 1832. The treaty stipulated that their Removal was contingent upon the tribe's approval of a selected site. The Seminoles sent a delegation of seven to explore the proposed area in the Indian Territory, accompanied by the maroon leaders and interpreters Abraham and Cudjo. On March 28, 1833, at Fort Gibson, Indian Territory, the delegates signed an agreement in the name of all the Seminoles, saying that they were satisfied with the land and willing to remove. Under the terms of the two treaties, the Seminoles agreed to settle among the slaveholding Creeks in the West and become a constituent part of that tribe.[67] That stipulation would become a bone of contention and complicate both Seminole relations with the maroons and the groups' joint resettlement in the Indian Territory for more than two decades.

In 1832, Yawohli, Asi Hacho (Davy Elliot), and some of the other leaders of bands on the Apalachicola agreed to remove to Texas. An 1833 census of the Apalachicolas listed nine blacks in Yawohli's town: one slave owned by Toney Hadjo and eight by Yawohli. In Waka Puchasi's town, there were five: one slave he owned and four free blacks, the family of Rose Sena Factor. In Ikonchatta Mikko's town were the mikko's twenty-four slaves. Yawohli's and Asi Hacho's bands emigrated in 1834, leaving around 600 Indians and the remaining blacks on the Apalachicola.

Americans referred to Seminoles who cooperated with the Removal program as "friendly Indians." The majority derived from the Apalachee region and the Apalachicola groups, although most of the former were "hostile" and favored war. In late September 1835, a party of Seminoles who were opposed to emigration executed the Apalachee Charley Emathla, leader of the Totolosi, as he was preparing to depart Florida voluntarily. Nevertheless, in 1836, bands of "friendly" Apalachees emigrated to the Indian Territory. Apalachicolas under John Walker and Ikonchatta Mikko, meanwhile, took up arms against "hostile" Seminoles in late 1835 and also were listed by Americans in the "friendly" category. Nevertheless, neighboring whites stole most of Ikonchatta Mikko's slaves. Ikonchatta Mikko and John Walker finally removed to the Indian Territory with their few remaining blacks in October 1838.[68]

Most of the Seminole bands repudiated the 1833 Treaty of Fort Gibson. They believed that their delegates had been bribed and that the maroon interpreters had misrepresented the wishes of the Indians while secretly pursuing their own agenda. Nevertheless, U.S. officials ordered the Seminoles to prepare to remove within the three years provided by the treaty. Instead, the maroons and Seminoles prepared to engage the United States over their proposed Removal to the Indian Territory. American attempts to extend the southeastern frontier contributed to Seminole maroon ethnogenesis by fostering independent group activities, including diplomatic initiatives. Fearing for their safety, freedom, and continued existence as a people, the maroons vehemently opposed Removal and helped strengthen Seminole resolve to remain in Florida. Seminoles also began to fear for their slave property and tributary rights, if they settled among Creeks in the West. The maroons were afraid that, under the Creeks, they would be returned to their former owners or reenslaved, and they exerted considerable influence on the Seminoles to oppose emigration.

In January 1834, Thompson observed that one of the major causes of Seminole hostility to Removal was "the influence which it is said the negroes, the very slaves in the nation, have over the Indians." Governor DuVal concurred, noting, "The slaves belonging to the Indians have a controlling influence over their masters, and are utterly opposed to any change of residence." In March 1835, General Richard Call made the following recommendation to President Jackson: "The negroes have a great influence among the Indians [and] are violently opposed to leaving the country. If the Indians are permitted to convert them into specie, one great obstacle in the way of removal may be overcome." The opposition of the maroons paved the way for the onset of the Second Seminole War.[69]

When Thompson called the Seminole mikkos together on October 21, 1834, they challenged the validity of both the treaties of Payne's Landing and Fort Gibson, charging the government with trickery. After that, diplomatic relations deteriorated rapidly. Agitation from white settlers to seize the maroons increased during the spring of 1835. In an attempt to force him to adhere to the terms stipulated at Payne's Landing, Thompson then imprisoned Asin Yahola. Maroon and Indian depredations escalated, culminating in Emathla's and John Caesar's raids on the Saint John's River plantations the two days after Christmas.

On December 28, 1835, the Second Seminole War officially began. At Fort King, Abayaca (Arpeika; Sam Jones), a Seminole medicine man and prophet, assassinated Thompson. Meanwhile, fifty miles away, north of the Withlacoochee River near the Wahoo Swamp, the black guide Louis Pachecho led a relief column under Major Francis Dade into an ambush of Africans and Seminoles. During the so-called Dade Massacre, the allies annihilated the infantry unit, killing Dade and ninety-five of his command.[70] Survivor Ransom Clark recounted that after the Indians withdrew,

> forty or fifty negroes, on horseback, galloped up and alighted, tying their beasts, and commenced, with horrid shouts and yells, the butchering of the wounded, together with an indiscriminate plunder, stripping the bodies of the dead of clothes, watches and money, and splitting open the heads of all who showed the least signs of life with their axes and knives, and accompanying their bloody work with obscene and taunting derisions and with frequent cries of "what have you got to sell?"[71]

The maroons might have ridden over from their settlements on the Withlacoochee, or from Pilaklikaha, less than ten miles east of the battlefield. Realizing there would be reprisals, the Alachua maroons abandoned Pilaklikaha soon afterward. On March 30, 1836, General Abraham Eustis arrived at the town, and the following day his forces torched the maroons' homes.[72] Eustis documented the scene by ordering a drawing of the inferno that later appeared in print as a hand-colored engraving.

The Second Seminole War cost the United States over $20 million and the lives of 1,500 members of its armed forces. Countless other fatalities occurred among white settlers and militia before the conflict ended in August 1842. Seminole resistance to Removal would not have been so fierce or prolonged had it not been for maroon involvement. When General Thomas Jesup assumed command of the U.S. forces in early December 1836, he quickly differentiated between his adversaries: "This, you may be assured is a negro and not an Indian war; and if it be not speedily put down, the south will feel the effects of it before the end of next season."[73] The following spring, Jesup remarked, "Throughout my operations I found the negroes the most active and determined warriors; and during the conference with the Indian chiefs I ascertained that they exercised an almost controlling influence over them."[74]

During the first two years of the war, the maroons typically fought in their own companies, under maroon leadership, and played a significant role as warriors. They took part in all the major engagements: the Withlacoochee campaign in March 1836, the Battle of Wahoo Swamp in November of that year, John Caesar's raid outside Saint Augustine in

Burning of the Town Pilak-li-ka-ha by Gen. Eustis. Lithograph, 1837. (Library of Congress)

January 1837, and the Battle of Okeechobee the following December. Should they lose the war, the maroons knew to expect reenslavement, the breakup of their families, and the destruction of their civilization. They were every bit as firm in their resistance as the Seminoles. The most expensive "Indian" war in the history of the United States involved maroons as much as Seminoles.[75]

Recruited by maroons, refugees from Florida plantations as well as other blacks captured by Indians joined the allies. Giddings estimated that by 1836 fully 1,400 Africans were associated with the Seminoles.[76] Although that figure is far too high, the U.S. Army eventually sent nearly 500 of the maroons to the Indian Territory. Many other blacks either were killed during the war or were returned to slavery.

General Jesup instigated the policy of removing maroons to the West with the Seminoles as a matter of military expediency to conclude the war as quickly as possible. On March 6, 1837, at Camp Dade, he concluded a treaty with representatives of Principal Chief Mikkoanapa and Hulbutta Harjo (Alligator). John Horse, who by that time headed the Oklawaha maroons, served as the interpreter for the delegation. Under the terms of the Camp Dade accord, the Seminoles agreed to cease

General Thomas S. Jesup. (U.S. Army Quartermaster Museum)

hostilities, make their way to Tampa Bay by April 10, and board transports to the West. They surrendered hostages to ensure their compliance.

Through the bargaining of Abraham, the agreement included important provisions affecting the maroons: "Major General Jesup, in behalf of
the United States agrees that the Seminoles and their allies who come in,

and emigrate to the West, shall be secure in their lives and property; that their negroes, their bona fide property, shall accompany them to the West."[77] The Seminole mikkos apparently interpreted this to mean that both their slaves and their tributary rights had been secured. In other words, virtually all of the blacks associated with the tribe now would be considered the "bona fide property" of Seminoles. The maroons, however, had other ideas.

Jesup at first intended to carry out his part of the agreement. He reasoned, "The negroes rule the Indians and it is important that they should feel themselves secure; if they should become alarmed and hold out, the war will be renewed."[78] But legally, most of the Seminole maroons still belonged to white planters. Under pressure from Florida slave owners, Jesup made the mistake of entering into an agreement with Coi (Cae) Harjo and other Seminole leaders to surrender the blacks they had taken during the war. The maroons banded together in opposition and were supported by some of the more militant Seminoles. When several Florida planters arrived at the emigration camp to search for runaways, the maroons and many of the Seminoles fled. On June 2, moreover, Asin Yahola, Kowakochi, and John Horse seized and carried off the Seminole hostages surrendered under the terms of the truce.[79]

The American commander then reintroduced the old "divide and rule" policy to separate the Indians and maroons. That strategy proved successful and caused a rift between the allies that widened during the post-Removal period. In direct contradiction to the Camp Dade accord, Jesup began to offer freedom to the maroons, should they separate from the Seminoles and surrender. If it would put an end to their harboring runaways, he even proposed to reverse Jackson's Removal policy by allowing the Seminoles to remain in Florida:

> The two races, the Negro and the Indian, are rapidly approximating; they are identified in interests and feelings. [Should] the Indians remain in this territory, the negroes among them will form a rallying point for runaway negroes from adjacent states, and if they remove, the fastnesses of the country would be immediately occupied by negroes. I am very sure that they could be confined to a small district near Florida Point and would accept peace and the small district referred to as the condition for the surrender of all runaway negroes.[80]

But the question remained of how to dispose of the Seminole maroons.

Jesup did not intend to disperse maroons among southern plantations. They had shown their resolve to escape from servitude; they knew the way to Florida and had become accustomed to freedom. Moreover, they were trained in the use of arms, had proven to be fierce warriors during the recent conflict, and could assume leadership roles in slave insurrections. To prevent that, Jesup engaged the U.S. government in slave trading ventures in September 1836. To put a stop to the sale of ninety Seminole maroons captured by Creeks to slave traders in Georgia, Jesup purchased them. That one action created a myriad of problems during and after Removal as the original owners and other opportunistic interlopers pressed claims for those blacks. Not wishing to allow the maroons to remain among the Seminoles or be returned to southern plantations, Jesup initially favored expelling them from the United States and recommended Africa as a destination.[81] Realizing the impracticality of his suggestion, he then returned to his earlier position by proposing to send the maroons to the Indian Territory with the Seminoles as part of the Removal program.

At the beginning of 1838, believing that the more militant maroons would not surrender until their freedom was assured, and that Seminoles would hold out as long as the blacks, Jesup sought a new treaty that would solve both problems. In early February, from Fort Jupiter, Jesup appealed through African emissaries to the leading maroons, August, July, and John Horse, "to whom, and to their people, I promised freedom and protection on their separating from the Indians and surrendering." Jesup's emancipation proclamation granted freedom to the Seminole maroons, but perhaps two-thirds were runaways, captives, or their descendants and still legally the slaves of white owners. This latest initiative also ran counter to the Camp Dade accord, in which the general had promised the Seminole mikkos that the maroons were to be considered their bona fide property and would accompany them to the West. Jesup's action led to a plethora of disputed slave claims that would plague Seminole-maroon relations in the Indian Territory until the outbreak of the Civil War.

In view of Jesup's refusal to return the maroons to southern plantations, "it was stipulated that they should be sent to the West as part of the Seminole Nation." Black emancipation and Removal had become the policy of the U.S. Army.[82] To give his new initiative legal justification, Jesup resorted to the fiction that all the maroons were legitimate Seminole property. As a result, he dispatched to the West all the blacks who appeared at the emigration camps. With the onset of that policy, the Second Seminole War effectively came to an end for the maroons. Most of those remaining in the field took the opportunity to sue for peace under Jesup's promise of liberty and Removal. During the campaign of September 1837 to March 1838, some 250 Africans either had surrendered or had been captured. Under the counsel of Abraham, Hulbutta Harjo surrendered with John Horse, the two bringing in 61 Indians and 27 blacks.[83] The allies were transported quickly to the West. Hulbutta Harjo's capitulation led to the surrender of 360 more Indians and maroons in April. If recent runaways and slaves the Seminoles and maroons had captured from local plantations managed to hold out until 1838, the U.S. government deemed them free. Those blacks boarded transports to the West alongside Seminole maroons of longer standing.

After 1838, having attained such favorable terms for themselves, blacks took on a new role as U.S. government agents who induced militant Seminoles to surrender and remove west. Maroon guides, interpreters, and intermediaries, such as Sandy Perryman and Sampson, became indispensable to the army in establishing contact with Seminoles who had yet to capitulate. Most important of all was John Horse, who returned to Florida from the Indian Territory and played a significant role in negotiating between U.S. officials and Seminole leaders remaining in the field. By 1842, General William Worth, the last of the U.S. commanders in the Second Seminole War, estimated that only 301 Seminoles remained in Florida. Realizing the futility of trying to force those resourceful Indians to remove, Worth met with their leaders in council at Cedar Key on August 14. The general informed them that they could remain in Florida on a swampland reservation deep within the southern section of the peninsula.[84] Maroon Removal ultimately had superseded Seminole Removal on the American list of priorities.

By the time the Seminole maroons prepared to leave Florida for the Indian Territory, they clearly had emerged as a separate and distinct people. Europeans and Americans had named them "Seminole Negroes," and U.S. army officers had treated them as an independent group during the Second Seminole War. The maroons had developed a sense of "peoplehood."[85] They knew what it meant to be a member of their community and the boundaries—ancestral, historical, racial, ethnic, and cultural

—that separated them from others. That is what gave the group identity and strength.

Having secured promises of freedom from the Americans, the Seminoles' slaves and tributary allies had become more assertive. Although the Indians and maroons had joined in fierce resistance to American expansionism during the Second Seminole War, they had different motives. The Seminoles wished to retain their homelands and property and remain separate from the Creeks. The maroons, however, were battling reenslavement and fighting for their freedom. American Removal policies helped further divisions between the two, but Seminoles and maroons already were divided. Tributary allies now were classified as property, and property could be sold. And no matter how benevolent indigenous Seminole slavery might be, freedom offered the maroons a much brighter future. In Florida, Seminoles and maroons had elected to live mostly apart, building separate communities and establishing distinctive cultures. They tended to interact substantially only during periods of stress or in warfare. That pattern would be repeated in the Indian Territory.

Jesup's initiatives drove a deep wedge between Seminoles and maroons that would lead to serious problems after Removal. He had assured the Indians that their property rights would be secure, yet he had promised many of the maroons their freedom. Adding to the complications, blacks had surrendered at different times and under differing circumstances. Some the Americans classified as slaves; others were deemed to be free. Then there was the whole question of slave ownership. A maroon runaway or captive from a southern plantation, legally owned by a European or white American, claimed as a slave or tributary by a Seminole, apprehended by Creeks, and asserting freedom under Jesup's emancipation proclamation, could give rise to a plethora of conflicting claims. Such cases could drag on for years, involving heirs and descendants, testing both American and Indian legal systems, and trying the patience of claimants, U.S. government officials, and Seminole mikkos. For now, however, the American commanders in Florida chose simply to export the problem to the West.

Seminole-maroon relations had become strained after the First Seminole War. The allies came to distrust each other. Seminoles began to sell some of their slaves, and at Moultrie Creek the mikkos agreed to prevent more runaways from entering their settlements and to return those already living among them. A decade later, Seminoles suspected that maroon interpreters had secured a good deal for their people at the Indians' expense when they facilitated the signing of the unfavorable treaties of Payne's Landing and Fort Gibson. During the Second Seminole War, blacks chose American promises of freedom over continued resistance, and they separated from the Indians to secure that goal. Beginning in 1838, maroons aided the Removal program by bringing in Indians. Their helping the U.S. Army seemed to confirm Seminoles' suspicions that their allies had sold them out. The maroons, meanwhile, treasured their hard-won liberty and would fight hard to retain it. Although claimed by whites, Creeks, and Seminoles, many of the maroons vowed that, in the West, they would be slaves no more. The whole made for a sea of troubles that faced the Florida emigrants once they arrived in the Indian Territory.

CHAPTER THREE

Post-Removal Upheavals

The traumas of the Second Seminole War and Removal to the West were followed by further upheavals during the late 1830s and 1840s. Mutual suspicion and resentment dominated interactions between Seminoles and maroons during the immediate post-Removal period. Some Seminoles were unaware of the promises of freedom that the U.S. Army commanders had made to their slaves and tributaries, while others chose to ignore those promises, but all assumed ownership rights in the Indian Territory. Many of the maroons possessed emancipation documents signed by generals, and they resented the stance adopted by the Indians. Both slaves and tributary allies feared that they would be sold to whites or members of the other slaveholding tribes. Seminoles also believed that maroons had betrayed them during Removal negotiations by procuring better terms for themselves at their expense. Some gave vent to their anger by attacking the lives, families, and property of the leading black interpreters. Many maroons felt that they had no further obligation to the mikkos and now came to view them as adversaries. The most militant sought to separate from the Indians and move off by themselves.

The terms of the 1832 Treaty of Payne's Landing and the 1833 Treaty of Fort Gibson stipulated that the Seminoles would settle among the Creeks in the West and become a constituent part of that larger tribe. The 1833 treaty designated the Seminoles a tract of land lying between the Canadian River and the North Fork to the western extremities of Little River. After the Apalachicola emigrations of 1834, bands of Apalachees were the next to arrive in the Indian Territory in 1836. They and their blacks settled along the Canadian beside already established Creek towns. Then, in late October 1838, the remaining Apalachicola bands in Florida removed to the Indian Territory with their blacks and settled among the Creeks on the Little River between the North Canadian and the Canadian. The Apalachees who settled on the Canadian were mostly former Red Sticks who had cooperated with the United States and were considered "friendly" by the Americans. Apalachicolas under John Walker and Ikonchatta Mikko also had taken up arms against Seminoles in late 1835 and were included in the "friendly" category. By 1844, the "friendly" Apalachees had settled in five bands on the Canadian, and five bands of Apalachicolas were living on the Little River. While maintaining their separate identities, those Seminole bands apparently integrated with the Creeks without significant difficulties.[1]

When Hopothli Yahola (Opothleyohola; Gouge) and his Upper Creek Tuckabatchee band removed to the Indian Territory in 1837, they settled in the eastern part of the Seminoles' designated tract near the confluence of the North Fork and the Canadian. Fear of and opposition to Creek domination had been a major cause of Seminole resistance to Removal. Indeed, the two had been armed antagonists during the Second Seminole War. Hopothli Yahola, Echo Harjo, and other Tuckabatchee warriors had fought on the side of the U.S. Army in Florida.[2] The prospect of settling close to their recent adversaries was abhorrent to the "hostile" Seminoles. But for the maroons, proximity to slaveholding Creeks would present a major risk to their freedom.

As the Tuckabatchees had occupied the proposed Seminole lands, U.S. officials and Creek leaders selected a new tract for the immigrant Florida Indians and blacks between the Deep Fork and the North Fork of the Canadian. Seminoles and maroons began settling on those new lands as early as the spring of 1839. The conciliatory Principal Chief Mikkoanapa led his Alachua band and his blacks there soon after arriving in the Indian Territory. They were late planting a crop and could not raise enough corn to see them through that first winter. In his annual report for 1839, Commissioner of Indian Affairs T. Hartley Crawford observed, "They are indisposed to labor; their negroes are equally so, who, unfortunately, have great control over them. It is to be deeply regretted that their slaves were ever permitted to enter the Indian country." The following year, their situation improved, yet acting Superintendent of Indian Affairs for

Micanopy, a Seminole chief (Mikkoanapa). Lithograph after Charles Bird King, published ca. 1836–44. (From McKenney and Hall, *The Indian Tribes of North America*)

the Western Territory William Armstrong still echoed Crawford's belief that the maroons "exercise an improper influence over them, and show a bad example to other slaves."[3]

The remaining "friendly" Indian immigrants followed Mikkoanapa's lead to the Creek country. The Deep Fork settlements came to include eleven bands of Alachua, Apalachee, and Red Stick derivation, led by Mikkoanapa, Coi Harjo, and Holatoochee. Associated Seminole maroons also founded a community on the Deep Fork around that time. But other less "friendly" or conciliatory Seminoles, who had held out the longest in Florida and were the most vehement in their defense of a separate identity, refused to remove to their assigned lands among the Creeks and instead remained in the Cherokee country around Fort Gibson.[4]

Creeks threatened the Seminoles' indigenous customs and practices, and they laid claim to their blacks. Intermarried whites and their accul-turated mixed-race offspring had come to dominate the leadership of the Lower Creeks. That wealthy, elite group of Lower Creek plantocrats also operated a system of institutionalized black slavery. In the West, the Upper and Lower Creeks united under a general tribal council. Roley McIntosh, a Creek-white and the wealthy and acculturated head of the Lower towns, became principal chief of the entire nation, and his party came to dominate the Creek government. The Seminoles believed that if a union of the two tribes came about, the more numerous Creeks, led by the McIntosh party, would insist on their acculturation. That would result in the subjugation of Seminole interests and the loss of their sepa-rate identity.[5]

Creek individuals also claimed many of the maroons. Seminole mikkos feared that once the tribes were united, Creeks would seize their blacks. Seminoles traditionally associated ownership of slaves and tributary rights with leadership status. Following the upheavals of Removal, mikkos were anxious to strengthen and consolidate their power by retaining their blacks within their parties.

Seminole spokesmen most often cited the fear that Creeks would rob them of their slaves as the source of their opposition to unification with the larger tribe. Either because they understood that whites appreciated slave ownership but not tributary ally status, or because something was lost in translation, the mikkos now referred to almost all of the maroons as their slaves. The maroons also opposed the proposed union. The Creeks had adopted institutionalized bondage, after the southern white model, with harsh black codes. Under the Creeks, the maroons could expect to be kidnapped, sold, or subjected to a far harsher form of slavery.[6]

Kowakochi had continued the struggle in Florida until March 1841 and was the last important Indian leader to surrender in the Second Seminole War. When he removed to the Indian Territory in November, he refused to settle among the Creeks and instead remained a squatter on Cherokee land for more than three years. Kowakochi and his band made camp opposite the mouth of the Grand River, just below the garrison at Fort Gibson.[7] As early as November 28, using as his interpreter "the celebrated Negro Abram," Kowakochi was complaining to Major Ethan Allen Hitchcock about the treatment he had received.[8]

Representing more than half the total number of Florida Indian immigrants, 1,646 Seminoles were camped on Cherokee land around Fort Gibson under Kowakochi, Hulbutta Harjo, and other leaders by early 1842. Though destitute, they steadfastly refused to remove to their assigned lands.[9] In his annual report for 1842, Armstrong noted the reasons for the Seminoles' reluctance to move to the Creek country:

> [There] is danger of the Creeks oppressing the Seminoles whenever difficulty about the right of property arises, and unfortunately there are too many fruitful sources of disputed property, especially about Negroes. In many cases the Creeks claim Negroes which are in the possession of the Seminoles. [The] question as to the right of these Negroes should be adjudged as early as possible, as it is one now calculated to produce and keep up a bad state of feeling.[10]

Those Seminoles remained firm in their resolve not to relocate among the Creeks and risk losing their blacks.

John Horse had become associated with Kowakochi and Hulbutta Harjo in Florida. In the Indian Territory, he became recognized as the spokesman for the maroons. From the time of his final Removal to the West in 1842 until the treaty of 1845, Horse remained closely allied with the Seminoles residing in the Cherokee country. At that time, he likely hoped for a return to the relationship that had existed between the Seminoles and maroons in Florida. Seeing that Seminole opposition to the Creeks furthered the interests of the maroons, Horse followed Kowakochi's lead.

Horse had been the last maroon leader to surrender in Florida. After his capitulation with Hulbutta Harjo in April 1838, he was shipped immediately to the West. But Horse returned to Florida in 1839, became well known to the U.S. Army as a guide and interpreter, and assisted in bringing in recalcitrant Seminoles and maroons during the last two years of the war.[11]

In the summer of 1842, John Horse left Florida for the last time. On July 22, he sailed out of New Orleans on the steamboat *Swan* in a party of 102 Seminole captives under the charge of Lieutenant E. R. S. Canby. On August 5, because of low water in the Arkansas River, they landed at La Fourche Bar, six miles below Little Rock. Emigration officials were anxious to remove new arrivals immediately to the Creek country south of the Arkansas to avoid adding to the numbers of those already settled on Cherokee lands, but Canby was unable to negotiate a draft to conduct the party farther.

John Horse had managed to accumulate a substantial amount of property in Florida. He had acquired more than ninety head of cattle in a single herd and also owned a saddle, three pots, four tin pans, two tin kettles, and a tool kit containing two handsaws, an auger, and chisels. Horse was able to loan Canby $1,500 for the costs of transportation so that the party could proceed. On August 12, Canby secured wagons and teams, and the party set out, finally arriving at the Creek Council grounds on September 6, where he delivered the emigrants to Creek agent John McKee. John Horse subsequently made his home on the Deep Fork and helped establish the Seminole maroon community at that location. Upon the death of his Indian owner, Charles Cavallo, in Florida, Horse had become the property of the Seminole mikkos. In February 1843, for his services in providing funds for Canby's party, the mikkos in council declared Horse to be free.[12]

As a free black living among the Seminoles, John Horse lived in constant danger of being kidnapped by Creeks or whites and returned to slavery. Although he made his home on the Deep Fork, he was not safe in the Creek country and spent much of his time at Fort Gibson. Cherokee agent Pierce Butler reported in April 1845, "During the residence of the Seminoles in the Cherokee Nation, John has been called on almost daily for the last two years [to] interpret, and attend to their calls and wishes." Although frequently the only interpreter at the post, Horse was not hired officially, but Butler felt that his services were so important that he ought to be paid.[13] As the interpreter, intermediary, and adviser of Kowakochi, Hulbutta Harjo, and their supporters at Fort Gibson, John Horse assumed a powerful position to advance the interests of the maroons and sustain the Seminoles in their opposition to the Creeks.

During the spring of 1844, Creek speculators instigated a kidnapping campaign to capture Seminole maroons. In one such incident, Siah Hardridge stole Dembo, a slave of Sally Factor, a Creek woman who lived with the Seminoles. Hardridge claimed that he had purchased thirty of Sally Factor's slaves for $2,000 prior to Removal. Kowakochi, representing Mikkoanapa, tried to enlist the aid of the military at Fort Gibson in recovering Dembo. According to Kowakochi, Seminoles were enraged over the incident, and he feared an outbreak of hostilities with the Creeks if thieves like Hardridge went unpunished. Combined pressure from Seminoles, Creeks, and U.S. military officials finally forced Hardridge to release Dembo.[14]

In April, Kowakochi organized a Seminole delegation to Washington hoping to find a solution to the difficulties. John Horse served as interpreter and doubtless represented the interests of the maroons to the Seminole delegates. Mikkoanapa and other Seminole leaders protested against Kowakochi's initiative, stating that they would not be bound by the actions of the delegation, which did not have their authority.[15] Nevertheless, the delegates claimed to speak for all the Seminoles in seeking fulfillment of the treaty obligations and promises the U.S. commanders had made to them in Florida. Through John Horse, Kowakochi and Hulbutta Harjo explained the situation to Jesup:

> [On] arriving at Fort Gibson [we] were told [that] a large portion of the country designed for us had been taken possession of by the Creeks, and believing if we settled among the Creeks (who were desiring we should do so and come under their laws) they being the strongest party, that they would take by force our Negro property from us, as many bad men among them were setting up unjust claims to many of our Blacks on which account we still remain in the Cherokee Nation.[16]

The threat of losing slave property to the Creeks remained the main reason the delegates put forward for their refusal to remove to their assigned lands.

When the delegates returned home in July 1844, they met with trouble. John Horse had been back at Fort Gibson only a few days when "a Seminole, in the immediate vicinity of this Post, fired at him with a rifle, and killed the horse upon which he was riding. His friends on the 'Deep Fork' where he resides, have sent him word to remain here; that, if he goes home, he will certainly be killed."[17] Colonel Richard Mason, in command at Fort Gibson, believed the attack resulted from Horse's service to the U.S. troops as a guide and interpreter during the late stages of the Second Seminole War. Butler, however, reported that upon his return, Horse had become "obnoxious to many of the Seminoles, particularly his former owners who in consequence of some offensive language shot his horse under him and would have taken his life if not prevented."[18] Jesup, meanwhile, believed that the Seminoles were hostile to Horse and other leading maroon interpreters because they suspected them of having deceived the Indians during treaty negotiations and held them responsible for the failure of the government to keep its promises.[19]

Seminoles earlier had attacked and killed other maroon interpreters and intermediaries for aiding the U.S. forces in Florida.[20] Moreover, Horse had sided with the independent initiatives pursued by Kowakochi and his followers. Perhaps flushed with a sense of his own importance, upon his return Horse had criticized his former owners, Seminole mikkos who had settled amongst the Creeks and disapproved of the Washington delegation. Seminoles living in the Creek country also likely suspected that, when he visited the capital, Horse had served as an advocate only for the interests of the maroons. As the delegation went in the name of Principal Chief Mikkoanapa, any agreements favorable to the maroons would be binding on the whole tribe. Some Seminoles resorted to force in an attempt to halt those developments and terminate the diplomatic career of the talented John Horse.

The attempt on his life meant that Horse no longer could reside safely among Seminoles in the Creek country. Colonel Mason told him to remain at Fort Gibson, where the military would furnish him and his family of three with rations until the post commander received further instructions from Washington. Horse had more than fifty head of stock, a wagon, and other farm equipment on the Deep Fork. As he was unable to return home to take care of it, Mason was certain that Horse would lose his property. On August 2, 1844, acting on advice from Jesup, Secretary of War William Wilkins instructed General Matthew Arbuckle, "Let

John remain under the protection of the garrison and furnish him and his family with rations etc. Let the proper chiefs be advised that they are held accountable for his property in the Indian Country and will be made responsible for any injury he or his family may receive from the Indians."[21] Later that month, the Seminoles sent an apology, disapproving of the actions of this "one man" and offering to pay for the animal that was shot. But no funds were available, and Horse was not reimbursed.[22]

Although his home was on the Deep Fork, John Horse had chosen to spend much of the period as an interpreter and intermediary at Fort Gibson. In that capacity, he stayed in close contact with Seminole affairs and advanced the interests of the maroons. Following the attempt on his life, however, he was forced to reside under the protection of the military at the post from July 1844 until January 1849. At Fort Gibson and in Washington, John Horse pursued an independent course of action for the maroons.

During the winter of 1844, U.S. commissioners entered into negotiations with the Creeks and Seminoles to try to settle the differences between them. As historian Grant Foreman suggested, "the real bone of contention, the source of nearly all the bitter hostility, the controversy revolving round the Seminole Negroes," dominated the discussions.[23] On December 28, 1844, Kowakochi and other Seminole leaders submitted a memorial that once more expressed the sincere hope that Creeks would not interfere with their blacks:

> [We] wish our Brethren the Creeks will not permit any of their citizens to interfere with any of our Negro property; this description of property was put under our protection by the Government (at least much the largest number of Negroes with us are so under the above circumstance) and in no case can be taken out of our possession, without instructions from the Government to that effect.[24]

Kowakochi and his followers had determined not to submit to Creek law on any terms, but they eventually relented.

Kowakochi was a signatory to the tripartite treaty of January 4, 1845, between the United States, the Creeks, and the Seminoles. The destitution of his band members and increased incentives were the deciding factors that persuaded him to sign. As Armstrong recalled, "what was of most consequence" was that the military would issue the Seminoles with rations during their removal to the Creek country and for six months after their emigration had been completed.[25]

The 1845 treaty addressed the controversy surrounding the Seminoles' blacks in Article 3: "It is mutually agreed by the Creeks and Seminoles, that all contested cases between the two tribes concerning the right of property, growing out of sales or transactions that may have occurred previous to the ratification of this treaty, shall be subject to the decision of the president of the United States." The Seminoles could settle in any part of the Creek country, and those who had not already done so were to remove there immediately. The Seminoles could make their own town regulations, but subject to the general control of the Creek Council, to which they would send representatives. There was to be no distinction between the two tribes in any respect, except that neither could interfere with the pecuniary affairs of the other.[26] In theory, the treaty united the tribes, but in practice the Seminoles remained separate, independent, and clearly distinguishable.

During the spring, most of the Seminoles removed to the Creek country. They established twenty-seven towns in the Little River region some miles distant from each other and planted new fields in the bottomlands. Kowakochi and Mikkoanapa established their bands about five miles below the mouth of Little River on Wildcat Creek. By the fall, the Seminoles were well established in their new homes.[27]

The treaty spelled disaster for both Seminoles and maroons. The Seminoles were able to maintain their social organization only at the cost of their independence. They had only minority representation on the Creek Council, and the more-numerous Creeks would subsume their interests. Seminoles were not even secure in their property. The treaty contained no provision dealing with title to, or control over, slaves. Article 3 referred to contested cases between the tribes; Creek individuals still could press fraudulent claims to the Seminoles' blacks. That had been the most frequently expressed source of Seminole opposition to the Creeks and would remain so after 1845.

Siah Hardridge quickly resumed his slaving activities. In March, Dembo Factor stated at Fort Gibson that Hardridge was trying to capture him again to run him off to Texas. Hardridge also had acquired some slaves from Nelly Factor in 1843. Hardy, one of Nelly Factor's slaves, also sought protection from the military at Fort Gibson under Jesup's emancipation

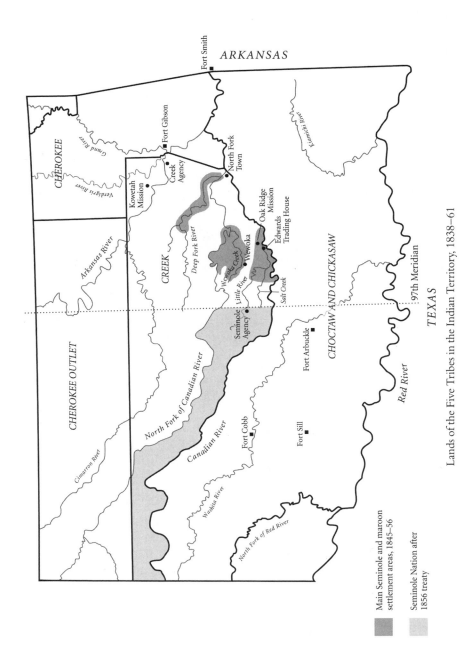

Lands of the Five Tribes in the Indian Territory, 1838–61

ARKANSAS

Fort Smith

CHEROKEE

Grand River

Fort Gibson

Verdigris River

Kowetah
Mission

Creek
Agency

North Fork
Town

Oak Ridge
Mission

Edwards
Trading House

CREEK

Deep Fork River

Wewoka Creek

Wewoka

Little River

Salt Creek

Kiamichi River

Arkansas River

CHEROKEE OUTLET

Seminole
Agency

CHOCTAW AND CHICKASAW

97th Meridian

TEXAS

Fort Arbuckle

North Fork of Canadian River

Canadian River

Cimarron River

Fort Cobb

Fort Sill

Washita River

Red River

North Fork of Red River

Main Seminole and maroon
settlement areas, 1845–56

Seminole Nation after
1856 treaty

63

proclamation. In addition, the opportunistic Hardridge had managed to purchase Sarah and Linus—two children of Juana (Wannah), John Horse's older stepsister—from a Seminole-black named Jim and had mistreated them. Juana and her husband, Sam Mills, sought refuge at the post with their remaining children, but during the summer of 1847 Hardridge sold Sarah and Linus at Fort Smith and they were never heard of again. In May 1845, Rose Sena Factor and August, a brother of Dembo Factor, also sought military protection from Hardridge for themselves and Rose's children. General Arbuckle eventually warned Hardridge to stop kidnapping blacks, putting a stop to his slaving activities for a while.[28]

John Horse had remained at Fort Gibson since July 1844. From mid-October of that year until mid–April 1845, Seminoles often called upon him to interpret, and "frequently different bands would send for him a dozen times a day." He was especially active from the signing of the treaty to the relocation of the main body of Seminoles on February 9, 1845. For sixty days, from February until early April, Horse drove his wagon and three yoke of oxen in the train that removed Seminoles and their baggage from their camps near Fort Gibson to the Little River. But his position among the Seminoles remained precarious. During the removal to the Creek country, there was a second attempt on his life, and Seminole subagent Thomas Judge believed his assailants would try again.[29] Once more, Horse took refuge at Fort Gibson. On April 16, 1845, Butler reported, " 'Gopher John'—A Seminole Black [is] now living under the flag of the military."[30]

The Seminole maroons faced a desperate situation. The treaty gave the Creeks dominance over the Seminoles. Whites and Creek-whites could reenslave free blacks, such as John Horse, through questionable or fraudulent claims or kidnapping. Slaves of Seminoles faced similar dangers that could result in their subjection to a much harsher form of slavery. And claimants and slave hunters did not distinguish between slaves and tributary allies. With the unification of the tribes, Creek slave laws applied to the Seminole maroons. Those laws, formulated as part of the Creek Constitution of 1825, affected free blacks as well as slaves. Under the Creeks, the maroons faced inequality before the law, legislation preventing them from marrying Indians, and confiscation of personal property. Later additions to the Creek law forbade blacks from living in separate towns or bearing arms.[31] Under the Creeks' black codes, which came to resemble those operating in the South, the maroons could expect loss of liberty and personal property, and the destruction of their families and communities.

John Horse determined upon a new initiative. Following the attempts on his life and the treaty of 1845, he had lost faith in Seminoles. In April, he accompanied General John T. Mason to Washington as a servant, "with the view of obtaining permission of the Government to return and settle in Florida."[32] Horse arrived in Washington on May 18, and from then until June 22 he stayed at Galabrun's European Hotel on Pennsylvania Avenue between Fourteenth and Fifteenth Streets, near the White House. He probably slept in the servant's quarters.[33] On May 28, he again applied for compensation for his loss of property the previous summer.[34] Horse spent the next year promoting the interests of the maroons in the capital.

After the treaty of 1845, the maroons who had settled in the Cherokee Nation removed to the Little River country and in their customary fashion established communities separate from the Indians. They settled mostly on Wewoka Creek and two of its tributaries. Another community was situated to the west of Wildcat Creek. The residents of a maroon settlement on the east bank of a tributary of the Canadian, near Edwards's trading house, had established a communal town field nearby to the south. Trails connected the black and Seminole settlements. But many of the maroons who earlier had settled on the Deep Fork remained there with Seminoles who also chose to stay. Following the signing of the 1845 treaty, Creeks proceeded to present claims and assert jurisdiction over the Seminole maroons.[35]

Meanwhile, in Washington, John Horse separated from General Mason. Horse would not perform a servant's duties, and a lawsuit resulted. He moved out of Galabrun's, and from June 23 until September 2 he lived with Francis Selden, a free mulatto who kept a "refectory" on the north side of Pennsylvania Avenue between Fourteenth and Fifteenth Streets West and charged him a dollar a day for rent. From September 2 to December 2, Horse paid $20 to stay at the establishment of one Alcock, and from December 2 to February 25, 1846, he paid George Brown $28 for room and board.[36]

During the summer of 1845, Horse was successful in soliciting the support of Quartermaster General Jesup for the maroons' cause. On July 17, Jesup visited Fort Gibson to direct the construction of new stone buildings. He sent word to the maroons, many of whom Seminoles still

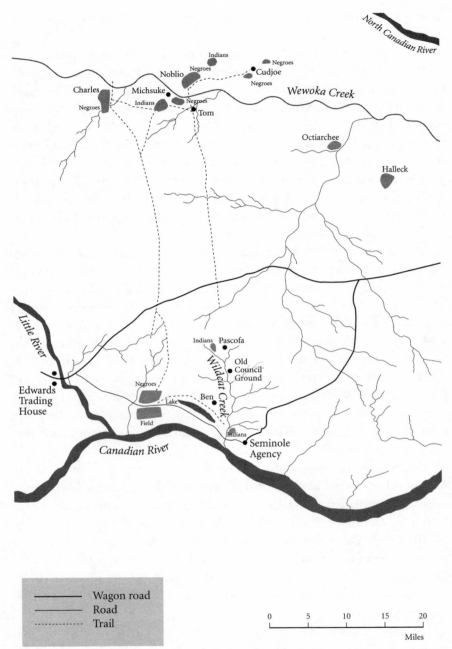

Indians

Negroes

Noblio

Negroes

Cudjoe

Negroes

Charles

Michsuke

Wewoka Creek

Negroes

Indians

Negroes

Tom

Octiarchee

Halleck

North Canadian River

Indians

Pascofa

Old
Council
Ground

Wildcat Creek

Little River

Negroes

Edwards
Trading
House

Lake

Ben

Field

Indians

Seminole
Agency

Canadian River

——— Wagon road
——— Road
·········· Trail

0   5   10   15   20

Miles

"Map Showing Free Negro Settlements in the Creek Country." Circa 1852. Based on an unidentified sketch map locating maroon communities among the Seminoles, reproduced in Abel, *The American Indian as Slaveholder and Secessionist* (1919).

claimed as slaves, that they were free under the promises he had made to them in Florida and that they should meet him at the post. The maroons arrived after Jesup had returned to Washington, but he had left behind a list of those he considered free. During the summer, many of the men, some with their families, sought refuge under the protection of the military at Fort Gibson. In 1845 and 1846, the military employed some sixty or seventy of them in constructing a commissary building and other stone structures at the fort.[37]

John Horse continued to advocate the maroons' cause in Washington, and on April 8, 1846, Jesup informed General Arbuckle: "The case of the Seminole Negroes is now before the President." Jesup requested Arbuckle to prevent any interference with the maroons at Fort Gibson until the president determined whether they were to remain in the Seminole country or be allowed to remove elsewhere. Horse then prepared to return to the Indian Territory. During his year in Washington, he had been responsible for Jesup's intervention, the protection of the maroons by the military at Fort Gibson, and the referral of the case to the president. Jesup wrote to Arbuckle, "John Cowayee has been so long here waiting a decision that he thinks it necessary to return to his family, leaving the business of himself and his people in my hands."[38]

Horse recalled his previous return to the Indian Territory in July 1844 and tried to prevent a recurrence of those events. He had Jesup prepare a statement that, during his stay in Washington, he had not interfered in Indian affairs but had concentrated only on matters affecting the maroons. Furthermore, he had acted only in the capacity of interpreter to Kowako-chi's delegation during his previous visit. Nevertheless, Horse found more problems awaiting him upon his return: Kowakochi's "brother" had stolen a horse from Susan, Horse's wife, during his absence. Horse dare not retrieve the animal, as he feared for his life among the Seminoles. Moreover, Indians began to kill his livestock on the Deep Fork. Horse instigated claims for his losses but never received compensation. Then, in early June 1846, slavers attacked the Deep Fork settlement, hoping to seize children, but seventy-two of the maroon men managed to turn back the kidnappers by force of arms.[39]

In spite of those problems, the large number of maroons who had settled on the Deep Fork remained firm in their wish to stay there, provided they could have a tract of their own. The land was not the best available, but they had managed to build cabins and plant fields. By the summer of 1846, they had accumulated more than a thousand head of stock. An army officer at Fort Gibson described the maroons living there as being as "honest, temperate, and industrious as could be expected from the habits which they acquired living with the Indians in Florida."[40] Unlike John Horse, those maroons did not seek protection at Fort Gibson, for they realized that would necessitate leaving behind their cattle, horses, and improvements, which then would be lost, stolen, or destroyed. Instead, they stayed put, farmed, raised families, and defended their community against slavers.

The maroons at Fort Gibson remained under the protection of the military and awaited the decision of the president amid Seminole slave claims and kidnappers' raids. Fearing attack or abduction, they would not venture outside the fort for provisions. When the men's employment on construction projects ended in late 1846, they had no further means of support, and Colonel Gustavus Loomis, the commander at the post, had to issue them with rations to prevent their starvation. The following summer, to force the U.S. government to make a decision in the case, Creeks threatened to seize and reenslave all the maroons at Fort Gibson. As the threat of Creek aggression increased and kidnapping ventures and sales mounted, more maroons traveled to the post for "free papers" and protection during the fall. Creeks and Seminoles engaged in slave raids at the fort during the spring and summer of 1848, but the maroons remained firm in their resolve to retain their freedom and independence.[41]

During those slave-hunting campaigns, John Horse again sought permission to remove the maroons from the Indian Territory. In early December 1847, he and fellow maroon Tony Barnet told Loomis that they never would be allowed to enjoy their freedom among the Seminoles in the Creek country. They were "willing and desirous to emigrate to any place where they can be free and unmolested." Loomis suggested to Jesup that they be transported to Africa, "where they can be free and this they desire: or to any place separate from the Indians."[42] Arbuckle recommended that government agents immediately adopt measures "for the removal of these unfortunate people from the vicinity of the Indian country [to] Liberia." He suggested that they travel to New Orleans, and from there sail to Africa. If it was considered inadvisable to remove the group at public expense, the Colonization Society might agree to take charge of the maroons at New Orleans.[43] But Loomis's and Arbuckle's recommendations fell on deaf ears.

Loomis praised the maroons residing at Fort Gibson. They attended Sunday school and during the summer of 1847 had raised large quantities of corn and rice.[44] But Creeks held a different view of the maroons on the reserve. In April 1848, the Creek delegation in Washington stated that the group had become a "positive nuisance":

> As things now exist they are apparently subject to no control, they violate the laws of the United States and the laws of the Creek nation with perfect impunity. They are idle and worthless constantly engaging in bringing whisky into the nation stealing and rioting, and offering inducements to the slaves belonging to the various surrounding tribes of Indians to run away and when they are detected in crime, they at once take protection on the Government reservation where they are sustained by the commanding officer at the post.

The Creeks demanded the "removal of these Negroes from their country," or their placement "under the control of their laws."[45]

On June 10, 1848, John Horse sent a list of the maroons' complaints to Jesup:

> We have great many enemies, great many who think only of doing us injuries—many who fabricate false claims and who for a few goods or a little whisky make false titles to our great annoyance. [We] are much annoyed, our people carried away, and our horses an object for many bad persons—so much so that we are now reduced to great poverty.[46]

From his strategic position as interpreter to the Seminoles at Fort Gibson, Horse heard that it was probable that the maroons would be turned over to the Seminoles as slaves. To cover himself against that possibility, he sought to establish his free status "on another title" by reverting to the decision of the Seminole Council to free him. He anxiously requested Jesup to trace his emancipation papers of 1843. Later, he tried to establish the freedom of other members of his family. In late 1848, he sought to buy the freedom of his wife Susan and their children from Nelly Factor. And in January 1849, Horse purchased the freedom of his stepnephew Andrew, Juana's son, from Chitto Harjo (Crazy Snake).[47]

John Horse's assumptions proved to be correct, and his preparation timely. On June 28, 1848, Attorney General John Y. Mason delivered the opinion that would determine the fate of the Seminole maroons. Jesup had based the authority for his emancipation proclamation on the convention of war that held that captured movable property was at the disposal of the captor. To the attorney general, the legal principles were clear: regarded as people, slaves had no power to contract and could not enter into any treaty or convention; regarded as property, when captured from an enemy in a land war, they were to be treated as any other movable property, and not subject to the law of prize. Whether they were prisoners of war or booty, the executive department of the U.S. government, under whose authority they were captured, would decide their disposition. Therefore, on consideration of public policy or for other reasons satisfactory to the executive, the maroons could be restored and their antebellum status reestablished.

J. Y. Mason was of the opinion that there was no precedent for the qualified freedom Jesup had promised the maroons. The U.S. government had no right to incorporate freed blacks with the Seminoles without their consent given by treaty. Hence, there was no authority for such a promise. The opposition of the Creeks to such a settlement of free blacks being established in their country also pointed to the impracticality of such an arrangement. "My opinion is," the attorney general wrote, "that the Military authorities should be instructed to restore the Negroes to the condition in which they were with the Seminoles, prior to the date of Major General Jesup's letter of the 8th of April 1846." President James Polk approved the opinion on July 8.[48]

During the first week of August, Arbuckle received instructions to deliver the maroons to the Seminole mikkos. Seminoles now would own their former tributary allies, like slaves. Arbuckle should report any not belonging to Seminoles, along with any claims made to them. The post commander at Fort Gibson should not issue rations to the maroons, except to prevent them from starving. John Horse still was trying to establish his free status, as U.S. officials were having problems locating his emancipation papers. He asked Kowakochi to make a statement that the Seminole chiefs had granted him freedom, and Kowakochi complied on August 21.[49] Realizing that the maroons could expect no further help from the U.S. government, Horse established his base as a free black and sought to renew his alliance with Kowakochi to achieve freedom for all of his people.

The removal of the Seminole maroons on the reserve to the Creek country was delayed for several months. A Creek raid on a maroon settlement in September and continuing plots of slave speculators persuaded Arbuckle to instruct the commander at Fort Gibson to keep at the post all the blacks who had been reported free on Jesup's list. They should not be allowed to leave without permission. Moreover, the military should bring in and protect other blacks not on Jesup's list or residing on the reserve, and not claimed by Seminoles, until their disposition was decided. Those either were free blacks or were runaways who had fled from Florida plantations during the latter stages of the Second Seminole War, had removed with the Indians, and had continued to reside among them. A summer drought had stricken the maroons at Fort Gibson by severely reducing their harvest. By the late fall, their provisions had run out and they were destitute. In mid-November, the military had to issue rations to almost all the maroons living on the reserve to prevent them from starving. The Seminole leaders met in council and decided to receive the blacks at Fort Gibson on December 22. They would take them back to their settlements and turn them over to Seminole owners.[50]

The decision of the attorney general and their impending distribution to Seminole owners meant that the maroons living at Fort Gibson were on their own. For more than three and a half years they had lived apart from the Indians. The followers of John Horse had become more militant and increasingly saw themselves as independent. They were about to be transferred to a hostile environment and subjected to Creek aggression, sale, kidnap, and harsh black codes with little hope of support from the U.S. government or the army. But the attitudes and roles that Seminole owners would adopt toward their former slaves and tributaries remained to be determined, and there lay the key to their future. Within the year, both the Indians and the maroons would divide and separate, each seeking their best interests via a different path.

Kowakochi remained fiercely opposed to Creek dominance of Seminole affairs and only grudgingly had signed the tripartite treaty of 1845 to end the destitution of his followers. After removing to the Creek country, however, the Seminoles encountered more problems, experiencing drought, starvation, and dependence on agency officials.[51] As early as

1845, Kowakochi began to seek an alternative to a life of misery in the Indian Territory.

In May 1845, Kowakochi participated in the Grand Council on the Deep Fork as the "counsellor and organ" (or speaker) of Mikkoanapa. Representatives of twelve tribes attended the council, and Kowakochi came into close contact with delegates from the southern plains.[52] In the winter of 1845–46, the Butler-Lewis peace mission to the Comanches offered him the opportunity to explore Texas and build on his relationship with the Plains tribes.[53] During 1846, Kowakochi engaged in exploratory hunting and trading expeditions on the southern plains, meeting with southwestern Indian leaders in council.[54] Around that time, he began to formulate the idea of creating a new confederacy outside the Indian Territory. Based on the Florida model, that alliance would include bands of Seminoles, Plains Indians, and blacks, linked by trade, true to indigenous practices, and opposed to white acculturation and American expansionism. During 1847 and 1848, Kowakochi and his followers continued to complain about the treatment the Seminoles had received since Removal, to resist Creek influence over Seminole affairs, and to organize and promote the new confederacy.[55]

In 1849, two significant events took place that dramatically affected the history of Seminole-maroon relations. On or before December 22, 1848, Mikkoanapa had died after arriving at Fort Gibson to participate in the restoration of the maroons to the Seminoles. His demise and bad weather delayed the transfer until the New Year. The Seminoles chose Mikko Mucasa (Jim Jumper), a nephew of Mikkoanapa through the maternal line, to succeed him as principal chief. Kowakochi, also a nephew of Mikkoanapa through the maternal line, might have held hopes of attaining the office, especially as he had served the tribe as speaker. Like his uncle, Mikko Mucasa was more accommodating to Creeks than his cousin Kowakochi. He also associated closely with Marcellus Duval, an Alabamian Democrat who supported slavery and had succeeded Judge as Seminole subagent in late 1845. The scheming Duval had a personal interest in the Seminole maroons. Indeed it has been suggested that he might have influenced the selection of Mikko Mucasa as principal chief.[56] With Mikko Mucasa's accession, Kowakochi determined to resist all operation of Creek laws, especially those affecting the maroons. He also planned to establish his new confederacy outside of the Indian Territory, across the Rio Grande in Mexico.[57]

Earlier in the New Year, on January 2, the military had handed over the maroons on Jesup's emancipation list to the Seminole mikkos. However, the transfer took place only after the Seminoles had given certain assurances. The commanding officer at Fort Gibson notified all persons concerned that any sales made prior to the transfer would not be recognized. Nevertheless, Creek, Cherokee, and white speculators purchased around one-third of the maroons affected by the decision from Seminoles who frequently had no legitimate claim. Some Seminole owners, becoming influenced by more acculturated Lower Creeks, began to consider their slaves as property and disposed of them cheaply. The mikkos also had promised a further one-third of the maroons in question to William J. Duval, a brother of the subagent, for his services as attorney in causing the blacks to be restored to them. The maroons heard that Seminoles had disposed of two-thirds of their number to whites and Indian slaveholders from other tribes and that they would be distributed among the various claimants and "scattered" as soon as they left the military reserve. They declared that they sooner would die where they were than submit to such a fate after being promised their freedom.[58]

Arbuckle was apprehensive that many of the maroons would make their escape and that others would oppose the transfer by force of arms. Lieutenant F. F. Flint, assistant to General William Belknap, the post commander at Fort Gibson, therefore reached the following agreement with the Seminole mikkos:

> When the Negroes were turned over to the Chiefs at Fort Gibson, it was with the express understanding that they would be permitted to live in "towns," as they had formerly done, and that they should not be sold, or otherwise disposed of, to either white men or Indians, but be kept in the Seminole country. The chiefs were told that the Negroes would be turned over with this expectation, to which they assented; thereby virtually making a promise to the same effect. Had they not done so, the Blacks never would peaceably have returned to the nation.[59]

The mikkos gave the maroons to understand that they would not distribute them among the various claimants but would allow them to remain with the Seminoles and would treat them kindly. The maroons stated that they were perfectly satisfied to live among the Indians, as they had before.[60] The day after the transfer, Belknap reported, "No difficulty has arisen in the performance of this duty, either from the Indians, negroes or claimants, nor do I anticipate any. As soon as the weather permits, I shall send the negroes to the Indian country."[61]

General Jesup's 1845 list of emancipated slaves had included 313 names. By the time of the transfer, 34 had died, 3 were described as "no such person," 11 had been sold out of the country, 3 were "free" and uncontested, and 6 others were listed without a claimant. The military turned over to Seminole owners as slaves 256 maroons promised freedom by Jesup. Of those, more than half had been living on the reserve, the remainder mostly on the Deep Fork and at Little River. One group of 9, listed as belonging to Charley Emathla, was residing on the North Fork. The list included a total of 14 free blacks, although 11 had a Seminole claimant. Only 3—John Horse, Romeo, and Judy—were listed as free and without a claimant.[62] Arbuckle suggested that one-third of all of the Seminole maroons had been living at Fort Gibson at the time of the transfer,[63] putting their entire population at close to 400. That would mean that around 130 of the maroons were not listed. But lacking detailed census information on maroons that had not removed to the military reservation, the general likely underestimated the overall total.

Although deaths and sales would have reduced the maroon population after Removal, those losses probably were offset by natural increase and an infusion of runaways and free blacks from the other slaveholding tribes and from Arkansas and Texas. The maroon population likely would have remained close to the 500 who had removed to the West. If that supposition is correct, around 225 to 250, or close to half of all the maroons living in the Creek and Seminole country in 1849, had not been included in Jesup's list, had not sought refuge at Fort Gibson, and were not included in the transfer to the Seminoles.

Because almost all of the attention and documentation on the maroons at that time focused on those affected by Jesup's emancipation promise, especially the ones who took up residence at Fort Gibson, little is known of this other group. Those maroons removed to the Creek country with Mikkoanapa and his followers, formed separate settlements on the Deep Fork and at Little River, and carved out new lives for themselves in the Indian Territory. By the summer of 1846, the Deep Fork maroons herded more than a thousand head of stock and were able to muster a force of seventy-two men to defend their settlement against slavers. They apparently reestablished their former relationship with Seminole mikkos in the West, offering an annual tribute but enjoying a great deal of independence and autonomy. That group seems to have been less affected by the troubles experienced by the maroons on the reserve. Instead of the instability of residing temporarily at Fort Gibson, they built farms, raised livestock, and grew crops in their settlements. They were more prepared to accept the indigenous form of tribute and deference practiced by Seminole mikkos. Those more accommodating maroons would form a significant majority of the group that remained behind in the Indian Territory after 1850, and their history helped determine the group's future relations with Seminoles.

Owing to the severity of the winter, the maroons did not remove from Fort Gibson to the Seminole country until the early spring of 1849. They were armed, and the military advised them to defend themselves against slave hunters during their journey. Mikko Mucasa and other Seminole leaders wanted the group to relocate to a site they had selected, some twelve miles from the subagency. Upon reaching the Seminole country, however, the maroons began to defy the authority of the mikkos. John Horse led his followers to Wewoka Creek, about thirty miles from the subagency, where they settled at some distance from the Seminoles. The community became known as Wewoka, meaning "barking waters," after a small falls that broke over the rocks just north of the present-day town of the same name. But other maroons, who had not moved to Fort Gibson, remained on the Deep Fork and at Little River. Wishing to avoid an armed confrontation, the mikkos determined not to interfere until they decided the various claims, but then they planned to turn the maroons over to Seminole owners.[64]

In keeping with custom, the Seminole maroons established their communities at a distance from the Indian settlements. Fearing kidnap, they armed themselves heavily for protection. Recounting those events in November 1854, Lieutenant Francis Page observed:

> They retained their arms, and lived under no restraint whatever from their owners; in fact they seemed to be regarded by the Chiefs as common property, and the negroes considered themselves free, and merely under the guardianship of those Indians who claimed them as property in Florida before the emigration west.[65]

John Horse's position in the Seminole country remained precarious, and he sought to ensure his mobility to protect and advance his own personal interests and those of his people. On April 8, 1849, he had the army issue a pass allowing him to travel anywhere in the Indian Territory "where his necessary business might take him."[66] Horse apparently used that privilege to advantage to recruit support for Kowakochi's confederacy within the Seminole maroon settlements and among Creek and Cherokee blacks.

Before their transfer, the maroons living at Fort Gibson stated that they were prepared to live among the Seminoles as they had before. But since Removal, events had taken place that made such reconciliation unlikely. By then, the Seminoles were subject to Creek law that contained no provision for the indigenous form of tributary obligations they practiced or its resultant social arrangements: separate and independent settlements of armed and mounted maroons. Moreover, some Seminole owners had become influenced by the likes of Marcellus Duval and by their more acculturated Lower Creek neighbors and were more amenable to selling slaves outside the tribe. Meanwhile, the maroons who had resided at the post had grown increasingly insubordinate and militant under the promise of freedom and their three-and-a-half-year separation from the Indians. Unlike those not included on Jesup's list, they no longer were prepared to offer the same tribute and deference to Seminole mikkos that they had in Florida, and they would not adhere to the Creeks' black codes.

In June 1849, the Seminole mikkos sent two men to Wewoka to apprehend Walking Joe, an alleged horse thief. When they tried to arrest the suspect, Joe pulled a knife, but the Indians succeeded in disarming and capturing him. Before they could leave, however, all of the maroon men in the town arrived armed with knives and guns. Threatening the two Indians, they set Joe free. They then sent Cuffy, an interpreter and intermediary, to the mikkos with a message: to avoid injury, Seminoles should not travel to Wewoka to arrest anyone without first consulting with the town's leaders. Asked to explain the incident, John Horse blamed the "young and unmanageable negroes,"[67] but all of the maroons were prepared to defend their liberty and communities by force, if necessary.

In early July, the mikkos ascertained the original owners of slaves and tributary rights before the army had offered the maroons protection, and they also determined the current owners whose right and title derived from Seminole law. Mikko Mucasa and the Creek leaders wished to comply with Creek law by disarming the maroons, breaking up their settlements, and distributing them to Seminole owners throughout the country. The maroons on Jesup's list knew that Seminoles already had disposed of a large percentage of their number to white, Creek, and Cherokee claimants. They positively refused to be separated or to allow the Indians to destroy their settlements, and they told the Seminoles that the military would support them. Described as "well-armed, rebellious and living chiefly in one town," the maroons were able to offer powerful resistance to Seminoles and Creeks attempting to enforce the law. The militants also refused to recognize the right of their owners to dispose of them as they wished.[68]

The Seminoles did not want to confront the maroons and sought the aid of subagent Duval. As the mikkos had promised around ninety of them to his brother, he had a personal interest in seeing the safe transference of the maroons to Seminole owners. On July 16, Duval wrote to Arbuckle: "The Negroes will most assuredly resist the Creeks in the execution of their laws, and unless assisted by the government, would also resist the Seminoles. They have already resisted the laws, and will, I believe, continue to oppose them, so long as they are allowed to remain armed. [It] is absolutely necessary that these negroes should be disarmed."[69] Although John Drennen, the Western Superintendent, supported Duval's request, Arbuckle and his aide-de-camp Flint opposed it. Arbuckle had learned of Duval's interest in the maroons and would not help him.[70]

In early August, Flint wrote to Belknap, expressing his belief that the principal object of disarming the maroons was to enable purchasers, speculators, and other claimants to take possession of them.[71] Later he wrote to Drennen, "[The] promises to them have been violated on all sides, and the present state of affairs is principally attributable to the Indians themselves."[72] Arbuckle observed, "[The] Seminoles are sufficiently numerous to properly control their negroes, without the assistance of the military, and it is clearly their duty to keep them in subjection themselves."[73] Drennen, however, believed that the maroons would not resist U.S. troops but certainly would oppose any attempts by Seminoles and Creeks to disarm them. "[I] then conceive it to be the imperative duty of the government to protect the Indian and quell domestic strife," Drennen concluded.[74]

After J. Y. Mason's decision and the removal of the group living at Fort

Gibson to the Seminole country, the army was powerless to offer the maroons effective aid and could not for long maintain its policy of noninterference in the face of rising pressure from the Indian office. The Seminole subagent had a personal interest in seeing the maroons disarmed, reduced to slavery, and dispersed, and the powerful Western Superintendent supported him. The maroons also could expect no help from Mikko Mucasa, who had sided with the Duvals, and Creeks threatened to enforce their black codes themselves. In desperate need of a viable alternative, John Horse and his followers once again turned to their old ally Kowakochi.

The increasingly disaffected Kowakochi had determined to obstruct all operation of Creek laws as they affected his people: "He was strongly influenced by Gopher John and others of the chief negroes, to resist any interference in reference to the condition of the negroes, and was urged by them to resist all influence of the Creeks over the Seminoles. [The] negro chiefs have exercised a controlling influence over the Seminoles, and have induced them to resist the government and laws of the Creek nation."[75] On September 8, Kowakochi and some of his followers called on Arbuckle. They stated that the Seminoles had no complaints against the maroons the military had turned over to them at Fort Gibson, and they refuted Duval's charges that the maroons were disorderly, rebellious, and insubordinate. The maroons had settled in three towns sufficiently convenient to the Indians. As they were very poor, the Seminoles wished them to retain their arms for hunting purposes and to support their children. Kowakochi also expressed his hope that the maroons would be allowed to remain where they were without being disturbed any more.

Although they claimed that Mikko Mucasa had sent them, Kowakochi and his supporters acted independently and did not represent the views of the principal chief. They stated that Mikko Mucasa, who owned no slaves himself, had promised one-third of the transferred maroons to William J. Duval without even conferring with their owners or gaining their consent. Moreover, Marcellus Duval recently had told them that one-third was not sufficient remuneration. If the Seminoles did not give up more blacks, the subagent would withhold their annuity payments. He had informed Roley McIntosh that if the Creeks approved of disarming the maroons, the Seminoles would assist them. The subagent had arranged a council under the Creek leader Jim Boy for September 3 near the maroon settlements to achieve that objective. But Kowakochi claimed that the Seminoles were opposed to any interference by the Creeks and had boycotted the council. Accepting Kowakochi's account, Arbuckle delayed military intervention until he received further instructions.[76]

By that time, Kowakochi was finalizing his plan to remove from the Indian Territory and establish a new confederacy in Mexico. During his exploring, hunting, trading, and diplomatic trips to the southern plains, he had become familiar both with the southwestern territories as far as the Rio Grande and with Plains Indian relations with Mexico. Kowakochi also had learned of Mexican colonization schemes aimed at attracting immigrants to populate the vast expanses of the Republic. Those culminated on July 20, 1848, when President José Joaquín de Herrera signed a bill entitled "Military Colonies: A Project for Their Establishment on the Eastern and Western Frontiers of the Republic," which provided the guidelines for directing Mexican colonization. Mexico would provide immigrants with land, tools, food, livestock, and other incentives to establish military colonies on its frontiers as buffers against the incursions of depredating Indian bands. The organization of the colonies would be left largely to the discretion of the inhabitants, and immigrants would enjoy freedom of religion and trial by jury.[77] Of greatest significance to Seminole maroons, however, Mexico had outlawed slavery twenty years earlier and now offered them freedom.

During the summer of 1849, much to the dissatisfaction of the Creeks, some of the recently transferred maroons again fled the Seminole country for Fort Gibson. Further collusion between those Seminole maroons and free blacks of the Creek and Cherokee nations who resided in the vicinity of the military reserve likely took place at that time. In October, there were more kidnapping raids around the post. Accompanied by his brother, Siah Hardridge again sought out Dembo Factor. Factor drew a pistol and a knife to defend himself, but Hardridge's brother blasted him with a shotgun and inflicted a serious wound. At the post hospital, the surgeon declared the wound to be mortal. The next day, however, Hardridge abducted Factor and took him to the Creek Nation. By the end of October, Factor was said to be recovering. Soon, he would be free of his oppressor.[78] The situation was becoming intolerable for many of the maroons. Working closely with John Horse and Kowakochi, they prepared to quit the Indian Territory for Mexico.

In mid-October, a Seminole delegation headed by Halleck Tastanaki and accompanied by subagent Duval assembled at North Fork Town to travel to Florida. Its intention was to persuade Holata Mikko and the remaining Seminoles and maroons there to remove to the Indian Territory. Foreseeing a new Creek initiative to disarm the maroons and enforce their black codes, Kowakochi sent a proposition to the subagent that he wished to have communicated to the president: he proposed to remove the whole tribe to Mexico. It was the Seminoles' wish, Kowakochi asserted, as they were tired of living among the Creeks and the country there would suit them better. If the president favored his enterprise, Kowakochi would persuade Holata Mikko and the remaining Seminoles in Florida to remove to Mexico, whereas they never willingly would agree to relocate among the Creeks. Duval believed, however, that Kowakochi had secretly told members of the delegation to advise Holata Mikko to remain in Florida until he could persuade the government to make a treaty allowing them to remove with him to Mexico. In all likelihood, the subagent referred to Jim Bowlegs, Tom, and Tony Barnet, three maroons who had accompanied the delegation as interpreters. Jim Bowlegs was a former slave and adviser of Holata Mikko in Florida prior to Removal and likely could exert influence over the Seminole leader.[79]

Kowakochi took the opportunity to put his plan into action when the Seminole delegation left North Fork Town for Florida. Capitalizing on Duval's absence, he mobilized the emigrants. Kowakochi told his Seminole band members that everything was suited to their needs in Mexico and informed the maroons that the Plains tribes had agreed to allow them to pass unharmed if they followed him. Facing more slave raids, John Horse's followers hurriedly gathered their belongings and made ready to leave. One night around November 10, the Seminole and maroon allies, numbering about two hundred, hastily rode out of the Indian Territory and crossed the Red River into Texas. The wounded Dembo Factor somehow managed to escape from Siah Hardridge and join John Horse. Sampson July and Jack Bowlegs, meanwhile, had to depart so quickly that they left their wives and some of their children behind.

The Indians and blacks were represented in approximately equal numbers. They included around twenty-five Seminole families under Kowakochi, a few dissatisfied traditionalist Creeks, twenty maroon families under John Horse, and some Creek and Cherokee blacks. Many of the maroons were closely related. John Horse's stepsister Juana and her children were among the emigrants, and Sampson July, Dembo Factor, and Thomas Factor—the brother and uncles, respectively, of Horse's wife Susan—also made the journey and became maroon leaders in Mexico and

Texas.[80] Despairing of ever finding peace or happiness in the Indian Territory, the two groups prepared to open another chapter of Seminole-maroon relations on the Texas-Mexico border.[81]

The spring and summer of 1850 were difficult times for the maroons who had remained behind in the Indian Territory. In April, Jim Bowlegs returned with the Florida delegation. His former owner, Holata Mikko, sent a letter to the Seminole mikkos, placing Jim in charge of his fifty slaves in the Indian Territory during his absence.[82] Jim Bowlegs thus acquired considerable influence among the remaining maroons and became a natural successor to John Horse. In early June, Creek slave hunters entered the Seminole country and took Jim Bowlegs and two other maroons. General Belknap rescued them, but Roley McIntosh protested the military's once again offering maroons protection. McIntosh informed Belknap that because Jim Bowlegs was a slave, Creek law prohibited him from owning arms and horses.[83] More likely, however, the Creeks were anxious to remove this new threat to their authority.

Matters came to a head on June 24 when a party of Creeks led by Hardridge, Cherokees, and whites arrived in the vicinity of Wewoka, armed and equipped to take by force the maroons they claimed as slaves. When the Seminoles in the area learned that it was the party's intention to attack Wewoka, many of them decided to assist the maroons in defending themselves. Duval arrived the following day and prevented a clash by ordering the slave hunters to return to the Creek country north of the North Fork. Seminole mikkos later met the Creek leaders of the party in council, where they agreed to assist the group in capturing a number of blacks. Around 180 of the maroons were taken and held at the Seminole subagency.[84] Likely, those included most of the remaining maroons on Jesup's list. That number, when added to the 100 emigrants in John Horse's party, approximates the 256 maroons transferred to the Seminoles in January 1849, plus the 9 listed as free or without a claimant.

That proved to be the last straw for Jim Bowlegs and his followers. Immediately after the seizure, he forsook the protection of the military reserve to gather his supporters for an attempt to join John Horse in Mexico.[85] By early July 1850, around 180 maroons under his leadership "were en route for Texas, armed, and bidding defiance to any person or persons who should attempt to take them."[86] They split into parties of between 40 and 80 and made their way south across the plains toward the Mexican border.[87] But despite Kowakochi's assurances to the contrary,

Comanches attacked the emigrants while they were traveling through Texas. The Indians captured Jim Bowlegs's party, hoping to sell them into slavery, and they put to death another entire group of maroons, except for two girls they mutilated.[88]

After successfully negotiating a favorable agreement and seeing his followers settled on their new lands in Coahuila, Kowakochi returned to the Indian Territory. He arrived on September 18 and called a council nine days later to discuss the prospect of removing all the Seminoles to Mexico. He told slave owners that their runaways were living there and that if they emigrated with him they again could control their blacks. He also stated that he had arranged to have the Seminole annuity paid out on the Rio Grande. Duval informed the mikkos, however, that Mexico had abolished slavery and that their blacks were now free. Duval also told them that Kowakochi's statements concerning the annuity were false and that he, as their subagent, was opposed to their removal. Most of the Seminoles apparently remained unimpressed by Kowakochi's enterprise.[89]

In contrast, some of the remaining maroons and other blacks in the Indian Territory were attracted by the Mexican colony. Kowakochi's return caused great excitement among the Creeks, who feared losing their slaves. On September 23, McIntosh wrote to Belknap, "Now he come back with enticing news, and want to carry his people in that nation; and the negroes, he told them if they emigrate to that country, they will be all freed by the government. This is good news to the negroes. I am told some are prepared to go."[90] That same day and the following week, Creek leaders in council adopted measures to foil Kowakochi's plans, and Duval feared a clash over the maroons. Three hundred Creek warriors rode into the Seminole country with instructions to prevent any blacks from leaving the nation and to detain Kowakochi until they could ascertain the object of his mission. At Wewoka, the party halted after learning that Kowakochi was present in the Seminole country and that a number of maroons were preparing to leave, but then the Creeks returned home.[91]

Kowakochi learned from Duval that McIntosh had ordered his arrest for conspiring to entice away the maroons and create disorder in the nation, and that he had ordered out the Creek lighthorse (mounted law enforcement officers) to capture and convey him to the Arkansas District of the Creek Nation. Kowakochi again expressed his hatred of the Lower Creeks but decided to withdraw south of the Canadian River, outside

Seminole and Creek limits. In early October 1850, under threat of arrest, Kowakochi left the Indian Territory for the last time. He took with him only some thirty to forty Seminole men and their families, numbering in all around one hundred Indians, together with a handful of maroons.[92]

Lower Creek lighthorsemen pursued Kowakochi and his followers across the Canadian, but near Camp Arbuckle they encountered the band of Comanches that had captured Jim Bowlegs's party as it was crossing the southern plains to Mexico. The lighthorse paid the Comanches a ransom for delivering the runaways and set off back to the Seminole country. The maroons refused to return peaceably and tried to escape their captors, resulting in a bloody battle and casualties on both sides.[93] Dr. Rodney Glisan observed that the prisoners had fought bravely but largely in vain, when he remarked upon the number of wounded among the sixty captive maroons in the party that passed by his camp on October 23 on its way to the Seminole country.[94] But a few of the maroons apparently managed to escape from their Creek captors and make their way to Mexico.[95]

Most of the Seminole maroon emigrants from the Indian Territory had been included on Jesup's list. Whether they were slaves Jesup wished to emancipate or free blacks such as John Horse, those maroons had become the objects of slave claims and kidnapping raids. They were the most militant in their search for unqualified freedom, and to attain it, they had sought refuge at Fort Gibson for years. When Attorney General Mason's decision resulted in the transfer of most of that group to the Seminoles as slaves, not only their freedom but also their lives, families, and property became endangered. Rather than risk sale or abduction and reenslavement, they had preferred to take their chances in Mexico. Of all the maroons, the emigrants felt that they faced the gravest danger if they remained behind in the Indian Territory.

But around 225 to 250 Seminole maroons had not appeared on Jesup's list and had not taken up residence at Fort Gibson. Since Removal, they had kept a much lower profile, and their experiences are harder to trace in the documentary record. Despite the upheavals of the post-Removal period, those maroons had managed to create new lives for themselves in the West. Only a handful of that group had chosen to flee the Seminole country for Mexico. Rejoined by kinsmen who attempted to escape but were captured and brought back, the remainder formed the community that stayed behind in the Indian Territory and set about reestablishing relations with Seminoles during the 1850s.

CHAPTER FOUR

Seminole Slave Owners

Accurate statistics on the number of Seminole maroons living in the Indian Territory during the 1840s are lacking, and contemporary estimates varied widely. Almost 500 maroons had removed west with the Seminoles between 1838 and 1843.[1] A few had been sold or kidnapped out of the Seminole country, while some others had fallen victim to disease and death during and after Removal. Clearly, N. Sayer Harris's estimate that there were 1,000 blacks among the Seminoles in 1844 was much too high.[2] But the losses seem to have been offset by natural increase and by an infusion of free blacks and runaways from other slaveholding tribes, particularly the Cherokees and Creeks, and from neighboring Arkansas and Texas. Arbuckle would appear to have underestimated, therefore, when he suggested that there were only around 400 blacks associated with the Seminoles in the Indian Territory in 1848.[3] On the eve of the migrations to Mexico, the Seminole maroon population likely remained about the same size as at the time of Removal.

Some 280 of the 500 Seminole maroons tried to escape to Mexico in 1849–50, and around 180 successfully crossed the border. Of the other 100, some were killed or sold into slavery by Comanches, but the Creek lighthorse eventually returned most of the others to the Seminole country. Around 220 maroons did not leave for Mexico, and some 60 to 80 others who did were returned. An estimated 300 Seminole maroons, therefore, remained in the Indian Territory after the migrations to Mexico. Although sales reduced their number somewhat during the 1850s, natural increase and immigration apparently counterbalanced those losses, and the size of the maroon population probably remained fairly constant throughout the decade. Fearing that enumeration would lead to more claims to their blacks from outsiders, the Seminole mikkos forbade any census of the maroons in 1860. However, an 1867 census of the Loyal Seminoles listed 335 freedmen.[4] Allowing both for an infusion of new immigrant blacks from neighboring tribes and states during and immediately after the Civil War, and for losses incurred during the conflict, that figure supports the estimate that around 300 Seminole maroons were living in the Indian Territory in 1861.

The Seminole Indian population experienced a sharp reduction between Removal and the Civil War. Due largely to disease, the Seminole population declined by 61 percent in less than twenty years, from 4,883 at the time of Removal to 1,907 in 1857. Between 1857 and 1860, owing mainly to an influx of Seminole immigrants from Florida and Mexico, their numbers increased by 38 percent to 2,630, yet the Indian population still showed a 46 percent decline since the Seminoles' arrival in the Indian Territory.[5] The ratio of blacks to Seminoles was fairly high, as it was within the other slaveholding tribes, at about one to six or seven in 1857–58.[6] As John Horse's followers also discovered in Coahuila,[7] the maroons seemed less susceptible to epidemics than their Seminole Indian associates, and better able to offset losses through immigration and natural increase. That difference would emerge most dramatically after the Civil War. While Seminole population growth remained stagnant, the number of freedmen increased at a prolific rate during the forty years between emancipation and Oklahoma statehood.

The maroons who remained behind in the Seminole country after the migrations to Mexico faced many problems. Attorney General Mason had overruled Jesup's emancipation proclamation and directed the military to turn over the maroons to the Seminole mikkos as slaves.[8] The maroons were now subject to Creek codes and could expect to become objects of slave claims and targets for speculators and kidnappers, with no hope of further support from military officials. They also had lost many talented leaders to Coahuila. John Horse, John Kibbetts, Dembo Factor, Hardy Factor, and Cuffy had all gone. Gone, too, were some of their strongest supporters among the Indians, and leadership of the Seminoles now was in the hands of Mikko Mucasa, who was collaborating with white slaveholders. Some Seminole owners might seek to compensate for

three years of lost tributes. Many maroons had remained fiercely independent and had refused to heed the mikkos, to the point of armed
rebellion and defection. Those developments did not bode well for the
future of Seminole-maroon relations in the Indian Territory.

Yet contrary to what might have been expected, the Seminole maroons fared relatively well during the 1850s, and certainly much better
than most blacks associated with the other Civilized Tribes. Littlefield
goes too far when he suggests that "[Wild] Cat's scheme had been disastrous for the blacks who had remained behind."[9] Owners were more
likely to sell slaves out of the Seminole country than before, and both
slaves and free blacks alike lived under the constant threat of Creeks or
whites presenting claims or kidnapping them, but the Seminole maroons'
quality of life remained comparatively high. Most continued to enjoy a
great deal of independence and autonomy. In fact, the 1850s saw a re-
emergence of many of the characteristics of pre-Removal Seminole-
maroon relations.

Four reasons best explain this. First of all, the ethnohistorical experience of the Seminoles, which largely determined the course of their
relations with the maroons, was fundamentally different from that of the
other slaveholding tribes. Long after Removal, they held fast to their
indigenous beliefs and practices. The Seminoles had the lowest rate of
white intermarriage and were the least acculturated of the Five Tribes.
Consequently, the system of tribute and deference the mikkos employed
changed little after Removal.

During the antebellum period, as Native customs went into decline
due to both internal and external pressures, slaveholding elites composed
of wealthy intermarried whites and their mixed-race offspring emerged
among the Cherokees, Creeks, Choctaws, and Chickasaws. Those elites
assumed positions of economic, social, political, and cultural leadership
and came to direct tribal policy regarding Indian-black relations. That
highly acculturated plantocracy instigated the adoption of capitalist economies, democratic elections, constitutional governments, Christianity,
school-based education, written laws and law enforcement agencies, institutionalized slavery, and severe black codes.[10] In contrast, the Seminoles experienced few of those changes. They remained a nation of
subsistence farmers and hunters maintaining a southeastern indigenous
culture governed by hereditary chiefs.

Seminoles opposed white intermarriage and resisted interference in their internal affairs. Sattler has suggested that, during the first half of the nineteenth century, they apparently prohibited marriage with whites, and the Brown family had to live outside the Seminole Nation before the Civil War.[11] Consequently, no internal catalyst for change emerged, and the Seminoles successfully withstood external pressures to adopt elements of white civilization. Between 1810 and 1858, the Seminoles and maroons allied in opposition to white expansionism in Florida in three protracted wars against the United States, and the main body removed only after inflicting considerable damage on the financial resources and manpower of the enemy. Long after their Removal to the West, Seminoles continued to harbor resentment against whites for the loss of loved ones and lands.

The story was much the same in the Indian Territory. Seminoles did not forgive their former adversaries or wish to adopt their culture. White agents of acculturation, meanwhile, tended to ignore the uninterested Seminoles and instead concentrated their efforts on the more receptive members of the other slaveholding tribes. By 1860, only thirty-five whites were living among the Seminoles in the Indian Territory,[12] and there were so few Seminole-whites that the small population of Seminole-maroons outnumbered them. The Seminoles also experienced many problems in adjusting to life in the Indian Territory. Frequent removals, isolation, factionalism, leadership changes, protracted slave claims, unification with the Creeks, and the defections to Mexico all worked against their acceptance of white agents of change. The Seminole country was an infertile area for the growth of white acculturative influences during the antebellum period.

Typically, Seminole slave owners were traditionalists who adhered to aboriginal notions of servitude. As a whole, Seminoles showed little interest in plantations, manufacturing, or other capitalist ventures and did not develop commercial agricultural enterprises after Removal. Rather, they engaged in subsistence farming on small acreages, raising corn, potatoes, rice, melons, pumpkins, and beans; keeping cattle, hogs, horses, and chickens; and producing modest surpluses for trading purposes. As late as 1846, some were living "solely by the 'hunt,' " and Marcellus Duval predicted that, thereafter, many would become completely dependent on the chase for their livelihood. Not until 1857 could it be said that hunting had been reduced to a supplementary source of subsistence.[13]

With the exception of the hereditary mikkos and their relatives, wealth seems to have been fairly equally distributed, and Seminole social organization remained based on the clan and band rather than class. Pascofar, a slaveholding mikko, claimed only $4,726 compensation for property losses during the Civil War, yet his compatriots considered him "rich."[14] No equivalent of a "Rich Jim" Vann, Benjamin Marshall, Pittman Colbert, or Robert McDonald Jones—wealthy slaveholding plantocrats of white descent who assumed positions of power and influence among the Cherokees, Creeks, Chickasaws, and Choctaws, respectively—emerged among the Seminoles.

Not being so concerned with profit, Seminole slave owners had no need for either the cheap labor force provided by institutionalized bondage or the rigid control structure usually erected to preserve it. Because of the continuing strength of Native traditions within the tribe, slavery never assumed the same connotations among Seminole owners that it did among the Indian-white elites of the other Civilized Tribes. Right up to the Civil War, Seminole slaveholders continued to practice the system they had developed in Florida. The maroons offered tribute and deference to their owners or associated mikkos but otherwise controlled most aspects of their daily lives.

In 1844, the informed Major Ethan Allen Hitchcock astutely observed that, within the Five Tribes, to be a slave of a "full-blood" meant something quite different from being a slave of an intermarried white or "half-breed":

> The full-blood Indian rarely works himself and but few of them make their slaves work. A slave among wild Indians is almost as free as his owner, who scarcely exercises the authority of a master, beyond requiring something like a tax paid in corn or other product of labor. Proceeding from this condition, more service is required from the slave until among the half-breeds and the Whites who have married natives, they become slaves indeed in all manner of work.[15]

More than ninety years later, New Thompson, a man with firsthand experience as a former Cherokee slave, echoed Hitchcock's statement: "The only negroes who had to work hard were the ones who belonged to the half-breeds. As the Indian didn't do much work he didn't expect his slaves to do much work."[16] Seminole slavery in the Indian Territory was similar to that practiced by other indigenous traditionalists among the Cherokees, Creeks, Chickasaws, and Choctaws, but it did not resemble the institution developed by the Indian-white elites within each of those tribes.

Not only the economy but also the lifestyle, government, and institutions of the Seminoles remained indigenous after Removal. Most lived in log cabins with only the most basic of furnishings. In 1846, the Seminole subagent reported, "Their cabins are much better than those they have heretofore lived in . . . a stool or two, pestle and mortar, 'hominy baskets,' two or three pots or kettles, with 'sofky' spoons, and a beef hide in the corner, which serves as a bed."[17] Those homes contrasted sharply with the plantation mansions constructed by Indian-white slaveholders of the other Civilized Tribes during the antebellum period. Even after having achieved their independence from the Creeks in the late 1850s, Seminoles again elected to build log cabins in their "new country" farther west.[18]

Few Seminoles could speak English, and Creek continued to be the first language of the majority. Throughout the 1840s and 1850s, both U.S. officials and Seminole mikkos employed maroon interpreters in official capacities. White missionaries also viewed the maroons as vital to establishing channels of communication with the Indians. Roads and bridges were few and of poor quality, making travel within the Seminole country difficult. The great majority of Seminoles continued to wear their traditional dress and eat Native foods. They used calico and skins extensively, and the men generally preferred the hunting shirt, leggings, and turban to the clothes of the white frontiersman. In the Seminole diet, Native meat and corn dishes—especially sofky—predominated. The Indians showed little interest in the written word or white institutions. Newspapers, museums, improvement societies, and other such symbols of white acculturation did not emerge within Seminole society prior to the Civil War, as they did among the other Civilized Tribes.

Christianity and school education, two of the great pillars of white civilization that the Indian-white elites of the other slaveholding tribes embraced so eagerly, made little headway among the Seminoles. In 1845, Presbyterian minister Robert Loughridge, hoping to establish a church, visited the Seminoles. Though some welcomed him, the majority opposed having "schools, preaching, fiddle-dancing, card-playing and the like" brought among them.[19] James Factor, an Indian-black, had become a leading slaveholder, council member, and interpreter among the Seminoles. He replaced Abraham as official interpreter to the council. A Baptist minister later recalled the reaction to Factor's conversion to Christianity in the 1850s: "The Seminoles were very indignant. Factor was arrested and brought before a large council. Some advocated that he be shot; others that he be expatriated; and others, that he be severely beaten and compelled to renounce Christianity."[20] Only through the machinations of his friend Heniha Mikko did Factor escape punishment. As their Native religion remained strong and their opposition to white acculturation ran high, clearly, the path of the early missionaries to the Seminoles was strewn with obstacles.

The Presbyterians, Methodists, and Baptists all were active in the Seminole country between Removal and the Civil War, but their efforts met with little success among the Indians, maroons constituting the majority of their congregations. In 1843, Talomas Mikko (John Bemo), a Presbyterian of Seminole extraction, traveled west from Philadelphia to serve as a missionary to the tribe.[21] A year later, however, his congregation included only "several Seminoles."[22] Rev. John Lilley and his family joined Talomas Mikko in October 1848, and a year later they opened a Presbyterian mission at Oak Ridge on the Little River.[23] But the mission served mainly as a school, with only a small congregation meeting for preaching on Sundays.

In 1854, Loughridge held a meeting at the Oak Ridge Mission and received two Native members into the first Seminole Presbyterian Church. The following year, William Templeton of the Creek Presbyterian Church added another twenty Seminole converts.[24] Rev. James Ross Ramsay received the appointment of missionary to the Seminoles in the early spring of 1856. The congregation rose steadily, with the number of communicants peaking at forty-three the following year. Heniha Mikko was Ramsay's most notable Seminole convert, joining the church in the winter of 1857–58. But having to remove farther west after the 1856 treaty disrupted the Presbyterians. They never regained the numerical strength at their new Prairie Mission, at Pond Creek near Wewoka, that they had enjoyed at Oak Ridge. And in 1860, Heniha Mikko became a Baptist and took with him a large percentage of the Presbyterian congregation.[25]

The first Methodist congregation among the Seminoles included just sixteen Indian members in 1848, and Rev. James Essex reported considerable opposition within the tribe to his Little River Mission.[26] The first Baptist contact with the Seminoles came with the arrival of Joseph Smedley, a general Indian missionary of the American Mission Association, in 1842. But Baptist missionary activity was confined almost entirely to maroons during the 1840s and 1850s, and Seminoles began to take an interest only after Rev. Joseph Samuel Murrow (Morrow) arrived in January 1860. In the new Seminole Nation, Murrow quickly established the Little River Station. During early February, with the help of Talomas Mikko, who had converted some years earlier, Murrow organized the first Seminole Baptist congregation at Ash Creek Church, near Sasakwa. He received seven initial members and added two more that same day, but in spite of the Presbyterian defections, the congregation increased to only thirty by 1861.[27] At the outbreak of the Civil War, therefore, there were only around fifty Christian Seminoles, representing just 2 percent of the Seminole population, living in the Indian Territory.

Moreover, few Seminoles attended school during the antebellum period. From the time of Removal until they became independent of the Creeks, the Seminoles had no funds set aside for educational purposes. Christian missionaries alone were responsible for the few schools that opened among them. Under the terms of the 1856 treaty, the Seminoles were to receive $3,000 annually for ten years for the support of schools.[28] Although their agent reported a year later that the Seminole Council was "very much alive to the importance of the speedy establishment of schools," it instigated no public program, and school education remained marginal.[29]

Talomas Mikko opened the first school to operate among the Seminoles at Prospect Hill, near the Creek Agency, on March 15, 1844. Fifteen boys initially enrolled,[30] but the institution failed to flourish, and in 1846 Duval reported that the tribe neither had nor wanted a school.[31] The following year, the Seminole subagent observed:

> The subject of education is thought about as little of, as if it was only intended for White people. They feel themselves, and desire to be considered, as decidedly beyond the pale of civilization, perfectly satisfied to walk in the "footsteps of their predecessors," showing, as far as mental improvement is concerned, a philosophy in being satisfied with their present state.[32]

Undaunted, John Lilley opened a second Presbyterian school, at Oak Ridge, in October 1849. Fashioned after the manual labor institutions operating in the other slaveholding tribes, the school accepted both boarders and day students and had an initial enrollment of eleven.[33]

Held in a small, one-room log cabin, the Oak Ridge Mission School ran for ten years and constituted the principal center of white learning in the Seminole country prior to the Civil War. Although Lilley was hopeful that this school would succeed, Duval remained skeptical, commenting in 1851, "There is little or no disposition among the Seminoles to have their children educated; if they are willing to send them to school, it is to have them clothed and fed."[34] Lilley's optimism proved unwarranted, as documented by the low enrollment at the school. The number of Seminole children attending Oak Ridge rose by just two in four years, from seventeen in 1853 to nineteen in 1857, and enrollment peaked at a mere twenty-two in 1859.[35]

The educational efforts of the Methodists and Baptists also met with little success. Just fifteen students attended the Methodist school at the Little River Mission in 1848.[36] And when Clara Murrow, the reverend's daughter, opened a Baptist neighborhood school near the Ash Creek Church in 1860, she could attract only "several children" to its sessions.[37] Throughout the antebellum period, Seminoles remained largely uninterested in the history, culture, and institutions of white civilization.

Unlike the other slaveholding tribes, the Seminoles did not adopt a constitution or written laws after Removal. Other mainstays of white society, such as democratic elections, centralized government, and institutionalized legal systems and law enforcement agencies, also failed to take hold within the tribe. The clan and the band, the two most dynamic political, social, cultural, and economic units within Seminole civilization, continued to predominate. Consequently, the Seminoles remained content to practice a confederate form of government, under hereditary leaders.

Though technically subject to the Creek Council for a decade from the mid-1840s to the mid-1850s, the Seminoles continued to manage most of their own affairs. Following the 1845 treaty, the Seminoles settled in twenty-seven towns, organized into bands led by mikkos and having their own local laws. The leading tribal officers were the principal chief and an executive council, both deriving their position from lineage. The

Seminole Council was composed of the mikkos, and it had the power to pass laws for all the tribe.[38] In practice, however, the bands held most of the power. The Seminoles had no written laws,[39] no court system or justices, and no law enforcement officers. In legal cases of national importance, the council served as both judge and jury. Behavior was viewed as a moral and ethical question, beyond the limits of written rules of conduct. The Seminoles relied on the honor system, and deterrents employed to control crime were restricted to the local level.

In keeping with their Native customs, the Seminoles developed few rules to regulate the behavior of slaves or the remainder of their black population. They had no equivalent of the black codes operating in the other slaveholding tribes. Indigenous practices benefited the maroon community by discouraging the sale of blacks out of the Seminole country.

After achieving independence from the Creeks in 1856, the Seminoles had the opportunity to create a centralized, federal government. In the summer of 1859, they held a general council in which they discussed the possibility of establishing a national government similar to those operating in the other slaveholding tribes. As the Seminoles had no funds set aside for such purposes, those in favor wanted U.S. officials to withhold from their annuities, and turn over to the mikkos, a sum sufficient to meet the expenses of the new government. That group stressed the need for education and favored the establishment of a national manual labor school with funds accruing from the tripartite treaty. They also suggested creating a lighthorse company to enforce national laws, establishing other paid national offices, and making the chief executive and council membership salaried positions. But those propositions were not approved, the more traditional majority preferring, the agent observed, "their former habits and customs."[40]

In view of the wide-ranging differences between their experience and that of the Cherokees, Creeks, Choctaws, and Chickasaws, it could be argued that the Seminoles should not be classified as one of the Civilized Tribes. In contrast to the others, the Seminoles remained a nation of traditionalists. Although they were sedentary town dwellers and had slaveholders, their economy, lifestyle, political system, and institutions remained indigenous. Nowhere were the differences between the Seminoles and the other Civilized Tribes more pronounced than in the type of servitude practiced by the majority of slave owners. Seminole slavery in the Indian Territory retained most of its pre-Removal characteristics; it did not incorporate the main features of the system adopted by the Indian-white elites within the other slaveholding tribes.

White contemporaries were quick to point out the differences between the Seminoles and their more "civilized" Indian neighbors. In their correspondence and reports, the agents, superintendents, and commissioners of Indian affairs frequently listed the progress the Cherokees, Creeks, Choctaws, and Chickasaws were making. Then they either would mention the Seminoles briefly, stressing their problems and lack of advancement, or omit them completely. One example is the commissioner's annual report for 1854, in which he first praised the achievements of the other four and then described the Seminoles as being "ignorant, more or less debased, idle and addicted to dissipation."[41] In their massive 1861 history of the United States, John Barber and Henry Howe lauded the progress the four tribes were making in "the arts of civilization" but did not even mention the Seminoles in that context.[42] The *Southern Literary Messenger* clarified the argument: For an Indian tribe to be considered civilized, it had to have adopted institutionalized slavery. The system of servitude employed by the Seminoles was so unlike the "Southern Institutions" incorporated by the other slaveholding tribes that the *Messenger* did not consider them worthy of being considered alongside the Cherokees, Creeks, Choctaws, and Chickasaws as one of the Civilized Tribes.[43]

The Seminoles' retention of an indigenous civilization and their resistance to white agents of acculturation largely explain why the maroons associated with them fared so well during the 1850s. A second reason was that, although technically united with the Creeks for much of the period, the Seminoles acted independently and refused to apply Creek codes to their blacks. As early as 1847, Duval reported Seminole opposition to the 1845 treaty and to Creek hegemony,[44] and that proved to be one of the main reasons behind the defections to Mexico in 1849–50. But the departure of Kowakochi and his band did not weaken the resolve of the Seminoles who remained behind to manage their own affairs. They continued to assert their independence, and in 1851, Duval noted "their unwillingness to submit to Creek laws or Creek authority."[45]

In the fall of 1852, Duval traveled to San Antonio in an attempt to recover maroons who had been promised his brother by Seminoles but had escaped to Mexico. He was unsuccessful in his mission and started back to the Indian Territory, but in Austin, Duval learned that charges were being brought against him for his slaving activities. Before he could return to the Seminole country, the subagent was removed from office for having been absent from his post too often. With the removal of Duval from the subagency, the death of Mikko Mucasa soon afterward, and the accession of Heniha Mikko to principal chief, Seminoles became more vehement in their opposition to the Creeks, and the maroons' prospects improved.[46] One of the remaining problems was that Creeks continued to interfere with the maroons. In his annual report for 1853, Bryan Smithson, the new Seminole subagent, wrote:

> Their unwillingness to submit to Creek laws or Creek authority, still continues, and there is at present the appearance of a difficulty between them and the Creeks in regard to the right of sale of some negroes belonging to the Seminoles. The Creeks claiming the right of having the matter investigated by and through the Creek council, whilst the Seminoles claim the right of settling the same by their own laws.[47]

After 1853, believing that they constituted too small a minority to influence its decisions, the Seminoles stopped sending representatives to the Creek Council. They also deprived those choosing to live among the larger tribe of a share in their annuities.[48]

Throughout the period of their unification with the Creeks, the Seminoles sought to determine the course of their relations with the maroons independently. They allowed their blacks to live apart, with few restraints, and own arms, livestock, and other property, all of which were prohibited by Creek law. This proved to be a constant source of friction between the two tribes, punctuated by Creek attempts to enforce their laws and dispossess the blacks and by armed resistance on the part of Seminoles and their maroon associates. The maroons remained major beneficiaries of Seminole independence.

Due largely to the escalating slaving activities of individual Creeks pursuing dubious or fraudulent claims to blacks living in the Seminole country, matters came to a head in 1855. In that year, Seminole subagent Josiah Washbourne reported that, as they no longer had a voice on their councils, the Seminoles did not consider themselves bound by the Creeks' "domineering, unequal and unjust" laws. The status of the maroons remained a significant issue. The Creeks sought to subject the Seminoles to their will, but the Seminoles reserved the right to decide all claims to blacks associated with them independently, ignoring the findings of the Creek Council. Seminoles took delight in defying or evading the laws of the Creeks "as often as possible," and were "practically without government or law." By 1856, the unification of the two tribes was no longer viable.[49]

Creek and Seminole delegations traveled to Washington, D.C., in the spring of 1856 to engage in new treaty negotiations. During the discussions, the Seminole delegates focused attention upon one of their major concerns. They requested, "That a plan be agreed upon, in the present convention, whereby all contested claims for negroes, or other property, between the Seminoles and Creeks, may be clearly, satisfactorily and finally adjusted, agreably [sic] to both parties."[50] But there was no need for such a provision to be included in the treaty that eventually emerged on August 7, 1856. On that date, the Seminoles finally regained their political and territorial independence, and the right to manage their own internal affairs.

Under the terms of the new treaty, the Creeks ceded to the Seminoles over two million acres of land, between the North Fork and South Canadian, to the west of where they were settled, in return for a payment of one million dollars from the U.S. government. The Seminoles were to remove to their new domain as soon as was practicable and there would constitute an independent, sovereign nation with the "unrestricted right of self-government, and full jurisdiction over persons and property" within its boundaries. The Seminoles would have their own agency and receive funds for educational purposes, agricultural assistance, the support of blacksmiths' shops, and per capita payments in the form of annuities. For the first time, the treaty made provision for a separate, clearly defined, Seminole Nation in the Indian Territory.[51]

The 1856 treaty must have come as a considerable relief to the Seminole maroons, who stood to benefit greatly from its stipulations. For the previous eleven years, they had been subject to Creek codes. Although these had not been in operation in the Seminole country, Creeks had retained the right to enforce them, and on several occasions had attempted to do so. Because of their geographical proximity to interested parties, the maroons also had lived under the constant threat of being fraudulently claimed and carried off, or kidnapped, by Creek slave hunters. The treaty of 1856 finally placed the Seminole maroons outside the sphere of Creek jurisdiction, and actually encouraged them to remove further west, away from their potential enemies. From that point on, the maroons would be subject to Seminole not Creek law. Unlike the Chickasaws, who adopted many of the laws of the Choctaws after they separated from that larger tribe in 1855, the Seminoles did not copy the Creeks' black codes after they had gained their independence. Instead, the maroons retained a great deal of independence.

The Creeks continued to exercise jurisdiction over those Seminoles and maroons who did not remove to their new country after the treaty. In the late 1850s, the Creek codes became increasingly severe, and in 1860 the Seminole agent reported renewed difficulties arising from "the stringent exercise of the Creek laws over the Seminoles and their property." He then correctly predicted that this would provide the stimulus for those that remained behind "to move and settle in their own country" once they had gathered their crops.[52]

A third reason why the lot of the maroons continued to be better than that of most blacks associated with the other Civilized Tribes resulted from the response of the mikkos and other Seminole slave owners to the migrations to Mexico. Throughout the 1850s, rumors circulated that more maroons were preparing to leave for Coahuila, and they reached a peak during periods of intense activity by Creek and white slave hunters. In the fall of 1854, for example, at the height of a disputed claim involving a great many of the maroons, reports suggested that a large number planned to run away the following spring to either Mexico or Canada, and U.S. military officials made ready to prevent their escape.[53] There were few restrictions on black mobility operating in the Seminole country, and some owners occasionally responded to the threat of further defections by selling their slaves. But that was unusual, and most seem to have employed persuasion and protection rather than coercion to keep their slaves in the Indian Territory. Rather than trying to exert stricter control over the black population, Seminole owners instead continued to demand little of their slaves. They had little choice, if they wished to keep their slaveholdings intact and still abide by their Native traditions.

A fourth and final reason why the maroons fared so well stemmed from the makeup and approach of the group members themselves. After the migrations to Mexico, those who remained behind in the Indian Territory tended to be less militant than those who had chosen to leave, facilitating a reestablishment of their former relationship with Seminoles during the 1850s. The supporters of John Horse had used Jesup's emancipation proclamation as a springboard to unqualified freedom. For three years, they had defied the mikkos by taking up residence at Fort Gibson. Upon being turned over to the Seminoles as slaves, they had refused to subject themselves to greater control, had continued to assert their right to independence, and had been prepared to defend it by force of arms. When their situation deteriorated still further in the late 1840s, they had elected to bolt for Mexico. They had risked the perils of the southern plains for the promise of liberty in an unknown and dangerous land. Those maroons had proved they were willing to go to any lengths to attain unqualified freedom.

Others were not prepared to go so far. Most had not removed to Fort Gibson in the mid-1840s but had stayed among the Seminoles on the Deep Fork and at Little River. Those people had continued to live in much the same way as they had before, with slaves and tributaries raising crops and livestock and giving a percentage to their owners or associated mikkos, and free blacks without tributary obligation being subject to even fewer restraints. They had chosen not to defy the Seminole mikkos by pressing for their freedom and asserting their independence, but to comply with the few demands placed upon them. During the 1850s, most of the maroons who had remained behind in the Indian Territory would continue in their compliance and derive benefit from its results.

Given the lack of restrictions on black mobility and the absence of an effective police force in the Seminole country, it seems clear that most of the maroons who stayed in the Indian Territory chose to do so. Likely, they were not prepared to face the possibility of reenslavement by whites or death at the hands of Plains Indians while en route to the mere prospect of freedom in a strange and distant land. Better the devil they knew; they had learned through hard experience that they could do far worse than live among the Seminoles. Those maroons were tired of wars, removals, and other traumas. During the 1850s, they attempted to create a more settled lifestyle by building farms, planting gardens, and raising crops and herds. If they could secure peace and stability by paying a small tribute to an Indian mikko, so be it. The tactic paid dividends. Seminole owners continued to demand little and generally left the maroons to their own devices.

But who were those Seminole slave owners? From the available evidence, it emerges that there were relatively few slaveholders within the tribe, and those few were either mikkos or their heirs. Seminole mikkos also held tributary rights over most of the remaining maroons. Serving in the role of guardians, those same mikkos also controlled the slaveholdings and tributary rights of others. In effect, only a few members of a small leadership elite had any stake in the tribe's blacks. Most Seminoles had no direct interest in slavery or owning tributary rights, and the few who did were held in check by the strength of Seminole indigenous customs. Mikkos were the very people expected to display the greatest diligence in guarding and preserving the tribe's cultural traditions.

Seminole property ownership was determined largely by custom. A Seminole's allegiance lay first with his or her clan, then with his or her band, and finally with the tribe as a whole. That was reflected in the way Seminoles bequeathed and inherited slaves and tributary rights. Every effort was made to retain the owner's blacks and other property within his or her matrilineal clan, and that resulted in a fairly complex system of inheritance. When a male died, his slaves or tributary rights generally would pass not to his children but to his nearest clan relatives, usually his sister's offspring. If he lacked such nephews or nieces, his property might pass to a sister, a maternal aunt, or her offspring (the deceased's cousins). Further removed heirs might include children of a son with a female member of the clan (the deceased's grandchildren) or occasionally a brother or maternal uncle, but rarely their offspring. Female slaveholders could leave slaves or tributary rights to their children, but if they died without issue, their property also would pass through the maternal line to their closest clan relatives.

In April 1850, Holata Mikko provided an example of how property could be bequeathed to more-distant female heirs when he asked that, after he died, his slaves be given to the nieces of his "poor brother Holatoochee."[54] Due to matrilineal inheritance, substantial numbers of blacks passed into the hands of Seminole women. Included among prominent Seminole slave owners of the post-Removal period were Nelly Factor, the niece of Black Factor;[55] Mahpahyistchee and Mahkahtistchee (Molly), the granddaughters of the Mikasuki mikko Kapichee Mikko;[56] and Harriet Bowlegs and Eliza Bowlegs, descendants of the late principal chief Hothli Hopoya and relatives of Holata Mikko.[57]

The Seminole custom of retaining property within the clan had two important effects. First of all, it derived from the system of matrilineal descent and was the means by which hereditary leaders kept the slaves and tributary rights of their predecessors. Seminole mikkos tended to be succeeded by the same nephews who inherited their blacks. Descent and inheritance worked together to preserve the leadership positions, propertied interests, and economic and social hegemony of the tribe's chieftain elite. Second, although the ties linking male heirs with their inherited blacks usually were strong, those between female heirs and the slaves they inherited frequently were weak. Seminole slave ownership continued to be associated with leadership and status. While that was of great importance to male heirs, it had less relevance to women, particularly those without male offspring. Evidence suggests that whereas male Seminole heirs tended to retain their blacks, female inheritors were more likely to sell or manumit their slaves. Those two factors bore heavily on Seminole-maroon relations after Removal.

Most of the Seminoles' slaves either were owned outright or were controlled by their leaders, and tribal mechanisms worked to keep it that way. If a slaveholder died without heirs, most often his blacks would revert to the band or, more precisely, the mikko. The Seminoles also employed a system of guardianship whereby slaves were given over to the protection of leaders if the heirs were minor, infirm, or incompetent. During their guardianship, Seminole mikkos had complete control over their wards' property and could derive substantial benefit by way of tribute. Having weaker ties to those slaves, some chose to abuse the privilege by selling their black charges for personal gain. Because of the strength of the guardians' control, U.S. officials, Indians, and maroons alike frequently referred to guardians as being the actual owners. But for all practical purposes, it made little difference if the Seminole mikko were a slave owner or a guardian.

Sometimes proctorship over slave property lasted for many years, and if the ward died without issue, the guardian eventually assumed full rights of ownership. The guardian selected usually was a mikko. However, mikkos often needed to seek guardians themselves, in which case the position typically fell to the principal chief. Mikkoanapa, for example, reportedly owned only one slave of his own but acted as guardian over many other maroons (or perhaps their tributary obligations).[58] In that way, mikkos came to own or control a large percentage of the Seminoles' slaves and tributary rights. Included among this elite were Mikkoanapa, Mikkopotokee, Mikko Mucasa, Heniha Mikko, and Holata Mikko.

Statistics relating to Seminole slave ownership clearly reflect the continuing strength of Native traditions within the tribe. Through ownership or guardianship, a small elite group, composed of hereditary mikkos and their close relatives and descendants, controlled most of the Seminoles' slaves. Due to matrilineal descent, moreover, many of the maroons paid tribute to Seminole women.

In the summer of 1845, 313 Seminole maroons were named in conjunction with Jesup's emancipation proclamation of 1838.[59] The list accounts for the majority of the Seminole maroon population at that time. It identified only slaves and free blacks and did not distinguish tributary allies. Claimants were included for all but 9 of those listed. Without those 9—John Horse, Romeo, and Judy; Tom Mills's wife Limas and 4 of his children, Sarah, Juana (Wannah), Dephney, and Andrew; and Abraham's son Washington—the total came to 304. The list included seventeen claimants, with fifteen named individuals. The Seminole Nation and the Creek Nation claimed 7 on the list. Those fifteen individuals claimed a total of 297 maroons, but the nine largest owners accounted for 279, or 94 percent of them.

The largest claimants were Mikkoanapa with 84, Nelly Factor with 57, Holata Mikko with 45, Mikkopotokee with 23, Holatoochee with 19, Echo Hadjo (Echo Hadjochee) with 17, A Halleck Hadjo with 12, Harriet Bowlegs with 11, and Charley Emathla, also with 11. Thus a very small number of Seminoles claimed the great majority of the maroons. This elite consisted mostly of principal chiefs, bandleaders, and their relatives, descendants, and heirs. Mikkoanapa and Holata Mikko, for example, principal chiefs in the Indian Territory and Florida after the main Removals, between them accounted for more than 42 percent of the maroons listed with a named claimant. Mikkopotokee, the nephew of Kapichee Mikko, acted as guardian for his deceased uncle's two granddaughters Mahpahyistchee and Mahkahtistchee. If the 23 under his protection are added to those held by Nelly Factor and Harriet Bowlegs, it emerges that a further 91 maroons, or 31 percent of those on the list with named claimants, belonged to Seminole women. In July 1850, in fact, Mahkahtistchee claimed to be the owner of 79 blacks "besides many infant children,"[60] a figure that would have made her the largest Seminole slaveholder at that time.

Information compiled by the Dawes Commission during tribal enrollment at the end of the century casts additional light on the makeup of

Seminole slaveholders.[61] If applicable, the commissioners asked the maroons to name their former owners. Excluding Newborns, who were not alive during slavery and were categorized separately, the Dawes Commission enrolled 857 Seminole freedmen and freedwomen. Of those, 164 were born before or during 1865, making them eligible to have been slaves. Fifty-five claimed to have been born free (most, probably, tributary allies) or did not specify who had owned them, leaving 109 listed as having a named owner.

Those 109 Seminole freedmen and freedwomen claimed to have been owned by thirty-four separate individuals,[62] but the three largest slaveholders accounted for 57, or 52 percent, of them. They were Heniha Mikko, with 25 slaves; Eliza Bowlegs, with 19; and Holata Mikko, with 13. Other principal chiefs listed as owning slaves included Hothli Hopoya, Payne, and John Chupco, who held 4 blacks between them. If these are added to those owned by the three largest slaveholders, Seminole principal chiefs and their descendants were responsible for 61, or 56 percent, of the sample. Three other owners of 7 blacks were acknowledged as having been Creek. If those are excluded from the calculation, the share held by the Seminole chieftain elite jumps to almost 60 percent. That leaves a total of 41 other blacks claiming twenty-five different owners. Some of those names are recognizable as Seminole (likely mikkos or their heirs), but others, though not identified as such, clearly were of Creek, Cherokee, or white extraction, while still others are unidentifiable. Thus, the number of slaves in the sample owned by Seminoles likely was much less than 109, raising substantially the percentage held by the elite. This furthers the argument that a small group of hereditary leaders and their heirs owned the great majority of Seminole slaves.

Information relating to the mothers and fathers of enrolled Seminole freedmen and freedwomen, who were reported to be citizens but were not included in the Dawes rolls, provides further insight. Most of those individuals were deceased. Others were said to be living but, for reasons such as residence elsewhere, were not enrolled. Whenever possible, however, the commissioners provided information about an enrollee's parents, including the name of their former owner. This information is less reliable than that provided by the enrollees about themselves, yet it provides supplementary evidence and supports the findings.[63]

The rolls listed thirty-five named former owners for the 156 unenrolled freedman mothers and fathers said to be Seminole citizens. Again, the three largest slaveholders were Eliza Bowlegs, with 36; Heniha Mikko, with 24; and Holata Mikko, with 12. Their combined holdings accounted for 46 percent of the sample. Other principal chiefs listed were Payne, with 6; Hothli Hopoya, with 4; and Mikkoanapa, with 2. Pin (King) Bowlegs (Hothli Hopoya or possibly Holata Mikko) had 3, while Eliza Bowlegs and Holata Mikko both were listed as the owner of one particular black. If those are added to the holdings of the three largest slave owners, the share of the principal chieftain elite rises to 56 percent, the same as among the enrollees. Six owners of 20 other blacks in the sample were identified as Creeks. If those are excluded from the calculation, the share of the elite rises to 65 percent. The remaining 48 blacks in the sample listed twenty-two different owners, but again, many of those clearly were not of Seminole extraction. These numbers therefore support the findings among the enrollees.

A profile of a typical Seminole slave owner, which stands in stark contrast to that in the other slaveholding tribes, emerges from these statistics. Whereas one could expect a Cherokee, Creek, Choctaw, or Chickasaw slaveholder to be a well-to-do Indian-white plantocrat or industrialist, a Seminole slave owner usually was not of white descent or wealthy but a "fullblood" farmer with few material assets. The typical slaveholder among the four tribes wore the clothing of whites, had a Christian education, spoke English, and lived in elegant style in a large house surrounded by improvements. A typical Seminole slaveholder wore native garb, did not attend school or church, spoke Creek, and lived in a basic log cabin with a small garden. Male slaveholders predominated within the other four tribes, but after Removal, Indian women owned one of every three slaves among the Seminoles.

Like the Seminoles, most Cherokees, Creeks, Choctaws, and Chickasaws did not possess slaves. In 1860, just 12 percent of families within those four tribes living in the Indian Territory owned any blacks.[64] They usually were members of the new capitalist order that had emerged within each of the tribes. They viewed institutionalized slavery controlled by severe black codes as the key to both individual and group success, and they had promoted its incorporation, preservation, and expansion within their tribes. Seminole slave owners typically were members of the hereditary ruling elite. Other Seminoles expected them to preserve native practices and oppose the type of changes that facilitated the adoption of institutionalized slavery within the other four tribes. Seminole owners tended to hold on to a worldview that demanded that slavery retain its traditional forms.

The system of tribute and deference the mikkos had employed in Florida continued in the Indian Territory until the Civil War. After Removal, however, some owners became more open to selling their slaves outside the tribe. Seminole slaveholders had become cognizant of the concepts of personal property and profit in Florida and were prepared to defend their rights as owners in the Indian Territory, but in practice they could exercise little control over their blacks. Slave owners faced the choice of whether to realize the highest returns for their property through sale or to retain their blacks and continue to receive their traditional annual tributes. It was in this regard that Seminole slaveholders divided.

Some owners, epitomized by the Bowlegs family, remained unwilling to sell their blacks. The ties that bound those Indians and maroons tended to be strong, spanning years and sometimes generations. They were based on a shared history of alliance and kinship. The Bowlegses enjoyed both the tributes and the status that the association brought them, and they tended to retain their blacks. Even when ties appeared less strong, as when they assumed the role of guardian or the owners were female inheritors, they retained their traditional approach and would not sell.

Harriet Bowlegs provided an excellent example. After Removal, her blacks stayed with her until Jesup visited the Indian Territory in the summer of 1845, when they fled to Fort Gibson. In September 1846, Harriet complained to Duval that she was impoverished and that her house was falling into ruin. The maroons on the military reservation refused to help her, stating that they were now free, yet she did not attempt to sell them. She held on to her slaves throughout her life, freeing some, and emancipated all that remained at her death, becoming the leading manumitter among the Seminoles.[65] The Bowlegs family remained constant to Native customs that guided slaveholding practice and owners' relations with their blacks.

Other Seminole slave owners had weaker ties with their blacks. Those included Mikko Mucasa and Heniha Mikko—brothers who owned few slaves of their own but acted as guardians over many others—and some female inheritors. Usually, those individuals had acquired their property recently, were acting as guardians, or were women who had inherited their slaves from a distant relative. Those owners had only a short history of association with their blacks. Some became susceptible to the influence of outsiders and compromised their Native beliefs for monetary gain by selling their slaves.

Financial considerations were becoming more important to some Seminole owners, who realized that they could derive more material benefit by selling their blacks. In the Indian Territory during the 1850s, the customary annual individual tribute of ten bushels of corn was worth only $5, but the going rate for a healthy black ranged from $250 to $1,200 for an individual with special talents or skills. If a slave of a Seminole paid tribute his entire lifetime, he never would come close to producing for his owner the equivalent of his market value. Assets in slave property also were a liability, especially for those owners who lacked a history of strong allegiance from their blacks. Their slaves might run off to join John Horse's band of maroons on the Rio Grande, or they might be claimed or kidnapped by whites or Creeks. Seminole customs tended to hold those owners in check, and they were unable to impose stricter controls over their slaves. One solution some chose was to hire out their blacks to traders, military officials, and missionaries, but others turned to sales for greater financial gain. Heniha Mikko, for example, sold several slaves to non–tribal members during the 1840s and 1850s.[66] In that way, some owners made money from their property by dispatching a number of the maroons from the Seminole country.

Some Seminole leaders, acting as guardians over a great many more slaves than they owned, occasionally chose to dispose of their wards' property and keep the proceeds. Southern Superintendent Charles Dean reported in June 1856 that, as there was "no inducement" to retain their blacks, "the shrewder of the Indians" were engaging in speculative enterprises with whites:

> Many cases of oppression and spoliation, in which women and orphan children suffer the loss of property, are produced by this cause. [The] relationship of guardian as it exists among them is simply a means whereby the guardian, if so disposed, possesses himself of the property of the ward. In cases like this the White speculator too frequently becomes the possessor of the slaves to the loss of the real owner.[67]

Mikko Mucasa provided the best example of such exploits in the early 1850s. He worked in cahoots with the Duvals to run off and sell a number of blacks belonging to his wards and to Seminoles absent in Florida to prevent them from fleeing to Mexico.[68] Dean believed that trend to be "on the increase."[69] The threat of sale by money-seeking Seminole owners and guardians proved to be a source of considerable concern to some of the maroons during the 1840s and 1850s.

Some female owners, with only loose ties to their blacks, also disposed of slaves to non–tribal members. Seminole women were less affected by the prestige attached to slave ownership. They also could not offer maroons the same protection as a mikko and might have experienced difficulty collecting their tributes. Consequently, women tended to be more open to offers from outsiders than their male counterparts. While female inheritors with stronger ties to their blacks tended to retain or manumit their slaves, those with weaker ties and more interest in financial considerations were more likely to dispose of them. The latter consisted of women who were serving as guardians for heirs or who only recently had inherited their property from a distant relative. Prior to Removal, for example, Sally Factor had sold ten of her own slaves and twenty others belonging to her nephews and nieces, for whom she had acted as guardian, to Siah Hardridge.[70] And in 1843, Nelly Factor also sold Hardridge a number of her inherited slaves.[71] But the most important instance of a female owner selling her property outside the tribe took place in the early 1850s when Mahkahtistchee sold her slaves to Daniel Boone Aspberry, a Creek-white. Various claimants pursued Mahkahtistchee's blacks throughout the decade, and the information that emerged from the ensuing testimony provides the principal body of evidence pertaining to Seminole slave ownership at that time.

Kapichee Mikko originally had owned the blacks in question. Most were the descendants of Pompey and his two wives, Melinda and Dolly, whom Kapichee Mikko had purchased near Saint Augustine during the English period in Florida. When Kapichee Mikko had died, Mikkopotokee, his sister's son, had inherited his slaves. For unknown reasons, Mikkopotokee had refused to accept the property and had given the blacks to Kapichee Mikko's son, Tuskeneehau, and his sisters. Prior to Removal, however, Tuskeneehau had committed suicide, and his sisters also had died. The property then had returned to Mikkopotokee, who had acted as guardian for Tuskeneehau's daughters, Mahpahyistchee and Mahkahtistchee.[72]

During the 1830s and 1840s, Hugh Love, a white Georgian and a licensed trader to the Creeks in the West, and his heirs laid claim to a number of those blacks. The claim was based on Love's supposed purchase of the slaves in 1835 from members of a Creek-white family named Gray. The Grays claimed to be the original owners of the slaves and stated that Seminoles had stolen them in or around 1795. Love had died shortly after making his purchase, and his brother, John, and other heirs took up the claim.[73]

John Love had traveled to New Orleans with the intention of apprehending the blacks he claimed en route to the Indian Territory. In May 1838, he had persuaded the local courts to prohibit the army from removing those sixty-seven slaves outside the city limits. Shortly afterward, however, he was forced to reduce his claim. Love had been able to identify thirty-two of the blacks, but the other thirty-five had camped elsewhere. When they had heard of Love's pending arrival, all of the maroons in the camp had disguised themselves with paint, rendering positive identification impossible. Love had apprehended the thirty-two he could identify and had them transported from Fort Pike to the local jail. There they had remained while the other emigrant maroons and Seminoles sailed up the Arkansas to Fort Gibson. On June 17, the U.S. district attorney had obtained an order demanding that the local authorities deliver the incarcerated slaves to the emigration agents and that Love drop the suit. Love had been given ten days to appeal, but he had not. On June 27, therefore, the authorities handed over the thirty-two maroons to Lieutenant John Reynolds to be dispatched to Fort Gibson. The blacks had arrived safely in the Indian Territory on August 5, and the Love claim temporarily fell into abeyance.[74]

During the summer of 1840, John Love had tried to enlist the aid of some leading Creeks and Seminoles in acquiring the slaves he claimed. On July 3, Arbuckle had met in council with Creek and Seminole leaders, and they had agreed that Love's claim was good. Later, however, Mikkoanapa, Cloud, and Nocose Yahola had informed Arbuckle that the blacks were the property of Mahpahyistchee and Mahkahtistchee. That change of heart had resulted from the death of Mikkopotokee, leaving the slaves under Mikkoanapa's guardianship. The principal chief thus had a direct interest in retaining his wards' property in the Seminole country.

According to the three leaders, some of the blacks had been living among the Seminoles for more than fifty years, and their owners never had agreed to sell them. Thus, when Love had presented his claim in Washington in May 1841, it had come to nothing.[75] Undaunted, Love again had raised the claim in the spring of 1842 and in 1844, when it had gone before the Creek Council. But again the Seminole mikkos had declared the blacks to be the property of Tuskeneehau's daughters.[76] When the maroons who had been residing at Fort Gibson had been turned over to the Seminoles in January 1849, W. E. Love, another heir to the original claimant, had demanded to receive the slaves he allegedly had inherited. The military officials in charge of the transfer had refused his demands, however, and the Love claim had come to an end.[77]

With the death of Mikkoanapa in December 1848, Mahkahtistchee came into possession of her grandfather's blacks with the understanding that when she died, they would pass to her sister, Mahpahyistchee. Their number evidently had increased since the death of Kapichee Mikko, for in August 1850, Mahkahtistchee claimed to be the owner of seventy-nine slaves and a number of small children. Mikko Mucasa and several other Seminole mikkos agreed, however, that she should give thirty-four of them to William J. Duval, the brother of the subagent. Those slaves would serve as partial compensation for the services he had rendered as attorney in securing the return of the maroons residing at Fort Gibson. Thirty-one women and children belonging to Mahkahtistchee were seized, and just three men escaped capture. Mahkahtistchee complained that her blacks had not even fled to the post but had continued to live near to her. Moreover, she never had agreed to part with any of her slaves, and the Seminole leaders had assumed the right to dispose of them without her consent.[78] But Mahkahtistchee's protests fell on deaf ears, and those dealings substantially reduced her slaveholdings.

By the early 1850s, Mahkahtistchee was "very considerably advanced in years" and unable to control her blacks. Dean described the relationship between the Seminole owner and her slaves:

> Her negroes, as far as the disposition of their own time and labor was concerned, were only nominally in a state of servitude; they did not, nor was she able to compel them, to labor regularly for her, neither did they pay her for the liberty of disposing of their own time and labor; they would not support her in an establishment, residence or home of her own, or cultivate fields separately

for her. But if she would reside or live with any of them they would support her, and in this way she passed from one family of her slaves to another,—now with one—now with another. As the infirmities of age increased she grew more dissatisfied with the state of things, and sought means by which she could more effectually control her servants and force them to maintain her in comfort.[79]

What Dean described appears to have been a remnant of an earlier form of kinship slavery. There is also a strong suggestion that Harriet Bowlegs had enjoyed a similar relationship with her blacks prior to their removing to Fort Gibson. As Saunt explains, "Kinship slaves were to some extent family members. They cooked, cleaned, collected firewood, farmed, provided sexual services, and were a lot like any other family member. [In] kinship societies, the line between slave and family was frequently murky."[80] But while the maroons wished to preserve the old ways and maintain their traditional relationship with their owner, Mahkahtistchee sought to derive more material benefit from her property. And she was prepared to dispose of her inheritance to do so.

Mahkahtistchee was a prime candidate to become involved in the sale of blacks outside of the tribe. She was a female inheritor who stood to gain little status or financial remuneration from keeping her slaves. Also, she was only distantly related to the person from whom she had inherited the property. Because of Mikkopotokee's refusal to accept his inheritance, Mahkahtistchee had acquired the slaves through the male line. It is unlikely that she would have enjoyed a close relationship with Kapichee Mikko, her paternal grandfather, so the ties binding her to her inherited blacks would have been weak. Furthermore, those slaves had a long history of guardianship, and Mahkahtistchee's ownership had been short, so few obstacles prevented her from disposing of them. Finally, they seemed a liability; at any time, Mahkahtistchee might lose her assets altogether. Hugh Love and his heirs already had coveted her blacks, and Seminole leaders had disposed of almost half of them without her consent and without compensating her for the loss. She had no guarantees that the Loves would not revive their claim, that Seminole leaders would not give away or sell more of her property, or that kidnappers would not steal her slaves. Mahkahtistchee was receiving little material benefit from owning her blacks, and there remained the distinct possibility that they might elect to quit the Indian Territory and join their kinsmen in Mexico.

Deciding that she needed more tangible means of support in her old age and infirmity, Mahkahtistchee broke with Seminole custom by selling her slaves outside the tribe. In the spring of 1853, Aspberry persuaded her to part with the property. On April 7, the two reached an understanding whereby Aspberry would capture as many of Mahkahtistchee's blacks as he could, pay her the bargain price of $100 for each one taken, and sell them outside the Seminole country for whatever they would fetch. Although he paid her no money at that point, Mahkahtistchee gave Aspberry a bill of sale. Later he would use the bill as evidence of his right to her property. During the summer, her sister, Mahpahyistchee, died without issue, and other slaves she owned passed to Mahkahtistchee. In September, she sold them to Aspberry. But before he could capture any of those blacks, Mahkahtistchee died, leaving the way open for Aspberry to claim sole possession of the rights of ownership to her property.[81]

Mahkahtistchee's death opened up a Pandora's box of disputed claims to her slaves. The resultant speculation lasted for six years and suggested a wide circle of dealings in blacks associated with Seminoles. Other speculators from neighboring tribes and states became involved and added further complications to existing claims, either by purchasing slaves who still were residing in the Seminole country or disposing of them before their title was clear and undisputed. There were conflicting reports on the number of blacks included in the various claims and their rightful owners. And unsubstantiated accusations of bribery, corruption, and complicity leveled at both Indian agents and Seminole and Creek leaders alike by interested parties, further clouded the issues.[82] But what clearly emerges from the disputed claims to Mahkahtistchee's slaves is an image of the speculator in diametrical opposition to the Seminole mikko. The one attempted to remove the blacks from the Seminole country and sell them for profit, the other sought to utilize his position and indigenous practices to retain them within his sphere of influence.

With Mahkahtistchee's demise, Aspberry determined to move immediately to capture her slaves before the bill of sale could be disputed. Hearing of the circumstances of the "sale," however, the blacks refused to accept him as their owner "and notified him that they would resist unto death any attempt by him to seize them;—and in this determination they appear to have been supported by some of the Seminole Indians."[83] Un-

daunted, Aspberry sought the aid of the Creek authorities. Soon afterward, Creek leaders in council decided that his claim was good and
ordered the lighthorse to assist him in securing his property.

One night during early November 1853, Aspberry, together with
thirty Creek lighthorsemen and several white associates, rode over to
Mahkahtistchee's last residence, about twelve miles from the Oak Ridge
Mission. There, they captured twenty-seven of her slaves, most being
members of one large family, while they slept.[84] Mary Ann Lilley, the
wife of the Presbyterian minister, recounted the scene: "The Father belonged to another person and they tore them all away from him leaving
him wounded and bleeding behind. He tried to rescue them and they cut
him down with their knives, poor fellow he died not know[ing] that the
law gave them a right to his flesh and blood."[85] The alarm soon spread to
the maroons living close by, and Aspberry and his men beat a hasty retreat
from the Seminole country, carrying their captives with them.[86]

The kidnapped blacks were taken to North Fork Town in the Creek
Nation and sold to various white residents of Arkansas. A black man who
was there told Talomas Mikko:

> [It] was heart rending to see the mother of the large family. [It]
> was all scattered and she would walk from one to another putting
> her hand on their heads saying in a pitiful tone, 'Oh! Lord, Oh
> Lord!' untill [sic] she fell down in a swoon and in that state she
> was put in a wagon by a white Baptist minister, and drove off.[87]

But Aspberry had not secured all the slaves he claimed were his. In
February 1854, he suggested that sixteen of them still were at large in the
Seminole country. In view of the danger involved in trying to capture
Seminole maroons, however, his two leading associates apparently retired
from the enterprise, and Aspberry sold his title to those remaining to
Cornelius Pryor, a white U.S. citizen and trader at North Fork Town.[88]

Aspberry's involvement in the affair did not end there, for he was
behind a second kidnapping venture in April 1854. This time the raid
aimed to capture the family of George Noble, a free maroon. George
appears to have been the son of Noble and the nephew of Polly, a wife of
former Seminole principal chief Hothli Hopoya. Noble and Polly were
children of Beck, a slave of Hothli Hopoya. In 1819, the mikko had
emancipated his wife and her two children, Margarita and Martiness, but

Beck's other children, including Noble, and their offspring had been bequeathed to Harriet Bowlegs. Sometime after Removal, Harriet Bowlegs manumitted George, and he continued to reside among the maroons as a free black.[89]

Although George Noble was a free man, his wife and children became targets for speculators. In the fall of 1853, U.S. government officials made plans to send a delegation to Florida to persuade Holata Mikko and his band to remove to the Indian Territory. Knowing of his close association with the Bowlegs family, in early December they asked George to participate in the expedition as an interpreter and intermediary. Aware that Aspberry possessed a bill of sale for his family, and knowing the circumstances surrounding the recent kidnapping raid into the Seminole country, he at first refused. But after Lieutenant John Gibbons and Seminole subagent Bryan Smithson assured him that his family would not be molested during his absence, George relented and traveled to Florida with the delegation.

In the meantime, Aspberry sold his title to the family to other parties in the Creek Nation. Taking advantage of his absence, one night in mid-April 1854, a company of Creeks attacked George's wife and children. The eldest son tried to defend the family, but they killed him and carried off the rest. They also stole or destroyed property valued at $370. Fifty bushels of corn were lost, and a "fine brooding sow" killed, while "one very fine horse" and three ponies were taken away. George Noble's wife and children later were "sold into slavery in Louisiana," and although he petitioned for redress for the outrage, government officials took no action on his behalf to recover his family or property.[90]

Pryor, meanwhile, expanded his interests in Seminole slave property. During the spring of 1854, a number of Seminole maroons who had been claimed by Aspberry urged Pryor to purchase title to them all. They either would buy their freedom from him or find other purchasers of their choice in the Seminole and Creek Nations. Their response emphasizes the comparative laxity of Seminole slavery. While they were prepared to live as slaves among the Seminoles, those maroons preferred to buy their freedom rather than allow non–tribal members to purchase them. That they had accrued enough funds to purchase their freedom also suggests that they were keeping most of what they produced—and that they produced a lot.

Pryor favored the agreement. On November 24, 1854, he gave Aspberry a promissory note for $7,800 for the maroons. With this latest purchase, Pryor claimed to own the title to twenty-five slaves associated with the Seminoles, as well as five others living in the Creek country. He proceeded to the Seminole country to dispose of the blacks, as arranged, but when he arrived there, he learned that some Seminole leaders were opposed to the arrangement and disputed his title.[91] Pryor's main opponents turned out to be Halleck Tastanaki, Necksucky, and Heniha Mikko. Shortly thereafter, those three commenced a prolonged campaign of obstructionism aimed at frustrating Pryor's efforts to dispose of the maroons, in order to retain them within their own spheres of influence.

Because she had died without issue, the Seminole leaders claimed that they should either inherit Mahkahtistchee's slaves or act as guardians over them for her yet-to-be-determined heirs. Under Seminole law, these leaders stated, the property should pass first to Mahkahtistchee's band-leaders and then to the principal chief, Heniha Mikko. In his capacity as her mikko, Halleck Tastanaki informed Pryor that he and Necksucky were the guardians of Mahkahtistchee's blacks "and would not suffer them to be taken from the country." Pryor suggested that they bring the matter before the Creek authorities for a ruling, and Halleck Tastanaki concurred. When the council met on December 26, however, Halleck Tastanaki failed to appear. In January 1855, Pryor turned to Superintendent Thomas Drew for assistance.[92] That began a four-year period of personal appeals and written petitions to government officials for redress of his grievances. Pryor's industry produced a mountain of correspondence and a plethora of conflicting reports, contradictory testimony, and personality clashes, but it failed to deliver the blacks he claimed. In the end, the efforts of the Seminole mikkos were rewarded with their retaining the disputed slaves within the tribe.

Though the Seminole mikkos nominally accepted Pryor's title, they used various tactics to frustrate his attempts to secure Mahkahtistchee's blacks. First, they claimed to have opposed the original sale. At the time of his death, Kapichee Mikko had "enjoined upon the town chiefs to see that the property was kept together, and that the negroes made corn for his children, which they had always done."[93] Heniha Mikko had advised Mahkahtistchee not to sell her slaves, but she had ignored him. Not only that, but she also had not complied with the old Seminole custom of obtaining the consent of the bandleaders before making the sale. The mikkos also claimed to be unhappy with Aspberry's subsequent conduct in the affair and were distressed over his kidnapping incursions into their country.[94] They stalled for time and would not allow Pryor to remove or dispose of Mahkahtistchee's blacks.

The Seminole mikkos next used tribal customs to obstruct Pryor's efforts. They claimed that, under Seminole law, if a slaveholder died without heirs, his or her property would pass to the bandleaders. If the heirs were minor, "in all cases" the mikkos would assume the role of guardian. It also was reported to be general practice for Seminole mikkos "to levy a tribute upon large estates in their country." As Mahkahtistchee's bandleader, Halleck Tastanaki now demanded $100 for each black claimed by Pryor before he would allow them to be removed from their present location.[95] Even if he did not qualify as either the owner or guardian of Mahkahtistchee's slaves, Halleck Tastanaki still stood to gain a substantial amount in taxes. But Halleck Tastanaki likely inflated the figure applied to each black to make payment impossible. His intent was not to extract taxes from Pryor but to force him to drop his claim.

The persistent Pryor would not be put off easily, and he forced the mikkos to resort to still other methods to thwart the stubborn claimant. Their next ploy was to introduce other heirs to Kapichee Mikko's property. Halleck Tastanaki and Passock Yohola now claimed that the blacks belonged to two minor children of Charley Brown, who had died a few years earlier. They stated that Charley Brown was the same Kapichee Mikko who originally had owned the slaves and that Mahkahtistchee had acted as guardian of the property for his children because he had not removed to the Indian Territory. Later, Halleck Tastanaki and other Seminole leaders claimed that no division of Kapichee Mikko's estate ever had taken place and that others of his grandchildren were entitled to a share of his property equal to that of the children of Tuskeneehau. At various times, the mikkos mentioned six, seven, eight, and even fourteen other heirs.[96] But again, that was a ruse. Charley Brown was not Kapichee Mikko but a distant relative with no claim to his property. That merely added to the complexity of the case and prevented Pryor's claim from being brought to a speedy conclusion.

But by far the most effective tactic the mikkos employed was their not cooperating with Pryor to have the case formally decided. The chiefs would arrange to meet with Pryor at a certain time and place and then fail to show up. If Pryor attended one of their council meetings, they would appear to comply with his requests but later would decide differently. At that time, the Seminoles still were subject to the authority of the Creek Council. On several occasions, Pryor arranged for his claim to be decided by that body. The Seminole mikkos attended only once, stating that "they would not hold themselves bound by the decision of the Creek Council, and that the proper place to try the matter was before the Seminole agent and council." Then they left.

The case dragged on through the mid-1850s until, except for Pryor's incessant petitioning, it fell into abeyance. Pryor might have continued to speculate in Seminole slaves, given that in April 1856 he claimed to be the owner of thirty-seven of them, the largest number mentioned until then.[97] He raised his claim again in February 1857[98] and April 1859[99] but to no avail. After six years, the case drew to a close, with the Seminole mikkos and the maroons in dispute the clear victors.

The information that emerged during the various claims to Mahkah-tistchee's blacks adds substance to our knowledge and understanding of Seminole slave ownership in the Indian Territory. It clearly was unusual for an owner to sell so many slaves outside the tribe, and Seminole mikkos frowned on the practice. Mahkahtistchee's circumstances were unusual in that she held most of the qualifications associated with amenability to disposing of slave property, and she became particularly susceptible to the influence of speculators. But Mahkahtistchee displayed poor business sense and a lack of understanding of the potential value of her property in her sales. Aspberry stood to make a fortune on the deal. Mahkahtistchee cannot be described as a typical Seminole slaveholder. She ignored traditional practices when choosing to dispose of her blacks in that way. The Seminole mikkos then acted to preserve tribal customs by retaining the property within their sphere of influence.

It also emerged that Seminole owners were not at complete liberty to dispose of their slaves to whomever they pleased, whenever it suited them. They were held in check by indigenous practices designed to retain blacks within the tribe. Seminole mikkos assumed a patriarchal role in such matters. They expected slave owners to seek their advice before entering into transactions and to gain their consent before engaging in large sales. If slaveholders ignored those traditional practices or conducted a sale in a manner unacceptable to them, Seminole mikkos were prepared to exert their considerable influence to prevent any transference of property from taking place. Furthermore, although Seminole mikkos supposedly were subject to the overall authority of the Creek Council from

1845 to 1856, they clearly refused to accept its findings and rulings in such matters. They insisted on having the right to investigate and decide all claims to slave property owned by Seminoles, and they went to great lengths to protect it.

Finally, Seminole customs relating to slave ownership were intended to retain blacks not just within the tribe but within the grasp of the leadership elite. The system of taxation, guardianship, and inheritance the Seminoles employed enabled the mikkos to gain possession of the great majority of slaves held by the tribe. Nowhere was this more clearly illustrated than in the case of Mahkahtistchee's blacks. A Mikasuki mikko originally had owned the slaves in question, and Seminole bandleaders and a principal chief had become their guardians. When Mahkahtistchee died without issue, other mikkos stood to become inheritors, guardians, or eventual owners of her property. Those individuals built obstacles to frustrate the efforts of speculators and prevent the blacks from leaving the tribe. Among the Seminoles, power and status continued to be attached to slaveholding after Removal, and indigenous practices helped strengthen the position of the leadership elite by consolidating its monopoly of the tribe's slave property.

CHAPTER FIVE

"Only Slaves in Name"

Although the threat of sale and kidnapping of slaves became more prevalent, slavery among the Seminoles changed little after Removal. That resulted from the continuing strength of indigenous practices within the tribe, and the leadership status of its slaveholders. In the Indian Territory the Seminoles resisted white acculturative influences and tenaciously retained their Native traditions. As in Florida, almost all Seminole slave owners were mikkos or their heirs. Leaders more concerned with status and tradition than profits owned most of the slaves. Consequently, the system of slavery they employed remained aboriginal, featuring tribute and deference. Seminole owners placed as few demands on their blacks in the West as they had in Florida, and the maroons continued to enjoy a great deal of independence.

Contemporary descriptions of Seminole slavery in the West closely resemble those of the pre-Removal period. Many "slaves" likely remained tributary allies. Upon arriving in the Indian Territory, Indian-white owners among the Cherokees, Creeks, Choctaws, and Chickasaws put their slaves to work clearing land, building houses and improvements, planting fields and gardens, and tending to livestock. In terms of the resources available to them, the largest slaveholders held a clear advantage over the other tribal members. In contrast, Western Superintendent Armstrong reported in 1839 and 1840 that the Seminole maroons who had settled between the Arkansas and the Deep Fork were "indisposed to labor" and that they exercised "an important influence" and "great control" over their Indian owners.[1]

By 1842, the maroons had become much more productive. In his annual report, Armstrong observed: "That portion of the Seminoles who have settled on the Deep Fork of the Canadian have raised a surplus of corn, beans, pumpkins, melons, all of which grow to great perfection, and a few have raised small patches of rice. The labor, however, is principally performed by the Seminole negroes, who have thus far conducted themselves with great propriety."[2]

Two years later, on a tour through the Indian Territory, N. Sayer Harris reported that slaves of Seminoles paid merely a "small tribute to their master, say two or three bushels of corn, or when they raise stock a beef or two."[3] It appears that, prior to the tripartite treaty of 1845, Seminole slave owners and maroons attempted to reestablish their pre-Removal relationship in the Indian Territory.

Following the traumas of the late 1840s and early 1850s, which had resulted in the followers of Kowakochi and John Horse migrating to Mexico, Seminole slaveholders and maroons who remained behind again attempted to reconstruct their former relationship. During the 1850s, Seminole owners made no more of a sustained effort to exert greater control over their slaves than they had before. Nor did they attempt to punish blacks for the actions of their kinsmen by placing more demands on them. After so much upheaval, they embarked on a period of consolidation and appear to have been content to exact tributes, much as they had in Florida.

In June 1856, Dean penned the most detailed contemporary description of Seminole slavery as it then was being practiced in the Indian Territory:

> It is well known that the slaves are only slaves in name. In nine cases out of ten they live with their masters or not as they please; work, if they work at all, when and where they please, and make their own bargains; come and go according to their own inclination, sit at the table with their masters, and speak to them as tho' they were equals. I have seen some exhibitions of these traits that would scarcely be believed without being witnessed. It is very rare indeed that the Indian owner of this class of property holds them

in proper subjection to himself. The consequence of this condition of things is that no profit is derived from the property; the slaves are really of no value to their owners beyond the imaginary distinction that attaches to the name of master; and hence when the Indians are removed from intercourse with the Whites there is no trouble among them about titles &c., to their negroes.[4]

Those comments echoed Gad Humphreys's 1827 observation that blacks associated with the Seminoles were "slaves but in name." Dean's description vividly illustrates the consistency and continuity inherent within Seminole-maroon relations.

Although airing typical southern white sensibilities, Dean's comments fairly accurately described Seminole slavery at that time. Seminole freedman Primus Dean later recalled another example of kinship slavery. His mother told him that the Seminoles "didn't consider them slaves" but members of the family, and that Indians and blacks ate together and worked and slept side by side.[5] Dave McIntosh, another Seminole freedman, recounted that the maroons' forebears had enjoyed so much freedom as slaves that emancipation hardly had affected their daily lives.[6] But perhaps most remarkably, the census takers of 1860, although carefully enumerating both slave owners and bondsmen in the Cherokee, Creek, Choctaw, and Chickasaw tribes, were led to believe that slavery did not exist at all among the Seminoles. They incorrectly but tellingly concluded, "The small tribe of Seminoles [hold] no slaves, but intermarry with the colored population."[7]

Seminole slaves continued to live apart from their owners, to own property, including horses and firearms, and to conduct their own bargains, free from restraints of trade. Creek law forbade slaves from owning guns and horses, and that tribe took exception to the Seminoles' allowing their blacks to do so. In the first week of September 1848, Creek and Cherokee slave hunters kidnapped Clary and her five children, all under the protection of Mikkoanapa. During the raid, the kidnappers took a gun from Thomas, Clary's husband, and a horse, a saddle, and a bridle belonging to a free black named Margaret. The raiders claimed that they were acting under orders from Roley McIntosh and that, according to Creek law, they had the right to dispossess the blacks of such property. But the Seminoles demanded that the party return the blacks' property.

That affair helped add to the friction between Seminoles, Creeks, and maroons and kept tensions high during the period just prior to Kowako-chi's and John Horse's defection.[8]

Under the terms of the 1866 Reconstruction treaty, those Seminoles and maroons who had remained loyal to the Union were to receive monetary compensation for property lost or destroyed during the Civil War. U.S. officials set aside $50,000 for the purpose and determined to adjust all claims accordingly.[9] The claims compiled for assessing who was eligible to participate in the award reveal important information on the property holdings and lifestyle of the Seminole maroons living in the Indian Territory at the onset of the Civil War. It also is possible to use the claims to compare maroon and Loyal Seminole property holdings at that time.[10]

Fifty-nine Seminole maroon heads of household claimed a total of $27,640 for property lost during the Civil War.[11] Their claims ranged from $76 to $1,322 and averaged $468 per household. Ben Bruner, inter-preter and adviser to Holata Mikko, submitted the largest maroon claim. His property included 60 head of cattle worth $428, 20 horses worth $400, and farming tools valued at $186.[12] Prior to the Civil War, the Bruners established themselves as the most affluent of the maroon fam-ilies, their wealth being based on livestock holdings. Five members of the Bruner family—Affy, Ben, Caesar, John, and Sancho—claimed a total of 53 head of horses worth $1,210, 11 head of cattle worth $783, and 33 cows and calves valued at $495. Between them, they claimed $2,488 in livestock alone. Each of the five Bruner claims was far higher than the maroon average. Their totals averaged almost $800 per claimant, 70 per-cent higher than the average maroon claim.[13]

During the postbellum period, the Bruners used the compensation they received under the 1866 treaty to rebuild their livestock holdings and become the wealthiest dynasty among the Seminole freedmen. Ben Bruner became leader of the Jim Lane band during Reconstruction. Soon afterward, it became known as the Ben Bruner band. Caesar Bruner later took over and became the most famous of the Seminole freedman bandleaders. It became known as the Caesar Bruner band, and his de-scendants have retained the name into the early twenty-first century.

Surprisingly, the maroons do not appear to have engaged in as much agricultural diversification as the Loyal Seminoles. While the maroons concentrated almost exclusively on staples such as cattle, corn, hogs, and poultry, the Loyal Seminoles claimed for such items as beans, beehives, cabbage, Hungarian grass, Irish potatoes, onions, peanuts, peas, pumpkins (fresh and dried), rice, salt, sheep, and wheat. But many of the Indians also claimed only for staples, and most of the Loyal Seminoles' property was concentrated in horses, cattle, and hogs. One of the most interesting maroon claims was that of Rebecca Payne, a close associate of the Bruners. Besides the customary staples, Payne's property included 2 yoke of oxen, 8 bushels of peanuts, 11 bushels of potatoes, 3 bushels of onions, 3 bushels of beans, 60 pounds of bacon, and a wagon and horses, the whole valued at $1,174.[14] But Rebecca Payne's claim was exceptional.

The claims vividly document the maroons' lack of diversification. Ten items accounted for all of fifty-one of the fifty-nine maroon claims, and their combined value represented more than 99 percent of the total amount of property the maroons claimed to have owned. In order of their total value, those items were horses; cattle, cows, and calves; hogs; corn; household goods; farm tools; yokes of oxen; firearms; poultry; and potatoes. Only eight, or less than 14 percent, of the maroon claims included anything other than those ten items. Interestingly, although rice was listed among the Loyal Seminole property losses, it was not included in any of the maroon claims. The group grew the crop in Florida prior to Removal, at Fort Gibson in the summer of 1847, and in the Seminole Nation after the Civil War, so it seems unusual that the maroons did not claim for rice.[15]

Of the eight maroon heads of household listing property other than the standard ten items, three claimed for bacon, three for peanuts, two for beans, two for fodder, and one each for beehives, oats, onions, and wheat. The summed value of those articles was $135, or less than one-half of one percent of the total the maroons claimed. Of the eight claims, only five individuals listed items other than bacon or fodder. They included Ben Bruner, who grew wheat and oats; Daily Davis, who grew peanuts; Davy Dilley, who grew peanuts and kept bees; Rebecca Payne, who grew peanuts, onions, and beans; and Jack Shortman, who grew beans.[16] Observers in Florida, the Indian Territory, Coahuila, and Texas often noted that the maroons were skilled in agricultural techniques. They also engaged in diversified farming both before and shortly after Removal. It would appear, therefore, that the lack of diversification and innovation apparent in the group's property returns resulted from the constant disruption and removals that dogged their progress in the late 1840s and 1850s. The maroons seem to have become more conservative agriculturists, relying on livestock and crop staples to meet their needs.

The four most valuable items owned by maroon claimants were horses; cattle, cows, and calves; hogs; and corn. Fifty-five of the fifty-nine maroon heads of household claimed for horses. The claims ranged from Calina Payne's single mare to Abram Payne's 34 head.[17] The maroons claimed 447 horses in all, an average of 8 head per owner. In addition, three claimants listed 39 yearlings. The value of the horses and yearlings represented 38 percent of the total maroon claim. Cattle, and cows and calves, which were differentiated in the claims, came next. Only eleven of the fifty-nine heads of household did not claim for one or the other, and four claimed for both. Eighty-one percent of the maroon claimants, therefore, owned either cattle or cows and calves, or both. The claims ranged from Adoca Coody's and Calina Payne's 2 head each to Ben Bruner's 60 head.[18] Forty-two maroons claimed a total of 643 head of cattle, an average of 15 head per owner. Seven maroons claimed just for cows and calves, and four more for cows and calves in addition to cattle. They claimed 79 head of cows and calves in all, an average of 7 head per owner. The value of the cattle, cows, and calves listed represented 20 percent of the total maroon claim.

Hogs and corn came next. Fifty-four of the fifty-nine maroon heads of household listed hogs. They claimed a total of 1,577 hogs, an average of 29 head per owner. Their value represented 14 percent of the total maroon claim. Forty-three maroons listed corn. They claimed for 4,640 bushels, an average of 108 bushels per household. A 10-bushel tribute to a Seminole mikko, therefore, would have accounted for less than one-tenth of the corn produced by most maroon households.[19] Although crucial to their subsistence, corn had a low market value of just 50 cents per bushel, and it amounted to just 8 percent of the total maroon claim.

Household goods, farm tools, yokes of oxen, guns, poultry, and potatoes came next in order of value. Fifty-five of the fifty-nine maroon claimants listed household goods at an average of $34 per owner. Forty-eight claimed for farm tools, at an average of $38 per owner. Of those, Swamp William Bowlegs, Caesar Bruner, Abram Payne, Cathrine Payne, Rebecca Payne, and Philip Sayers claimed for wagons and horses lost during the Civil War.[20] Seventeen of the maroons claimed for yokes of oxen. Eleven claimed one yoke, five claimed two yokes, and Jim Bowlegs,[21] claimed three. Twenty-two of the maroons listed guns, and Ned Cudjo and Robert Johnson claimed two guns each.[22] Thirty-six claimed for poultry, an average of $5 worth of birds per owner. And fifteen of the maroons claimed for potatoes, an average of 10 bushels per owner. The combined value of the household goods, farm tools, yokes of oxen, guns, poultry, and potatoes listed accounted for the remaining 20 percent of the property claimed by the maroons.

The property returns document that both slaves of Seminoles and free blacks owned horses and firearms. A number, in fact, owned large herds of horses and must have been raising the animals as a commercial venture. The maroons also possessed weapons. Twenty-two of the fifty-nine heads of household claimed to have lost guns during the Civil War, but that figure is probably far below the number who owned firearms in 1861. Although the Confederates forced them to abandon property at the onset of the war, the maroons would not have surrendered their guns easily. Firearms were vital for food and defense and easily portable. The great majority would have packed their guns along with other necessary belongings when they were forced to leave their homes and property behind.

Prior to the war, the maroons needed firearms for hunting and for defense against speculators and kidnappers. Unarmed blacks made easy targets, and the gun became the family's most important possession. The Seminoles either permitted the maroons to own firearms or were unable to prevent them from doing so. Evidence suggests the former scenario. Seminoles actually opposed Creek efforts to remove guns from their blacks. In September 1849, Kowakochi informed Arbuckle that the Indians were willing to allow the maroons to retain their arms. Although he cited hunting purposes as the reason, the disaffected leader likely was concerned that his black allies could defend themselves when they fled with him across the southern plains to Mexico.[23] Seminoles would have met with resistance had they attempted to take the maroons' guns and horses from them, but the situation never arose. Seminole slaveholders seemed unconcerned that their slaves might use their horses to run off, and they did not feel threatened by the proximity of armed blacks. If the maroons were defenseless, they were more likely to be stolen from the Seminole country and lost to their owners.

The Loyal claims also show that the Seminoles allowed the maroons to use tribal lands for their own benefit prior to the Civil War. Throughout the antebellum period, Seminole land was not owned by individuals but held in common. Each Indian town had a communal field that everybody worked for the good of the community. Each tribal member had the right to claim sole usage of unclaimed acreage as long as it was not within a short distance of another person's lot. The products of the land, and all improvements placed upon it, became the personal property of the individual working it. Most Seminoles remained uninterested in profits, opposed to institutionalized slavery, and content to stay subsistence farmers. Consequently, their individual acreages were small, and plenty of land remained available for the maroons.

Slave owners made no attempt to stop their blacks from using Seminole lands or settling apart from them in what amounted to autonomous maroon townships. Except for the small annual tribute to their owners, Seminole slaves kept the products of their labor. Free blacks, meanwhile, went about their business unhindered by property taxes. Both slaves and free blacks appear to have been as free of restrictions as Seminoles, and a number of them worked large acreages, raised substantial herds and crops, and became comparatively wealthy. By including the group in the award to the Loyalists in 1867, the Seminole authorities and the U.S. government formally recognized that the maroons had enjoyed the right to use tribal lands and own property during the antebellum period.

The property returns tell us a great deal about the lifestyle of the Seminole maroons. The chances were better than nine in ten that a maroon family kept horses and hogs and possessed household goods; better than eight in ten that it owned cattle, or cows and calves, and farm tools; better than seven in ten that it grew corn; and better than six in ten that it kept poultry. Only one family in four raised potatoes or owned oxen, however, and far fewer still engaged in any other agricultural pursuits. The maroons' main assets were in horses, cattle, cows and calves, hogs, and corn, and the value of those items amounted to more than 80 percent of the total they claimed. But although corn accounted for only 8 percent of the total, it held an importance to the maroons far in excess of its market value and was central to their existence. Corn was foundational to their diet, it constituted the tribute they usually gave to the mikko, and it served as a staple source of animal feed. Farm tools and firearms also appeared down the list of the most valuable commodities claimed, but they were of equally vital importance to the maroons' welfare and survival.

A picture begins to emerge of a Seminole maroon household on the eve of the Civil War. The family lived in a basic one- or two-room log cabin, containing kitchen utensils and other household goods. It kept a gun for hunting and defense. Chickens ran around in the yard outside. The family owned several horses, small herds of hogs and cattle, around a hundred bushels of corn, and an array of farm tools. If it did not grow corn, the family would have traded livestock for it. It was unlikely to grow potatoes, but if it did, it would raise around ten bushels. If it were doing well, the maroon family might own a yoke of oxen for plowing or heavy lifting, or a wagon and horses for transportation. It might also diversify by keeping bees or by growing small patches of beans, oats, peanuts, or wheat. But the family was far more likely to concentrate on tried and trusted products. Its main asset was livestock, which it traded for other necessities, and corn was its most important staple.

The family's diet would be tied to its livestock and produce. The maroons also hunted for game and fished in the local rivers and creeks, but their meals normally would feature beef, pork, and especially southern and Indian corn dishes. Although subsistence farming was how it supported itself, the family was not poor but rapidly acquiring assets. Each family member had chores and expected to work hard. The frontier lifestyle was rugged, demanding, and fraught with danger, yet it had compensations. The sense of family and community was strong, and industry could lead to success.

The wealth of the maroons compared quite favorably to that of the Loyal Seminoles. For property lost during the war, 281 Loyal Seminole heads of household claimed a total of $185,565. The claims ranged from $55 to $5,375. The Loyal Seminole average of $660 per household exceeded the maroon average by 41 percent. That figure is somewhat misleading, however. Wealth was quite evenly distributed among both the Indians and the maroons, but a small elite group of mikkos and other leading individuals held a disproportionate share of the total held by the Loyal Seminoles. In fact, 254 of the 281 Loyal Seminole claims fell within the maroon range. Of the 27 that fell outside it, 24 were larger and only 3 smaller. Those 24 included 10 Loyal Seminole mikkos, who also accounted for 3 of the top 5 claims. The largest Seminole claim, that of the mikko Fos (Foos) Harjo,[24] was more than eight times the Seminole average, whereas the largest maroon claim was less than three times the maroon average. If the claims of the top 10 Seminole claimants and those of the 7 remaining mikkos are excluded from the calculation, the average claim of the remaining 264 Loyal Seminole heads of household exceeded the maroon average by just 17 percent. Close examination of the individual claims reveals that most Loyal Seminole families were not much better off than the maroons.

A number of the maroons used the opportunity afforded them by the lack of restrictions on land usage and property ownership to become quite affluent. Ten maroons claimed more than the Loyal Seminole average—even including the Indian elite. Three owned more than $1,000 worth of property, and the Bruner and Payne families, especially, took full advantage of the opportunities offered. Only 24 of the 281 Loyal Seminole heads of household claimed more property than Ben Bruner, a free black.

The most remarkable statistic to emerge from the claims is that slaves of Seminoles sometimes owned more property than their owners. Jim Bowlegs, a slave of Nancy Chupco, provided the best example. Bowlegs acted as a witness in Chupco's claim and testified, "She was my mistress—I belonged to her." As was typical for the Loyal Seminoles and maroons, the Confederates drove Chupco from her home in September 1861 and forced her to abandon all her property, save that which she could carry with her. Later, she and her sister Nellie were captured at Bird Creek, where "the rebels took her horse and bundles and money (in a tin box)—took everything from her." Therefore, Chupco likely included all of her property in her claim for $626.[25] Jim Bowlegs, meanwhile, claimed to have lost $758 worth of property; he owned property valued at 21 percent more than that of his owner.[26]

Jim Bowlegs, in fact, had done very well for himself and had acquired extensive livestock holdings. His property included 7 horses, 40 head of cattle, 50 hogs and pigs, and 3 yoke of oxen. His owner, by comparison, owned just 9 horses, 9 head of cattle, 14 pigs, and a work steer. No example better illustrates the differences between Seminole slavery and the system practiced by the slaveholding elites in the other Civilized Tribes. The relationship of Jim Bowlegs and Nancy Chupco highlights the equality of opportunity and potential for economic advancement afforded slaves of Seminoles.

In keeping with their largely independent status, slaves of Seminoles enjoyed a high level of personal mobility. The maroons continued to live apart from the Indians, own horses, and be subject to few formal controls. As a result, they were able to travel around at will. The ease with which slaves eluded their owners in the 1840s, first by removing to Fort Gibson and later departing for Mexico, points to the lack of laws or other deterrents operating among the Seminoles to restrict their movement. Seminole owners also allowed their slaves to seek paid employment outside the tribal domain. Joe—son of Primus, the striker in the Seminoles' blacksmith's shop—and Joe's wife Hannah, for example, waited on several officers at Fort Gibson and in 1848 worked for Lieutenant F. F. Flint at Fort Smith.[27]

At harvest time, slaves of Seminoles would journey to the garrisons looking for work. Before setting out, they were supposed to obtain a pass from their owner stating that they had permission to seek employment, and the military did not permit blacks without passes to remain around the posts.[28] Seminole owners did not care for that practice, however, and their lack of concern led to its abuse. Just prior to the Civil War, the lack of restrictions limiting black mobility in the Seminole country came to light during a dramatic incident involving a runaway slave from the Creek Nation. The event caused a great deal of controversy, threatened the position of Presbyterian missionaries among the Creeks and Seminoles, and led to drastic changes in the Creeks' black code.

In the summer of 1860, Luke, the slave of a Creek-white, ran away from his owner and headed for Mexico.[29] During the course of his escape, he killed one of his pursuers, a white man named West, and by the time he reached the Oak Ridge Mission in the Seminole country, Luke was wanted by the Creek authorities as a runaway and a murderer. Luke was the cousin of Robert Johnson,[30] Ramsay's black interpreter, and the brother of a "noted preacher in the *Baptist Church*." Luke's wife, Hannah, who accompanied him, was a half-sister of Ramsay's black nurse. The couple purported to be visiting Johnson and stayed at the mission for several days.[31] At that stage, Ramsay had no way of knowing what had transpired and no reason to suspect that anything was amiss.

After a short stay with his cousin, Luke sought to obtain a pass from Ramsay. Luke told the reverend that he had his owner's permission to find work gathering hay at one of the southwestern garrisons, either Fort Cobb, Fort Sill, or Fort Arbuckle. He said that he had forgotten to obtain a pass from his owner and asked the minister to issue him one. As Johnson vouched for his cousin and supported his application, Ramsay made a decision he would come to regret and agreed to provide Luke with a pass. Ramsay's statements, offered later in his own defense, give a clear insight into how easy it was for blacks to travel at will in the Seminole country.

Because few of the Indians could read or write, the reverend often was called upon to provide such written authorization:

> [It] is well known in that region especially among the Seminoles that I have been in the habit of writing passes for their slaves when they are about starting to the garrisons to hunt work. They have been so accustomed to this that their slaves often come and get passes without any written order from their owners. [This] is the way in which I was betrayed into the present difficulty.[32]

Luke made his way to Fort Cobb and found work at the post. Soon afterward, however, word arrived that he was wanted by the Creek authorities. A force of militiamen set out from the garrison and found Luke hiding in a hayfield. As Ramsay later learned, "they had arrested him, and sat him on a horse; and on the way, he had pulled out a knife, and had cut his own throat, from ear to ear. And when the surgeon came and sewed up his throat, in order to save his life: he had torn it open again, and had thus bled to death."[33] Though Luke's life had ended, Ramsay's problems were just beginning.

Luke's pursuers found the pass that Ramsay had issued him in his pocket. The minister had not signed his name to the document, but they threatened Luke's wife with "instant death" if she did not divulge the author. Hannah named Ramsay and then was returned to the Creeks, who whipped her as a runaway. Upon seeing Luke's pass, Moty Kennard, the principal chief of the Creeks, called a council, and it demanded retribution. Since Luke's departure, the Presbyterian Board had granted Ramsay timely permission to return to the East for a visit. At North Fork Town, the minister learned of Luke's crimes and the circumstances surrounding his death. Ramsay immediately wrote to Kennard, exonerating both himself and Johnson, who had signed the pass, by claiming they had been duped. The Creeks, however, believed that Ramsay was an abolitionist, and they determined "with violence, Even to Tar and Feather Him." Fearing the worst, Ramsay hastily fled North Fork Town, but in less than an hour "a band of Creek men, painted and whooping," started after him. Fortunately for the minister, he took a wrong turn outside the town and unwittingly escaped his pursuers without being harmed.[34] Ramsay remained in the East until after the Civil War, when he finally felt it safe to return to the Seminole country.

Creek slave owners were outraged by this tampering with their property and were determined that similar meddling would not happen again. The deeper issue lay not with the Presbyterian minister, however, but with the Seminole system of slavery that encouraged such behavior. Seminole slaveholders apparently did not object to their blacks traveling to procure work, and they allowed individuals such as Ramsay to issue them with passes without their owner's consent. By that time, the Seminoles were independent of the Creeks and in control of their own internal affairs. Members of the Creek slaveholding elite, however, clearly wished to disassociate themselves from such practices and prevent similar occurrences from taking place again. Consequently, the Creeks passed a series of laws that placed more restrictions on the movements of their slave population than any other Indian nation.

Beginning in 1860, Creek codes required slave owners to keep their blacks "immediately around their improvements." They prohibited slaves from hiring themselves out to employers during their free time and imposed a fine of $50 per offense on those who did not obey. Slaves were not to travel more than two miles from their owners' premises at any time, or any distance at night, without a written pass from their owner. Any slave violating that law would receive twenty-five lashes. Owners issuing passes, meanwhile, should state the slave's destination or face a $10 fine. Another law resulting from Luke and Hannah's escape forbade individuals to issue passes to slaves they did not own. Anybody doing so would receive a $100 fine and a hundred lashes; inability to pay would result in another hundred lashes. If the slave were to escape, the individual issuing the pass would receive a hundred lashes and be required to pay the owner the full value of the escapee. Failure to pay would result in death. Runaways, moreover, would receive a hundred lashes, while those found harboring them would be fined $50 or receive a hundred stripes. The Creeks also created a reward system for those who captured runaways.[35]

Those laws, which so drastically increased the severity of the Creeks' black codes, were a direct response to the independence slaves enjoyed in the Seminole country. Significantly, the Seminoles did not respond to the Luke episode in a similar manner. They passed no regulatory legislation restricting slaves' mobility, and blacks associated with the tribe continued to enjoy freedom to travel.

Slaves of Seminoles also could acquire their freedom through manumission or purchase. The Seminoles apparently had no laws prohibiting owners from emancipating their slaves. From the Florida emigration rolls, we learn that Sawakee freed "Wann 1st" before her death,[36] that Hothli Emathla (Jumper) manumitted Long Bob, a leading black partisan during the Second Seminole War,[37] and that "Holatoochee was to retain his negroes during his life, but they were never to be sold or separated and were to be ultimately free."[38] This suggests that emancipation was not an unusual practice for Seminole owners.

Slaves of Seminoles became good candidates for manumission if they were included in one or more of three categories. First were those related to their owner through either marriage or descent. In 1819, for example, Hothli Hopoya emancipated his wife, Polly, and her two children, Margarita and Martiness.[39] Then there were those inherited by owners whose families had a long history of close association with their blacks. Leaders occasionally would bequeath their slaves to heirs with the understanding that they would be freed upon the inheritor's death. Other inheritors, particularly females without male heirs, stipulated that, upon their demise, their slaves should be freed. Harriet Bowlegs provided the best example of that by emancipating at her death all the slaves she had inherited from Hothli Hopoya.[40] Finally, there were those who had performed an outstanding service for either their owner or the tribe as a whole. Holata Mikko's interpreter and counselor Ben Bruner, for instance, appears to have been manumitted for services he rendered his owner prior to and during his Removal to the Indian Territory. And earlier, the Seminole chiefs had freed John Horse for providing the cost of transporting a party of Seminoles from the Arkansas River to their assigned lands in 1842.[41] Seminole owners emancipated their slaves at various times and for a number of reasons.

Seminole slaves also could buy their freedom or that of others. Given that Seminole owners allowed their slaves to own property and raise crops and livestock of their own, such purchases became quite feasible. So little hardship was attached to Seminole slavery, however, that few seem to have taken advantage of that opportunity. Besides no longer having to give a small annual individual tribute to their owner, the only real benefit slaves stood to gain by buying their freedom was that they no longer could be sold legitimately. But the door to fraudulent claims and kidnapping still remained open for free blacks. Consequently, although a number were wealthy enough to purchase their freedom, most Seminole slaves chose to continue in their state of limited servitude and retain their assets.

The slaves who became most interested in acquiring their freedom, or that of family members, were those in immediate danger of being sold by Seminoles or claimed and forcibly seized by non–tribal members. Polly, the widow of Hothli Hopoya, for instance, purchased the freedom of her husband, the interpreter Tony Barnet, who had become the object of a number of Creek claims.[42] Abraham bought his son Washington from Mikkoanapa and later emancipated the youth as claimants from outside the tribe were pursuing both.[43] And John Horse acquired his step-nephew Andrew from Chitto Harjo after the military turned over the maroons residing at Fort Gibson to the Seminole mikkos in January 1849.[44] But the slaves purchased by Cornelius Pryor provided the best example of that practice. Rather than face removal from the tribe, they asked to be allowed to find Seminole owners or purchase their own liberty. One of them, a black named Bob, actually bought his freedom for $300. Seminole leaders sanctioned the transaction and "expressed them-selves highly gratified" that Pryor had agreed to allow the maroons to remain associated with the tribe.[45] Presumably, the mikkos intended them to retain tributary ally status. By allowing owners to emancipate slaves and blacks to purchase their freedom, the Seminoles illustrated that they had no problem with the idea of a large free black population existing within their midst.

Although free blacks could not be bought or sold legitimately, they remained targets for kidnappers and slave hunters pursuing fraudulent claims. During the 1850s, Denis and Abraham, two free black leaders asso-ciated with the Seminoles, became objects of speculative enterprises and kidnapping ventures. Their involvement suggests that no black living in the Seminole country at that time was entirely safe. Jesup had included Denis and his wife in his emancipation proclamation, and Denis had a doc-ument signed by General Zachary Taylor to prove it. His former owner, Harriet Bowlegs, also had manumitted him along with her other blacks. Nevertheless, when his Indian "protector" traveled to Florida with a Seminole delegation to try to persuade Holata Mikko to remove to the Indian Territory, Mikko Mucasa and Marcellus Duval carried off Denis's wife to Arkansas. The mikko and the subagent, with the assistance of a store-keeper named Aird, also planned to capture Denis, and on May 9, 1852, he was forced to seek protection at Fort Arbuckle. What became of his wife is unknown, but Denis's statements became the focus of charges filed against Duval that led to his eventual removal from the Seminole subagency.[46]

In the mid-1850s, the family of the famous Florida maroon leader, Abraham, became the object of a claim pursued by William Sena (Billy) Factor. The son of Rose Sena Factor, "a mixed blood Seminole and negress,"[47] Billy and his mother themselves had been targets for claimants and slave hunters in Florida and the Indian Territory. In 1821, Matteo Solano and Miguel Papy had purchased Rose near Saint Augustine. After living for about a year with Solano, she had escaped and run away to the Indians. Captain William Miller, a Creek-white, eventually captured Rose with a child near Tampa Bay. Miller took the two fugitives to the Creek country and there sold them to Chilly McIntosh. Rose subsequently became the property of Black Factor, and she and her family began an association with the Apalachicolas.

Black Factor later gave Rose to his son Sam for a wife. When Black Factor died, however, his niece and legitimate heir, Nelly Factor, claimed his property. Nelly Factor disputed her cousin's right to own Rose and her family, but in September 1828 the Apalachicola mikkos decided that Sam Factor was their rightful owner. Sam later claimed that he had bought Rose and her two children, Billy and Sarah, from Nelly. In 1832, he manumitted Rose, Billy, Sarah, and Sarah's sons Daniel and Paladore, granting them the right "to enjoy all the freedom and privileges of the tribe." The mikkos sanctioned the emancipation, and Sam reaffirmed it before Seminole agent Wiley Thompson in February 1835.[48]

Levin Brown, a white resident of Jackson County, Florida, subsequently claimed Billy Factor. In July 1834, the claimant's brother, Isaac Brown, and a man named Douglas led a party of slave hunters and two trained dogs to take Factor from his home, but the raid was unsuccessful. Sometime afterward, a white raiding party led by Ezekiel Robertson took Rose Sena Factor and her family captive. Rose and Billy managed to escape, but the slavers took Sarah and her sons up river to Stewart County, Georgia, and they were never heard of again.

By the outbreak of the Second Seminole War, Rose, Billy, and his wife, Nancy, owned a substantial amount of property in herds and crops that they subsequently lost, in part to Seminoles and in part to the American forces. Rose and Billy served the United States in a number of capacities during the war. In 1837, Billy found work as an army herdsman and later served as a guide, courier, and interpreter for the Creek regiment and the U.S. Navy. Most significantly, he acted as an intermediary during the negotiations with Kowakochi and played an important role in persuading the Seminole mikko to remove west. Rose, meanwhile, was employed as an interpreter at Tampa Bay. On October 11, 1841, Rose, Billy, Nancy, and two children left Florida for the Indian Territory.[49]

After Removal, Billy Factor acquired a bad reputation in the Indian country. In December 1855, Washbourne, referring to Factor as a "hybrid Seminole and negro," observed: "He is a scoundrel unwhipt of justice, or rather he has been whipped several times by both Creeks and Seminoles, once in my presence, for horse-stealing. He has also murdered a Cherokee, and many years ago burned a Creek woman to death. He is an outlaw and dare not show his head by daylight in the Seminole country."[50] Because of his record, Factor and his wife settled outside the Indian Territory in Sebastian County, Arkansas. He also was heavily in debt. In 1852, Factor claimed $2,000 for the property he and his mother had lost during the Second Seminole War. In 1854, he received $300 of it, but Superintendent William Drew was sent $700 more to pay Factor's creditors, and the remaining $1,000 was set aside for Joseph Vandever, the administrator of Rose Sena Factor's estate.[51] Desperate to secure more funds, Billy Factor began to pursue additional slave claims.

One of Factor's schemes involved Abraham. In 1855, he accused the former leader of Pilaklikaha of selling five slaves belonging to Black Factor to a white man named Hansom some thirty years before. Billy previously had sold any interest he had in those slaves several times over, but he now actively sought compensation for his "loss." During the harvest period, Abraham and his family were working at Fort Arbuckle in the Chickasaw Nation and living close to the post. Abraham had purchased and emancipated the members of his family and was himself a free black. Nevertheless, one night in mid-September, Billy and a party of "wild young Creeks," attacked his family and carried off his wife and three of his children. Billy still was not satisfied, for he later brought a suit against Abraham before the Creek Council. But his plan misfired. The Creek authorities decided that Abraham was not liable for the blacks sold in Florida and returned his family to him.[52]

The matter did not end there. In late December, Abraham left his family at home and fled to Fort Arbuckle for protection, stating that Factor was after him again. But agent Washbourne was unsympathetic, believing he was in no further danger. If Factor was pursuing him, why did Abraham leave his family behind for the kidnappers? Washbourne noted,

He did not fly to Fort Arbuckle for protection but for something to eat; having raised no corn for the past season because, at the time he should have been planting corn, he was constrained to appear before the United States' District Court at Van Buren Arks., whither his sons had been taken on a charge of selling whiskey to the Indians. He is a wily old negro and his influence upon the Seminoles is bad. I have been obliged to reprimand him more than once for inebriety.[53]

The subagent concluded that Abraham considered himself "a personage entitled to great attention" and had been "spoiled by notice paid to him by U.S. officers heretofore."[54]

This affair brought to light the perils facing all blacks living in the Seminole country, no matter their status or how well known they were. In the late 1850s, the decisions passed down in the case involving the Beams family, free blacks living in the Indian Territory, might have alleviated the threat slightly, yet it remained severe.[55] Kidnapping continued to be a source of great danger to free blacks until emancipation.

A number of free Seminole maroons became quite wealthy. Abraham's son Washington recalled, for example, that his father was a successful cattle raiser and would return from market "with a sack full of gold and silver" that he kept under the floorboards of his cabin.[56] Free blacks also held positions of importance as interpreters. John Horse, Cudjo, Tony Barnet, Abraham, George Noble, and Ben Bruner all interpreted for the Seminoles in an official capacity during the 1840s and 50s. In 1852, for example, Abraham interpreted for a delegation of mikkos that sought to negotiate the Removal of the remaining Seminoles in Florida to the Indian Territory. Some maroons also acted as counselors to Seminole mikkos and advised the Indians on important matters affecting the tribe.

In contrast to the actions the Cherokees took after the slave revolt of 1842, the Seminoles did not pass punitive legislation against the free black population after the defections to Mexico in 1849–50, even though a free black, John Horse, organized and led the exodus. Nor did free Seminole blacks come under the yoke of property or poll taxes, or the threat of removal or reenslavement, as they did in the other slaveholding tribes. Seminole owners seem not to have viewed free blacks as subversive, and they continued to allow them to reside among the slave population. The

Seminoles were able to accept different classes of blacks being associated with the tribe. Although all slaves were black, not all blacks were slaves.

Because of the similarities in their lifestyles, it is often difficult to differentiate between Seminole slaves and free (but tributary) blacks. The group included only a small number of free nontributary blacks. During the post-Removal period, slaves and free blacks continued to live together in maroon communities under black leadership. After the military transferred them to the Seminoles in 1849, the blacks settled apart from the Indians in three towns, their principal settlement being on Wewoka Creek under the leadership of John Horse.[57] Mary Ann Lilley penned the following description of the Wewoka community:

> [Mr.] Lilley used to go to a place called Rocky mountain, it was a high rocky bluff, and then went down a long distance to the river bottom, to where they lived and cultivated the river bottom. The colored people lived there and Uncle Warren was the patriarch of the clan.[58] Their masters were scattered all around there. Uncle Warren was set free by the Seminoles before they came here and all his children were slaves save Catherine who was born free.[59]

Wewoka continued to serve as a maroon settlement after John Horse and his followers left for Mexico. It likely included several black communities (see the map on page 66). Ramsay referred to "an African town over on the Wewoka, called Uncle Charles town" being in existence in the summer of 1856.[60] And a 1932 article in the *Daily Oklahoman* stated that prior to the Civil War, the *Arkansas Gazette* had made "frequent mention of Wewoka as a place of refuge for runaway slaves from Creek, Seminole and Cherokee masters, where they joined free negroes."[61]

Primarily for safety and protection, slaves, free blacks, and runaways from elsewhere banded together to form such maroon communities in remote and defensible locations in the Seminole country. The Seminoles could exert little control over those black towns and were unable to enforce their laws there. When they attempted to do so, as in the case involving the accused horse thief Walking Joe, the maroon residents gave them short shrift.[62] As in Florida, those towns came to constitute settlements of armed maroons under free black leadership.

Although the maroons utilized tribal lands for their own benefit, the

Seminoles did not consider them members of the tribe. In 1857, Southern Superintendent Elias Rector made a surprising observation: "Among the Creeks and Seminoles, in particular, are also many negroes of unmixed African blood, and many persons partly of that blood free, and enjoying the rights among the Indians themselves of citizenship, intermarrying with the latter and, sharing their annuities and other moneys."[63] But Rector's statement was largely inaccurate.

There is no evidence to support the contention that free blacks enjoyed the rights associated with Seminole tribal membership. Seminole law did not protect them, and they lived outside the jurisdiction of tribal justice, as Rector himself recognized: "[An] offence committed by one of these against the person or property of an Indian, and vice versa, is, by the letter of the law, punishable, under the laws of the United States."[64] Nor were free blacks as a group included in Seminole annuity payments. Maroon names do not appear on the annuity rolls of the late 1850s, and the 1860 roll does not list the likes of Abraham or Ben Bruner.[65] Of greatest importance, no evidence can be produced to show that the Seminoles included free blacks in their polity at that time. There is no indication that the Indians afforded the maroon communities political representation or that black mikkos sat on the Seminole Council. The signatures or marks of maroon leaders do not appear on official tribal documents of the 1850s. Although blacks frequently acted as interpreters and advisers and could, at times, exert great influence over the mikkos' decision making, Seminoles did not consider maroons to be an integral part of their political process. Maroons remained closely associated with the Seminole Nation, but not part of it.

Elias Rector in the late 1850s and the U.S. census takers in the early 1860s intimated that intermarriage between Seminoles and blacks was fairly common prior to the Civil War.[66] In her influential 1915 study, *The American Indian as Slaveholder and Secessionist,* Annie Heloise Abel supported that notion, and it became the standard interpretation.[67] But the prominence of a few maroon leaders in Seminole circles appears to have influenced Rector and his contemporaries unduly. The unprecedented degree of economic opportunity, personal mobility, and independence enjoyed by maroons in the Seminole country, and the stark contrast that presented with the experience of blacks owned by members of the slaveholding elites in the other Civilized Tribes, added to their misperception.

They mistook residential proximity for assimilation, and association for miscegenation.

Due to a lack of substantial evidence, it is impossible to make conclusive statements on the amount of Seminole-maroon intermarriage that took place between Removal and the Civil War. During the postbellum period, however, there was a remarkably low incidence of such unions.[68] The upheavals of the post-Removal period—the assassination attempts on maroon leaders, the Seminole union with the Creeks, the maroons' self-imposed exile at Fort Gibson and their forced transference to Seminole owners, the migrations to Mexico, the slave sales, the legitimate and fraudulent claims, and the kidnapping ventures—all served to undermine Seminole-maroon relations. That would suggest that mixed marriages likely were an equally unusual occurrence prior to the Civil War.

With few exceptions, maroons continued to be excluded from Indian clans and bands. In earlier times, the Seminoles had incorporated Indian slaves into their clan system, and they and their children eventually would become members of the tribe.[69] But no evidence has been found to suggest that it was Seminole practice to incorporate black slaves in a similar fashion, and everything points to the opposite. Seminoles might have been influenced by European and southern white racism, or by racial and cultural differences they perceived distinguishing them from Africans, in deciding that they would not assimilate black slaves into the tribe as they had other Indians. Nor did Seminoles typically adopt blacks into their clans following manumission. The Seminoles occasionally allowed leading maroon males to join a clan, perhaps in appreciation for outstanding service or because of intermarriage or a familial relationship, but that was not usual. Even children of Seminole fathers and maroon mothers were born outside of Indian society. The only exceptions were the small number of offspring of Indian mothers and maroon fathers. Those Indian-maroons were born members of their mother's clan and band and enjoyed the rights and privileges of Seminoles.

The clan was the core, the very fabric, of Indian society. As Miller has suggested, the clan was fundamental to the Seminole cosmos.[70] Membership in a Seminole band, meanwhile, brought with it community, shared cultural ties, protection under tribal law, political representation on the council, and the right to receive annuities. To live outside of the clan and band system meant exclusion from almost every facet of Seminole economic, social, and political life. Instead, displaced Africans and their descendants formed their own remote and isolated communities on a hostile frontier. Even though the Seminoles afforded them certain privileges, maroons became members of no society but their own.

Although obliged to pay an annual tribute to an absentee mikko, the maroons' settlements were self-governing communities with independent economic, social, and political systems. Their towns were well organized, with the residents choosing their own leaders. When experiencing an external threat, the maroons acted in concert for the good of the community. Their settlements enjoyed strong internal channels of communication and also interacted substantially with other black communities in the Indian Territory. Seminole maroons from different locations were able to overcome geographical separation and congregate at Fort Gibson in 1845. Seminole, Creek, and Cherokee blacks also were able to meet at a prearranged time and place before leaving for Mexico in 1849. And during Aspberry's slave hunting raid in 1853, the maroons quickly spread the alarm and forced the kidnappers to withdraw in haste.

As in Florida, slaves and tributaries of the same owner tended to congregate together. That fostered a strong sense of community within the maroon settlements that persisted beyond the Civil War. For example, of the ninety-seven enrolled and unenrolled maroons whose names appeared on Seminole freedman census cards and who claimed to have been a slave of members of the Bowlegs circle—Hothli Hopoya, Payne, Eliza Bowlegs, and Holata Mikko—ninety-two were members of the Dosar Barkus band.[71] Residents of Seminole maroon settlements traded with each other, helped one another at harvest time and during other busy or difficult periods, and interacted socially. Their society featured large extended families living in fairly small areas, so most residents were related in some way. Members of Seminole maroon communities became bound together by ties of kinship and interdependence.

A separate, vital, and clearly identifiable Seminole maroon culture emerged within their communities during the antebellum period. The maroons adopted some things they liked or found useful from the Seminoles, such as food preparations and items of clothing, but their society mostly reflected their African heritage and history of enslavement under both Europeans and southern whites. Consequently, maroon culture differed substantially from that of the Seminoles. Three key elements—language, naming practices, and religion—highlight those differences.

Each reflected the uniqueness of maroon culture, and each in some way was transmitted to Seminoles.

The maroons' first language was what linguist Ian Hancock has termed Afro-Seminole Creole. The Creole evolved in Florida prior to Removal and is related to Gullah, its lexicon containing mostly English-sounding words but also some African, Spanish, and Creek expressions. It has been identified among the Texas, Coahuila, and Oklahoma Seminole maroon communities.[72] The Seminole Indians' native tongues were Creek and Hitchiti. Although some leading African males could converse fluently in Creek and assumed important roles within the tribe as interpreters, the first languages spoken within the maroon and Seminole communities in the Indian Territory were completely different.[73] Maroons did not need interpreters when addressing whites and often served as translators for Seminoles. While each of the Loyal Seminoles required an interpreter when filing their claim for compensation in 1867, for example, not once did a maroon use one.

There is no greater signifier of a group's sense of cultural identity than its language. Afro-Seminole was alien and unintelligible to the maroons' Indian neighbors. By speaking it rather than Creek as their first language, the maroons asserted their independence and trod a path to linguistic distinctiveness. Afro-Seminole spoke to the maroons' unique heritage and helped preserve their culture. It also gave them an inestimable advantage over the Indians in dealing with whites. Significantly, the Seminoles' principal contact with "English" came through maroons. That might have resulted in the development of a pidgin among them. Linguist Joseph Dillard has argued, "[There] is a clear African-to-Indian transmission in the case of the Seminoles. [We] find Pidgin and Creole English spoken by the Seminoles and the African slaves who escaped to them, respectively."[74] Unfortunately, Dillard restricted his argument almost entirely to Florida. How much and for how long Afro-Seminole influenced the use of English of Seminoles living in the Indian Territory remains to be determined.

Naming practices were another manifestation of the Seminole maroons' unique historical experience and cultural heritage. Maroon naming patterns suggest that their society was very different from that of the Indians. From the late eighteenth to the early twentieth century, they employed a Kongo/Angolan naming system. Males were given double names, arranged to show their descent, and namesaking became a pronounced pattern.[75] That suggests that the group placed more importance than Seminoles on the male line.

The maroons utilized African-derived names, such as "Dembo" and "Dindy," and widely incorporated West African day names, such as "Cudjo" and "Cuffy" and their English equivalents "Monday" and "Friday."[76] Men with untranslated African day names tended to attain positions of high standing within the maroon community. Cudjo headed a settlement in Florida and became one of the leading maroon interpreters prior to Removal, while Cuffy played the role of interpreter and intermediary between maroons and Seminoles in 1849 and later became a prominent member of the Nacimiento community. The modern-day place-names of Cudjoe Key in Florida and Cudjo Creek in Seminole County, Oklahoma, bear witness to the importance of that African name among the maroons. "Cudjoe" has remained a prominent surname among the Oklahoma group. During the 1980s and early 1990s, twin brothers Lance and Lawrence Cudjoe represented the Caesar Bruner band and were considered the ablest of the Seminole freedman leaders.[77]

The maroons also used the English names for the two full summer months. Men named July and August had been prominent at Pilaklikaha and played important roles as guides, interpreters, and leaders during the Second Seminole War. The Julys later became a leading family among the Coahuila and Texas maroons.[78] The use of famous biblical and ancient historical names, such as "Abraham," "Caesar," "Rebecca," "Sampson," "Sarah," and "Titus," dates back to the experience of blacks on southern plantations when slaveholders forced them to drop their African names and take those chosen by their owners. The maroons passed down those "slave names" to their descendants, along with the names of former Seminole owners, such as "Bowlegs," "Bruner," "Factor," and "Payne."

Some geographic names, such as "Carolina," "Lousanna," "Tennessee," and "Swamp" referred to the state or place the individual or his or her ancestors were born or raised. Others, like "Slavery" and "Guide," related to a forebear's status or function. The group also employed nicknames similar to Gullah "basket names." Some, such as "Hard Times," "Plenty," and "Poor Gal" appear to have reflected conditions at the time the child was born. Others, likely given later, portrayed a personal attribute. Examples of that practice include "Dancer" and "Whistler." Often, maroon names included an exotic mixture of those diverse elements. Members of the Indian Territory and Oklahoma groups included, for example, Dindy Adam, Swamp William Bowlegs, Lousanna Cudjoe, Rebecca Payne, and Slavery Pompey.

Naming practices like those were unknown among the Seminole Indians. There was minimal maroon-to-Indian transmission in naming, and vice versa. Maroon names such as "Scipio," "Sampson," "Caesar," and "Nero" appear on the Final Rolls of the Seminole Indians, likely as a result of earlier intermarriages. Moreover, several maroons took the busk name "Warrior," the English translation of the Seminole title *tastanaki*. In the 1840s, John Horse at times was referred to as John Warrior;[79] in 1870, John Kibbetts, a maroon leader in Coahuila and Texas, signed himself as Snake Warrior;[80] and in 1875, Sergeant John Ward (Warrior) of the Seminole Negro Indian Scouts won the Congressional Medal of Honor.[81] The surname "Warrior" also appeared on the Final Rolls of the Seminole freedmen at the time of allotment, with Jack Warrior and his sons Amos and Levy being listed.[82] In the late 1970s and early 1980s, Ben Warrior of Sasakwa led the Dosar Barkus band and was the longest-serving freedman on the Seminole Council.[83] And William "Dub" Warrior, currently president of the Seminole Indian Scouts Cemetery Association, has remained a prominent leader within the Texas group into the early twenty-first century.[84] But those are isolated examples confined to particular individuals and their descendants. Outside the small minority of intermarried families, evidence does not suggest that the maroons or Seminoles influenced the naming practices of the other.

Cultural differences between Seminoles and maroons also manifested themselves in the groups' attitudes toward Christianity. While the great majority of Seminoles continued to practice their Native religion and were either opposed or indifferent to the efforts of missionaries after Removal, many of the maroons came to embrace Christianity in some form or other. Although the ratio of blacks to Indians was only around one to six, by the outbreak of the Civil War there were more maroon than Seminole Christians. In contrast to the situation that existed in the other slaveholding tribes, blacks associated with the Seminoles could receive religious instruction and practice Christianity in their towns. Consequently, Christian religions became incorporated into maroon culture between Removal and the Civil War, and the church has continued to play a central role in Seminole freedman society into the twenty-first century.

The maroons were exposed to Christianity long before the Seminoles.

Many had received religious instruction on British, Spanish, or American plantations. That, together with their familiarity with English, made them more amenable than Seminoles to the overtures of Christian missionaries in the Indian Territory. Baptists, Presbyterians, and Methodists were the most active among them, and the maroons who became Christian invariably joined one of those churches. The Methodists met with only limited success, counting just four blacks among their Seminole converts in 1848.[85] The Baptist faith, however, appealed greatly to the maroons. Most of their initial contact with that religion came through Creek black missionaries, and the Presbyterian ministers lamented the group's attraction to its simple yet dramatic ceremonies, epitomized by immersion. Consequently, most maroon converts joined that faith, while others joined the Presbyterians. Thereafter, as interpreters and instructors, maroons played a vital role in transmitting their own version of Christianity to the Indians. Without their efforts, few Seminoles would have become Christian prior to the Civil War.

Blacks played an important role in helping to establish the Baptist religion among the Creeks.[86] After Removal, the Creek authorities passed laws against preaching, but blacks illicitly kept the faith and were responsible for many conversions at North Fork Town. In the summer of 1842, Baptist missionary Charles Kellum suggested that a meeting took place almost every night at "that Hell upon earth."[87] As North Fork Town was so near to the Seminole country, and mobility was not an issue, maroons likely attended the illegal meetings black preachers held there. The community subsequently became the home base for missionary operations among the maroons, and the Creek black preachers Joseph Islands and Monday Durant became largely responsible for establishing the Baptist faith within the group.

The earliest known Baptist missionary contact with the Seminoles dates from the arrival of Joseph Smedley in 1842. In 1846, Smedley was planning to establish a church of thirty to forty members called the Deep Fork or Seminole Church. A year later, the American Indian Mission Association announced that Joseph Islands had organized a Seminole Baptist church of fifty members.[88] But that early Seminole congregation was composed almost entirely of maroons.

Shortly after Presbyterian minister John Lilley had established the Oak Ridge Mission, John Horse visited him. As the maroons living at Wewoka "called themselves Baptists," Horse was anxious to learn the missionary's religious affiliation. Horse later added to the Lilleys' surprise by demonstrating knowledge of the Bible, which he referred to as "de big book."[89] In all likelihood, maroons had attended services at North Fork Town or Creek black preachers had traveled to Wewoka and introduced the Baptist religion to the community there.

In 1852, Monday Durant, a free Creek black began visiting and preaching to the maroons living in the Seminole country. Durant owned a store at the mouth of the Little River and thus lived close by.[90] On December 1, 1853, Henry Buckner, Baptist missionary to the Creeks, reported from North Fork Town, "Monday preaches on Little River to the Seminoles every fourth week; and had baptized four the last time I saw him."[91] In 1854, Durant organized his converts into a church that Murrow described as being "composed wholly of negroes."[92]

Although the nation had no official prohibition on Christianity at that time, individual Creeks persecuted black Baptists, and preachers faced constant danger. Echo Harjo, chief of the Upper Creek Canadian District, for example, wished to stamp out Christianity in his province and threatened Durant's life.[93] The maroon Baptists would have taken strong precautions to remain undiscovered. As Robert Hamilton, a historian of Baptist faith among the Indians, has suggested, the maroons would have "secretly held their meetings, baptizing after midnight in the streams, with guards posted to keep from being surprised and arrested."[94]

Monday Durant's black church was directly responsible for the Baptist religion's spreading to the Seminoles. Though wishing to maintain secrecy, the maroon Baptists became overenthusiastic about their new religion, and "there was much shouting among them." Seminoles were deeply suspicious of those black assemblies and believed that their behavior resulted from "bewitchment." Consequently, they sent the Indian-black James Factor—one of the few English-speaking Seminoles, a tribal interpreter, and Heniha Mikko's closest adviser—to investigate. At the meeting, Factor fell under the influence of the black preachers and converted. The Seminole mikkos debated the case for some time but finally expelled Factor from the council. Adoniram Holt, a Baptist missionary to the Seminoles during the 1870s, recalled, "John Jumper, telling me of this later, said he was sure James Factor was a better man than he. John Jumper was dissatisfied with what the council had done and resolved that he would investigate for himself concerning this bewitchment. The result [was] that he himself in turn became bewitched."[95]

The principal chief of the Seminoles and his interpreter and adviser both converted to Christianity because of the influence of Creek black and Seminole maroon Baptists. Heniha Mikko at first became Presbyterian, but with the coming of Murrow to the Seminole country, he changed his religious affiliation to Baptist. Heniha Mikko and Factor both were ordained to the ministry in 1865, and they became leading lights in the Seminole Baptist church during Reconstruction.

In the mid-1850s, Talomas Mikko came under the influence of Buckner and switched from being a Presbyterian to a Baptist preacher. That weakened the Presbyterians and aided the Baptists, because, as Ramsay later lamented, Talomas Mikko was so successful in gaining black converts:

> [He had] a great facility of interesting Colored people; and he became our great opponent in that field of labor. Wherever we went preaching, he went also and immersed the Colored people. And Mr. Lilley supposed that he had got all the people of Charles Town to be willing to be Presbyterians; and went over there one day for the purpose of trying to organize them into a church [but] he found when he got there, that Bemo had been there, and had got them all persuaded to go under the water, and that they were Baptists.[96]

The Seminole maroon Baptist church grew rapidly in the late 1850s. When Murrow visited the Seminole country for the first time in 1859, Talomas Mikko informed him that more than one hundred members were participating in services.[97]

It is ironic that the religion maroons so firmly embraced and passed on to Indians would become associated with segregation and the Confederacy. When Murrow arrived in the Seminole country to assume his missionary duties in January 1860, he immediately set about organizing a separate Seminole Indian congregation at the Ash Creek Church. Later that year, he formally divided the Seminole Baptist Church into Indian and black congregations, each with its own structure, "to benefit [the] church in its church capacity, and also [the] community in its social relationships."[98] Although they shared a common religion, from then on, maroons and Seminoles were to practice it in segregated congregations. By the early 1860s, the Baptist religion had become a rallying cry for

Talomas Mikko (John Bemo). Daguerreotype. (Florida Department of State)

Heniha Mikko's followers. Murrow became a fierce Confederate supporter, and he undoubtedly influenced Heniha Mikko to side with the South. During the war, Murrow became the Confederate agent to the Seminoles, and his position expanded to include commissary duties for the refugee Indians.

The Presbyterians also were active in the Seminole country between Removal and the Civil War, but they did not enjoy as much success among the maroons as did the Baptists. A number of maroons did embrace Presbyterianism, however, and they again played an important role in spreading the religion to the Seminoles. In 1844, subagent Judge reported that Talomas Mikko preached regularly once or twice per week "to full houses." His congregation included only a few Seminoles, however, and was composed almost entirely of blacks.[99] The growth of the Baptist religion among the maroons severely hampered the efforts of the Presbyterian missionaries. By the time John Lilley arrived in the Seminole country in 1848, it already was established as the group's principal Christian religion. Nevertheless, the Presbyterians attempted to make inroads into the maroon community.

Although the people of John Horse's community professed to be Baptist, the Lilleys "often hired them and had preaching there."[100] During a visit to the Lilleys in early September 1849, just a few weeks prior to the Seminole and maroon migrations to Mexico, Ramsay, together with Talomas Mikko and the Lilleys' two daughters, organized a service at Rocky Mountain, near Wewoka. Ramsay recalled, "We had a very pleasant meeting, Africans and Indians made the house full. Mr. Bemo remarked if I had given each of those people ten dollars apiece, I could not have pleased them as well as by giving them the sermon which I gave."[101]

In spite of their Baptist leanings, John Lilley still was preaching to maroons at Wewoka in the summer of 1856. Ramsay remarked, "The colored people professed to have a great deal of confidence in Mr. Lilley. They got him to do all their writing for them; and said that they loved to hear him preach." It was only through the influence of the newly converted Talomas Mikko, Ramsay believed, that the maroons at Charles Town became Baptist rather than Presbyterian. Even after that setback, however, the Presbyterians maintained close ties with the maroons. When Ramsay left the Oak Ridge Mission to establish a station in the new Seminole country, he was accompanied by Robert Johnson, Big Jim, and Short Billy, three blacks he subsequently employed in building the cabins for the new Prairie Mission at Pond Creek. Ramsay also hired a number of black horse thieves, who had moved into the surrounding area to hide out from their owners, to build a second house, haul rails, and build a fence around his ten-acre lot.[102] On that rugged frontier, law and order frequently took a backseat to practicality, even among Christian missionaries.

With the exception of Talomas Mikko, the Presbyterian missionaries sent to the Seminole country were white and in great need of reliable interpreters. Talomas Mikko also spoke English as his first language and used an interpreter when preaching to Seminoles. At various times, John Lilley employed "a half African and half Indian" named Willis and "an old colored man, named Uncle Fay." By the summer of 1856, however, the situation had reached a crisis, for Willis had died, Uncle Fay "understood both languages imperfectly" and could not be trusted, and Talomas Mikko had defected to the Baptists.[103] As a matter of necessity, the newly arrived Ramsay secured the services of Robert Johnson, a black interpreter with whom he had become familiar at the Kowetah Mission in the Creek country.

Robert Johnson was a colorful character and lived a most interesting life. In time, he became the most frequently used and influential interpreter among the Seminoles and played an important role during the Civil War and the negotiations leading up to the treaty of 1866. He also fathered a son, James Coody Johnson, who, as an interpreter, attorney, and politician, became one of the most influential and powerful black leaders in the Indian Territory and Oklahoma during the early years of the twentieth century.

Robert Johnson was born in Alabama in December 1824 and traveled to the Indian Territory with Creeks along the Trail of Tears. The slave of a Creek named A. Foster, Johnson lived at Econchata town on the Arkansas River. During the late 1840s, he became a member of the predominantly black Presbyterian congregation at the nearby Kowetah Mission. There he became familiar to the Lilleys and Ramsay before they went out to the Seminole country. Mary Ann Lilley recalled that she tried to teach Johnson how to spell in the class she held on Sunday mornings. At first, he "was very anxious to learn [but] after he learned a little he stopped." The novelty indeed had worn off, as he still was unable to read or write in 1869, although by 1860 he could sign his name. Up to that point, Johnson never had tried his hand at translating, but one day John Lilley persuaded him to accompany the missionary to an Indian settlement across the Arkansas from Kowetah that had no meeting.[104] Robert Johnson then commenced a career that led to his becoming the most sought-after interpreter in the Creek and Seminole nations.

Soon after his initial introduction to translating, Robert Johnson began work on the farm at Kowetah and trained to be an interpreter. His owner would receive $8 per month in consideration for Johnson's working five days each week. At that time, Creek owners afforded their slaves the privilege of working Saturdays for themselves. The Presbyterians trained Johnson on Saturdays and paid him for his time. He moved into a small cabin in the southwest corner of the mission station and soon became a familiar figure about the place. As "Robert" also was the name of both the Presbyterian minister Loughridge and his son, the mission's new interpreter usually went by "Robin" to avoid confusion. During his time at Kowetah, he was known as Robin Foster, but after he left Loughridge and traveled to the Seminole country, he again became known as Robert Foster. He took the surname Johnson sometime during the Civil War, probably after emancipation. From then until his death on December 13, 1893, he became known as Robert Johnson.[105]

Johnson worked at the Presbyterian mission as both a farmhand and handyman. Indeed, according to this contemporary description by Augustis Loomis, he was an industrious jack-of-all-trades:

> [One] of our stated interpreters at the Kowetah Mission, was Robin, a negro, and he occupied the cabin in the corner. Robin was also a man of all work, and very "handy" at repairing tools, and preparing many little "make shifts," which cannot be obtained in that far off country, except by making. Within, his cabin was like a boatswain's locker, having a great many things, but all in confusion. Under the window was the tool chest, which served also for a seat, and sometimes for a table; there was a stool, and one chair with a piece of green cowhide, with the hair still on, drawn on it for a seat. Hanging about, you see scraps of old harness, buckles, spurs; and there are hatchets and hoes, axe-helves, broom-handles and brooms, and some of these in process of construction; for this man occupies himself at such labour in the evening, by way of overwork, to earn pocket money for himself.[106]

Skills such as those, especially at so low a price, were at a premium in the Indian Territory at that time. Given his additional potential as an interpreter, Johnson presented an impressive package, and the mission became anxious to retain his services.

Ramsay first became acquainted with Robert Johnson shortly after the missionary arrived in the Creek country in the summer of 1849. One summer day, during the harvest, Johnson was cutting hay with Daniel Carr, another hired slave. Ramsay and Rev. Hamilton Ballentine, his associate, determined to teach them how to build a Pennsylvania haystack. But the prairie hay did not bind together as well as timothy and the stack fell apart, with Ramsay tumbling to the ground. At that, the two blacks let out a knowing laugh.[107] Ramsay and Johnson soon grew to be friends, and the missionary came to rely heavily on him to interpret his message to the Indians.

Ramsay set about training Johnson as an interpreter on his free Saturdays and paid him for his time. The minister recalled:

> He was unable to read, and of course at that time was very ignorant. When he first began, he made a great many mistakes and as a part of the congregation understood both English and Creek, they would laugh at his mistakes; so that he grew discouraged; and it was only after much praise on our part, that he was induced to persevere; and after a few months, he became a very proficient interpreter. We paid him for interpreting and he received the money himself.[108]

In his new capacity as a trusted interpreter, Johnson soon made himself indispensable to the Presbyterians. In 1851, Ramsay wrote to Walter Lowrie, the corresponding secretary of the Presbyterian Board of Foreign Missions, asking his permission to purchase Johnson, if he could obtain him for $600 or $700 or less, "in order that he may work out his time and at length become a free man." That idea was not unprecedented, for a year earlier Loughridge had bought his black cook, Celia, from William Drew for $400 with the understanding that she could earn her freedom. Ramsay described Johnson as "a young, healthy man and one of natural talent" and proposed that he employ both his brain and muscle power to earn his freedom.[109] Although it would have represented little financial risk, the board did not approve purchasing Johnson at that time. Ramsay did not abandon the idea, however, and only awaited an opportune moment to reintroduce his proposal.

During the early 1850s, as they rode along on their "long missionary excursions" to the Indians, Johnson, who "was fond of talking," explained to the Presbyterian ministers the Creek version of the origin of the races and the reasons why they were employed in their chosen fields of labor. The missionaries also learned from him "many facts concerning the country, and the habits of the people, their civil polity, and religious superstitions; as well as many things relating to the extent and influence of Christianity amongst the Indians." During those sessions, Loomis remarked upon "that large and intelligent eye of the interpreter, rolling quicker as some new idea enters his understanding, or a new thought springs up in his own mind."[110]

On one occasion, Johnson saved Ramsay from being physically abused by an inebriated Indian. While Ramsay was escaping, Johnson picked up half a fence rail and challenged the attacker, but the Indian just laughed and went back to his house, whooping.[111] Sharing such experiences, a strong bond grew between the missionary and the interpreter. When the board ordered him to take up his duties in the Seminole country in the spring of 1856, Ramsay determined, once again, to secure Johnson's services.

Sometime during the late 1830s or early 1840s, Johnson had fathered a daughter, Kitty, with Nancy, an Indian-black. Nancy's descendants suggested that she had removed from New Orleans to the Indian Territory with four children. Nancy and Kitty emigrated to Mexico with John Horse's group in 1849. Kitty Johnson's daughters later recalled that, as a young girl on the journey, Kitty had shared a horse at the front of the party with Kowakochi's son, Billy. Nancy married John Kibbetts, who became a leader of the maroons in Coahuila and later a sergeant in the Seminole Negro Indian Scouts in Texas.[112]

While serving as the interpreter at Kowetah, Robert Johnson had married Elizabeth Hawkins, a Creek black. His wife did not live with him at the mission, however, and every other Saturday he rode off to spend the day with her. A female associate of Loomis once asked Johnson how he passed the time on the long journeys: "He answered, 'Why, ma'am, some of the way I prays, and some of the way I preaches.' 'Preach, Robin! And to whom do you preach?' she asked. 'Oh, to myself, ma'am.'" Johnson soon would put the oratorical skills he had worked on perfecting to full use in his dealings with Seminoles and cause a great deal of concern for Ramsay. In the early summer of 1856, the reverend asked the Creek slave owner Foster to let him hire Robert as an interpreter. Soon afterward, Robert Johnson and his wife, Elizabeth, moved out to the Oak Ridge Mission and commenced their association with the Seminoles.[113]

Ramsay was unhappy with having to rely so heavily on his interpreter and wished to communicate personally with the Seminoles. The minister determined to learn Creek himself, and soon after the interpreter's arrival, he set about creating a dictionary of the language. Ramsay would ask Johnson the Creek equivalent of common English words and set his answers down on paper. Though the reverend found this interesting, the interpreter considered translating dull and frequently fell asleep during the sessions. Ramsay next worked at constructing sentences. He would read the English to Johnson, then his translation, and the interpreter would correct his grammatical errors.[114] This early attempt to produce a Creek dictionary became possible only through the collaboration of an illiterate and enslaved black translator.

Ramsay's worst fears about his reliance on the black interpreter were realized. In December 1857, the missionary wrote an important letter to the Presbyterian board in Pennsylvania. Ramsay complained that Johnson was transmitting Africanisms along with Presbyterianism to the Seminoles and that his "interpretive notions and prejudices" had influenced the Indians greatly. He continued:

> Our interpreter at present is an African [and] he will have African ways and will try to lead our people in the same way. And they most willingly follow him as all the Creeks do the negroes among them in such things as having frequent fasts followed by feasts, great camp meetings, observing Christmas which they call 'Big Sunday' with a great fast and sitting up all Christmas night singing and shouting and praying.

Such goings-on could prove subversive to the church. Johnson was "almost adored" by the Indians he spoke to, and Ramsay felt himself "pretty much at his mercy." The minister could preach only when the interpreter had the notion and even then could discuss only "what he loves to talk about." Ramsay concluded by stating that he was more determined than ever to learn the Creek language.[115]

Ramsay's statements tell us something of the influence blacks had in the transmission of Christianity to the Seminoles, but they suggest a great deal more. Creek blacks and Seminole maroons modified the religion to include elements of their African heritage. There would have been substantial differences between the orthodox Presbyterian and Baptist religions and the versions practiced in the maroon communities. Those modified versions were the ones first accepted by the Indians. Just as James Factor was "bewitched" by black Baptists, so other Seminoles became entranced by the Africanized Presbyterianism that Robert Johnson preached. The concern expressed by the white missionaries suggests the extent of the problem. Murrow elected to segregate the Seminole Baptist church into Indian and black congregations, and in February 1858, Ramsay was relieved to report, "Our interpreter, Robert, was called home to the Creek agency by his master and soon after he left our people began again to return to order."[116] Christianity seems to have appealed to blacks primarily through its colorful, evocative, and mysterious ceremonies, rituals, and observances. Seminoles appear to have taken to the more extreme Africanized versions of the Presbyterian and Baptist religions for the same reasons.[117]

Although he was unhappy with the influence his interpreter was exerting over the Indians, Ramsay was unable to preach to Seminoles without Johnson's help. Consequently, the minister paid Johnson's owner $150 for the slave's services and "Robin received nearly the same for interpreting." By March 1858, Johnson had returned to the Oak Ridge Mission.[118] In the winter of 1859, Ramsay sought to put an end to future outlays by making arrangements to purchase Johnson from Foster. Buying slaves represented but one of several compromises that Presbyterian missionaries working in the Indian Territory were prepared to make to win the battle for souls.[119] Nor was the idea unheard of at the Seminole Mission. In November 1853, Mary Ann Lilley had written to the Presbyterian board requesting that it provide the money needed to buy her black cook, Mary, who lived "in constant dread for fear her owners will sell her off."[120] Ramsay had tried to secure Johnson's services on a permanent basis as early as 1851, but his proposal had fallen through. By 1859, however, Johnson had become a much more accomplished and sought-after interpreter, and his owner could command a higher price.

By December 1859, Ramsay felt that purchasing Johnson had become a necessity. It had become increasingly more expensive to hire him, his

owner might order him to return at any time, leaving the mission without an interpreter, and most importantly, Buckner was trying to secure
his services for the Baptists. Ramsay observed, "[Although] he is not in
every respect what we could wish him to be, yet he is a very popular
interpreter and the best we are at all likely to get." The reverend informed
the board that Foster had agreed to sell Johnson for $1,200, and that he
had the means to complete the purchase. Ironically, Heniha Mikko, who
shortly thereafter converted to the Baptist faith himself, provided most of
the money. He furnished an interest free loan of $800, and Ramsay's
"brethren, and other missionaries," would provide the balance. On January 19, 1860, the minister triumphantly reported that he had completed
the purchase. Johnson was faced with the burden of repaying the sale
price to his creditors, but Ramsay was of the opinion that "by industry
and economy" he could achieve that within five years and obtain his
freedom.[121]

Ramsay was delighted with the purchase. He had concluded it just in
time. Shortly afterward, Murrow rode out to the Seminole country to
team up with Talomas Mikko without an interpreter. John Read, who
had been interpreting for Talomas Mikko, had taken to drink, and the
ministers were prepared to offer Foster $400 per year for Johnson's ser-
vices. The Baptists were forced to hire Sancho, another black, as their
interpreter at $150 per year. Sancho and his wife, who was hired as a
domestic at $6 per month, moved out to the Little River Station with the
Murrows.[122] By the beginning of the 1860s, therefore, African interpreters were playing important roles, and exerting considerable influence,
in spreading both the Baptist and Presbyterian religions to the Indians.

His acquisition by the Presbyterians also must have come as a considerable relief to Robert Johnson. No longer could Foster subject him to his
whims or sell him away from his wife and family. Instead, Johnson could
go about his work as an interpreter and handyman at the Seminole Mission, knowing that he was gradually earning his freedom. Yet events soon
made the enterprise turn sour. First, Ramsay fled from the Indian Territory following the affair involving Johnson's runaway cousin, Luke; then
Heniha Mikko became a Baptist; and finally the Civil War broke out
before Johnson had a chance to repay his debt. As the majority shareholder, Heniha Mikko assumed the rights of ownership over him, and
thus would begin a new and dangerous chapter in the life of the black
interpreter.

By the beginning of the new decade, dark clouds had begun to gather on the maroons' horizon. As the national debate over the future of slavery and states' rights turned into war, the group once more became involved in a military conflict. With the coming of the Civil War, Seminoles and maroons again were forced to flee from their communities. Just as maroons had participated in the First and Second Seminole Wars in Florida to prevent being returned to southern plantations, so would they fight for their freedom in the "White Man's War" in the Indian Territory. This time, however, they would be asked to fight not only whites but also Seminoles. The Civil War would prove to be the most important watershed in their history, as it would lead to the maroons' eventual emancipation and incorporation into the Seminole Nation.

CHAPTER SIX

The Civil War

In the spring of 1858, Holata Mikko's band of Okonis and Fushachi Hacho's band of Mikasukis removed from Florida to the Indian Territory. Holata Mikko had become principal chief of the Seminoles who had remained in Florida after the Second Seminole War. His followers had managed to avoid the main Removals of the late 1830s and early 1840s by remaining secluded in the Everglades. U.S. officials had tried to persuade the reluctant mikko to remove. Several delegations of Seminoles, employing maroon interpreters familiar to him, had been dispatched from the Indian Territory to negotiate, but each had proven unsuccessful. Beginning in 1855, however, the United States made a final effort to remove by force this final obstacle to its mastery of the southern peninsula. The resultant Third Seminole War, 1855–58, lacked the drama of the first and second, but several significant skirmishes did take place, and maroons again assumed a leading role in the hostilities.

Holata Mikko, realizing that his force of fewer than 100 warriors was hopelessly outnumbered, employed hit-and-run tactics in a guerrilla campaign against the U.S. Army. His followers were described as a "treacherous, troublesome set of Seminoles and escaped Negro slaves."[1] Although few in number, the maroons' bravery in battle was noted by their adversaries, with General Rufus Saxton observing, "The negroes would often stand fire when the Indians would run away."[2] Holata Mikko's resistance to Removal was softened somewhat when he learned of the treaty of 1856, under the terms of which the Seminoles living in the West gained their

Holata Mikko (Billy Bowlegs). Daguerreotype, 1852. (Florida State Archives)

independence and a tract of land separate from the Creeks. He also received generous inducements from U.S. officials to leave Florida. Holata Mikko finally agreed to remove to the Indian Territory in March 1858.[3]

In early May, after formal ceremonies and iced champagne, Holata

Mikko, dressed in "red leggings, silver crown, and feathers," left Tampa Bay with his followers for the Indian Territory on board the portentously named U.S. steamer *Grey Cloud*. The party of 165 Indians included 39 warriors and 126 women and children, accompanied by only 2 maroons, one being described as an old man in Holata Mikko's band.[4] En route to the West, the emigrants stopped in New Orleans and spent a week there. The Seminoles were seen as something of a curiosity and newsworthy. An article appearing in *Harper's Weekly* shortly after the Seminoles had left New Orleans described Holata Mikko as having "two wives, one son, five daughters, fifty slaves, and a hundred thousand dollars in hard cash." His "Privy Council" consisted of his "brothers-in-law" John Chupco (Long John) and Nokos Harjo—described as his "Lieutenant" and "Inspector General," respectively—and Ben Bruner, a black slave belonging to the mikko.[5]

Ben Bruner was said to be the "guide, philosopher and friend [and] the interpreter, adviser, confidant and special favorite of King Billy."[6] It had been reported as early as 1846 that Holata Mikko spoke English fluently.[7] Bruner, therefore, likely served in the role of counselor rather than interpreter. The *Harper's* article continued:

> Ben Bruno [is] a fine, intelligent-looking negro. Unlike his master, he shows a decided predilection for civilized life, and an early visit to a ready-made clothing establishment speedily transformed him into a very creditable imitation of a 'white man's nigger.' He has more brains than Billy and all his tribe, and exercises almost unbounded influence over his master. [I] would advise any one who wishes to get into the good graces of Billy Bowlegs to pay special attention to Ben Bruno.[8]

Elsewhere, Bruner was described as a "huge negro, typical of the African race," whose father had "run away from his owner and escaped to the indians [*sic*]."[9]

By the time he left Florida, Ben Bruner already owned considerable assets. In the West, he used those as a springboard to acquire substantial livestock holdings. By the outbreak of the Civil War, Bruner had become the wealthiest Seminole maroon in the Indian Territory.[10] He also was employed in the salaried position of U.S. interpreter to the Seminoles at the subagency.[11] From there he was able to keep in close touch with

Ben Bruno, Negro Slave and Favorite (Ben Bruner). Lithograph published in *Harper's Weekly*, June 12, 1858.

affairs affecting his people. Consequently, Ben Bruner became one of the most influential maroons. After the Civil War, he would become a freedman bandleader and sit on the Seminole Council.

The Florida immigrants arrived at Fort Smith on May 28, 1858. A week later, they made their way to the Little River country by horse and wagon.[12] Holata Mikko's arrival led to a resurgence of factionalism within the tribe. Heniha Mikko had become principal chief of the Seminoles living in the Indian Territory, but Holata Mikko had led those who had remained in Florida. As the son of a sister of Mikkoanapa, Holata Mikko had a strong claim to be considered overall leader. The Florida immigrants were reported to be unhappy with the new country the Seminoles had acquired from the Creeks and wished instead to settle in the Little River area.[13] Holata Mikko had his slaves who were already residing there construct houses for him near their settlement on the Wewoka.[14] He then headed a Seminole delegation to Florida in an attempt to persuade those remaining to remove west. Although he received $200 for his efforts, Holata Mikko likely would have been concerned most with adding to his base of support. The venture was partly successful. On February 15, 1859, a party of seventy-five Seminoles left Florida for the Indian Territory, completing the last of the major Removals.[15]

A rivalry developed between Holata Mikko and Heniha Mikko over who should be principal chief and chart a future for the Seminoles. The contest stemmed from hereditary rights and history, but philosophical differences also separated the two. After the treaty of 1856, Heniha Mikko supported agents of white acculturation. He favored the adoption of Christianity, clothing and education favored by whites, and a centralized, constitutional form of government. In 1860, Heniha Mikko became a Baptist and fell under the influence of the minister Murrow, who espoused many of the ideals of the Old South. Under Murrow's leadership, the Seminole Baptist church became a vehicle for acculturation. In an attempt to bring the Seminoles into line with the other Civilized Tribes, one of Murrow's first moves was to divide the church into Indian and black congregations. Heniha Mikko's supporters embraced the Baptist religion, and later the Confederacy.

In contrast, Holata Mikko wanted to retain the old ways and did not favor the white road. While his rival had begun accepting elements of southern white culture, Holata Mikko had been fighting U.S. troops in the Florida swamps. Whereas Heniha Mikko engaged in speculative enterprises involving slave property and later supported segregation in the church, Holata Mikko employed the son of a runaway as his counselor. White associates and more acculturated Indian neighbors within the other Civilized Tribes were influencing Heniha Mikko's views on blacks. His actions suggest that he came to see slaves as property meant primarily to make their owners money. Holata Mikko, although a slave owner, treated his blacks more as associates, allies, and tributaries than monetary assets. His family had a long history of close ties with maroons, and bonds of shared experience and kinship cemented the relationship. That difference added fuel to the fire and further alienated the two rivals. Soon Holata Mikko would challenge Heniha Mikko for the principal chieftainship.

Events at first moved rapidly. On March 10, 1859, Murrow wrote to a friend from North Fork Town, "Billy Bowlegs and his party are still in the Creek country and he acts and speaks very independently. He has written word to the Creek Chief that he is not ready to move and does not intend to move until he does get ready. Billy is very popular among his own people who speak very strongly of turning their present Chief, John Jumper, out of office and making Billy chief." But less than a month later, Holata Mikko was dead. Murrow reported on April 2:

> Billy Bowlegs [is] dead. He died a few days since while on a visit to the "New Country" for the purpose of selecting a place to settle. A few of his followers were with him and buried him in the true old Seminole style: viz, with everything he had with him. They first killed his pony, and were hardly prevented from killing a negro man who he had with him in attendance. His rifle, money, and everything else, were buried. Billy was very wealthy, owning, it is said, more than one hundred negroes, besides large herds of cattle, ponies etc. He was very popular with the Seminoles, who spoke frequently of raising him to the office of principal chief.[16]

In his annual report for 1859, Southern Superintendent Elias Rector confirmed Holata Mikko's death.[17]

Sonaki Mikko succeeded him and was listed as leader of the Florida immigrant Okoni band on the Seminole annuity roll of 1860. Sonaki Mikko also came to be known as Billy Bowlegs, leading some to confuse him with the deceased Holata Mikko. Sonaki Mikko and the other Florida immigrant leaders continued to oppose Heniha Mikko and the actions of the Seminole Council.[18]

As a result of the political events of 1860, by late January 1861, six states had seceded from the Union, and Arkansas was considering joining them. The Federal government treated the Indian Territory as a low priority, but politicians in Arkansas and Texas quickly realized the strategic importance of the area and actively courted Indian support. On January 29, Governor Henry Rector of Arkansas wrote to John Ross, principal chief of the Cherokees, "Your people, in their institutions, productions, latitude, and natural sympathies are allied to the common brotherhood of the slaveholding States. Our people and yours are natural allies in war and friends in peace. Your country is salubrious and fertile, and possesses the highest capacity for future progress and development by application of 'slave labor.' " Rector explained that the Lincoln administration viewed the Indians' land as "fruitful fields ripe for the harvest of abolitionism, free soilers, and northern mountebanks." He pledged the South to the protection of the tribes' territorial integrity and monetary interests and requested their support in the forthcoming struggle.[19]

The Civilized Tribes were mostly receptive to the Confederates' overtures. With the exception of the Seminoles, the leadership of each was in the hands of wealthy Indian-white slaveholders, who identified their political, economic, social, and cultural interests with the South. Southern sympathizers also held, or had access to, every governmental position in the Southern Superintendency of Indian Affairs and controlled all sources of official information available to the tribes. All of the Indian agents and the Superintendent himself were supporters of the South, and they exerted strong influence over the tribes' leaders. As if that were not enough, Southern postmasters told the Indians that the Confederates were winning the war and that the Lincoln administration had fallen.[20]

At first, the Seminoles were unimpressed by the Confederate overtures. They were the only one of the Five Tribes without an Indian-white planter elite. Their leadership and institutions remained indigenous. They were largely unacculturated, and they had not adopted chattel slavery. There seemed to be fewer advantages to a Confederate alliance for Seminoles than for any of the other Civilized Tribes. During March 1861, therefore, the Seminole Council voted not to meet with the Confederates but to remain neutral and honor the tribe's existing treaties.[21]

However, Heniha Mikko's supporters soon would be drawn into the Confederate camp.

Heniha Mikko had fallen under the influence of his minister and friend Joseph Murrow and Seminole agents Josiah Washbourne and Samuel Rutherford, who all were deeply sympathetic to the South. As early as March 1860, Murrow had observed: "If this country belongs to any part of the union, that portion is the South. The Indians are all slave-holders and their feelings and sympathies are all southern. The soil and climate both are altogether suited for slaves. Negroes are healthier here, and there are more cases of longevity among them than either Whites or Indians. Let southern champions stand ready then to defend their just title to this territory."[22] Later, he made reference to "Black Republican Kansasites." Murrow subsequently was appointed Confederate agent to the Seminoles.[23] A Union intelligence report described Washbourne, the Seminole agent from 1854 to 1857, as one of the most die-hard Southerners in the Indian Territory. He subsequently worked hard for the Confederacy among the Seminoles, helped divide the tribe, and persuaded many of the Indians to organize militarily in support of the South. Rutherford, his successor, had been prominent in Arkansas politics. He put his considerable talents to work for the Confederacy, arguing that the Seminoles were slaveholders, of southern origin, and inhabitants of the South.[24] Heniha Mikko was won over by his influential white associates.

The Federal government had not paid the Seminoles their annuities for 1860.[25] That coincided with the worst drought in the Indian Territory in thirty years. By the spring of 1861, many Seminoles were destitute, and the Confederates were promising to honor the obligations of the U.S. government. As expected, the Choctaws and Chickasaws went over to the Confederacy. Then, in late April and early May, the Federal forces relinquished their control over the military posts in the Indian Territory and beat a hasty retreat to Fort Leavenworth, Kansas.[26] More promises were broken as treaty stipulations had provided that those posts would protect the Indians from attack. It now appeared that the Federal government had abandoned the Five Tribes. In his annual report for 1861, Commissioner of Indian Affairs William Dole ascribed the defection of the tribes to the Lincoln administration's failure to explain "its intended policy in relation to slavery" and to its withdrawal of military support from the Indian Territory.[27] By the late spring, the secessionists were at the Seminoles' door.

Soon after the Federal retreat, troops from Texas occupied Forts Wash-ita, Cobb, and Arbuckle. On May 13, the Confederate States created the military district of the Indian Territory and placed it under the control of Benjamin McCulloch. They also established a Bureau of Indian Affairs, with David Hubbard as commissioner, and on May 17 annexed the Indian Territory. The Confederacy extended its protection over all the Indians in the territory, and Albert Pike of Arkansas was sent out to negotiate treaties with each of the tribes.[28] Pike proved to be a wise choice as commissioner. Shrewd and effective, he was well known to the Indians and convinced that the Confederacy needed their support. By the end of the year, he had negotiated treaties with all of the major tribes in the Indian Territory.

In June 1861, an intertribal council of Choctaws, Chickasaws, Semi-noles, and Creeks sympathetic to the Confederacy met at North Fork Town, and on July 1, a "United Nations of the Indian Territory was formed." Included in the constitution was a provision granting the Grand Council of Delegates the right to raise Indian troops to oppose "invading forces of Abolitionist hordes under Abraham Lincoln."[29] Between July 10 and 12, the Choctaws, Chickasaws, and Creeks signed treaties with Pike at North Fork Town.[30] Heniha Mikko recently had received a letter from George Welch, who signed himself "Capt.—Commanding the Texas troops in the service of the Southern Confederacy."[31] Welch emphasized the themes that the Confederacy had stressed throughout: the Union would take away the tribe's land and slaves, the Federal government could not meet its treaty obligations, and the Seminoles' best interests lay with the South.[32] Heniha Mikko duly decided to throw in his lot with the Confederacy.

Pike, together with Elias Rector, Rutherford, and Moty Kennard, principal chief of the Confederate Creeks, traveled to the Seminole coun-try and concluded a treaty with Heniha Mikko at the tribal council house on August 1. Like the Creeks, the Seminoles as a whole had not agreed to support the Confederacy. E. H. Carruth later stated that Pike had con-ducted his negotiations with Heniha Mikko and four of his cohorts in secret and that they were bribed for their support.[33] Twelve mikkos, representing only around half of the Seminole population, signed the treaty. Sonaki Mikko, John Chupco, and the other Seminole mikkos refused to sign and stood in opposition to Heniha Mikko's Confederates.

A remarkably progressive document, the treaty with the Confederacy contained the most favorable terms the Seminoles ever had received from a foreign government.[34] Their territorial and political integrity were guaranteed. The treaty granted the Seminoles the right to unrestricted self-government, full jurisdiction over persons and property within their borders, and sole control over tribal membership. The legal rights of Indians in the Confederate States were to be increased greatly, and they would be subject to no discrimination before the law because of race. The Seminoles and Creeks each could send a delegate to the Confederate Congress to represent their interests. The Confederacy also agreed to assume responsibility for past and present U.S. monetary obligations to the Seminoles, and Indians were not to bear any expense of the war. The tribe was set to receive many more benefits from its alliance with the Confederacy than it ever had from its association with the Federal government. The Confederate commissioners also had treated the Seminole mikkos as peers.

The Confederate treaty contained clauses recognizing the importance of slavery to Heniha Mikko and his associates. Black slavery was acknowledged and declared to be legal. Slaves were defined as personal property, and the Seminoles could determine both individual titles and rights of inheritance according to their own laws and customs. The treaty extended the fugitive slave laws to include the Seminole country. The laws applied both to slaves fleeing to the Indian Territory and to Seminole slaves who might escape to other Indian nations or to the Confederate States. The treaty also included very specific clauses relating to slavery among the Seminoles. Owners would be reimbursed for slaves illegally seized during their Removal from Florida. The Confederacy agreed to investigate claims and determine settlements, to be paid either to the owners or their heirs. The Seminoles' claim for $52,650 for the loss of slave labor during the maroons' three-year residence at Fort Gibson, 1845–48, also would be settled.[35] Finally, the Confederacy agreed to pay $5,000 to the heirs of Sally Factor for the services of her slaves July and Murray, who had served the U.S. Army as interpreters for four years during the Second Seminole War without their owner receiving payment.

The Seminoles were not the only tribe to be rent apart by the Civil War. Except for some traditionalists, the Choctaws and Chickasaws solidly backed the Confederacy, but the Cherokees and Creeks were divided in their allegiance. The tribes split along old factional lines. On October 7, 1861, the Cherokees became the last of the Five Civilized Tribes to sign a Confederate treaty.[36] The National Party under John Ross subsequently supported the Union, while the old Treaty Party under Elias Boudinot and Stand Watie sided with the Confederacy. Battle lines were drawn between the more traditional Keetoowahs, who supported the North, and the Indian-white Knights of the Golden Circle, who sided with the South. Among the Creeks, ancient divisions also resurfaced. The Confederate treaty was the work of acculturated Lower Creek leaders. Traditional Upper Creeks quickly took exception to the treaty and banded behind the Tuckabatchee mikko Hopothli Yahola.

Hopothli Yahola was a wealthy slaveholder, but he also opposed white acculturation. He had fought at the Battle of Horseshoe Bend, had resisted Removal, and now stood against the Confederate blueprint for his tribe's future.[37] The division within the Seminoles appears to have followed similar lines. The issue of slave ownership does not explain the rift. The owners of the largest numbers of slaves, accounting for half of all Seminole slaves with identifiable owners, became Loyalists.[38] The factionalism that arose after the arrival of the Florida immigrants in the late 1850s better explains the split. Like Hopothli Yahola, Loyal Seminoles might have owned slaves, but they favored traditionalism over the kind of rapid acculturation an alliance with the South seemed to offer. Old alliances also came into play. Nogusa Emathla's band of Seminoles returning from Mexico in 1861 joined Heniha Mikko's towns on the Canadian and fought with the Confederacy. As Miller explains, "Coacoochee's italwa simply resumed their place at the Alachua fire."[39]

During the summer and early fall of 1861, Hopothli Yahola ignored the pleas of Confederates to join them. Instead, he massed his followers into camp near the junction of the Deep Fork and the North Fork, around the site of present-day Eufaula, and prepared to quit the Creek country by heading northward. He was joined by Loyal Seminoles under Sonaki Mikko, John Chupco, Halleck Tastanaki, Fos Harjo, and Pascofar; Seminole maroons and Creek blacks; runaway slaves from other parts of the Indian Territory; and refugees from various other Indian tribes.[40] At its peak, Hopothli Yahola's force included more than 2,000 warriors, in excess of 3,000 women and children, and some 300 blacks, totaling around 5,500.[41]

Seminole maroon heads of household known to have made the journey north with the Loyalists at that time include three Bowlegses—Cyrus, Dolly, and Hagar—as well as Hattie Charles, Sam Cudjo, Jacob Davis,

O-Poth-Le-Yo-Ho-Lo, speaker of the councils (Hopothli Yahola). Lithograph after Charles Bird King, published ca. 1836–44. (From McKenney and Hall, *The Indian Tribes of North America*)

Betsy Miller, and Jack Shortman. With their families and other unnamed maroons, they left their homes to flee toward the Union lines. But not all slaves of Loyal Seminoles joined their owners. For example, Jim Bowlegs, a slave of Nancy Chupco, who emigrated at that time, remained behind in the Seminole country for another year.[42] The Loyal Seminoles and maroons took with them all that they could carry. They gathered together supplies of food, clothing, blankets, guns, tools, and cooking utensils and loaded them into wagons or onto horses, or carried them by hand. The emigrants also took their livestock, driving horses, cattle, hogs, sheep, and chickens before them. Some of the Indians and maroons rode in wagons, but most were on horseback.

On November 5, the Loyalists broke camp and headed in the direction of Kansas.[43] Although evidence is sketchy and interpretations vary, they apparently split into three groups.[44] The first, headed by Hopothli Yahola, contained most of the Creek Indian and Creek black men in the party. That group needed to get north in the fastest time possible. On October 31, Kennard and other Lower Creek mikkos had written to former Choctaw agent Colonel Douglas Cooper, informing him of their intention to put down Hopothli Yahola's movement. All free blacks in the party and every slave they captured that did not belong to Lower Creeks in the expedition would be sold. Runaways from other nations would be "dealt with according to Creek laws."[45] The apparent intention of Hopothli Yahola's vanguard was to act as a decoy for the rest of the party, rebuild old Fort Arbuckle for protection against attack and as a possible base for guerrilla operations in the Indian Territory, and later assist other Loyalists with crossing the Arkansas. The second group contained mostly Creek Indian women, children, old people, and their slaves. The third group, including the Seminoles, Seminole maroons, and members of the other tribes, brought up the rear.

Cooper led an armed force into the Creek country to apprehend Hopothli Yahola, but by the time he reached North Fork Town on November 15, the emigrants had gone long ago. Cooper sent a message to the Loyalists to stop with "a McIntosh negro slave," but it was ignored.[46] Cooper then set out in pursuit. Except for a detachment of Texas Cavalry, Indian troops accounted entirely for his force of 1,400. Cooper's command included the First Seminole Battalion of Mounted Volunteers, mustered into service on September 21 under the command of Heniha Mikko (Major John Jumper). Meanwhile, the second and third groups in Hopothli Yahola's train prepared to cross the Arkansas, likely in flat boats made and operated by blacks from the first group. While the Indians and blacks were crossing, Hopothli Yahola's command acted as a decoy, leading the Confederates away. On November 19, Cooper came upon that vanguard at Round Mountain, just north of the Cimarron River, near its confluence with the Arkansas. The two engaged, but without clear result. Under the cover of darkness, the Loyalists crossed the Arkansas into the Cherokee country and rejoined their kinsmen. Cooper later deemed

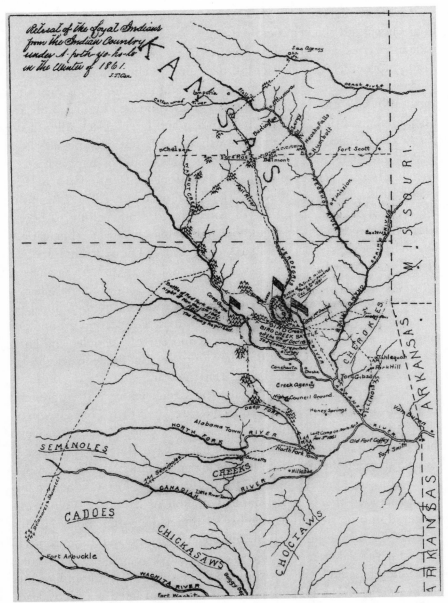

"Retreat of the Loyal Indians from the Indian Country under A-poth-yo-ho-lo in the Winter of 1861." Sketch map by J. T. Cox, reproduced in Abel, *The American Indian as Shareholder and Secessionist* (1919).

Heniha Mikko's conduct at Round Mountain, the first Civil War battle in the Indian Territory, "worthy of high commendation."[47]

The Confederates believed Hopothli Yahola to be heading for Walnut Creek, Kansas. Instead, he moved south down the Arkansas and took up a strong position at the Horseshoe Bend of Bird Creek, at Chusto-Talasah (Caving Banks). Cooper finally engaged the Loyalists on December 9, with Heniha Mikko leading the Creek-Seminole column on the Confederate left wing against his fellow tribesmen and the Seminole maroons. Again the action was indecisive, and the Loyalists were able to slip away. The frustrated Cooper then retired his force to Fort Gibson to pick up reinforcements and supplies.[48]

On December 26, a second Confederate force of 1,600 white troops under Colonel James McIntosh attacked the Loyalists at Chustenahlah, on Hominy Creek just west of present-day Skiatook. The Confederates' superior arms, equipment, and fresh horses, combined with the Loyalists' shortage of ammunition and overall exhaustion following their long trek and previous two engagements, proved decisive. Although the Seminoles under Halleck Tastanaki fought bravely and bore the brunt of the attack, they and their maroon allies eventually were driven from the field, and the engagement became a rout. Sonuck Harjo (Harjochee), said to be a "brother" of Sonaki Mikko, and a participant in the battle, reported, "In this third fight we were whipped and our people cut to pieces badly. During this fight our men were killed and women and children were not spared. Those that escaped death did not escape without some wound being inflicted on them and all our horses and provisions were captured."[49] McIntosh later claimed that his troops had killed upward of 250 Loyalists and captured 160 women and children and 20 blacks.[50] Betsy Miller was one of the Seminole maroons captured. She was imprisoned and later returned to the Seminole country.[51]

The Loyalists were put to headlong flight and headed north for Kansas in disarray. They resumed their journey under terrible conditions and suffered unimaginable hardship. In their panic, the Indians and blacks had left everything behind and were forced to journey on through the bitter winter cold without food, clothing, shelter, or horses. Many were practically naked and totally without subsistence. Almost all were on foot, and few had shoes. To add to their misery, a blizzard blew into their faces out of the northwest and further slowed their progress. Watie, McIntosh, and Cooper, meanwhile, commenced mop-up operations and pursued the

Loyalists to within ten miles of the Union lines, killing some, wounding others, and capturing more women and children.[52]

Some of the emigrants froze or starved to death, and bodies littered the trail. Others contracted frostbite and later had limbs amputated. Women gave birth on the open snow without blankets or shelter. Still others were "reduced to such extremity as to be obliged to feed upon their ponies and their dogs."[53] In that desperate state, the depleted, forlorn, and destitute Indian and black refugees struggled across the Union lines into Kansas early in the New Year. The country they left behind was decimated. In January 1862 the minister Murrow observed, "The western portions of the Indian Territory are all ruined and laid waste. All improvements are burned, stock all driven off or killed, and the entire western settlements are deserted."[54]

The Loyalists went into camp on the bleak Kansas plains between the Verdigris and Fall Rivers, and between Walnut Creek and the Arkansas, with the Seminoles and maroons settling near Fort Roe.[55] By February 5, 1862, the refugees included 3,168 Creeks, 53 Creek slaves, 38 free Creek blacks, 777 Seminoles, 136 Quapaws, 50 Cherokees, 31 Chickasaws, and perhaps 300 Indians from various other tribes, totaling some 4,500.[56] The Seminole population included both Indians and maroons. Conditions in the camps were dreadful, the emigrants being "destitute of clothing, shelter, fuel, horses, cooking utensils and food."[57] Many were starving, naked, suffering from wounds, frostbite, or disease, and in desperate need of medical attention. They faced the harsh winter without shelter or blankets. Within two months of their arrival, 240 Creeks alone had died, and 100 frozen limbs were amputated. Union officials and Kansas residents were unprepared for the problems posed by the refugees, whose "number was being constantly augmented by the daily arrival of other camps and families."[58] Already, the Creek and Seminole Loyalists began clamoring to return to their homes in the Indian Territory.[59]

To prevent the risk of disease arising from the presence of hundreds of dead and rotting ponies around the campgrounds, Union officials decided to move the emigrants to a new location in the Neosho River Valley, some 130 miles to the northeast. There, the refugees would be closer to the Sac and Fox Agency, a center of administrative control. George Snow, appointed the Union Seminole agent on January 7, prepared to move his charges in early March. Many were unable to make the journey unaided. Hired Kansas teamsters piled the sick, the women and children, and their few remaining effects into wagons and hauled them away. The men followed along behind, usually on foot. On March 6, the Seminoles refused to go any farther and made camp near Le Roy in Coffey County.[60] Their stay there would be short, however, and soon they would move on again.

In mid-April, special agent George Collamore visited the refugee Indians and blacks and described the scene:

> [I] found them encamped upon the Neosho river bottom, in the timber, extending a distance of some seven miles. Not a comfortable tent was to be seen. Such coverings as I saw were made in the rudest manner, being composed of pieces of cloth, old quilts, handkerchiefs, aprons and c & c. Stretched upon sticks and so limited were many of them in size that they were scarcely sufficient to cover the emaciated and dying forms beneath them.

Consumption, pneumonia, and exposure were prevalent, and the death rate was extremely high. By that time, 7,600 refugees, including 1,096 Seminoles and maroons were camped on the Neosho. Many were almost naked, deprived of shelter, and starving. Collamore observed, "I went from lodge to lodge, and tribe to tribe, and the suffering of the well to say nothing of the sick is beyond description."[61]

Food remained scarce. On March 3, Congress had passed an act providing that the annuities of "hostiles"—Indians who had sided with the Confederacy—should be applied to the relief of refugees from the Indian Territory.[62] For the Indians, that translated into a per capita weekly ration of one pound of flour, a piece of spoiled bacon, and a little salt. The mikkos described the bacon as "not fit for a dog to eat." It had been condemned at Leavenworth, and many who ate it became ill.[63] The lot of the Seminole maroons was even worse. Benjamin Van Horn, who contracted to supply cattle to the refugees, noted, "[The] Government did not make any allowance, all they got to eat was what the Indians gave them, consequently they were on short rations."[64] Many of the other goods distributed to the Indians were unsuitable and had to be traded for green corn, chickens, and eggs for half their value. Collamore reported that the refugees "ardently desire to return to their farms, rebuild their cabins, renew their fences, [and] plant the seed."[65]

The Northern Seminoles reorganized and selected Sonaki Mikko as their principal chief. On April 14, Sonaki Mikko and the other Loyal Seminole mikkos informed Dole that they were "as fully prepared to do business as we were before the rebellion." They asked to be recognized formally as the Seminole Nation and that the tribe's annuities be paid to them. The Confederate Seminoles had "forfeited all right and claim to any annuities or any property belonging to the Seminole Nation" and were "no longer entitled to be considered part of the Seminole Nation." A year later, Sonaki Mikko was signing himself "Head Chief Seminole Nation" and "King of the Seminoles."[66]

Under pressure from irate local inhabitants, on April 24 Snow persuaded his charges to remove farther downstream from Le Roy to Neosho Falls in Woodson County.[67] There, as customary, the maroons and Seminoles made camp a short distance from each other in the woods just below the dam.[68] Most would remain in that location until they returned to the Indian Territory in 1864 and 1865. Although conditions improved steadily as rations became more substantial and medical attention more available, the maroons and Seminoles continued to suffer. Disease constituted the biggest problem in the camps and would plague the lives of the refugees until the end of the war.

Northern officials realized that it would be cheaper to enlist the able-bodied men than subsist them as refugees in Kansas. On March 13, Dole proposed that Indians and blacks help regain the Indian Territory for the Union. Within a week, he was promised an expeditionary force of two white regiments and 2,000 Indians, appropriately armed. Once the emigrants had recovered their homes, they would be given the means to defend themselves. Consequently, during spring 1862, able-bodied male refugees were mustered into a new unit—the Union Indian Brigade, or Indian Home Guard—to participate in a Federal invasion of the Indian Territory planned for that summer.[69]

The First Regiment of the Union Indian Brigade came to include eight companies of Creeks and two of Seminoles. The two Seminole units were Company A, which had 100 members under Captain Halleck Tastanaki and Lieutenant Fos Harjo, and Company B, which had 106 members under Captain Sonaki Mikko (by then known to whites as Billy Bowlegs) and Lieutenant John Chupco.[70] Indian Territory blacks also enrolled in the brigade as both soldiers and interpreters, providing a bridge between the Indians and white officers. Historian Gary Zellar notes, "They served as negotiators, clerks, orderlies, medicine men, soldiers and scouts."

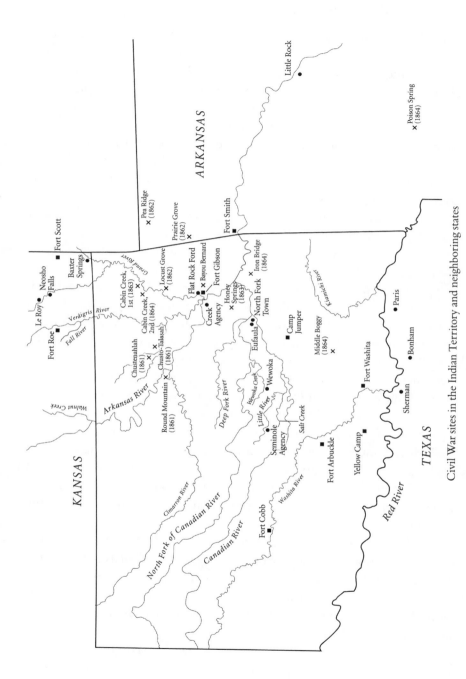

Civil War sites in the Indian Territory and neighboring states

KANSAS

ARKANSAS

TEXAS

Little Rock

Poison Spring
× (1864)

Fort Scott

Pea Ridge
× (1862)

Prairie Grove
× (1862)

Fort Smith

Le Roy
Neosho
Falls
Baxter
Springs

Grand River

Cabin Creek
1st (1863)
Locust Grove
(1862)
Flat Rock Ford
Bayou Bernard
Fort Gibson

Iron Bridge
(1864)

Paris

Fort Roe

Verdigris River

Fall River

Cabin Creek,
2nd (1864)
Creek
Agency
Honey
Springs
(1863)
North Fork
Town

Camp
Jumper

Bonham

Walnut Creek

Chustenahlah
(1861)
Chusto-Talasah
(1861)

Middle Boggy
(1864)
×

Fort Washita

Kiamichi River

Arkansas River

Round Mountain
(1861)

Deep Fork River

Eufaula

Wewoka

Wewoka Creek

Little River

Sherman

Cimarron River

North Fork of Canadian River

Seminole
Agency

Salt Creek

Fort Arbuckle

Yellow Camp

Fort Cobb

Canadian River

Washita River

Red River

173

Union cavalry sergeant Wiley Britton recalled, "Nearly all the negro men fit for the military service who had belonged to the Cherokees and Creeks joined the Indian regiments." Littlefield has named fifteen Creek blacks, apart from interpreters, who served in the First Regiment.[71] Seminole maroons also served in the brigade. Jim Bowlegs, for example, later stated that he had been a member of the same unit as his owner's husband,[72] and Robert Johnson subsequently became the main interpreter for the Seminole companies. Seminole maroons and Creek blacks thus became the first African American Union soldiers to be mustered into combat units during the Civil War.[73]

From its inception until it was mustered out of service in the spring of 1865, the Union Indian Brigade took part in more than thirty actions in Missouri, Arkansas, and the Indian Territory, frequently in concert with black regiments.[74] Seminole maroons and other Indian Territory blacks also participated in many of those engagements. As Porter has remarked, "Since Creek, Seminole and Cherokee Negroes served in the Union Indian regiments on equal terms with the Indians, when one reads of an action in which Union Indians were involved one should envisage black as well as brown faces in the ranks."[75] In the spring of 1864, the blacks were mustered out of the Union Indian Brigade and into separate regiments. John Cox, special Indian agent in the Indian Territory, lamented the loss: "It is well known that the interpreters in the Indian regiments, especially the Creeks, are almost exclusively colored persons, residents in the Indian Country; they are therefore indispensable for the maintenance of discipline and good service." "Those of the most active and efficient of the First Regiment," the Seminole and Creek companies, were the first to be mustered out.[76] Thereafter, they became part of the history of the black Union regiments.

As fellow members of the Union Indian Brigade, Seminoles and maroons took part in the First Federal Invasion of the Indian Territory in the summer of 1862. Except for a white auxiliary, the Union force was composed entirely of Indians and blacks. The Indian brigade included more than one thousand Creeks and Seminoles with their black associates, Cherokees, Quapaws, and "full companies of wild Delawares, Kechees, Ironeyes, Cadoes [sic] and Kickapoos [besides] sixty Delawares from the Delaware Reservation, and about two hundred Osages."[77] The expedition set out on June 28 and met with quick success, defeating Confederates at the Battles of Locust Grove, July 3, and Bayou Bernard, July 27.

The Union force quickly established dominance north of the Arkansas, and it looked as though the Confederates would be swept south to the Red River. However, dissension among the officer corps resulted in the arrest of the expedition commander, Colonel William Weer, and an eventual retreat to Baxter Springs, Kansas, in August.[78] For the time being, the Indian Territory remained in the hands of the Confederacy.

Some 1,500 Indian and black refugees followed the expedition into the Indian Territory in the hope of returning to their homes. They were forced to retreat north with the Union army and spend another winter in the camps in Kansas. Most of the other Loyalists who had remained behind in the Indian Territory also followed the army north during the coming months, and a large refugee camp sprang up around Baxter Springs.[79] A second wave of Seminole maroons fled to Kansas in October 1862. Heads of household known to have made their way north at that time included three Bowlegses—Jim, Mollie, and William—and Tom Noble and Polly Sayers. Other Seminole maroon heads of household who journeyed to Kansas during the Civil War, but at an unknown date, include Johnson Bowlegs, Tony Bowlegs, Caesar Bruner, Bob Davies, and Calina Payne.[80] Their families would have accompanied them. Some of those heads of household joined the Union Indian Brigade, others later enlisted in black regiments, and still others spent the rest of the war in the Seminole maroon refugee camp at Neosho Falls.

On September 29, 1862, Seminole agent Snow reported on the Indians and maroons under his care. The Loyal Seminole population included 107 men, 372 women, and 440 children—919 total—in camp at Neosho Falls. Most of the men were old or otherwise unfit for military duty. In addition, 193 Seminole warriors had joined the Union Indian Brigade. The Seminoles, he observed:

> [Have] brought with them about sixty colored people, and over one hundred have come from the nation since and joined them. These colored people are generally intelligent and talk the English language, and understand how to do common work on a farm, but it is evident that they have not been brought up to labor like those among the Whites. The greater portion of them, however, claim to be free, under the pretext that their masters were secesh.[81]

The following year, after the arrival of the second wave of Seminole and maroon emigrants, the agent reported, "[Nearly] two-thirds of these Indians, as well as all their negroes, have left their country and come here to be protected by the government."[82] Snow exaggerated the percentages of both Indian and maroon emigrants. Sattler has suggested that, by that time, the total Seminole population and band distribution had divided equally between the North and the South.[83] And only a large majority, but not all, of the Seminole maroons made their way to Kansas during the course of the Civil War.

On December 7, Indian Territory blacks in the Union Indian Brigade engaged Confederates at the Battle of Prairie Grove. Zellar suggests that those were the first regularly mustered African Americans to participate in a major Civil War engagement and that Southern newspapers reported with alarm seeing "Negroes in federal uniforms" at the battle.[84] Following another severe winter in the camps, plans were made in the spring of 1863 to return the refugees to their homes in the Indian Territory.[85]

After the Union had secured its position in northern Arkansas and southern Missouri, on April 18 the Indian brigade occupied Fort Gibson in what became known as the Second Federal Invasion of the Indian Territory.[86] The Union troops then fortified the post as a base of operations against the Confederates. Many refugees from the Neosho camps followed the Federal advance. Britton noted that "these families were mostly Creeks and Seminoles, the families of the soldiers of the First and Second Indian regiments."[87] Seminole maroons and Creek and Cherokee blacks also journeyed south: "Most of the colored men who had belonged to Indian masters had enlisted in the Indian regiments, and of course their families encamped with the Indian families. There was no recognized difference of social status between the Indians and negroes, so they mingled together on terms of perfect equality."[88] Other Loyal Indians and blacks, who had taken refuge in the Cherokee country during the Confederate ascendancy in the Indian Territory, also flocked to the post.[89]

The refugees planted fields around Fort Gibson, but following repeated attacks by Stand Watie's guerrillas, they were forced to retire within the confines of the fortifications. By early June, some 3,000 Indian and black soldiers and 6,000 refugees, including 500 or more blacks, were living in a one-and-a-half-square-mile area within the fort. A recent smallpox epidemic, combined with the usual problems of dysentery, un-

sanitary conditions, and lack of food, clothing, shelter, and medical attention, led to still more suffering. The soldiers and refugees were dependent
upon supplies sent from Kansas posts.[90] As members of the Kansas Colored Regiments, blacks from the Indian Territory would play a vital role
in keeping those supply lines open.

Although the First South Carolina Colored Volunteers had been the
first to recruit, organize, and arm a separate African American military
unit for the Union during the early summer of 1862, it had disbanded
quickly, due to political pressure and lack of official sanction. The First
Kansas Colored Volunteers Infantry Regiment, mustered into service that
winter, was the first unit of black troops to receive Federal recognition and
approval. On July 22, 1862, Senator James Lane, a strong proponent of
utilizing black troops, had become recruiting agent in the Department of
Kansas. During the fall, African Americans were enlisted rapidly. By the
early New Year, six of the ten companies needed to create an infantry regiment had been enlisted, and on January 13, 1863, the First Kansas Colored
was mustered into service. During the next three months, recruitment
continued until the four remaining companies were complete.[91]

Company I, mustered into service on May 2, included most of the
eligible Indian Territory blacks. Benjamin Van Horn, who earlier had
taken a contract to supply cattle for the refugees camped on the Neosho
and at the Sac and Fox Agency, recruited them. He was given "full
company cooking utensals [sic] and camp equipage and rations, six new
wall tents, 80 guns, some ammunition, two wagons and teams for transport, and a drill master." Between mid–March and late April, Van Horn
enlisted the full company quota of eighty men and marched them to Fort
Scott to join the regiment. The men were mustered in as Company I, and
Van Horn became captain and the company commander. The blacks
exchanged their "old rags" for new uniforms and "were as proud as a little
boy with a red wagon." They then marched to Baxter Springs to commence drilling exercises prior to receiving orders to support and reinforce
the Union Indian Brigade at Fort Gibson.[92]

Many of Van Horn's recruits were Seminole maroons and Creek
blacks. James Goodin, Scipio Gouge, Elias Hardridge, and Thomas Herrod, four of the Creek blacks, had enlisted in the Indian brigade the
previous year. Van Horn was not choosy in his recruiting. Elias Hardridge
and Nero Hardridge, for example, were both minors enlisted without
their parents' consent. Some might have been forced to enlist, helping to

account for the high desertion rate within the company during 1863. But desertion became far less prevalent as time went by. The Seminole maroon recruits included three Bowlegses—Cyrus, George, and Robert—and Sam Cudjo and Simon Noble. The service records of those five men suggest the diversity of experience and fortune that soldiers of Company I encountered. Sam Cudjo was promoted to corporal and later claimed to have become a sergeant before being mustered out with the regiment on October 1, 1865. Cyrus Bowlegs was discharged for disability at Fort Smith, Arkansas, on December 4, 1863. George Bowlegs deserted at Fort Gibson on December 8, 1863. Robert Bowlegs died of disease at Fort Smith on May 26, 1864. And Simon Noble was killed in action at the Battle of Poison Spring, near Camden, Arkansas, on April 18, 1864.[93] Seminole maroon Union troopers would experience victory, defeat, promotion, honorable discharge, disability, disease, and death during the course of the Civil War.

The First Kansas Colored Infantry soon played a large role in the Battles of Cabin Creek and Honey Springs, the two most important Civil War engagements in the Indian Territory.[94] In late June, a large wagon train left Fort Scott with supplies for the troops and refugee Indians and blacks at Fort Gibson. Around 600 mounted men of the Union Indian Brigade strengthened the escort. As the train moved into the Indian Territory, however, news came to Baxter Springs that Watie and a large force of Confederate Indians and Texans were preparing to attack before the supplies could reach their destination. The First Kansas Colored marched out of Baxter Springs on June 26 and came upon the wagon train the same day. On July 2, Watie's Confederates attacked the train when it attempted to cross the swollen Cabin Creek. In what became the turning point in the engagement, the First Kansas Colored opened fire and drove the Confederates from their position. The Union troops then crossed and attacked the enemy, one contemporary noting that the blacks, "charged through the water up to their necks, holding guns over their heads and firing."[95] The Confederates were put to flight, and the engagement quickly became a rout.

The Battle of Cabin Creek represented a major victory for the Federal forces. The Union losses were 3 killed and 30 wounded, while the Confederates had around 50 killed, the same number wounded, and nine taken prisoner. The wagon train completed the journey to Fort Gibson on July 5. The military and refugees at the post received their much-needed supplies, and the reinforcements strengthened the garrison. The Union victory was due largely to the performance of the First Kansas Colored. The blacks were reported to be anxious to prove themselves in battle. Confederate officers' statements that the South would give no quarter to the Colored Regiments and would take no black prisoners only strengthened their resolve.[96] The battle marked the first Civil War engagement in which black, Indian, and white units fought together. Watie disparagingly referred to his opponents as "this mongrel force."[97] William Burke commented that the black troops "evinced a coolness and true soldierly spirit which inspired the officers in command with [confidence]."[98] And Wiley Britton praised "their soldierly appearance and splendid conduct at Cabin Creek," which helped reduce prejudice within the Union army against using black troops.[99]

The Confederates regrouped at Honey Springs depot, some twenty-five miles south of Fort Gibson. The Union commanders wished to press home their advantage and sent out a force of nearly 3,000, including the First Kansas Colored, the First and Second Regiments of the Union Indian Brigade, and some white artillery and cavalry units. The Confederates included two Cherokee and two Creek regiments and a reserve of the Choctaw and Chickasaw Regiment, as well as Texas Rangers and cavalry and artillery units. In total, the Confederate force amounted to more than 6,000 men. During the ensuing engagement, Union black and Indian troops fought side-by-side against Confederate Indians and Texans for control of the Indian Territory. Despite being outnumbered by more than two to one, the Union forces again emerged victorious.

The Battle of Honey Springs, July 17, 1863, actually took place at Elk Creek, about three miles north of the depot. The Confederates had taken a strong position, but the turning point came when the First Kansas Colored broke through the center of their line, causing them to retreat. The blacks even shot down the standard-bearer and captured the Confederates' colors. The First Regiment of the Union Indian Brigade, including the Seminole companies, then helped drive the enemy across the creek. The Confederates were put to headlong flight, with the Union blacks and Indians in hot pursuit, and the engagement turned into another rout. At the Honey Springs depot, the Union forces discovered some 300 to 400 sets of handcuffs. Captured prisoners informed them that the Confederates had intended to shackle black captives before carrying them off to slavery in the South as the spoils of victory. The discovery would only have added to the black troops' resolve to defeat the enemy.[100]

The battle left the northern Indian Territory firmly in the hands of the Union. The Federal losses at Honey Springs were 14 dead and 62 wounded, while the Confederates had 150 killed, 400 wounded, and 77 captured. The list of Union casualties reflected that the blacks and Indians had borne the brunt of the fighting. The First Kansas Colored had 2 men killed and 30 wounded, and the First Regiment of the Union Indian Brigade had 2 killed and 6 wounded. Captains Nokos Alochee and Sonaki Mikko were commended for "efficient service" and "gallant conduct" during the campaign.[101]

Their commanding officers also lavished praise on the black infantrymen. Lieutenant Colonel John Bowles reported, "[The] officers and men throughout the entire regiment behaved nobly, and with the coolness of veterans. Each seemed to vie with the other in the performance of his duty, and it was with the greatest gratification that I witnessed their gallant and determined resistance under the most galling fire."[102] General James Blunt, in overall command of the Union forces at Honey Springs, further observed:

> The First Kansas (colored) particularly distinguished itself; they fought like veterans, and preserved their line unbroken throughout the engagement. Their coolness and bravery I have never seen surpassed; they were in the hottest of the fight, and opposed to Texas troops twice their number, whom they completely routed. One Texas regiment (the Twentieth Cavalry) that fought against them went into the fight with 300 men and came out with only 60.[103]

Blunt later informed his department commander that he would prefer one black soldier to ten Indians and concluded, "The question that negroes will fight is settled; besides they make better soldiers in every respect than any troops I have ever had under my command."[104] Bowles's and Blunt's allusion to "veterans" is suggestive. Maroons in the First Kansas Colored had battled U.S. forces to a standstill during the Second Seminole War in Florida and indeed qualified as seasoned campaigners.

The Battle of Honey Springs was the largest and most significant military engagement ever to be fought in what is now the state of Oklahoma. It took place in the same month as the fall of Vicksburg and Lee's defeat at Gettysburg and exerted so profound an influence on the Civil War in the Indian Territory that it has been called "the Gettysburg of the trans-Mississippi West."[105] Six weeks later, Federal forces captured Fort Smith.[106] By the end of the year, the Confederates had been swept far south into the Choctaw and Chickasaw Nations, almost to the Red River. Black and Indian soldiers deserve much of the credit for the Union's ascendancy in the Indian Territory.

In early September 1863, the First Kansas Colored was ordered to Fort Smith. The newly formed Second Kansas Colored Volunteers Infantry Regiment joined it there. The Second Kansas Colored also included Seminole maroons, such as Private Aaron Sanco of Company G, and Creek blacks.[107] On November 2, Brigadier General John McNeil wrote of the First Kansas Colored, "The negro regiment is a triumph of drill and discipline, and reflects great honor on Colonel Williams, in command. Few volunteer regiments that I have seen make a better appearance. I regard them as first rate infantry."[108] The two black regiments conducted various operations deep within Confederate Indian Territory, but in early December, they were transferred to Arkansas.[109]

In the late winter and early spring of 1864, the First Kansas Colored became involved in heavy fighting in Arkansas. As part of the Camden Expedition, the black regiment participated in the disastrous Battle of Poison Spring, April 17, 1864, when a superior Confederate force attacked and overwhelmed a Federal supply train and escort.[110] The Confederates included the Twenty-ninth Texas and Tandy Walker's Choctaw Indian Brigade, two of the units humiliated by the blacks at Honey Springs. They were bent on revenge.

The First Kansas Colored fought gallantly at Poison Spring. The commanding officer of Company I, which contained most of the Indian Territory blacks, later commended his men for the "coolness, bravery, and promptness with which they obeyed and executed orders."[111] But the weight of numbers proved decisive, and the Confederates inflicted terrible retribution on the Union troops. The black regiment suffered its heaviest losses of the war, having 117 killed and 65 wounded. Company I lost 11 killed and had 6 wounded.[112] The Confederates showed no mercy. They took only four black prisoners, with other captured blacks being "murdered on the spot."[113] Britton reported that the Confederates, "with a wild hurrah and war whoop of the Indians," shot and bayoneted the black soldiers where they fell. Some feigned death, then crawled off the battlefield after dark to try to reach the Union camp. Snakes bit several who hid in the weeds, and by the time they reached camp, their bodies were swollen with the poison.[114] Suffering from exhaustion and their numbers badly depleted, the men of the First Kansas Colored returned to Fort Smith in May, but they soon would see further action in the Indian Territory.

In February 1864, detachments of the First and Third Regiments of the Indian brigade joined a Union expedition into Confederate Indian Territory. The commanding officer carried copies of Lincoln's emancipation proclamation translated into the various languages of the Confederate Indians and distributed them freely. He also sent messages of goodwill and encouragement to Heniha Mikko and other prominent Indian leaders, urging them to surrender and transfer their allegiance to the Union. On February 13, the Federal force came upon Heniha Mikko's Seminoles and other Confederates in camp at Middle Boggy in the Choctaw Nation. In the ensuing battle, the Seminole members of the Union Indian Brigade punished their Confederate tribesmen. John Chupco reported, "We met our old chief 'John Jumper' in the Chickasaw Nation, he had with him all the Rebel Seminoles. He gave us fight—we whipped him—we killed many."[115]

The goodwill messages to Heniha Mikko fell on deaf ears. Since first signing the treaty with Pike, he had remained true to the Confederacy. He first commanded the Seminole Battalion and then, when it was raised to a regiment, the First Seminole Regiment. Heniha Mikko fought at the Battles of Round Mountain, Chusto-Talasah, and Pea Ridge. On November 21, 1862, he became an honorary lieutenant colonel. After Pea Ridge, he, together with his fellow Seminole officers—Major James Factor, Captain Fos Hatchee Cochuehue, and Lieutenants John F. Brown, George Cloud, and Thomas Cloud—actively participated in the Confederate guerrilla campaigns in the Indian Territory.[116]

Following the Battle of Middle Boggy, Heniha Mikko renewed his pledge of allegiance to the Confederacy. On July 6, 1864, he delivered a speech to the First Seminole Regiment, urging his men to reenlist: "I do not think we have any cause to regret our choice. Our interests and feelings are Southern. Our homes, our families, everything we have in short, is in the South."[117] His speech proved persuasive, and the Confederate Seminoles subsequently played an important part in the Second Battle of Cabin Creek.

During June and September 1864, the Kansas black regiments pitted their might against Confederate Indian troops in two more battles that proved to be the last major Civil War engagements in the Indian Territory. The Second Kansas Colored won a convincing victory over Watie's guerrillas at Iron Bridge, Choctaw Nation, on June 16.[118] But it would be a different story a few months later at the Second Battle of Cabin Creek.

On September 14, the First Kansas Colored received orders to reinforce Fort Gibson and keep open the supply routes. Thirty-seven men were sent to help operate a hay station at the Union outpost at Flat Rock Ford, a few miles north of the post, on the Grand River. Meanwhile, the Confederates had determined to close the Federal supply lines and assembled a large force of 2,000, including the First Seminole Regiment under Heniha Mikko. On the sixteenth, Confederates attacked the hay station at Flat Rock. By nightfall, only four of the blacks were still alive. They escaped certain death by hiding in the prairie grass and water holes. After dark, they slipped through the Confederate sentries and alerted the garrison at Fort Gibson.[119]

While the action at Flat Rock was taking place, an immense Federal wagon train was making its way south from Fort Scott to Fort Gibson along the old Texas Road. On September 18, the train arrived at the Federal stockade at Cabin Creek, where it was joined by reinforcements from Fort Gibson. Although the Federal troops were aware of the coming onslaught, they were hopelessly outnumbered. Moving up from Flat Rock, the Confederates mounted a night attack during the early morning of September 19. The Confederate Indians fought with great enthusiasm, routed the Union forces, and captured the entire train, chalking up the greatest Confederate military victory in the Indian Territory.[120]

The Second Battle of Cabin Creek marked the last major campaign for the black troops in the Indian Territory. Immediately after the battle, most of the black units were transferred to neighboring states. During the summer of 1864, the black regiments had been reorganized, the First Kansas Colored becoming the Seventy-ninth U.S. Colored Infantry and the Second Kansas Colored becoming the Eighty-third U.S. Colored Infantry. The Seventy-ninth and Eighty-third were mustered out of service on October 1 and 9, respectively, and the men received their final pay and discharges at Leavenworth later that month.[121] Some of the Indian Territory blacks reenlisted in black regiments after the war, but most made their way home to begin new lives as freedmen.

Clashes between Confederate Indians and Loyal Indians and blacks dominate the history of the Civil War in the Indian Territory. The antagonists took the field against each other in all of the major campaigns there. Blacks and Indians fought in the engagements involving Hopothli Yahola's followers, the First and Second Federal Invasions of the Indian Territory, and the Battles of Cabin Creek, Iron Bridge, and Honey Springs. In each, one or the other played a decisive role. The Loyal Indians and blacks played a vital part in regaining and holding the Indian Territory for the Union, and without the participation of the Confederate Indian troops, the Southern forces would have been pushed across the Red River into Texas long before the end of the war.

As fellow refugees in Kansas and the Indian Territory, and as soldiers in the Union army, the Loyal Seminoles and maroons continued their long tradition of alliance. Yet the relationship remained one of close association rather than integration. During the flight northward to Kansas in 1861, the maroons and Seminoles traveled in separate groups, as had the followers of John Horse and Kowakochi when they rode out of the Indian Territory for Mexico twelve years earlier. When attacked by the Confederates, moreover, the maroons fought in their own units under maroon leadership, as they had in Florida during the Seminole Wars and as would their kinsmen in Coahuila during Indian campaigns. In Kansas, the Seminoles and maroons settled apart from each other on the Neosho. Some of the maroons joined the Union Indian Brigade alongside Seminoles, but eventually almost all of the Indian Territory blacks were mustered into the Kansas Colored Regiments. As in Florida and Mexico, maroons and Seminoles supported a common cause, but mostly fought in separate units.

The Loyal Seminoles and maroons allied in opposition to the Confederates and ultimately emerged victorious. They shared the experience of losing loved ones, homes, and property in the Indian Territory, their horrific flight to Kansas, life in the refugee camps, and service in the Union army. But even more significantly, the two fought together against Heniha Mikko's Confederate Seminoles at Chusto-Talasah, Middle Boggy, and the Second Battle of Cabin Creek. The Loyal Seminoles considered the maroons allies and Heniha Mikko's Confederates the enemy. As the Loyalists would lead the nation for many years after the war, that helps explain why the Seminole freedmen fared so well during Reconstruction.

By summer 1863, the Loyal Seminole and maroon refugees had been split into two groups: one living at Neosho Falls and the other with the Union Indian Brigade and the black regiments at Fort Gibson. In August, newspaper correspondent Charles Monroe Chase visited the Seminoles and maroons in their camps on the Neosho. He wrote of the Seminoles, "By treaty the Government provides for their necessary wants. All they do is draw their rations and cook them, occasionally catching fish or picking a few blackberries, which they sell in the village for rum money. Their time is spent in lounging in the shade or tents supplied by the Government." Chase then visited "the slave camp a few rods away from the camp of the Indians" and noted, "The negroes were very sociable, I could not help but observe the contrast between the negro and Indian characters. The little darkeys at our approach, would run towards us with open ivory, and dance for joy at our notice. The older ones were pleased and so anxious to answer our questions, that one was scarcely asked before 'yes massa' or 'no massa' was out of a half dozen mouths at a time."[122] From Chase's comments, we catch a rare glimpse of life in the Seminole and maroon refugee camps in Kansas at the height of the Civil War.

The situation of the refugees at Neosho Falls had improved since the previous winter. On July 29, Pascofar, "Business Chief" of the Loyal Seminoles, wrote to Commissioner Dole, asking for more sugar, coffee, tents, and heavy clothing for the women and children. But he added, "[I] am not going to complain of our treatment. We have had plenty the most of the time of good substantial food."[123] In September, Seminole agent Snow reported, "The general health of the Indians has been remarkably good and the mortality among them quite small. [They] have been well fed, clothed and their medical needs well attended to."[124]

Matters soon took a turn for the worse. In the fall of 1863, smallpox struck the Seminole and maroon camps at Neosho Falls. The Indian office immediately vaccinated the refugees; nevertheless, the virus spread quickly to all the camps along the Neosho and at the Sac and Fox Agency. The disease hit the Seminoles particularly hard. By the end of the year, only 622 Seminoles remained in camp at Neosho Falls, a reduction of 106 since the summer. While some had followed the Union forces to Fort Gibson, most had fallen victim to the virus. Agent Snow later claimed that 80 Seminoles had died of smallpox during the winter of 1863–64.[125] A census of the Seminole maroon camp on the Neosho, taken in late December 1863, listed a population of 112, plus 69 Cherokee black and Creek black women who were living with the maroons for protection, as their husbands had joined the Union army.[126] But how badly the epidemic hit the maroon camp is unknown.

Sonaki Mikko was one of the victims of the smallpox outbreak. Like Kowakochi before him, he had avoided enemy bullets but finally succumbed to disease and died in exile. The precise date of his death is unknown, but it took place between September 1863 and March 1864, probably in November 1863.[127] The mikko was buried on the military reservation at Fort Gibson, and a stone marking his grave was placed in the officers' circle.[128] John Chupco, a matrilineal heir to Mikkoanapa through Holata Mikko, succeeded Sonaki Mikko.[129] By March 1864, Chupco was signing himself "Head Chief of the Seminole Nation." Pascofar assumed Chupco's former position as second chief of the Loyal Seminoles.[130]

The refugees at Fort Gibson also lived in poor conditions. Overcrowding, lack of sanitation, disease, and malnutrition continued to dog the Seminoles and maroons, who became almost entirely dependent upon the Federal supply trains coming from Fort Scott. Chupco related that the Seminole troops stationed at the post constantly went hungry and were forced to forage for food or compete with Confederates for stray cattle.[131] Union officials became concerned about the shortage of food and medical supplies. On March 16, 1864, Cox complained to William Coffin that the black refugees who had fled to the post for protection were consuming large amounts of supplies that could otherwise have been used to subsist the Indians there. Inducements were presented to those refugees to remove farther north, but "their attachment to the Indian race and the Indian country, together with the discouragements presented by those who express apprehension that the north will be overrun by a dependent non-producing class, render it almost impossible to shake them off."[132] Yet plans already were afoot to remove the remaining refugees in Kansas to the Indian Territory.

Senator Lane had proposed the idea in a joint resolution in early March. By that time, the refugees numbered around 9,200 and cost $60,000 per month to maintain. Congress appropriated the necessary funds for an immediate removal so that the Indians and blacks could plant a crop that season. When the train finally left Kansas in mid-May, it included nearly 5,000 refugees, mostly Creeks. Because of the persistence of the smallpox epidemic at Neosho Falls, most of the Seminoles were unable to make the journey, and 470 of them remained behind.[133]

Those maroons and Seminoles who were able to travel arrived at Fort Gibson on June 15. As it still was unsafe to return to their homes, they settled within the confines of the military reservation with the army and the other refugees. The numbers within the fort swelled to such an extent that the refugee population alone reached 16,000. The latest arrivals came too late to plant a crop and became completely dependent on Federal rations.[134] Confederate seizures of the Union supply boat *J. R. Williams* on the Arkansas River in June and the Federal wagon train during the Second Battle of Cabin Creek in September, coupled with a general crop failure in the Indian Territory that summer, resulted in widespread destitution among the refugees at Fort Gibson. Crime increased, with one report suggesting that the blacks, in particular, stole food, livestock, and other items, pillaging "indiscriminately, as well as from the union Indians as from the rebels."[135] The situation was even worse at Neosho Falls. Because of the smallpox epidemic, the maroons and Seminoles there had been forced to burn most of their clothing and, by the summer of 1864, they were naked and starving.[136]

Throughout the winter of 1864–65, the maroon and Loyal Seminole refugees remained in camp at Neosho Falls and Fort Gibson. They continued to live off Federal rations, which remained in short supply and of poor quality, together with what little they could raise themselves. George Reynolds, the latest Seminole agent, reported in 1865 that he had rented fifty acres of land for the group at Fort Gibson and had furnished seed and farming implements to some 500 refugees. The maroons and Seminoles then were able to raise corn and garden produce worth $2,500.[137] But even after the threat from Confederate guerrillas disappeared, the refugees continued to lose tools, crops, and livestock to Kansas jayhawkers, Texas bushwhackers, and renegade Indians and blacks, and still considered it unsafe to venture outside the confines of the military reservation. The maroons and Loyal Seminoles would spend one last problem-ridden winter in the camps at Fort Gibson and Neosho Falls before they were able to return home.[138]

Although most had managed to escape northward to Kansas, the Cherokee country, or Fort Gibson during the early stages of the Civil War, some of the maroons had remained behind among the Confederate Semi-noles. Adhering to the treaty they had signed with Pike, Heniha Mikko's supporters retained black slavery throughout the war. The Confederate Seminoles bought and sold blacks and profited from their labor.[139] Soon after the outbreak of hostilities, moreover, Heniha Mikko's followers adopted sections of the Creek code in passing a law aimed at reenslaving all free blacks associated with the tribe and confiscating their property. Later, it was estimated that "about seventy" were reenslaved under that law. Given their large number, those free blacks likely were former tributary allies of Seminole mikkos. They were "distributed [among] the Nation" and made to work for the Confederate Seminoles.[140] Heniha Mikko and his followers had wasted little time in adopting the racial tenets of their new allies. From that point on, all blacks would be slaves.

The experiences of three individuals—John Bruner, Ben Bruner, and Robert Johnson—provide important information on relations between Confederate Seminoles and maroons during the Civil War. John Bruner was born a Creek black in Alabama. After removing to the Indian Terri-tory, he married Grace Bowlegs, "a full blood Seminole," and they had children together. John was a slave, but because Grace was Indian, both she and the children were free. During the Civil War, John's brothers Perry, Caesar, and Will escaped to the North with the Seminoles and maroons and later served with the Union army. However, John and another brother remained behind. James Factor, Heniha Mikko's inter-preter and chief adviser, bought John for $3,000 in Confederate money and later took the Bruner family south to the Seminole refugee camps. Black slavery among the Confederate Seminoles continued to feature tribute and deference. John's son, Benjamin F. Bruner, later reported that Factor, a "big slave owner," was "very kind and good to his slaves." In a system similar to sharecropping, Factor allowed John to "rent land" and by way of payment, give his owner "part of what he made." After the war, the Bruner family returned to the Seminole Nation and became part of the freedman community.[141]

By 1861, Ben Bruner, Holata Mikko's former counselor, had become the wealthiest of the Seminole maroons and a free man. He also served as the U.S. interpreter to the Seminoles at an annual salary of $400.[142] At the outbreak of the Civil War, Seminole agent Rutherford left his post and instructed Bruner to remain at the agency and maintain the buildings, tribal records, and other government property until he returned. In September 1862, Murrow, the new Confederate agent to the Seminoles, arrived at the agency to assume his duties and reported, "The buildings, archives, &c., were then in the charge of a free mulatto man. He had done all he could to preserve them, but everything was in confusion, the old agent having been absent nearly a year."[143] But Bruner's devotion to duty would cost him his freedom.

It is uncertain when Ben Bruner left the agency. Conflicting dates of October 1863, July 1864, and the end of 1864 later were given for his departure. But it is certain that Heniha Mikko's Confederates reenslaved him and confiscated his property. Although he was free, Bruner stated that he was "forcibly taken away in bondage" and "compelled to go south by the Southern Forces commanded by John Jumper." The Confederate Seminoles took his livestock from him and drove it off. Although he was the tribe's official interpreter, a wealthy, intelligent man, and a former counselor to a Seminole mikko, Bruner was treated like any other black. He later claimed that he had received payment for his services at the agency only until January 1860, and in 1866, 1870, and 1879 he petitioned for back pay. Though Heniha Mikko and John F. Brown supported his statements, however, his petitions were ignored. The Indian bureau argued that there was no more reason for settling his claim than for paying all interpreters of Confederate Indian agents, and Ben Bruner's loyalty went unrecognized and unrewarded.[144]

Robert Johnson also found himself in a difficult position at the outbreak of the Civil War. Johnson, it will be recalled, had been bought from his Creek owner to serve as the interpreter for Rev. James Ramsay, the Presbyterian minister to the Seminoles. Heniha Mikko had contributed $800 toward the cost of the purchase, with the understanding that Johnson would repay him from his wages and earn his freedom. Although Ramsay was Johnson's employer, therefore, Heniha Mikko was the majority shareholder and had the strongest claim to ownership. Following the affair involving Robert's runaway cousin, Luke, Ramsay remained in the East, for fear of his life, and Johnson was left without an employer. Heniha Mikko immediately assumed ownership rights over the black interpreter and, during the early stages of the war, "took him wherever he went, as waiting boy." Johnson then determined upon a daring plan to attain his freedom by fleeing across the Union lines.

Johnson's wife, Elizabeth, worked as a cook at the Presbyterian mission for Rev. John Lilley and his family, who had remained behind in the

Seminole country. Confederate Seminole slaveholders continued to allow their slaves a great deal of freedom and mobility, and Johnson was able
to secure a furlough from Heniha Mikko to visit Elizabeth at the mission.
The interpreter saw his chance and launched his bid for freedom.

Early one morning, he rode out of the Seminole Mission toward the
Creek Agency. His mother-in-law, "Big Sarah" Davis, lived near there. In
the evening, he stopped for a while at the home of Timmy Barnett, a
Creek black, but the area was teeming with Confederates, so he continued his journey under the cover of darkness. Some time later, he
arrived at Big Sarah's and slept for a few hours. Early the next day, Big
Sarah awoke him, saying, "Bob, now is your time or never." Johnson
dressed quickly, saddled his horse, and headed for the Arkansas River,
about a mile distant. He plunged his horse into the water, pushing him
along with all his might, all the while looking behind for pursuers. When
he reached the opposite bank, he found a group of Union soldiers in the
river bottom, whereupon "he took off his hat, whirled it round and
round, and said; 'Hurrah! Hurrah!! HURRAH!!! He was in the land of
freedom." Johnson had made a narrow escape, for Heniha Mikko and his
men had found him missing and set out in hot pursuit. On that occasion,
however, the Confederates returned empty-handed.[145]

The very day he crossed the Arkansas, Johnson enlisted in the Union
army. As he was an excellent interpreter, the officers at Fort Gibson
employed him to translate for the Seminole and Creek companies of the
First Regiment of the Union Indian Brigade stationed at the post. Because of the importance of his position, Johnson was not mustered into
the Kansas Colored regiments with the other Indian Territory blacks but
remained as an interpreter at Fort Gibson until the end of the war.[146]

Shortly after Union forces occupied Fort Gibson at the onset of the
Second Federal Invasion of the Indian Territory, more than one hundred
Confederate Seminoles and Creeks defected and immediately joined the
First Regiment of the Indian brigade.[147] Johnson interpreted the oath of
muster to the new recruits.[148] During the winter of 1863–64, he accompanied a Seminole rescue party that succeeded in bringing in the Lilley
family and Talomas Mikko, who had remained loyal to the Union.[149] In
1864, a son, James Coody Johnson, was born to Robert and Elizabeth at
Fort Gibson.[150] After the war, Robert Johnson acted as tribal interpreter
during the conference at Fort Smith in 1865, the negotiations in Washington leading up to the Reconstruction treaty of 1866, and the hearings

on the claims for compensation pressed by the Loyal Seminoles and maroons in 1866–67. He and his family returned to the Seminole Nation after the war and eventually made their home near Wewoka, the site of the Seminole Agency.

Under the Confederate Seminoles, slaves remained slaves, free blacks were reenslaved and had their property confiscated, and runaways were hunted down, incarcerated, and returned to slavery. Most of the blacks associated with Heniha Mikko's party continued to reside in the Seminole country until 1863. Following the reoccupation of Fort Gibson by the Union forces in April and the defeats at Cabin Creek and Honey Springs in June and July, however, the position of the Confederates in northern and central Indian Territory became untenable, and they were forced to flee south. The Southern Seminoles, Creeks, and Cherokees left their homes and retreated to the Choctaw and Chickasaw nations, taking their blacks with them. They established refugee camps on the Blue, Boggy, Red, Washita, and Kiamichi rivers, while some settled even farther south in northern Texas, near the towns of Sherman, Bonham, and Paris. But by far the heaviest concentrations of Confederate Indians and their blacks were in the south of the Indian Territory.[151]

Following the Union forces' incursions into the southern Indian Territory and the Battle of Middle Boggy, in early 1864 Confederate Seminole slaveholders were reported to be running their blacks into Texas, as far south as the Brazos, for safety.[152] However, those Indians and blacks appear to have returned to the Choctaw Nation soon after the danger had passed. The main Confederate Seminole refugee encampment was situated in the woods near Oil Springs, some fifty miles west of Fort Washita. It came to be known as Yellow Camp. In August 1864, 574 Seminole and 441 Creek refugees were living at Yellow Camp.[153] The blacks' encampment probably was situated close by. Camp Jumper, located by a spring about five miles north of McAlester, also is listed as a Civil War site by the Oklahoma Historical Society.[154]

The Southern refugees seem to have fared somewhat better than their Northern counterparts, at least until the later stages of the war. The Confederate government subsisted those living in the refugee camps. Their rations consisted of one and one-eighth pounds of flour or one and one-quarter pounds of cornmeal, one and one-half pounds of beef, and two quarts of salt per hundred rations. Private contractors supplied the Seminoles. Although those contractors occasionally failed to deliver the goods, the Seminoles were fortunate to have an honest and efficient issuing agent and administrator in Murrow. In the summer of 1864, Heniha Mikko commented, "The Confederate States have not deserted us; we have been provided for; our women and children are fed."[155]

The Confederate Seminoles also were able to produce food of their own, mainly by means of slave labor. The blacks did not receive Confederate rations and were completely reliant on what they could raise themselves, plus the few supplies their owners furnished them. The Cherokee and Chickasaw slaveholding elites used their blacks to raise crops and livestock, weave clothing, and generally supply their needs and those of the men serving in the Confederate army. There also is a suggestion that Confederate Seminoles might have employed slaves in commercial agricultural pursuits, given that on July 6, 1864, Heniha Mikko applied for a permit to export two hundred bales of cotton to Mexico.[156] While the lot of the Confederate Indians might have been superior to that of their Union counterparts, the blacks associated with them suffered as many hardships as their kinsmen to the North.

By the spring of 1865, the resistance of the Confederacy was virtually at an end. In the Indian Territory, desertions were frequent, supplies scarce, and conditions in the refugee camps rapidly deteriorating. On April 9, Lee surrendered the Army of Northern Virginia to Grant at the Appomattox Court House and soon after the other Confederate units capitulated. On May 26, General Kirby Smith surrendered the Trans-Mississippi Department, bringing to an end armed resistance in the West. In early June, Cooper surrendered the white Confederate troops stationed in the Indian Territory, but the Indian nations reserved the right to capitulate independently. The Choctaws and Chickasaws formally laid down their arms on June 19 and July 14, respectively. Watie, meanwhile, had under his immediate command the Cherokee, Creek, Seminole, and Osage troops, and those he surrendered on June 23.[157] With that, the war in the Indian Territory officially drew to a close.

At the end of the Civil War, the Loyal Seminole and maroon refugees still were divided into two groups: one at Fort Gibson and the other at Neosho Falls. Both were destitute, disease-ridden, exhausted, and, in spite of their victory, low on morale. Meanwhile, the situation among the Southern Seminoles and their blacks had worsened dramatically. Crude shelters, disease, and acute shortages of food, clothing, and medicine had begun to take their toll. According to Tatekke Tiger, the Seminole refugees at Yellow Camp, like their Loyal compatriots, were smitten by a smallpox epidemic "which caused lots of sickness and deaths."[158] Although the Southern Seminoles and their blacks raised a good crop in 1865, it was insufficient to meet their needs. Shortly afterward, Superintendent Elijah Sells described them as "poor," "destitute of subsistence and clothing," and totally lacking in "all kinds of farming implements."[159]

The Federal government subsequently took up the burden of caring for the estimated 950 Southern Seminoles, along with the other Confederate Indian refugees. The commissioner of Indian affairs established supply depots, wrote contracts for feeding the destitute, and appointed a special agent to ensure that those contracts were carried out in good faith. The indigent of both factions thus received at least partial support from the government, but starvation remained a major problem among both maroons and Loyal and Confederate Seminoles until they were able to return home and reap a harvest in 1866.[160]

Although the Civil War had ended, many important issues remained to be resolved for the divided Seminoles and the newly freed maroons. Top of the postbellum list of priorities for the Federal government would be establishing a new set of diplomatic relations with each of the Five Tribes, all of whom, to a greater or lesser extent, had supported the Confederacy. It would involve negotiating new treaties and determining the status of the freedmen within each of the tribes, and that would become the main business of Reconstruction in the Indian Territory.

CHAPTER SEVEN

Reconstruction

During the Civil War, factional divisions among the Seminoles had widened as Indians and blacks engaged each other in mortal combat on the battlefields of the Indian Territory. Although the Loyalists had fought on the winning side, there were no Seminole or maroon victors in the "White Man's War." Lives and property had been lost, wounds inflicted, the land ravaged, and the Seminole Nation divided. The future seemed uncertain, at best.

When the war ended, the federal government quickly sought to reestablish relations with the Five Tribes by negotiating new treaties. In September 1865, it sent a distinguished board of commissioners to Fort Smith, Arkansas, to meet with their leaders.[1] As the conference prepared to open, the Seminoles, Creeks, and Cherokees were divided. The Loyal and Confederate parties had differing viewpoints, and establishing consensus would prove challenging. While the U.S. commissioners were well-organized, experienced negotiators with clear and far-reaching objectives, the Indian delegates were ill-prepared to make important decisions affecting the future of their people.

Secretary of the Interior James Harlan instructed the board to submit seven major propositions to the Indian delegates as the agenda for the negotiations. The government's position rested on the premise that although some of the Indians had remained loyal, each of the Five Tribes had sided with the Confederacy. They should be punished and forced to agree to various demands. Two of the most controversial propositions concerned the position of blacks within the nations. Slavery would be abolished and never again "exist among them, otherwise than in the punishment of crime," and immediate steps should be taken for the incorporation of former slaves into the tribes "on an equal footing in all respects with the original members."[2] The former Confederates found that a hard pill to swallow.

When the Fort Smith Council opened on September 9, the Confederate Seminoles had not yet arrived. The Loyal delegation, consisting of John Chupco, Pascofar, Fohutshe, Fos Harjo, and Chutcote Harjo, represented the nation. Robert Johnson and Caesar Bruner, two important leaders in the maroon community, served as interpreters. Commissioner of Indian Affairs Dennis Cooley opened the conference with a message from the president, stating that he wished to renew the government's alliances with the Indian nations. By supporting the Confederacy, they had forfeited their former treaty rights and should be prepared to accede to the government's demands. However, the commissioners assured the Loyal parties that they would receive compensation for losses they had suffered during the war. That afternoon, Pascofar spoke for the Seminoles. He stated that the Loyal delegates had traveled to Fort Smith to make peace with the Confederate Seminoles and were not prepared to make new treaties or conduct other business. They would need more time to consider the proposals put before them.[3]

The following day, Cooley reiterated the need to negotiate new treaties. He included in the requirements the stipulation that the Five Tribes incorporate the freedmen on an equal footing with Indian members. On September 12, the Loyal Seminole delegates addressed the commissioners. They were fully prepared to accept all the requirements put to them, except the one relating to the freedmen. They asked the commissioners to change the wording to make it clear that only "colored persons lately held in bondage by the Seminole people, and free persons of color residing in the nation previous to the rebellion," would be adopted as freedmen. The Loyal delegates then explained their position: "We are willing to provide for the colored people of our own nation, but do not desire our lands to become colonization grounds for the negroes of other States and Territories."[4]

The Loyal Seminoles did not consider themselves authorized to sign new treaties but suggested that they refer the propositions to the nation as a whole, come to an understanding with the Confederate party, and appoint delegates to engage in further negotiations at a later date. The commissioners concluded that treaties could not be finalized at Fort Smith and instead drafted preliminary agreements to be signed by those delegates present at the council. Under the terms of those agreements, the tribes rescinded their treaties with the Confederacy, reaffirmed their allegiance to the United States, and stated their intention to live in peace from then on. The Loyal Seminoles signed on September 14.[5]

On September 16, the Confederate Seminole delegation, consisting of Heniha Mikko, George Cloud, Fos Hatchee Cochuehue, Passock Yohola, James Factor, and John F. Brown, arrived at Fort Smith. The Loyal and Confederate delegates immediately began to reconcile, and the Southern Seminoles signed the agreement.[6] Later that same day, however, Confederate party members issued a statement regretting their action, for they had not completely understood the terms. They agreed to all the propositions except two. They did not support a consolidated government for the Indian Territory, but their strongest opposition focused on the requirement that the Seminoles adopt the freedmen.

The Southern Seminole delegates were willing to accept the abolition of slavery and the unconditional emancipation of the nation's blacks, but they delivered this pointed statement regarding the status of the freedmen:

> [The] proposition to "incorporate" the free negro with us on "equal footing with the original members" of the Seminole tribe, is presented to us so suddenly that it shocks the lesson we have learned for long years from the white man as to the negro's inferiority. We honestly think that both the welfare of the Seminole and the freed negro would be injured if not destroyed by such "incorporation." The emancipated black man must, of necessity, be "suitably provided for." Such provision requires time and consultation as to how it shall best be done, and we, consequently, beg the indulgence of further time before we decide.[7]

It was clearly too early to ask the Confederate Seminoles to set aside their acquired southern racial notions and put behind them the bitterness of their Civil War experiences and accept the freedmen as equals.

On September 18, the two Seminole parties presented a joint resolution to the commissioners. They stated that they both had signed the agreement and subscribed to all of its provisions. They were determined to settle their differences, meet with their people, and elect delegates empowered to enter into treaties with the U.S. government. They then requested permission to return home to their families until called upon by the president to negotiate a new treaty. However, the Confederate Seminoles reiterated that they did not accept all of the government's stipulations. John F. Brown delivered an address restating that the Southern Seminole delegates did not agree to the two propositions. He also requested that their earlier statement be read before the council. The Fort Smith conference adjourned two days later. Its main accomplishments were that it had begun the process of reconciliation, familiarized the Indians with the government's intentions, and arranged for delegates to proceed to Washington to negotiate new treaties.[8]

The differing attitudes of the Loyal and Confederate Seminoles toward adopting the freedmen found expression in late 1865 and early 1866. In October 1865, Southern Superintendent Elijah Sells reported that the Loyal Seminoles and Creeks had "a large number of negroes—their former slaves—living with them and they desire to have them incorporated into their tribes as citizens, with equal rights."[9] But on December 5, Seminole agent George Reynolds stated, "The Seminoles lately in Rebellion are not acting in good faith towards the Freedmen, in every instance they are holding them as slaves as long as they can. They have taken from them their crops they had made and left them entirely destitute of everything."[10]

Following the Fort Smith Council, U.S. government officials felt concern for the safety of freedmen in the Indian Territory. Most worrisome was the situation among the Indians who had been strongest in their support for the Confederacy. In November, Major General John Sanborn was appointed commissioner for "regulating relations between Freedmen in Indian Territory and their former masters." He was instructed not to interfere where relations were satisfactory to both parties but to assist the freedmen and furnish relief when they were subject to abuse. The commissioner arrived at Fort Smith on December 24 and distributed a series of circulars in the Indian Territory to communicate his policies.[11]

On January 1 and 2, 1866, Sanborn met with Loyal Seminole representative Pascofar at Fort Gibson. Pascofar informed the commissioner: "I understand what you want to accomplish in regard to the Coloured folks. This has been accomplished. We receive them as brethren on the same footing and rights. [We] are not willing to receive the coloured folks of other tribes. [We] can take care of the Negroes of our own Nation, without any aid from the Federal Government." Asked if the Southern Seminoles were abusing the freedmen, Pascofar intimated that the former Confederates still held some of their blacks as slaves while others had been set free. Given that they were drawing the same government rations as the Loyalists, the Southern Seminoles did not feel compelled to free the blacks.[12]

On January 5, Sanborn reported: "The Creek nation look upon the freedmen as their equals in rights, and have, or are in favor of, incorporating them into their tribe with all the rights and privileges of native Indians. The Seminoles entertain the same or nearly the same sentiments and feelings as the Creeks. The freedmen of the Seminole and Creek tribes believe that the national laws and customs of their tribes are sufficient for their protection."[13] The freedmen presumably were referring to "laws and customs" operating among the Loyal Seminoles and Creeks. With slavery abolished, the Seminole freedmen, at least, had good reason to feel confident that they would fare well.

Sanborn's first report included some general observations on the freedmen, resulting from his initial tour of the Indian Territory. He found them "the most industrious, economical, and in many respects the more intelligent portion of the population of the Indian Territory." They all wished to remain in the area "upon lands set apart for their exclusive use." The Indians who were willing to let the freedmen remain also felt "they should be located upon a tract of country by themselves."[14] Sanborn remained in and around the Indian Territory until spring, but his other reports were either general in nature or dealt with the difficulties encountered by Indians and freedmen in adjusting to the dismantling of plantation slavery—problems alien to the Seminoles and maroons.[15]

Sanborn never understood the complexities inherent in his task or came to terms with the problems he faced. Preconceived notions and a naive approach led to suggestions for sweeping remedies removed from reality. On April 13, he asked to be relieved from duty, believing his job was done. The rights of the freedmen were "fully acknowledged," and he recommended that the commission discontinue its work.[16] Yet with the exception of the Seminoles, and to a lesser extent the Creeks, that assessment was wrong. The status of the freedmen associated with the Cherokee, Choctaw, and Chickasaw nations would prove problematic until and beyond Oklahoma statehood. At a critical juncture, the U.S. government divested responsibility for the future of freedmen living in the Indian Territory, leaving their fate to the nations themselves.

In December 1865, Cooley instructed Reynolds to select a delegation composed of both Loyal and Confederate Seminoles and travel immediately to Washington to take part in treaty negotiations with the U.S. government. The two Seminole factions held a joint council, but friction occurred over the choice of delegates and the Loyalists' insistence that the Southern Seminoles adhere to the principal chieftainship of John Chupco. The two sides failed to reconcile, and the Loyalists assumed overall leadership of the nation. The Northern party then chose three of the four delegates—Chupco, Fos Harjo, and Chutcote Harjo—with only John F. Brown representing the Southern faction. Robert Johnson accompanied the delegation in the official capacity of tribal interpreter and also acted as adviser to the Loyal Seminoles.[17]

The Seminole delegates traveled to Washington with the Creek delegation. The Creek delegation consisted of three Indians—Oktarharsars Harjo, Kawita Mikko, and Kotchoche—and Harry Island, an influential black interpreter. The Seminole and Creek agents had overall responsibility for the group. The party of seven Indians, two blacks, and two whites arrived in St. Louis on January 8, 1866, and the agents purchased first-class rail tickets for each of them. Things went smoothly until they reached Bellaire on the Ohio River. There the conductor allowed the agents into the first-class compartment but sent the Indians and blacks to the second-class car. The agents informed him that the Indians were Creek and Seminole leaders ordered to Washington by the government, but the conductor's objections stemmed from their association with the two blacks. They pointed out that Johnson and Island were interpreters, members of the Indian nations, and in possession of first-class tickets, but to no avail. The Indians and their interpreters traveled the rest of the way in second class.[18]

In Washington, the government paid for the Seminole delegation to stay in a hotel, at a cost of $2 per person per day.[19] The Northern and Southern Seminole delegates did not act in unison during the treaty negotiations but followed independent courses of action. The Loyal Seminoles were more willing to comply with the government's demands. On January 30, the three Northern delegates informed the commissioner of Indian affairs: "We have agreed in council to recognize the colored people formerly belonging to the Seminoles as a part of us with equal rights among us in property protection and the enjoyment of all the benefits arizing [sic] out of treaty stipulations made or to be made with the United States Government."[20] Brown was not a party to that communication and entertained different sentiments, but the Loyalists had a majority. Given that the incorporation of the freedmen was the most controversial requirement they faced, negotiations proceeded quickly, and the Seminoles became the first of the Five Tribes to come to terms.

The Reconstruction treaty, signed on March 21, marked a watershed in the history of Seminole-maroon relations. After stipulating that slavery and involuntary servitude would be abolished "except for and in punishment of crime," Article 2 continued:

> And inasmuch as there are among the Seminoles many persons of African descent and blood, who have no interest or property in the soil, and no recognized civil rights, it is stipulated that hereafter these persons and their descendants, and such other of the same race as shall be permitted by said nation to settle there, shall have and enjoy all the rights of native citizens, and the laws of said nation shall be equally binding upon all persons of whatever race or color, who may be adopted as citizens or members of said tribe.[21]

But indiscriminate use of the terms "citizens," "members," "nation," and "tribe" led to differences in interpretation of this important article.[22] U.S. officials did not intend any distinction, but Seminole Indians distinguished between incorporating the freedmen as "citizens" of their new "nation" (polity) and including them as "members" of their "tribe" (society), an important difference that has exercised a profound effect on relations between the two groups ever since.

Nevertheless, freedom finally had arrived for the maroons, and they would be slaves no more. The treaty removed forever the threat of sale, kidnap, breakup of families, forced labor, and persecution. Henceforth, the freedmen could keep all the products of their labor. The terms also stipulated that they would enjoy all the rights of Native citizens in the Seminole Nation. The 1866 treaty signaled the beginning of a truly remarkable era for the Seminole maroons.

The treaty contained other provisions that greatly affected the future of both Indians and freedmen. The Seminoles agreed to "cede and convey to the United States their entire domain" in the Indian Territory. The Seminoles were paid 15 cents per acre for 2,169,080 acres, a total of $325,362. Following an accurate survey of the land, it was discovered in 1889 that the ceded tract actually had consisted of only 2,037,412.62 acres. Nevertheless, the Seminole Nation received an additional $1,912,942.02 in return for relinquishing "all claims of every kind and character" to the land. The bulk of the award, $1.5 million, would be held in trust and the interest paid semiannually to the Seminole national treasurer to disburse as per capita payments to both Indian and freedman citizens.[23]

Having ceded their entire domain, the Seminoles were permitted to purchase a much smaller tract farther east from the government. The land formed part of the Creek cession and consisted of 200,000 acres lying between the North Fork and South Canadian, east of the old Seminole reservation. The Seminoles paid the United States 50 cents per acre for the new land, a total of $100,000.[24] In February 1881, the Seminoles managed to purchase an adjoining 175,000 acres to the east from the Creek Nation, at $1 per acre.[25] With that addition, the Seminole Nation's landholdings remained at 375,000 acres until statehood, when the tract increased slightly to become Seminole County, Oklahoma.

The U.S. government foresaw the ceded Seminole lands being utilized to "locate other Indians and freedmen thereon."[26] The Seminoles' and freedmen's new neighbors to the west would be bands of Pottawatomies and Shawnees. The "unassigned lands" farther west were opened to white settlement in the run of 1889 and became part of the Oklahoma Territory. In 1869 and again in 1883, Choctaw and Chickasaw freedmen asked to be resettled on the old Seminole reservation.[27] In November 1880, "quite a large number" of freedmen in southern Kansas asked to relocate there the following spring, and in 1886 some blacks in Topeka made a similar request.[28] Although nothing came of those ideas, they added support to the freedman colonization programs of the late 1880s that sought to create an all-black state of Oklahoma. Those programs culminated in Edwin P. McCabe's movement and the founding of the black town of Langston in the Oklahoma Territory.[29]

The balance between what the nation received for its old reservation and what it paid for its new lands would benefit both Seminole Indian and freedman citizens. The U.S. government set aside $40,362 to deal with the immediate problem of subsistence, allowing discrimination only

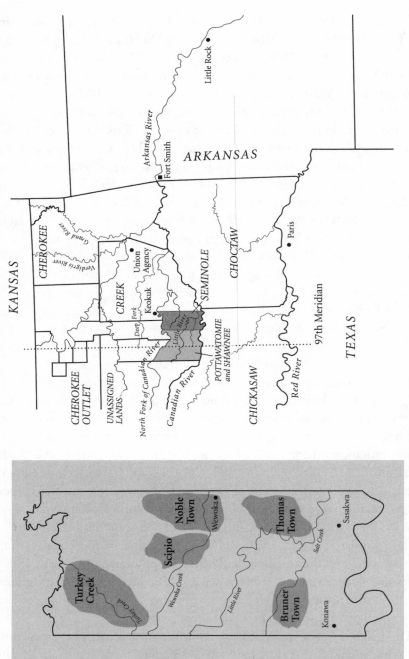

Freedman townships in the Seminole Nation around 1885

"in favor of the destitute." Citizens would receive $30,000 to "occupy, restore and improve their farms, and to make their nation independent and self-sustaining," and $20,000 for agricultural implements, seed, and stock. A new mill would cost $15,000. The government took $70,000 to create a permanent trust fund for the new nation. Of that, $50,000 would support education, and $20,000 government. The Seminole treasurer would use the yearly interest payments to support schools and pay the government officers. The remaining $50,000 would compensate "loyal members of said tribe, irrespective of race or color, whether at the time of said losses the claimants shall have been in servitude or not; provided said claimants are made members of said tribe by the stipulations of this treaty." Finally, the United States reassumed its former treaty obligations and agreed to renew all annuity payments, but the recipients now would include Seminole freedmen as well as Indians.[30]

Robert Johnson and Harry Island, the two black interpreters, probably helped gain such favorable terms for the Seminole and Creek freedmen. Through interpretation, mediation, and counsel, Johnson and Island worked outside traditional political channels and likely exerted considerable influence on the delegates' diplomatic negotiations. With the exception of John F. Brown, the Seminole and Creek delegations were composed of Loyalists who spoke Creek and "Mikasuki"[31] (Hitchiti) and had a history of reliance on black interpreters and advisers. Johnson had developed strong diplomatic skills and powers of persuasion by that time, and Island was considered "as sharp as tacks."[32] A Creek Nation newspaper later claimed that Island had obtained "the most favorable concessions for the negroes, and that he misrepresented to the Creeks what was in the agreement, and they did not know at the time they agreed that the negro had been given equal rights with the Indians."[33]

The Loyal Creeks also signed the Seminole treaty, with Johnson and Island acting as interpreters for the combined delegation.[34] Brown opposed the clause requiring the Seminoles to adopt the freedmen, and similar protests came from a Southern Creek delegation sent to Washington to try to prevent ratification of the Creek treaty.[35] The Southern parties subsequently adopted the line that the black interpreters had influenced the outcome of the treaty negotiations to the benefit of the freedmen and the detriment of the Indians, a view long held by some Creeks and Seminoles.

The three Loyal Seminole delegates signed the treaty in Brown's presence, but the representative of the Southern party clearly remained unhappy with many of its provisions. The day of the signing, he penned a three-point protest to the commissioner of Indian affairs and asked that it be filed on record with the treaty. Brown believed that the price paid for the Seminoles' former lands was too little and that the tribe's new reservation was too small. He also protested against "any interference with the internal and municipal officers and regulations of the Seminole Nation heretofore recognized by the United States."[36] On March 23, Brown engaged one E. B. Grayson to work against the ratification of the treaty. Grayson would receive 15 percent of whatever monies the Southern Seminoles would be awarded under the new treaty. That same day, Brown addressed a second letter of protest to President Andrew Johnson. He reiterated his earlier complaints but now also disapproved of the incorporation of the freedmen on equal terms and the use of Seminole Nation funds to compensate the Loyal Indians and maroons.[37]

On April 26, Sells and Reynolds issued a joint rebuttal to Brown's protests. Fifteen cents per acre for the old reservation was reasonable, as it was among the worst land in the Indian Territory. The purchase price of 50 cents per acre also was fair, as the new reservation included the very best lands the Creeks had ceded. Sells and Reynolds also insisted that the vast majority of the Seminoles favored equal rights for the maroons. The freedmen, moreover, were the most enterprising people in the Seminole Nation. If granted equality, they could assist the Indians in their "march towards civilization." Finally, it was right and fitting that the nation should indemnify those Seminoles and maroons who had remained loyal to the Union.[38] Whether Brown was convinced or had other reasons is unclear, but he added his signature to the treaty sometime prior to its ratification by the U.S. Senate on July 19. That marked the beginnings of reconciliation between the Loyal and Confederate factions and the Southern Seminoles' coming to terms with the freedmen's equal status within the nation.

The Seminoles abided by their treaty obligations, incorporated the freedmen into the nation, and granted them equal rights. U.S. government officials were quick to remark how well the Indians were accepting the maroons' new status. As early as fall 1866, Commissioner Cooley reported, "Slavery is entirely abolished, and the freedmen placed upon an equal footing with the remainder of the people."[39]

Referring to Indian Territory freedmen in 1869, the commissioner of

Indian affairs observed, "With the Seminoles they seem to find the most favor, as that tribe has accorded to them unconditional citizenship."[40] In his annual report for that year, Reynolds wrote: "They formed new treaties; they complied with all the conditions imposed upon them; they adopted their former slaves, and made them citizens of their country, with equal rights in the soil and annuities. Their Negroes hold office and sit on their councils. They took hold of the question of reconstruction and settled it at once, practically, peaceably, and firmly."[41] In 1870, the Bureau of Indian Commissioners reported that among the Seminoles "there are 400 negroes having all the rights of citizens,"[42] and in 1882 the commissioner of Indian affairs noted that "no distinction" was made in the Seminole Nation between Indians and freedmen.[43] In 1885, the Mikasuki leader Hulbutta Mikko (Alligator), described as the second chief of the Seminole Nation, testified that the freedmen voted and had the same rights as Seminoles. Asked if freedmen intermarried with Seminoles, Hulbutta Mikko answered that he did "not know of any case of that kind," but he noted that the nation was experiencing no trouble arising out of prejudice against blacks.[44] In 1890, the U.S. census commissioners' report on the Seminole Nation stated, "The adopted freedmen are the most progressive, and here, as in the Creek Nation, they enjoy every right of native born Indians; some of them are quite wealthy, dress well, take an active interest in education, and in advancing the moral and social condition of their people."[45]

Throughout the Reconstruction period and beyond, white observers made note of the way Seminoles treated the maroons. The freedmen attained equal political, economic, social, and cultural rights in the Seminole Nation. They were protected by and treated equally before the law and were granted equal opportunity. The freedmen received the franchise and could vote during Seminole elections for the offices of principal and second chief. No law prevented a freedman from standing for Seminole principal chief, but as the traditional ruling clans continued to dominate the leadership of the tribe, that never happened. Nevertheless, the freedmen became an important political factor,[46] and the traditionalists actively courted their support. The freedmen played a large part in allowing Chupco to retain power until his death in 1881[47] and Hulbutta Mikko to defeat John F. Brown in 1902. As interpreters and advisers to Chupco and Hulbutta Mikko, the Johnsons came to exert considerable political influence in Seminole national affairs for almost half of the forty-two-year period between the end of the Civil War and Oklahoma statehood. Other Seminole freedmen became government officers or otherwise held positions of importance within the nation. The careers of those enterprising and talented individuals illustrate the potential for freedman advancement in the Seminole Nation during the postbellum period.

Robert Johnson remained the most influential and powerful freedman in the Seminole Nation during Reconstruction. Following the signing of the 1866 treaty in Washington, Johnson returned to the Indian Territory and helped Elijah (E. J.) Brown, a white trader from Kansas, remove the Loyal refugee Seminoles and maroons from Neosho Falls and Fort Gibson to the new reservation. As reward, the Seminoles formally adopted both men into the nation.[48] Johnson's wife, Elizabeth, remained a Creek freedwoman and retained her association with Arkansas Colored Town.[49] Her mother, Big Sarah Davis, who had helped Robert escape across the Union lines during the Civil War, continued to live there and kept an inn near the Creek Agency.[50] Because of the Creeks' and Seminoles' system of matrilineal descent, Robert and Elizabeth's son Coody would be enrolled and allotted land as a Creek freedman.[51] Due to his father's adoption and powerful position, however, Coody Johnson moved easily within Seminole Indian and freedman circles and later became an influential leader within the nation himself.

Although he still could not read or write, Robert Johnson remained the U.S. interpreter to the Seminoles at a salary of $400 per year.[52] In January 1871, Seminole agent Henry Breiner described him as a man of "truth and honesty" who could "speak the english [sic] language as well as any of the colored or Indian citizens of the Seminole Nation."[53] From his position as interpreter at the agency, Johnson came to exert considerable influence over Seminole affairs. In November 1869, for example, Reynolds, who had been replaced as Seminole agent by Captain T. A. Baldwin, asked Johnson, Chupco, and the Upper Creek chief Sands "to use their influence with the National authorities to have a certain steam mill purchased and erected under his supervision, accepted by the Nation." Baldwin opposed the scheme, and Reynolds sought his removal. Johnson then helped circulate a petition that led to Breiner's replacing Baldwin as Seminole agent.[54]

Robert Johnson served not only as the U.S. interpreter to the Seminoles but also as the interpreter and adviser of Principal Chief John Chupco. In that role, Johnson acted in an official capacity on a number of occasions, secured other important offices for himself, and came to exert even more influence over Seminole national affairs. During the winter of 1872–73, in the capacity of delegate and interpreter, Johnson accompanied Chupco, Heniha Mikko, James Factor, and Elijah Brown to Washington to try to purchase more land for the Seminole Nation west of the new reservation. When the party returned to the Indian Territory, Johnson received $46 for using his team to transport two of the other delegates from the Seminole Agency to their homes. In January 1874, Johnson served as interpreter to another Seminole delegation that traveled to Washington to try to procure an amendment to the 1856 treaty so that all national monies would be paid to the Seminole treasurer instead of per capita. Two years later, he was back in Washington again on official Seminole business. Besides his duties as interpreter, adviser to the chief, and delegate, at various times Johnson acted as guard at the Seminole Agency (probably to protect the annuity payment) and superintendent of the nation's blacksmith shops. The freedmen also elected him as a representative of the Jim Lane band (later the Bruner band), and he sat on the Seminole councils.[55]

As Chupco's right-hand man, Johnson's influence grew until, by 1875, he had become one of the five most powerful leaders in the Seminole Nation. In August of that year, Special Commissioner John Shanks wrote to Commissioner of Indian Affairs E. P. Smith: "Robert Johnson is a negro, and is interpreter to the chief. [The] truth is that though they have a council, John Jumper, James Factor, John Chupco, E. J. Brown, and Robert Johnson together, and they work together, are in fact the Government of the Seminoles. [These] men control the council."[56] From his various salaried positions and landholdings, Robert Johnson became quite wealthy. In March 1875, for example, he received $623 for claims against the Seminole Nation.[57] In his later years, Johnson remained prominent in the Presbyterian Church, stayed active in the affairs of his band and nation, and remained an important and well-respected figure until his death in 1893.

Caesar Bowlegs was another important freedman to rise to prominence in the Seminole Nation during the late nineteenth century. Born in 1843 or 1844, the son of Sharper Bowlegs and Chosto, he was a slave of Eliza Bowlegs, as were both his parents.[58] By his late teenage years, he had acquired three horses and fifteen hogs and pigs valued at $114.[59] During the Civil War, Caesar went north to Kansas with the Loyal

Caesar Bowlegs. (Western History Collections, University of Oklahoma Libraries)

Seminoles and maroons. After the war, he carried the mail from Fort Gibson to Wewoka when the post office opened there in 1867.[60] He emerged from the war a member of the John Chupco band, an affiliation he retained through 1870.[61] Why he became a member of Chupco's band is unknown, but perhaps it came as a reward for a service he had rendered the mikko. By 1890, however, Caesar had become a member of the Seminole freedman Joe Scipio band, and later he enrolled as a member of the Dosar Barkus band.[62]

After the Civil War, Caesar Bowlegs made his home at Wewoka and a few years later had a child with Dolly. Dolly had migrated to Kansas with the Loyal Seminoles and maroons in the fall of 1861. After the war, she had a son, Billy Bowlegs, with George Bowlegs, also a former slave of Eliza Bowlegs, and had a second son, Peter Cyrus, with Paldo Cyrus. In 1870, Dolly gave birth to Caesar's son, Jack Bowlegs, but then died later that year. Jack Bowlegs later married Rina King, a daughter of Jim King, a noncitizen, and Dora, a Seminole freedwoman and former slave of Mikkoanapa. Jack and Rina Bowlegs gave Caesar two grandsons who appear on the Seminole freedman rolls—August and Bud, aged four and two in 1898. The couple apparently separated soon afterward, however, as in 1898 Rina had a daughter, Dora, by Simon Noble, a Creek freedman, the child dying in the summer of 1902. Rina also had a son, Lou, by Mike Charles, a noncitizen, in March 1902. In 1901, Jack Bowlegs was reported to be living in Columbus, Ohio.[63]

Caesar then married Lessie Rentie, a Creek freedwoman several years his senior. The couple had four children, Amy, Jimmie, Johnie, and Stella. Through matrilineal descent, Caesar Bowlegs's children later enrolled and were allotted land as Creek freedmen and freedwomen. Caesar and Lessie were still together at the turn of the century. His was the first name to appear on the Seminole freedman rolls, and he selected his allotment just north of the Wewoka townsite. Lessie was listed on the Creek freedman roll and chose her lands near the Creek-Seminole border.[64]

In the 1880s and 1890s, Caesar Bowlegs operated and maintained a toll bridge over Wewoka Creek.[65] He provided a vital service in linking Indian and freedman citizens living in the north of the nation with the important trading center of Wewoka, located south of the creek. The Seminoles also employed him, together with an Indian named Checote, to bury criminals after they had been executed by the lighthorsemen, the nation's mounted law enforcement agency established during Reconstruction.[66] But Caesar would acquire his reputation as an interpreter, and in that capacity he made his biggest contribution to Seminole and freedman history.

Through his association with the John Chupco band, Caesar Bowlegs became well acquainted with both the languages and the ways of Seminoles. In the 1870s, agent Breiner, a doctor himself,[67] had petitioned for a national physician for the Seminoles. In the early 1880s, one finally was appointed. Dr. C. P. Lynn became the first white physician to practice medicine among the Seminoles, and in the late 1890s Dr. Virgil Berry succeeded him.[68] The physicians made Wewoka their home base. Because he was bilingual, known to both Seminoles and freedmen, and familiar with the country, Bowlegs was appointed the physician's interpreter and guide, a position of considerable importance. He accompanied Lynn every time he was called out to a patient. By the 1890s, Caesar also was serving as interpreter "for all the white men who have business with any members of the tribe unless the governor [John F. Brown] is present." It was said that he knew "personally every family of the tribe" and was "highly regarded by everybody for his courtesy and intelligence."[69] Dr. Berry described him as "faithful and efficient" and noted, "In all the time I was with Caesar I never knew him do a mean act."[70] The freedman interpreter became a familiar and respected figure in both the Seminole and maroon communities.[71]

As recounted by the physician, Caesar Bowlegs and Dr. Berry developed a very close relationship.[72] Berry began his duties in May 1898 and served the Seminoles and freedmen for three years. Bowlegs proved invaluable as a guide, interpreter, intermediary, expert on Indian and maroon mores, and medical assistant. The black interpreter escorted the white doctor on all his calls. As they drove along in their buggy, Bowlegs would tell Berry stories about the Seminoles, using animated gestures, just as Robert Johnson had done for the Presbyterian ministers half a century earlier. One familiar with him observed, "Caesar loved to talk about the subject he knew best, for he was as much like the Seminoles as it was possible to be."[73]

Sometimes the doctor and his interpreter would be caught at nightfall far away from Wewoka and with another full day's work ahead of them. In summer, they would drive off the road and feed the team, then Bowlegs would produce a snack of chitlin cornbread or jerky from the sack of essential supplies he always carried with him. At times, he would kill a rabbit or quail and roast it over the open fire. When they grew tired, Berry would sleep under the buggy while Bowlegs, preferring the open ground, slept under a nearby tree.[74]

Bowlegs had acquired a sound medical knowledge over the years, and he helped the physician attend to patients, even administering anesthetics. During Berry's term, a devastating smallpox epidemic hit the Seminole Nation, and the two men were in constant action. After first inoculating themselves, Berry and Bowlegs set out to vaccinate the entire nation. They each kept two sets of white canvas overalls and gloves. While they wore one set, they soaked the other in disinfectant, then boiled and laundered it to prevent infection. The two worked day and night, returning to Wewoka only for a fresh team, food, and a change of suits. At last they completed their massive task, but then they were faced with combating the disease when it broke out. The Seminole population was devastated by the outbreak. The physician and his assistant worked hard to fight the disease, but the epidemic still was raging when Berry left the Seminole country to take up private practice at Wetumka in the Creek Nation in the summer of 1901.[75] It was four more years before the disease ran its course and the Seminole death rate returned to its 1898 level.[76]

Caesar Bowlegs died soon after Dr. Berry's departure,[77] but he had lived a remarkable life and had become an important figure in the Seminole Nation. Berry described him as being "as black as pitch," yet Indians accepted him and he accompanied white men of standing. He lived in a maroon community and married a Seminole freedwoman and a Creek freedwoman, yet he also had a deep knowledge of Indian customs. As a slave of Eliza Bowlegs, a Loyalist, and an adopted member of John Chupco's band, Caesar Bowlegs enjoyed a long history of close association with Seminole traditionalists. He became familiar with Native practices and fluent in Creek. That came to light during one particular incident. Following the untimely death of a child of the Seminole bandleader Kinkehee, Bowlegs consoled the father in his Native language and later drew on his experience as a gravedigger in helping the mikko bury his child.[78]

Bowlegs facilitated the process of white acculturation within the tribe. He was educated and "a pillar in the colored Presbyterian church."[79] He could read, and he carried a Bible with him at all times. He also favored the clothing of whites. In an undated photograph, he appears wearing a three-piece corduroy suit and a straw boater.[80] When the first white

Seminole Indian and freedman lighthorsemen, Wewoka. (Oklahoma Historical Society)

physician arrived in the early 1880s, Indian and maroon medicine men were the doctors practicing in the Seminole country. Even at the turn of the century, many Seminoles still were afraid to go against the advice of their medicine men. But Berry and Bowlegs began an education program, and soon the physician "was seldom refused permission to use 'the white man's medicine.'" As the communicator between doctor and patient, Bowlegs played a vital role in that process. "His persuasive powers were considerable,"[81] and he deserves credit for gaining widespread acceptance of scientific principles and medical technology among the Seminoles and maroons.

A number of freedmen served with the Seminole lighthorse. The force of ten included a captain, a lieutenant, and eight privates. The Indian and freedman bands nominated suitable candidates, and the council elected officers to four-year terms. Should a lighthorseman resign, be found guilty of a crime, or die in office, the council would fill the vacancy. The officers received an annual wage. By the end of the century, the rates stood at $500 for the captain, $450 for the lieutenant, and $300 for privates.[82] Although never attaining either of the top positions, freedmen always were well represented on the Seminole lighthorse, usually supplying two of the eight privates.

Those freedman officers were better able than Indians to combat crime in the maroon communities, as they spoke Creole and were familiar with both the inhabitants and the terrain. They also could speak Creek and thus could deal with Indian criminals and their victims. Like the Seminole Negro Indian Scouts, who saw service against Indian raiders on the borders of Texas and Mexico at that same time,[83] the freedman lighthorsemen were excellent riders, experts with firearms, and seasoned campaigners and were familiar with Indian customs and languages. They were well suited to enforcing the laws of the Seminole Nation.

The duties of law enforcement officers were essentially threefold—to transport and guard funds, to apprehend suspected criminals and take them to trial before the council, and to administer punishment to those found guilty. Seminoles and freedmen received their annuity payments every three months. The lighthorse met the shipment of money at the Creek Agency and hauled it out to the Seminole Nation in a covered wagon. One officer drove, one rode in front, two behind, two on each side, and two in the wagon with the shipment. Joe Grayson recalled, "All were heavily armed. Nobody ever had the courage to attack them so they were never robbed." Seminole freedwoman Carrie Cyrus added, "All of the people feared them."[84]

Like the Royal Canadian Mounted Police, the Seminole lighthorsemen were known for always getting their man.[85] Because there were no tribal jails, the officers sometimes kept prisoners in their homes until they could be tried. If the council was not due to meet for some time, several lighthorsemen each would keep the prisoner for a month. On such occasions, the officers received compensation for their outlay and inconvenience. But employing a code of honor, convicted criminals generally went free with the understanding that they would return to receive their punishment at an assigned time. The lighthorsemen administered the punishment, invariably a whipping unless the offense was murder. The criminal generally received fifty lashes for a first offense, one hundred for the second, and so on. Two or more officers administered the stripes. Murderers were shot by two of the lighthorsemen, the privates serving as executioners in rotation.

Both the Indian and freedman lighthorsemen subscribed to the power of Seminole medicine men and sought their aid during difficult or dangerous times. Before they set out in search of a notorious outlaw, the officers would meet with the snake doctor. Carrie Cyrus, whose husband, Dennis Cyrus, served with the lighthorse for many years, described the ensuing ceremony:

[The] Snake Doctor [would] mix a quantity of herbs together; such as, Devil shoe string, Conquer John and others not known. He would put these into a big kettle and put a fire under it and boil this all together until it looked like tea. Then the Horsemen would gather around the fire and spit till they put the fire out. But during this time the Snake Doctor was spitting in their faces with the medicine that was in the pot. This was supposed to carry them through battle without getting shot.[86]

The lighthorsemen selected to execute a criminal were given notice so they could receive "ministration by the medicine man." After the execution, the two officers repaired to a nearby pool, and each dived in four times "to cleanse them of the death of their fellow man at the hands of the law."[87] The freedman lighthorsemen spoke Creek, served alongside Indian officers, interacted substantially with Seminoles, and subscribed to Native beliefs and customs. But they were members of a small, elite group of freedmen whose experiences were exceptional rather than typical of the Seminole maroon population as a whole.

Freedmen who served with the Seminole lighthorse included Cumsey (Tecumseh) Bruner, Grant Bruner, Thomas Bruner, Sam Cudjo, Dennis Cyrus, Pompey Davis, John Dennis, Caesar Payne, and Thomas Payne. First Kansas Colored Infantry veteran Sam Cudjo was killed in a shootout with an outlaw in a black settlement on the south side of the Canadian in March 1885. But Dennis Cyrus, Caesar Payne, Pompey Davis, and Cumsey Bruner are the best remembered. Cyrus received fifty lashes himself for stealing before becoming a lighthorseman. He served as an officer for twenty-five years and was still with the lighthorse at statehood, along with Tom Bruner and Caesar Payne. Cyrus also worked as a deputy U.S. marshal for five years, serving under John Cordell, who was stationed at Wewoka. Dennis Cyrus died on Christmas Eve, 1912. Like John Horse before him, Caesar Payne rode a white horse. Payne also was a long-serving member of the lighthorse.

Together with Pompey Davis, Caesar Payne frequently accompanied criminals to Wewoka for trial before the Seminole Council. When his turn came, a freedman lighthorseman would administer the stripes or put to death a convicted murderer with either an Indian or another freedman officer. Pompey Davis and Chuckaleese, a Seminole officer, for example, were responsible for executing Lige Brown, said to be a "fullblood." In

Dennis Cyrus, Seminole freedman lighthorseman
and deputy U.S. marshal. Courtesy of Lily Wright
Jefferson. Copy photograph by Rebecca Bateman.

the summer of 1896, two other freedmen officers carried out the last
execution administered under Seminole law.[88] That case involved Pulmusky, an Indian who had murdered John Factor during a drunken
brawl. The lighthorsemen apprehended the accused and brought him
before the council. He was found guilty and sentenced to death. Pulmusky was released and told to return at the appointed time for his
execution. One who attended described the scene:

> When the time, day and hour, came the prisoner was there
> among the crowd and he walked forward. He was blindfolded
> and he sat on a rock by a tree; a white paper heart was cut and
> placed over his heart and then two light-horsemen were selected
> to shoot him. Cumsey Bruner and Caesar Payne were the ones
> and they were negroes.[89]

The last execution in the Seminole Nation, 1896. Freedman lighthorsemen shot Pulmusky, an Indian, for the murder of John Factor. (Oklahoma Historical Society)

That maroons were empowered to whip and execute Indians says much about the status of freedmen within the Seminole Nation after the Civil War.

The freedman lighthorsemen worked alongside black deputy U.S. marshals in helping to maintain law and order in the Seminole Nation during the late nineteenth century.[90] The lighthorse had jurisdiction over cases involving Seminole citizens, but the federal government exercised jurisdiction where crimes involving noncitizens or both citizens and noncitizens took place in the Indian nations. U.S. marshals transported arrested suspects to either the Court for the Western District of Arkansas at Little Rock or the Court for the Eastern District of Texas at Paris. Finally, a federal court was established within the Indian Territory at Muskogee in 1889. Like the freedman lighthorsemen, the black deputies were hired because they knew Indian languages and customs and were familiar with the terrain in the nations. A number were freedmen of the Five Tribes, while others hailed from neighboring Arkansas or Texas. Indians and freedmen also were said to prefer black to white law enforcement officers.[91] A number of black deputy U.S. marshals rode the Indian Territory trails in the years prior to Oklahoma statehood, concentrating mostly on capturing Indian and freedman criminals.

Grant Johnson and Bass Reeves became the most famous of the black deputies. Both spoke Creek and worked extensively in the Creek and Seminole nations. Johnson, the son of a Chickasaw freedman and a Creek freedwoman, became a deputy in the late 1880s and served with distinction until 1906. Born in 1824 near Paris, Texas, Reeves spent the early part of his life as a slave in Texas and Arkansas. His career as a law enforcement officer began in 1875 and by the time he retired in 1907, he had served under seven different marshals.

Between 1875 and 1889, Bass Reeves rode out of Fort Smith and concentrated heavily on the "Seminole whiskey trail" that ran from Denton, Texas, via Sasakwa, into the very heart of the Seminole and Pottawatomie reservations. On one occasion, he rode after thieves who had robbed John F. Brown's store at Sasakwa, apprehending them in the Creek Nation, east of Keokuk. Reeves later stated that, of all the criminals he had encountered, Seminole Indian and freedman fugitives proved the most difficult to catch.[92]

From 1882 until the opening of the Oklahoma Territory in 1889, detachments of the Ninth and Tenth cavalries, or "buffalo soldiers," also

Bass Reeves. (Butler Center for Arkansas Studies, Central Arkansas Library System, Little Rock)

were active in the Indian Territory. They prevented intruders from entering the unassigned lands ceded by the Seminoles.[93] As lighthorsemen, deputy marshals, and soldiers in the U.S. Army, freedmen played a vital role in combating crime in and around the Seminole Nation during the postbellum period.

A number of other freedmen assumed positions of importance within the Seminole Nation after the Civil War. In 1870, Joseph McGillrey, a Civil War veteran, became the nation's blacksmith. Tom Noble and Dan Marshall were other freedmen who became blacksmiths. By 1886, Isaac Bottley was carrying the mail from Wewoka to Sasakwa, a position later filled by Dave McIntosh, another freedman. Bottley became well known in Wewoka, and businessmen visiting the area often called on him to interpret. Caesar Bruner, employed as an interpreter during the Fort Smith negotiations, became a clerk and interpreter at the Wewoka Trading Company and later came to own and operate a store himself in the north of the Seminole Nation. He also became a prominent freedman bandleader and religious leader. A freedman with strong Indian connections—being an adopted member of the Simon Brown (Newcomers) band and having children on the Creek Indian rolls—Caesar Simon was elected to the office of janitor of the Seminole Nation capital in 1894.[94]

Seminole freedmen became delegates, interpreters and politicians, advisers to principal chiefs, blacksmiths and superintendents of blacksmith shops, agency guards, toll bridge operators, gravediggers, medical assistants, guides and mediators, law enforcement officers, mail carriers, clerks, shopkeepers, and janitors. Still others became teachers and religious leaders in the freedmen's neighborhood schools and churches. Their careers spoke volumes for the opportunities that opened to maroons after the Civil War.

The freedmen were afforded equal political rights in the Seminole Nation from Reconstruction to Oklahoma statehood. They received the franchise and were permitted to vote for the principal chief and second chief in popular elections every four years. The Seminoles made no effort to disfranchise the freedmen at any time during the period. The Indians also allowed the maroons to organize politically and send representatives to the council. The band remained the central political constituency within the Seminole Nation. Earlier, each band had represented a community of one or more towns. But in time, members relocated for economic or social reasons, and a band's constituency could span several communities.

Right up to allotment, however, freedman band membership tended to remain associated with residence in a particular community.

After the Civil War, the Seminole Nation divided into twenty-three bands, twenty-one of which were Indian and two freedman. Each band sent three representatives to the council—a bandleader and two council members. In 1870, there were 2,336 members of the Seminole Nation, with 1,952 in Indian bands and 384 in the two freedman bands. Freedmen, therefore, were underrepresented on the council. Although they constituted more than 16 percent of the total population, they had less than 9 percent of the council members. But representation on the council was not proportional. Okfusky's band, with 29 members, sent three representatives, the same as Short Bird's band, which had 178 members. Of the two freedman bands, only the William Noble band, with 274 members, was underrepresented. Six of the Indian bands, in fact, had more members than the Ben Bruner band.[95] No known law or custom prevented the freedmen from organizing into more than two bands, had they wished. Therefore, it cannot be argued that the freedmen were subjected to discrimination when it came to political representation.

During the early 1870s, the inequity in band membership was addressed as the Seminole Nation moved toward a more centralized constitutional form of government.[96] The Indians reorganized into twelve bands, while the freedmen remained in two. This new political arrangement more accurately reflected the composition of the population.[97] The council's new structure of thirty-six Indian and six freedman representatives would remain until the Seminole national government was dissolved at statehood.

By the turn of the century, the freedmen again were underrepresented. Their population had risen dramatically against that of the Seminoles so that freedmen came to constitute almost one-third of the nation, yet they had only one-seventh of the representatives on the council. But demography, traditionalism, and conservatism rather than discrimination account for that inequity. The Seminoles neither had increased the number of Indian representatives nor reduced the number of freedmen on the council. The government of the Seminole Nation was not responsive to population shifts, and the freedmen would have needed to create four new bands to receive proportional representation. Again, some of the Indian bands contained twice as many members as others. The Seminole Nation's institutions remained essentially indigenous. They were designed neither to support proportional representation nor to discriminate against freedmen.

Each band elected a leader and two council members by a popular vote of its members every four years. Six freedman representatives sat on the council and participated in the decision-making process that affected many aspects of citizens' lives in the Seminole Nation. The council assumed the duties of both the legislative and judicial branches of the Seminole government. Council members fulfilled five main duties: they represented the views, wishes, and needs of their constituents before the principal chief and council; they created and codified laws; they tried criminal cases and passed sentence on those found guilty; they appointed officers whose positions were not decided by popular elections; and they furnished advice to the principal chief and helped formulate Seminole national policy. Among the important officers the council appointed were the treasurer, the superintendent of schools, two schools trustees, the superintendent of blacksmith shops, and the lighthorsemen. From their involvement in rebuilding the nation during Reconstruction to their engagement in enrollment and allotment at the end of the century, freedman bandleaders and representatives actively participated as Seminole Council members during one of the most important periods in that nation's history.

Not only were the freedmen granted equal political rights, but they were also protected by Seminole laws that their band representatives helped create and administer. The laws of the Seminole Nation governed the conduct of Indian and freedman citizens with regard to other Seminole citizens, but when U.S. citizens became involved, Seminole Indians and freedmen became subject to the laws of the United States.[98] There is no evidence to suggest that freedmen were treated differently from Indians before Seminole law. Moreover, the freedmen were represented on the council and the lighthorse, the nation's judiciary and law enforcement agency. Friction between Seminoles and freedmen appears to have been minimal. There was no "Negro baiting" or persecution of freedmen by Indians in the Seminole Nation, and racial violence between the two appears to have been rare.

The freedmen attained equal economic rights and equality of opportunity in the Seminole Nation during the postbellum period. They quickly partook in Seminole Nation monetary awards by sharing in the compensation the United States awarded Loyalists for their property

Seminole Indian and freedman council members and lighthorsemen, ca. 1875. John Chupco is seated third from right. (Oklahoma Historical Society)

losses during the Civil War.[99] Throughout the period from Reconstruction to enrollment and allotment, the freedmen received per capita annuity payments as citizens of the Seminole Nation. The Seminoles made no attempt to deprive them of that benefit. Freedman council members and other government officers also received identical salaries to Seminoles in the same positions. In 1870, for example, each Indian and freedman bandleader received $90 per annum for his service.[100] By 1908, bandleaders' salaries had risen to $350 per year, with the other freedman and Indian council members each receiving $250.[101] There was no discrimination based on race in the disbursement of Seminole Nation funds or government officers' salaries.

The freedmen also utilized Seminole Nation lands for their exclusive benefit and kept the products of their labor. Until allotment, the Seminoles retained their indigenous system of communal landholding. Any Indian or freedman could use as much land as he wished, provided he did not infringe on the rights of others. He could make improvements and keep as his own the crops and livestock he raised on the land. Unlike the Chickasaws and Choctaws, the Seminoles made no effort to limit the amount of acreage available to the freedman population. Consequently, a number of the more industrious and enterprising Seminole freedmen came to acquire substantial holdings. The Bruners, for example, became veritable cattle barons during this period, with large landed interests at Bruner Town and Turkey Creek. Even as slaves or tributaries, the maroons had used Seminole lands and kept most of what they produced. After the Civil War, however, the freedmen truly gained a stake in the Seminole Nation's landholdings. The Seminole national authorities and the U.S. government recognized their right to own land as citizens when they received individual allotments equal in value to those of Indians at the turn of the century. As a result, one-third of the Seminole Nation passed into the hands of the freedmen.

Finally, the Seminole freedmen attained equal social and cultural rights. They attended schools supported by Seminole Nation funds, and some became teachers. They were free to practice their various religions under black ministers and, in general, were left to their own devices. The freedmen had their own bandleaders, religious leaders, medicine men, and educators. They practiced an Africanized form of Presbyterian and Baptist religions, and they retained their distinctive Creole language and system of naming practices. The unique Seminole maroon culture the group had developed in Florida and the Indian Territory during the antebellum period continued to thrive in the Seminole freedman townships after the Civil War.

A number of Seminole freedmen later intimated that they "scarcely knew the difference between being free and being in slavery," but there were several important differences.[102] They no longer had to offer tribute to Seminole mikkos, and the threat of sale and kidnap finally had disappeared. The freedmen, moreover, acquired political representation, access to salaried national offices, protection by the law, freedom to practice their religions, equality of educational opportunity, and a share in the nation's land, annuities, and other monetary awards. They enjoyed all the rights of Seminole Nation citizens and were able to control their own destinies, free of interference, for the first time on American soil. Bearing in mind the problems they already had overcome and the challenges they would face later after Oklahoma became a state, it is no overstatement to suggest that the postbellum period in the Indian Territory represented a golden age in the history of the Seminole freedmen.

CHAPTER EIGHT

Intermarriage

The Seminoles emerged as the most successful of the Five Tribes in abiding by the terms of their Reconstruction treaty. The Seminole freedmen had good reason to be thankful for their affiliation. Next to the Seminoles, the Creeks fared best in that regard, followed by the Cherokees, then the Choctaws; the Chickasaws lagged far behind.[1] The antebellum and Civil War experiences of each directly and dramatically affected the course of its relations with freedmen during the postbellum period. The stronger the tribe's history of white intermarriage and acculturation, the greater the problems the freedmen faced during Reconstruction. Those that had embraced the South and its institutions most closely felt the strongest antipathy to freedmen; those less affected by such influences found the adjustments easier to make and experienced a smoother transition.

Besides the Seminoles, the Creeks proved the most successful in accommodating emancipation and incorporation.[2] Acculturated and wealthy Indian-white Lower Creeks had assumed leadership positions within the nation during the antebellum period and had sponsored the adoption of institutionalized slavery and black codes. Most Upper Creeks, however, had resembled Seminoles in their lack of acculturation; indigenous beliefs and customs remained strong among that group. Upper Creek Loyalists emerged from the Civil War victorious and led the nation during Reconstruction.

During the 1866 treaty negotiations, the Loyal Creeks stated that

Hopothli Yahola had promised equality to all the slaves who supported him during the conflict, and they wished to abide by that pledge. The Northern faction signed the ensuing treaty of June 14 without the approval of the Confederates. Like the Southern Seminoles, however, the Confederate Creeks were anxious for peace and compromise. The Creek Reconstruction treaty abolished slavery and stipulated that the nation's freedmen would enjoy all the rights of Indian citizens, including an equal interest in lands and national funds. The Creeks mostly abided by the treaty's provisions.

Like the Seminole maroons, Creek freedmen were granted rights equal to those of Indian citizens. They received the franchise and political representation, and their council members came to constitute an influential voting bloc in the Creek legislature. Creek freedmen also could hold government office. A number assumed important positions within the nation as interpreters, judges, delegates, law enforcement officers, and politicians. The Creeks gave them an equal stake in the land, annuity payments, and tribal monies. The freedmen had equal economic opportunity and access to education and were treated equally before the law. They settled in black towns and there practiced their religions and maintained their cultural traditions. In 1882, the commissioner of Indian affairs reported, "These Indians have respected their treaty stipulations relating to their freedmen, and have granted them every right of other citizens."[3]

Ethnohistorian Katja May has suggested that some Creeks and Cherokees "impeded the political and social equality of the African American citizens."[4] There were reports of friction between the Indian and freedman townships throughout the period, and at the time of enrollment, Chief Isparhecher tried to limit freedman allotments to forty acres. Although the freedmen ultimately received sixty acres, the same as Indian citizens, the Creek leadership also questioned their right to share in the nation's equalization funds. But all in all, the Creeks accommodated their freedmen quite well.

In contrast to the Seminoles and to a lesser extent the Creeks, the other three tribes—the Cherokees, Choctaws, and Chickasaws—experienced far more difficulty in coming to terms with the challenges posed by emancipation and incorporation. During the antebellum period, intermarried white and Indian-white elites had come to power in each of those tribes. They had sponsored a program of rapid acculturation based on adopting the institutions, attitudes, and lifestyle of the white South. As incorporating agents of white civilization had gained widespread acceptance, Native beliefs and practices had declined. The three nations had developed advanced capitalist economies, featuring plantation agriculture, substantial industries, and large-scale commercial enterprises. To supply the labor force, they had adopted institutionalized slavery featuring harsh black codes. Their slaves had enjoyed little independence. As racial attitudes hardened, moreover, the three had prohibited Indian-black intermarriage and had reenslaved free blacks.

Of the Five Tribes, the Chickasaws, Choctaws, and Cherokees had been strongest in their support for the South. The Choctaws and Chickasaws had been the first to conclude treaties with the Confederacy and proved to be the most committed in their allegiance, placing large numbers of troops in the field. Although the Cherokees had divided, most of the leading Indian-whites had followed Stand Watie into the arms of the South. During Reconstruction, the three nations all had systems of institutionalized slavery and black codes to dismantle, and they needed a new labor force. The Chickasaws, Choctaws, and Confederate Cherokees also were bitter in defeat and resentful of having to emancipate their former slaves and incorporate the freedmen on equal terms. Many former Confederates regained political power in those nations during Reconstruction and brought with them their racial attitudes and policies. Being situated next to the former slave states Arkansas and Texas only made matters worse, as ex-Confederate settlers and Southern white rhetoric exerted their influence. In dealing with their freedmen, the Cherokees, Choctaws, and Chickasaws faced problems that were alien to the Seminoles.

The Cherokee freedmen struggled for their rights, and many were denied citizenship.[5] Under the terms of the treaty of August 11, 1866, only former slaves and free blacks who were associated with Cherokees at the start of the Civil War and residing in the nation at that time, or who returned within six months, would be entitled to citizenship rights. Many either did not hear about that clause or could not return in time and missed out. Those lacking recognition as Cherokee freedmen had no legal rights or clearly defined status in the nation. They could cultivate land, but their improvements were never secure, and they were denied access to the courts, the political system, and the tribal schools. Freedman claims to Cherokee citizenship, and the innumerable suits that resulted, dominated relations between the two groups during the postbellum period. In the end, the Dawes Commission would have to decide which freedmen were entitled to land as Cherokee citizens.

Freedmen who were recognized as citizens of the Cherokee Nation eventually received some benefits. Cherokee law protected them, and they sat on juries, served as elected officials, rested secure in the ownership of improvements, and had access to limited, segregated public school facilities. But they experienced discrimination when it came to land and money. Between 1883 and 1888, the Cherokees excluded them from per capita payments for land cessions and leases. Their leaders reasoned that freedmen had no legal or equitable claim to the public property of the Cherokee Nation. At the time of allotment, they clung to that line, hoping to grant each freedman just forty acres. The Dawes Commission reverted to the wording of the Reconstruction treaty and enrolled only those freedmen who had returned to the nation within the specified six months, together with their descendants. Many freedmen who had been associated with Cherokees since the antebellum period and had been living in the nation for forty years since the end of the Civil War were deprived of land and lost ownership rights to their improvements. Due to the insistence of the Dawes Commission, however, freedmen fortunate enough to have enrolled as Cherokee citizens received land allotments equal in value to those of Indians.

Not surprisingly, the Choctaws and Chickasaws were the least accommodating toward their freedmen.[6] For twenty years after the Civil War, the Choctaw freedmen had no clearly defined status within the nation. They were treated as U.S. citizens, both as individuals and before the law. They had no rights in the public domain but were permitted to use land for their own benefit. In effect, they were tenants without any rights of tenure. The Choctaws finally adopted the freedmen as citizens in 1885 but granted them only limited rights. They had no share in Choctaw monies, per capita annuity payments, or the national domain. In the event of allotment, each freedman would receive just forty acres. Although the Choctaw freedmen could vote in elections, they could not sit on the council or stand for office, as those positions were restricted to citizens classified as Indian.

The Choctaw freedmen received equal but separate educational opportunities, and little social interaction took place between Indians and blacks. As soon as the Choctaws adopted the freedmen, they passed a law prohibiting Indian-black intermarriage. The Choctaws viewed adoption as granting specific privileges to the freedmen and not a gateway to assimilation. The Choctaw freedmen lived in separate towns, attended their own schools, and constituted an independent voting bloc. At the time of allotment, the Choctaws enforced the clause restricting the freedmen's acreage. The freedmen received the equivalent value of forty acres of Choctaw land while Indian citizens received eight times that amount.

The Chickasaws were even less accommodating than the Choctaws and never incorporated their former slaves. Under the terms of their 1866 treaty, joint Chickasaw-Choctaw action was required before either could adopt the freedmen. The Chickasaws effectively prevented the Choctaws from adopting their freedmen earlier. Only after taking special measures could the Choctaws independently incorporate their former slaves. But the Chickasaw legislature rejected adopting their freedmen and instead requested their removal from the nation. One of the biggest problems was the sheer number of freedmen involved. No census of the freedmen had been taken after the Civil War, the Chickasaws hoping that they soon would be removed. A flood of black immigrants into the nation during Reconstruction made impossible the positive identification of those entitled to consideration. The fear of freedman dominance underpinned Chickasaw reticence. By 1893, freedmen in the Chickasaw Nation outnumbered Indians.

The Chickasaw freedmen experienced hard times from the end of the Civil War to Oklahoma statehood. For forty years, they lived in the Chickasaw Nation without any rights. The Indians treated them like black U.S. citizens, but U.S. government officials treated them as citizens of the Chickasaw Nation. Freedmen could use Chickasaw lands, but they held no rights of tenure and faced the constant threat of forcible removal from the nation. They could not vote or hold office and were not protected by Chickasaw law. They suffered ill treatment and educational deprivation. They were outcasts, caught between two worlds, belonging to neither. On February 12, 1890, Union agent Leo Bennett reported: "The close of twenty-five years of 'freedom' (?) finds the Chickasaw Freedmen the most wretched people in this Western Country. They are poor, deplorably ignorant, and are buffeted around from pillar to post, abused, degraded, debased and denied. No home, no country, no government, no schools; it is impossible for them to be lower in the moral scale."[7]

At the time of allotment, the Chickasaws objected to sharing their lands with the freedmen. Only through the insistence of the Dawes Commission did they receive their forty acres. The Chickasaws later brought suit against the U.S. government and received compensation for lands allotted to the freedmen.

The question quickly arose as to how and why the Seminoles had incorporated the maroons so successfully when the Cherokees, Choctaws, and Chickasaws, in particular, experienced problems similar to those of the Deep South in accommodating freedmen within their societies. In his annual report for 1866, Commissioner of Indian Affairs Dennis Cooley wrote of the Five Tribes, "Slavery is entirely abolished, and the freedmen placed upon an equal footing with the remainder of the people. This equality was the more easily accomplished in the case of the Seminoles, since there had already been a considerable intermingling of the races before the tribe removed from Florida."[8]

During the next forty years, others expanded upon Cooley's assessment. The argument came to include three main elements: both before and after Removal, maroons had intermarried with Seminoles freely and extensively; their fertile unions had produced large numbers of "half breeds"; and those offspring had integrated easily within Seminole society, blurring distinctions between Indians and blacks. For most white observers, this intermarriage theory proved compelling. It best explained why race relations seemed so different in the Seminole Nation.

In 1890, the federal census commissioners reported on the Seminoles: "[The] negroes constitute a very considerable portion of the nation, with whom many Indians are intermarried."[9] The contemporary writer J. A. Newsom concurred, noting that "many" of the Seminoles "were crossed with the Negro race."[10] In an article that appeared in the popular *Harper's New Monthly Magazine* in November 1893, Rezin McAdam argued that the Seminoles had become "negroized," having only a few Indians that could "boast of blood uncontaminated by that of the African."[11] At the time of tribal enrollment and allotment, commentators seeking to explain relations between Indians and freedmen within the Five Tribes seized upon that notion.

The Dawes Commission created separate rolls for Indians and freedmen in each of the five nations, but observers usually contrasted the experience of the Seminoles and Creeks with that of the Cherokees, Choctaws, and Chickasaws, who, they argued, did not intermarry with blacks. In June 1901, the *El Reno (Oklahoma Territory) News* reported, "There are few fullblood Seminoles. There are but two white men married to Indians, but the admixture with negro blood is very large. About half of the citizens of the nation are mixed Indian and negro blood."[12] Three years later, after noting that, generally speaking, "Indians dislike Negroes," the *Vinita (Cherokee Nation) Weekly Chieftain* observed, "The prejudice against the negro is less severe among the Creeks and Seminoles, because many of the members of these tribes have negro blood in their veins."[13]

In an influential 1907 article on race in the new state of Oklahoma published shortly after statehood, Professor L. J. Abbott provided the most extreme example of that view. Abbott appeared to have reached his conclusions only after extensive research:

> Soon after the Five Civilized Tribes settled in Indian Territory, the negroes were accepted as an integral portion of the Creek and Seminole tribes, for, long previous to their settlement in the Indian Territory, members of these tribes had intermarried with the Negroes. Intermarriage became common so that now (on the writer's authority) there is not a Seminole family that is entirely free from Negro blood; and there are but three Creek families (some make it two) that are pure blood.

According to Abbott, the Cherokees, Choctaws, and Chickasaws "seldom or never mixed their blood with the Negro" but intermarried extensively with whites. In "a generation or two," those three tribes would lose their identity among whites, "but the Creeks and Seminoles, except a few instances where Caucasian blood largely predominates, will be counted as negroes."[14]

The belief that black blood ran in the veins of most Seminole Indians certainly prevailed among white residents of the Indian Territory and, later, Oklahoma. In general, white renters in the Indian nations loathed the reversal of economic roles based on race, but they considered Seminole landlords the most "uncivilized" of all. Among the Five Tribes, they opined, the Seminoles suffered from being the least mixed with whites and the most mixed with blacks. White renters in the Seminole Nation found that both humiliating and galling.[15]

Several better-informed or more perceptive contemporaries challenged the prevailing view and more accurately described Seminole-freedman relations prior to statehood. In 1870, in regard to the Seminole Nation, the Board of Indian Commissioners reported, "There are 400 negroes having all the rights of citizens. The Indians and negroes do not intermarry."[16] Seven years later, in an important revisionist article entitled "The Seminoles, or History Corrected," the *Indian Journal* observed:

> It is a mistake that the Seminoles intermarried with the negroes who ran to them from Southern slave owners. There is not among all the five civilized tribes a purer Indian stock than the Seminoles. [If] they had married negroes, then bees wax and tallow would have been in demand to this day, to keep their hair straight. For pure blooded unmixed Indians, of the finest type, commend me to the Seminoles.[17]

In 1896, John Thornton wrote in the same journal:

> The Seminole people are mostly full-blood Indians or full-blood negroes, there being very little perceptible admixture. The slaves owned by these people prior to emancipation become [*sic*] Indian citizens with freedom and they now constitute about 500 of the total population of 2,900 and enjoy all the educational, annuity and governmental privileges accorded other citizens.[18]

Charles Coe took up that theme two years later when he described the Seminole population as including "several hundred negroes, most of them descendants of the famous Maroons, who are recognized as Seminoles by the tribe, and who enjoy all rights of the others except intermarriage with the Indians, although there are some admixtures."[19] In 1901, D. C. Gideon observed, "The Seminoles have not largely intermarried with the white man, and there are but few half-breed negroes,"[20] a notion echoed by Ora Eddleman Reed five years later.[21]

Yet after Oklahoma entered the Union in 1907, scholars and other commentators reasserted that a high rate of miscegenation had accounted for the nature of relations between Seminoles and freedmen during the postbellum period. Between statehood and World War II, that myth became entrenched. Smithsonian anthropologist Frederick Hodge in his 1910 *Handbook of American Indians, North of Mexico,* wrote of the Seminoles, "In 1908 they were reported officially to number 2,138, largely mixed with negro blood, in addition to 986 freedmen."[22] Hodge's *Handbook* became the standard reference in the field. In 1920, U.S. probate attorney Florence Etheridge, shortly after being assigned to work among the Seminoles in Oklahoma, reported to the Superintendent for the Five Civilized Tribes, "With practically all the Seminoles, it is, of course, merely a question of degree of Indian and negro blood."[23] And in 1931, in a paper prepared for the federal census, G. E. E. Lindquist reported, "There does not seem to be a tendency to intermixture of white and Indian among the Seminoles as it is true among the Five Civilized Tribes as a whole. This may be due, in part at least, to instances of intermarriage with Negroes."[24]

In 1932, in a pioneering and highly influential article published in the *Journal of Negro History,* Kenneth Porter suggested that interaction between blacks and Seminoles and Creeks had led to "the Africanizing of two of the principal Indian tribes."[25] This theme dominated his subsequent work, and Porter became the leading historian of Indian-black relations on the American frontier for the next forty years. In 1934, Otis Duncan argued in another scholarly journal that while intense antagonism had characterized relations between blacks and Cherokees, Choctaws, and Chickasaws during the postbellum period, "The Creeks and Seminoles [admitted] the freedmen into their tribes and intermarried with them rather freely."[26] The press also adopted that interpretation. In 1939, the *Daily Oklahoman* recounted that, after the Civil War, the freedmen "[entered] into the tribal life of the Indians, sat in their councils, became interpreters, and especially among the Creeks and Seminoles, through marriage, formed blood relationships."[27]

The myth of massive Seminole-maroon intermarriage has shown remarkable resilience. Of the leading twentieth-century historians working in the field, only Joseph Thoburn and Muriel Wright questioned the prevailing view, and then only fleetingly. They argued that although the Seminoles accepted the freedmen into the tribe after the Civil War, "The majority [did] not accept the Negroes socially."[28] Much more common has been the interpretation adopted by the popular historian William Loren Katz: "Seminoles, whose blacks often had been dear friends and family members, quickly accepted emancipation and equality."[29] Only since 1990 have researchers begun to publish work that has challenged that conventional wisdom.[30]

Surprisingly, the myth persists, even in academia. In a 2004 article on emancipation and Reconstruction in the Indian Territory, Saunt observed:

> The meaning of freedom gained the most currency among the Seminoles and Creeks, partly because marriage between people of Indian and African descent was more common in these nations, making kinship a fact difficult to deny. As early as 1842 one army officer reportedly had predicted "that in a few years the Creeks would be all black" because of the rate of intermarriage. One observer noted that by 1870 the Creeks were "largely amalgamated with the African." The Seminoles, after fighting three wars with the help of their slaves, intermarried even more frequently.[31]

And in the winter of 2005, legal historian Carla Pratt concluded, "The African influence among these southeastern Indians was considerable and is evidenced by the black skin and African facial features of many Seminole Indians."[32]

How, then, did this intermarriage myth arise, and why has it proven so enduring? First of all, it provided a simple answer to a complex problem. Social integration through miscegenation offered a plausible explanation as to why Seminoles were able to incorporate freedmen so successfully into their nation when the other Civilized Tribes experienced such difficulties. On a sliding scale, it appeared, the tribe with the highest rate of black intermarriage did the best, the one with the lowest the worst. But that scale used the wrong measures: the one with the lowest rate of white intermarriage did the best, and the one with the highest the worst.

Second, the argument was both persuasive and compelling, appearing to be based on solid fact. Some Seminoles and maroons had intermarried in Florida prior to Removal. More importantly, high-profile individuals had been among those engaging in such unions. U.S. government officials knew, for example, that Hothli Hopoya had married Polly, of African descent, and had freed her and her children in 1819.[33] The Apalachicola leader Waka Puchasi was described as "half negro and Indian," and Asin Yahola, the most prominent Seminole opposed to Removal at the start of the Second Seminole War, also was reported to be part African. Abolitionists even circulated propaganda suggesting that this

THE NATION ROBBING AN INDIAN CHIEF OF HIS WIFE.

The Nation Robbing an Indian Chief of His Wife. Published in the *American Anti-Slavery Almanac,* 1839, this lithograph purported to document the kidnapping of Asin Yahola's (Osceola's) black wife. A piece of abolitionist propaganda, it contributed to the myth of massive Seminole-maroon intermarriage. (Walter Havighurst Special Collections, Miami University)

famous Seminole leader had been driven to hostility by the seizure of one of his wives, the daughter of a Seminole mikko and a runaway African woman.[34] Government agents also noted that the Seminoles had rewarded Abraham, the leading maroon interpreter in Florida, with a wife, "the widow of the former chief of the nation."[35] Still other unions came to public light during slave claims involving maroon participants or their mixed-race offspring. The marriage of Black Factor's son, Sam, and Rose Sena Factor, for instance, had become known during Nelly Factor's claim to Rose and her children.[36] Unions between Seminoles and maroons tended to be conspicuous. By their very nature, they seemed to curious whites exotic, forbidden, and noteworthy. While never common, such intermarriages usually were noticed.

Third, the nature of Seminole-maroon relations seemed to support the argument. By the time of the Second Seminole War, U.S. government and military officials concluded that Indians and blacks had identical interests and were integrating. General Jesup had suggested that Seminoles and maroons were "rapidly approximating."[37] That appeared to have been confirmed after their joint Removal to the Indian Territory. Instead of adopting institutionalized slavery or black codes like the other Civilized Tribes, Seminoles allowed the maroons large measures of independence. Surely, it seemed, widespread miscegenation was a necessary ingredient in that formula. The joint emigration of Kowakochi's and John Horse's supporters to Coahuila in 1849–50 and the exodus of the Loyal Seminoles and maroons to Kansas in 1861 apparently backed the theory. So did the tribe's low rate of white intermarriage, its aversion to agents of white acculturation, a lack of detailed knowledge on the nature of Seminole-maroon relations, and a general feeling of fear and suspicion on the part of white observers. That both Seminoles and freedmen practiced polygyny became apparent during enrollment and only added weight to the argument. It seemed entirely reasonable to assume that those primitive and promiscuous Indians and Africans frequently engaged in plural intermarriages.

Fourth, the large and ever-increasing number of freedmen living in the Seminole Nation and enjoying the same rights as Indians gave rise to the belief that many were the offspring of mixed unions. During the postbellum period, the Seminole freedman population tripled while the number of Seminole Indians remained, at best, constant. By the early 1900s, when the intermarriage theory was being promoted most strongly, freedmen constituted one of every three Seminole citizens, and a good number had attained important positions within the nation. Mixed marriages and social integration seemed to explain why so many black faces appeared among the Seminole population, and why they were faring so well.

Fifth, for decades after statehood, whites portrayed Seminole Indians as a "mongrelized" population, tainted by black blood. Criminal tendencies, laziness, drunkenness, and backwardness all could be attributed to their African admixture. That helps explain why some Seminoles tried so hard to rid themselves of their association with the freedmen. Even the perception of black admixture was a serious liability in Jim Crow Oklahoma. Similarly, whites attributed what they perceived as wild, aggressive, and violent tendencies in the freedmen to their "Indian blood." As Bateman has argued, mixed-race Indian-blacks were thought to possess "the worst traits of both groups, resulting in a criminal type more ruthless than any other known."[38] Miscegenation not only helped explain race relations in the Seminole Nation but also helped rationalize and sustain white prejudice toward both Seminoles and freedmen.

Finally, during and after the civil rights movement of the 1950s and 1960s, advocates for multiculturalism appropriated the intermarriage myth. The situation in the Seminole Nation has been portrayed as a refreshing exception to the violence, segregation, and prejudice African Americans experienced elsewhere and as a model for emulation. Miscegenation could lead to racial integration and to social and cultural assimilation, resulting in a better society.

But the documentary record does not support the myth of massive Seminole-maroon intermarriage. Family information that Indians and freedman divulged to the Dawes Commission during enrollment provides clues to the true nature of relations between Seminoles and maroons after the Civil War.[39] By analyzing the Seminole Indian and Seminole freedman census cards, important conclusions relating to miscegenation in the Seminole Nation can be drawn.[40] First and foremost, there appears to have been a very low rate of intermarriage between Indians and freedmen, resulting in only a small population of mixed-race Seminole-maroons.

Second, intermarriages involving Seminole freedmen and Indian women were more common than between Indian men and Seminole freedwomen, but both types of union were rare. The census cards indicate just thirty mixed-race Seminole-freedmen on the Indian rolls and fifteen on the freedman rolls. A further twenty-three individuals on the Seminole Indian rolls are known to have been mixed-race Seminole–Creek freedmen.[41] The rolls indicate that only five Seminole freedmen of no known Indian admixture had children with seven Seminole Indian women of no known freedman admixture. Moreover, just two men of no known freedman admixture on the Seminole rolls fathered children by Seminole freedwomen. One of those was an adopted white; the other, an Indian who died before allotment.

Because of the inadequacies of the raw data, these figures should be viewed not as definitive but as indicative of trends. Yet even allowing for a wide margin of error, the numbers clearly point to a very low rate of Indian-freedman miscegenation within the Seminole Nation during the postbellum period. Even including Seminole–Creek freedmen, only sixty-eight Indian-freedmen could be identified through the census cards, representing just 2 percent of the total population.

Clearly, that figure is lower than it should be. Seminoles had reason to hide black admixture, most of which derived from earlier intermarriages. To give just three examples, many Factors were listed on the Seminole Indian rolls as "fullbloods," while the Harrison and Caesar families,[42] although not listed as such, probably also were of Indian-black descent. Among freedman enrollees, Indian admixture also could go unacknowledged. For instance, if Benjamin F. Bruner's claim that his deceased mother, Grace Bowlegs, had been "fullblood" Seminole Indian was correct, he, his brother Thomas Bruner, his sister Annie Payne, and Annie's eight children all should have enrolled as Seminole Indians, not freedmen. But after the Civil War, Grace's children joined the Jim Lane band (later the Bruner band), that of her husband, and became members of the freedman community.[43]

The number of people of mixed race in the Seminole Nation at the time of enrollment probably amounted to just over 200, or 7 percent of the total population. That figure includes the families of a handful of intermarried whites, but most individuals of mixed race were Indian-black. Sattler is the only other researcher to have analyzed the Seminole rolls in this way, and he reached the same conclusions:

> Black and Indian Seminoles [maintained] a marked degree of social distance and seldom intermarried. Only about one percent (12 out of slightly over 1200) of the verifiable unions listed on the Final Roll of the Seminole in 1898 reflected such marriages. This rate was less than half that for marriage to United States citizens in either group. Most of these cases involved Indian women and Black men. The Indians and Blacks clearly maintained separate identities and a degree of social distance.[44]

Based on her analysis of archival sources and information she obtained from Seminole freedman descendants in the mid-1980s, Bateman agrees that "black-Indian miscegenation was far less common than many whites, and Freedmen, assume."[45]

A low incidence of Indian-black intermarriage also occurred among Cherokees and Creeks after the Civil War, and the rate was probably even lower among Choctaws and Chickasaws.[46] Historian Circe Sturm has calculated that, among the 4,208 adult Cherokee freedmen the Dawes Commission enumerated, only around 300, or 7 percent, claimed any degree of Cherokee Indian ancestry on their census cards.[47] May also conducted random sampling from the 1900 censuses of the Cherokee and Creek nations. Among the Cherokees, she found that fewer than 2 percent of "fullbloods" had a "black Indian" or "black immigrant" spouse. And among the 533 Creek households she sampled, May documented fewer than 2 percent of "fullbloods" as having married "black Indians."

The same number had married "black immigrants," and only 5 percent of "black Indians" were married to "fullbloods." As with the Seminoles and maroons, most of those unions involved freedman males entering into unions with Indian women. May concludes, "Surprisingly, the reputation of frequent intermarriage among Creeks and African Americans was not substantiated by the census figures."[48]

The third conclusion relating to miscegenation in the Seminole Nation to be drawn from the enrollment records is that it was usually prominent freedmen who participated in the few intermarriages with Indian women. Tom Noble and Grant Bruner, sons of the postbellum band-leaders William Noble and Caesar Bruner, for example, were two of the freedmen of no known Indian admixture who had children with "full-blood" Seminole women. Those maroons spoke Creek and held important positions within the nation, Tom Noble being a blacksmith and Grant Bruner a council member and lighthorseman.[49] They would have experienced extensive contact with Seminoles through their fathers and their positions. An Indian marriage likely brought increased status for freedman males within the maroon community. Their children would be included in Indian clans and bands and considered to be Seminoles. Yet a maroon marriage brought no such advantage for Indian males, offspring of such unions being considered freedman and excluded from Seminole society.[50]

Fourth, freedman names were carried into Seminole Indian society through intermarriage. Although the offspring of maroon men and Indian women usually seem to have been considered Seminole, they took the surname of the father. Occasionally, parents of those families also gave their children characteristic freedman first names, such as "Nero."

Finally, mixed-race Seminole-maroons were far more likely to engage in further intermarriages than other Indians or freedmen. A study of landholding in the Seminole Nation at the time of allotment, drawn from the records of the Dawes Commission, suggests that Indian-blacks tended to live on the fringes of Seminole and freedman communities, where the two intersected. This was especially noticeable at the Scipio and Turkey Creek settlements, but no intermarriages could be traced in or around Thomas Town (chart 1).[51] Children of unions between maroon men and Indian women grew up to marry both Seminoles and freedmen, as did offspring of marriages between Indian men and maroon women. Mixed-race Seminole-maroons also tended to have close family ties and marry

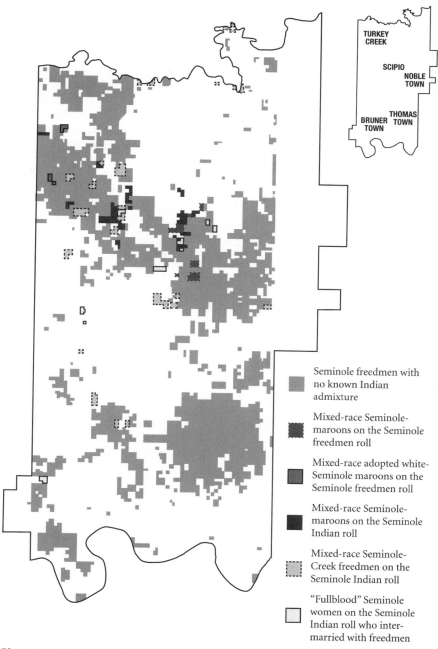

TURKEY
CREEK

SCIPIO

NOBLE
TOWN

BRUNER   THOMAS
TOWN   TOWN

Seminole freedmen with
no known Indian
admixture

Mixed-race Seminole-
maroons on the Seminole
freedmen roll

Mixed-race adopted white-
Seminole maroons on the
Seminole freedmen roll

Mixed-race Seminole-
maroons on the Seminole
Indian roll

Mixed-race Seminole-
Creek freedmen on the
Seminole Indian roll

"Fullblood" Seminole
women on the Seminole
Indian roll who inter-
married with freedmen

Chart 1. Landholdings of Seminole freedmen and mixed-race Seminole maroons at the time
of allotment.

each other. That led to a significant development. Due to the nation's adherence to matrilineal descent, some individuals of mixed race but of predominantly maroon descent were enrolled as Seminoles, while some of predominantly Indian admixture were enrolled as freedmen.

The Nobles were the largest of the mixed-race Seminole-maroon families.[52] Tom Noble, son of the freedman bandleader William Noble and Dinah, a Seminole freedwoman, married Wasutke, a "fullblood" Seminole, prior to the Civil War. By the late 1870s, the couple had five children: Rinah, Albert, Nero, Logan, and Leah. The Noble children were half-Indian and half-maroon, but because of matrilineal descent they became members of their mother's Indian band, the Oktiarche band, and eventually were enrolled as Seminoles. The marital experiences of those five individuals furnish important insights into the status of mixed-race Indian-maroons within the Seminole Nation prior to Oklahoma statehood.

At the time of enrollment, Rinah Noble had nine children by five different husbands. At least four of her spouses were of African but no known Indian descent. Rinah married two Seminole freedmen, Robert Davis and March Doser; two Creek freedmen, Jim Carter and Philip Eleck; and Prairie Bill, a noncitizen whose race was not indicated. Six of Rinah's children by her husbands of known African descent were three-quarters freedman and just one-quarter Seminole, while her three with Prairie Bill were at least one-quarter freedman, yet all nine were enrolled as one-quarter Seminole through their mother.

Albert Noble had children with both a maroon and an Indian. He fathered a daughter with Rebecca Andrews, a Seminole freedwoman, and the child was enrolled as a freedman. He also had four children with Lousianna, a "fullblood" Seminole. Those children became members of their mother's Oktiarche band and later were enrolled as three-quarter Seminole. Interestingly, after Albert Noble's death in 1903, Lousianna had a daughter with a "fullblood" Seminole.

Nero Noble married Rachael Carter, a daughter of one of his sister Rinah's husbands, Jim Carter, and a Seminole freedwoman. Nero and Rachael had three daughters. Although those children were one-quarter Seminole, the same as Rinah's, they became members of a freedman band and were enrolled as freedmen through their mother. Logan Noble had two children with Seminole freedwoman Susie Mills, the half-sister of Rebecca Andrews, one of his brother Albert's wives. Those offspring also

"Uncle Scipio Noble, 1904." A son of the freedman bandleader William Noble, Scipio came from a prominent family in the Seminole Nation. His half-brother Tom married the "full-blood" Seminole Wasutke and gave rise to a mixed-race dynasty. Born in the early 1840s, Scipio is wearing the traditional turban documented in earlier images of Seminoles and maroons, but rarely seen in the Indian Territory so late. Although the photograph is dated 1904, *Campbell's Abstract* reported that Scipio Noble died on October 10, 1901. (Western History Collections, University of Oklahoma Libraries)

were enrolled as freedmen. Leah Noble married Seminole freedman Bob (Bud) Carter, another of Jim Carter's children, and had three children with him. Like most of Rinah's progeny, Leah's offspring were three-quarters freedman and only one-quarter Indian, yet they became members of her Oktiarche band and were enrolled as Seminoles. Leah also had a daughter, Polly, with Seminole freedman Bob Bowlegs, a former husband of Rebecca Andrews. Polly, also three-quarters freedman, apparently lived with her "fullblood" Seminole grandmother, Wasutke.

By the time the Dawes Commission compiled the census cards, the one Indian-maroon intermarriage between Wasutke and Tom Noble had resulted in twenty-eight mixed-race Seminole-freedmen. Six of those were enrolled as freedmen and twenty-two as Seminoles. Of the

"Uncle" Isaac Bottley *(left)* and "Uncle" Jim Carter *(right),* ca. 1930. Bottley became a leading Seminole freedman interpreter at the time of enrollment and allotment. Carter, a Creek freedman, and two of his children married mixed-race Nobles on the Seminole Indian rolls. Detail of photograph from the *St. Petersburg (Fla.) Times,* January 4, 1931. (Western History Collections, University of Oklahoma Libraries)

latter, at least ten were of three-quarters freedman descent and another five were one-half freedman. The six enrolled as freedmen were one-quarter Indian, the same as the ten enrolled as Seminoles. Depending on the status of the mother, cousins and half-sisters of the same racial admixture were classified as either Indian or freedman.

Band affiliation suggests that Seminole and maroon society considered some of mixed race to be Indian and others freedman. How they considered themselves is another matter. The census cards document eleven marriages for the children of Wasutke and Tom Noble, but only one involving a Seminole Indian. At least nine of the other ten unions involved freedmen or freedwomen. The twenty-two of mixed race who were enrolled as Seminoles also might have experienced fairly extensive social and cultural interaction with Indians, but their level of involvement in the Oktiarche band and with their mothers' clan is unknown. The Nobles and their offspring maintained close links with other intermarried and mixed-race families. Their marital partners and settlement patterns point to close kinship ties and complex family networks within the Seminole freedman, Creek freedman, and mixed-race Indian-freedman communities.

The Coody and Warrior families displayed similar traits and became closely linked.[53] Seminole freedman Dosar Coody, a former slave of Bill Coody, married Tarthloga (Tuthoka; Toth-hoga), a "fullblood" Seminole, sometime before 1870 and probably shortly after the Civil War. By the mid-1880s, the couple had four sons and one daughter: Tom, Daniel, Sarah, Joseph, and Bob. All five became members of the Echoille band, that of their Indian mother, and later were enrolled as Seminoles. Their marital experiences were similar to those of the Nobles.

Tom Coody, the eldest, married Jennie, a Seminole "fullblood," the daughter of Hulbutta Harjochee and Lucy. Tom and Jennie had two daughters, Amey and Nellie. Amey and Nellie became members of the Echoille band, that of their mother and also of their mixed-race father. This union suggests that at least one mixed-race Seminole-freedman member of the Echoille band interacted substantially with other Indian members, to the point of marrying a "fullblood" Seminole woman. Amey and Nellie would have enrolled as three-quarters Seminole, but both died in August 1899. While the mixed-race brothers Tom and Joseph shared a census card, Jennie, Amey, and Nellie were listed on the census card headed by Lucy. This suggests that Jennie and her daughters were considered members of Lucy's rather than Tom's household. Daniel Coody, meanwhile, also married a Seminole "fullblood," Wisey, but the young couple died before having any children.

Sarah Coody, the only daughter, married Jack Warrior in what was perhaps the most interesting union of all, as Jack was also of mixed race. Jack Warrior's father, John Factor, was a member of the Seminole Thomas Palmer band, but given his family background, Factor likely was of mixed race himself. He also could have been the man Pulmusky murdered in the drunken brawl mentioned in chapter 7. Freedman lighthorsemen later executed Pulmusky. Jack Warrior's mother, Seminole freedwoman Dicey Harred, was a former slave of Lucinda Edwards. Like his mother, Jack became a member of the Caesar Bruner band and later enrolled as a Seminole freedman. How he became a Warrior (*tastanaki*) is unknown, but his father's clan probably gave him that title.

Jack and Sarah (née Coody) Warrior had a daughter, Stella, who was born in 1898 and enrolled as one-quarter Seminole. But that classification ignored her father's Indian admixture, listing Jack, like all others of mixed race on the Seminole freedman rolls, simply as freedman. Stella should have enrolled as one-half Seminole and one-half freedman. Jack Warrior previously had three other children with two Seminole freedwomen. He and Sarah Cudjoe had two sons, Amos and Levi Warrior; then he and Affie Davis had another son, Mattea Davis, all of whom enrolled as freedmen.

Joseph Coody, the fourth child, died on May 31, 1900, without issue. In 1898, the twelve-year-old Bob Coody was living as the ward of the Seminole "fullbloods" Nocosilla Thlocco and his wife Tina. Tarthloga had died sometime earlier, leaving Bob without a mother. Her husband, Dosar Coody, already had two other children with Creek freedwoman Louvina Roberts. After Tarthloga's death, Dosar married Hannah, a Seminole freedwoman and the daughter of Pompey and Hester. It would appear, therefore, that when Dosar Coody chose to marry into the freedman community, relatives or fellow clan members of his late Indian wife adopted his mixed-race minor son into their Seminole family.

Historians Tiya Miles and Claudio Saunt have produced detailed studies of two mixed-race families among the Cherokees and Creeks. Among the Cherokees, Miles suggests, "Race as we understand it now was not the determining factor in a person's tribal identity or tribal membership. Instead, lineage determined belonging. A person who appeared 'Black' and had a Native American mother would have been defined and accepted as Indian."[54] If the Indian parent was female, data drawn from the Seminole and Seminole freedman annuity and Final Rolls and land allotment records support that assertion. However, if the Indian parent was male, mixed-race Indian-maroon offspring in the Seminole Nation appear to have become part of the freedman community. Miles concludes her book-length study of the descendants of Shoe Boots and his African wife, Doll, by suggesting the complexities of identity and status faced by mixed-race Cherokee-blacks:

> The Shoeboots family members seem to have been racially mixed and culturally Cherokee, having lived in Cherokee communities throughout most of their lives. They spoke Cherokee, lived Cherokee, and probably dreamed Cherokee, even as their experience of being racialized as black set them apart, texturing and modifying what being Cherokee meant for them.[55]

Saunt's study of the Indian-white-black Grayson family suggests that race ultimately trumped lineage and kinship, at least among the Creeks. He portrays a family rent asunder by the all-pervasive issue: "[Race] drove a wedge between family members, separating those with African ancestry from those without, and driving the two sides apart until they denied their common origins." The children of the Creek Sinnugee and her Scottish husband, Robert Grierson, married both Indians and Africans, creating a triracial family. As the tragedy unfolded: "[Her] children would disown their offspring, abandon their spouses, and repudiate their siblings. Her descendants would enslave their own relatives, and brothers would go to war against brothers. By the end of the nineteenth century, Sinnugee's grandchildren would deny each other's existence." After statehood, "the color line separated people who were often distantly and sometimes closely related." Saunt concludes, "In black and white Oklahoma, the Graysons lived on opposite sides of the tracks."[56]

Fascinating and important though these studies of mixed-race families might be, more data will be needed to detect trends and patterns within the Five Tribes. We do not know yet, for example, whether there might have been "a groupness to mixedness."[57] Within the Seminole Nation, Indian-freedman unions were rare, producing only a small mixed-race population. Most involved the offspring of a handful of earlier intermarriages. By the 1890s, hardly any freedmen without Indian admixture were marrying Seminoles without African admixture. While mixed-race family members tended to have close ties, the classification of their offspring by the Seminole Nation as either Indian or freedman depended on how the mother was identified. In any case, their numbers were too small to serve as a bridge between the Seminole and maroon communities.

The reasons why the Seminoles were able to incorporate the freedmen into their new nation more successfully than the other Civilized Tribes were multifaceted. They had deep roots within the history of relations between Indians and maroons in the antebellum period and during the Civil War. Intermarriage was only one factor in that complex equation, and five others ultimately proved more important.

First of all, unlike the other Civilized Tribes, the Seminoles had not adopted a capitalist economy in the years prior to the Civil War. No Indian-white elite had arisen to lead the tribe, and there had been no plantations, industries, or commercial enterprises of substance in the Seminole country. Some Seminole slave owners, becoming increasingly aware of the value of their property, had adopted the rhetoric of Indian-white plantocrat neighbors and had engaged in buying and selling blacks. But the tribe's indigenous customs typically had worked to hold such owners in check; most retained their blacks and treated them well.

Seminole slavery had included none of the stereotypes associated with the "Peculiar Institution." Owners had placed few demands on their slaves. The maroons had used Seminole land and kept most of the products of their labor. They had owned arms and horses, had lived apart from the Indians in their own communities headed by maroon leaders, had traveled freely both within and outside the Seminole country, and had maintained a separate and unique culture. Manumission had not been unusual, and some Indian-black marriages had taken place. Both slaves and free maroons had attained positions of importance within the tribe as interpreters and advisers to mikkos and as religious leaders. Then the arrival of Holata Mikko and his followers from Florida had strengthened Seminole-maroon relations just prior to the Civil War. The Seminoles' retention of their Native beliefs and practices had prevented the culture and attitudes of the white South from taking a firm hold, preparing the way for their successfully incorporating the freedmen during Reconstruction.

As a result of their antebellum experience and the events of the Civil War, the Seminoles found themselves particularly well prepared to deal with the challenges of emancipation and Reconstruction. The Loyal Seminole leaders were sympathetic to the freedmen, and incorporating them into the new nation required relatively few adjustments. The Seminoles had no system of institutionalized slavery or black codes to dismantle. Though they had lost assets in slave property, Seminole owners were less concerned with profit than most of their counterparts among the other Civilized Tribes and so felt less resentment. As there was no planta-tion agriculture or industry to support, former Seminole owners lacked incentive to create a freedman labor force to take the place of their slaves. Thus, the Seminoles were removed from the economic pressures that dogged relations between Indians and freedmen in the other Civilized Tribes during Reconstruction. Before the Civil War, the maroons had used land in the Seminole country almost exclusively for their own bene-fit. Now they effectively owned it. Likewise, their move from inter-preters and advisers to Seminole Council members appears to have been accommodated fairly easily.

Second, everybody living in the Seminole Nation was tired of wars and strife and anxious for peace and stability. Nobody, including Confed-erate Seminoles and other former slaveholders, wanted racial conflict after the Civil War. For most of their lives, Seminoles and maroons had suffered through trauma. Alone among the Five Tribes, they had engaged the United States in prolonged wars to oppose Removal. Many had fought in the Second Seminole War; some also had fought in the first and third. Seminole and maroon armed resistance to white encroachment lasted for almost half a century. In the end, most had been uprooted from their homes, removed to a distant territory in the West, and resettled there upon the land of others.

In the Indian Territory, many of the maroons had separated from the Seminoles and taken refuge at Fort Gibson. More problems arose due to dubious or fraudulent slave claims, kidnappings, and an unsympathetic Creek government. Such post-Removal upheavals led to the eventual emigration of the supporters of John Horse and Kowakochi to Mexico. The 1850s continued to be troubled times for both Seminoles and ma-roons. Those who had remained behind acquired their own land, but only by removing farther west, and the maroons continued to live under the threat of sale and kidnap. The last of the Florida immigrants and the returnees from Mexico had arrived just in time to participate in the American Civil War. That conflagration had proven disastrous for both Loyal and Confederate Seminoles and for the maroons. Property losses, intense hardship, dislocation, military casualties, starvation, disease, and death had marked their experience. By the end of the war, many sur-vivors had suffered personal injury or the loss of loved ones. Their homes had been destroyed, their livestock stolen, and the land ravaged. Most had lost everything.

By 1866, all parties within the Seminole Nation united in a wish for peace. Although factionalism continued to play an important role in the political life of the nation, it did not hinder Seminole Reconstruction. The former Loyalists and Confederates both showed a willingness to put the past behind them and embrace the process of building new lives for themselves. Seminole leaders repeated that theme constantly after the Civil War. In December 1874, James Factor observed, "I am safe in saying I and my people are satisfied—we have no trouble; all our Indians are obedient to the law. [It] is my business to report my people peaceable. We make our meat and our bread—we have churches and schools. [We] have tried to live in peace."[58] In May 1885, Heniha Mikko summarized the Seminoles' position: "Our people in the past have seen enough of turmoil and strife and greatly desire peace. We are enlarging our farms, our stock is increasing, our people are more industrious and prosperous."[59] Seminoles had no interest in battling freedmen.

Third, Loyalists led the Seminole Nation during Reconstruction, facilitating the incorporation of the freedmen. John Chupco, who had fought with Holata Mikko during the Third Seminole War and with Sonaki Mikko during the Civil War, became principal chief of the reunited nation after peace was declared.[60] Chupco and his followers, who had fought alongside the maroons in Florida and during the Civil War, supported incorporating the freedmen. The Union faction dominated the Fort Smith Council and 1866 treaty negotiations and oversaw the adoption of the freedmen. Robert Johnson served as Chupco's interpreter and main adviser, and contemporaries noted that the principal chief counted freedmen among his strongest supporters.[61] By the time of Chupco's death in 1881, the freedmen had been incorporated in the nation for fifteen years and were in possession of all the rights of Seminole citizens.

For the first few years of Reconstruction, the former Confederate Seminoles functioned as a separate entity in the south of the nation. Heniha Mikko served as their leader, and they had their own council. The Southern Seminoles were based around present-day Sasakwa, with Middle Creek, some six miles south of Wewoka, serving as the nation's Mason-Dixon Line.[62] Little is known of relations between those former Confederates and freedmen at that time. Initially, they experienced more difficulty than their Northern compatriots in coming to terms with the maroons' new position within the nation, but evidence suggests that

John Chupco. (National Anthropological Archives, Smithsonian Institution)

relations improved somewhat thereafter. The freedmen moved off by themselves and established townships north and west of the Southern Seminole settlements. No reports of interference or conflict circulated. Like the Loyalists, the former Confederate Seminoles appear to have adopted a "live and let live" attitude toward the freedmen.

Heniha Mikko (John Jumper). (National Anthropological Archives, Smithsonian Institution)

Although Heniha Mikko was referred to as "Chief of the Southern band" in the late 1860s and worked with John Chupco on matters of national concern, the U.S. government recognized Chupco as principal chief and it was he who made the executive decisions affecting the course of Seminole-freedman relations. During their reorganization in the early 1870s, the Seminoles reunited under one government, with Chupco as principal chief and Heniha Mikko as second chief. By 1875, however, the Seminole government again had a decidedly Southern slant, with many former Confederates in positions of power. Besides Heniha Mikko, James Factor was a council member and delegate, the superintendent of black-smiths' shops, and the tribal treasurer; Thomas Cloud was the superin-tendent of schools; and John F. Brown was a delegate and the clerk of the council.[63] Heniha Mikko succeeded Chupco in 1881 and continued in office for five years. His son-in-law John F. Brown succeeded him and remained principal chief until 1902, when Hulbutta Mikko, a traditional-ist, defeated him. Upon the death of Hulbutta Mikko three years later, Brown again became principal chief. Thus, former Confederates con-trolled the leadership of the nation for all but three of the twenty-six years between Chupco's demise and statehood, yet they offered no challenge to the position of the freedmen within Seminole society.

By the time the Southern faction returned to power in the Seminole Nation, Reconstruction was a fait accompli. The Seminoles had incor-porated the freedmen, and the former Confederates had to come to terms with it. But the contrasting reactions of the Southern Seminole leadership and the freedmen to the proposed and actual immigration of maroons from West Texas in the 1880s and 1890s points to a continuing racial tension between the two groups. In the summer of 1881, Sergeant David Bowlegs rode out of the Seminole Negro Indian Scouts' settle-ment at Las Moras Creek on the Fort Clark military reservation to visit his kinsmen among the freedmen in the Indian Territory. Liking what he saw, he took a favorable report back to Texas:

> If I had no one but myself and my wife I would rather soldier than do anything else I know of, but I have a large family growing up and we are here where we own nothing, and can get no work. My children will grow up idle and become criminals on this frontier. I have been raised like an Indian, but want to go to my people and settle in a home, and teach my children to work, and most of my people are like me.

By mid-June 1882, fifty-seven of the Texas maroons were prepared to leave.[64]

Learning of that development, Heniha Mikko called a meeting of the Seminole Council and delivered its verdict to Union agent John Tufts on

August 2: "The Council are unanimously opposed to the coming of the said Bowlegs and party. [There] is no foundation in fact for the assertion that the Seminoles here were willing for them to come among them to settle." Those maroons had "voluntarily abandoned their Tribe" many years before and had no just claim to the rights and benefits of Seminole citizenship under the 1866 treaty. Moreover, the group contained individuals of "doubtful identity" and notorious outlaws who were deemed undesirable immigrants.[65] Despite the opposition of Heniha Mikko and the Indian bureau, Bowlegs, his wife Fanny, and their nine children removed independently to the Seminole Nation in December. Relatives welcomed the immigrants, who settled so easily into the isolated freedman community that Seminole and U.S. authorities failed to detect their presence for more than a year.[66]

In May 1883, it was reported that more of the scouts wished to return to the Indian Territory with their families the following spring.[67] The proposal again provoked a negative reaction from Heniha Mikko. On September 17, he explained to Tufts why the Seminoles would not welcome the return of the Texas maroons. Most had been owned by Seminoles, they had chosen freely to leave for Mexico, and they had become citizens of that country. Since they had emigrated before the 1856 and 1866 treaties that had created separate Seminole reservations, they had not been included in their provisions. The emigrants could not claim Seminole citizenship by "blood, tribal organization or treaty" and had no right to land or other benefits in the nation. Heniha Mikko portrayed the immigrant maroons as "turbulent," "lawless," and a threat to the already troubled nation: "To sum it all up, they have no rights here, we have no room for them, and we protest against their being sent here as we have done before."[68]

Despite Heniha Mikko's protestations, in October 1883, another party of twenty-seven maroons removed independently from west Texas to the Seminole Nation. That made a total of thirty-eight who had immigrated without permission in less than a year. This second group included Joseph Bagby (Bagly), his "state-raised" wife, their ten children, and their two sons-in-law, Henry Coleman and Thompson; David Bowlegs's sister Dolly, her state-raised husband, and their nine children; and Polly Marshall and her Creek black husband. The latest arrivals settled among their kinsmen and immediately began to make improvements on the land. Their presence became known to Heniha Mikko only in the late winter, and on March 1, 1884, he demanded that Tufts eject them as intruders. Secretary of the Interior Henry Teller supported that decision. Yet although Tufts ordered them to leave forthwith, the maroon immigrants remained within the freedman communities in the Seminole Nation. Still other returnees from Texas joined them; members of the Bruner and Wilson families resettled in the nation around that time and added to the freedman population.[69]

Although they continued to reside in the Seminole Nation, the immigrants from Texas effectively disappeared within the freedman communities. None was included in Seminole Nation census records for the 1890s, compiled for annuity payments, or indeed in the Final Rolls of the Seminole Nation, drawn up for allotment purposes under the auspices of the Dawes Commission. That would suggest that they never became Seminole citizens or derived any direct benefit from their association with the nation in the way of monetary awards or land ownership. Rather, they seem to have lived upon and worked the land of relatives.[70]

But the immigrants left behind some faint tracks for researchers. On May 16, 1885, Brigadier General David Stanley, in command of the Department of Texas, reported that they had been welcomed into the Seminole Nation and were living there still. And recounting their numbers in February 1888, the maroons at Fort Clark stated that three families were living in the Indian Territory. In 1942, Seminole freedman George Noble recounted that David Bowlegs often told stories of his scouting exploits before he died near Noble Town. Bowlegs's army discharge papers were filed with the Seminole County clerk in Wewoka in 1935. In 1951, Porter reported that the descendants of the immigrants in Seminole County still maintained visiting relations with the Texas and Mexico maroon communities.[71]

The differing reactions to the immigrants from Texas shed light on aspects of relations between Seminoles and maroons at that time. By then, Heniha Mikko was a Baptist minister, with white associates and Indian-white family members. John F. Brown was his son-in-law. Heniha Mikko favored Seminole acculturation. During the antebellum period, he had acquired substantial holdings in slave property and had dealt widely in blacks. He had become a Confederate colonel during the Civil War and had led the Seminole Battalion against Union black troops during military engagements in the Indian Territory. Defeated and exhausted, the Southern Seminole party he headed could only watch as the Loyalists oversaw the incorporation of the freedmen into the nation during Reconstruction. Although he did not contest the rights of the freedmen to Seminole citizenship, Heniha Mikko clearly was no friend to the maroons. He responded to the potential immigrant crisis by giving vent to the racial consciousness of his supporters and opposing the return of the Texas group. By that time, the freedman population already was increasing rapidly, and Heniha Mikko likely feared that blacks would overrun the Seminoles.

The freedmen were the ones who wanted the Texas maroons to return to the Indian Territory. The immigrants were "well received" by freedmen, not Indians. Heniha Mikko stressed that several of their number had been slaves, labeled them "persons of African descent and blood," and referred to them as "these negroes."[72] Apart from Heniha Mikko, an axis of former Confederate sympathizers headed by delegate John F. Brown dominated the Seminole leadership by that time. The acculturated son of an intermarried Scotsman, Brown had led Seminole opposition to the incorporation of the freedmen during the 1866 treaty negotiations. In 1885, he succeeded Heniha Mikko as principal chief and dominated Seminole affairs for the next twenty years. Brown adopted the Heniha Mikko line as his own. He acknowledged the citizenship rights of the freedmen but opposed the efforts of the Texas maroons to return to the nation. Racial tension and mutual suspicion continued to feature in relations between freedmen and the former Confederate Seminole leadership during the postbellum period.

Significantly, the immigrants chose to return during a period when the Choctaw and Chickasaw freedmen, in particular, were experiencing widespread discrimination, segregation, the threat of ejection from those nations, and outright persecution. The Texas maroons clearly perceived the Seminole Nation to be a safe and desirable place to live after the Civil War. But it was the freedman settlements that attracted them. They wished to reestablish relations with their kinsmen, not with Seminoles. The freedmen and Indians continued to see themselves as separate and distinct groups. In fact, the freedman communities were so independent and isolated that they continued to constitute maroon communities in the Indian Territory, with Seminoles being generally unaware of what happened within them. It took an entire year for the Indians to realize that illegal borderlands immigrants had made their homes there. Both the Seminole and the federal authorities then proved powerless to eject them

John F. Brown. (Oklahoma Historical Society)

from the freedman townships. The freedmen, meanwhile, welcomed the immigrants, fought for their right to remain, hid and supported them in their settlements, and risked censure by the Seminole national and federal authorities for doing so. The ties that bound members of the freedman community to their long-departed Texas cousins remained stronger than those linking them to neighboring Seminole Indians.

Yet the Southern Seminole leaders only opposed what they perceived to be illegal freedman immigration. The affair took place at a time when intruders were invading the other Indian nations in massive numbers. The nations' governments had the right to call upon their Indian agents to have such persons expelled, but in reality, enforcing removal orders in the Indian Territory at that time proved next to impossible. White squatters were especially numerous, but freedman intruders also were proving troublesome.[73] Although the Seminoles suffered less than the other Civilized Tribes in that regard, their leaders wished to put a stop to the problem before it escalated. Heniha Mikko argued that there was insufficient arable land for the population already living in the Seminole Nation and that the residents could not afford to make room for the immigrants. The former Confederates never challenged the position or rights of freedmen citizens within the nation. They tacitly agreed to coexist peacefully. Significantly, it was during Brown's administration that the freedmen received land allotments equal in value to those of Indians, with no protest being voiced by the Seminole leadership.

The fourth reason why the Seminoles proved to be the most accommodating in incorporating the freedmen stemmed from their remaining by far the least acculturated of the Five Tribes. Throughout the period from Reconstruction to Oklahoma statehood, Seminole relations with freedmen remained more indigenous and less discriminatory than their more acculturated neighbors'. The Seminoles' political institutions, economic and legal systems, social organization, cultural manifestations, and overall lifestyle continued to be essentially aboriginal. Although it began to adopt elements of the federal system operating among the Cherokees, Choctaws, and Chickasaws, the Seminole Nation remained a fairly loose confederacy of bands, based on the Florida model. There was an incomplete separation of powers within the government, the council serving as both the legislative and judicial branches. Although the Seminoles introduced popular elections, the traditional ruling clans continued to exert considerable political influence, and hereditary mikkos dominated the leadership and the councils. During the late nineteenth century, John F. Brown exploited that and exercised considerable power in his position of governor (principal chief). By 1900, the Seminoles were the only one of the Five Tribes not to have a written constitution or their acts of council published.[74]

The economy also remained undeveloped. Most Seminoles continued to be subsistence farmers, producing small surpluses for trade during good years. With their per capita annuity payments, they purchased necessities they could not produce, plus other items. The great majority lived in log cabins with basic furnishings and owned few personal possessions. There was little large-scale agriculture and few industries or exports. Communications were poor, with only a system of rough trails and loose dirt roads linking the various settlements. Bridges across rivers and creeks were scarce and often washed away during heavy rains. Little money was available, and barter prevailed.[75]

John F. Brown and his brother, Andrew J. Brown, came to dominate Seminole economic life. They owned the only two substantial stores in the nation, at Sasakwa and Wewoka, and established a commercial monopoly. The brothers issued scrip against each citizen's annuity payment, and that came to be the main currency in circulation in the Seminole Nation. Because the Browns gave credit in advance and the scrip was redeemable only at their stores, that kept most Seminole citizens in perpetual debt and stunted economic growth. The Browns pocketed most of the available money in the nation and became quite wealthy, building a financial empire based on commerce, industry, and agriculture that became known throughout the Indian Territory.[76] Most Seminoles, meanwhile, continued to farm their small holdings and live modestly.

The Seminoles created a judiciary and a unit of law enforcement officers but did not produce written laws until the early twentieth century.[77] Their system of justice continued to rely heavily on honor and trust. The Seminoles frequently left convicted criminals unguarded, expecting them of their own accord to appear for a whipping or execution on the day appointed. Incarceration and other less violent forms of punishment rarely, if ever, were employed.

Native practices continued to dominate the Indians' social organization and cultural manifestations. Seminole society remained matrilineal, with both clan and band affiliation being determined through the female line. The clan continued at the center of a Seminole's existence. Few Seminoles were intermarried or of mixed race; only a small percentage could read, write, or speak English; and many continued to wear elements of their traditional dress. Indians and freedmen both practiced polygyny. Only a small percentage of Seminoles accepted Christianity and school education, most preferring their Native religion and teachings. There were few schools or churches in the nation. Square grounds, busk ceremonies, stickball games, and medicine men remained at the heart of Seminole civilization until statehood and beyond. At the turn of the century, contemporary white observers agreed that the Seminoles lagged far behind the other Civilized Tribes in their level of "advancement."

The great majority of Seminoles remained unaffected by white acculturative influences. The main advocates of white civilization and catalysts of change in the other Civilized Tribes—Indian agents, missionaries, educators, intermarried whites and their offspring, traders, and settlers—made no significant impact on the Seminoles during the postbellum period. Littlefield has suggested, "Before the 1890s, the Seminoles had been perhaps the least touched of the five tribes by the importation of American-based social, religious, and economic practices."[78] But there is no perhaps about it. Sattler concludes, "Most aspects of Seminole sociopolitical organization changed relatively little in Indian Territory during the nineteenth century. [Overall] the Seminoles remained a culturally conservative people until after allotment in 1905."[79] Between 1866 and 1874, the Seminoles had their own Indian agent, stationed at Wewoka, but then the agencies of the Five Tribes were consolidated into the Union Agency, with headquarters at Muskogee in the Creek Nation. The postbellum Seminole agents did not exert much influence in their affairs or accelerate the process of acculturation. Henry Breiner, for example, failed to implement a plan for a hospital and a physician.[80] Muskogee was more than one hundred miles away by rough wagon road, and the Union agent was too remote to have a great impact on Seminole affairs.[81] As catalysts of acculturation in the Seminole Nation, Indian agents proved largely ineffective.

Missionaries and educators again met with little success. Reverend Murrow did not return to the Seminole Nation after the Civil War, and the Baptist ministry was left in the hands of Native preachers. Heniha Mikko and James Factor were ordained as ministers, and later John F. Brown and Andrew J. Brown joined them. Those four individuals dominated the leadership of the Seminole Baptist Church from the Civil War to statehood. Except for brief spells when white missionaries were stationed in the nation, Native ministers led the Baptist congregations throughout the period. Consequently, the vehicle with perhaps the strongest potential for accelerating Seminole acculturation stalled. In 1866, there were 150 Seminole Indian Baptists, and two years later that number had grown to 250 members, attending three churches. However, Seminole Baptist membership appears to have peaked at 367 in 1883. Its staunchest support lay with former Confederates or those who already had accepted elements of white culture. The great majority of Seminoles remained unaffected by Baptist influence.[82]

Presbyterianism again offered the main Christian alternative to the Baptist religion in the Seminole Nation. The Presbyterians had the advantage of a resident white minister in Rev. James Ramsay, but ironically, as it had before the Civil War, the denomination continued to attract more traditional Seminoles. Seminole Christianity continued to reflect the factionalism present in the nation's politics and society; former Confederates supported the Baptist religion, and Loyalists Presbyterianism. The Presbyterians experienced some success at first, their membership rising from 66 in 1867 to 110 two years later.[83] In 1870, however, many of the Seminole Presbyterians returned to their former ways by participating in a stickball game near Wewoka. Afterward, many "remained in their heathenish course," and church membership declined from 150 to 30.[84] Ramsay remained in the Seminole Nation until the 1890s, but the Presbyterians never recovered. By 1902, the Seminoles had only one Presbyterian church, under a Native licentiate, with a membership of just fifty-five.[85]

At the time of statehood, around 20 to 25 percent of the Seminole Indian population was Christian, but many of those also continued to practice their Native religion and could not be described as regular churchgoers. As anthropologist Alexander Spoehr observed, "[The] situation may be envisaged as a small nucleus of devout Christians, containing a number of the most influential men of the tribe, surrounded by several hundred followers of varying degrees of faithfulness, while the remainder of the people preferred to follow in the footsteps of their forefathers."[86] The sustained growth of Christianity among the Seminoles would be a post-statehood development.

School education similarly failed to make major inroads among the Seminoles between the end of the Civil War and statehood. Only nine schools were established in the nation during that period: five day schools, two boarding schools, and two academies. Only six ever operated at any one time. Two of the day schools, moreover, were situated in maroon townships and catered to children of Seminole freedmen. The Indian day schools were small scale and poorly attended, generally averaging only twenty students each. The teachers concentrated on teaching English, but they met with little success. In 1876, only ninety-five Seminole Indians could read. Eight years later, it was estimated that among the total Seminole Nation population of 3,000, only 800 citizens could speak English.[87] Of those, 70 to 75 percent were freedmen.

White teachers tended to stay but a short while in the Seminole Nation before moving on. Consequently, they had little opportunity to make a lasting impact on Seminole society. Interestingly, Antoinette Snow Constant, a white day-school teacher, sang the praises of integrated education and taught Indian, freedman, and white children in the same classroom. Ramsay did the same at the Presbyterian boarding school. It could not be argued then that those teachers were attempting to seduce the Seminoles with southern white segregationist racial notions. Significantly, the Seminoles eventually evicted Mrs. Constant from the nation for interfering with their indigenous customs, in particular their punishment for witchcraft.[88] Traditionalism continued to outweigh the Seminoles' hunger for white knowledge.

Throughout the period, the nation supported schools from its annuity payments. Moreover, school education received a considerable boost during Governor Brown's administration with the opening of the Seminole Female Academy, the Mekasukey Academy for boys, and its twin the Emahaka Academy for girls, in the 1880s and early 1890s. But those institutions arrived too late to transform Seminole society before statehood. With the exception of former Confederate sympathizers, most showed little interest in school education. By the turn of the century, the Seminoles had a lower percentage of students and English speakers, a lower level of literacy, and fewer schools per head of population than any of the other Civilized Tribes.

The majority of Seminoles remained opposed to whites intermarrying or settling among them. For many years, Elijah Brown was the only adopted white in the nation.[89] Although he was joined later by intermarried whites such as Alexander Crain,[90] adoption continued to be a rare occurrence throughout the period. Moreover, intermarriage did not automatically confer citizenship in the Seminole Nation. Unless they were adopted formally, intermarried whites enjoyed only the barest rights of residency, were regarded as U.S. citizens, and were not protected by Seminole law.[91]

Because traditionalism and the clan system remained so strong among the Seminoles, most scorned white intermarriage. The few unions that took place typically involved members of the Southern party; James Factor, for example, married a white woman.[92] And the Seminole participants usually were of white descent; John F. Brown's sisters, Lucy and Alice, for instance, took white men for husbands.[93] At the time of allotment, the initial Seminole Indian roll showed 1,256 "fullbloods" and 643 "mixed bloods" and adopted citizens. But those figures are misleading, as the figure for the "mixed bloods" included individuals of mixed Indian descent. The great majority of Seminole "mixed bloods" were "fullblood" Indian, usually a mixture of Seminole and Creek. "Fullbloods" thus composed almost the entire Seminole Indian population. Seminole-blacks actually outnumbered intermarried and adopted whites and Seminole-whites on the Indian rolls, but their combined totals included only around 100 individuals, or less than 5 percent of the Seminole Indian population.[94]

Not only was there a low rate of white adoption and intermarriage among the Seminoles, but also few white residents lived in the nation. Just thirty-one noncitizens were living among the Seminoles in 1876, for example, their number including teachers, missionaries, government employees, and traders.[95] The following year, Union Agency statistics showed just one adopted white citizen in the nation, 35 whites residing on the reservation by permission of the Seminole authorities, and 6 by permission of the U.S. authorities.[96] By 1890, there still were fewer than 100 whites residing in the Seminole Nation, while 48,421 lived among the Chickasaws.[97] The experience of the Seminoles was fundamentally different from that of their neighbors, who were swamped by white settlers. In 1890, it was estimated that the total population of the Five Tribes in the Indian Territory was 180,000, of which 110,000 were whites. The ratio within the combined tribes was approximately 60 percent white to 30 percent Indian and 10 percent freedman.[98] Moreover, many of the Indians had white admixture. Among the Seminoles, however, the ratio was closer to 63 percent "fullblood" Indian, 30 percent freedman, and just 7 percent adopted and intermarried white, Seminole-white, and Seminole-freedman.

There were reasons for that on both sides. The Seminole Nation was not an attractive location for white settlers. The reservation was small, remote, difficult to reach, and dangerous, having a reputation as a hideout for notorious outlaws and desperadoes. It had nothing to compare with the rich bottomlands prevalent within the Cherokee, Choctaw, and Chickasaw nations. Moreover, Seminole citizens already had taken most of the desirable land. Communications were poor. There were no major roads or waterways and few bridges. The Seminole Nation also was distant from supply depots, commercial outlets, and industrial centers. The Seminole economy remained undeveloped. There was little money in circulation, a scarcity of capital for investment, and a poor labor supply. Most Seminoles seemed uninterested in wages or profits. Language constituted a major problem, as most of the inhabitants did not speak English and freedman interpreters were considered a necessity. And schools and churches were few and far between. There was little to recommend the Seminole country to white immigrants. It would take the prospect of cheap or free land, opened up under allotment, and the discovery of oil to tempt them to settle there in large numbers.

Intermarriage was a similarly unattractive proposition, offering few economic or social incentives to prospective white candidates. Cultural differences and the prospect of social ostracism by the majority of the population also presented large obstacles. In contrast, in 1888 it was reported that "a White intermarried man in the Cherokee Nation has all the privileges substantially that a Cherokee has" and "his rights in the Choctaw Nation and Chickasaw Nation are as if he were a native Choctaw or Chickasaw."[99] Those nations had plenty of good land available, excellent communications, links with important commercial centers, and developed, capitalist economies. There was a large freedman labor supply and a pool of capital for investment, and intermarried white and Indian-white leaders sponsored agricultural and commercial enterprises. Those three nations were close to white settlements, and English was spoken widely. Christianity was accepted, and school education was easily available. No surprise then that most white settlers chose the Cherokee, Choctaw, and Chickasaw nations. Few were prepared to live in virtual isolation, outside the pale of American civilization, among the Seminoles. Those who did, typically, were rugged frontier types unlikely to serve as powerful agents of acculturation.

For their part, Seminoles hardly encouraged white settlement. Their previous dealings had left the Indians suspicious of whites' motives and intentions. Whites had engaged them in three wars and forcibly removed them from their Florida homeland. Slave hunters, kidnappers, and fraudulent claimants had tried to rob them of their blacks, and the American Civil War had divided the nation, taken a heavy toll on their numbers, and seen the destruction of their homes and property. Wishing to preserve their customs and traditions, most Seminoles continued to shun what whites had to offer.

The Seminoles' fears were realized when white cattle rustlers from the Pottawatomie country and Oklahoma Territory conducted raids into the nation and made off with their livestock. To prevent further losses, the Seminoles built a barbed-wire fence along the entire western border of the nation, further isolating themselves from white encroachment.[100] Some of the younger Seminoles fell prey to white liquor stores, saloons, and gambling dens that arose along their borders in the 1880s and 1890s, and that led to further resentment within the nation. Mutual suspicion, conflict, and friction characterized relations between Seminoles and their white neighbors during those years. The explosion came in 1898 during the notorious Mont Ballard case, when a white mob burned alive two young Seminoles accused of raping and murdering a white woman in the Pottawatomie country. Racial tension ran high, and for a time there was talk of a fourth Seminole war on the frontier.[101] Although it came to nothing, the affair vividly illustrated the bad feeling and distrust that existed between Seminoles and whites during the postbellum period. As late as 1903, it was noted that Seminoles "wouldn't talk to white settlers."[102] They clearly didn't listen to them either.

White agents of acculturation made little headway in bringing the Seminoles into line with the other Civilized Tribes. Instead, most Seminoles retained their Native customs, institutions, and philosophy. That extended to their views on the freedmen. Seminoles clearly saw maroons as different from themselves. Based on Heniha Emathla's version of the origin and roles of the various races, slave ownership by Seminole mikkos and other tribal members, and the proslavery actions of the Southern party during the Civil War, it emerged that at least some Seminoles considered blacks inferior to themselves. During the 1866 treaty negotiations, former Confederate Seminoles suggested that they had acquired such racist notions from whites. But after the end of the Civil War, they saw no need to discriminate against the freedmen to maintain a work-force or bolster their own status. That helps explain why Seminoles afforded the maroons equality of opportunity and left them to their own devices. The freedmen derived immeasurable benefit from the Seminoles' retention of their indigenous ways.

The fifth and final reason for the successful incorporation of the freedmen into the Seminole Nation lay with the continued pattern of social separation the Indians and maroons had established during the antebellum period. That reduced the potential for racial friction. During Reconstruction and beyond, Indians and maroons lived much as they had before, farming their small acreages in separate townships and keeping themselves to themselves. Seminoles and freedmen did not integrate, instead they left each other to their own devices.

Although the freedmen were incorporated into the nation and given equal rights, they typically were not adopted into Seminole clans or bands. That substantially reduced social relations and the likelihood of intermarriage between Seminoles and maroons. As the two groups lived within a small geographical area, some interaction naturally occurred. Observers made occasional reference to Seminoles and freedmen attending religious meetings and stickball games together.[103] Seminole and freedman sympathizers also allied in support of Creek traditionalist followers of Isparhecher during the Green Peach War.[104] White teachers ran some integrated schools in the Seminole Nation, and both Indian and freedman representatives sat on the tribal councils and served on the lighthorse. But the freedmen who moved most easily within Seminole circles were members of a small elite. Those maroons usually had a long family tradition of close association with Seminoles, spoke Creek, and held positions of power and influence within the nation. Members of that group were far more likely to marry Indians than were most freedmen. Meanwhile, most maroons centered their lives within the freedman townships and interacted with Seminoles only occasionally.

During the period from the end of the Civil War to Oklahoma statehood, the Seminole freedman population rose dramatically while that of the Seminole Indians remained static. From 1870 to 1875, for example, the freedman population increased more than 20 percent, while that of the Seminoles rose less than 2 percent. Between 1870 and 1905, the freedman population increased by more than 150 percent, from 384 to

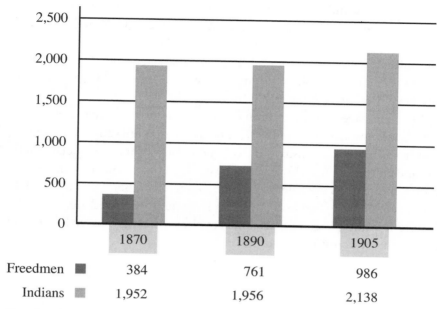

Chart 2. Indian and freedman populations in the Seminole Nation, 1870–1905.

986, while that of the Seminoles rose less than 10 percent, from 1,952 to 2,138 (chart 2). In 1870, freedmen constituted one-sixth of the total population; by 1905 they accounted for almost one-third.[105]

The huge rise in the freedman population was attributable not to miscegenation with Seminoles or other Indians, but to a high birth rate and low death rate within the group and to a large number of unions with Creek freedmen. The immigration of the maroon families from west Texas also bolstered their numbers. After the Civil War, Seminole freedmen produced children at a prolific rate, and their townships came to be composed of large, extended families. Throughout the period, the average freedman household size ranged from 18 to 30 percent higher than that of the Seminoles. In other words, Seminole freedmen were raising many more children than Seminole Indians.[106]

The maroons' resistance to disease also played an important role. During the smallpox epidemic of the late 1890s and early 1900s, the Seminole Indian population was ravaged, but the disease made little headway among the freedmen.[107] The maroons often engaged in unions with Creek freedmen during the period but only occasionally intermarried with Creek Indians. Thus, an infusion of male Creek freedman admixture helped stimulate Seminole freedman population growth. Meanwhile, Seminole Indians only rarely intermarried with Creek freedmen, and only a small number of offspring of such unions were listed during enrollment. Only through a high rate of marriage with Creek Indians were the Seminoles able to counter a low birth rate and high death rate and keep their population stable.[108]

Intermarriage and integration did not account for why the freedmen were accommodated so easily within the Seminole Nation during Reconstruction; instead, history and other complex economic, social, political, and cultural factors should take the credit. There came to be many maroons among the Seminole population, but most of their faces were black, not Black Indian. Far from being one society of mixed heritage, the Seminole Nation became a place where clearly distinguishable Indian and freedman communities peacefully coexisted.

CHAPTER NINE

Language, Society, and Culture

After the Civil War, Seminoles and freedmen, in their customary fashion, chose to settle apart in separate communities. The freedmen established four towns: Thomas Town, on the northern banks of Little River, situated between present-day Sasakwa and Wewoka; Noble Town, just north of Wewoka; Bruner Town, on Salt Creek to the south of Little River, between present-day Konawa and Seminole; and Pompey Town, said to be situated "some 20 miles from [the] Seminole agency," but not given a precise location.[1] Pompey Town probably was near Bruner Town. Unlike the Seminoles, the freedmen named their towns after the most prominent men in the communities: Thomas Joe (also known as Thomas Payne),[2] William Noble, Ben Bruner, and Pompey Payne.

Three major developments took place in the freedman townships between Reconstruction and statehood, and Thomas Town was the only community unaffected. First of all, Pompey Town proved to be a short-lived settlement, and most of its residents apparently moved to Bruner Town in the late 1860s, leaving three freedman communities. Second, in the early 1880s, Caesar Bruner took most of the residents of Bruner Town and moved north of present-day Seminole to establish a fourth freedman settlement at Turkey Creek. Finally, prior to 1890, Scipio, a fifth freedman township, was established. That settlement, located just west of Noble Town, appears to have been named after Scipio Davis. The two communities were situated close together, suggesting that the residents of Scipio formerly had resided in Noble Town. That suggestion is supported by family residence patterns and commonality in band membership at the time of allotment.[3]

The most significant of those developments was the establishment of the Turkey Creek settlement. The Bruners had engaged in stock raising prior to the Civil War and had increased their holdings substantially at Bruner Town during Reconstruction. But cattle rustlers, based across the Seminoles' western border in the Pottawatomie country, caused them to remove north. As Caesar Bruner explained, his followers were "much troubled by parties stealing their stock."[4] Turkey Creek offered a safer environment and plenty of good open country for grazing. The Bruner families established large-scale ranching operations in the northwest corner of the Seminole Nation, and the Turkey Creek settlement assumed a character different from that of the other freedman townships, which were based on farming and crop raising. The Bruner cattle barons also outstripped the Little River and Wewoka Creek farmers in wealth, but that had little effect on the freedmen's sense of community, and relations between the various maroon settlements remained close.

By the time of allotment, the Seminole Nation included five freedman townships. The largest, Thomas Town—or, as it had become more commonly known, Little River—constituted a heavily populated area of around four square miles; the smallest, Bruner Town, included only a few families who had elected not to move north to Turkey Creek with the other residents. In between them in size were the neighboring communities of Noble Town and Scipio and the thriving settlement at Turkey Creek.

In Seminole fashion, the freedmen also divided into bands after the Civil War. Although they initially settled in four towns, they organized into just three bands: the Jim Lane band, the John Brown band, and the Pompey Payne band. The Jim Lane band had 124 members and was dominated by the Bruner families and their associates; the John Brown band had 149 members, including the Nobles and 65 members of the various Bowlegs families; and the Pompey Payne band had 62 members, including Robert Johnson and his family and 29 Paynes. The Pompey Payne band proved to be as short-lived as Pompey Town, its base. By spring 1868, its members had joined the Jim Lane band, leaving just two freedman bands in the Seminole Nation.[5]

The freedmen had named their remaining two bands after the famous abolitionists John Brown and James Lane, suggesting that they identified themselves as emancipated African Americans, not Indians. Lane also had organized the First Kansas Colored Infantry Regiment, in which a number of the maroons had served with valor. There was considerable realignment within the freedman bands in the late 1860s, anticipating the reduction in the number of Indian bands that took place during the reorganization of the Seminole Nation in the early 1870s. When joined by the Pompey Payne band, the Jim Lane band had thirty-seven members more than the John Brown band. In 1868, Holata Mikko's former adviser Ben Bruner was leading the Jim Lane band, and William Noble the John Brown band. By 1870, the band names had changed to those of their new leaders, a trend that would continue into the 1890s, and membership had shifted dramatically from the one to the other. The membership of the Ben Bruner band had been reduced to 110, while that of the William Noble band had grown to 274.[6]

Anthropologist Art Gallaher suggested that, during the realignment, Little River served as a dividing line between the two freedman bands, with maroons residing to the south constituting the Bruner band and those to the north the Noble band.[7] The Noble band thus would have included three freedman townships to the Bruner band's one, accounting for their disproportionate memberships. Freedman band membership patterns at the time of allotment support Gallaher's theory. At the turn of the century, the great majority of freedmen living in Noble Town, Scipio, and Thomas Town were members of the Dosar Barkus band (formerly the William Noble band), while most of the Caesar Bruner band (formerly the Ben Bruner band) lived at either Turkey Creek or Bruner Town (chart 3).

The two freedman bands went through several leadership and name changes between the end of the Civil War and Oklahoma statehood. The Seminole Indian bands also experienced numerous name changes during the period. Ben Bruner remained the leader of his band in 1879. In that year, Caesar Bruner was a council member. Shortly afterward, he removed most of the band to Turkey Creek and likely assumed the leadership at that time. He remained leader of the Caesar Bruner band through allotment. By 1906, Ucum Bruner had replaced his aging father as leader, but the band retained the Caesar Bruner name. William Noble also remained the leader of his band in 1879. By 1890, however, Scipio Davis's son Joe Scipio (enrolled as Joe Davis) was the bandleader. In 1892, Dosar Barkus assumed the leadership and retained it through allotment. Al-

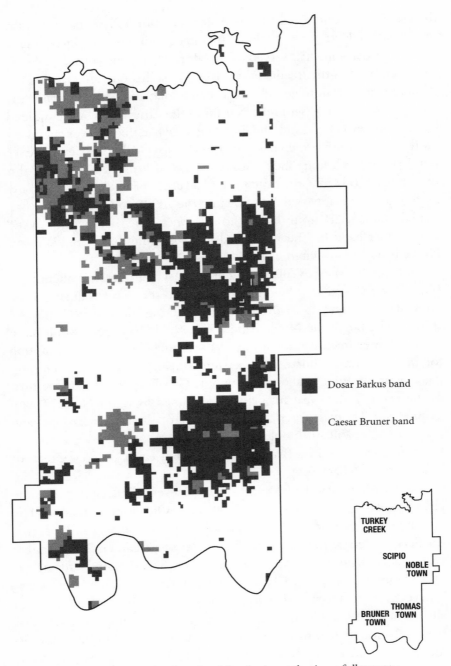

Chart 3. Seminole freedman band distribution at the time of allotment.

though Reynolds Cudjo had succeeded him by 1906, the band kept the Dosar Barkus name and, like the Caesar Bruner band, has done ever since.[8]

Freedmen bandleaders and council members formed part of a small maroon elite that moved easily within Seminole Indian society. The bandleader wielded considerable power at both local and national levels and was expected to possess certain talents and qualities. Consequently, the office fell to the person the group considered to be the outstanding individual in the community. He had to be of good character, honorable, experienced, familiar with the other band members, and physically able. He also needed to speak and understand Creek, as council meetings were conducted in the Seminole language. Freedman bandleaders and their offspring assumed prominent positions within Seminole society, interacted substantially with Indians, and sometimes engaged in intermarriage.

Caesar Bruner furnishes an excellent example of a freedman bandleader. A onetime tribal interpreter and clerk at the Wewoka Trading Company, Bruner became one of the leading freedmen in the Seminole Nation during Reconstruction. He married Seminole freedwoman Nancy Lincoln. The couple had eight children and gave rise to a dynasty that dominated freedman economic, social, and political life. With the profits from his cattle interests and the store and post office he established at Heliswa, three miles south of present-day Seminole, Bruner sent his children to eastern colleges. His son George Washington Bruner and his daughter Louisa became teachers; his son Ucum a bandleader and preacher; and his son Grant a lighthorseman and council member. Caesar Bruner practiced polygyny and had children with several other women. He and Grant both fathered children by women enrolled as Seminoles.[9]

Freedman townships and bands became a prominent feature in the Seminole Nation between the end of the Civil War and Oklahoma statehood. The Seminole freedman town had its own leaders, doctors,[10] preachers, economic arrangements, system of law enforcement, cultural institutions, and social activities. The freedman communities consisted of large, closely knit, extended families living on farms or ranches within a relatively small area around a nucleus of a church, a school, a store, and a cemetery. The residents were self-sufficient, requiring little from outside the town. Typically, they interacted mostly with each other, with Seminole maroons from other settlements, and with neighboring freedmen residing among the other Civilized Tribes, but only occasionally with

Caesar Bruner. Courtesy of Charles Etta Bruner McMillon and "Pompey" Bruner Fixico.

Seminoles, other Indians, or whites. Again, the Seminole freedman towns in the Indian Territory most closely resembled other maroon communities throughout the Americas.

The annuity rolls of the period, which subdivided the population under heads of household, throw additional light on the Seminole freedman family unit. In 1870, the Ben Bruner band included 100 individuals divided into 19 family units headed by that of the bandleader, his wife Rachael, and their 7 children. Two males, Fred Cuffee and Washington Abraham, the latter the son of Florida Alachua maroon leader Abraham, were listed alone. The smallest family units included 3 people; one of those consisted of Robert Johnson, his wife, Lizzie (Elizabeth), and their young son, Coody. The largest unit, headed by Matt Bowlegs, had 10 members and was more typical of the extended freedman family. Listed with Matt Bowlegs were his sister Lydia and her daughters Delilah, Sarah, and Hattie; Lydia's sons Mack and Jake; Delilah's daughter Martha; Matt's nephew Guss; and Gracy, whose relationship to the family was not specified. The William Noble band included 274 individuals divided into 40 units, with 17 people listed alone. The largest of the extended families was headed by Joseph Barkus and consisted of 15 members, including the future bandleader Dosar Barkus. Thomas Payne's family had 14 members, and those of Scipio Davis and Lottsy had 13 each. Many of the maroons' names told of their past: included in the freedman rolls were Gibson Payne and Ransom Tecumseh.[11]

The pattern of large, extended maroon families emerges in all the annuity rolls of the period and in the Final Rolls of the Seminole freedmen. The freedman townships were dominated by a handful of large families, notably the Barkuses, Bowlegses, Bruners, and Davises. Offspring also tended to settle near their parents, producing remarkably tight-knit settlement patterns. For many years, freedman marriages usually involved members of the same town or, if not, then the same band. It was possible to change band affiliation, but few of the freedmen chose to do so. As a result, the freedman townships proved to be demographically very stable. Although Seminole freedman society was becoming more mobile, with Scipio fast advancing on Turkey Creek, the old town and band affiliations remained strong, especially in the Little River, Noble Town, and Scipio settlements.

With few exceptions, maroons never became members of Seminole Indian society. Once again, only a few elite leaders seem to have been included in Indian clans or bands. The maroons' kinship system—based on intragroup marriages, the consanguineal household, and endogamous residential patterns, and not upon the matrilineal clan—differed fundamentally from that of the Seminoles.[12] That led to complex kinship ties linking a series of large extended families within the maroon community. It also led to a sense of ethnic distinctiveness and the growth of group identity.

Some prominent freedman leaders continued to practice polygyny, fathering children by different women they maintained in separate households. Some leading Seminoles also retained this domestic organizational pattern. The practice dated back to pre-Removal times, but it became prominent among the Seminole freedmen in the Indian Territory and Oklahoma after the Civil War. It appears to have peaked during the period 1880–1920, explaining the high incidence of female-headed households on the freedman Final Rolls. During that time, men participating in polygynous unions usually were prominent and wealthy. They included bandleaders, council representatives, lighthorsemen, and leaders in freedman churches.[13] Polygyny also was the prerogative of maroon leaders in Jamaica, French Guiana, Suriname, and Brazil and was reported among the Black Caribs from as early as the late eighteenth century.[14] Among the Seminole maroons, the practice might have had African precedents, but it appears to have developed independently among the Seminole Indians.

Until long after Oklahoma statehood, the maroons' first language remained Afro-Seminole Creole, and the Seminole Indians' native tongues remained Creek and Hitchiti. Although some leading freedman males could converse fluently in Creek and assumed important roles within the Seminole Nation as interpreters, the first languages spoken within the maroon and Seminole communities continued to be completely different.[15] Until the early twentieth century, the freedmen also continued to employ their unique naming system. The father's line remained important. Sattler argues that the maroons' naming practices "showed a distinct patrilineal bias" that was absent in Seminole Indian society.[16] But after the Civil War, freedmen traced their band membership and rights to land through the maternal line, according to Seminole practice. Bateman has suggested that the group could be described best as "bilateral with a certain patrilateral bias."[17]

The threat of being kidnapped or sold into slavery was gone, and now they could keep all the fruits of their labor, but otherwise the daily lives of Seminole freedmen changed little after the Civil War. The great majority lived in log cabins of native timber chinked with clay. Some had a continuous roof, while others utilized clapboards. A rock chimney held together with mud served as the fireplace and stove. A porch usually was attached to the front of the house, and if the cabin belonged to a bandleader or preacher, this often served as a venue for informal meetings. Should a freedman require shelter but lack the tools or timber to build a cabin quickly, he generally lived in a dugout, roofed over with wooden

"Log home of Caesar Bruner near Seminole, Oklahoma." Although abandoned, the band-leader's home at Turkey Creek was still standing in the mid 1950s. (Western History Collections, University of Oklahoma Libraries)

poles and soil. A few are said to have lived in sod houses. Frame houses appeared among the Seminoles by 1880, but because the nation lacked lumber mills, and materials had to be hauled long distances over poor roads, those dwellings were expensive, impractical, and thus rarely built.[18]

The Seminole freedman family owned few household goods or personal possessions, concentrating its resources on agricultural equipment, improvements, seed, and livestock. Consequently, the interiors of their homes tended to be Spartan. Newsom, who as a young boy settled in the Seminole Nation around 1880, described one of the freedman cabins in Bruner Town. Although beautifully situated on a small prairie amid a cluster of trees, the home had only the most basic furnishings and utensils:

> The household goods consisted of two chairs with rope bottoms, a small bench and spring seat. Their bedding consisted of a pile of sage grass in two corners of the hut and two or three well worn quilts for covering. Their cooking utensils consisted of a water

bucket, the old time bake oven, a frying pan, a few tin cups, and some knives and forks without handles. The floor and the yard were used for the table.[19]

Although they fared much better than most freedmen associated with the other Civilized Tribes, the lot of the Seminole maroons was never easy.

Each freedman household owned a cabin and fields. Invariably, the maroons built their homes close to the nearest available water supply, and the freedman townships extended along the banks of rivers or creeks. At first, their cabins were situated fifty to one hundred yards apart, but as the community cultivated more land, those distances widened progressively. Their fields were not contiguous but scattered, single units usually consisting of two to three acres and rarely exceeding five. Because of the uneven quality of the land, the freedmen tended to concentrate their efforts on small, fertile areas of bottomland. A family's fields, therefore, were often a half-mile or more from its cabin. The Bruners proved the exception, as they engaged in range cattle raising and built ranches in more open-prairie, grazing country. Yet the need for water remained, and the Bruner families eventually populated both banks of Turkey Creek. The country was free range for much of the period. Cattle, horses, and sheep were branded, and hogs were pierced through the ears or nostrils. The freedmen erected a stray pen in each of the towns. But after allotment, with its resultant influx of new settlers, most of the maroons built rail fences around their farms and ranches.[20]

The freedman farm was a cooperative family enterprise. Rice and corn were the main crops grown in the fields, but the family also raised some barley, cotton, oats, and wheat. The women planted the rice and worked it with hoes. When the rice came to head, the children scared away the birds. The women then harvested the rice with butchers' knives and thrashed out the seed in a hollow tree stump, using fans to blow away the husk. The children prepared the cottonseed by rolling it in damp ashes. The men then planted the seed in rows by hand and later thinned it with hoes. Only enough cotton was grown to make the family's clothes. The cotton was seeded by hand, spun into thread, then woven into cloth. All of the family members assisted at sowing and harvesting time and helped tend to the livestock and farm animals, which usually consisted of cattle, hogs, horses, and chickens, with perhaps a yoke of oxen, a mule or two, or a few sheep.

The Seminole freedman family was almost completely self-sufficient.

Besides its crops and livestock, the family invariably kept a garden and orchard. It grew beans, peanuts, peas, pumpkins, squash, sweet and Irish potatoes, and turnips in the garden. Family members preserved the harvested turnips and potatoes by burying them in pits underground. They grew apples, apricots, cherries, gooseberries, melons, peaches, and quince in the orchard and dried some of the fruit as preserves. The freedwomen and children also picked wild fruits, herbs, and vegetables. Fish thrived in the many rivers and creeks that threaded through the Seminole Nation. Game also was plentiful during those years, and the men engaged in hunting and fishing. Deer, prairie chickens, quail, rabbits, raccoons, squirrels, and wild turkey all were easily available. The names of Coon Creek and Turkey Creek, which supported two of the freedman towns, derived from the preponderance of wildlife in those areas.[21] As Seminole freedman Dave McIntosh explained later, "There was plenty in the country, plenty. [Now] you could eat meat of a different kind every day, if you wasn't too lazy to get out and kill it."[22]

Although the freedmen grew some small patches of tobacco, they generally purchased it and other luxury items, such as coffee, sugar, wool, and calico, at the nation's stores. Money was scarce, and the family used its annuity payments, together with whatever it could earn by trade or industry, to buy those goods. Men tanned cowhides and buffalo hides for quilts and rugs. Women made the family's clothes by hand, using cotton, hides, wool, and calico. Again, cooperation proved key, with men, for example, tanning squirrel hides for the palms of gloves knitted by women. Women also prepared the food with help from the children. This consisted almost entirely of whatever the family had managed to produce, gather, hunt, or catch. Sofky and other Indian corn dishes remained prevalent in the freedman diet. The corn was soaked in water until soft, then dried, and finally pounded on a rock to produce flour. Freedwomen then prepared sourdough cornbread and blue-corn fry bread. Fresh seasonal fruit and vegetables and either fresh or dried meat were the family's other staples.[23] The diet of the maroons was substantial, varied, and healthy, contributing to their longevity.

The Seminole freedman townships became known for criminal activity, but most crime was committed outside the perpetrator's community. That is best explained by respect for family, neighbors, and friends and fear of discovery and reprisals. Most criminals were convicted of horse stealing; Reynolds Stewart and Stephus Cudjo were two maroons who were whipped for that offense. Wallace Stone and the mixed-race Amos Warrior were other freedmen who received whippings during the period. One old maroon, aged eighty-four, was found guilty of stealing a hog and sentenced to fifty lashes. He died while receiving his punishment. It was said that Seminole Indians took their whippings stoically, making only deep groans, but the pleas and cries of freedman criminals could be heard a mile away. The last freedman to be whipped in the Seminole Nation was Harry Thomas for the attempted rape of Adeline Foster, who later married Ned Cudjo.[24]

The most notorious maroon outlaws of the period were the members of the Bob Dosar gang, who based their operations at Little River. Among his other crimes, Dosar had murdered his brother and was considered extremely dangerous. Caesar Payne, a Seminole freedman lighthorseman, was hired to kill him for a reported fee of $1,000. Payne, a cousin of Dosar's, was able to trick and kill the outlaw, but in doing so he gained many enemies in the Little River community. Soon afterward, Joe Barkus, another of Dosar's relatives, murdered Payne. Barkus was sentenced to the penitentiary at McAlester and served his time. He died shortly after returning to the Seminole Nation.[25]

Individuals who committed crimes in the Seminole Nation against persons who were not Seminole citizens were tried before the federal courts. James Mills, a freedman, appeared before "Hanging Judge" Isaac Parker at Fort Smith and was executed on April 19, 1889, for murdering John Windham, another freedman, in one of the Seminole maroon townships on December 15, 1887.[26] Mills joined other notorious freedman criminals given the death sentence by Parker. Those included members of the mixed-race Creek-freedman Rufus-Buck gang. Parker convicted the gang of robbery, rape, and murder in the Creek Nation. After his execution, the body of one of the outlaws, Buss Luckey Davis, a cousin of Seminole freedwoman Carrie Cyrus, was sent to Wewoka for burial.[27]

The most famous freedman criminal given the death sentence by Parker was Crawford Goldsby, or Cherokee Bill, the son of a former buffalo soldier. Goldsby, of Cherokee and freedman descent, operated out of the Cherokee, Creek, and Seminole nations. He was convicted of robbery and multiple murders and hanged in 1896 at the age of twenty.[28] One maroon murderer did not make it to the scaffold. In May 1880, Charley Bowlegs, a freedman, led a party of four Indians on a horse-stealing raid into the Chickasaw Nation and murdered two white settlers. Hunted down by deputies and realizing the fate that awaited him, Bowlegs committed suicide. Of his fellow criminals, one of the Indians was killed in a quarrel, two escaped from justice, and the fourth, Tulwa Harjo, was captured and convicted of murder but later released.[29]

One particular crime involving Seminole freedmen highlights the strong sense of community inherent in the maroon townships. In the early 1890s, Philip (alias George) Lincoln, Renty Scipio, and Esau Gardiner were convicted of stealing horses in the Chickasaw Nation by the U.S. Court, Eastern District of Texas, in Paris and sentenced to five years' imprisonment in the house of correction in Detroit, Michigan. Lincoln died in prison on June 25, 1896, but still was enrolled as a member of the Dosar Barkus band and allotted land in the Seminole Nation. That was the result of a successful ploy by his bandleaders. Though they knew of Lincoln's death, they said nothing of it to the Dawes Commission so that his "old" and "needy" mother, Eliza, could use or sell the land. The plan proved successful. Not only did his mother inherit the allotment, but also, in 1934, the commissioner of Indian affairs decided that Lincoln's heirs were entitled to his per capita annuity payments.[30] Whenever and however they were able, freedman bandleaders took care of their members.

Some of the most notorious outlaws in the history of the American West rode through the Seminole Nation during those years. They included the James and Younger gang, the Daltons, and Henry and Belle Starr. After robberies, outlaws would divide their loot in the Indian nations. One of the main hideouts was on Big Creek, near Chimney Mountain, nine miles north of Wewoka; another was west of Konawa. A number of outlaws hid out in the maroon townships. They were attracted by the remoteness of the settlements and their lack of contact with the outside world. Just as the freedmen had secreted the David Bowlegs party of immigrants from Texas, so would they, at various times and for rich rewards, hide the Daltons, the Youngers, and Dick Glass.

Dan Marshall, the father of Carrie Cyrus, was a blacksmith in Wewoka. The outlaws would have him put their horses' shoes on backwards to outfox the deputies. A number of outlaws also came to the Marshalls' home for food. They would tie their horses in the woods and await the signal that it was safe to come in. As money was no object, the outlaws sometimes would pay $25 for one meal. Carrie baked bread and cookies for Cole Younger and his gang, while the freedman boys took care of their horses. The outlaws sometimes would pay a dollar for every ear of corn the boys fed to their mounts. Carrie became the sweetheart of Gypsy Bill, a member of the Bob Dosar gang, but she later married Dennis Cyrus, who became one of the leading freedman lighthorsemen and a deputy U.S. marshal.[31]

The notorious Creek freedman murderer Dick Glass also "holed up" among the Seminole maroons in 1885. At one time, Glass appears to have been at the Little River settlement, giving Sasakwa as an address, and at another he seems to have sought refuge with associates at Bruner Town.[32] It also was said that the Dalton gang sometimes hid out with the Caesar Dindy family at Little River.[33]

Because of those clandestine activities, the Seminole maroon townships acquired the reputation of being lawless communities and the dens of outlaws and murderers.[34] Newsom observed that the residents of Bruner Town "were noted, at least a number of them, as being very desperate, they having committed a number of murders and other minor crimes."[35] The Little River community, meanwhile, acquired legendary notoriety. Even lawmen dared not enter the settlement, for fear of their lives. In a 1914 article entitled "Indian Standard Lowered by Seminole Negroes Sent to Oklahoma," E. A. Macmillan referred to "the unenviable reputation [for] criminality [of] that band of outlaws," concluding that it resulted from heredity, the freedmen being descendants of "the cannibalistic clans that infested the west African coast."[36] Macmillan merely was expanding on notions that had circulated in and around the Indian Territory during the late nineteenth century. The freedmen likely relished and embellished the unsavory reputation their settlements acquired. Maroon communities enjoyed isolation, and being seen as dangerous kept uninvited guests away.[37]

The Seminole freedman bandleader was responsible for seeing that life in the township ran smoothly. One of his main functions was to coordinate community action. There is no evidence that the maroons worked communal fields during this period, but rail splitting, road maintenance, church construction, and similar projects were group activities. The freedmen also would have helped each other out when building homes, at harvest time, and in the calving season. Local law enforcement featured occasional community mobilization against criminal activity, as in the raising of posses. The freedmen would have had some kind of alarm when the town came under threat, the men meeting in an agreed-upon place. They had to deal with cattle and horse thieves and murderers in the

1870s, 1880s, and 1890s as they had with slave hunters and kidnappers in the 1840s and 1850s. The bandleader would have arranged and organized most of those activities.

The bandleader acted as a clearinghouse for local problems, either deciding issues himself or referring them to the Seminole Council. He also served as a justice of the peace, enforcing local laws, determining rights of inheritance, and deciding land or property disputes. He was responsible for keeping records of his members and disbursing annuity payments. He also made decisions regarding requests for changes in band affiliation, though those were few. Usually, the bandleader also served as the town's religious leader, preaching, instigating and coordinating social events, and relating news to the populace from the pulpit. In such ways, he came to know each of the families in his band and came to be treated as a trusted adviser. Band members even would seek his advice on personal matters, such as choosing between suitors. At the turn of the century, bandleaders put this knowledge and experience to good use by facilitating the process of enrollment and allotment.[38]

One of the most important institutions to arise in the Seminole maroon townships during Reconstruction was the neighborhood school. Although freedmen were permitted to attend Indian schools, they rarely did. The freedmen preferred to construct schools in their own settlements and send their children there. The freedman neighborhood school would remain the pillar of maroon education in the Seminole Nation throughout the period.

After the Civil War, some of the interest on awards accruing from the Reconstruction treaty of 1866 funded the beginnings of a system of education in the Seminole Nation. In the summer of 1867, two new schoolhouses were built; one for freedmen at Noble Town and the other for Indians at Wewoka.[39] Following agent Reynolds's suggestion, the Presbyterian Home Mission Board provided teachers for the schools, with Rev. James Ramsay initially assuming control at Noble Town and Mary M. Lilley at Wewoka. Although both the freedman and Indian children were beginners, it quickly emerged that the freedman students held an enormous advantage. Much of the curriculum focused on teaching the English language. Seminoles experienced great difficulty with that requirement, "but few knowing even the alphabet, and none speaking English."[40] Because they spoke an English-based Creole, the freedman children fared much better, as Ramsay reported in 1868:

[Nearly] all commenced with the alphabet, but some of these could read well in Wilson's second reader before school closed. Such eagerness to obtain an education as they manifested is rarely seen. Although very destitute of clothing, and the winter very severe, they would not miss a day from school, many of them coming through the snow on bare feet.

The Noble Town school ran for six months and averaged thirty pupils in its first year.[41]

In the summer of 1868, Ramsay took over at the Wewoka school, and Cora Shook, born in Maryland and appointed from Fort Smith, became the teacher at Noble Town.[42] On May 27, 1870, she reported:

The scholars have progressed very well; behaviour generally good. Average attendance per day, 20; more girls than boys. Different studies, First, Second, and Third Readers, geography, arithmetic, spelling and writing. Most of the scholars and people have taken an interest in the school, and some of them have taken a great deal of interest in their studies.[43]

Shook remained at the Noble Town school until 1871, when she was dismissed for incompetence and replaced by Maggie Washburn (Washbourne), a daughter of the Lilleys and the wife of a brother of the former Seminole subagent.[44] That same year, a second freedman school opened at Bruner Town. Agent Breiner furnished around $70 from the school fund to purchase flooring, windows, and rails, and the residents of Bruner Town completed the construction. By 1872, two Indian schools were in operation, as well as the two freedman schools, but Breiner considered the Bruner Town school "the most complete and comfortable schoolhouse in the nation."[45]

In that latter year, J. L. Lilley, a brother of Maggie Washburn's, was the teacher at the Bruner Town school. Lilley also conducted a Sunday school for the local residents that both children and parents attended. Agent Breiner considered that to be "a very important branch of education, for, although many of them profess to be Christians, and no doubt desire to conform to its rules, yet their knowledge of its teachings and requirements is very limited, and so much mixed with superstition and heathenish customs that it would be very difficult to determine whether

they have built upon the rock or the sand."[46] Breiner's statement echoed
Reverend Ramsay's concern in the late 1850s that Robert Johnson was
imparting "heathenish" ideas to the Indians along with his Presbyterian
teachings. Apparently, African and perhaps Indian practices still featured
in the Seminole maroons' version of Christianity.

In his annual report for 1872, Breiner made some important observations on the state of Indian and freedman education in the Seminole
Nation. The neighborhood schools had made commendable progress
during the last session, "especially the colored schools." The Indian children were hampered by not speaking English as their first language or
having teachers who spoke Creek. As the freedmen could "all speak a
jargon English," their children held a great advantage over the Indian
children in acquiring an education. Both of the teachers in the freedman
schools spoke encouragingly of their students' progress, and they hoped
and believed that some would become qualified to assume "useful and
important stations among their people." Breiner believed that the educated freedman children would grow up to become "the principal men
and women of the nation." Their success would be attributable not to "a
superior intellect or greater aptitude to learn than the Indian" but to their
"partial knowledge of English."[47] Breiner's prediction saw at least some
fulfillment in the early twentieth century when the educated Coody
Johnson came to dominate Seminole national affairs during the principal
chieftainship of Hulbutta Mikko, who did not speak English.

Once the freedmen had acquired equal educational opportunity, reports on the Seminole Nation tended not to differentiate between Indian
and freedman schools or students. Consequently, detailed information on
the history of the two freedman neighborhood schools during this period
is lacking. But at least a partial picture can be pieced together from
various sources. In the fall of 1874, Presbyterian missionary David Constant was assigned to the Noble Town school, and he apparently continued to teach there until around 1878. In the spring of 1886, Mrs.
Junkin of Columbus, Ohio, took over the running of the school, and
afterward her husband, Dr. Junkin, assisted her. The two remained at the
school until 1888, when they resigned and returned to Ohio. In 1890,
Louisa Bruner, a Seminole freedwoman, was teaching the Noble Town
school in the church house. The school ran for nine months that year.
The children attended school for part of the day and then returned home
to work in the fields, especially at harvest time. Pupils at the Noble Town

school at that time included Joe Allen, Ned Allen, Harry Cyrus, Dave McIntosh, John Noble, and Whistler Noble. All of the students at the school were freedmen except for two Indians, Robert and Millie, the son and daughter of Este Larney, captain of the Seminole lighthorse.[48]

When the Bruners moved to Turkey Creek, they built there the Mount Zion Baptist Church at a cost of $600. The Seminole Council contributed $200 from the nation's school fund, with the provision that the church be used for educational purposes. Consequently, the Turkey Creek school met in the church through allotment.[49] Five neighborhood schools were operating in the Seminole Nation in 1877, one having recently opened at Wewoka.[50] By 1881, however, just two Indian and two freedman schools were in operation again. The census takers of 1890 reported that four neighborhood schools were running in the Seminole Nation: "Two of these public schools are set apart for the education of negro [sic] children, and have an average attendance of 47 pupils, as against 34 for the Indian schools."[51]

Although freedmen constituted only between one-sixth and one-third of the total population during the period 1866–1907, half of the neighborhood schools in the Seminole Nation were located in their communities. The average daily attendance in the freedman schools also was higher than in the Indian schools. Their speaking an English-based Creole added to their interest in white education and contributed to their success at school. The neighborhood school, in close association with the local church, became an integral part of the Seminole freedman township prior to statehood.

Missionaries made some attempt to integrate education in the Seminole Nation during the period. The most notable effort was the school established by Antoinette Snow Constant at Wewoka. During the summer of 1873, the Constants left their home in Labelle County, Kansas, for a tour of Presbyterian missionary duty in the Seminole Nation. They arrived at the old Oak Ridge Mission near Wewoka in early September. Soon afterward, they opened their first school "in a log cabin near the mission," but it met with little success. The following year, Mrs. Constant opened a school in the basement of the new Presbyterian church in Wewoka, some two miles south of her home at the mission. Each day, she rode to the school by pony or buggy.[52] The school included both Indian and freedman students. Moses Chapone, later enrolled as a Seminole, attended the school. He described it as "a mixed school for the Indians and a few Negro children."[53] That same fall, David Constant became a teacher at the Noble Town school.

The basement in the Presbyterian church was dark and damp, having no stove or fireplace to provide heat and light. Consequently, in the winter of 1875, Mrs. Constant moved the school to the nearby and recently vacated Seminole Agency. The Constants also used the building as their home and base of operations. In one of the rooms, they installed modern desks and chairs, decorated the walls with scripture texts and mottoes, and added a small Mason and Hamlin rosewood organ, the music giving the children great pleasure. In no time, it became "one of the best equipped and attended school-rooms among the Seminoles." At its peak, more than fifty Indian, freedman, and white students enrolled at the school. The age range was broad. Some of the pupils were children, while others were young men and women. Among the Seminole pupils were Anna Nulcup Harjo and Billy, a nephew of John Chupco. The freedman students included Carrie Cyrus, Coody Johnson, Benjamin F. Bruner, and Louisa Bruner, the daughter of freedman bandleader Caesar Bruner.[54]

Because their fathers held prominent positions in the Seminole Nation, Coody Johnson and Louisa Bruner had learned Creek at an early age, and they assumed the role of interpreter in class. Johnson was a young teenager at that time and said to be "bright and always ready to do his part in the school." When Louisa Bruner first entered the school, "she came barefooted, with a kerchief on her head, thinly clad but neat and clean," and knowing "but little of civilized life." Mrs. Constant described her as "a mixed blood, tall, with negro features," adding, "In appearance the Indian predominated, but she claimed the negro race." Bruner had an insatiable thirst for knowledge: "She early accepted Christianity and became a great help in Bible-work and in the class-room in our school. She was the first girl among the Seminoles to learn to play the organ; and with her fine voice became a leader in the school." For several years, Louisa Bruner lived in Mrs. Constant's home, serving as the teacher's interpreter in all her dealings with Seminoles.[55]

Contrary to prevailing white attitudes at that time, Mrs. Constant had some remarkably liberal views on race. She wrote in her journal, "I make no differentiation in my work on account of race or color. They are all bright children. All must be educated and christianized." And later: "There was *ostracism* on the part of many because of the education of the

Antoinette Constant's integrated Presbyterian mission school at the old Seminole Agency in Wewoka, ca. 1880. Mrs. Constant is standing in the rear to the left. Louisa Bruner is sitting at the organ to the right. James Coody Johnson, who would have been about sixteen years old, likely is the tallest youth standing in the rear. (Oklahoma Historical Society)

two races together, 'But God, that made the world, made of one blood, all nations of men.' " Mrs. Constant held firm to her belief that integrated education benefited both the Indian and freedmen children. She later recalled, "The two races, educated together, made greater progress in learning the English language, in school work, and in Bible Study." Including the freedmen "proved to be helpful to the Indians and a blessing to both races."[56] Mrs. Constant corresponded on the subject with Chapman Armstrong, president of the Hampton Normal Institute for the Education of Indians and Freedmen in Hampton, Virginia. The two exchanged notes based on their personal experiences, and their relationship led to some Seminole and freedman students attending the Hampton Institute.[57]

The Wewoka school closed for good on May 30, 1880. Mrs. Constant became involved in a case of alleged witchcraft in the Seminole Nation. The council found an old Indian woman guilty and ordered her to be shot. Only through Mrs. Constant's personal appeal to Union agent Tufts was the woman spared. But that intercession cost the teacher her job. Chupco and the Seminole Council ordered her to leave the nation for interfering with their system of justice.[58]

Before leaving the Seminole Nation, Mrs. Constant urged many of her students to enroll at the Hampton Institute under her mentor, Chapman Armstrong. In her early twenties by that time, Louisa Bruner had expressed a strong interest in becoming a student at Hampton. The women of the Presbyterian Board raised money for her travel expenses, and she enrolled. The journey east itself was an education for the young Seminole freedwoman, who knew little of life outside the Indian Territory. She put the same energy into her studies at Hampton as she had at Wewoka. Armstrong suggested that "among all his five hundred Indian and Colored girls, he could *trust Louisa most.*" She remained at Hampton Institute for more than four years. After her graduation, she wrote to Mrs. Constant, "*The happiest day of my life* was when I stepped upon the rostrum to receive my Diploma in my *simple* calico dress!" Louisa Bruner returned to the Seminole Nation, and by 1890 was running the Noble Town school. She became the first freedwoman teacher in the Seminole Nation.[59]

Benjamin F. Bruner was another of Mrs. Constant's students who made the journey east to Hampton. By that time, Benjamin was in his late twenties, married to Jeanetta Shields, and the father of three children. He separated from his wife and family to further his education. Benjamin returned to the Seminole Nation in 1885 and taught school—presumably at Bruner Town or Turkey Creek—until 1890. In so doing, he became the first citizen of the Seminole Nation to run one of its schools. He married Creek freedwoman Ellen Rentie, and together they had six children. From 1890 to 1905, Benjamin served on the Seminole Council as a representative of the Bruner band. He then moved to Holdenville in the Creek Nation, where his wife and their children owned 640 acres in allotments. Bruner became a wealthy landowner. He built a large home, a school for black sharecroppers in the area, and the Unity Baptist Church, serving on the deacon board for many years. Benjamin F. Bruner died in 1939 at the age of eighty-seven. He was interred in the Turkey Creek community cemetery.[60]

When Mrs. Constant left the Seminole Nation, a number of her Indian and freedman pupils enrolled at the Ramsay mission school in Wewoka. The school had opened in the late fall of 1871 with twelve Seminole boarders and a total enrollment of sixteen. It closed for five years, beginning in 1872, but in fall 1877 it reopened with twelve Indian pupils and the missionaries' children. In the fall of 1879, Maggie Ramsay—the daughter of the missionary and his Seminole wife, Eliza Chupco—became the principal teacher at the school, and the enrollment rose to thirty-three. Soon afterward, however, she was transferred to the Bogotá mission in Colombia, South America. As Maggie Ramsay was about to leave the Seminole Nation, "many were the calls made on her by different individuals, both Indians and Africans expressing their regrets at her departure, and asking God's blessing on her."[61]

Following the influx of Mrs. Constant's former students, the enrollment at the Ramsay mission school rose to sixty-three in 1883. Again, both Indians and freedmen attended the school. Prominent Seminole students included Thomas McGeisey, later to become the superintendent of public schools, and Alice Brown Davis, who during the early twentieth century became the first woman to be elected principal chief of the Seminoles. The leading freedman students at the school were Isaac Bottley, King Cudjo, and Coody Johnson. The Ramsay mission school finally closed in 1894, and both teachers and pupils transferred to Nuyaka in the Creek Nation.[62]

Several freedmen attended the Sasakwa Female Academy, the Emahaka Academy, and the Mekasukey Academy—the other three pillars of school education established in the Seminole Nation prior to Oklahoma statehood. Between 1880 and 1887, the Methodist Episcopal Church, South, ran the Sasakwa Female Academy, but then it turned over control to the Baptists. In January 1888, Baptist missionary William Blake reopened the school and found both Indians and freedmen among its thirty enrollees. Blake later observed, "The laws of the Seminoles extends [sic] the same privileges to the Negro people among them as to the Seminoles, and so we had negro [sic] children from two bands of the Nation."[63] In 1893, the Sasakwa Academy was enlarged into the Emahaka Academy for girls, located nearby. Mary McIntosh, Jeanetta Wisner, and a daughter of Dan Brown were three of the freedman girls who attended the school. A few Indian and freedman boys also attended Emahaka for a while, as Newman Jacobs, John Goat, Ezra (Israel) Dean, and Willie and Jonas Barkus were included among the students.[64]

A few of the freedman boys also attended the male equivalent of Emahaka, the Mekasukey Academy, located five miles northwest of Wewoka, which opened in October 1891. For the Seminole students, the language problem remained. While many of the freedmen could speak "Indian," the Seminoles found English difficult and received demerits if they were caught speaking their native tongue. That might help explain the friction that marred relations between Indian and freedman students. Billy Spencer, a Seminole student at Mekasukey later recalled:

> [We] tried to get along with them as good as we know how to get along, but it seems like there was something there that it never could be solved, which the Indians and the colored people there could never get along. And there was always a fight and it came to where they got to stabbing each other with knives and so on.[65]

Beginning in 1906, Seminole freedman Primus Dean attended Mekasukey for four years. In 1910, however, he and the other freedmen were "Jim-Crowed" out of the academy. Some went to Boley to attend the Creek-Seminole College and Agricultural Institute for freedmen and Indian-blacks founded by John C. Leftwich in 1905.[66] Several were killed in a fire at that school. But most of the freedman Mekasukey Academy students "went back to their localities to go to school,"[67] and "the colored never did go back up there to school any more."[68]

Although missionaries introduced integrated education into the Seminole Nation in 1874 and it continued through Oklahoma statehood, few freedmen other than children of the elite were included. At times it proved successful, Mrs. Constant noting the benefits to both Indians and freedmen. But at others, it triggered racial friction, as witnessed by the knife fights at Mekasukey. The local neighborhood schools in the freedman townships continued to be the main source of education for Seminole maroons until the end of the century and remained so after statehood. With the rapid influx of new settlers into the Seminole Nation and then Seminole County in the early 1900s, the number of neighborhood schools increased to twenty: fifteen for Seminole Indians and whites and five for Seminole freedmen and noncitizen blacks.[69] The process of formally separating the races had begun. The peaceful coexistence that had characterized Seminole-freedmen relations in the Indian Territory became enforced racial segregation in the new state of Oklahoma.

The neighborhood schools in the freedman townships were tied to local churches that also became central to the maroon community. Each of the Seminole freedman settlements built a church after the Civil War.

The Thomases founded the Thomas Town Church in 1867. Ben Warrior, a Thomas descendant, suggested that Seminoles and maroons at first worshipped together at the Spring Creek Baptist Church, but "the freedmans had some trouble with the Indians" and so built their own. Likely, the trouble began because of Seminole Baptist support for the former Confederacy. In 1983, the Thomas Town Church still held a service one Sunday each month. The Middle Creek Church also was founded during Reconstruction, after splitting off from the Thomas Town Church. The residents of Noble Town established a second Spring Creek Church, and the freedmen at Scipio built a church that also remained active in the early 1980s.[70]

Shortly after the Civil War, the Bruners built the Salt Creek Church at Bruner Town. When most of those families moved north, they constructed the Mount Zion Baptist Church at Turkey Creek. The new community hauled the lumber for the building a considerable distance, dug a deep well, established a cemetery, split rails and made fences, and raised outbuildings. Completed in 1896, the Mount Zion Church also served as a neighborhood school, and it remained the focus of community life at Turkey Creek until statehood and beyond.[71]

Little is known of the activities of the Seminole freedman churches during this period. As they were so remote, the maroon townships received only occasional visits from passing missionaries, and reports were few and far between. The freedmen themselves led their churches, with the bandleader usually adopting the role of minister. Caesar Bruner, Ucum Bruner, and William Noble served in that capacity between Reconstruction and statehood. Between 1880 and 1900, the leaders of the Noble Town Church were John Stepney, first deacon; Sauree Boley, deacon; Dick Bruce, Bob Davis, William Noble, July Sango, and Fred Stepney, deacons and leaders; Rina Henderson, first mother; Hagar Syms, second mother; Ann Timon, third mother; Iza Winters, first missionary; and August Bruner, second missionary.[72] The Seminole freedman churches were well organized, with both men and women holding important positions. They also served as pillars of the community. Church was where residents of freedman townships gathered, worshipped, and socialized on a regular basis.

The Seminole freedman churches were based on the Baptist faith, but they differed substantially from traditional Southern Baptist churches. In the absence of white missionaries, maroon ministers leaned heavily on what they had learned from Creek black preachers prior to the Civil War, plus customs and practices that had survived through oral tradition. The Seminole freedmen practiced a syncretistic form of the Baptist religion, featuring Africanisms and elements of Seminole culture, and perhaps including aspects of Presbyterianism. During the summer, the maroons held camp meetings as well as religious services. At those meetings, participants would camp out for about a week and conduct various open-air services and ceremonies. In 1983, the Scipio Church still held an annual camp meeting during the first week of September.[73]

The Seminole freedmen's religion did not conform to white Baptist standards. Bandleaders, who also typically served as preachers, practiced polygyny. The maroons' burial practices also reflected their diverse heritage. Nightlong wakes, with prayer, singing, periods of prolonged wailing and mourning, and food and drink, preceded burial. An "Indian doctor" frequently treated the grave dirt, and the maroons often would bury a deceased male with his worldly possessions. A small "house" sometimes would be built over the grave for protection.[74] Thus, Africanisms and Indianisms permeated the Seminole freedmen's Baptist religion.

After the Civil War, some of the Seminole maroons continued to embrace Presbyterianism. Leading freedman Presbyterians during the period included Caesar Bowlegs and the Johnson family. Presbyterians also taught in the neighborhood schools and conducted Sunday school in the freedman townships. The Methodists were not active among the maroons for most of the period, and it was not until 1898 that Seminole freedwoman Viola Chandler established a Methodist church and Sunday school for freedmen in Wewoka.[75]

Most of the Seminole freedmen remained Baptist. In 1883, there were reported to be 125 freedman Baptists in the Seminole Nation, and four years later there were eight Baptist church buildings among the Indians and maroons. In 1888, twenty black Baptist churches, with twenty ordained ministers and 1,261 members, were reported in the Seminole and Creek nations.[76] And in March 1896, Murrow wrote, "There are now four Indian, and two or three negro churches, with about four hundred members, among the Seminoles."[77] But Murrow underestimated. By that time, the Seminole freedmen had built five Baptist church buildings in their townships, and most of their population of 850 likely were members. Although only a minority of Seminoles accepted Christianity, most of the freedmen became Baptist. Yet the form of the religion that they practiced was a unique cultural manifestation, restricted solely to the maroon communities.

The freedmen also observed several holidays that were not recognized by Seminoles. They celebrated the Fourth of August, the forerunner of the Emancipation Proclamation and considered by the group to be of great importance. The holiday typically featured a large gathering and picnic, followed by dancing that continued through the night. The maroons also continued to celebrate Christmas—or Big Sunday, as they called it—and Easter. All-night prayer meetings preceded the main celebrations, which again consisted of feasting and dancing.[78] Those freedmen celebrations and Christian ceremonies meant nothing to most Seminoles. The language, society, and culture of the Indian towns, populated mostly by traditionalists practicing Native customs, contrasted sharply with those of the maroon communities.

Some freedmen and Seminoles traded quite extensively with each other. The two also interacted substantially at times and for specific purposes. For example, joint Indian and freedman posses sometimes would chase and apprehend dangerous criminals who had entered the nation.[79] But social interaction between maroons and Seminoles in general appears to have been minimal. Much has been made of freedmen joining Seminole clans and participating in stomp dances at Indian square grounds. That this occasionally happened is undeniable, but such participation was unusual. Proponents of the myth of massive Seminole-maroon intermarriage have made the exception the rule. Anxious to maintain Indian connections during a period of rapid decline in status after statehood, some freedmen also exaggerated the extent of their interactions with Seminoles. Most socialized primarily with other freedmen, and only occasionally with Indians or whites. The Indians and freedmen respected each other's independence and group integrity, their separation kept conflict to a minimum, and the period came to be characterized by both parties' willingness to abide by the status quo.

For forty years after emancipation, Seminole freedmen enjoyed rights and privileges equal to those of Indians—rights and privileges unknown to most African American populations at that time. Yet most freedmen did not participate in Seminole indigenous practices, and the maroons' language, society, and culture remained alien to the Indians. The Seminoles incorporated the freedmen into the nation—the entity created after the Civil War to govern Seminole and maroon citizens and deal with the

United States; they never adopted them, as a group, into their indigenous tribe. The tribe was where the Seminole clans and bands resided, and most freedmen were excluded from those. That distinction would emerge dramatically after enrollment and allotment. Throughout the century following Oklahoma statehood, differing interpretations of what had been agreed to in 1866, and what had taken place since, dominated relations between Seminoles, freedmen, and agencies of the U.S. government.

CHAPTER TEN

Relations with Seminoles
in Oklahoma

At no time was the contrast between the Seminoles and the other Civilized Tribes more marked than during enrollment and allotment at the turn of the century. The Cherokees, Creeks, Choctaws, and Chickasaws attempted either to reduce their freedmen's landholdings to a disproportionate forty acres or to exclude them from the allotment process altogether. The Seminoles, meanwhile, quietly agreed to share their land with the freedmen on an equal basis.

The Seminoles were the first of the Five Tribes to come to an agreement with the Dawes Commission, and the first to complete the process of allotment. They raised no protest against the rights of the freedmen as a group, and there were very few individual contests over allotments or rights to citizenship. The process of parceling the Seminole Nation into individual pockets of land owned by Indians and maroons went through quickly and smoothly, whereas the Cherokees, for example, faced a mountain of contests regarding freedman citizenship. Again, the way was much clearer for the Seminoles than the other Civilized Tribes. The freedmen had been citizens of the nation for more than thirty years, and at no time had the Indians contested their right to own land.

The opening of the Oklahoma Territory in 1889 signaled the beginning of concerted efforts to make the remaining Indian Territory available for settlement through the dissolution of tribal lands. In the early 1890s, the U.S. government appointed the Dawes Commission to enroll the members of the Five Tribes prior to allotting their lands in severalty. The intention was to free up large land surpluses for sale to white immigrants. The Dawes Commission arrived in the Indian Territory in January 1894 and opened negotiations with each of the Indian nations. After initially rejecting the commission's proposals, the Seminoles signed an agreement on December 16, 1897, that became the basis for their enrollment and allotment process. Although the Chickasaws, Choctaws, and Creeks also came to terms early with the Dawes Commission, the Seminoles were the only nation to ratify their agreement. The Curtis Act of June 1898 signaled the beginning of that process for the other Civilized Tribes, but by then, the Seminoles were ready to commence enrollment.[1]

The Seminole agreement stipulated that land "shall be divided among the members of the tribe so that each shall have an equal share thereof in value." It included no discretionary clauses regarding the rights of the freedmen. Maroons were to receive acreages equal in value to those of Indians. The commission would divide the land into classes arbitrarily with a fixed value placed on each. Each member of the nation could select an allotment that would include his or her improvements, and each would have an equal share "so far as may be, the fertility of the soil and location considered." Allotments would be of different size, according to quality, but equal in monetary value. For their own protection, each Seminole and freedman allottee would select a forty-acre homestead that would remain inalienable and non-taxable in perpetuity.[2] The commission's intent was eventually to free the surplus lands of individual allottees for sale and thereby facilitate settlement of the area by whites. In that regard, it would prove most successful.

Enrollment ran very smoothly in the Seminole Nation. The commissioners used the 1897 annuity roll to determine citizenship, and the bandleaders provided additional information on questionable applicants, recent births and deaths, and other issues. The Dawes Commission encountered few problems. There were comparatively few Seminoles and freedmen to enroll, their government was free of corruption, applicants filed few fraudulent claims, and there was relatively little land to allot, the nation being only sixteen miles wide and forty long at its furthest points. The main challenges were that most Seminoles did not speak English, and there were few established surnames among the Indians.[3] But one can imagine the problems the white commissioners faced in attempting to enroll a complex population composed of American Indians and maroons, with each employing its own language, social organization, and naming practices.

Intermarriage did not automatically confer Seminole citizenship, and there were few intruders, so the Dawes Commission avoided two of the problem groups encountered within the other Civilized Tribes. Because the freedmen enjoyed equal landholding rights in the nation, the commissioners treated them the same as Indian citizens but enrolled the group separately. Neither the Seminole agreement of 1897 nor the Curtis Act of 1898 called for separate rolls of Indians and freedmen. While the latter act required separate rolls for the freedmen of the other Civilized Tribes, it adhered to the myth of massive intermarriage by specifying only one for the "Seminoles, Indians and Freedmen." But the commissioners soon found it expedient to create two Seminole rolls, one for Indians "by blood" and one for freedmen. Creating separate rolls recognized the social organization that existed within the nation and likely reflected the wishes of the delegates and bandleaders who assisted the commission with its work.

The Dawes Commission quickly completed the main enrollment in the Seminole Nation. It took less than two months, beginning in July and ending in August 1898, and the rolls were closed on December 31, 1899. There were few citizenship contests.[4]

The commission rejected five applicants for enrollment on the grounds of nonresidence. Of those, four—Henry Bowlegs, Jim Brown, Ed Stewart, and Dickey Wiley—were freedmen. Their histories make fascinating reading. Seminole freedman Dickey Wiley had left the nation in 1873 and last had been seen driving an oxcart to Fort Arbuckle in the company of white men.[5] As a young boy, Jim Brown was "sent off" by his father, John Brown. around 1880. Jim "went west and was with the wild Injuns somewhere." When his sister Charlotte Davis last heard from him in July 1898, "He was at Fort Sill, married to a tribe woman."[6] Ed Stewart, a Civil War veteran, had moved to Fort Smith around 1895, leaving behind a wife and at least five children in the Seminole Nation. At first, he returned periodically and spoke of building a home, but later he became a porter in a store at Fort Smith and married again. He then wrote to his wife in the Seminole Nation, telling her that "if she wanted to marry again to go ahead and marry."[7]

Henry Bowlegs was the son of John Bowlegs, a former slave of Holata Mikko and Eliza Bowlegs. In 1862, John had fled to Kansas with his wife,

Bess, and their family. Bess had died at Fort Scott, and John had remained there with the children. He visited the Seminole Nation occasionally, but did not return to settle there until 1891. Henry remained behind in Kansas City with his nephews and cousins. By 1900, aged about twenty-seven, he was reported to be "living in the States somewhere . . . St. Louis or Chicago, Kansas City, some place in there. He travels all the time." When his father last heard from him in 1898, Henry Bowlegs "was in Nebraska, just from one town into another, travels all de time with the minstrels."[8]

Two of the other Seminole citizenship cases involved a freedman and a freedwoman. Sam Mahardy, an Indian–black, filed the first. Sam's father, Wyatt McHardy, although described as a "living Chickasaw Freedman," was enrolled as a Chickasaw "by blood." That came about because McHardy's mother was at least part Chickasaw Indian on her maternal side, while his father was a Chickasaw freedman. Sam's mother, Betsy Mahardy, was a Seminole freedwoman, and following the system of matrilineal descent, he was enrolled as a Seminole freedman.

Sam lived in the Chickasaw Nation, and Chickasaws recognized him as a freedman. He married into the Chickasaw freedman community, as did his brother, Lyman Mahardy. Sam contested his enrollment as a Seminole freedman and wished to enroll as a Chickasaw "by blood." Under the terms of the Curtis Act, when applicants claimed dual citizenship, the two nations involved had the right to determine the case. If they could not agree, the claimant had the right to choose. The Chickasaws contested Mahardy's claim, and it emerged that he always had been recognized as a Seminole citizen, drawing annuity payments as a member of the Caesar Bruner band. Because the Seminoles did not contest the claim, Mahardy was enrolled as a Seminole freedman.

But the matter did not end there. Mahardy insisted that he was a Chickasaw "by blood" and appeared before the Dawes Commission on at least three occasions to try to effect a transfer. On June 28, 1902, the commission arbitrarily allotted him a homestead and surplus, and on November 19 it turned down his appeal for a transfer. In December, Mahardy appealed directly to the secretary of the interior, but without success. When allotment restrictions on freedmen were lifted in 1908, he leased, mortgaged, and disposed of his lands in the Seminole Nation. In 1911, however, he again sought further investigation of the case. As late as 1928, Mahardy still was seeking to be recognized as a Chickasaw. On

April 24, he wrote to the secretary of the interior requesting further investigation, but again nothing came of it.[9]

Sam Mahardy preferred to be considered Chickasaw Indian than Seminole freedman. If his appeal were successful, Mahardy stood to gain a larger allotment and higher-quality land. But other evidence also suggests that people with African and Indian admixture saw advantage in enrolling as citizens "by blood" rather than as freedmen. Jenetta Eleck, for example, the daughter of Creek freedman Phillip Eleck and the mixed-race Seminole-maroon Rinah Eleck (née Noble), originally appeared on both the Creek freedman and Seminole Indian rolls. But "both parents expressed a desire that if it was found Jenetta had rights in both Nations, she should be enrolled as a Seminole and given rights as such." Jenetta and her brother and sister subsequently appeared on the Seminole Indian rolls.[10] African Americans typically attach status to Indian heritage. That was always true for the Seminole freedmen, and it is still true in the early twenty-first century. In the waning days of the old Seminole Nation, and with the prospect of Jim Crow Oklahoma rapidly approaching, when offered a choice of classification, people of African and Native American extraction typically preferred Indian to black.

The other freedman citizenship case involved Eliza Lottie, a Seminole freedwoman. Lottie's mother and father had been slaves of Holata Mikko. In the Indian Territory, her parents had been "run off by slave drivers" when she was about ten or eleven years old. Eliza and her sister had been sold to a slave dealer and had tried to run away to Mexico but had been overtaken by Heniha Mikko's men and brought back to the Indian Territory. Heniha Mikko then had sold the sisters to a slave trader from Missouri. After the Civil War, Eliza married and moved to Kansas. She lived there until 1891, when she returned to the Seminole Nation with John Bowlegs. One of her brothers and a sister were enrolled but because she had not become a citizen of the Seminole Nation in 1866 and had not returned until twenty-five years later, Eliza Lottie was classified as a "Missouri freedman" and her application for enrollment was denied.[11]

By an act of March 3, 1905, Congress authorized the enrollment of children born to Seminoles and freedmen between the time the rolls first were made and the day following the act.[12] As a result, the Dawes Commission completed two more rolls, the Newborn Seminole roll and the Newborn freedman roll, adding 248 Seminole and 129 freedman children to the roster of Seminole citizens. Those figures maintained the trend toward a one-freedman-to-two-Indians ratio in the Seminole Nation at that time.

The commissioners rejected a number of applicants for enrollment as Newborn freedmen because they were born too late. Those included Florence Cudjo, Josephine Cudjo, Sam Dindy, Osceola Glass, John Willis Moore, Angeline Payne, and Luther Whitfield. For some, the deadline came only just too early. Both Luther Whitfield and Sam Dindy were born on March 4, but because they were not born prior to that date, they were not entitled to enroll. Dindy, in fact, was born around 6:00 a.m., missing out on forty acres of land and a share in Seminole annuity payments and other monies by just a few hours.[13] The Final Rolls of the Seminole Nation included 1,890 Seminoles "by blood," 248 Newborn Seminoles, 857 freedmen, and 129 Newborn freedmen, for a grand total of 3,124 citizens.[14]

The appraisal and allotment of lands in the Seminole Nation proceeded as quickly and smoothly as enrollment. The appraisal began on April 15, 1899, and took only seven months to complete. The commission assigned arbitrary values of $5 per acre for first-class land, $2.50 per acre for second-class land, and $1.25 per acre for third-class land. The vast majority of acreage in the Seminole Nation was classified as second-class land. The Seminoles and freedmen were in possession of more than 365,850 acres valued at close to $860,000. By 1902, all of the original Seminole and freedmen enrollees had received their allotments.[15]

Each Seminole Indian and freedman citizen received an average of 120 acres, with 40 acres designated as a nontaxable and inalienable homestead. The few problems that arose mostly involved enrollees filing for the same acreage or owning improvements on another's allotment.[16] The commission resolved those quickly, and by June 30, 1902, no Seminole or freedman allotment contests were pending or on appeal.[17] In 1903, the U.S. inspector for Indian Territory reported that initial enrollment and allotment had been completed and that "matters in general in this nation [are] progressing satisfactorily."[18] Insufficient land remained to grant the Newborn Seminoles and Newborn freedmen their full quota. To prevent the charge of unfairness, the commission apportioned each of those children a 40-acre tract by drawing their names randomly.[19] With that, the Dawes Commission completed the allotment of the nation, communal landholding became a thing of the past, and Seminole Indians and maroons became individual landowners. Equally quickly, it seemed, many freedmen became dispossessed sharecroppers working the land of others.

Three key features that had characterized relations between freedmen and Seminoles after the Civil War—a low rate of intermarriage, their geographic and social separation, and the alliance of freedmen and unacculturated Seminole leaders—all emerged in dramatic fashion at the time of enrollment and allotment. The Seminole Indian and freedman census cards strongly indicate that little intermarriage between the two groups had taken place during the postbellum period. The records of the Dawes Commission also clearly document the existence of separate maroon communities within the Seminole Nation at that time. The maroons took their allotments in and around the freedman townships, illustrating both their then current and planned future settlement patterns. The third development emerged in the early 1900s, when enrollment and allotment were virtually complete. Reacting against the dissolution of the nation and an increase in white influence and activity, freedmen and unacculturated Seminoles revived their historic alliance. This time, it manifested in their joint participation in the Crazy Snake Rebellion, and the rise to prominence of the talented freedman leader Coody Johnson.

There appears to have been considerable support for the Creek Chitto Harjo (Crazy Snake) among unacculturated Seminoles, freedmen, and Indian-blacks. Chitto Harjo, a former supporter of the traditionalist Isparhecher during the Green Peach War, attempted to turn back the hands of time by calling a halt to white acculturative influences and the allotment process and returning to Native values. For a decade, 1899–1909, his followers instigated a separatist movement among the Creeks and Seminoles, punctuated by violent outbursts. They hoped to create a new nation with a traditional constitution. The movement relied heavily on the hopes and dreams of nostalgic traditionalists and freedmen wishing to return to a mythical past, and it rapidly became a vehicle for the disillusioned and dispossessed.

Many of the "Snakes" had been cheated or robbed of their allotments. Others sold all they had and gave the proceeds to the new prophet. By 1909, Chitto Harjo's followers had camped out in shantytowns at the Hickory stomp grounds, the capital of their new nation. Most were poor and hungry. By that time, Chitto Harjo's freedman supporters outnumbered the Indians, and the latter appear to have become disillusioned with the movement and scattered. The freedman settlement attracted criminal elements and soon acquired notoriety with law enforcement officers. Some of the residents took to stealing from local farms and ranches to feed their starving families, leading to an outbreak of violence. Freedman Snakes stole some barbecued bacon, and officers were dispatched to arrest the guilty parties. A fight broke out, and in what became known as the Smoked Meat Rebellion, several from both sides were killed. Chitto Harjo fled with his right-hand man, Charles Coker, a freedman, but whether he was killed or managed to escape across the Canadian River remains unclear. What is clear is that his disappearance or demise resulted in the end of the Crazy Snake movement.[20]

The dramatic rise to power of Coody Johnson was the second man- ifestation of the reinvigorated alliance between freedmen and unaccultu- rated Seminoles. Born at Fort Gibson in 1864, Coody had learned the Creek language as a young boy from his father, Robert Johnson. By the age of fourteen, he was an interpreter at Mrs. Constant's school in We- woka. After that, he attended the Ramsay mission school, where he was noted as being a bright student.[21] Coody then traveled east to attend Lincoln Academy in Chester, Pennsylvania. After that, he returned west and served as an interpreter for two years at "Hanging Judge" Parker's federal court at Fort Smith. While there, he read law and was admitted to the bar. He became an excellent trial attorney, and it was reported that "no Indian that Coody defended was ever convicted." Through his Creek freedman mother, Elizabeth, he became a member of Arkansas Colored Town and represented that community in the Creek House of Warriors. Because of his intelligence, and his legal and language skills, his influence and reputation grew rapidly: "When Coody announced that he was going to speak on some policy or problem of government, [the] full blood Creeks from all over the nation gathered in to hear his speech." John F. Brown, himself fluent in Creek, described Coody Johnson as "the finest interpreter of the Creek language or Seminole language that has ever lived."[22] By the turn of the century, whites, Indians, and freedmen alike already considered Johnson a powerful figure within the Creek and Seminole nations.

Although he was a Creek freedman and held considerable political power in the Creek legislature, Coody Johnson succeeded his father as the leading freedman in the Seminole Nation and established his law office in Wewoka. In 1902, Hulbutta Mikko defeated John F. Brown in

James Coody Johnson *(left)* with Hulbutta Mikko *(seated)* and Okchar Harjo, ca. 1903. Johnson literally became the principal chief's right-hand man. (Oklahoma Historical Society)

the Seminole election for principal chief. Hulbutta Mikko could not speak English and lacked the administrative skills and experience required to deal with the complex challenges of enrollment, allotment, and the dissolution of the Seminole Nation. According to C. Guy Cutlip, a prominent white resident of Wewoka at that time, Hulbutta Mikko's first executive decision was to appoint a personal secretary "with full powers to transact all business and sign the Chief's name, and this power and authority was delegated to Coody Johnson by the Council and by the Chief, and Coody, in fact, became the Chief."[23]

The "intelligent and shrewd" freedman secretary came to dominate Seminole national affairs for three full years. Johnson interpreted to the chief, traveled to Washington on his behalf, attached his own signature to official documents, and concluded most aspects of important Seminole Nation business.[24] During February and March 1905, Hulbutta Mikko traveled to Mexico with a Seminole delegation to investigate the possibility of reclaiming Kowakochi's land grant at Nacimiento, Coahuila. While Hulbutta Mikko was away, Johnson, in effect, was left in sole control. During one of the most crucial phases in their history, the Seminoles placed their national affairs in the hands of a freedman. Just as Mikkoanapa had Abraham; Kowakochi, John Horse; Holata Mikko, Ben Bruner; and John Chupco, Robert Johnson, so Hulbutta Mikko had Coody Johnson. The consistency and continuity inherent in Seminole-maroon relations prior to Oklahoma statehood were truly remarkable.

When Hulbutta Mikko died in 1905, Jacob Harrison succeeded him. Although Harrison enrolled as a "fullblood" Seminole,[25] there is a strong suggestion that he was of Indian and African admixture. F. G. Alex, a Creek, was told that, during the Civil War, "when the Southern soldiers found a negro with the Indians they always took them if possible. The Southern soldiers started to take four children from their mother, the oldest boy Jacob Harrison was taken they thought he was a negro boy. A meeting was called and proved he was Indian."[26] In the early 1870s, the Presbyterian minister John Gillis hired Harrison to interpret his sermon and lessons to the Seminoles, showing that he both understood and spoke English.[27] Dr. Virgil Berry described Harrison, who also had served as captain of the Seminole lighthorse, as "a tall, athletic type, part Indian, part negro, and part white."[28] The South McAlester (Choctaw Nation) Capital referred to him as "a man of negro blood."[29] He gave two of his sons the characteristic freedman names "Sampson" and "Jefferson," and a stepson, Chepon Moses (Moses Chapone), lived with the family. Harrison also fathered children on the Creek freedman roll.[30]

Hulbutta Mikko died on March 24. On May 2, a special session of the Seminole Council impeached Harrison for incompetence, ousted him from office, and appointed John F. Brown to take his place. During Harrison's brief tenure, Coody Johnson kept a firm grip on the affairs of the Seminole Nation.[31] For almost six weeks during the spring of 1905, therefore, the Seminole Nation appears to have been run by a freedman and an Indian-black.

When John F. Brown returned to office, Johnson reverted to his Wewoka-based law practice and represented a great many Indians and freedmen in legal battles against land grafters. He supported the creation of the Indian state of Sequoyah from out of the old nations and attended the ensuing Sequoyah Convention as a freedman delegate. He also became president of the Negro Protective League of Oklahoma and Indian Territory, which fought, unsuccessfully, to prevent Oklahoma from entering the Union as a segregationist state. On March 27, 1907, Johnson presided over a convention of delegates representing 75,000 Oklahoma Territory and Indian Territory freedmen. The convention, which included fifteen Seminole freedman delegates, met to discuss issues arising out of Oklahoma's impending statehood.

Johnson became quite wealthy, owning a number of farms in the Creek and Seminole nations and a 560-acre ranch northeast of Wewoka. He also owned a thriving law practice, a hotel, and other properties in the town. He built the first high school for blacks in Seminole County at Wewoka, and the school bore his name. In his will, Johnson also left provision for the establishment of an industrial training school "to be dedicated and conducted purely for Negro youths" of Oklahoma. He became involved in the Barney Thlocco land claim and reaped considerable financial benefit from his interests in the Black Panther Oil Company during the 1910s and 1920s. Cutlip described Johnson as a great friend of Booker T. Washington, who visited him in Wewoka and at his ranch on several occasions. Through his dealings in the courts, with oil companies, and with prominent black educators and politicians, Coody Johnson attained celebrity and national importance as one of Oklahoma's foremost freedman leaders. He died in February 1927 and was buried in the Johnsons' cemetery, one mile north of Wewoka.[32]

The allotment of the Seminole Nation threw the Indians and freedmen into a strange world they knew little about. Both were ill-equipped to cope with either its complexities or its predators. The U.S. government moved quickly to facilitate the purchase of their lands by white settlers. An April 21, 1904, act of Congress removed restrictions on the surplus lands of all allottees of the Five Tribes (except for minors) who were not of Indian extraction. For citizens "by blood," sales were left to the discretion of the Department of the Interior. Then, on April 26, 1906, a second act removed restrictions from the surplus lands of all allottees, save for "fullbloods," who were not permitted to dispose of their lands for another twenty-five years. Finally, on May 27, 1908, Congress passed an act removing restrictions from all lands, including homesteads, of allottees enrolled as less than one-half "blood" Indian. That act also removed restrictions from the surplus lands of one-half to three-quarter "blood" Indians, but the lands of "fullbloods" remained fully restricted.[33]

In other words, after March 1904, even though they might have had some Indian admixture, Seminole maroons listed on the freedman rolls could sell all but their forty-acre homestead. After May 1908, they were free to dispose of all of their lands. Homesteads of mixed-race Seminole-maroons who were half or more Indian and appeared on the rolls of citizens "by blood" remained restricted, but their surpluses could be sold. And mixed-race Seminole-maroons listed as less than one-half Indian on the rolls of citizens "by blood" could sell everything.

Seminoles and freedmen became easy prey for land sharks and grafters who moved into their former nation. Many were cheated out of their land by fraudulent methods. Others sold all they had, sometimes for a trifle. The Indians and maroons knew nothing of the concepts or laws governing individual land ownership or conveyances and could not comprehend what was happening to them. Although leaders like Coody Johnson attempted to protect the freedmen, the sheer scope of the problem and the guile of the grafters rendered the task impossible. Many lost all of their lands and died in poverty.

In May 1906, Violet Crain, likely of mixed race and a resident of Earlsboro, just west of the old Seminole Nation border, wrote to the secretary of the interior, "explaining as near as possible the condition of things here in the Seminole Nation among the Freedmans and mix-bloods":

> It's a burning shame in the sight of God the way these people are being treated in this land buying business. This Country is made up of a class of cold hearted Land Grabbers who've left all thoughts of fair dealing behind, and are here for no other purpose than to rob and cheat these ignorant people out of their homes, for a few baubles barely enough to cover notary fees and paper which the so-called deeds are written upon. Can nothing be done to stop

this? I appeal to you dear sir in behalf of these people. They are not capable of controlling their own affairs. They are more to be pitied than blamed. They are all uneducated. It is true they've had schools but the faculties were either of a class that was all for the money or they were uneducated themselves. They are no more capable of controlling their affairs than a child.

The "Freedmans and mixbloods" were selling second-class land to grafters for as little as twenty-six cents per acre. A month earlier, Seminole freedman Witty Cudjo had made a similar plea for assistance: "The young men are ignorant and having been beset by temptations are induced to give deeds to the sale of their lands receiving little in return and that quickly wasted. Others are led into making what they believe is advantageous leases and it turns out to be a warranty deed to they land. [The] sales are generally entered into secretly." Yet the U.S. government provided the freedmen no help.[34]

In her classic work *And Still the Waters Run,* Oklahoma historian Angie Debo described in detail the various methods by which grafters cheated Indians and freedmen of the Five Civilized Tribes out of their land. The Seminoles and the Seminole freedmen were among the worst affected. In 1911, cases of alleged fraud in Seminole County were so numerous that Congress made provision for the employment of a special assistant to the attorney general to help with prosecutions.[35] A special report of the Bureau of Indian Commissioners, written in 1917, stated the case bluntly, "[Probate] matters in Seminole County are in a deplorable condition and [the] graft perpetuated around Wewoka has made that particular section of the country notorious above all the notorious graft centers of the Indian portions of Oklahoma." The commissioners concluded, "The Seminole situation is so bad it could scarcely be worse and [radical] measures must be taken at once if anything at all in the way of relief is to be accomplished."[36] But measures were not taken, and the Seminoles and freedmen received no relief.

By an act of Congress of March 3, 1901, all members of the Five Tribes became U.S. citizens in preparation for Oklahoma statehood.[37] Under the terms of the earlier agreement of 1897, moreover, the Seminole national government officially ceased to function on March 4, 1906. Almost overnight, it seemed, the Indians and freedmen went from being

Seminole citizens to U.S. citizens, and from residents of the Seminole Nation, Indian Territory, to residents of Seminole County, Oklahoma. With poor preparation, little education, and scarcely time for reflection, the Seminoles and maroons were thrust into the mainstream of American society.

Racism was fundamental to the founding of the new state of Oklahoma. During the election campaign for delegates to the Constitutional Convention to be held in Guthrie, Oklahoma Territory, commencing in November 1906, race became a major issue. The Democrats subsequently won a landslide victory on a platform featuring support for separate schools, coaches, and depots, and opposition to mixed marriages and the election of blacks to public office. They also favored inserting a Jim Crow provision in the state constitution, and were prevented from including one only by the threat of a presidential veto from Theodore Roosevelt. Instead, on December 5, 1907, the Democrats sponsored the passage of a Jim Crow law during the very first legislative session of the forty-sixth state. The law went into effect on February 16, 1908, and the state legislature subsequently passed other laws prohibiting mixed marriages and segregating public institutions. Finally, in 1910, in a move that graphically illustrated the strength of racism running through southern progressivism, Oklahoma adopted a grandfather clause that, at a stroke, effectively disfranchised the entire freedman population of the Sooner State.[38]

Legislated and discriminated against, the maroons entered a segregated society. They were feared and loathed by many elements within it. While Oklahoma's state constitution classified Indians as white, freedmen were deemed to be Negroes.[39] But the Seminole maroons saw themselves as more than that and different from other African Americans. Most initially tried retreating into their isolated central Oklahoma communities and kept apart from whites and "state-raised" blacks who immigrated to Seminole County. The freedmen were afraid that the presence of black immigrants would jeopardize their status as "Natives" or "Indian Negroes." Nevertheless, they helped the black immigrants by providing them with seed, tools, and teams for plowing and by allowing them to sharecrop on freedman land. During those early years of Oklahoma statehood, the Seminole freedmen would not marry state blacks and even maintained separate sections in their cemeteries for the immigrants. As time went by, however, those social boundaries faded and marriages increased as the freedmen and black immigrants realized they shared much in common as a segregated minority. Nevertheless, both Bateman and anthropologist Olatunde Bayo Lawuyi have reported that in the early to mid-1980s, elderly Seminole freedmen still distinguished between "Natives" and "state-raised" blacks, not always pejoratively, but mostly to distinguish their heritage.[40]

Loss of land led to emigration from the freedman communities. Some of the maroons elected to follow the example of their forbears, who had crossed borders into Florida, Cuba, the Bahamas, and Mexico to remain beyond the reach of oppressors. Between 1908 and 1912, hundreds of disillusioned Seminole and Creek freedmen fled north of the border to Canada with other Oklahoma blacks and established homesteads on the Alberta plains. But they were not welcomed there.[41] Other Seminole freedmen supported Alfred "Chief" Sam's separatist back-to-Africa movement in Oklahoma during 1913–14, and a few sailed with him to the Gold Coast.[42] Still others sought to return to simpler times by supporting dissident reactionary causes, such as the Crazy Snake Rebellion and the short-lived and ill-fated Green Corn Rebellion of 1917.[43]

The oil boom of the 1920s saw freedmen again cheated out of their lands. Cotton tenant farming, on which they depended, also went into decline as farmland gave way to oil derricks. The Ku Klux Klan became active in Seminole County during the 1920s, adding lynching to the freedmen's problems. A steady stream of out-migration, especially of the young, began after World War I, peaked during the exodus of "Okies" in the 1930s, continued during World War II as freedmen sought work in defense industries in California and elsewhere, and eventually resulted in a substantial depopulation of the historic maroon communities. For those who remained behind, Prohibition led to bootlegging in the Little River country and a resultant rise in alcohol-related crimes. The Dust Bowl and the Great Depression only added to their difficulties.[44] In December 1937, it was suggested that members of the Caesar Bruner band were considering rejoining their kinsmen in Coahuila, but this came to nothing.[45]

The patterns of separatism and cultural distinctiveness that had defined Seminole-maroon relations in the Indian Territory continued in Oklahoma during the twentieth century. The freedman community remained centered on the bandleader, the church and its officers, and the cemetery. In 1999, anthropologist Jack Schultz suggested:

At statehood, the once amicable relationship between Seminoles and freedmen were strained, and in many instances relations ceased. The split was evident in the churches as well. At statehood, Seminole churches became strictly Seminole, and freedman churches likewise segregated into black churches. [Today] there is no interaction between freedman and Seminole Baptist churches.[46]

The matrilineal clan also remained at the heart of Seminole Indian civilization, but remained absent among the freedmen.

Maroon children continued to settle near their parents in communities composed of large families closely tied together by endogamous unions and residence patterns. Leading freedmen practiced polygyny until at least 1920. After statehood, polygyny became evermore problematic legally as new inheritance laws went into effect. Within the group, acceptance of polygyny as an alternative to monogamy also declined over time. Freedmen inherited their band membership and in-group identity through the mother. As time passed, their two bands cut across communities and tied the maroons even more closely to one another. The generation born in the 1880s continued to speak Afro-Seminole Creole and engage in African naming practices. Some also retained the ability to converse with Seminoles in Creek. The maroons retained a strong sense of pride in their ancestry, history, traditions, and culture, allowing them to maintain an ethnic group identity that has survived into the twenty-first century. Though a great deal changed for the Seminole freedmen when Oklahoma entered the Union, much remained the same.[47]

Faced with racial prejudice as African Americans in Jim Crow Oklahoma, participation in Seminole affairs assumed added importance for the freedmen. But segregation had separated still further Seminoles from maroons. In March 1930, the Seminole Nation of Oklahoma filed a petition in federal court challenging the right of freedman citizens to its property and funds. The petitioners argued that the 1866 treaty had intended to confer such rights only on Seminoles "by blood," and not on freedmen. They suggested that the treaty distinguished between the right to participate in the Seminole polity as a citizen of the nation, intended for both Indians and freedmen, and the right to participate as a tribal member, intended only for Indians "by blood."[48] In effect, those Seminoles argued that they had incorporated the freedmen into the nation but not into their tribe.

Recognizing the distinction Seminoles make between "nation" and "tribe" is crucial to an understanding of the current conflict between the Indians, the freedmen, and agencies of the U.S. government.[49] Seminoles have made the following argument consistently since the 1930s: The freedmen became citizens of the Seminole Nation, a political and geographical entity the United States created in 1866. They became part of a new Seminole polity, even to the extent of sitting on the council. As citizens of the Seminole Nation, they received rights, benefits, and an equal share in the land. But the Seminoles never included the freedmen, as a group, in their indigenous society. The maroons lived outside of the Seminole cosmos and were excluded from Indian culture. They never were adopted into the "tribe," and they did not become Indian. Only Seminole Indians should be eligible to participate in tribal benefits.

In 1933, in *Seminole Nation v. United States,* the U.S. Court of Claims decided that no such distinction was intended or contained in the 1866 treaty. Nor could the court discover any evidence that the Seminoles had discriminated against freedman citizens prior to enrollment. Such attitudes had appeared only when the question of land allotment arose.[50] The Seminoles later filed at least two more suits against the federal government for lands the Dawes Commission allotted to the maroons, both resulting in the denial of their claims.[51]

Relations continued to deteriorate during the New Deal as Seminoles tried to disfranchise the freedmen and deny them political representation on the council. The Indian Reorganization Act of 1934 and the Oklahoma Indian Welfare Act of 1936 led the Seminoles to seek federal recognition as a tribe. Self-styled "progressive" Indians made freedman exclusion from the proposed Seminole constitution a priority. Indeed, in 1934 the young Seminole attorney Charles Grounds stated that they preferred no tribal government at all to one shared with blacks. Constitutional drafts excluding the freedmen were formulated but not approved. The freedman bands continued to function, but in an unofficial capacity. Although they were unable to agree on articles of incorporation or a constitution, the Seminoles resumed national elections in 1936. Documentation produced at that time provides valuable insights into the nature of Seminole-freedman relations during the mid- to late 1930s.[52]

In response to a 1934 Office of Indian Affairs questionnaire seeking their opinion on tribal reorganization, Seminole leaders replied:

There is much resentment on the part of progressive Seminole Indians because the Department has seen fit to regard the Freedman (former slaves of the Indians) on an equal par and with the same civil and tribal rights as that of the Seminole Indians by blood. In the election of the Chief and in matters pertaining to the Tribe in common the Indians by blood feel they only should have sole jurisdiction. This desire is based on the original treaties and now under State laws. It will be remembered that the Government caused the negroes to attend Indian Government schools with the Indians. This demoralizing system was corrected by the Laws of the State of Oklahoma in prohibiting same.[53]

Those Seminoles argued that segregation in the new state of Oklahoma had saved them from forced integration in schools.

In 1937, anthropologist Charles Wisdom produced an important but unpublished "Report on the Social Condition of the Oklahoma Seminole," designed to inform the implementation of the 1934 and 1936 acts. Wisdom devoted a considerable portion of his report to relations between Seminoles and freedmen at that time. Many Seminoles felt that the freedman population was growing exponentially in relation to their own and that blacks soon would overrun them.[54] That perception had strong historical precedent. Although Indians always had outnumbered maroons in the Seminole Nation, massive freedman population growth had colored Heniha Mikko's and John F. Brown's reaction to the proposed immigration of the Texas maroons in the 1880s and 1890s. The fear that blacks would overwhelm Indians and take over the nation continued to influence the attitude of some Seminoles toward the freedmen to the end of the twentieth century.

Wisdom noted a basic division between younger "progressive" and older "conservative" factions among the Seminoles. Men under forty, literate in English, who supported the Office of Indian Affairs and its programs, constituted the "young progressives." Those Indians had lived in a segregated state all of their lives and were the most opposed to freedman participation in Seminole affairs. Wisdom summarized the complaints they aired to him: "Why doesn't the Government stop treating us like Negroes? We're not Negroes, and we don't want to have anything to do with them. Why doesn't the Government let us organize and carry on our business as Indians?" Other Seminoles told Wisdom that they wanted "an organized tribe of Indians, not a tribe of Indians mixed up with a bunch of niggers. If we take the niggers into our organized tribe we'll just be niggers and nothing else, and we're tired of having the Government treat us like that."[55] The progressive faction had strong representation on the Seminole Council elected in 1936. However, the council also included some older Seminoles who were more favorably inclined toward the freedmen. The progressives referred to that group as "nigger men." One of those older conservatives was George Jones, who was elected principal chief in 1936 and served until 1942.[56]

The Seminole election of 1936 pointed to the divisions that dominated Seminole-freedman relations during the New Deal. During the buildup to the election, the freedmen had been prevented from participating in Seminole housing and construction projects. When it came time to cast their ballots, the freedmen voted as a bloc for Jones, their political ally. Their support proved pivotal to his electoral success. All of the one hundred freedman votes cast went to Jones, while the progressive candidate received only fifty of the sixty-five Seminole ballots cast. The young progressives then protested the election and demanded that the freedmen be barred from voting in the future. Wisdom concluded that, among the freedmen, real interest in Seminole affairs was confined to the older generation, who remembered the days before statehood and were the most anxious to retain their history and an identity apart from other blacks.[57]

The freedmen continued to take an active role in Seminole elections, voting for Indian candidates they felt would represent their interests best. As African Americans, they had been denied the franchise in Oklahoma for many years, so their participation in Seminole political affairs took on even more importance. Their involvement often made the difference in Seminole elections. Largely due to freedman support, and over the opposition of the progressives, for example, Waddy Gibbs was elected as principal chief in 1944. The turnout was low; only seventy voters participated in the election. All thirty-two of the freedman votes were cast for Gibbs, while the Seminole vote was split between Gibbs and the more progressive Ben Walker. Gibbs apparently bused freedman supporters to Wewoka to vote for him. He was a former Snake who also had taken part in the Green Corn Rebellion. The progressives considered him uneducated and backward, and they contested the election. Their biggest com-

George Jones. Detail of a photograph. (Seminole Nation Museum)

plaint stemmed from Gibbs's association with the freedmen. Around that time, apparently discouraged by the progressives, freedmen band representatives also stopped attending Seminole Council meetings.[58]

In 1954, a Seminole suit seeking to recover lands allotted and annuities paid to the freedmen was before the Indian Claims Commission. C. O. Talley, the Bureau of Indian Affairs (BIA) acting area director of the Five Civilized Tribes in Muskogee, invited Seminole representatives to explain to him how they elected their officials. Included in Talley's invitation were representatives of the two freedman bands. Seven of the Seminole representatives, headed by Marcy Cully, opposed the participation of the freedmen in the meeting. They wrote to the commissioner of Indian affairs:

> The negro has no place in our Indian Council because there are no Federal laws specially affecting the Indians that will affect the negroes. [The] undersigned Seminole Indian leaders who were at this meeting do not recognize the Freedman (Negro) as Members of the Tribe or that they have any place in our tribal set up at this time. [There] is now on file in the Indian Court of Claims a suit attempting to recover monies wrongfully paid to the Freedmen by this Government which rightfully belongs to the Seminole Indians.[59]

Those Seminole leaders realized that, by including their representatives, Talley had recognized the two Seminole freedman bands. Acting Commissioner of Indian Affairs W. Barton Greenwood confirmed the Seminoles' fears. Responding to their letter, Greenwood asserted that, based on the provisions of the 1866 treaty, the freedmen had the same right to participate in Seminole affairs as "Seminole citizens by blood."[60] That set a precedent, leading to later struggles between Seminoles and freedmen.

In the mid-1960s, the Seminoles again sought federal recognition in order to conduct business with the U.S. government. In 1964, the twelve Indian and two freedman bands in existence at the time of allotment were called upon to name representatives to a constitutional committee. In various constitutional drafts produced over the next five years, some of the Seminoles again proposed excluding the freedmen. One proposal called for instigating a degree-of-Indian-blood criterion that would eliminate the great majority of freedmen from eligibility. Another sought to create two constitutions, one for Indians and one for freedmen. Interestingly, the maroons showed some interest in that idea. If passed, a separate freedman constitution, in effect, would have created the first black tribe in America and could have allowed the maroons to seek federal recognition as a tribal or indigenous people in their own right.[61] But the proposal went nowhere.

In theory, at least, the U.S. government recognizes Indian nations, such as the Seminoles, as having sovereign status with the authority to determine their own criteria for membership.[62] However, since the U.S. government also had recognized the freedmen as citizens of the Seminole Nation since 1866, the BIA would not sanction Seminole attempts to base tribal membership on blood quantum. The Seminole Constitution finally approved by the commissioner of Indian affairs in 1969 included the freedmen and granted them equal political rights in the Seminole Nation. Article II stated that members consisted of "all Seminole citizens whose names appear on the final rolls of the Seminole Nation of Oklahoma" and their descendants. Moreover, Article IV, which contained a clause requiring one-quarter blood quantum as eligibility to vote in Seminole elections, also included a specific exemption for freedman members. Freedmen subsequently exercised their right to vote in tribal elections, but as Seminoles and the federal government both did not consider them Indian, they were excluded from most other benefits associated with membership. In 1978, responding to a large judgment award, Seminoles again attempted to exclude the freedmen from the political process. This time they tried a constitutional amendment, but it failed to gain approval.[63]

Since the 1930s, Seminoles have attempted on many occasions to prevent the freedmen from participating in the Seminole Nation's political affairs. They also have sought to deprive the freedmen of benefits associated with Seminole citizenship and to obtain recompense for lands and funds the freedmen received as Seminole citizens prior to 1907. The U.S. Congress has denied the freedmen the right to participate in the $16 million settlement the Indian Claims Commission awarded the Seminoles on April 27, 1976, for loss of lands in Florida under the terms of the 1823 Treaty of Moultrie Creek and the 1833 Treaty of Fort Gibson. At times, the freedmen looked likely to be included in the award. On June 20, 1983, for example, Principal Chief James Milam opined, "In my estimation, the Freedmen ought to share [in the judgment fund]. They are in the Constitution; they are members of the Seminole Nation as constituted today. [I] heartily encourage and endorse the Freedman's inclusion."[64] But the freedmen were not included.

In a scene reminiscent of nineteenth-century Seminole delegations, Lance and Lawrence Cudjoe, twin brothers and freedman council members, accompanied Milam to Washington on an official visit at that time. The Cudjoes had historic African names and strong African American profiles, having excelled as student athletes at Langston University and barnstormed with the Harlem Globetrotters before becoming educators and freedman leaders. In an act that bound them to their ancestors and to the history of marronage throughout the Americas, those descendants of Seminole maroons journeyed to the nation's capital to advocate for their people's rights by treaty.[65]

In 1990, after years of wrangling over who should be included, Congress passed the Distribution Act, detailing the disposition of the judgment fund award. The Seminole Nation of Oklahoma would receive 75 percent, and Seminoles and Mikasukis in Florida the remaining 25 percent. The BIA ruled that the freedmen could not participate in those funds because they were not recognized members of the Seminole tribe at the time the land was taken. The Seminoles argued that even if the freedmen were entitled to allotments in the Seminole Nation, they had no right to land lost before they became citizens in 1866. The freedmen countered that they, too, had lost lands in Florida and had as much right to share in the award as Indians. By the early 1990s, the Seminole trust fund emanating from the award had grown, with interest, to some $56 million. The freedmen sued to be included in the award as a group, to no avail.[66]

When the Seminole Nation of Oklahoma received its share, it established its 1991 Usage Plan. The nation paid out a small per capita cash payment but invested most of the funds and established food, health, housing, elderly, and child assistance, as well as education benefits supported by income from the trust.[67] To participate, freedmen must be able to prove descent from an individual listed on the Final Roll of Seminole Indians "by blood," compiled by the Dawes Commission. To add to the freedmen's frustration, because of the matrilineal system of descent operating in the Seminole Nation, the Dawes Commission listed a number of predominantly Indian Seminole-maroons on the freedman rolls and a number of predominantly freedman Seminole-maroons on the Indian

Lance *(top)* and Lawrence Cudjoe
as student athletes at Langston
University. (Langston University
Athletics Hall of Fame)

rolls. Descendants of predominantly Indian Seminole-maroons who appeared on the freedman rolls are excluded from benefits accruing from the award, while descendants of predominantly freedman Seminole-maroons on the Indian rolls are included.

The BIA's long and unfortunate history of interfering in Seminole affairs and in relations between Indians and maroons has continued unabated. The bureau insisted that the Seminoles accept the freedmen as citizens, yet until fall 2003 it also held the position that freedmen were ineligible to receive Certificate of Degree of Indian Blood (CDIB) cards. The BIA issued the cards as proof of descent from individuals listed on the Final Rolls of Seminole Indians "by blood." The Seminole Nation accepted them in lieu of proof of Seminole Indian descent to 1823. The cards entitle their holders to participate in federally funded Seminole programs. In February 1995, around 300 Seminole freedmen descended upon the BIA offices in Wewoka, seeking CDIB cards. They were denied. By not permitting them to hold cards, the BIA prevented the freedmen from receiving federal benefits targeted at Seminoles. In 1996, in a case entitled *Davis v. United States,* Seminole freedwoman Sylvia Davis, a descendant of Scipio Davis, and herself a Dosar Barkus band council member, challenged that administrative determination by bringing suit against the BIA for failing to issue her with a CDIB card. Davis claimed benefits for her son, Donnell E. Davis, deriving from the Seminole Nation's judgment fund.[68]

In January 2000, reportedly as a consequence of the pending Davis suit, the BIA threatened to cease any further payments to Seminoles from the judgment fund. Soon afterward, the Seminoles undertook to deny the freedmen inclusion in the nation. On July 1, the Seminole Nation voted in a referendum to amend its 1969 constitution by including a blood quantum requirement for tribal membership of one-eighth. Most controversially, the exemption from the requirement that had allowed the freedmen to vote in Seminole elections also was removed. Those amendments effectively disqualified freedmen from membership, voting rights, and holding government office in the Seminole Nation, and the Dosar Barkus and Caesar Bruner bands' seats in the council were abolished.[69]

The BIA informed the Seminole Nation that it would not approve the constitutional amendment that excluded the freedmen. Nevertheless, the Seminoles refused to recognize the freedmen as members or allow their bandleaders to sit on the council. When the BIA ceased payment to the

Sylvia Davis and her family (Donnell Davis at right). Photograph courtesy of *Newsday*.

Seminoles in October, they sued in U.S. District Court for the District of Columbia in a case entitled *Seminole Nation of Oklahoma v. Babbitt* (later *Seminole Nation of Oklahoma v. Norton*). The suit asserted that, as a sovereign entity, the Seminole Nation has the right to determine its own membership and that the BIA had no right to challenge its constitutional amendments. The freedmen petitioned to enter the case as intervenor-plaintiffs, but their motion was denied.[70]

It remained unclear whether the Seminoles would enforce the constitutional amendments excluding the freedmen from their general elections. However, it was reported widely that the freedmen were not allowed to vote in the July 2001 election for Seminole principal chief. Then, on September 27, a year after the suit had been filed, the U.S. District Court for the District of Columbia upheld the decision of the BIA not to approve the membership amendment. The BIA immediately attempted to nullify the results of the election and declared the Seminole government invalid. That caused a series of political crises that included efforts by the BIA to wrest control of the government of the Seminole Nation from its opponents. Seminoles saw that as an attack on their sovereignty and sought media attention, prompting the national coverage that began in April

2002. But as Kelly concludes, the strategy backfired: "What the press ultimately saw, however, wasn't federal overreaching, but what appeared to it to be tribal racism and an attempt to subvert the law."[71]

In September 2003, the BIA decided to issue CDIBs to the freedmen, and on October 24 it provided them with access to some federally funded benefits. Approximately two thousand Seminole freedmen became eligible to receive burial assistance, disaster relief, assistance to needy families, and child and adult protective services from the BIA. But the Seminoles continued to deny benefits deriving from nation-administered programs to any who could not trace descent from an individual listed on the Final Rolls of Seminole Indians "by blood." Basing membership on blood quantum, Indians effectively have excluded the freedmen by erecting racial boundaries around the Seminole Nation. Facing a similar situation in the Cherokee Nation, a frustrated Marilyn Vann, president of the Descendants of Freedmen of the Five Civilized Tribes Association, exclaimed: "Is the Cherokee nation a 'race' or a 'nation'? The Federal government does not have government to government relations with 'races' but with 'nations.' "[72]

The Davis suit, meanwhile, made its way through the federal court system until it reached the U.S. Supreme Court. On June 28, 2004, the justices refused to hear the freedmen's appeal of a lower court decision holding that they could not sue without including the Seminole Nation of Oklahoma among the defendants. The Seminole Nation is protected against such suits by sovereign immunity. The attorneys for the Seminole freedmen remained determined to continue the fight in the courts.[73]

It has been suggested that Seminole freedmen use genetic testing to prove Indian descent. In 1984, anthropologist James Howard suggested that likely would be difficult:

> Until quite recently Negroes continued to reside among the Seminoles, acting as interpreters and liaison with whites. There was some intermarriage, but in almost all cases the mixed off-spring became a part of the black communities rather than of the Seminole towns. Blood group frequencies, for example, prove that the modern Florida Seminoles have almost no Negro ancestry, and observations of Oklahoma Seminole phenotypes indicate this to be true for that portion of the tribe as well.[74]

Using genetics to trace ancestry has become more common. Between 1998 and 2000, anthropologists and scientists published findings of studies showing that the African Lemba might be Jewish, that African Americans could identify their ancestral homelands, and that some descendants of the enslaved Sally Hemings could claim Thomas Jefferson as an ancestor.[75] So far, the Seminole freedmen have not used genetic science to try to prove their right to participate in Seminole Nation benefits as Indians. With blood quantum becoming a requirement for membership, however, they soon might. Were they to do so, evidence suggests that they would be disappointed. Only sixty-eight mixed-race Indian-freedmen in the Seminole Nation could be traced through the census cards. Of those, just fifteen appeared on the freedman rolls, the others being listed on the Seminole rolls and recognized as "Indians." Moreover, geneticist Rick Kittles conducted DNA testing in 2004 on one hundred descendants of freedmen associated with the Five Tribes in Oklahoma. Although he hypothesized that the group's DNA would be around 20 percent American Indian, Kittles reported in June 2005 that he had found it to be just 6 percent.[76] That figure represents less than half of a one-eighth-blood quantum requirement, and the origin of the Indian DNA is not identified.

Bioethicist Josephine Johnston suggests that genetic testing is not yet sufficiently sophisticated to provide freedmen with the evidence they would need to prove blood quantum rights to Seminole citizenship, even if they could show sufficient Indian ancestry. Moreover, she notes: "Freedmen do not appear to hinge their identity as tribal members on possession of Indian blood. In fact, their identity persists in spite of many having no proof of Indian genealogy. Instead, they rely on a history of comradeship and inclusion in the tribe to justify their membership in the Nation."[77] As ethnohistorian Kimberly TallBear concludes, "Science cannot prove an individual's identity as a member of a cultural entity such as a tribe; it can only reveal one individual's genetic inheritance or partial inheritance. The two are not synonymous."[78]

Through blood quantum restrictions, Indians have refused the freedmen membership in the Seminole Nation. The freedmen argue that their heritage and rights are being denied. They remain locked in seemingly endless legal combat with agencies of the U.S. government and with Seminole Indians over issues of race, ethnicity, national sovereignty, membership rights, eligibility requirements, and historical interpretation. The older maroons still proclaim their Seminole citizenship and defend their right to participate in the political process, but the young see less meaning or relevance in the group's Indian associations. "It takes your pride away," said the eighteen-year-old freedman Donnell Davis in January 2001. "You know they don't want you to be a part of them. They tell you you're nothing to them."[79]

In the early 1990s, large crowds recognized and celebrated the maroon heritage of the Brackettville and Nacimiento groups on the National Mall in Washington, D.C., during the "Maroon Culture in the Americas" component of the 1992 Smithsonian Institution Festival of American Folklife. The Seminole maroons of west Texas and Coahuila took their rightful place alongside maroon community representatives from Jamaica, Columbia, Mexico, French Guiana, and Suriname. But Seminole freedmen from Oklahoma did not participate. Sylvia Davis later described her group as "a forgotten tribe of people."[80] The associated traveling exhibition "Creativity and Resistance: Maroon Culture in the Americas" and its accompanying Web site added to the recognition of the Brackettville and Nacimiento groups,[81] and book-length studies have followed.[82] Unfortunately, such recognition has eluded the Seminole freedmen, who continue to be represented negatively as not "blood Seminoles" ("bloods") or misrepresented positively as Black Indians.

The Seminole freedmen of Oklahoma are not Black Indians; they are maroon descendants. When freedmen describe themselves as Seminoles or Natives, they are affirming their history, culture, and identity by distinguishing themselves from other African Americans. But like the Texas and Coahuila maroons, who also call themselves Seminoles, freedmen understand that they are not Seminole Indians. They know the difference between freedmans and bloods.

Although their communities were in proximity and their histories partially shared in Florida and the Indian Territory, Seminoles and maroons remained culturally distinct. After the Civil War, the freedmen established their own townships and bands in the Seminole Nation. They had their own leaders, economic and social arrangements, and cultural life. The majority interacted mostly with other freedmen. The maroons had their own schools, churches, language, and naming practices. Intermarriage with Indians was rare and usually involved only members of a few elite families. Offspring of those unions accounted for only a small percentage of the overall Seminole and freedman populations. Seminoles and freedmen were able to live in peace during the period from Reconstruction to Oklahoma statehood, but they also chose to live apart. The coming of Jim Crow laws to the Sooner State replaced that separation with segregation.

Cultural transmission between maroons and Seminoles certainly occurred. In Florida, the maroons had influenced Seminole beadwork and music. In the Indian Territory, they affected the Seminoles' use of English, transmitted Africanisms to the Indians along with Christianity, and added to their choices for personal names. Joseph Dillard has argued that the Seminoles' introduction to "English" came through African interpreters. As they actually were hearing Afro-Seminole Creole, the Indians initially spoke a pidgin English. "English" became the lingua franca between Seminoles and whites, Seminoles and freedmen, freedmen and whites, and freedmen and other African Americans.[83] There was also clear maroon-to-Indian transmission in the way Seminoles first accepted Christianity in the Indian Territory. The Presbyterian minister James Ramsay lamented that his black interpreter, Robert Johnson, was passing along Africanisms to his Seminole congregation. "Bewitched" maroons, meanwhile, acquired their Baptist religion from Creek black missionaries acting out of North Fork Town and passed along an Africanized form of the religion to the likes of Seminole converts James Factor and Heniha Mikko. The Seminole Indian rolls also include isolated examples of individuals with typical freedman first names and surnames. But there is no evidence that the Seminoles ever employed the maroons' naming practices.

Cultural transmission from Seminoles to maroons also took place in a number of areas. In Florida, according to Simmons, the maroons had lived and dressed "pretty much like the Indians."[84] They ate Indian dishes, dressed in Seminole fashion, lived in similar dwellings, and practiced a communal form of agriculture. A number of Africans also learned the Seminoles' native languages. If they were living in Indian villages, that would facilitate personal communication. Other maroon leaders acquired power and influence by learning to interpret between Seminoles and speakers of English and Spanish. Freedmen retained as surnames the names of former Seminole slave owners, such as Bowlegs, Factor, and Payne. No evidence suggests that the maroons ever adopted the Seminole clan system, but they organized into bands, both in the Indian Territory and Oklahoma and in Texas. The freedmen also adopted the Seminole practice of determining band affiliation through the mother.

In 1951, Gallaher suggested a number of other areas where he perceived Seminole cultural transmission to the freedmen, including marriage customs and superstitions. He argued that burial customs among the freedmen were "essentially the same as those found among the Creek and Seminole Indians of today."[85] But given their long history of geographical proximity and close association, it is all the more remarkable that the Seminoles' and freedmen's cultural transmissions were not more extensive and systemic. Gallaher concluded, "Although becoming somewhat acculturated to this group, indications are that the Freedmen were never completely culturally identified with the Seminoles. It appears that they accepted several aspects of the Seminole culture, perhaps those which were the most useful to them in their association with the latter group, but overall they appeared to retain much of their original culture."[86]

The freedmen added select Seminole transmissions to African and plantation slave society retentions to form a unique and complex cultural whole. Similar retaining, borrowing, adapting, and synthesizing behaviors have been documented in other maroon communities throughout the Americas. That is a far cry from the idea that Africans who associated with Seminoles became Indian.

In the first decade of the twenty-first century, Seminole Indians and freedmen remain culturally distinct ethnic groups. Seminoles certainly see it that way. Miller suggests, "The argument that Freedmen are not Seminoles because they do not participate in Seminole culture seems conclusive from an indigenous perspective." Jerry Haney, principal chief from 1989 to 2001, has stated, "They were always looked on as non-Indian. They were always a separate people." Jackie Warledo, a Seminole Council member, analogized, "Our history is being rewritten here. We were two different races. We had two different cultures and we still do. Just because you go to a Polish festival doesn't mean you are Polish." And Patricia Wickman, director of the Department of Anthropology and Genealogy, Seminole Tribe of Florida, is of this opinion: "The entire subject of the Black Seminoles makes no sense. A person with a black parent and a Seminole parent is either black or Indian, depending on how they were raised culturally. They could not be a black Indian. It's like saying cat dog."[87]

Bud Crockett. Photograph courtesy of *Newsday*.

In the July 2002 *60 Minutes II* television story, the strongest voice of reason came from Seminole freedman Bud Crockett, who stated, "It's not all about the money. It's about setting the history records straight about our ancestry and our history. And what legacy we intend to leave for our kids."[88] A decade earlier, during and after the Festival of American Folklife, leaders of the Texas and Coahuila groups poignantly stated that they had not realized they were maroons.[89] They always had known that they had "never been slaves," that they were different from other African Americans, and they felt vindicated. Now they could take pride in a "new" identity that helped explain a complex past. The Texas and Coahuila group leaders enjoyed meeting the other maroon representatives in

Washington. No longer were they isolated and alone; there were others out there like them. As Miss Charles Emily Wilson eloquently wrote in the festival program:

> Today there are few of us left who know our history and speak our language. It may be that too much time has already passed to get those things back. Some of the young people leave our small community and return to Brackettville only to visit. But perhaps this recognition of who we are and what we have done may stir in their hearts a sense of pride and may move them to learn from us while they can, and they may yet pass on our story to their own children. We have given our loyalty and our skill to our country, and we have contributed to its history. I can rest now, knowing that this has been recognized at last, and that future schoolchildren, both American and Seminole, will learn about the part we have played in the growth of our great nation.[90]

It is now time to recognize the maroon heritage of the Seminole freedmen of Oklahoma—to celebrate the group's ancestry and history, to heal relations between Seminole Indians and freedmen, to restore Donnell Davis's pride, and to let Bud Crockett rest.

Notes

PREFACE

1. Kenneth W. Porter, *The Negro on the American Frontier* (New York: New York Times, Arno Press, 1971), 331 (first quote), 461 (second).

INTRODUCTION

1. CBS TV, "A Nation Divided," *60 Minutes II* story, http://www.cbsnews.com/stories/2002/07/01/60II (July 12, 2002).

2. Brent Staples, "The Seminole Tribe, Running from History," Editorial Observer, *New York Times,* April 21, 2002. Staples's opinion piece followed shortly after John Keilman's article "Bloodlines Drawn over Money" had appeared in the *Chicago Tribune,* April 4, 2002. The following month, Megan K. Stack authored an article with a similar slant, "Tribal Rift Is a Matter of Blood," *Los Angeles Times,* May 16, 2002. Staples since has written two more editorials in the same vein: "When Racial Discrimination Is Not Just Black and White," *New York Times,* September 12, 2003, and "The Black Seminole Indians Keep Fighting for Equality in the American West," *New York Times,* November 18, 2003. For the first piece, Staples recruited the eminent historian John Hope Franklin, of African and Choctaw descent and raised in Tulsa. Franklin argued that African Americans and Indians in Oklahoma were "very much involved with each other, not only in terms of friendship but in terms of marriage," and concluded: "It is perfectly absurd to talk about dividing Indians and blacks. Any Indians who speak in exclusionary terms do not represent the historic interests or the historic relationships of Indians and blacks." In October 2003, Jon Velie, an attorney for the Seminole freedmen, picked up on Staples's theme and extended the argument back to 1699: "There have been blacks among the Seminole tribe all along. It's a totally multiracial tribe" (Mac Bentley, "Seminole Freedmen Recognized," *Daily Oklahoman,* October 25, 2003). In his editorial of the following month, Staples described the Seminoles as both "the blackest of all the Indian tribes" and "white Indians in the American West." Matthew Kelly, an anthropologist at the

University of Chicago who has assisted the Seminoles in their legal battles against the federal government and the Seminole freedmen, accurately describes such media coverage as "a hodge-podge of historical inaccuracies, gross oversimplifications, or moral indignation that did neither the Freedmen nor the Seminoles justice" (Matthew Kelly, pers. comm., February 3, 2003). For some American Indian reactions to Staples's opinions, see Denny McAuliffe (Osage), "African American Indians," http://www.reznetnews.org (September 17, 2003); Susan A. Miller (Seminole), "Seminoles and Africans under Seminole Law: Sources and Discourses of Tribal Sovereignty and 'Black Indian' Entitlement," *Wicazo Sa Review* 20 (2005): 23–47; and David Wilkins (Lumbee), "Red, Black, and Bruised," http://www.alter net.org/rights/17111/ (November 4, 2003).

3. Stack, "Tribal Rift." That notion had been suggested a year earlier by the indignant popular historian and freedman advocate William Loren Katz, who wrote: "Those Seminoles who today oppose the racial equality, brotherhood and sisterhood pioneered by their glorious warrior ancestors, are advocating a crude version of 'ethnic cleansing.' It is all the more repugnant because its sponsors represent in lineage the first victims of racism and genocide in the Americas" (William Loren Katz, "Justice and African Seminoles," *Black World Today,* March 15, 2001, http://www.tbwt.com/content/article.asp?articleid=221 [March 16, 2001]).

4. Jeff Guinn, *Our Land Before We Die: The Proud Story of the Seminole Negro* (New York: Jeremy P. Tarcher/Putnam, 2002); Rosalyn Howard, *Black Seminoles in the Bahamas* (Gaines-ville: University Press of Florida, 2002); Kevin Mulroy, *Freedom on the Border: The Seminole Maroons in Florida, the Indian Territory, Coahuila, and Texas* (Lubbock: Texas Tech University Press, 1993); Kenneth W. Porter, *The Black Seminoles: History of a Freedom-Seeking People,* Alcione M. Amos and Thomas P. Senter, eds. (Gainesville: University Press of Florida, 1996).

5. Daniel F. Littlefield, Jr., *Africans and Seminoles: From Removal to Emancipation* (Jackson: University Press of Mississippi, Banner Books, 2001), ix–xii. This is the first paperback edition of Littlefield's indispensable 1977 work, published by Greenwood Press in Westport, Conn.

6. Claudio Saunt, "The Paradox of Freedom: Tribal Sovereignty and Emancipation during the Reconstruction of Indian Territory," *Journal of Southern History* 70 (2004): 91n90.

7. Kenneth W. Porter, "Relations between Negroes and Indians within the Present Limits of the United States," *Journal of Negro History* 17 (1932): 287–367; Laurence Foster, *Negro-Indian Relationships in the Southeast* (Philadelphia: published by the author, 1935); John M. Goggin, "The Seminole Negroes of Andros Island, Bahamas," *Florida Historical Quarterly* 24 (1946): 201–206.

8. In order of term listed: Kevin Mulroy, "Relations between Blacks and Seminoles after Removal," Ph.D. thesis, University of Keele (England), 1984; Ian F. Hancock, *Creole Features in the Afro-Seminole Speech of Brackettville, Texas,* Society for Caribbean Linguistics Occasional Paper no. 3 (Mona, Jamaica: University of the West Indies, 1975); Rebecca B. Bateman, "Africans and Indians: A Comparative Study of the Black Carib and Black Seminole," *Ethno-history* 37 (1990): 1–24; James Leitch Wright, Jr., *Creeks and Seminoles: The Destruction and Regeneration of the Muskogulge People* (Lincoln: University of Nebraska Press, 1986).

9. Robert M. Loughridge and David M. Hodge, *English and Muskokee Dictionary: Col-lected from Various Sources and Revised; Dictionary of the Muskokee or Creek Language in Creek and English* (Okmulgee, Okla.: Baptist Home Mission Board, 1964 [1890]), 132; Richard Sattler, pers. comm., May 9, 2002 (citing a late eighteenth- or early nineteenth-century Creek word list).

10. Lucinda Davis interview from the Works Progress Administration's Oklahoma Slave

Narratives Project. Reprinted in Patrick Minges, ed., *Black Indian Slave Narratives* (Winston-Salem, N.C.: John F. Blair, 2004), 118.

11. Sattler, pers. comm., May 9, 2002.

12. See, for example, Minnie Moore Willson, *The Seminoles of Florida* (New York: Moffat Yard and Co., 1920 [1896]), 106–108.

13. D. F. Littlefield, *Africans and Seminoles*, 4.

14. Richard Price, ed., *Maroon Societies: Rebel Slave Communities in the Americas*, rev. ed. (Baltimore: Johns Hopkins University Press, 1979), 1–30. See also, generally, Alvin O. Thompson, *African Runaways and Maroons in the Americas* (Kingston, Jamaica: University of West Indies Press, 2006).

15. Kevin A. Yelvington, foreword to *True-Born Maroons*, by Kenneth M. Bilby (Gainesville: University Press of Florida, 2005), xi.

16. Joshua R. Giddings, *The Exiles of Florida; or, The Crimes Committed by Our Government against the Maroons, Who Fled from South Carolina, and Other Slave States, Seeking Protection under Spanish Laws* (Columbus, Ohio: Follett, Foster, and Co., 1858).

17. Herbert Aptheker, "Maroons within the Present Limits of the United States," *Journal of Negro History* 24 (1939): 167–84.

18. William C. Sturtevant, review of *Africans and Seminoles: From Removal to Emancipation*, by Daniel F. Littlefield, Jr., *American Anthropologist* 81 (1979): 916–17. See also Kevin Mulroy, "Seminole Maroons," in *Handbook of North American Indians*, vol. 14, *Southeast*, Raymond D. Fogelson, ed. (Washington, D.C.: Smithsonian Institution Press, 2004), 475.

19. Bateman, "Africans and Indians"; Rebecca B. Bateman, "Naming Patterns in Black Seminole Ethnogenesis," *Ethnohistory* 49 (2002): 227–57; Rebecca B. Bateman, "Slaves or Seminoles?" 12 pp. typescript (2002), copy provided by Bateman; Rebecca B. Bateman, "We're Still Here: History, Kinship, and Group Identity among the Seminole Freedmen of Oklahoma," Ph.D. dissertation, Johns Hopkins University, 1990, passim; Susan Miller, *Coacoochee's Bones: A Seminole Saga* (Lawrence: University Press of Kansas, 2003), 55–71, 183–88; Miller, "Seminoles and Africans"; Kevin Mulroy, "Ethnogenesis and Ethnohistory of the Seminole Maroons," *Journal of World History* 4 (1993): 287–305; Mulroy, *Freedom on the Border;* Mulroy, "Seminole Maroons," 465–77; Richard A. Sattler, "Siminoli Italwa: Socio-political Change among the Oklahoma Seminoles between Removal and Allotment, 1836–1905," Ph.D. dissertation, University of Oklahoma, 1987. Bateman has preferred the term "Black Seminole" but subscribes to the argument that the freedmen are maroon descendants.

20. William Loren Katz first coined the term "Black Indians" in the late 1960s and used it in *The Black West: A Documentary and Pictorial History* (Garden City, N.Y.: Doubleday, 1971). In the late 1980s, Katz included it as the title of his widely read *Black Indians: A Hidden Heritage* (New York: Atheneum, 1986) and in the revised and expanded third edition of *The Black West* (Seattle: Open Hand, 1987). Since then, the term has gained widespread popularity in both academia and the popular media, even being used as the title for a documentary film aired on public television: *Black Indians: An American Story* (executive producer Steven R. Heape, Riche-Heape Films, 2000). The term "Black Indians" usually is employed in one of two ways: (1) to describe individuals who are descendants of unions between people of African ancestry and American Indians, or (2) in a broader sense, to describe Africans or African Americans who simply had or have strong associations with American Indians. The latter category includes people of African descent who, supposedly, adopted most elements of Native American culture, to the point of their actually becoming Indian. This second classification typically includes individuals also listed in the first category. Those using the term "Black Indians" tend to include Seminole maroons in the all-encompassing second category.

For an interesting perspective on the term from an individual of Assateague Gingaskin, Cherokee, and African American descent, see Ron Welburn, "A Most Secret Identity: Native American Assimilation and Identity Resistance in African America," in *Confounding the Color Line: The Indian-Black Experience in North America,* James F. Brooks, ed. (Lincoln: University of Nebraska Press, 2002), 292–320, esp. 306–307.

21. Charles W. Dean to George W. Manypenny, June 24, 1856, National Archives Microfilm Publications, M234, Record Group 75, Records of the Bureau of Indian Affairs, 1824–81, 962 rolls (hereafter cited as M234), roll 802, Seminole Agency 1856–58, D180-56.

22. D. F. Littlefield, *Africans and Seminoles,* 174.

23. Surprisingly, given the thrust of his own work, Kenneth Porter in his review of *Africans and Seminoles* subscribed to Littlefield's aberration argument. The First and Second Seminole Wars and Removal "virtually destroyed" the relationship between blacks and Seminoles. After the Civil War, however, "the triumphant Seminole Unionists immediately freed and adopted their Negroes, granting them full rights of citizenship. The half-century struggle had ended happily—at least for those who had survived the years of war and enslavement." Kenneth W. Porter, review of *Africans and Seminoles: From Removal to Emancipation,* by Daniel F. Littlefield, Jr., *Pacific Historical Review* 48 (1979): 423–24.

24. Thomas L. McKenney and James Hall, *The Indian Tribes of North America,* 3 vols., new ed., Frederick W. Hodge and David I. Bushnell, eds. (Edinburgh: John Grant, 1933–34), vol. 2, 264–69.

25. U.S. Commissioner of Indian Affairs, *Annual Report of the Commissioner of Indian Affairs* (hereafter cited as *ARCIA*) *1847,* Doc. 20, Report of Marcellus Duval, 889.

26. Staples, "Black Seminole Indians Keep Fighting." Staples's editorial appeared in 2003, but Seminoles had been hearing similar sentiments since the United States annexed Florida in 1821.

1. BEGINNINGS IN FLORIDA

1. The following discussion of the origins of the Seminoles is drawn primarily from Howard F. Cline, *Notes on Colonial Indians and Communities in Florida, 1700–1821; Notes on the Treaty of Coweta,* vol. 1 of *Florida Indians,* 3 vols. in *American Indian Ethnohistory: Southern and Southeast Indians,* David A. Horr, comp. and ed. (New York: Garland, 1974); Howard F. Cline, *Provisional Historical Gazeteer, with Locational Notes on Florida Colonial Communities, 1700–1823,* vol. 2 of *Florida Indians;* Charles H. Fairbanks, *Ethnohistorical Report on the Florida Indians, Commission Findings by Indian Claims Commission,* vol. 3 of *Florida Indians;* Richard A. Sattler, "Remnants, Renegades, and Runaways: Seminole Ethnogenesis Reconsidered," in *History, Power, and Identity: Ethnogenesis in the Americas,* Jonathan D. Hill, ed. (Iowa City: University of Iowa Press, 1996), 36–69; Sattler, "Siminoli Italwa," 1–107; William C. Sturtevant, "Creek into Seminole," in *North American Indians in Historical Perspective,* Eleanor Burke Leacock and Nancy Oestreich Lurie, eds. (New York: Random House, 1971), 92–128; William C. Sturtevant and Jessica R. Cattelino, "Florida Seminole and Miccosukee," in *Handbook: Southeast,* 429–49; John R. Swanton, "Early History of the Creek Indians and Their Neighbours," *Bureau of American Ethnology Bulletin* 73 (Washington, D.C.: Government Printing Office, 1922), 120–23, 389–99, 414; and Willard B. Walker, "Creek Confederacy before Removal," in *Handbook: Southeast,* 373–92.

2. Francis Harper, ed., *The Travels of William Bartram: Naturalist's Edition* (Athens: University of Georgia Press, 1998 [1791]), esp. 59–60 [93], 122–23 [191–94], 325–26 [511–13]. Harper's page references in square brackets refer to William Bartram, *Travels through North & South Carolina, Georgia, East & West Florida, the Cherokee Country, the Extensive Territories of the*

Muscogulges, or Creek Confederacy, and the Country of the Choctaw, 1st ed. (Philadelphia: James and Johnson, 1791).

3. Sturtevant and Cattelino, "Florida Seminole," 432.

4. Harper, *Travels of William Bartram,* 326 [512–13]. On the sabana system, see Amy Turner Bushnell, "Ruling 'the Republic of Indians' in Seventeenth-Century Florida," in *Powhatan's Mantle: Indians in the Colonial Southeast,* Peter H. Wood, Gregory A. Waselkov, and M. Thomas Hatley, eds. (Lincoln: University of Nebraska Press, 1989), 134, 140, 142–43.

5. Harper, ed., *Travels of William Bartram,* 118–19 [186].

6. William McLoughlin was one of only a few scholars to raise the point that, no matter how mild the form of slavery they practiced, Indians were the slave owners, blacks were the enslaved, and they were not equal. See William G. McLoughlin, "Red Indians, Black Slavery, and White Racism: America's Slaveholding Indians," *American Quarterly* 26 (1974): 367–85. Historian John Nelson has argued, "Slavery among the Seminoles, though moderate compared with slavery on Southern plantations, was still slavery. The Seminoles expected service and tribute from their slaves." John C. Nelson, "An Alliance Asunder: The Dissolution of the Seminole-Black Partnership," *Michigan Journal of History* (Fall 2004): introduction, 7–8, http://www.umich.edu/historyj/papers/fall2004/nelson.htm (November 1, 2005).

7. Irene Wright, "Dispatches of Spanish Officials Bearing on the Free Negro Settlement of Gracia Real de Santa Terese de Mose, Florida," *Journal of Negro History* 9 (1924): 145–46, 150–53; Verne Elmo Chatelain, *The Defenses of Spanish Florida, 1565 to 1763,* Carnegie Institute of Washington Publication 511 (Washington, D.C., 1941), 160–61n4.

8. Jane Landers, "Black Society in Spanish St. Augustine, 1784–1821," Ph.D. dissertation, University of Florida, 1988, 14–15.

9. Jane Landers, "African Presence in Early Spanish Colonization of the Caribbean and Southeastern Borderlands," in *Archaeological and Historical Perspectives on the Spanish Borderlands East,* vol. 2 of *Columbian Consequences,* David Hurst Thomas, ed., 3 vols. (Washington, D.C.: Smithsonian Institution, 1990), 321.

10. Governor José de Zuniga y Cerda, Orders for Apalachee Province, 1704. I am grateful to Amy Turner Bushnell for providing this reference. On black runaways to Spanish Florida, see Jane G. Landers, "Spanish Sanctuary: Fugitive Slaves in Florida, 1687–1790," *Florida Historical Quarterly* 62 (1984): 296–313; and John J. TePaske, "The Fugitive Slave: Intercolonial Rivalry and Spanish Slave Policy, 1687–1764," in *Eighteenth-Century Florida and Its Borderlands,* Samuel Proctor, ed. (Gainesville: University of Florida Press, 1975), 1–12.

11. Jane Landers, "Gracia Real de Santa Terese de Mose: A Free Black Town in Spanish Colonial Florida," *American Historical Review* 95 (1990): 19–22; Porter, *Negro on the American Frontier,* 169–70.

12. Quoted in Porter, *Negro on the American Frontier,* 170.

13. Landers, "African Presence," 323.

14. Quoted in Daniel L. Schafer, "St. Augustine's British Years," special issue, *El Escribano: The St. Augustine Journal of History* 38 (2001): 96.

15. Patrick Riordan, "Finding Freedom in Florida: Native Peoples, African Americans, and Colonists, 1670–1816," *Florida Historical Quarterly* 75 (1996): 37, 38 table 1.

16. John K. Mahon, *History of the Second Seminole War, 1835–1842,* rev. ed. (Gainesville: University of Florida Press, 1985 [1967]), 20.

17. Riordan, "Finding Freedom," 38.

18. Porter, *Negro on the American Frontier,* 187.

19. Claudio Saunt, " 'The English Has Now a Mind to Make Slaves of Them All': Creeks, Seminoles, and the Problem of Slavery," *American Indian Quarterly* 22 (1998): 167.

20. Quoted in ibid., 167.

21. Ibid., 167–68. See also Claudio Saunt, *A New Order of Things: Property, Power, and the Transformation of the Creek Indians, 1733–1816* (Cambridge: Cambridge University Press, 1999), 129–34.

22. Theda Perdue, *"Mixed Blood" Indians: Racial Construction in the Early South* (Athens: University of Georgia Press, 2003), 4; Saunt, "The English," 167–68; James Leitch Wright, Jr., *The Only Land They Knew: The Tragic Story of the American Indians in the Old South* (New York: Free Press, 1981), 76. Kathryn E. Holland Braund, in "The Creek Indians, Blacks, and Slavery," *Journal of Southern History* 57 (1991): 609n31, suggests that it is unlikely that Black Factor was of African descent. But the Factors owned slaves and otherwise became closely involved with the maroons, both before and after Removal. Black Factor's son, Sam, probably fathered Rose Sena Factor's son Billy, described by the Seminole agent in 1856 as "a hybrid Seminole and negro." J. W. Washbourne to Charles W. Dean, January 24, 1856, M234-802, D92-56.

23. D. F. Littlefield, *Africans and Seminoles*, 30, 53–55, 65–67n60.

24. John C. Casey to Isaac Clark, July 11, 1838, *Negroes, etc., Captured from Indians in Florida*, 25th Cong., 3d sess., H. Doc. 225, 1839 (hereafter cited as H. Doc. 225), 51; D. F. Littlefield, *Africans and Seminoles*, 41–42, appendix lists J and L. Porter claimed to have traced twenty-two variants of Kapichee Mikko's name. Porter, *Negro on the American Frontier*, 223–24.

25. James W. Covington, *The Seminoles of Florida* (Gainesville: University Press of Florida, 1993), 29.

26. Canter Brown, Jr., *Florida's Peace River Frontier* (Orlando: University of Central Florida Press, 1991), 6; Jedidiah Morse, *A Report to the Secretary of War of the United States on Indian Affairs* (New Haven, Conn.: Southern Converse, 1822), 306–309; Sattler, "Siminoli Italwa," 73, 83–84, 98 fig. 2.6, 99; Swanton, "Early History of the Creek Indians," 400n1, 406–407.

27. Affidavit of Edward M. Wanton, Alachua County, enc. in Wiley Thompson to Elbert Herring, March 25, 1835, M234-800; William Hayne Simmons, *Notices of East Florida, with an Account of the Seminole Nation of Indians* (Gainesville: University of Florida Press, 1973 [1822]), 75.

28. Saunt, "The English," 168–69, 179n113.

29. Jane G. Landers, introduction to *Colonial Plantations and Economy in Florida*, Jane G. Landers, ed. (Gainesville: University Press of Florida, 2000), 1.

30. Description of Abraham's Old Town collection (8SM136), Florida Archeology Collection, Florida Museum of Natural History, University of Florida, http://www.flmnh.ufl .edu/flarch/collections.htm (June 14, 2005); Scott McCabe, "Searching for Peliklakaha, Land of the Forgotten Seminoles," *Palm Beach (Fla.) Post*, August 20, 2001; Terrance M. Weik, "A Historical Archaeology of Black Seminole Maroons in Florida: Ethnogenesis and Culture Contact at Pilaklikaha," Ph.D. dissertation, University of Florida, 2002, chaps. 5 and 6; Brent R. Weisman, "The Plantation System of the Florida Seminole Indians and Black Seminoles during the Colonial Era," in *Colonial Plantations*, 136–37.

31. Jane G. Landers, *Black Society in Spanish Florida* (Urbana: University of Illinois Press, 1999), 91–93; Susan R. Parker, "The Cattle Trade in East Florida, 1784–1821," in *Colonial Plantations*, 154–55; Susan R. Parker, "Success through Diversification: Francis Philip Fatio's New Switzerland Plantation," in *Colonial Plantations*, 76. On Seminole livestock raising and trading in Florida and the Indian Territory, see Richard A. Sattler, "Cowboys and Indians: Creek and Seminole Stock Raising, 1700–1900," *American Indian Culture and Research Journal* 22 (1998): 79–99.

32. Saunt, *New Order,* 134.

33. Richard A. Sattler, pers. comm., June 8, 2002.

34. Landers, "Black Society," 74–77; Parker, "Cattle Trade," 154–55.

35. Myer M. Cohen, *Notices of Florida and the Campaigns, by an Officer of the Left Wing* (Charleston, S.C.: Burges and Honour; New York: B. B. Hussey, 1836), 78–79.

36. Rebecca B. Bateman, pers. comm., August 9, 2004; Bilby, *True-Born Maroons,* 350 (quote).

37. The notion of "new people" is drawn from Jacqueline Peterson and Jennifer S. H. Brown, eds. *The New Peoples: Being and Becoming Métis in North America* (Lincoln: University of Nebraska Press, 1985), 3–4. See also Bateman, "Africans and Indians," 1. For a discussion of the Seminole maroons as a new people, see Mulroy, "Ethnogenesis and Ethnohistory," 287–305.

38. Daniel L. Schafer, "Zephaniah Kingsley's Laurel Grove Plantation, 1803–1813," in *Colonial Plantations,* 110–11. Kingsley produced a detailed descriptive inventory of the slaves seized by the Seminoles. It is reproduced in the appendix to *Colonial Plantations,* 198–202. Bilby notes that a similarly "complex spectrum of geographical and cultural regions" resulting in "many different African languages and cultural backgrounds" was represented among the early Jamaican Maroon population. Kenneth Bilby, "Ethnogenesis in the Guianas and Jamaica: Two Maroon Cases," in *History, Power, and Identity,* 120.

39. The suggestion that ethnicity can serve as an early and important structural principle in the formation of new societies is taken from Nancie L. Solien González, *Sojourners of the Caribbean: Ethnogenesis and Ethnohistory of the Garífuna* (Urbana: University of Illinois Press, 1988), 6. Jane Landers, citing Peter Wood's evidence that most slaves arriving in the English colony of South Carolina in the mid-eighteenth century came from Kongo/Angola, notes, "Given that most of the Florida maroons were runaways from the Carolinas, it can be assumed many were from Central Africa; however, even in Spanish documents, ethnicity is much harder to trace beyond urban centers. Only occasional references surface." Jane G. Landers, "The Central African Presence in Spanish Maroon Communities," in *Central Africans and Cultural Transformations in the American Diaspora,* Linda M. Heywood, ed. (Cambridge: Cambridge University Press, 2002), 232; Peter Wood, *Black Majority: Negroes in Colonial South Carolina from 1670 through the Stono Rebellion* (New York: Knopf, 1974), appendix C, 334–41.

40. This notion is drawn from many studies of maroon history and culture throughout the Americas. On African organizational principles and cultural retentions among the Guianese and Jamaican Maroons, for example, see Kenneth Bilby, "Swearing by the Past, Swearing to the Future: Sacred Oaths, Alliances, and Treaties among the Guianese and Jamaican Maroons," *Ethnohistory* 44 (1997): 655–90; and Barbara K. Kopytoff, "Colonial Treaty as Sacred Charter of the Jamaican Maroons," *Ethnohistory* 26 (1979): 45–64.

41. Quoted in Julius W. Pratt, *Expansionists of 1812* (New York: Macmillan, 1925), 117.

42. Quoted in T. Frederick Davis, "United States Troops in Spanish East Florida, 1812–1813," *Florida Historical Quarterly* 9 (1930): 107.

43. Charles H. Coe, *Red Patriots: The Story of the Seminoles* (Cincinnati: Editor Publishing Co., 1898), 11–13; Landers, "Black Society," 85–89; Porter, *Negro on the American Frontier,* 183–203; Pratt, *Expansionists,* 202–209.

44. Quoted in Nicholas Halatsz, *The Rattling Chains: Slave Unrest and Revolt in the Antebellum South* (New York: McKay, Van Rees, 1966), 108.

45. James G. Forbes, *Sketches, Historical and Topographical, of the Floridas, More Particularly of East Florida* (Gainesville: University of Florida Press, 1964 [1821]), 121, 200–205. See also Mark F. Boyd, "Events at Prospect Bluff on the Apalachicola River, 1808–1818," *Florida*

Historical Quarterly 16 (1937): 55–96; William S. Coker and Thomas D. Watson, *Indian Traders of the Southeastern Spanish Borderlands: Panton, Leslie and Company, and John Forbes and Company, 1783–1847* (Pensacola: University of West Florida Press, 1986), 302–308; James W. Covington, "The Negro Fort," *Gulf Coast Historical Review* 5 (1990): 79–91; and James Leitch Wright, Jr., "A Note on the First Seminole War as Seen by the Indians, Negroes, and Their British Advisers," *Journal of Southern History* 34 (1968): 567.

46. Brown, *Peace River,* 6; Coker and Watson, *Indian Traders,* 309; George Klos, "Blacks and the Seminole Removal Debate, 1821–1835," *Florida Historical Quarterly* 68 (1989): 60–61.

47. Canter Brown, Jr., *African Americans on the Tampa Bay Frontier* (Tampa: Tampa Bay History Center, 1997), 9–20; Brown, *Peace River,* 7–10; Canter Brown, Jr., "The 'Sarrazota, or Runaway Negro Plantations': Tampa Bay's First Black Community, 1812–1821," *Tampa Bay History* 12 (1990): 5–19. In early 2005, the "Looking for Angola" project began archaeological excavations on the Little Manatee River at East Bradenton, Manatee County, at a site thought to be the location of the Angola plantation. Marcus Franklin, "Excavators Seeking Freedom Pioneers," *St. Petersburg (Fla.) Times,* February 7, 2005; "Looking for Angola," *Quest (Magazine of the University of Central Florida, College of Arts and Sciences)* (Spring 2005): 20.

48. Porter, *Negro on the American Frontier,* 221–36 (quote on 236). Historian Y. N. Kly has described the long series of campaigns in which the maroons engaged American forces as "the Gullah War" or "the African role in what is popularly called the Seminole Wars." Y. N. Kly, "The Gullah War, 1739–1858," in *The Legacy of Ibo Landing: Gullah Roots of African American Culture,* Marquetta L. Goodwine, ed. (Atlanta: Clarity Press, 1998), 21. Joseph Opala also led efforts in the late 1990s to have the Seminole maroons' Gullah connections recognized. See Herb Frazier, "Seminole, Gullah Ties Traced," *Charleston (S.C.) Post and Courier,* November 14, 1998; and Herb Frazier, "Gullah-Seminole Link Comes to Light," *Charleston (S.C.) Post and Courier,* July 6, 1999.

49. Horatio S. Dexter to William P. DuVal, August 20, 1823, reproduced in Mark F. Boyd, "Horatio S. Dexter and Events Leading to the Treaty of Moultrie Creek with the Seminole Indians," *Florida Anthropologist* 11 (1958): 89, 92; Brown, *Peace River,* 21; C. Brown, "Runaway Negro Plantations," 14–15; Toni Carrier, "Black Seminoles, Maroons, and Freedom Seekers in Florida," part 3, "The Destruction of Angola," University of South Florida Africana Heritage Project, 2005, http://www.africanaheritage.com/black_seminoles_angola .asp (June 25, 2005); Simmons, *Notices of East Florida,* 41.

50. Horatio S. Dexter, "Observations on the Seminole Indians, 1823," National Archives Microfilm Publications, M271, Record Group 75, Records of the Office of the Secretary of War, Letters Received by the Secretary of War Relating to Indian Affairs, 1800–1823, 4 rolls (hereafter cited as M271), roll 4, 1822–23, 505–19, frame 506 (first quote); Dexter to DuVal, August 20, 1823, in Boyd, "Horatio Dexter," 92 (second quote). See also Brown, *Peace River,* 13, 23–29, 371n24; Cohen, *Notices of Florida,* 238; and Larry E. Rivers, *Slavery in Florida: Territorial Days to Emancipation* (Gainesville: University Press of Florida, 2000), 195.

51. Quoted in Klos, "Blacks and the Seminole Removal Debate," 61. See also Canter Brown, Jr., "Tales of Angola: Free Blacks, Red Stick Creeks, and International Intrigue in Spanish Southwest Florida, 1812–1821," in *Go Sound the Trumpet: Selections in Florida's African American History,* David H. Jackson, Jr., and Canter Brown, Jr., eds. (Tampa: University of Tampa Press, 2005), 7–8, 12.

52. Landers, *Black Society in Spanish Florida,* 237.

53. Clarence Edwin Carter, comp. and ed., *Territorial Papers of the United States: The Territory of Florida, 1821–1824* (New York: AMS Press, 1956), 745.

54. C. Brown, "Runaway Negro Plantations," 14–16; John M. Goggin, "An Anthropo-

logical Reconnaissance of Andros Island, Bahamas," *American Antiquity* 5 (1939): 21–26; Goggin, "Seminole Negroes of Andros Island," 201–206; Rosalyn Howard, "The Promised is'Land: Reconstructing History and Identity among the Black Seminoles of Andros Island, Bahamas," Ph.D. dissertation, University of Florida, 1999, esp. 42–49, 83–124, 134–42, 148–52; Harry A. Kersey, Jr., "The Seminole Negroes of Andros Island Revisited: Some New Pieces to an Old Puzzle," *Florida Anthropologist* 34 (1981): 169–76; Bertram A. Newton, "A History of Red Bays, Andros, Bahamas," 5 pp. typescript, 1968, copy provided by William Sturtevant; Kenneth W. Porter, "Notes on the Seminole Negroes in the Bahamas," *Florida Historical Quarterly* 24 (1945): 56–60; William C. Sturtevant, "Seminole Maroons, Andros Island, Bahamas, 8–11 March 1977," field notes, copy provided by Sturtevant.

2. REMOVAL TO INDIAN TERRITORY

1. Morse, *Report to the Secretary of War,* 149–50.

2. Simmons, *Notices of East Florida,* 76.

3. Dexter, "Observations on the Seminole Indians," frame 513. Boyd published an incomplete version of this document in "Horatio Dexter," 81–85. That is the version typically used by scholars. Unfortunately, Boyd omitted Dexter's important observation that "they [the Negroes] give the master half what the lands produce; he provides them nothing."

4. Gad Humphreys to William McCarty, September 6, 1827, in *Territorial Papers of the United States,* Clarence E. Carter, comp. and ed., 28 vols. (Washington, D.C.: Government Printing Office, 1934–75), vol. 23, 911.

5. Woodburne Potter, *The War in Florida: Being an Exposition of Its Causes and an Accurate History of the Campaigns of Generals Clinch, Gaines, and Scott, by a Late Staff Officer* (Baltimore: Lewis and Coleman, 1836), 45.

6. Wiley Thompson to Lewis Cass, April 27, 1835, M234-806, Seminole Agency Emigration, 1827–46, frame 103.

7. George A. McCall, *Letters from the Frontiers: Written during a Period of Thirty Years' Service in the Army of the United States* (Philadelphia: J. B. Lippincott and Co., 1868), 160.

8. Sattler, pers. comm., June 8, 2002.

9. Sattler, "Siminoli Italwa," 26.

10. Harper, *Travels of William Bartram,* 59–60 [93]; Sattler, "Siminoli Italwa," 24.

11. Gary W. McDonogh, ed., *The Florida Negro: A Federal Writer's Project Legacy* (Jackson: University Press of Mississippi, 1992), 38, quoting from Zephaniah Kingsley, *A Treatise on the Patriarchal, or Co-operative System of Society as It Exists in Some Governments and Colonies in America, and in the United States, under the Name of Slavery, with Its Necessity and Advantages, by an Inhabitant of Florida* (1829).

12. Dexter to DuVal, quoted in Boyd, "Horatio Dexter," 88; Dexter, "Observations on the Seminole Indians," frames 507–508.

13. Weisman, "Plantation System," quotes on 136, 143–44, 146. Weisman acknowledges that that the evidence supporting his arguments with regard to the Seminole Indians is "minimally adequate" and for the Black Seminoles "far less so" (137). Nevertheless, this long-overdue questioning of old assumptions regarding Seminole slave ownership in Florida by encompassing archaeological findings is both refreshing and persuasive, and he has opened up fertile areas for further investigation.

14. U.S. Congress, *American State Papers,* 38 vols. (Washington, D.C.: Government Printing Office, 1832–61), vol. 7, *Military Affairs,* 427.

15. Porter, *Negro on the American Frontier,* 302–303.

16. Simmons, *Notices of East Florida*, 76; Thompson to Cass, April 27, 1835, M234-806, frame 103; John L. Williams, *The Territory of Florida* (Gainesville: University of Florida Press, 1962 [1837]), 239–40. See also Cohen, *Notices of Florida*, 78.

17. Mulroy, "Seminole Maroons," in *Handbook: Southeast*, 475–76.

18. Simmons, *Notices of East Florida*, 76.

19. Dexter to DuVal, August 20, 1823, in Boyd, "Horatio Dexter," 88. In the Indian Territory, at least one of the maroon communities in the Little River country retained a communal town field into the early 1850s (see "Map Showing Free Negro Settlements in the Creek Country" on page 66). After the Civil War, the freedmen replaced their communal town fields with larger individual acreages, but the Seminoles kept theirs until around 1890. See chap. 9, and Sattler, "Siminoli Italwa," 288–89.

20. Frank Laumer, ed. *Amidst a Storm of Bullets: The Diary of Lt. Henry Prince in Florida* (Tampa: University of Tampa Press, 1998), 92–93 and illus. 31.

21. Thompson to Cass, April 27, 1835, M234-806, frame 103; McCall, *Letters from the Frontiers*, 160.

22. Jacob R. Motte, *Journey into Wilderness: An Army Surgeon's Account of Life in Camp and Field during the Creek and Seminole Wars, 1836–1838*, James F. Sunderman, ed. (Gainesville: University of Florida Press, 1953), 210.

23. Simmons, *Notices of East Florida*, 76–77.

24. Dexter, "Observations on the Seminole Indians," frame 513.

25. Simmons, *Notices of East Florida*, 50; Thompson to Cass, April 27, 1835, M234-806, frame 103; Potter, *War in Florida*, 45–46; J. L. Williams, *Territory of Florida*, 239–40.

26. Mulroy, "Seminole Maroons," 467 fig. 3.

27. Thomas Larose, "The African Influences on Seminole Beadwork," paper presented at the twelfth Triennial Symposium of the Arts Council of the African Studies Association, St. Thomas, U.S. Virgin Islands, April 25–29, 2001, copy provided by Larose.

28. Dorothy Downs, *Art of the Florida Seminoles and Miccosukee Indians* (Gainesville: University Press of Florida, 1995), 155–56 and fig 6.2, 166–67 and plate 24; Dorothy Downs, "Possible African Influence on the Art of the Florida Seminoles," in *African Impact on the Material Culture of the Americas*, Conference Proceedings, Diggs Gallery, Winston-Salem State University (Winston-Salem, N.C.: Winston-Salem Museum of Early Southern Decorative Arts, 1996), 1–10; Larose, "African Influences"; Marcilene Wittner, "African Influences on Florida Indian Patchwork," *Southeastern College Art Conference (SECAC) Review* 11 (1989): 269–75.

29. Babatunde Lawal, "Reclaiming the Past: Yoruba Elements in African American Arts," in *The Yoruba Diaspora in the Atlantic World*, Toyin Talola and Matt D. Childs, eds. (Bloomington: Indiana University Press, 2004), 303–304.

30. Frances Densmore, "Seminole Music," *Bureau of American Ethnology Bulletin* 161 (Washington, D.C.: Government Printing Office, 1956), 203, 213, 215.

31. Quoted in Saunt, *New Order*, 35.

32. Ibid., 19.

33. Betty Mae Tiger Jumper and Patsy West, *A Seminole Legend: The Life of Betty Mae Tiger Jumper* (Gainesville: University Press of Florida, 2001), 12–13; Miller, *Coacoochee's Bones*, 1–6, 55–68, 186–87; Miller, "Seminoles and Africans," 30.

34. Tolagbe Ogunleye, "The Self-Emancipated Africans of Florida: Pan-African Nationalists in the 'New World,'" *Journal of Black Studies* 27 (1996): 24–38. See also Foster, *Negro-Indian Relationships*, 51–57. Ogunleye considers "maroons" a derogatory term used by "enraged enslavers" and prefers "self-emancipated Africans" (35n3). Unfortunately, that term

describes only some of the Seminole maroons. In addition to self-emancipated individuals (runaways), the maroons also included persons not yet emancipated (slaves of Seminole Indians or of other maroons), persons emancipated by Indian or maroon owners, and persons born free in Florida. Also, besides displaced Africans, the maroon community included a sizable population of African Americans and a much smaller number of mixed-race Indian-blacks.

35. See chapters 5 and 9.

36. See chapter 8. Braund suggests that mixed-race marriages were much more common among Creeks than Seminoles prior to Removal: "So pervasive was miscegenation, both in the European colonies surrounding the Creek country and in the Creek towns themselves, that a variety of descriptive terms emerged to describe the multihued result of this intimate racial mixing." Braund, "Creek Indians, Blacks, and Slavery," 615–16.

37. Abraham to Coi (Cae) Harjo, September 11, 1837, quoted in full in Porter, *Negro on the American Frontier*, 333–34. Porter (ibid., 304) suggests that "Souanaffe Tustenuggee" could be interpreted as "Shawnee Warrior," but that it also might have meant "Suwannee Warrior."

38. Giddings, *Exiles of Florida*, 324.

39. Morse, *Report to the Secretary of War*, 306–309; Swanton, "Early History of the Creek Indians," 400n1, 406–407.

40. Simmons, *Notices of East Florida*, 41.

41. Richard A. Sattler, "Women's Status among the Muskogee and Cherokee," in *Women and Power in Native North America*, Laura F. Klein and Lillian A. Ackerman, eds. (Norman: University of Oklahoma Press, 1995), 220.

42. Brown, *Peace River*, 26. As early as 1922, anthropologist John Swanton made reference to Buckra Woman's being the mother of Holata Mikko. See Swanton, "Early History of the Creek Indians," 407.

43. Kenneth W. Porter, "Billy Bowlegs (Holata Micco) in the Seminole Wars," part 1, *Florida Historical Quarterly* 45 (1967): 221–23; Kenneth W. Porter, "The Cowkeeper Dynasty of the Seminole Nation," *Florida Historical Quarterly* 30 (1952): 346n21; Sattler, "Siminoli Italwa," 98 fig. 2.6.

44. Brown, *Peace River*, 26–27, 35–36, 39–40; Brown, *Tampa Bay Frontier*, 13, 16–18; Rivers, *Slavery in Florida*, 195–96.

45. Annie H. Abel, *The American Indian as Slaveholder and Secessionist: An Omitted Chapter in the Diplomatic History of the Southern Confederacy* (Cleveland: Arthur H. Clark, 1915), map on 25 (Ben; Charles; Cudjo; Noblio; Tom); Mary Ann Lilley, "The Autobiography of Mary Ann Lilley," 64 pp. typescript, n.d., sec. X, case 5, drawer 3, Seminole Indian file 1, 3a-522-a-1, Indian Archives, Oklahoma Historical Society, Oklahoma City, 47–48 (Juan: "Uncle Warren"); Rev. James Ross Ramsay, "Autobiography," 100 pp. typescript (Santa Paula, Calif.: James Robinson Ramsay, 1939), 33, reproduced on microfilm by the American First Title and Trust Company of Oklahoma City (1 reel, 1970), copy in the Western History Collections, University of Oklahoma Libraries, microfilm 42–66 ("Uncle" Charles). The sketch "Map Showing Free Negro Settlements in the Creek Country," which is reproduced in Abel's *Slaveholder and Secessionist* and forms the basis of the illustration on page 66, contains many geographical inaccuracies. Its primary value lies in naming and roughly locating maroon communities among the Seminoles shortly after mid-century.

46. Dexter to DuVal, August 20, 1823, in Boyd, "Horatio Dexter," 89; Laumer, *Diary of Henry Prince*, 92–93; Brent R. Weisman, *Like Beads on a String: A Culture History of the Seminole Indians in North Peninsular Florida* (Tuscaloosa: University of Alabama Press, 1989), 78, 103, 128, 136, 173–74; Weisman, "Plantation System," 139 map 6, 142.

47. Like Mulatto Girl's town and Buckra Woman's town, that maroon community was named after the Seminole to whom the residents paid tribute, in this case Kapichee Mikko. Simmons, *Notices of East Florida,* 41–42. See also Landers, *Black Society in Spanish Florida,* map on 236.

48. John Bemrose, *Reminiscences of the Second Seminole War,* John K. Mahon, ed. (Gainesville: University of Florida Press, 1966), 70; Dexter, "Observations on the Seminole Indians," frames 507–508; Mark F. Boyd, "The Seminole War: Its Background and Onset," *Florida Historical Quarterly* 30 (1951): 14; Cohen, *Notices of Florida,* 78–79; Porter, *Black Seminoles,* 33, 39, 46; Porter, *Negro on the American Frontier,* 339–56.

49. During his Florida years, John Horse was known as John Cavallo, John Cowaya (and variants), or the nickname "Gopher John." After Removal, in addition to Gopher John, he also became known as Juan Caballo. "Horse," by which he came to be known in Mexico and Texas, was a translation of his owner's surname. Dexter, "Observations on the Seminole Indians," frames 507–508; McCall, *Letters from the Frontiers,* 164; Mulroy, *Freedom on the Border,* 188n57; Kevin Mulroy, "John Horse," in *American National Biography Online* (Oxford and London: American Council of Learned Societies; Oxford University Press, 1999), http://www.anb.org/articles/20/20-01870.html, December 2003 update (January 20, 2004); Porter, *Black Seminoles,* 3, 29–30, 37, map on 38; Kenneth W. Porter, "Davy Crockett and John Horse: A Possible Origin of the Coonskin Story," *American Literature* 15 (1943): 10–15; Kenneth W. Porter, "Thlonoto-sassa: A Note on an Obscure Seminole Village of the Early 1820s," *Florida Anthropologist* 13 (1960): 115–19; Sattler, "Siminoli Italwa," 119.

50. Dexter, "Observations on the Seminole Indians," frames 507–508.

51. Sattler, "Siminoli Italwa," 118–19.

52. McCall, *Letters from the Frontiers,* 160.

53. Miller, *Coacoochee's Bones,* 42–43; Sattler, "Siminoli Italwa," 170.

54. U.S. Congress, *American State Papers,* vol. 7, *Military Affairs,* 825–26; Laumer, *Diary of Henry Prince,* 92–93; Porter, *Negro on the American Frontier,* 280; Kenneth W. Porter, "Osceola and the Negroes," *Florida Historical Quarterly* 33 (1955): 237; Weisman, *Beads on a String,* 128.

55. Sattler, "Siminoli Italwa," 117–18.

56. Ibid., 118.

57. Richard Sattler, pers. comm., May 3, 2002.

58. Ibid., April 4, 2005.

59. Landers, "Black Society," 96.

60. Tuckose Emathla et al. (Florida delegates), talk of May 18, 1826, M234-800 (quote); Sattler, "Siminoli Italwa," 102–103.

61. Charles J. Kappler, comp., *Indian Affairs: Laws and Treaties,* 3 vols. (Washington, D.C.: Government Printing Office, 1904–13), vol. 2, 141–44; Porter, *Negro on the Frontier,* 111 (quote).

62. McKenney and Hall, *Indian Tribes of North America,* vol. 2, 264–69.

63. Perdue, *"Mixed Blood" Indians,* 77.

64. Claudio Saunt, *Black, White, and Indian: Race and the Unmaking of an American Family* (New York: Oxford University Press, 2005), 61.

65. Miller, *Coacoochee's Bones,* 56.

66. Sturtevant and Cattelino, "Florida Seminole," 433–34; Sattler, "Siminoli Italwa," 75, 92–96.

67. Kappler, *Indian Affairs,* vol. 2, 249–51, 290–91.

68. Ibid., 255–56; D. F. Littlefield, *Africans and Seminoles,* 49–50, 63n41; Miller, *Coacoochee's Bones,* 38, 200n15; Sattler, "Siminoli Italwa," 101, 112–13.

69. U.S. Congress, *American State Papers,* vol. 6, *Foreign Affairs,* 454, 458, 464.

70. Canter Brown, Jr., "The Florida Crisis of 1826–1827 and the Second Seminole War," *Florida Historical Quarterly* 73 (1995): 439–41; Grant Foreman, ed., "The Journal of Elijah Hicks," *Chronicles of Oklahoma* 13 (1935): 75; Frank Laumer, *Dade's Last Command* (Gainesville: University Presses of Florida, 1995); Kenneth W. Porter, "Louis Pachecho: The Man and the Myth," *Journal of Negro History* 28 (1943): 65–72; Potter, *War in Florida,* 106.

71. This quote is taken from Ransom Clark's first published account of the battle that appeared in the *Portland (Maine) Daily Advertiser,* March 13, 1836. Over the years, slight variations appeared in the survivor's account, as the details became more lurid with the retelling. In 1839, Clark hit the lecture circuit and also published the last of his descriptions of the battle in his *Narrative of Ransom Clark, the Only Survivor of Major Dade's Command in Florida: Containing Brief Descriptions of What Befel Him from His Enlistment in 1833, till His Discharge, in 1836; With an Account of the Inhuman Massacre, by the Indians and Negroes, of Major Dade's Detachment* (Binghamton, N.Y.: printed by Johnson and Marble, 1839). He died the following year. The taunting "what have you got to sell?" refers to the greeting maroons typically received from the U.S. Army when they visited forts in Florida. See Laumer, *Dade's Last Command,* 138; and Frank Laumer, *Massacre!* (Gainesville: University of Florida Press, 1968), 172.

72. Mahon, *Second Seminole War,* 156–57.

73. U.S. Congress, *American State Papers,* vol. 7, *Military Affairs,* 820–22.

74. Thomas Jesup to Roger Jones, March 6, 1837, H. Doc. 225, 51.

75. Mahon, *Second Seminole War;* Porter, *Black Seminoles,* 38–93; Porter, *Negro on the American Frontier,* 182–357.

76. Giddings, *Exiles of Florida,* 97.

77. "Capitulation of the Seminole Nation of Indians and Their Allies, March 6, 1837," H. Doc. 225, 52.

78. U.S. Congress, *American State Papers,* vol. 7, *Military Affairs,* 835.

79. Mahon, *Second Seminole War,* 201–205.

80. Jesup to Joel R. Poinsett, June 16, 1837, National Archives Record Group 94, Records of the Office of the Adjutant General, 1780s–1917, General Jesup's Papers (hereafter cited as Jesup's Papers), Letters Sent.

81. Jesup to Poinsett, September 23, 1837, ibid.

82. Jesup to William L. Marcy, April 3 and July 1, 1848, National Archives Microfilm Publications, M574, Record Group 75, Special Files of the Office of Indian Affairs, 1807–1904, 85 rolls (hereafter cited as M574), roll 13, file 96, "Seminole Claims to Certain Negroes 1841–1849."

83. Jesup to Poinsett, March 14, 1838; Jesup to William Wilkins, May 22, 1844; Jesup to Marcy, July 1, 1848, ibid.

84. Porter, "Billy Bowlegs in the Seminole Wars," part 1, 229.

85. Term coined by Robert K. Thomas in afterword to Peterson and Brown, *The New Peoples,* 247.

3. POST-REMOVAL UPHEAVALS

1. Kappler, *Indian Affairs,* vol. 2, 249–51, 290–91; D. F. Littlefield, *Africans and Seminoles,* 49–50; Miller, *Coacoochee's Bones,* 47, 49; Sattler, "Siminoli Italwa," 148–50, 170.

2. *ARCIA 1841,* Report 34, William Armstrong to T. Hartley Crawford, September 30, 1841, 327; *ARCIA 1842,* Report 25, Armstrong to Crawford, September 10, 1842, 450–51; Miller, *Coacoochee's Bones,* 47.

3. Crawford and Armstrong quoted in D. F. Littlefield, *Africans and Seminoles,* 71.

4. D. F. Littlefield, *Africans and Seminoles,* 107, 133; Miller, *Coacoochee's Bones,* 47–51; Sattler, "Siminoli Italwa," 170.

5. Perdue recently has argued against using race as the defining factor in interpreting the history of the Five Civilized Tribes. Perdue sees "the assumption that the presence of 'mixed bloods' made a society more 'civilized' [as problematic] on several levels." Perdue, *"Mixed Blood" Indians,* x. See also Theda Perdue, "Race and Culture: Writing the Ethnohistory of the Early South," *Ethnohistory* 51 (2004): 701–33, and Theda Perdue, "A Reply to Saunt et al.," *Ethnohistory* 53 (2006): 407. Perdue advocates for deeper understanding of the complexities inherent in Southeastern Indian societies but, surprisingly, downplays the importance of race. Far more persuasive is Saunt's argument: "[Race] was a central element in the lives of south-eastern Indians, not just as a marker of difference between natives and white newcomers but as a divisive and destructive force within Indian communities themselves." And: "By 1861, no corner of Creek society remained unaffected by race and slavery." Saunt, *Black, White, and Indian,* 4, 96, and also 11, 17, 158–60. See also Claudio Saunt et al., "Rethinking Race and Culture in the Early South," *Ethnohistory* 53 (2006): 399–405. Problematic though it might be, there is a strong correlation between the presence of intermarried whites and their "mixed-blood" offspring, on the one hand, and receptivity within the tribes to white ac-culturation, including the adoption of institutionalized black slavery, on the other. Almost entirely lacking an intermarried white and "mixed-blood" elite, the Seminoles, without question, remained the most indigenous and the least receptive of the Five Tribes.

6. *ARCIA 1841,* Report 34, Armstrong to Crawford, September 30, 1841, 327, and Report 36, J. Logan to Armstrong, September 30, 1841, 341; *ARCIA 1842,* Report 25, Armstrong to Crawford, September 10, 1842, 450–51, and Report 27, Logan to Armstrong, June 30, 1842, 456; *ARCIA 1845,* Report 17, Logan to Armstrong, September 20, 1845, 515–17; *ARCIA 1846,* Report 11, Logan to Armstrong, October 1, 1846, 274; *Arkansas Intelligencer,* August 2, 1845; Josiah Gregg, *Commerce of the Prairies,* 2 vols. (New York: H. G. Langley, 1844), vol. 2, 303; Daniel F. Littlefield, Jr., *Africans and Creeks: From the Colonial Period to the Civil War* (Westport, Conn.: Greenwood Press, 1979), 159–61; D. F. Littlefield, *Africans and Seminoles,* 176; Sigmund Sameth, "Creek Negroes: A Study of Race Relations," M.A. thesis, University of Oklahoma, 1940, 17–18, 20–21, 27–28.

7. D. F. Littlefield, *Africans and Seminoles,* 76; Edwin C. McReynolds, *The Seminoles* (Norman: University of Oklahoma Press, 1957), 232; Kenneth W. Porter, "Seminole Flight from Fort Marion," *Florida Historical Quarterly* 22 (1944): 132n4.

8. Ethan Allen Hitchcock, *Fifty Years in Camp and Field: The Diary of Major General Ethan Allen Hitchcock,* W. A. Croffut, ed. (New York: G. P. Putnam's Sons, 1909), 138.

9. Armstrong to Crawford, April 12, 1842, M234-800, Seminole Agency, 1824–45, A1223-42; Miller, *Coacoochee's Bones,* 49; Sattler, "Siminoli Italwa," 148–53.

10. *ARCIA 1842,* Report 25, Armstrong to Crawford, September 10, 1842, 450–51.

11. *Niles Weekly Register* 54, May 5, 1838; Porter, *Negro on the American Frontier,* 258–60; Porter, "Seminole Flight from Fort Marion," 129, 133n7; John T. Sprague, *The Origin, Progress and Conclusion of the Florida War* (New York: D. Appleton and Co.; Philadelphia: G. S. Appleton, 1848), 195.

12. W. W. J. Bliss to R. B. Mason, April 11, 1842, and Bliss to S. Kearny, May 13, 1842, National Archives Record Group 393, Records of the U.S. Army Continental Commands, 1821–1920, Fort Gibson, Letters Received (hereafter cited as Fort Gibson, Letters Received or Letters Sent), box 1; Mason to R. Jones, November 3, 1844, Fort Gibson, Letters Sent; L. Thomas to Mason, December 18, 1844, Fort Gibson, Letters Received, box 2; National

Archives Record Group 393, Records of the U.S. Army Continental Commands, 1821–1920, Fort Gibson, Indian Affairs (hereafter cited as Fort Gibson, Indian Affairs), 1–2, 8; Grant Foreman, *The Five Civilized Tribes* (Norman: University of Oklahoma Press, 1934), 226, 258; McReynolds, *Seminoles,* 259; John W. Morris, Charles Goins, and Edwin C. McReynolds, *Historical Atlas of Oklahoma* (Norman: University of Oklahoma Press, 1976 [1965]), no. 44, Seminole Nation 1889; Kenneth W. Porter, "O Freedom over Me: A Folk-History of the Wild Cat-John Horse Band of Seminole Negroes 1848–1882," Kenneth Wiggins Porter Papers, Manuscripts, Archives, and Rare Books Division, Schomburg Center for Research in Black Culture, New York Public Library, box 1; Porter, "Seminole Flight from Fort Marion," 133n7.

13. Report of Pierce M. Butler, Cherokee Agency, April 16, 1845, M234-800, B2452-45.

14. J. L. Belger to Gustavus Loomis, April 3, 1844, Fort Gibson, Letters Sent; J. L. Dawson to Captain Nathan Boone, April 10, 1844, Fort Gibson, Letters Received, box 2; Boone to Dawson, April 8, 1844, National Archives Record Group 393, Records of the U.S. Army Continental Commands, 1821–1920, Second and Seventh Military Departments (hereafter cited as Second and Seventh Military Departments), Letters Received, box 5; Bliss to Dawson, May 13, 1844, Second and Seventh Military Departments, Letters Sent; D. F. Littlefield, *Africans and Creeks,* 170–71; D. F. Littlefield, *Africans and Seminoles,* 84–85, 96n45.

15. Micco Nupper et al. to Commissioner of Indian Affairs, April 20, 1844, M234-800, M194-44.

16. Alligator et al. to Crawford, May 16, 1844, M234-800, M1624-44. See also Jesup to William Wilkins, May 30, 1844, M234-800, J1482-44; and G. Foreman, *Five Civilized Tribes,* 237.

17. Mason to Jones, July 10, 1844, M234-800, M1973-44. See also Porter, *Black Seminoles,* 113–14.

18. Butler to Crawford, July 25, 1845, M234-800, B2528-45.

19. Jesup, Endorsement of August 2, 1844, on Mason to Jones, July 10, 1844, M234-800, M1973-44.

20. Armstrong to Crawford, May 22, 1843, M234-800, A1457-43.

21. Wilkins's Instructions to General Matthew Arbuckle, August 2, 1844, M234-800, A1457-43.

22. Mason to Jones, July 10, 1844, and Thomas L. Judge to Boone, August 31, 1844, M234-800, M1973-44, J1684-45; Jones to Arbuckle, August 3, 1844, Fort Gibson, Letters Received, box 2; Statement of Boone, n.d., Fort Gibson, Indian Affairs, 25.

23. G. Foreman, *Five Civilized Tribes,* 243.

24. Seminole Memorial, December 28, 1844, M234-800, frame 626.

25. *ARCIA 1845,* Report 15, Armstrong to Crawford, September 30, 1845, 506–507.

26. Kappler, *Indian Affairs,* vol. 2, 407–409; National Archives Microfilm Publications, T494, Documents Relating to the Negotiation of Ratified and Unratified Treaties with Various Indian Tribes, 1801–69, 10 rolls (hereafter cited as T494), roll 4, Ratified Treaties 1838–53, Ratified Treaty no. 244, Documents Relating to the Negotiation of the Treaty of 4 January 1845 with the Creek and Seminole Indians, frames 235–43.

27. *ARCIA 1845,* Report 20, Marcellus Duval to Crawford, September 30, 1845, 530; Miller, *Coacoochee's Bones,* 95.

28. Mason to Jones, March 5, 1845, Mason to Lt. James H. Prentiss, May 21, 1845, and Captain A. Cady to Jones, March 18, 1846, Fort Gibson, Letters Sent; Prentiss to Mason, May 28, 1845, Second and Seventh Military Departments, Letters Sent; Statement of Mason, March 11, 1845, Loomis to McIntosh, July 20, 1846, and Kirkham to Jesup, August 20 and

26, 1846, Fort Gibson, Indian Affairs, 9, 18, 19; Jones to Arbuckle, April 22, 1846, and Captain J. Lynde to Flint, October 12, 1848, Second and Seventh Military Departments, Letters Received, boxes 6 and 7; D. F. Littlefield, *Africans and Seminoles,* 103–104, 108–109; Porter, *Black Seminoles,* 120–22.

29. Report of Butler, Cherokee Agency, April 16, 1845, Judge to Crawford, April 27, 1845, and Butler to Crawford, July 25, 1845, M234-800, B2452-45, J1684-45, B2528-45; G. Foreman, *Five Civilized Tribes,* 258; D. F. Littlefield, *Africans and Seminoles,* 104.

30. Report of Butler, Cherokee Agency, April 16, 1845, M234-800, B2452-45.

31. Janet Halliburton, "Black Slavery in the Creek Nation," *Chronicles of Oklahoma* 56 (1978): 303–305; Antonio J. Waring, ed., *Laws of the Creek Nation,* University of Georgia Libraries Miscellaneous Publications no. 1 (Athens: University of Georgia Press, 1960), 17–27.

32. Judge to Crawford, April 27, 1845, M234-800, J1684-45. General John T. Mason should not be confused with Colonel Richard Mason, the post commander at Fort Gibson, or with John Y. Mason, the attorney general whose opinion affected the maroons so dramatically in June 1848. See Porter, *Black Seminoles,* 116–17.

33. Kenneth W. Porter to Constance McLaughlin Green, June 18, 1973, included in "Seven Lean Years, 1842–1849," in Porter, "Freedom over Me," Porter Papers, box 2.

34. Application of Gopher John through J. C. Casey, Washington, May 28, 1845, M234-800, C2309-45.

35. Abel, *Slaveholder and Secessionist,* map on 25, and see the illustration on page 66 of the present work; Miller, *Coacoochee's Bones,* 95; Sattler, "Siminoli Italwa," 176–77.

36. Porter to McLaughlin Green, June 18, 1973, included in "Seven Lean Years, 1842–1849," and "Seven Lean Years," in Porter, "Freedom Over Me," 21–25, Porter Papers, box 2. See also Porter, *Black Seminoles,* 116–18.

37. Duval to William Medill, March 24, 1846, M234-801, Seminole Agency, 1846–55, D1059-46; Duval to J. K. Polk, December 21,1846, M574, roll 13, file 96, frames 194–200; G. Foreman, *Five Civilized Tribes,* 243; Grant Foreman, *Fort Gibson: A Brief History* (Norman: University of Oklahoma Press, 1936), 31. In 1978, a sign posted at the historic site of Fort Gibson read, "This Commissary Building was started by the U.S. Army in 1845 and many Seminole Negro Slaves were used in its construction. It is the oldest stone Military Building within the state. It is the property of Oklahoma."

38. Jesup to Arbuckle, April 8, 1846, M574, roll 13, file 96, frame 92.

39. William A. Gordon, Statement, April 13, 1846, Gustavis Loomis to Duval, May 3, 1846, and Ralph W. Kirkham to Jesup, August 20, 1846, Fort Gibson, Indian Affairs, 17–18; Duval to Medill, June 2, 1847, and Jesup to Medill, July 13, 1848, M234-801, D38-47, J96-48; Duval to Loomis, June 7, 1847, Fort Gibson, Letters Received, box 3; Loomis to Casey, June 11, 1847, Fort Gibson, Letters Sent; Porter, *Black Seminoles,* 121.

40. Kirkham to Jesup, August 20, 1846, Fort Gibson, Indian Affairs, 18.

41. Loomis to F. F. Flint, October 29, 1846, Second and Seventh Military Departments, Letters Received, box 6; Loomis to Flint, July 20, 1847, Fort Gibson, Indian Affairs, 26; D. F. Littlefield, *Africans and Seminoles,* 112–14.

42. Loomis to Jesup, December 7, 1847, M574, roll 13, file 96, frames 31–33.

43. Arbuckle to Jones, January 29, 1848, ibid., frames 28–29.

44. Loomis to Jesup, December 7, 1847, ibid., frames 31–33.

45. Benjamin Marshall, Tuckabatchee Micco, G. W. Stidham, and George Scott to Medill, April 26, 1848, ibid., frames 52–54.

46. Gopher John to Jesup, June 10, 1848, M234-801, J102-48.

47. Ibid.; Flint to William G. Belknap, December 19, 1848, Fort Gibson, Letters Re-

ceived, box 3; Receipts of Chitto Harjo, January 11, May 15, 1849, Fort Gibson, Indian Affairs, 44–46; Porter, *Black Seminoles,* 125.

48. John Y. Mason to President of the United States, June 28, 1848, M574, roll 13, file 96, frames 57–78, esp. frames 71, 73, 74, 77; *Official Opinions of the Attorneys General of the United States,* 112 vols. (Washington, D.C.: Farnham, 1852–70), vol. 4, 720–29.

49. Gopher John to Jesup, June 10, 1848, M234-801, J102-48; Jesup to B. L. E. Bonneville, July 28, 1848, Medill to Gopher John, August 2, 1848, and Statement of Coacoochee, August 21, 1848, Fort Gibson, Indian Affairs, 36–38; W. L. Marcy to Arbuckle, August 5, 1848, and Medill to Duval, August 5, 1848, Fort Gibson, Letters Received, box 3.

50. Flint to W. S. Ketchum, August 21 and September 25, 1848, Fort Gibson, Letters Received, box 3; D. S. Miles to Flint, November 17, 1848, and Duval to Arbuckle, December 1 and 11, 1848, Second and Seventh Military Departments, Letters Received, box 7; D. F. Littlefield, *Africans and Seminoles,* 131–32, 146.

51. *ARCIA 1845,* Report 15, Armstrong to Crawford, September 20, 1845, 506–507, and Report 20, Duval to Crawford, September 30, 1845, 529–31.

52. *ARCIA* 1846, Report 15, Duval to Medill, September 5, 1846, 278; *Arkansas Intelligencer,* May 24, 1845; *Cherokee Advocate,* May 22, 1845; Grant Foreman, *Advancing the Frontier 1830–1860* (Norman: University of Oklahoma Press, 1933), 229; Miller, *Coacoochee's Bones,* 97.

53. G. Foreman, "Journal of Elijah Hicks," 71, 75, 80–81. See also McReynolds, *Seminoles,* 256–57; and Miller, *Coacoochee's Bones,* 98–103.

54. *ARCIA 1846,* Report 9, Armstrong to Medill, October 10, 1846, 266, and Report 15, Duval to Medill, September 5, 1846, 279; *Arkansas Intelligencer,* October 3, 1846; *Cherokee Advocate,* July 30, 1846; G. Foreman, *Five Civilized Tribes,* 244–45, 260–61n12; Miller, *Coacoochee's Bones,* 103–105.

55. Coacoochee to Secretary of War, May 12, 1847, M234-801, C82-47; *ARCIA 1847,* Report 20, Duval to Medill, September 30, 1847, 888; *ARCIA 1848,* Report 22c, R. S. Neighbors to Medill, March 2, 1848, 576–86; Miller, *Coacoochee's Bones,* 103–105; Rupert N. Richardson, *The Comanche Barrier to South Plains Settlement: A Century and a Half of Savage Resistance to the Advancing White Frontier* (Glendale, Calif.: Arthur H. Clark, 1933), 170–71 and n317.

56. Mikko Mucasa appears to have been the son of Hothli Emathla (Jumper) and a sister of Mikkoanapa. Hothli Emathla was a Seminole leader during the Second Seminole War. Mikko Mucasa likely was the older brother of Heniha Mikko (John Jumper), who succeeded him as principal chief. Kowakochi was the son of Emathla and another sister of Mikkoanapa. See Carolyn T. Foreman, "The Jumper Family of the Seminole Nation," *Chronicles of Oklahoma* 34 (1956): 284; McReynolds, *Seminoles,* 260–61; and Kenneth W. Porter, "Seminole in Mexico, 1850–1861," *Chronicles of Oklahoma* 29 (1951): 154. Miller does not subscribe to the theory that Duval influenced the selection, seeing Mikko Mucasa as Mikkoanapa's rightful heir. See Miller, *Coacoochee's Bones,* 110–11.

57. Francis N. Page to D. E. Twiggs, November 18, 1854, *Indians—Creek and Seminole,* 33rd Cong., 2d Sess., H. Ex. Doc. 15, 1854 (hereafter cited *as Indians—Creek and Seminole*), 11.

58. Arbuckle to Jones, July 31, 1848, Flint to J. Drennen, September 10, 1849, and Page to Twiggs, November 18, 1854, ibid., 22, 29, 10; Miles to Flint, November 17, 1848, Second and Seventh Military Departments, Letters Received, box 7.

59. Arbuckle to Jones, July 31, 1849, *Indians—Creek and Seminole,* 22.

60. Belknap to Arbuckle, January 3, 1849, Arbuckle to Jones, January 8, 1849, M574, roll

13, file 96, frames 164, 140–41; Arbuckle to Jones, July 31, 1849, and Flint to Drennen, August 13, 1849, *Indians—Creek and Seminole,* 22, 26.

61. Belknap to Arbuckle, January 3, 1849, M574, roll 13, file 96, frame 164.

62. "List of Negroes who surrendered under a proclamation of Major General Jesup when in command of the Army in Florida, who were entitled to freedom or were to accompany the Seminoles as part of the Nation under the protection of the United States and were never to be separated or sold," Filed by Jesup in the Adjutant General's Office at Fort Gibson, Cherokee Nation, July 24, 1845, and "List of Negroes handed over to the Seminole Chiefs at Fort Gibson, Cherokee Nation, 2 January 1849," M574, roll 13, file 96, frames 143–54. Littlefield has reproduced the latter as List K in the appendix to his *Africans and Seminoles.*

63. Arbuckle to Jones, January 8, 1849, M574, roll 13, file 96, frames 140–41.

64. Duval to Belknap, June 7, 1849, Fort Gibson, Letters Received, box 3; Duval to Arbuckle, July 16, 1849, Arbuckle to Jones, July 31, 1849, and Page to Twiggs, November 18, 1854, *Indians—Creek and Seminole,* 19, 22, 10; " 'I'm in the Wewoka Switch': Heard in the Oil Fields over the World," *Chronicles of Oklahoma* 41 (1963): 457; D. F. Littlefield, *Africans and Seminoles,* 133–34.

65. Page to Twiggs, November 18, 1854, *Indians—Creek and Seminole,* 11.

66. "Pass," April 8, 1849, Fort Gibson, Indian Affairs, 45.

67. Duval to Belknap, June 7, 1849, Fort Gibson, Letters Received, box 3.

68. Duval to Arbuckle, July 16, 1849, Drennen to Arbuckle, July 20, 1849, and Arbuckle to Jones, July 31 and August 14, 1849, *Indians—Creek and Seminole,* 19–20, 22, 25.

69. Duval to Arbuckle, July 16, 1849, ibid., 19–20.

70. Drennen to Arbuckle, July 20, 1849, Flint to Drennen, July 26, 1849, and Arbuckle to Jones, July 31, 1849, ibid., 20, 21, 22–23.

71. Flint to Belknap, August 2, 1849, ibid., 23–24.

72. Flint to Drennen, August 13, 1849, ibid., 26.

73. Arbuckle to Jones, August 14, 1849, ibid., 25.

74. Drennen to Arbuckle, August 18, 1849, ibid., 27.

75. Page to Twiggs, November 18, 1854, ibid., 11.

76. Flint to Drennen, September 10, 1849, Flint to Colonel Raiford, September 10, 1849, Arbuckle to Jones, September 14, 1849, and Page to Twiggs, November 18, 1854, ibid., 28–29, 30, 31, 11.

77. Francisco F. de la Maza, *Código de colonización y terrenos baldíos de la República Mexicána 1451–1892* (Mexico City: Secretaría de Fomento, 1893), no. 120, Reglamento de 4 de Diciembre de 1846: Para la Direccion de Colonización, 347–59, esp. Article 45, 356, no. 125, Descreto de 19 de Julio de 1848, y Reglamento expedido el dia 20 del mismo mes, para el establecimiento de colonias militares en la nueva linea divisoria con los Estados Unidos de América, 400–406. See also Dieter G. Berringer, "Mexican Attitudes towards Immigration 1821–1857," Ph.D. dissertation, University of Wisconsin, 1972, 139–42; and Odie B. Faulk, "Projected Mexican Military Colonies for the Borderlands, 1848," *Journal of Arizona History* 9 (1968): 39–47.

78. J. Lynde to Flint, October 12, 1849, and Belknap to Flint, October 31, 1849, Second and Seventh Military Departments, Letters Received, box 7; Page to Twiggs, November 18, 1854, *Indians—Creek and Seminole,* 11.

79. Duval to O. Brown, November 5, 1849, M234-289, Florida Superintendency, 1838–50, D247-49; G. Foreman, *Five Civilized Tribes,* 248; McReynolds, *Seminoles,* 266.

80. Raiford to Drennen, November 15, 1849, M234-924, Western Superintendency, 1847–51, D274-49 enc.; Duval to Brown, May 30, 1850, M234-801, D392-50; Page to

Twiggs, November 18, 1854, *Indians—Creek and Seminole,* 11; Giddings, *Exiles of Florida,* 333; Miller, *Coacoochee's Bones,* 118–19; Mulroy, *Freedom on the Border,* 71, 143; Porter, "O Freedom over Me" and "They Packed Up at Night and Stole Away," in Porter, "Freedom over Me," Porter Papers, boxes 1 and 2; *San Antonio Western Texas,* June 6, 1850; Sattler, "Siminoli Italwa," 395–96n66; Frost Woodhull, "The Seminole Indian Scouts on the Border," *Frontier Times* 15 (1937): Statement of Charlie Daniels, 119.

81. For studies of the Seminoles and maroons in Texas and Mexico, see Miller, *Coacoochee's Bones;* Mulroy, *Freedom on the Border;* and Porter, *Black Seminoles.*

82. William Bowlegs to Seminole Chiefs, April 12, 1850, Second and Seventh Military Departments, Letters Received, box 8.

83. McIntosh to Belknap, June 12, 1850, *Indians—Creek and Seminole,* 16–17.

84. F. T. Dent to Flint, July 15, 1850, ibid., 17–18.

85. Duval to Arbuckle, July 29, 1850, and Belknap to Page, August 6, 1850, Second and Seventh Military Departments, Letters Received, box 8.

86. Dent to Flint, July 15, 1850, *Indians—Creek and Seminole,* 17–18.

87. Duval to Peter Hansborough Bell, October 20, 1850, Peter Hansborough Bell, Governors' Papers, 1849–53, Archives, Texas State Library and Archives Commission, Austin, folder 2, Correspondence: Indian Affairs 1850–52 (hereafter cited as Bell Papers); Walter Prescott Webb, *The Texas Rangers: A Century of Frontier Defense* (Boston: Houghton-Mifflin, 1935), 135.

88. Rodney Glisan, *Journal of Army Life* (San Francisco: A. L. Bancroft and Co., 1874), 65–66; Randolph B. Marcy and G. B. McClellan, *Exploration of the Red River of Louisiana in the Year 1852* (Washington, D.C.: R. Armstrong, Public Printer, 1853), 101; Randolph B. Marcy, *Thirty Years of Army Life on the Border* (New York: Harper and Bros., 1866), 30–31, 55–56; McReynolds, *Seminoles,* 263; Woodhull, "Seminole Indian Scouts," Statement of Renty Grayson 1927, 123. See also Grant Foreman, ed., *Adventure on Red River: Report on the Exploration of the Red River by Captain Randolph B. Marcy and Captain G. B. McClellan* (Norman: University of Oklahoma Press, 1937), 166.

89. Echo Hadjo et al. (Canadian Creek Chiefs) to McIntosh, September 20, 1850, and McIntosh to Belknap, September 23, 1850, *Indians—Creek and Seminole,* 31–32; Duval to Luke Lea, September 21 and 30, 1850, M234-801, D451-50, D455-50; Duval to Bell, October 20, 1850, and J. H. Rollins to Bell, October 30, 1850, Bell Papers.

90. McIntosh to Belknap, September 23, 1850, *Indians—Creek and Seminole,* 32.

91. Ibid.; Belknap to Page, October 15, 1850, ibid., 32; Duval to Lea, September 30, 1850, M234-801, D455-50; C. J. Atkins to Commander of Fort Gibson, September 30, 1850, Fort Gibson, Letters Received, box 3.

92. Duval to Bell, October 20, 1850, Bell Papers; Duval to Lea, December 9, 1850, M234-801, D481-50; *ARCIA 1851,* Report 40, Duval to Lea, October 25, 1851, 405; Page to Twiggs, November 18, 1854, *Indians—Creek and Seminole,* 13; Miller, *Coacoochee's Bones,* 132–38.

93. Page to Twiggs, November 18, 1854, *Indians—Creek and Seminole,* 12; *Cherokee Advocate,* November 19, 1850; *Fort Smith (Ark.) Herald,* November 1 and 11, 1850; McReynolds, *Seminoles,* 263.

94. Glisan, *Journal of Army Life,* 65–66.

95. Porter suggested that Jim Bowlegs was one of those who managed to elude his captors and escape to Mexico and that his descendants were living at Nacimiento, Coahuila, and in Brackettville, Texas, in the 1940s. Kenneth W. Porter, "Lament for Wild Cat," *Phylon* 4 (1943): 39. I accepted that suggestion in *Freedom on the Border,* 64, 71. However, in retracing

the documentary path, I have been unable to find support for the idea that Jim Bowlegs successfully emigrated to Mexico. It seems more probable that he returned to the Seminole country in the fall of 1850 and rejoined the maroon community there. While it is possible that the Jim Bowlegs who rose to prominence in the Indian Territory in the 1850s and during the Civil War (see ensuing chapters) was another person with the same name, that explanation is unlikely. More likely, the Bowlegs families in Nacimiento and Bracketville had descended from David, Friday, and Jack Bowlegs, maroons known to have made the journey to Mexico in 1849–50.

4. SEMINOLE SLAVE OWNERS

1. This total is based on an analysis of the various Seminole emigration rolls. D. F. Littlefield, in *Africans and Seminoles,* 176, arrives at the same figure.

2. N. Sayer Harris, *Journal of a Tour in the "Indian Country"* (New York: Daniel Dana, 1844), 16.

3. Arbuckle to Jones, January 8, 1849, M574, roll 13, file 96, frames 140–41.

4. "Claims of Loyal Seminole for Losses Suffered during the Civil War, Submitted under Provisions of the Treaty of March 21, 1866," M574, roll 11, file 87; D. F. Littlefield, *Africans and Seminoles,* 176.

5. *ARCIA 1857,* Doc. 58, Report of Samuel M. Rutherford, 184; Michael F. Doran, "Population Statistics of Nineteenth Century Indian Territory," *Chronicles of Oklahoma* 53 (1975): 497–98, 501.

6. Edward L. Carter, "The Seminole Nation after Leaving Florida, 1855–1860," *Chronicles of Oklahoma* 55 (1977): 452.

7. Mulroy, *Freedom on the Border,* 84.

8. J. Y. Mason to President of the United States, June 28, 1848, M574, roll 13, file 96, frames 57–78; *Official Opinions of the Attorneys General,* vol. 4, 720–29.

9. D. F. Littlefield, *Africans and Seminoles,* 155.

10. Information on the Cherokees, Creeks, Choctaws, and Chickasaws during the antebellum period is drawn from an extensive bibliography of primary and secondary sources. Surveys include Abel, *Slaveholder and Secessionist;* Angie E. Debo, *The Rise and Fall of the Choctaw Republic* (Norman: University of Oklahoma Press, 1934); G. Foreman, *Five Civilized Tribes;* Arrell M. Gibson, *The Chickasaws* (Norman: University of Oklahoma Press, 1971); D. F. Littlefield, *Africans and Creeks;* Daniel F. Littlefield, Jr., *The Cherokee Freedmen: From Emancipation to American Citizenship* (Westport, Conn.: Greenwood Press, 1978); Daniel F. Littlefield, Jr., *The Chickasaw Freedmen: A People without a Country* (Westport, Conn.: Greenwood Press, 1980); William G. McLoughlin, *After the Trail of Tears: The Cherokees' Struggle for Sovereignty, 1839–1880* (Chapel Hill: University of North Carolina Press, 1993); Theda Perdue, *Slavery and the Evolution of Cherokee Society 1540–1866* (Knoxville: University of Tennessee Press, 1979); Kaye M. Teall, *Black History in Oklahoma: A Resource Book* (Oklahoma City: Oklahoma City Public Schools—Title III, ESEA, 1971); and Morris L. Wardell, *A Political History of the Cherokee Nation 1838–1907* (Norman: University of Oklahoma Press, 1938).

11. Richard A. Sattler, pers. comm., January 30, 2006.

12. Doran, "Population Statistics," 501 table 3.

13. *ARCIA 1842,* Doc. 25, Report of Armstrong, 450–51; *ARCIA 1844,* Doc. 80, Report of Thomas L. Judge, 476; *ARCIA 1846,* Doc. 14, Report of Duval, 279–80; *ARCIA 1857,* Doc. 92, Report of Josiah Washbourne, 229.

14. M574, roll 11, file 87, frames 49 and 315.

15. Grant Foreman, ed., *A Traveller in Indian Territory: The Journal of Ethan Allen Hitchcock, Late Major-General in the United States Army* (Cedar Rapids, Iowa: Torch Press, 1930), 187.

16. Indian Pioneer Papers (a collection of oral history interviews conducted in Oklahoma under the auspices of the Works Progress Administration [WPA] during the 1930s), 116 vols., Indian Archives, Oklahoma Historical Society, vol. 108, 213. Many other contemporary observations support that idea. For example, on the eve of the Civil War, Charles Whipple reported on slavery among Cherokee-whites: "This institution was derived from the Whites. It has all the general characteristics of Negro slavery in the Southern portion of our union. In such a state of society as we find among these Indians, there must of necessity be some modification of the system; but in all essential features, it remains unchanged." Two years after the war ended, Albert Richardson wrote of Cherokee and Choctaw Indians without white admixture: "Slavery among them was farcical rather than tragical. The Negroes, far more intelligent than their masters, did much as they pleased, owning money, cattle and ponies; and as they made all purchases for the family, often feathering their own nests." Charles K. Whipple, *Relation of the American Board of Commissioners for Foreign Missions to Slavery* (Boston: R. F. Wallcut, 1861), 88–89; Albert D. Richardson, *Beyond the Mississippi* (Hartford, Conn.: American, 1867), 220.

17. *ARCIA 1846,* Doc. 14, Report of Duval, 281.

18. *ARCIA 1859,* Doc. 58, Report of Rutherford, 183–84.

19. Presbyterian Church in the USA, *Historical Sketches of the Missions under the Care of the Board of Missions of the Presbyterian Church* (Philadelphia: Woman's Foreign Missionary Society of the Presbyterian Church, 1886), 26–27.

20. Rev. Joseph S. Murrow to Rev. Walter N. Wyeth, March 10, 1896, quoted in Walter N. Wyeth, *Poor Lo: Early Indian Missions: A Memorial* (Philadelphia: Walter N. Wyeth, 1896), 113. Historian Robert Hamilton even suggested that the Seminoles enacted laws prohibiting the preaching or practice of Christianity within the tribe. Robert Hamilton, *The Gospel among the Red Men* (Nashville: Sunday School Board of the Southern Baptist Convention, 1944), 98. On Factor's being of Indian-black extraction, see Sattler, "Siminoli Italwa," 207.

21. *ARCIA 1843,* 271–72, and Doc. 73, Crawford to Armstrong, n.d., 372–73; G. Foreman, *Five Civilized Tribes,* caption for plate facing 240. On Talomas Mikko's unusual background, see Michael E. Welsh, "The Road to Assimilation: The Seminoles in Oklahoma," Ph.D. dissertation, University of New Mexico, 1983, 51–53.

22. *ARCIA 1844,* Doc. 80, Report of Judge, 477–78.

23. *ARCIA 1849,* Doc. 4A, John Lilley to Duval, September 19, 1849, 1128; *ARCIA 1869,* C3, W. Morris Grimes to Vincent Colyer, March 9, 1869, 79; Welsh, "Road to Assimilation," 55–57.

24. Presbyterian Church, *Historical Sketches,* 27.

25. Indian Pioneer Papers, vol. 104, no. 7727, Nettie Cain, 195; Ramsay, "Autobiography," 31, 38, 42–46, 58.

26. Roland Hinds, "Early Creek Missions," *Chronicles of Oklahoma* 17 (1939): 55–56.

27. William A. Carleton, *Not Yours, but You* (Berkeley, Calif.: William A. Carleton, 1954), 53–54; J. M. Gaskin, *Trail Blazers of Sooner Baptists* (Shawnee: Oklahoma Baptist University Press, 1953), 42; H. Glenn Jordan, "Joseph Samuel Morrow: The Man and His Times," Ph.D. dissertation, University of Oklahoma, 1982, 34–35, 272n82; James W. Moffit, "A History of Early Baptist Missions among the Five Civilized Tribes," Ph.D. dissertation, University of Oklahoma, 1946, 144–48; Eugene C. Routh, *The Story of Oklahoma Baptists* (Oklahoma City: Baptist General Convention of Oklahoma, 1932), 42–43.

28. Kappler, *Indian Affairs,* vol. 2, 573, Article 8.

29. *ARCIA 1857,* Doc. 92, Report of Washbourne, 228.

30. *ARCIA 1844,* Doc. 14, table on 356, and Doc. 31, Report of John D. Bemo, 379.

31. *ARCIA 1846,* Doc. 14, Report of Duval, 280.

32. *ARCIA 1847,* Doc. 20, Report of Duval, 889.

33. G. Foreman, *Five Civilized Tribes,* 246; Presbyterian Church, *Historical Sketches,* 27.

34. *ARCIA 1851,* Doc. 40, Report of Duval, 406.

35. John C. Lowrie, *A Manual of Missions, or Sketches of the Foreign Missions of the Presbyterian Church: With Maps, Showing the Stations and Statistics of Protestant Missions among Unevangelized Nations* (New York: A. D. F. Randolph, 1854), 22; *ARCIA 1857,* Doc. 93, Report of Lilley, 229; *ARCIA 1859,* Doc. 59, Report of Lilley, 186–87.

36. Hinds, "Creek Missions," 55–56.

37. Jordan, "Joseph Morrow," 35, 272n82.

38. *ARCIA 1845,* Doc. 20, Report of Duval, 529–30; *ARCIA 1846,* Doc. 14, Report of Duval, 278.

39. *ARCIA 1859,* Doc. 46, Report of Elias Rector, 159.

40. Rutherford to Elias Rector, August 15, 1860, quoted in G. Foreman, *Five Civilized Tribes,* 276.

41. *ARCIA 1854,* 12–13.

42. John W. Barber and Henry Howe, *Our Whole Country, or, the Past and Present of the United States, Historical and Descriptive,* 2 vols. (Cincinnati, Ohio: Henry Howe, 1861), vol. 2, 1477–78.

43. *Southern Literary Messenger* 28 (1859): 333–35.

44. *ARCIA 1847,* Doc. 20, Report of Duval, 888. See also *ARCIA 1848,* Doc. 13, Report of James Logan, 521–22; and *ARCIA 1849,* Doc. 4, Report of Duval, 1127.

45. *ARCIA 1851,* Doc. 40, Report of Duval, 406.

46. Drennen to Lea, September 27, 1852, Lea to A. H. H. Stuart, November 10, 1852, Duval to Lea, November 15, 1852, Duval to Commissioner of Indian Affairs, April 8, 1853, M234-801, I131-52 and enc., D223-52, D298-53; *ARCIA 1852,* Doc. 37, Report of Drennen, 103; Lilley, "Autobiography," 39; D. F. Littlefield, *Africans and Seminoles,* 157; McReynolds, *Seminoles,* 190.

47. *ARCIA 1853,* Doc. 63, Report of Bryan H. Smithson, 399. See also *ARCIA 1854,* Doc. 54, Report of Washbourne, 128.

48. *ARCIA 1855,* Doc. 47, Report of Dean, 120–21; *Arkansas Intelligencer,* June 29, 1855.

49. *ARCIA 1855,* Doc. 87, Report of Washbourne, 172 (first two quotes); and Report of Commissioner, 9 (third quote). See also Doc. 47, Report of Dean, 120–21; and Doc. 56, Report of W. H. Garrett, 136–37.

50. John Jumper, Tustenucochee, Parscofer (Pascofar), and James Factor to George W. Manypenny, May 3, 1856, M234-802, Seminole Agency, 1856–58, J151-56.

51. Kappler, *Indian Affairs,* vol. 2, 569–76.

52. *ARCIA 1860,* Doc. 51, Report of Rutherford, 126.

53. Major G. W. Andrews to Post Adjutant, November 23, 1854, Fort Gibson, Letters Received, box 3; Thomas S. Drew to Manypenny, March 14, 1855, M234-833, Southern Superintendency, 1851–56, D816-55; Cornelius D. Pryor to Dean, April 10, 1856, M234-802, D153-56; Foreman Transcripts, 7 typescript vols. containing transcribed copies of U.S. government documents on the Five Civilized Tribes, Indian Archives, Oklahoma Historical Society, vol. 7, 71.

54. William Bowlegs to Jim Jumper and the Chiefs, April 12, 1850, Second and Seventh Military Departments, Letters Received, box 8.

55. Decision of the Apalachicola Chiefs, June 15, 1827, Statement of Nelly Factor, September 4, 1828, Statement of DuVal, September 10, 1828, and DuVal to William J. Worth, December 22, 1842, M234-289, Florida Superintendency, 1838–50, S3398-43.

56. Deposition of Molly, Fort Smith, Arkansas, August 15, 1850, M234-802, D153-56 enc. E.

57. John C. Casey to Major Isaac Clark, July 11, 1838, H. Doc. 225, 119–21; Statement of Eliza, August 15, 1850, Second and Seventh Military Departments, Letters Received, box 8; Luther Blake to Luke Lea, November 18, 1852, M234-801, B149-52; Ramsay, "Autobiography," 46. Considerable confusion exists over the relationship between the various members of the Bowlegs family: Harriet, Eliza, Billy (Holata Mikko), and King (or Pin—Hothli Hopoya, but occasionally Holata Mikko). Harriet at times was reported to be the daughter of Hothli Hopoya but, given that she inherited his slaves, probably was his niece. Harriet could have been either the sister or, more likely, the aunt of Holata Mikko, but probably was not his niece, as was and is sometimes stated. If Harriet was his aunt, Holata Mikko probably was the great-nephew of Hothli Hopoya. Eliza would appear to have been either the cousin or the niece of Holata Mikko. Thus, Eliza possibly was the daughter, granddaughter, niece, or great-niece of Harriet, but probably was not her sister. For a discussion of the problems one will encounter in trying to trace the lineage of the Bowlegs family, see Porter, "Billy Bowlegs in the Seminole Wars," 221–23; and Porter, "Cowkeeper Dynasty," 346n21.

58. Deposition of Molly, August 15, 1850, M234-802, D153-56 enc. E.

59. "List of Negroes who surrendered under a proclamation of Major General Jesup when in command of the Army in Florida," Filed by Jesup in the Adjutant General's Office at Fort Gibson, Cherokee Nation, July 24, 1845, M574, roll 13, file 96, frames 143–54. Like so many censuses of the maroons, this list leaves questions unanswered, and the data are subject to a margin of error. For example, Echo Hadjo, listed as claiming six slaves, and Echo Hadjochee, listed as claiming another eleven, who appear on separate parts of the list, might have been the same person. If not, the latter likely was the relative and perhaps the heir of the former, supporting the argument. This Echo Hadjo might have been Echo Harjo, the mikko of the Upper Creek Canadian District. In that case, his slaves (and those of Echo Hadjochee?) should be removed from the sample, raising the percentage owned by the Seminole elite still higher. Charley Emathla was listed as owning eleven slaves. If he was the individual executed by Seminoles in September 1835, his heirs could have claimed his slaves or they would have become wards of a mikko.

60. Deposition of Molly, August 15, 1850, M234-802, D153-56 enc. E.

61. These statistics are based on information furnished in the 147 Seminole freedman census cards compiled under the direction of the Dawes Commission at the end of the century. National Archives Microfilm Publications, M1186, Enrollment Cards for the Five Civilized Tribes, 1898–1914, 93 rolls (hereafter cited as M1186), rolls 92–93.

62. Different names or spellings might have been used to refer to the same owner. Unknowingly, I might have listed one owner as two or more. But a reduction in the number of owners would only strengthen the argument.

63. Almost invariably, the Dawes Commission gathered information on unenrolled parents of enrolled Seminole freedmen and freedwomen from secondhand sources, usually their enrolled children. This information is far less reliable than that for enrollees, which typically was provided firsthand. Consequently, it should be treated with caution and weighed against more reliable sources. By definition, unlike the enrolled, the unenrolled did not receive a unique identifying number. Therefore, the chief danger in working with the unenrolled is the risk of duplication. The rolls include individuals engaging in plural marriages, experiencing

name changes, and having offspring with different spouses. Also, unenrolled freedmen and freedwomen sometimes were listed with only a first name. Another issue arises from the similarity of some freedman names. For example, the rolls list four different owners for individuals bearing the name "Betsey Bowlegs." Although this could seem suspect, both "Betsey" and "Bowlegs" were common names for Seminole freedwomen at that time, and plural marriages were common, so it might well be accurate. Another problem can occur when two individuals with a common name list the same owner. For instance, it is quite feasible that two Sam Bruners, formerly slaves of the same owner, married the same woman at different times. A final challenge is provided by the freedman practice of inverting males' first and second names to show lineage (see Bateman, "Naming Patterns," 227–57). In short, unknowingly I might have listed two people as one. Whenever possible, accuracy was checked against numerous additional sources, such as censuses taken between 1866 and 1898 and individual family genealogies, yet this still allows for a fairly wide margin of error. Because the commissioners gave each a unique number, the risk of duplication is removed when working with the enrollees. The statistics pertaining to the enrollees are far more reliable, and those pertaining to their unenrolled parents should occupy only a supporting role.

64. Saunt, "Paradox of Freedom," 67.

65. Harriet Bowlegs to Duval, September 26, 1846, and Duval to Medill, January 26, 1847, and enc., List of Negroes Claimed by Harriet Bowlegs, M574, roll 13, file 96; John C. Henshaw to Commissioner of Indian Affairs, June 7, 1853, and Drew to Manypenny, October 25, 1854, M234-801, H251-53, D709-54; D. F. Littlefield, *Africans and Seminoles,* 118n27.

66. John Q. Tufts to Hiram Price, March 25, 1884, National Archives Record Group 48, Records of the Department of the Interior, Indian Division, Special Files (hereafter cited as RG 48, SF), box 48, Indian Territory Division, Choctaw Freedman File, 6172–84, enclosed with Henry M. Teller to Commissioner of Indian Affairs, May 2, 1884, 8582–84; Pryor to Dean, April 10, 1856, M234-802, D153-56.

67. Dean to Manypenny, June 24, 1856, M234-802, D180-56.

68. Flint to Drennen, September 10, 1849, *Indians—Creek and Seminole;* Deposition of Molly, August 15, 1850, M234-802, D153-56 enc. E; Henshaw to Charles M. Conrad, May 9, 1852, and Secretary of War to Stuart, June 18, 1852, M234-801, W107-52 and enc.

69. Dean to Manypenny, June 24, 1856, M234-802, D180-56.

70. Dawson to Boone, April 10, 1844, Fort Gibson, Letters Received, box 2.

71. Lynde to Flint, October 12, 1849, Second and Seventh Military Departments, Letters Received, box 7.

72. "List of Seminole Negroe Prisoners turned over at Fort Pike, March 21, 1838, etc.," National Archives Record Group 75, Records of the Bureau of Indian Affairs, Miscellaneous Muster Rolls, 1832–36: Seminole (hereafter cited as RG 75, Seminole Muster Rolls); Casey to Clark, July 11, 1838, H. Doc. 225, 119–21; "List of slaves owned by Miccopotokee or Copiah Yahola, April 29, 1835," and "List of negroes belonging to Cubbitchar Micco," compiled by Duval, June 14, 1849, Deposition of So Nock Yohola, January 31, 1854, Deposition of Tuckabatchee Micco, August 7, 1855, Deposition of G. W. Stidham, n.d., Deposition of Benjamin Marshall, December 4, 1855, Deposition of Jacob Denisaw, April 2, 1856, and Deposition of James Logan, December 9, 1856, M234-802, D153-56 encs. J, M, F, G, H, T, I503-56.

73. John H. Love to Logan, July 3, 1840, M234-923, Western Superintendency, 1840–46, A899-40 enc.

74. Heirs of Love v. E. P. Gaines, n.d., Clark to C. A. Harris, May 3, 1838, Harris to Clark, May 11, 1838, Harris to Thomas Slidell, May 12, 1838, Lt. John G. Reynolds to Harris, May

15, 1838, Gaines to Jones, May 18, 1838, Reynolds to Harris, May 21 and June 28, 1838, Nathaniel F. Collins to Harris, July 29, 1838, and Tod Robinson to Reynolds, October 2, 1838, H. Doc. 225, 31, 47, 92, 124, 97, 104, 124, 30; Collins to Reynolds, June 25, 1838, Second and Seventh Military Departments, Letters Received, box 2; Reynolds's Journal, M234-291, Florida Superintendency Emigration, 1839–53, R415-39; "Muster Roll of Seminole Indians who arrived west of 5th August, 1838," M234-924, Western Superintendency Emigration, 1836–42, S1114-38; John Love to Logan, July 3, 1840, M234-923, A899-40 enc.

75. Arbuckle to Roley McIntosh, June 8, 1840, and Arbuckle to Logan, July 19, 1840, Second and Seventh Military Departments, Letters Sent; John Love to Logan, July 3, 1840, Armstrong to Crawford, October 17, 1840, and Mark A. Cooper to John Bell, May 17, 1841, M234-923, A889-40 and enc., C1411-41; Crawford to Bell, June 7, 1841, National Archives Microfilm Publications, M348, Bureau of Indian Affairs, Report Books, 1838–85, 53 rolls (hereafter cited as M348), roll 2, March 21, 1840–August 31, 1841, 420; Deposition of Dennisaw, April 2, 1856, and Pryor to Dean, April 10, 1856, M234-802, D153-56 and enc. T.

76. T. F. Foster to Secretary of War, January 7, 1842, M234-226, Creek Agency, 1839–42, F251-42; Crawford to Foster, January 21, 1842, National Archives Microfilm Publications, M21, Bureau of Indian Affairs, Letters Sent, 166 rolls (hereafter cited as M21), roll 31, August 2, 1841–February 23, 1842, 389; W. T. Colquitt to John C. Spencer, n.d., M234-289, C1710-42; Crawford to Spencer, May 13, 1842, M348-3, 142; Pryor to Dean, April 10, 1856, M234-802, D153-56.

77. W. E. Love to Belknap, January 3, 1849, and Belknap to Arbuckle, January 3, 1849, Fort Gibson, Letters Received, box 3.

78. Deposition of Molly, August 15, 1850, M234-802, D153-56 enc. E.

79. Dean to Manypenny, April 29, 1856, M234-802, D153-56. As she was "advanced in years" by the early 1850s, it is not clear why Mahkahtistchee's slaves had remained under guardianship so long. Likely, it was to protect her and her property from white claimants. Nevertheless, Mahkahtistchee still derived benefit from her association with her slaves during the guardianship of the Seminole mikkos.

80. Saunt, *Black, White, and Indian,* 16. See also Saunt, "Paradox of Freedom," 68. For a study of kinship slavery in the Southwest, see James F. Brooks, *Captives and Cousins: Slavery, Kinship, and Community in the Southwest Borderlands* (Chapel Hill: University of North Carolina Press, 2002).

81. Dean to Manypenny, April 29, 1856, M234-802, D153-56; Pryor to Drew, January 6, 1855, M234-833, D782-55.

82. For a thorough account of the role played by speculators, government agents, and military officials in the various claims to Mahkahtistchee's slaves, see D. F. Littlefield, *Africans and Seminoles,* 162–75.

83. Dean to Manypenny, April 29, 1856, M234-802, D153-56.

84. Smithson to Manypenny, November 24 and 27, 1853, and A. H. Rutherford to Manypenny, December 6, 1853, M234-801, D476-53 and encs.; Dean to Manypenny, April 29, 1856, and Rector to J. W. Denver, September 25, 1857, M234-802, D153-56, R341-57. Elias Rector estimated the number of abducted blacks to be twenty-three.

85. Mary Ann Lilley to Walter Lowrie, November 30, 1853, Letters from the American Indian Correspondence (Missions), 1841–87, in the Presbyterian Historical Society, Philadelphia, 7 microfilm rolls, Manuscripts Division, Western History Collections, University of Oklahoma (hereafter cited as Presbyterian Mission Correspondence), roll 7, box 12, vol. 2, 237.

86. Dean to Manypenny, April 29, 1856, M234-802, D153-56.

87. Mary Ann Lilley to Lowrie, November 30, 1853, Presbyterian Mission Correspondence, roll 7, box 12, vol. 2, 237.

88. Daniel B. Aspberry to W. Bright, February 16, 1854, and Dean to Manypenny, April 29, 1856, M234-802, M383-57 enc., D153-56.

89. "Registry of negro prisoners captured by the troops commanded by Major General Thomas S. Jesup, in 1836 and 1837, and owned by Indians, or who claim to be free," and Casey to Clark, July 11, 1838, H. Doc. 225, 66–69, 119–20; Statement of David Barnet, February 2, 1842, M234-226, H1047-42 enc.; Humphreys to R. B. Mason, December 5, 1845, Fort Gibson, Indian Affairs, 15; Statement of Washbourne, October 14, 1854, Deposition of George Noble, October 16, 1854, M234-801, D709-54 encs.

90. Deposition of George Noble, October 16, 1854, and see also Drew to Manypenny, October 25, 1854, M234-801, D709-54 and enc.

91. Pryor to Drew, January 6, 1855, M234-833, D782-55 enc.; Aspberry, Bill of Sale and Receipt, November 24, 1854, Pryor to Dean, April 10, 1856, and Chilly McIntosh to Commissioner of Indian Affairs, November 2, 1857, M234-802, D153-56 and enc. A, M383-57; Carolyn T. Foreman, "John Jumper," *Chronicles of Oklahoma* 29 (1951): 138.

92. Pryor to Drew, January 6, 1855, M234-833, D782-55 enc.

93. Pryor to Dean, April 10, 1856, M234-802, D153-56.

94. John Jumper et al. to President Franklin Pierce, n.d., and Washbourne to Manypenny, April 10, 1855, M234-801, D698-54 enc., G462-55 enc.; Washbourne to Drew, January 5, 1855, M234-802, D153-56 enc. A; Drew to Manypenny, January 27, 1855, M234-833, D782-55.

95. Drew to Manypenny, March 14, 1855, M234-833, D816-55.

96. Pryor to Dean, April 10, 1856, Deposition of Washbourne, n.d., M234-802, D153-56 and enc. N.

97. Pryor to Dean, April 10, 1856, and see also Dean to Manypenny, June 24, 1856, and Chilly McIntosh to Commissioner of Indian Affairs, November 2, 1857, M234-802, D153-56, D180-56, M383-57.

98. Pryor to R. N. Johnson, February 14, 1857, Jacob Thompson to Acting Commissioner of Indian Affairs, June 12, 1857, Pryor to Elias Rector, May 20, 1857, Elias Rector to Commissioner of Indian Affairs, June 21, 1857, and Elias Rector to Denver, July 7 and September 25, 1857, M234-802, I569-57 and enc., R270-57 and enc., R274-57, and R341-57; Charles E. Mix to Jacob Thompson, June 6, 1857, M348-10, January 2, 1857–May 31, 1858, 224; Denver to Elias Rector, June 17, 1857, M21-57, May 26, 1857–October 31, 1857, 57.

99. Mix to M. Thompson, April 7, 1859, M21-60, October 25, 1858–April 29, 1959, 415.

5. "ONLY SLAVES IN NAME"

1. *ARCIA 1838,* Doc. 43, Report of Armstrong, 472; *ARCIA 1840,* Doc. 17, Report of Armstrong, 314.

2. *ARCIA 1842,* Doc. 25, Report of Armstrong, 450–51.

3. Harris, *Journal of a Tour,* 16.

4. Dean to Manypenny, June 24, 1856, M234-802, D180-56.

5. Doris Duke Oral History Collection, 55 vols., Western History Collections, University of Oklahoma Libraries, vol. 43, interview T-280, Primus Dean, June 28, 1968.

6. Ibid., vol. 45, interview T-211, Dave McIntosh, 23–24.

7. *Preliminary Report of the Eighth Census, 1860* (Washington, D.C.: Government Printing Office, 1864), 10–11.

8. Captain W. S. Ketchum to Roley McIntosh, September 8, 1848, Roley McIntosh to Ketchum, September 14, 1848, William Whitfield to Ketchum, September 14, 1848, Flint to Ketchum, September 25, 1848, and Logan to Belknap, January 30, 1849, Fort Gibson, Letters Received, box 3; Ketchum to Roley McIntosh, September 11, 13, and 26, 1848, Fort Gibson, Indian Affairs, 39, 41, 40.

9. Kappler, *Indian Affairs,* vol. 2, 696–97; Wayne B. Lollar, "Seminole-U.S. Financial Relations 1823–1866," *Chronicles of Oklahoma* 50 (1972): 196. The Loyal Seminoles and maroons claimed a total of $213,205.20 in lost property but received just $50,000 in compensation.

10. The following statistics are based on information contained in "Claims of Loyal Seminole for Losses Suffered During the Civil War, Submitted under Provisions of the Treaty of March 21, 1866," M574, roll 11, file 87. This was found to be the most detailed and reliable source on the Loyal Seminole claims. See also "List of claims of Loyal Seminole Indians adjudged and determined by J. Tyler Powell and J. N. Caldwell—Commissioners—approved under the provisions of the treaty of the 21st March 1866" and "Pro rata computation of claims awarded by Commissioners Powell and Caldwell to Loyal Seminoles under the provisions of the treaty of March 21st, 1866," M234-803, Seminole Agency, 1859–67, P207-67 encs.; "List of Loyal Seminoles," Doc. 39522-A, Smn. 2-7, sec. X, file 2, Indian Archives, Oklahoma Historical Society; "Receipt Roll for $50,000 payment made to Loyal Seminoles, 1868," Doc. 100595-A-20-7 1868, National Archives, Southwest Region, Fort Worth, Tex.; and " 'Loyal Seminole Roll,' as prepared by Jas. E. Jenkins, Special Indian Agent, 8 March 1901," Grant Foreman Collection, box 49, R14, Archives, Gilcrease Museum, Tulsa (hereafter cited as Foreman Gilcrease). This last document traces the claimants and their descendants to 1901. Researchers should exercise caution when working with the Loyal claims. The claims were for losses incurred, and they did not necessarily represent all of the claimant's property. The commissioners asked claimants to provide witnesses to verify losses, so it is reasonable to assume that each claimant owned at least as much property as that for which he or she received compensation. Also, it would seem unlikely that the Indians lost a higher percentage of their property than the maroons overall, or vice versa. With so large a sample, the differences probably cancel out. Most of the Loyal Seminoles and maroons simply lost all, or almost all, they had. As Principal Chief John Chupco later observed, "Of their worldly goods all or nearly so, was left when we took our march northward. On our return after the war scarce a vestige of the property abandoned by us could be found" (John Chupco to Hayt, May 13, 1879, M234-871, Union Agency 1879, frames 523–25). Comparing property losses seems equitable to both the Indians and maroons. Although the commissioners accepted that all the blacks associated with the Seminoles were loyal, the only Seminoles they deemed eligible for the award were those who had actively supported the Union or who had been coerced into removing south by Confederates. The Loyal Seminoles tended to be members of the faction whose core was the most recent Florida immigrants. The claimants included half of the Seminole population.

11. The commissioners occasionally made errors in addition. The figures cited here are the results of my calculations and are rounded to the nearest dollar.

12. M574, roll 11, file 87, claim 291.

13. Ibid., claims 292, 291, 285, 290, 274.

14. Ibid., claim 280.

15. White observers made numerous references to the maroons' growing rice in Florida prior to Removal. The Fort Gibson reference is Loomis to Jesup, December 7, 1847, M574, roll 13, file 96, frames 31–33. And Bateman notes that, around the time of Oklahoma statehood, Seminole freedmen were raising rice in low-lying marshy areas of the Indian Territory. Bateman, "We're Still Here," 67.

16. Ibid., claims 291, 312, 306, 280, 307.

17. Ibid., claims 286, 282.

18. Ibid., claims 328, 286, 291.

19. In Gaines's and Porter's terms, this would have equated to a feudal tithe.

20. Ibid., claims 326, 285, 282, 318, 280, 327.

21. Ibid., claim 329.

22. Ibid., claims 268, 294.

23. Arbuckle to Jones, September 14, 1849, *Indians-Creek and Seminole,* 31.

24. M574, roll 11, file 87, claim 128.

25. Ibid., claim 173. The Loyal Seminoles and maroons did not claim for currency losses.

26. Ibid., claim 329. Likely this was the same Jim Bowlegs who had traveled to Florida in the attempt to persuade Holata Mikko to remove west in 1849. In 1850, Jim Bowlegs had fled to Texas, but Creek lighthorsemen had apprehended him and returned him to the Indian Territory.

27. Captain B. L. E. Bonneville to Flint, April 21 and May 3, 1848, Second and Seventh Military Departments, Letters Received, box 7; Flint to Bonneville, April 23 and May 1, 1848, Fort Gibson, Letters Received, box 3.

28. Ramsay to Rev. J. L. Wilson, October 19, 1860, and John Lilley to Wilson, November 3, 1860, Presbyterian Mission Correspondence, roll 2, box 6, vol. 3, 150, 152.

29. Rev. Robert M. Loughridge, Presbyterian minister to the Creeks, reported from Tullahassee Mission on August 6, 1860, "A Mexican was taken lately who was said to be the pilot for the negroes on their way to Mexico. The people met yesterday a few miles distant to hang the Mexican, but I understand they concluded to turn him over to the United States authority." Quoted in William G. McLoughlin, "Indian Slaveholders and Presbyterian Missionaries, 1837–1861," *Church History* 42 (1973): 546–47.

30. Robert Johnson at that time was known as Robert Foster. His name changes are documented later in this chapter. To avoid confusion, "Robert Johnson" is the form of his name used throughout this book.

31. Ramsay to Wilson, October 19, 1860, Presbyterian Mission Correspondence, roll 2, 150.

32. Ibid.

33. Ramsay, "Autobiography," 47.

34. Ibid.; Ramsay to Wilson, October 19, 1860, Presbyterian Mission Correspondence, roll 2, 150. Ramsay's reference to Robert Johnson's signing of Luke's pass is intriguing, especially as Johnson was still a slave himself. It reinforces the sense of laxity in control over blacks' mobility in the Seminole country, and of the influence Johnson enjoyed among the Presbyterian ministers.

35. "Laws of the Creek Nation," in "Creek-Laws," Manuscript File, Grant Foreman Collection, Indian Archives, Oklahoma Historical Society (hereafter cited as Foreman OHS), box 6, 83-229, laws 32, 33, 37, 112–15, 118, 119, second series beginning on 14, laws 110, 111, 115, 116; Loughridge to Ramsay, n.d., Presbyterian Mission Correspondence, roll 2, 161c.

36. "List of Seminole Negroe Prisoners turned over at Fort Pike, March 21, 1838, etc." RG 75, Seminole Muster Rolls.

37. "Negroes brought in by August and Latty at Fort Jupiter," included in "List of Negroes who surrendered under a proclamation of Major General Jesup etc.," M574, roll 13, file 96.

38. Jesup attached this as a footnote to "Negroes brought in by August and Latty at Fort Jupiter to General Jesup under a proclamation by him offering freedom to all who should separate from the Seminoles and surrender," Jesup's Papers, box 15.

39. Statement of Washbourne, October 14, 1854, based on "Manumission Document made before Edward Law judge of probate for the country of St. Johns, Territory of Florida, in 1821 and recorded in Clerk's office of said county 30 January 1822, Book 'B,' pp. 3–4," M234-801, D709-54 enc.

40. Henshaw to Conrad, May 9, 1852, and Henshaw to Manypenny, June 7, 1853, M234-801, W107-52 enc., H251-53.

41. Miscellaneous papers relating to Gopher John, and L. Thomas to R. B. Mason, December 18, 1844, Fort Gibson, Indian Affairs, 1–2, 8; R. B. Mason to Roger Jones, November 3, 1844, Fort Gibson, Letters Sent.

42. Armstrong to Seminole Agent, January 25, 1845, Second and Seventh Military Departments, Letters Received, box 6.

43. Porter, *Negro on the American Frontier,* 323–24.

44. Receipts of Chitto Harjo, January 11 and May 15, 1849, Fort Gibson, Indian Affairs, 44–46.

45. Pryor to Dean, April 10, 1856, M234-802, D153-56.

46. Henshaw to Conrad, May 9, 1852, Conrad to Stuart, June 18, 1852, Drennen to Lea, September 27, 1852, Lea to Stuart, November 10, 1852, and Duval to Commissioner of Indian Affairs, April 8, 1853, M234-801, W107-52 and enc., I131-52 and enc., D298-53.

47. M. Thompson to J. Thompson, December 6, 1858, M234-802, T346-58.

48. Decision of Apalachicola Chiefs, June 15, 1827, Statement of Nelly Factor, September 4, 1828, Statement of DuVal, September 10, 1828, Manumission Papers, May 27, 1832, Statement of Sam Factor, February 14, 1835, DuVal to Worth, December 22, 1842, Bill of Sale of Toney Proctor, April 26, 1841, T. S. Brown to Crawford, April 28, 1842, and Statement of Arbuckle, n.d., M234-289, S3398-43 and encs., B1773-43 and encs.; Crawford to Josiah Vose, September 16, 1842, M21-32, February 24, 1842–October 2, 1842, 463.

49. Chief John Walker to Wiley Thompson, July 31, 1834, and Wiley Thompson to Elbert Herring, September 23, 1835, M234-800, frame 429; Daniel Boyd to Harris, August 29, 1838, and John T. Sprague to Commissioner of Indian Affairs, April 30, 1843, M234-289, B576-38, S3398-43; Jesup to Richard K. Call, October 14, 1837, Jesup's Papers, Letters Sent; Worth to Commissioner of Indian Affairs, August 1, 1842, and Adjutant General to Commissioner, August 25, 1842, M234-291, A1282-42; Statement of General Zachary Taylor, n.d., Memorial of William Sena Factor, n.d., and W. K. Sebastian to Commissioner, May 1, 1852, M234-801, S90-52 and encs.; M. Thompson to J. Thompson, December 6, 1858, M234-802, T346-58; Potter, *War in Florida,* 15–16. At the time of, and subsequent to, the Factor family's emigration, Solano pressed for compensation for his losses, but his claim proved unsuccessful. See D. F. Littlefield, *Africans and Seminoles,* 65–67n60.

50. Washbourne to Dean, January 24, 1856, M234-802, D92-56.

51. Memorial of William Sena Factor, n.d., Drew to Manypenny, October 24, 1854, R. McClelland to Mix, July 5, 1855, and Mix to McClelland, July 9, 1855, M234-801, S90-52 enc., D708-54, I1053-55, I1068-55; M. Thompson to J. Thompson, December 6, 1858, M234-802, T346-58.

52. Washbourne to Dean, January 24, 1856, M234-802, D92-56.

53. Washbourne to Dean, December 20, 1855, and see also Dean to Commissioner of Indian Affairs, December 31, 1855, M234-802, D27-56 and enc.

54. Washbourne to Dean, January 24, 1856, M234-802, D92-56.

55. Daniel F. Littlefield, Jr. and Mary Ann Littlefield, "The Beams Family: Free Blacks in Indian Territory," *Journal of Negro History* 61 (1976): 16–35. The National Archives has gathered together much of the documentation pertinent to that case and reproduced it as "Beams Negroes, Suits for Freedom and Attorneys' Claims for Fees, 1854–1859," M574, roll 75, file 277.

56. Porter, *Negro on the American Frontier,* 329–30.

57. Flint to Drennen, September 10, 1849, *Indians—Creek and Seminole,* 28–29.

58. "Uncle Warren" (Whan; Juan) was Juan Caballo, or John Horse. Ramsay later referred to Horse's wife, Susan, as "Aunt Sue." See Ramsay, "Autobiography," 19. "Patriarch of the clan" should be read as "bandleader."

59. Lilley, "Autobiography," 47–48.

60. Ramsay, "Autobiography," 33. See also Abel, *Slaveholder and Secessionist,* map on 25; and the map on page 66 of the present work.

61. *Daily Oklahoman,* November 13, 1932.

62. Duval to Belknap, June 7, 1849, Fort Gibson, Letters Received, box 3.

63. *ARCIA 1857,* Doc. 82, Report of Elias Rector, 200.

64. Ibid.

65. Seminole Annuity Roll 1860, National Archives Record Group 75, Records of the Bureau of Indian Affairs, Seminole Annuity Rolls (hereafter cited as RG 75, BIA, Seminole Annuity Rolls).

66. *ARCIA 1857,* Doc. 82, Report of Rector, 200; *Preliminary Report of the Eighth Census,* 10–11.

67. Abel, *Slaveholder and Secessionist,* 23n14.

68. See chapter 8.

69. Harper, *Travels of William Bartram,* 118–19 [186].

70. Miller, *Coacoochee's Bones,* chap. 1.

71. Seminole freedman census cards, M1186, rolls 92–93. See also chart 3.

72. Hancock, *Creole Features in Afro-Seminole Speech;* Ian F. Hancock, *Further Observations on Afro-Seminole Creole,* Society for Caribbean Linguistics Occasional Papers no. 7 (Mona, Jamaica: University of the West Indies, 1977); Ian F. Hancock, "Texas Gullah: The Creole Language of the Brackettville Afro-Seminoles," in *Perspectives on American English,* Joseph L. Dillard, ed. (The Hague, Netherlands: Mouton, 1980), 305–33; Ian F. Hancock, *The Texas Seminoles and Their Language,* African and Afro-American Studies and Research Center, ser. 2, no. 1 (Austin: University of Texas, 1980).

73. Bateman, "We're Still Here," 292–93; *Daily Oklahoman,* January 1, 1922; Foster, *Negro-Indian Relationships,* 52; Arthur Gallaher, Jr., "A Survey of the Seminole Freedmen," M.A. thesis, University of Oklahoma, 1951, 4.

74. Joseph L. Dillard, *Black English: Its History and Usage in the United States* (New York: Random House, 1972), 150, and see also 86, 151–55.

75. Bateman, "Naming Patterns," 227–57; Bateman, "We're Still Here," 343–54.

76. Dillard, *Black English,* 124–27.

77. Bateman, "We're Still Here," 37n3; Lisa Beckloff, "Tribe's Freedmen Seek Share," *Daily Oklahoman,* February 21, 1992; William Dawson, pers. comm., January 13, 1982 and spring 1984; Ron Jackson, "Forefather Prepared Family for Challenge," *Sunday Oklahoman,*

November 7, 1999; Melinda B. Micco, " 'Blood and Money': The Case of the Seminole Freedmen and Seminole Indians in Oklahoma," in Tiya Miles and Sharon P. Holland, eds., *Crossing Waters, Crossing Worlds: The African Diaspora in Indian Country* (Durham, N.C., and London: Duke University Press, 2006), 127; personal observations as a consumer of the local press and popular media while living in Oklahoma, September 1978–January 1979 and February 1981–June 1984.

78. Mulroy, *Freedom on the Border,* 71, 114, 153, 163, 165.

79. Fort Gibson, Indian Affairs, 1–2.

80. Mulroy, *Freedom on the Border,* 114.

81. Ibid., 124–25.

82. Seminole freedman census card 625, enrollee 1945, and card 652, enrollees 2028 and 2029, M1186, roll 92.

83. Interview with Ben Warrior, January 24, 1979; interview with Ben Warrior conducted with Susan Miller, March 1, 1983.

84. Interview with "Pompey" Bruner Fixico, Los Angeles, November 11, 2005; interview with William "Dub" Warrior, Brackettville, Tex., September 15, 1990; Mulroy, *Freedom on the Border,* 175, 177.

85. Hinds, "Creek Missions," 55–56.

86. *ARCIA 1843,* Doc. 92, Report of J. L. Dawson, 423; *Baptist Missionary Magazine* 23 (1843): 33, 141; G. Foreman, *Advancing the Frontier,* 19; Hamilton, *Gospel among the Red Men,* 74; Hinds, "Creek Missions," 49–50; D. F. Littlefield, *Africans and Creeks,* 87; Isaac McCoy to *Baptist Weekly Journal,* January 18, 1833, reprinted in *Baptist Messenger* 19, no. 32, January 7, 1932, 1, 13; Isaac McCoy, *History of Baptist Indian Missions,* William M. Morrison, ed. (New York: H. and S. Raynor, 1840), 45; Isaac McCoy, *Periodical Account of Baptist Missions within the Indian Territory for the Year Ending December 31, 1836* (Shawnee Baptist Mission House, Indian Territory: Isaac McCoy, 1837), 39; Moffit, "Early Baptist Missions," 70; Solomon Peck, "History of the Missions of the Baptist General Convention," in *History of American Missions to the Heathen* (Worcester, Mass.: Spooner and Howland, 1840), 394–95; Carl Coke Rister, *Baptist Missions among the American Indians* (Atlanta: Home Mission Board, 1944), 68; Eugene C. Routh, "Henry Frieland Buckner," *Chronicles of Oklahoma* 14 (1936): 453, 459; Wyeth, *Poor Lo,* 70; Gary Zellar, "Europe Speaking to America through Africa: African Creeks and the Establishment of Christianity in the Creek Nation," Indigenous and African Experiences in the Americas Seminar, Hall Center for the Humanities, University of Kansas, Fall 2005, 31 pp., http://www.hallcenter.ku.edu/seminar/Africa (October 24, 2005).

87. Quoted in Zellar, "Europe Speaking," 23. See also Loren J. Belt, "Baptist Missions to the Indians of the Five Civilized Tribes of Oklahoma," Th.D. dissertation, Central Baptist Theological Seminary, 1955, 82, 85; Carolyn T. Foreman, "North Fork Town," *Chronicles of Oklahoma* 29 (1951): 81; Hamilton, *Gospel among the Red Men,* 78, 80–82; *Indian Advocate* 2 (April 1849): 2; Moffit, "Early Baptist Missions," 70; Routh, "Buckner," 459–60; Routh, *Oklahoma Baptists,* 34–36, 64; Wyeth, *Poor Lo,* 74.

88. Jordan, "Joseph Morrow," 34; Moffit, "Early Baptist Missions," 143.

89. Lilley, "Autobiography," 48–49.

90. National Archives Record Group 75, Records of the Bureau of Indian Affairs, Records Relating to Loyal Creek Claims, 1869–70, claim 177.

91. *Indian Advocate* 9 (1854): 7.

92. Murrow to Wyeth, March 10, 1896, quoted in Wyeth, *Poor Lo,* 112.

93. Carleton, *Not Yours,* 47–48.

94. Hamilton, *Gospel among the Red Men,* 98.

95. Adoniram J. Holt, *Pioneering in the Southwest* (Nashville: Sunday School Board of the Southern Baptist Convention, 1923), 110–11.

96. Ramsay, "Autobiography," 33.

97. Moffit, "Early Baptist Missions," 146.

98. Rehoboth Association, minutes, 1861, quoted in Jordan, "Joseph Morrow," 47.

99. *ARCIA 1844,* Doc. 80, Report of Judge, 477–78.

100. Lilley, "Autobiography," 48.

101. Ramsay, "Autobiography," 19.

102. Ibid., 33, 45–56; Mrs. Eliza Ramsay, letter to her parents in the form of a diary, ca. February 1860, Presbyterian Mission Correspondence, roll 2, 163½.

103. Ramsay, "Autobiography," 19, 33.

104. Ramsay to Wilson, December 28, 1859, Presbyterian Mission Correspondence, roll 1, box 6, vol. 1, 231; Statement of Loyal Seminoles through E. J. Brown, September 13, 1867, T. A. Baldwin, "Report of Employees in the Seminole Agency for the year 1869," and Baldwin to Ely S. Parker, October 31, 1869, M234-804, Seminole Agency, 1868–71, W777-67, B376-69, B459-69; Samuel S. Drake, *Indians of North America* (New York: Hurst and Co., 1880), 763–64; Otis Hume, "Cemeteries—Seminole; Johnson," June 21, 1937, Indian Pioneer Papers, vol. 56, 423–25A; Lilley, "Autobiography," 18–19, 21.

105. Indian Pioneer Papers, vol. 1, interview 55, F. G. Alex, 73; Lilley, "Autobiography," 29; Augustus W. Loomis, *Scenes in the Indian Country* (Philadelphia: Presbyterian Board of Publication, 1859), 52; Ramsay, "Autobiography," 18–19, 21. If Robert's father's name had been John, that would explain the Johnson surname. Other examples of that naming practice appear in the Seminole freedman census cards compiled by the Dawes Commission. Robert was buried in the Johnson Cemetery, situated about one mile north of present-day Wewoka in Seminole County, in sec. 17, township 8, range 8. Otis Hume, "Cemeteries—Seminole; Johnson," June 21, 1937, Indian Pioneer Papers, vol. 56, 423–25A.

106. Loomis, *Scenes,* 52–54.

107. "A Letter from Kowetah Mission, 1850," *Chronicles of Oklahoma* 46 (1968): 338; Ramsay, "Autobiography," 18–19.

108. Ramsay, "Autobiography," 21.

109. McLoughlin, "Indian Slaveholders," 539–40.

110. Loomis, *Scenes,* 54–57, 76.

111. Ramsay, "Autobiography," 21–22.

112. "My Mama Come with Wild Cat," in Porter, "Freedom over Me," Porter Papers, box 2; Mulroy, *Freedom on the Border,* 55, 71, 76, 81, 108, 109, 111–14, 139–43, 165.

113. Loomis, *Scenes,* 57–58; Ramsay to Wilson, July 9, 1856, Presbyterian Mission Correspondence, roll 1, 73; Ramsay, "Autobiography," 34.

114. Ramsay, "Autobiography," 37–38.

115. Ramsay to Wilson, December 7, 1857, Presbyterian Mission Correspondence, roll 1, 139.

116. Ramsay to Wilson, February 2, 1858, ibid., 151.

117. Sattler suggests that Seminoles also transformed Christianity radically to fit a Native cosmology. The Baptist religion particularly appealed because it offered more latitude for introducing Nativist elements. Sattler, pers. comm., January 30, 2006. See also Jack M. Schultz, *The Seminole Baptist Churches of Oklahoma: Maintaining a Traditional Community* (Norman: University of Oklahoma Press, 1999).

118. John Lilley to Wilson, March 11, 1858, Presbyterian Mission Correspondence, roll 1, 155.

119. On other compromises Presbyterian missionaries in the Indian Territory were prepared to make, see Robert T. Lewitt, "Indian Missions and Antislavery Sentiments: A Conflict of Evangelical and Humanitarian Ideals," *Mississippi Valley Historical Review* 50 (1963): 39–55; William G. McLoughlin, "The Choctaw Slave Burning: A Crisis in Mission Work among the Indians," *Journal of the West* 13 (1974): 113–27; and McLoughlin, "Indian Slaveholders."

120. Mary Ann Lilley to Lowrie, November 30, 1853, Presbyterian Mission Correspondence, roll 7, 237.

121. Ramsay to Wilson, December 28, 1859, January 19, 1860, and March 2, 1861, ibid., roll 1, 231, roll 2, 138, 1618; Ramsay, "Autobiography," 39–40.

122. Ramsay to Wilson, January 19, 1860, Mrs. Ramsay to her Parents, n.d., Presbyterian Mission Correspondence roll 2, 138, 163½.

6. THE CIVIL WAR

1. Quoted in Porter, "Billy Bowlegs in the Seminole Wars," 238n30.

2. Ibid. The number of maroons with Holata Mikko was small. In 1856, Special Indian Agent John C. Casey estimated that only three black warriors and four black women and children remained with the Seminoles in Florida. John C. Casey, "Linguistics Note Book," John C. Casey Collection, Archives, Gilcrease Museum, Tulsa, 73, 75.

3. McReynolds, *Seminoles,* 286–87.

4. Elias Rector to Mix, May 9, 1858, and L. B. Dunn to Mix, July 7, 1858, M234-802, R596-58, D560-58; *New York Herald,* May 27, 1858 (quote); Brown, *Peace River,* 117–18; Covington, *Seminoles of Florida,* 128–44. The small number of maroon emigrants meant that just a few others had remained behind. In 1883–84, anthropologist Clay McCauley conducted an exhaustive survey of the remaining Florida Seminoles for the Bureau of Ethnology. Among the Seminole population of 208, he discovered 3 black women and 7 offspring of Indian fathers and black mothers who had been adopted into the tribe. Clay McCauley, "The Seminole Indians of Florida," in *United States Bureau of American Ethnology, Fifth Annual Report, 1883–1884* (Washington, D.C.: Government Printing Office, 1887), 526.

5. "Billy Bowlegs in New Orleans," *Harper's Weekly,* June 12, 1858. Most of Holata Mikko's slaves had removed to the Indian Territory during the Second Seminole War and, by the time of his arrival, had established a maroon settlement in the Little River country.

6. Ibid.

7. Porter, "Billy Bowlegs in the Seminole Wars," 230.

8. "Billy Bowlegs in New Orleans."

9. Louis X. Eyma, *La vie dans le Nouveau-Monde* (Paris: Poulet-Malassis, 1862), 214. Author's translation.

10. "Return of property received and issued by Elias Rector, Special Agent and Commissioner for the removal of the Florida Indians in 1859," M234-834, Southern Superintendency, 1857–62, R1394-59; M574, roll 11, file 87, claim 291.

11. Samuel M. Rutherford to Mix, July 27, 1858, and Rector to Mix, August 23, 1858, M234-802, R824-58, R828-58; T. A. Baldwin to Ely S. Parker, April 26, 1870, M234-804, Seminole Agency 1868–71, B706-70.

12. *ARCIA 1858,* Doc. 51, Report of Rutherford. 152–53; G. Foreman, *Five Civilized Tribes,* 274; McReynolds, *Seminoles,* 287.

13. *ARCIA 1859,* Doc. 58, Report of Rutherford, 183–85.

14. John Lilley to Rev. J. L. Wilson, August 10, 1858, Presbyterian Mission Correspondence, roll 1, box 6, vol. 1, no. 169; Indian Pioneer Papers, vol. 52, interview 6950, Elizabeth Ross, 466–67; *Daily Oklahoman*, May 23, 1923.

15. G. Foreman, *Five Civilized Tribes*, 274–75; McReynolds, *Seminoles*, 287.

16. Quoted in Carolyn T. Foreman, "Billy Bowlegs," *Chronicles of Oklahoma* 33 (Winter 1955): 529–30.

17. *ARCIA 1859*, Doc. 46, Report of Rector, 161.

18. Seminole Annuity Roll 1860, RG 75, BIA, Seminole Annuity Rolls; Sattler, "Siminoli Italwa," 262–63, 268–71, 405n153. Carolyn Foreman correctly proposed that the celebrated Seminole Union leader was this second Billy Bowlegs. See C. T. Foreman, "Billy Bowlegs," 530. Porter argued that the two Billy Bowlegses were one and the same, suggesting that premature reports of the deaths of Seminole and maroon leaders were neither unprecedented nor unusual. See Kenneth W. Porter, "Billy Bowlegs (Holata Micco) in the Civil War," part 2, *Florida Historical Quarterly* 45 (1967): 394n3. The key to the respective identities of the two Billy Bowlegses lies with their indigenous names. The former principal chief of the Florida Seminoles who died in 1859 was Holata Mikko; the leader of the Seminole emigrants to Kansas and the principal chief of the Loyal Seminoles until his death in 1863 or 1864 was Sonaki Mikko. Sonaki Mikko also should not be confused with Sonuck Harjo (Sonuck Harjochee), who was said to be his "brother." Sonuck Harjo also emigrated with the Loyal Seminoles to Kansas in the winter of 1861–62 but was still corresponding in 1883 (see notes 49 and 127 below).

19. Henry M. Rector to John Ross, January 29, 1861, U.S. War Department, *The War of the Rebellion: A Compilation of the Official Records of the Union and Confederate Armies*, 4 ser., 130 vols. (Washington, D.C.: Government Printing Office, 1880–1901) (hereafter cited as *OR*), ser. 1, vol. 13, 490–91.

20. *ARCIA 1864*, no. 162B, John T. Cox to William G. Coffin, March 18, 1864, 333.

21. *ARCIA 1861*, E. H. Carruth to Major General D. Hunter, n.d., 46–49; Muriel H. Wright, "Seal of the Seminole Nation," *Chronicles of Oklahoma* 34 (1956): 266.

22. Rev. Joseph S. Murrow, Scrapbook, Rev. Joseph S. Murrow Collection, Bacone College Library, Bacone, Oklahoma, 29.

23. Carleton, *Not Yours*, 60–61. On Murrow's Southern sympathies, see Jordan, "Joseph Morrow," 38–40; and Alice H. Mackey, "Father Murrow: Civil War Period," *Chronicles of Oklahoma* 12 (1934): 58, 60–61.

24. T. E. Brown, "Seminole Indian Agents, 1842–1874," *Chronicles of Oklahoma* 51 (1973): 72, 74–75.

25. Elias Rector to A. B. Greenwood, August 4, 1860, and John Jumper et al. to Rutherford, November 15, 1860, M234-803, Seminole Agency, 1859–67, R1005-60, R1335-60.

26. *OR*, 1, 1, 647–68. To list all the relevant individual pieces of correspondence contained in the *OR* would take pages of footnotes. Except where a precise citation is required, therefore, page references only are listed.

27. *ARCIA 1861*, William P. Dole to Caleb B. Smith, November 27, 1861, 9–10.

28. Abel, *Slaveholder and Secessionist*, 83 et seq.; Walter L. Brown, "Albert Pike 1809–1891," Ph.D. dissertation, University of Texas, 1955, 539 et seq.

29. Angie E. Debo, *The Road to Disappearance: A History of the Creek Indians* (Norman: University of Oklahoma Press, 1941), 144–45.

30. *OR*, 4, 1, 426–66.

31. *Journal of the Provisional Congress of the Confederate States of America*, 7 vols., 58th Cong., 2d sess., S. Doc. 234, 1904–1905, vol. 1, 105; *OR*, 4, 1, 322–23.

32. Carruth to "Sir," July 11, 1861, quoted in Abel, *Slaveholder and Secessionist*, 84–86n122.

33. *ARCIA 1861,* Carruth to Hunter, November 26, 1861, 47.

34. *OR,* 4, 1, 513–27. For comparative context see, Kenny A. Franks, "An Analysis of the Confederate Treaties with the Five Civilized Tribes," *Chronicles of Oklahoma* 50 (1972): 458–73.

35. Abel, *Slaveholder and Secessionist,* 164–65n280.

36. *OR,* 4, 1, 669–87.

37. John B. Meserve, "Chief Opothleyohola," *Chronicles of Oklahoma* 9 (1931): 440–42.

38. Sattler, "Siminoli Italwa," 274.

39. Miller, *Coacoochee's Bones,* 181.

40. Debo, *Road to Disappearance,* 149–50; McReynolds, *Seminoles,* 297.

41. *OR,* 1, 8, 6–7, 23. Due to a lack of reliable documentation and the rapidly changing population of Hopothli Yahola's force, estimates of its size vary widely. Christine Schultz White and Benton R. White, in *Now the Wolf Has Come: The Creek Nation in the Civil War* (College Station: Texas A&M University Press, 1996), 150, estimate that as many as 9,000 emigrants from more than twenty nations made the trek north and that 7,000 reached Kansas. The 9,000 figure is also proposed by Willard B. Johnson in "Tracing Trails of Blood on Ice: Commemorating 'the Great Escape' in 1861–62 of Indians and Blacks into Kansas," *Negro History Bulletin* 64 (2001): electronic version, 3, 9n17. But that number does not tally with official reports of the casualties Hopothli Yahola's followers suffered en route or with the census taken soon after the survivors arrived on the Kansas plains. The figures cited here are more reasonable.

42. M574, roll 11, file 87, claims 300, 301, 299, 302, 322, 310, 289, 307, 329, 173.

43. Abel, *Slaveholder and Secessionist,* 254. See also Dean Trickett, "The Civil War in the Indian Territory," part 4, *Chronicles of Oklahoma* 18 (1940): 269–80.

44. This interpretation is based on Muriel H. Wright, "Colonel Cooper's Civil War Report on the Battle of Round Mountain," *Chronicles of Oklahoma* 39 (1961): 352–97. Angie Debo took strong exception to Wright's theory. See Angie E. Debo, "The Location of the Battle of Round Mountains," *Chronicles of Oklahoma* 41 (1963): 70–104. For a discussion of their heated debate, see Patricia Loughlin, "The Battle of the Historians of Round Mountain: An Examination of Muriel Wright and Angie Debo," *Heritage of the Great Plains* 31 (1998): 4–18.

45. Moty Canard, Echo Harjo et al. to Douglas H. Cooper, October 31, 1861, "Creek Nation—Civil War" file, sec. X, Indian Archives, Oklahoma Historical Society.

46. Angie E. Debo, "The Site of the Battle of Round Mountain, 1861," *Chronicles of Oklahoma* 27 (1949): 200.

47. *OR,* 1, 8, Report of Cooper, 5–7; "Enlistment Records 1st Seminole Mounted Volunteers," Foreman Gilcrease, box 34, vol. 73, 114 (21); Jessie R. Moore, "The Five Great Indian Nations: The Part They Played on Behalf of the Confederacy in the War between the States," *Chronicles of Oklahoma* 29 (1951): 330 and n12. The sites of Civil War engagements in Indian Territory listed here and elsewhere are the ones accepted by the Oklahoma Historical Society. See Muriel H. Wright and LeRoy H. Fischer, "Oklahoma Civil War Sites," *Chronicles of Oklahoma* 44 (1966): 158–215.

48. *OR,* 1, 8, 8–11; LeRoy H. Fischer and Kenny A. Franks, "Confederate Victory at Chusto-Talasah," *Chronicles of Oklahoma* 49 (1971): 452–76; McReynolds, *Seminoles,* 299–300.

49. Sonuck Harjo to Commissioner of Indian Affairs, October 3, 1883, National Archives Record Group 75, Letters Received by the Bureau of Indian Affairs, 1881–1907 (hereafter cited as RG 75, LR BIA 1881–1907), 18503-83.

50. *OR,* 1, 8, Report of Colonel James McIntosh, January 1, 1862, 22–25. See also accompanying reports, 26–31.

51. M574, roll 11, file 87, claim 289.

52. *OR,* 1, 8, 12–13, 24–25, 31–33.

53. *ARCIA 1862,* George W. Collamore to Dole, April 21, 1862, 156. For a vivid description of the journey by one who survived it, see *ARCIA 1865,* Statement of Sands, Chief of the Upper Creeks, 328–29.

54. Quoted in Mary Jane Warde, "Now the Wolf Has Come: The Civilian Civil War in the Indian Territory," *Chronicles of Oklahoma* 71 (1993): 64.

55. George C. Snow to William Coffin, February 13, 1862, M234-803, S307-62. See also Dean Banks, "Civil War Refugees from Indian Territory in the North, 1861–1864," *Chronicles of Oklahoma* 41 (1963): 286–98; Edmund J. Danziger, "The Office of Indian Affairs and the Problem of the Civil War Indian Refugees in Kansas," *Kansas Historical Quarterly* 35 (1969): 257–75; and Lela J. McBride Brockway Tindle, *Opothleyohola and the Loyal Muskogee: Their Flight to Kansas in the Civil War* (Jefferson, N.C.: McFarland, 2000), 175–76. 184–85.

56. *ARCIA 1862,* Archibald B. Campbell to Joseph Barnes, February 5, 1862, 151–52.

57. Hunter to Dole, February 6, 1862, quoted in Abel, *Slaveholder and Secessionist,* 272–73.

58. *ARCIA 1862,* Campbell to Barnes, February 5, 1862, 151–52. See also Reports of Dole and William Coffin in ibid., 27, 136–37.

59. *OR* 1, 8, Opothleyohola and Halleck Tustenuggee to President Abraham Lincoln, January 28, 1862, 534.

60. *ARCIA 1862,* Doc. 27, Report of Snow, 142; J. P. Hamilton, Sr., "Indian Refugees in Coffey County," reprinted in the *Le Roy (Kans.) Reporter,* August 14 and 21, 1931.

61. *ARCIA 1862,* Collamore to Dole, April 21, 1862, 156.

62. Abel, *Slaveholder and Secessionist,* 274–75.

63. *ARCIA 1862,* Collamore to Dole, April 21, 1862, 156.

64. Benjamin F. Van Horn, "Autobiography," Typewritten Statement Dictated in 1909, 30 pp., 21, Benjamin Van Horn Collection, misc. doc. 42706, Manuscripts Department, Kansas State Historical Society, Topeka.

65. *ARCIA 1862,* Doc. 27, Report of Snow, 143–44, and Collamore to Dole, April 21, 1862, 156 (quote).

66. Billy Bowlegs et al. to Dole, April 14, 1862, and Bowlegs (Sonukmekke) to Dole, March 2 and May 13, 1863, M234-803, C1594-62 enc., B131-63, and B317-63.

67. *ARCIA 1862,* Doc. 27, Report of Snow, 142.

68. Paskofar to Dole, July 29, 1863, M234-803, 76; Charles Monroe Chase to the editor of the *Sycamore (IL) True Republican and Sentinel,* August 21, 1863, "Letters from Kansas and Missouri to the *Sycamore (Ill.) True Republican and Sentinel,*" Charles Monroe Chase Collection, doc. 43207, Manuscripts Department, Kansas State Historical Society (hereafter cited as Chase Collection).

69. Annie H. Abel, *The American Indian as Participant in the Civil War* (Cleveland: Arthur H. Clark, 1919), 99–102. On the formation of the Union Indian Brigade, see Dean Trickett, "The Civil War in the Indian Territory, 1862," *Chronicles of Oklahoma* 19 (1941): 55–69.

70. Thomas to Dole, May 4, 1862, M234-834, F363-62. The regiment subsequently was reorganized. A year later, Sonaki Mikko signed himself as Captain of Company F. Bowlegs to Dole, May 13, 1863, M234-803, B317-63.

71. Wiley Britton, *The Union Indian Brigade in the Civil War* (Kansas City: Franklin Hudson, 1922), 179–80; D. F. Littlefield, *Africans and Creeks,* 239; Gary Zellar, "Occupying

the Middle Ground: African Creeks in the First Indian Home Guards, 1862–1865," *Chronicles of Oklahoma* 76 (1998): 49.

72. M574, roll 11, file 87, claim 173.

73. Gary Zellar, "First to Fight for Freedom: African Creek Soldiers Enter the Civil War," *Journal of the Indian Wars* 1 (2000): 1, 12.

74. Porter, "Billy Bowlegs in the Civil War," 397.

75. Porter, *Negro on the American Frontier,* 468.

76. *ARCIA 1864,* no. 162A, Cox to William Coffin, March 16, 1864, 332.

77. William Coffin to Dole, June 15, 1862, quoted in Abel, *Participant in the Civil War,* 115n.

78. *OR* 1, 13, 162, 475–512; Abel, *Participant in the Civil War,* 114–93; Britton, *Union Indian Brigade,* 61–73; G. N. Heath, "The First Federal Invasion of Indian Territory," *Chronicles of Oklahoma* 44 (1966): 409–19.

79. Wiley Britton, *The Civil War on the Border,* 2 vols. (New York: G. P. Putnam's Sons, 1890–1904), vol. 2, 3–7; Lary C. Rampp and Donald L. Rampp, *The Civil War in Indian Territory* (Austin, Tex.: Presidial Press, 1975), 16.

80. M574, roll 11, file 87, claims 329, 324, 296, 321, 325, 323, 250, 285, 313, 286.

81. *ARCIA 1862,* Doc. 27, Report of Snow, 142–43 (quote); "Census of Southern Refugee Indians belonging to the Southern Superintendency," December 13, 1862, M234-834, frame 1414.

82. *ARCIA 1863,* Doc. 86, Report of Snow, 185.

83. Sattler, "Siminoli Italwa," 229–30.

84. Zellar, "Occupying the Middle Ground," 59.

85. Annie H. Abel, *The American Indian under Reconstruction* (Cleveland: Arthur H. Clark, 1925), 36–39; Banks, "Civil War Refugees," 293–94.

86. *OR,* 1, 22, part 2, 224.

87. Britton, *Union Indian Brigade,* 257. See also *ARCIA 1863,* Doc. 86, Report of Snow, 185; and Wiley Britton, "Some Reminiscences of the Cherokee People—Returning to Their Homes the Exiles of a Nation," *Chronicles of Oklahoma* 6 (1928): 176–77.

88. Britton, *Civil War on the Border,* vol. 2, 17.

89. D. F. Littlefield, *Africans and Creeks,* 237.

90. Abel, *American Indian under Reconstruction,* 272; James G. Blunt, "General Blunt's Account of His Civil War Experiences," *Kansas Historical Quarterly* 1 (1932): 243–44.

91. Thomas J. Boyd, "The Use of Negro Troops by Kansas during the Civil War," M.A. thesis, Kansas State Teachers College, 1950, 1–21; William S. Burke, "Official Military History of the Kansas Regiments: During the War for the Suppression of the Great Rebellion," in *Report of the Adjutant General of the State of Kansas 1861–1865,* 2 vols. (Topeka: Kansas State Printing Co., 1896 [1867]), vol. 1, 246–47.

92. Van Horn, "Autobiography," 21–22.

93. Enlistment and Service Records, Company I, First Regiment Kansas Colored Volunteers, in *Report of the Adjutant General of Kansas,* vol. 1, 592–94; Special Order 33, by Command of Major General Blunt, Headquarters Army of the Frontier, August 22, 1863, "Regimental Letter and Order Book; 79th (New) U. S. Colored Troops," Microfilm, Records of the Department of War, National Archives, Washington D.C.; Deposition of Samuel Cudjo, July 26, 1869, and Baldwin to Parker, October 21, 1869, M234-804, Seminole Agency, 1868–71, B366-69 enc., B441-69.

94. The official reports on the Battles of Cabin Creek and Honey Springs are included in

OR, 1, 22, part 1, 341–42, 378–82, 447–62. For accounts of the battles, see Britton, *Union Indian Brigade,* 258–85; Annie R. Cubage, "Engagement at Cabin Creek, Indian Territory, July 1 and 2, 1863," *Chronicles of Oklahoma* 10 (1932): 44–51; Jess C. Epple, *Honey Springs Depot, Elk Creek, Creek Nation, Indian Territory* (Muskogee, Okla.: Hoffman Printing, 1964), 11–76; Charles R. Freeman, "The Battle of Honey Springs," *Chronicles of Oklahoma* 13 (1935): 154–68; McReynolds, *Seminoles,* 307–309; and W. A. Willey, "The Second Federal Invasion of the Indian Territory," *Chronicles of Oklahoma* 44 (1966): 420–30. On black participation in the battles, see Burke, "History of Kansas Regiments," 248–50; Dudley T. Cornish, "Kansas Negro Regiments in the Civil War," *Kansas Historical Quarterly* 20 (1953): 425–26; and Lary C. Rampp, "Negro Troop Activity in Indian Territory, 1863–1865," *Chronicles of Oklahoma* 47 (1969): 536–48. For an account of the role Company I played, see Van Horn, "Autobiography," 23–25. For reminiscences of the Battle of Honey Springs by Indian Territory blacks, see Teall, *Black History in Oklahoma,* 68–69, 71–74.

95. The source for this statement is Dr. D. D. Hancock, a surgeon at Fort Gibson at the time of the battle. "Notes and Documents: Fort Gibson in Early Days," *Chronicles of Oklahoma* 23 (1945): 292.

96. Britton, *Civil War on the Border,* vol. 2, 78; Dudley T. Cornish, *The Sable Arm: Negro Troops in the Union Army 1861–1865* (New York: Longmans, Green, 1956), 145–47.

97. Quoted in Saunt, *Black, White, and Indian,* 100.

98. Burke, "History of Kansas Regiments," 249.

99. Britton, *Union Indian Brigade,* 265–66.

100. Ibid., 282–83.

101. *OR,* 1, 22, part 1, 455–56.

102. Ibid., 450–51.

103. Ibid., 448.

104. Ibid., part 2, 465.

105. LeRoy H. Fischer, "Honey Springs Battlefield Park," *Chronicles of Oklahoma* 47 (1969): 516.

106. *OR,* 1, 22, part 1, 601–602.

107. On Sanco's involvement, see Affidavit of Aaron Sanco, December 11, 1869, Receipt Issued by John W. Wright, Cherokee Nation, May 2, 1866, and Baldwin to Parker, December 15, 1869, M234-804, B506-59 and encs. Littlefield includes fifteen Creek black members of the Second Kansas Colored, or Eighty-third U.S. Colored Infantry. D. F. Littlefield, *Africans and Creeks,* 238–39.

108. *OR,* 1, 22, part 2, General John McNeil to Major General John M. Schofield, November 2, 1863, 292.

109. Joseph T. Wilson, *The Black Phalanx: A History of the Negro Soldiers of the United States in the Wars of 1775–1812, 1861–1865* (Hartford, Conn.: American, 1888), 234–40.

110. For the official reports describing black participation in the Camden Expedition and the Battle of Poison Spring, see *OR,* 1, 34, part 1, 658, 734–56. For a concise account of the latter, see Ira D. Richards, "The Battle of Poison Spring," *Arkansas Historical Quarterly* 18 (1959): 338–49.

111. *OR,* 1, 34, part 1, 756.

112. Ibid., 754.

113. Ibid., 746.

114. Britton, *Union Indian Brigade,* 372–73.

115. *OR,* 1, 34, part 1, 108–109, 111–12, and part 2, 997; Speech of Long John, Head Chief of the Seminole Nation to the President of the United States, March 10, 1864,

M234-803, S291-64 (quote); Abel, *Participant in the Civil War*, 322–23; Frank Cunningham, *General Stand Watie's Confederate Indians* (San Antonio, Tex.: Naylor Co., 1959), 135; M. H. Wright and Fischer, "Oklahoma Civil War Sites," 161–62.

116. "Confederate Memorial Scroll to the Indian Officers in the War between the States," *Chronicles of Oklahoma* 28 (1950): 206 and facing plate; C. T. Foreman, "John Jumper," 142n17.

117. John Jumper, *Speech Delivered by Col. John Jumper to the Creeks and Seminoles Comprising the First Seminole Regiment, July 6th, 1864* (Fort Towson, Choctaw Nation, Indian Territory: Choctaw Government Printing Office, 1864), 3. See also Cunningham, *Watie's Confederate Indians*, 179.

118. *OR*, 1, 34, part 1, 1012–13; Lary C. Rampp, "Confederate Sinking of the J. R. Williams," *Journal of the West* 11 (1972): 43–50; Lary C. Rampp, "The Twilight of the Confederacy in the Indian Territory, 1863–1865," M.A. thesis, Oklahoma State University, 1968, 94–95.

119. *OR*, 1, 41, part 1, 771–72, 784–86; Britton, *Civil War on the Border*, vol. 2, 244–47; Britton, *Union Indian Brigade*, 436–40; Marvin J. Hancock, "The Second Battle of Cabin Creek," *Chronicles of Oklahoma* 39 (1961): 418; Rampp and Rampp, *Civil War in Indian Territory*, 102–106; Rampp, "Negro Troop Activity," 550–54.

120. *OR*, 1, 41, part 1, 766–92.

121. Boyd, "Use of Negro Troops," 47–48; Burke, "History of Kansas Regiments," 255; Cornish, "Kansas Negro Regiments," 429.

122. Chase to the editor of the *Sycamore (IL) True Republican and Sentinel*, August 21, 1863, Chase Collection.

123. Paskofar to Dole, July 29, 1863, M234-803, P76-63. The Seminole mikko emphasized the point in a similar letter a month later. See Paskofar to Dole, August 29, 1863, ibid., D235-63.

124. *ARCIA 1863*, Doc. 86, Report of Snow, 185.

125. *ARCIA 1864*, Archibald V. Coffin to William Coffin, August 26, 1864, and Doc. 149, Report of Snow, 307, 317–18; "Census of the Southern Refugee Indians in Kansas and the Cherokee Nation," Office of the Superintendent of Indian Affairs, Leavenworth, Kans., June 6, 1863, and William Coffin to Dole, January 26, 1864, M234-835, Southern Superintendency 1863–64, frames 231, 600–601.

126. "Number of Seminole Negroes together with the number of Cherokee and Creek Negro women and children, whose husbands and protectors are in the U.S. Army and who are under charge of Dec. 30th 1863," compiled by Snow at Neosho Falls, Kansas, M234-835, frame 601.

127. On September 4, 1863, Sonaki Mikko had signed a letter (as Billy Bowlegs) to the other Seminole mikkos and on March 10, 1864, both Chupco and Pascofar referred to his death. See Abel, *American Indian under Reconstruction*, 44–45n76–77; Paskofar to the President of the United States, March 10, 1864, and Speech of Long John, March 10, 1864, M234-803, S291-64. Klee Harjo, testifying after the war in the claim of Sonuck Harjo (Harjochee) for compensation for property losses as a Loyal Seminole, stated that Sonaki Mikko had "died of smallpox at Fort Gibson in November 1864." Although he mistook the year, Klee Harjo's recollection of the cause, place, and time of year probably would have been more accurate. That makes it likely that Sonaki Mikko died of smallpox at Fort Gibson in November 1863. See M574, roll 11, file 87, Claim 263.

128. *Fort Gibson (Okla.) Post*, April 22, 1909; Porter, "Billy Bowlegs in the Civil War," 400–401 and n. 23.

129. Richard A. Sattler, "Seminole in the West," in *Handbook: Southeast,* 461; Sattler, "Siminoli Italwa," 98, 334.

130. Paskofar to President of the United States, March 10, 1864, and Speech of Long John, March 10, 1864, M234-803, S291-64.

131. Speech of Long John, March 10, 1864, M234-803, S291-64.

132. *ARCIA 1864,* No. 162A, Cox to William Coffin, March 16, 1864, 332.

133. *ARCIA 1864,* Doc. 142, Report of William Coffin, 303–304, and Doc. 149, Report of Snow, 317–18; William Coffin to D. N. Cooley, December 15, 1865, M234-803, C1665-65; Abel, *American Indian under Reconstruction,* 49–62.

134. *ARCIA 1864,* William Coffin to Dole, June 16, 1864, 342–43.

135. Quoted in Abel, *American Indian under Reconstruction,* 75.

136. *ARCIA 1864,* Doc. 149, Report of Snow, 317–18, and Archibald Coffin to William Coffin, August 25, 1864, 451–52; Snow to Dole, August 8, 1864, M234-803, S428-64.

137. *ARCIA 1865,* Doc. 97, Report of George A. Reynolds, 281–82.

138. Laura E. Baum, "Agriculture among the Five Civilized Tribes, 1865–1906," M.A. thesis, University of Oklahoma, 1940, 18–20; Danziger, "Office of Indian Affairs," 272–75.

139. Indian Pioneer Papers, vol. 89, interview 12836, Ben F. Bruner, 259, and vol. 93, interview 13642, Carrie Marshall Pitman, 347; John Lilley to Lowrie, August 12, 1864, Presbyterian Mission Correspondence, roll 2, box 6, vol. 3, no. 175.

140. Reynolds to Elijah Sells, December 5, 1865, M234-837, Southern Superintendency, 1866–67, S13-66. Confederates from the other Civilized Tribes also maintained black slavery in the southern Indian Territory for the duration of the Civil War.

141. "Benjamin F. Bruner Obituary, Saturday, June 10, 1939," http://seminolenation-indianterritory.org/benjamin_f_bruner_obituary.htm (November 22, 2003); Indian Pioneer Papers, vol. 89, interview 12836, Ben F. Bruner, 259–60 (quotes); Seminole freedman census cards 699, 810, 828, enrollees 2220, 2631–37, and 2705, Newborn Seminole freedman census card 78, enrollees 84 and 85, M1186, roll 93.

142. John Jumper to Commissioner of Indian Affairs, January 11, 1876, M234-804, C71-76, enc.

143. Quoted in *ARCIA 1865,* Doc. 86, Report of Sells, 256.

144. Reynolds to Cooley, January 29, 1866, and reply written on same, M234-803, R21-66; Baldwin to Parker, April 26, 1870, Ben Bruner to Baldwin, April 27 and September 1, 1870, Elias Rector to A. W. Cram, August 31, 1875, and Jumper to Commissioner of Indian Affairs, January 11, 1876, M234-804, B706-70 and enc., B962-70, and C71-76 and enc.; Bruner to Col. A. B. Meacham, April 16, 1879, Statement of John F. Brown on same, and C. M. Carter to Commissioner of Indian Affairs, April 28, 1879, M234-871, Union Agency 1879, frames 492–95.

145. Ramsay, "Autobiography," 59–60.

146. Ibid., 60.

147. Britton, *Civil War on the Border,* vol. 2, 40.

148. M574, roll 11, file 87, claims 1, 2. See also claim 230.

149. Ramsay, "Autobiography," 58–59.

150. Abraham Hoffman, "Oklahoma's Black Panther," *War Chief of the Indian Territory Posse of Oklahoma Westerners* 6 (1972): 3; Creek freedman census card 1429, enrollee 4978, M1186, roll 88.

151. *OR,* 1, 48, part 1, 851.

152. D. F. Littlefield, *Africans and Seminoles,* 184–85.

153. Allan C. Ashcraft, "Confederate Indian Troop Conditions in August 1864," *Chroni-*

cles of Oklahoma 41 (1963): 279–82; C. T. Foreman, "John Jumper," 142; Indian Pioneer Papers, vol. 36, interview 12220, Tatekke Tiger, 482.

154. M. H. Wright and Fischer, "Oklahoma Civil War Sites," 204.

155. Ashcraft, "Confederate Indian Troop Conditions," 275, 279.

156. Angie E. Debo, "Southern Refugees of the Cherokee Nation," *Southwestern Historical Quarterly* 35 (1932): 262; LeRoy H. Fischer and William L. McMurry, "Confederate Refugees from Indian Territory," *Chronicles of Oklahoma* 57 (1979): 461.

157. *OR,* 1, 43, part 3, 600–602, *OR,* 1, 46, part 3, 665–66, and *OR,* 1, 48, part 2, 727, 1095, 1101, 1106, 1197, 1322.

158. Indian Pioneer Papers, vol. 36, interview 12220, Tatekke Tiger, 482.

159. *ARCIA 1865,* Doc. 86, Report of Sells, 255–56.

160. Ibid.; Debo, "Southern Refugees," 260–61; *OR,* 1, 48, part 2, 1096.

7. RECONSTRUCTION

1. The commissioners included Dennis Cooley, the commissioner of Indian affairs; Elijah Sells, the Southern Superintendent; Thomas Wister of the Society of Friends; Brigadier General William Harney of the U.S. Army; and Colonel Ely Parker of General Grant's staff, who later became commissioner of Indian affairs. Abel, *American Indian under Reconstruction,* 174–77.

2. Ibid., 221; *ARCIA 1865,* Doc. 105½, Report of Cooley, 298.

3. *ARCIA 1865,* Doc. 106, Official Report of the Proceedings of the Council with the Indians of the West and Southwest, Held at Fort Smith, Arkansas, in September 1865, 313–16.

4. Ibid., 318–25.

5. Ibid., 332–33.

6. T494, roll 8, Unratified Treaties 1821–65, frame 1260.

7. Southern Seminole delegates to U.S. Commissioners, September 16, 1865, ibid., frames 1270–73.

8. Address of John F. Brown to President of the Commission, September 18, 1865, ibid., frame 1283; *ARCIA 1865,* Doc. 106, 342, 350–51.

9. *ARCIA 1865,* Doc. 86, Report of Elijah Sells, 255–56.

10. George A. Reynolds to Sells, December 5, 1865, M234-837, Southern Superintendency, 1866–67, frames 551–55.

11. James Harlan to Cooley, November 18, 1865, M234-836, Southern Superintendency 1865, I1382-65; Harlan to John B. Sanborn, November 20, 1865, Sanborn Circular no. 1, January 1, 1866, Sanborn to Harlan, January 10, 1866, Sanborn Circular no. 6, March 27, 1866, and Sanborn to Major Pinkney Lugenbeel, April 7, 1866, M234-837, I56-66, S91-66, S203-66, S216-66.

12. "Statement of Indian Chiefs to Genl. Sanborn at Fort Gibson, Jany. 1st and 2nd, 1866," M234-837, frames 646–48.

13. *ARCIA 1866,* Doc. 147, Report of Sanborn, January 5, 1866, 284–85.

14. Ibid., 283–84.

15. See, for example, ibid., Doc. 148, Report of Sanborn, January 27, 1866, 285–86.

16. Ibid., Report of Cooley, 56, and Doc. 149, Report of Sanborn, April 13, 1866, 287.

17. Reynolds to Cooley, January 13 and February 16, 1866, John Chupco, Fos Harjo, and Chicote Harjo, Loyal Seminoles, to Commissioner of Indian Affairs, January 30, 1866, and Reynolds to Sells, April 6, 1866, M234-803, R14-66, R26-66, R23-66, S199-66 enc.;

"Statement of Indian Chiefs to Genl. Sanborn at Fort Gibson, Jany. 1st and 2nd, 1866," and J. Harlan (Creek agent) and Reynolds to Cooley, January 15, 1866, M234-837, frames 646–48, 212–14; Drake, *Indians of North America,* 763–64.

18. J. Harlan (Creek agent) and Reynolds to Cooley, January 15, 1866, M234-837, frames 212–14.

19. Reynolds to Cooley, February 16, 1866, M234-803, R26-66.

20. Chupco et al. to Commissioner of Indian Affairs, January 30, 1866, M234-803, R23-66.

21. Kappler, *Indian Affairs,* vol. 2, 695.

22. Matthew Kelly, "Naturalizing Seminole 'Racism' and the Multicultural Self," paper presented at the Human Rights Workshop, University of Chicago, May 25, 2004, 33 pp. http://humanrights.uchicago.edu/workshoppapers/kelly.pdf (February 8, 2006), 27.

23. Kappler, *Indian Affairs,* vol. 2, 695–96, and vol. 1, 340–41.

24. Ibid., vol. 2, 696.

25. *ARCIA 1882,* Report of Commissioner, lx.

26. Kappler, *Indian Affairs,* vol. 2, 695.

27. George W. Vann to Henry M. Teller, May 19, 1883, RG 75, LR BIA 1881–1907, 9445–83; T. F. Andrews, "Freedmen in Indian Territory: A Post–Civil War Dilemma," *Journal of the West* 4 (1965): 370.

28. B. H. Fisher to Secretary of the Interior, November 10, 1880, RG 48, SF, box 48; Nick Chiles to President Grover Cleveland, December 28, 1886, RG 75, LR BIA 1881–1907, 1661–87.

29. Teall, *Black History in Oklahoma,* 150–66.

30. Kappler, *Indian Affairs,* vol. 2, 696–97, 699.

31. Drake, *Indians of North America,* 763–64.

32. C. W. Turner, "Events among the Muskogees during Sixty Years," *Chronicles of Oklahoma* 10 (1932): 26.

33. *Holdenville (Creek Nation) Times,* August 17, 1906.

34. National Archives Microfilm Publications, M668, Records Relating to Ratified Indian Treaties, 1722–1869, 16 rolls, roll 14, Ratified Treaties, October 10, 1865–April 7, 1866, no. 352, frames 273–74.

35. D. F. Littlefield, *Africans and Creeks,* 247.

36. John F. Brown to Commissioner of Indian Affairs, March 21, 1866, M234-803, B86-66.

37. S. David Buice, "The Civil War and the Five Civilized Tribes: A Study in Federal-Indian Relations," Ph.D. dissertation, University of Oklahoma, 1970, 326–27.

38. Ibid., 328.

39. *ARCIA 1866,* Report of Commissioner, 8–9.

40. *ARCIA 1869,* Report of Commissioner, 9.

41. Ibid., Doc. 31, Report of Reynolds, 417–18.

42. U.S. Bureau of Indian Commissioners, *Annual Report of the Bureau of Indian Commissioners* (hereafter cited as *ARBIC*) *1870,* 139.

43. *ARCIA 1882,* Report of Commissioner, lx.

44. Testimony of Hulputter at Eufaula, Indian Territory, May 25, 1885, 49th Cong., 1st sess., S. Rep. 1278, part 2, 1886, 161–67.

45. U.S. Census Office, *The Five Civilized Tribes in Indian Territory: Extra Census Bulletin, Census Office, Department of the Interior* (Washington, D.C.: U.S. Census Printing Office, 1894), 69.

46. *ARCIA 1891,* part 1, 240.

47. D. B. Meacham to E. A. Hayt, November 20, 1878, M234-870, Union Agency 1878, frames 724–25.

48. Deposition of Robert Johnson, January 10, 1871, M234-804, Seminole Agency, 1868–71, B43-71 enc.

49. Creek freedman census card 1438, M1186, roll 88.

50. Helga H. Harriman, "Economic Conditions in the Creek Nation, 1865–1871," *Chronicles of Oklahoma* 51 (1973): 328.

51. Creek freedman census card 1429, M1186, roll 88.

52. "Statement of Loyal Seminoles," through Elijah J. Brown, September 13, 1867, and T. A. Baldwin to Parker, October 31, 1869, M234-804, W777-67 enc., B459-69. See also "Report of Employees in the Seminole Agency for the Year 1869," Baldwin to Parker, October 31, 1869, and October 25, 1870, "Abstract, Current Expenses, October 1869, Seminole Nation Agency," "Estimate of funds required for disbursement at the Seminole Agency, Indian Territory, for the 1st Quarter ending March 31st, 1870, by Capt. T. A. Baldwin, U.S.A. and I. At. [Indian Agent]," and "Estimate of funds required for disbursement at the Seminole Agency, Seminole Nation, for the 3rd Quarter 1870 by Capt. T. A. Baldwin, U.S.A. and I. Agt.," M234-804, B376-69, B458-69, B1058-70, B464-69, B588-70, B1058-70 enc.

53. Henry Breiner to Parker, January 25, 1871, M234-804, B43-71.

54. Baldwin to H. B. Hagan, January 20, 1870, M234-804, H805-70 enc.

55. "Abstract, Current Expenses, October 1869, Seminole Nation Agency," M234-804, B464-69; John Chupco, John Jumper, James Factor, and Robert Johnson, Delegates for the Seminole Nation, and E. J. Brown, Clerk of Delegation, to Breiner, December 27, 1872, and January 2 and 20, 1873, Breiner to H. R. Clum, January 20, 1873, Breiner to Ed. P. Smith, July 25, 1873, Nuthkup Harjo to Secretary of the Interior, December 30, 1873, Sanborn, Charles King, Chupco, and E. J. Brown, "Agreement" of January 31, 1874, John P. C. Shanks, special commissioner, "List of liabilities on Seminole Nation at 3 March 1875," and Chupco et al. to J. Smith, January 22, 1876, M234-805, Seminole Agency, 1872–76, B481-72 enc., B496-72/3 enc., B548-72/3 enc., B558-72/3 enc., B653-73, N11-74, S136-74, S1275-75 enc., C70-76; Seminole Delegates to Secretary of the Interior, January 12, 1876, M234-865, Union Agency, 1875–76, frame 596; Band Chiefs and Council Members, Seminole Nation, April 2, 1879, J. Ross Ramsey, Teacher, Mission School, Witness, M234-871, Union Agency 1879, frame 468.

56. Shanks to E. P. Smith, August 9, 1875, M234-805, S1275-75.

57. Shanks, "List of liabilities on Seminole Nation at 3 March 1875," ibid., enc.

58. Seminole freedman census card 608, enrollee 1900, M1186, roll 92.

59. M574, roll 11, file 87, claim 264.

60. *Wewoka (Okla.) Daily Times,* June 19, 1966. I am grateful to Richard Elwanger for providing this reference.

61. Seminole Annuity Roll 1870, RG 75, BIA, Seminole Annuity Rolls.

62. "Ledger" showing Seminole freedman family groupings and band affiliations in 1890 and 1892, 286 pp. holographic manuscript, C. Guy Cutlip Collection, Manuscripts Division, Western History Collections, University of Oklahoma (hereafter cited as Cutlip Collection), box 4, 79; Seminole freedman census card 608, M1186, roll 92.

63. Seminole freedman census card 629, enrollees 1949, 1950, and 1951, M1186, roll 92; Seminole freedman census card 782, enrollees 2509 and 2510, Newborn Seminole freedman census card 66, enrollee 73, M1186, roll 93; " 'Loyal Seminole Roll,' as prepared by Jas. E.

Jenkins, Special Agent, 8 March 1901," Foreman Gilcrease, box 49, R14, 58; J. B. Campbell, *Campbell's Abstract of Seminole Indian Census Cards and Index* (Muskogee, Okla.: Oklahoma Printing, 1925), 53, 62, 70. *Campbell's Abstract* is a useful aid for working with the Seminole and freedman census cards. Besides furnishing an index, it provides additional information on some of the enrollees by cross-referencing other rolls and including some death dates. Unfortunately, it does not include all the information the freedman enrollees furnished on the census cards. For complete documentation, the researcher must consult both the cards themselves and *Campbell's Abstract.*

64. Creek freedman census card 2, enrollees 6, 7, 8, and 9, and Creek freedman census card 3, enrollee 13, M1186, roll 85; J. B. Campbell, *Campbell's Abstract of Creek Freedman Census Cards and Index* (Muskogee, Okla.: Phoenix Job Printing, 1915), 9; J. Read Moore, *Moore's Seminole Roll and Land Guide* (Wewoka, Okla.: Lasiter, 1915), 3, 18, 25; Seaser Bolegs (Caesar Bowlegs) to Tams Bixby, November 28, 1899, Records of the Commission to the Five Civilized Tribes, Seminole File, 1897–1905, Letters Received, Letters Sent, and other papers, Indian Archives, Oklahoma Historical Society (hereafter cited as Dawes Commission, Seminole 1897–1905), 7094–99.

65. *Daily Oklahoman,* January 22, 1922; C. Guy Cutlip, "Wewoka—Barking Waters," 6 pp. typescript, Cutlip Collection, box 2, 1.

66. Indian Pioneer Papers, vol. 71, interview 12701, Moses Chapone, 457.

67. Bernice N. Crockett, "Health Conditions in Indian Territory from the Civil War to 1890," *Chronicles of Oklahoma* 36 (1958): 31–33.

68. Indian Pioneer Papers, vol. 71, interview 12701, Moses Chapone, 456; Margaret Berry Hand, "Necrology: Virgil Berry M.D.," *Chronicles of Oklahoma* 32 (1954): 236.

69. D. C. Gideon, *Indian Territory: Descriptive, Biographical, and Genealogical, Including the Landed Estates, Country Seats, etc.; with a General History of the Territory* (New York and Chicago: Lewis, 1901), 61. See also Duke Collection, vol. 51, interview T-243, Bettie Johnson, 16, and interview T-44, Lizzie Johnson Kernell, 2.

70. Virgil Berry, "Experiences of a Pioneer Doctor in Indian Territory," 35 pp. typescript, 1947, Virgil Berry Collection, Manuscripts Division, Western History Collections, University of Oklahoma Libraries, 13.

71. Indian Pioneer Papers, vol. 77, W. P. Blake to Grant Foreman, March 3, 1937, 213.

72. Berry, "Pioneer Doctor," 13 et seq.

73. Margaret Berry Blair with R. Palmer Howard, *Scalpel in a Saddlebag: The Story of a Physician in Indian Territory; Virgil Berry M.D.* (Oklahoma City: Oklahoma Western Heritage Books, 1979), 65.

74. Berry, "Pioneer Doctor," 13; Blair, *Scalpel in a Saddlebag,* 65.

75. Berry, "Pioneer Doctor," 13–20; Blair, *Scalpel in a Saddlebag,* 65.

76. This conclusion is drawn from information included in the Seminole Indian census cards, M1186, rolls 92, 93, and in *Campbell's Abstract of Seminole Indian Census Cards and Index.* It appears that, after a steep rise, the Seminole death rate began to flatten out in 1905.

77. Blair, *Scalpel in a Saddlebag,* 77.

78. Berry, "Pioneer Doctor," 13; Blair, *Scalpel in a Saddlebag,* 67–69.

79. Berry, "Pioneer Doctor," 13.

80. "Caesar Bowlegs, Seminole Indian," A. M. Seran Collection, Photographic Archives Division, Western History Collections, University of Oklahoma Libraries.

81. Blair, *Scalpel in a Saddlebag,* 66–69.

82. John M. Thornton, "The Seminole Nation: A Model Indian Government," *Indian Journal,* March 27, 1896; Laws of the Seminole Nation passed by the National Council,

January 28, 1903, Seminole Laws, July 1906, translated by George W. Grayson, Sem. vol. 4, Microfilm SMN 1, Indian Archives, Oklahoma Historical Society (hereafter cited as Seminole Laws 1903), chap. 6, secs. 1–15; Warrant Vouchers, Seminole Nation, Seminole Officers Payment for Quarters, April 1–June 30 and October 1–December 31, 1906, Acting Commissioner of Five Civilized Tribes to Dana H. Kelsey, January 12, 1909, J. G. Wright to Kelsey, April 20, June 22, July 8, and October 6, 1909, and Wright to A. J. Brown, June 10, 1909, Records of the Commission to the Five Civilized Tribes, Seminole Miscellaneous File, 1906–13, Indian Archives, Oklahoma Historical Society.

83. On the exploits of the Seminole Negro Indian Scouts, see Mulroy, *Freedom on the Border,* 107–73; Porter, *Black Seminoles,* 175–214; and Porter, *Negro on the American Frontier,* 472–91.

84. Indian Pioneer Papers, vol. 26, interview 12430, Joe M. Grayson, 373, and vol. 21, interview 6674, Carrie Cyrus, 400.

85. Carolyn T. Foreman, "Organization of the Seminole Light-Horse," *Chronicles of Oklahoma* 34 (1956): 340; Muriel H. Wright, *A Guide to the Indian Tribes of Oklahoma* (Norman: University of Oklahoma Press, 1951), 235–36; M. H. Wright, "Seal of the Seminole Nation," 268.

86. Indian Pioneer Papers, vol. 21, interview 6674, Carrie Cyrus, 400–401.

87. *Daily Oklahoman,* February 12, 1922.

88. Ibid.; Duke Collection, vol. 43, interview T-280, Primus Dean, 11, vol. 45, interview T-211, Dave McIntosh, 4, 14–15, and vol. 52, interview T-48, Billy Spencer, 4; Indian Pioneer Papers, vol. 21, interview 6674, Carrie Cyrus, 399–400, vol. 61, interview 7570, Harve Lovelday, 429, vol. 86, interview 7451, Robert Johnson, 181, and vol. 93, interview 13642, Carrie Marshall Pitman, 349; Harry H. Rogers to U.S. Indian Agent, Muskogee, February 23, 1906, and Grant Bruner to Kelsey, February 27, 1906, Dawes Commission, Seminole 1897–1905, 12281-06, 13427-06; Docs. 39518L, 39518M, Smn 2-7, sec. X, file 2, Indian Archives, Oklahoma Historical Society; Arthur T. Burton, "Seminole Light Horse Police," http://www.seminolenation-indianterritory.org/lighthorse.htm (July 7, 2005).

89. Indian Pioneer Papers, vol. 86, interview 7451, Robert Johnson, 180–81. See also "Tale of the Seminoles," unidentified press clipping, Foreman OHS, box 17, Seminole Indians.

90. See Daniel F. Littlefield, Jr., and Lonnie E. Underhill, "Negro Marshals in Indian Territory," *Journal of Negro History* 56 (1971): 77–87; Teall, *Black History in Oklahoma,* 122–27; and Nudie E. Williams, "Black Men Who Wore the 'Star,' " *Chronicles of Oklahoma* 59 (1981): 83–90.

91. Indian Pioneer Papers, vol. 70, interview 7855, Nancy E. Pruitt, 356.

92. Arthur T. Burton, *Black, Red and Deadly: Black and Indian Gunfighters of the Indian Territories* (Austin, Tex.: Eakin Press, 1991), chap. 16; Gideon, *Indian Territory,* 115–18; Littlefield and Underhill, "Negro Marshals," 80; Charles W. Mooney, *Localized History of Pottawatomie County, Oklahoma, to 1907* (Midwest City, Okla.: Lithographics Printers, 1971), 296–97; *Muskogee (Okla.) Phoenix,* July 13, 1910; *Oklahoma City Weekly Times Journal,* March 8, 1907.

93. William S. Savage, "The Role of Negro Soldiers in Protecting the Indian Territory from Intruders," *Journal of Negro History* 36 (1951): 32–34.

94. "Abstract of Disbursements made by T. A. Baldwin, Capt. U.S. Army and I. At. [Indian Agent] in the month ending April 30, 1870, for Treaty Stipulations," M234-804, B745-70; "List of Traders in Seminole Nation, licensed by the United States," enc. 3 with John Q. Tufts to Hayt, December 9, 1879, M234-872, Union Agency 1879, frame 1132;

Margaret A. Chaney, "A Tribal History of the Seminole Indians," M.A. thesis, University of Oklahoma, 1928, 84; *Daily Oklahoman,* October 9, 1921; Duke Collection, vol. 45, interviews T-210 and T-211, Dave McIntosh; *Muskogee (Creek Nation) Phoenix,* July 26, 1894; *Purcell (Choctaw Nation) Register,* August 3, 1894; Seminole freedman census card 609, enrollee 1901, M1186, roll 92; Wewoka Trading Company, Ledger, 1867–72, 182, Cutlip Collection.

95. Seminole Annuity Roll 1870, RG 75, BIA, Seminole Annuity Rolls.

96. "Act of Seminole Council relative to control of their annuity funds," passed May 12, 1871, M234-805, M782-72 enc.

97. "Voucher No. 2, Abstract E, 2nd Quarter 1875, Per Capita Roll of Seminole Nation," Foreman Gilcrease, box 49, R12.

98. Breiner to F. A. Walker, September 18, 1872, M234-805, B187-72; Memorandum relating to jurisdiction under the Seminole and Creek treaties of 1866, M234-867, Union Agency 1877, frame 922.

99. M574, roll 11, file 87.

100. "Abstract of disbursements made by T. A. Baldwin," M234-804, B724-70.

101. Rev. William Meyer to Secretary of the Interior, October 16, 1908, National Archives Record Group 75, Letters Received by the Bureau of Indian Affairs 1907–39 (hereafter cited as RG 75, LR BIA 1907–39), 655531-08, Sem. 211.

102. Foster, *Negro-Indian Relationships,* 65–66.

8. INTERMARRIAGE

1. For a good overview of how each of the Five Tribes dealt with emancipation and Reconstruction, see Saunt, "Paradox of Freedom," 63–94.

2. The most substantial studies of the Creek freedmen are Barbara Krauthamer, "Blacks on the Borders: African-Americans' Transition from Slavery to Freedom in Texas and the Indian Territory, 1836–1907," Ph.D. dissertation, Princeton University, 2000, chaps. 4 and 5; Katja May, *African Americans and Native Americans in the Creek and Cherokee Nations, 1830s to 1920s: Collision and Collusion* (New York and London: Garland, 1996); Sameth, "Creek Negroes"; and Gary W. Zellar, " 'If I Ain't One, You Won't Find Another One Here': Race, Identity, Citizenship, and Land; The African Creek Experience in the Indian Territory and Oklahoma, 1830–1910," Ph.D. dissertation, University of Arkansas, 2003, chaps. 3–7. See also relevant sections in Angie E. Debo, *And Still the Waters Run: The Betrayal of the Five Civilized Tribes* (Princeton, N.J.: Princeton University Press, 1940); Debo, *Road to Disappearance;* and D. F. Littlefield, *Africans and Creeks.* Saunt, in *Black, White, and Indian,* has traced the multigenerational history of one Creek family of African, Indian, and European descent—the Graysons—from the 1780s to the 1920s. That work includes a useful "Note on Sources and Historiography," 217–22.

3. *ARCIA 1882,* Report of Commissioner, lx.

4. May, *African Americans and Native Americans,* 4.

5. The standard work on the Cherokee freedmen remains D. F. Littlefield, *Cherokee Freedmen.* See also R. L. Ballenger, "The Colored High School of the Cherokee Nation," *Chronicles of Oklahoma* 30 (1952): 454–62; Tim Gammon, "Black Freedmen and the Cherokee Nation," *Journal of American Studies* 2 (1977): 357–64; Gary R. Kremer, "For Justice and a Fee: James Milton Turner and the Cherokee Freedmen," *Chronicles of Oklahoma* 58 (1980): 377–91; May, *African Americans and Native Americans;* relevant sections in McLoughlin, *After the Trail of Tears;* Tiya Miles, *Ties That Bind: The Story of an Afro-Cherokee Family in Slavery and Freedom* (Berkeley: University of California Press, 2005); Celia E. Naylor-Ojurongbe,

" 'More at Home with the Indians': African-American Slaves and Freedpeople in the Cherokee Nation, Indian Territory, 1838–1907," Ph.D. dissertation, Duke University, 2001; Circe Sturm, *Blood Politics: Race, Culture, and Identity in the Cherokee Nation of Oklahoma* (Berkeley: University of California Press, 2002); relevant sections in Wardell, *Political History of the Cherokee Nation;* and Walt Willson, "Freedmen in Indian Territory during Reconstruction," *Chronicles of Oklahoma* 49 (1971): 230–44.

6. The best study of blacks associated with the Chickasaws after the Civil War is D. F. Littlefield, *Chickasaw Freedmen.* That work includes discussion of the Choctaw freedmen. An extended study of the Choctaw freedmen has yet to be written. Other secondary accounts include Norman J. Bender, " 'We Surely Gave Them an Uplift,' " *Chronicles of Oklahoma* 61 (1983): 180–93; relevant sections in Debo, *Rise and Fall of the Choctaw Republic,* and Gibson, *Chickasaws;* Parthena L. James, "Reconstruction in the Chickasaw Nation: The Freedman Problem," *Chronicles of Oklahoma* 45 (1967): 44–57; Wyatt F. Jeltz, "The Relations of Negroes and Choctaw and Chickasaw Indians," *Journal of Negro History* 33 (1948): 24–37; and Krauthamer, "Blacks on the Borders," chaps. 6 and 7.

7. Quoted in D. F. Littlefield, *Chickasaw Freedmen,* 151.

8. *ARCIA 1866,* Report of Cooley, 8–9.

9. U.S. Census Office, *Five Civilized Tribes in Indian Territory,* 69.

10. J. A. Newsom, *The Life and Practice of the Wild and Modern Indian: The Early Days of Oklahoma; Some Thrilling Experiences* (Oklahoma City: Harlow, 1922), 75.

11. Rezin W. McAdam, "An Indian Commonwealth," *Harper's New Monthly Magazine* 87 (November 1893): 892.

12. *El Reno (Oklahoma Territory) News,* June 27, 1901. The *Alva (Oklahoma Territory) Review* also carried the story the same day.

13. *Vinita (Cherokee Nation) Weekly Chieftain,* March 17, 1904.

14. L. J. Abbott, "The Race Question in the Forty-sixth State," *Independent* 6 (July 1907): 206, 208.

15. Daniel F. Littlefield, Jr., *Seminole Burning: A Story of Racial Vengeance* (Jackson: University Press of Mississippi, 1996), 24.

16. *ARBIC 1870,* 139.

17. *Indian Journal,* April 12, 1877.

18. Ibid., March 27, 1896.

19. Coe, *Red Patriots,* 186.

20. Gideon, *Indian Territory,* 59.

21. Ora E. Reed, "The Passing of the Seminoles," *Sturm's Oklahoma Magazine* 3 (September 1906): 11–12.

22. Frederick W. Hodge, *Handbook of American Indians, North of Mexico,* 2 vols. (Washington, D.C.: Government Printing Office, 1910), vol. 2, 501, and see also 52–53, 600.

23. Quoted in Bateman, "We're Still Here," 254.

24. G. E. E. Lindquist, "Seminoles of Oklahoma," 2 pp. typescript, sec. X, case 5, drawer 3, Seminole Indians, file 1, 3a-522-a-1, Indian Archives, Oklahoma Historical Society.

25. Porter, "Relations between Negroes and Indians," 367.

26. Otis D. Duncan, "The Fusion of White, Negro, and Indian Cultures at the Converging of the New South and the West," *Southwestern Social Science Quarterly* 14 (1934): 359.

27. *Daily Oklahoman,* April 23, 1939.

28. Joseph B. Thoburn and Muriel H. Wright, *Oklahoma: A History of the State and Its People,* 4 vols. (New York: Lewis Historical, 1929), vol. 3, 390.

29. Katz, *Black Indians,* 144. Historian Gary Nash put a different spin on the argument by

suggesting that the Seminole maroons were "African Americans who became Indian without actually mixing their blood." Gary B. Nash, "The Hidden History of Mestizo America," *Journal of American History* 82 (1995): 948n16.

30. Bateman, "Africans and Indians," 8–18; Bateman, "Naming Patterns," 227–57, esp. 243; Miller, *Coacoochee's Bones*, 55–71, 183–88; Miller, "Seminoles and Africans"; Mulroy, *Freedom on the Border*, 159–62.

31. Saunt, "Paradox of Freedom," 83 (quote), and see also 91–92. After noting that Mulroy and Susan Miller have asserted that intermarriage between Seminoles and blacks was less common than other historians have suggested, Saunt nevertheless concludes: "All impressionistic evidence indicates, however, that Seminoles married blacks far more frequently than did the Creeks, Choctaws, Chickasaws, and Cherokees." Ibid., 83n64.

32. Carla D. Pratt, "Tribes and Tribulations: Beyond Sovereign Immunity and toward Reparation and Reconciliation for the Estelusti," *Washington and Lee Race Ethnic Ancestry Law Journal* 11 (2005): 94.

33. John C. Casey to Isaac Clark, July 11, 1838, H. Doc. 225, 119–20; Statement of Washbourne, October 14, 1854, M234-801, D709-54 enc.

34. Porter, *Negro on the American Frontier*, 111 (Waka Puchasi description). Porter suggests that the story concerning Asin Yahola's wife is "unsupported by trustworthy contemporary evidence" and "probably untrue." Kenneth W. Porter, "Osceola and the Negroes," *Florida Historical Quarterly* 33 (1955): 235–39 (quotes on 235, 239). See also Kenneth W. Porter, "The Episode of Osceola's Wife: Fact or Fiction?" *Florida Historical Quarterly* 26 (1947): 92–98.

35. Porter, *Negro on the American Frontier*, 305.

36. Decision of the Chiefs, June 15, 1827, Statement of Nelly Factor, September 4, 1828, Statement of DuVal, September 10, 1828, Manumission papers, May 27, 1832, Statement of Sam Factor, February 15, 1835, and DuVal to Worth, December 22, 1842, M234-289, S3398-43.

37. Jesup to Poinsett, June 16, 1837, Jesup's Papers, Letters Sent.

38. Bateman, "We're Still Here," 256–58. Historian Thomas Ingersoll has suggested that white prejudice made some Indian-blacks "among the most alienated and subversive of all mixed bloods." Thomas N. Ingersoll, *To Intermix with Our White Brothers: Indian Mixed Bloods in the United States from the Earliest Times to the Indian Removals* (Albuquerque: University of New Mexico Press, 2005), 110. The exploits of ruthless mixed-race criminals such as Billy Sena Factor, Cherokee Bill, and the members of the Rufus-Buck gang added support to the stereotype. Indian-blacks sometimes took pride in the meanness their mixed heritage supposedly bestowed. Although a former Confederate, Pleasant Porter, an Indian-black principal chief of the Creeks after the Civil War, bragged that he had the "meanest mixture of blood there was." Quoted in Saunt, *Black, White, and Indian*, 111. Seminole maroon communities, meanwhile, courted a reputation for being "mongrelized" and dangerous.

39. In 1930, physical anthropologist Wilton Krogman attempted a study of racial intermixture among the Oklahoma Seminoles. His original intention was to study the Seminole freedmen, but "the problem of legal status, the pride of race, the superstitious fear of 'bein' measured' (for one's coffin) and other factors entered in: we simply could not attempt a study of the Freedmen and their mixture in the Seminole Nation." As a result, Krogman fell prey to the usual generalizations: "The very number of Negroes associated with the Seminoles is almost *a priori* evidence of intermixture." He concluded, "Intermixture there has been, surely. Complete infiltration, no. The exact extent of crossing must remain a problem." Wilton M. Krogman, *The Physical Anthropology of the Seminole Indians of Oklahoma* (Rome: Failli, 1935), viii, 10, 13. No other anthropologist since has attempted such a study.

40. Although difficult to work with, prone to error, and sometimes providing insufficient detail for a thorough analysis, the census cards nevertheless constitute the largest and most useful body of information available on the genealogies of Seminoles and freedmen at that time. The ensuing figures are based on information contained in the Seminole Indian, Seminole freedman, Newborn Seminole Indian, and Newborn Seminole freedman census cards, M1186, rolls 92, 93. Genealogical information on Creek freedman participants in intermarriages with Seminole Indian women can be traced through the Creek Indian and freedman census cards, M1186, rolls 77–91. *Campbell's Abstract of Seminole Indian Census Cards and Index* provided a good starting point for tracing Seminole, freedman, and mixed-race Seminole-freedman genealogies. Whenever possible, additional information from other sources, such as Seminole annuity rolls, was consulted to increase accuracy.

Those designated "fullblood" on the Seminole Indian rolls were excluded from further investigation. Some of those might have had African admixture, but its source and extent would be impossible to trace. The study, then, was restricted to Seminoles classified as being of "mixed blood" and to Seminole freedmen. Band affiliation is the key to uncovering intermarriage. Although offspring typically became members of their mother's band, the census cards also list the father's band. Thus, an enrolled freedman father of an enrolled "Seminole" child, and an enrolled Indian father of an enrolled "freedman" child, can be detected. Because the Seminole census cards specified blood quantum, the task proved easier and probably produced more accurate results when tracing intermarriages involving freedmen and Indian women. Because the freedman rolls did not specify blood quantum, band affiliation is the only pointer to intermarriage in that source. A fairly wide margin of error should be factored into consideration of the results for the following reasons:

(a) The Dawes Commission compiled the rolls for the purpose of allotting land to legitimate Seminole citizens, not to provide researchers with a reliable genealogical resource. The census cards also reflect Indian and maroon social organization as interpreted and recorded by white U.S. government agents. Matrilineal descent, polygyny, and African-based naming patterns added layers of complexity to Seminole and freedman society that the Dawes Commission often overlooked, misunderstood, or misrepresented.

(b) Because it sought to establish legitimate claims to Seminole citizenship through lineage, the Dawes Commission concentrated on documenting unions that had produced enrollees. The census cards are not a reliable source for tracing childless intermarriages. Unless otherwise indicated, the following discussion uses the terms "intermarriage," "marriage," "miscegenation," "union," "husband," "spouse," and "wife" to refer to relationships and participants in relationships that produced children.

(c) Due to the complexities inherent in Seminole and freedman society, the cards contain errors. "Mixed bloods" sometimes were enrolled as "fullbloods" (and hence were not included in this study). Parents sometimes were listed as both "living" and "dead." A number of parents were said to be living Seminole citizens, but were not enrolled.

(d) The census cards often provide inadequate information for the purpose of this study. For example, they give no blood quantum for enrolled freedmen. Thus it was quite possible for a mixed-race Seminole-freedman and freedwoman, whose Indian admixture derived from their fathers, to parent children with high percentages of Seminole admixture who would be enrolled simply as freedmen. Also, the

simple listing "living Seminole" often disguised that the person in question was a
freedman citizen. Where parents were listed as dead or unknown, it is impossible to
trace lineage, except sometimes through other sources. And "non citizens" could
have been Indian, white, black, or Hispanic.

Therefore, the information contained in the census cards, and hence the results of this
analysis, should be treated with caution. The cards do not provide completely accurate
information on the racial makeup of Seminole society. Nor could the accuracy of miscegenation statistics be improved by tracing the rolls back to pre-Removal Florida. At no time could
individuals be classified with certainty as being "fully Seminole" or "fully African." Yet
despite their inadequacies, the census cards present a huge amount of useful genealogical
information on Seminole society at the turn of the century. They also allow researchers a rare
glimpse of the extent of Indian-freedman intermarriage within the Seminole Nation during
the period prior to Oklahoma statehood.

41. Some of the Creek freedman parents appearing on the Seminole Indian rolls were
designated as such. Others, however, were listed simply as "Creek," meaning Creek citizen,
not Creek Indian. The twenty-three individuals listed here are known to have had Creek
freedman fathers, either by their designation on the cards or by tracing them through the
Creek and Seminole freedman rolls and assuring accuracy with additional family information.
These twenty-three represent only those on the Seminole Indian roll known to have been of
mixed Seminole–Creek freedman extraction. There may have been more, but not many
more.

42. Seminole Indian census cards 9, 131, M1186, roll 92.

43. Indian Pioneer Papers, vol. 89, interview 12836, Ben F. Bruner, 259–60; "Ledger"
showing family groupings and band affiliations in 1890 and 1892, Cutlip Collection, box 4;
Loyal Seminole Roll, as Prepared by James E. Jenkins, Special Indian Agent, March 8, 1901,
and "Voucher No. 2, Abstract E, 2nd Quarter 1875, Per Capita Roll of Seminole Nation,"
Foreman Gilcrease, box 49, R14, R12; Seminole Annuity Roll 1870, RG 75, BIA, Seminole
Annuity Rolls; Seminole freedman census cards 699, 810, 828, enrollees 2220, 2631–37, and
2705, Newborn Seminole freedman census card 78, enrollees 84 and 85, M1186, roll 93.

44. Sattler, "Siminoli Italwa," 336–37.

45. Bateman, "We're Still Here," 254–55.

46. Among the Five Tribes, the Choctaws and Chickasaws had the highest rate of white
intermarriage, were strongest in their support for the Confederacy, and displayed the highest
levels of white acculturation. They also showed, by far, the most antipathy toward their
freedmen after the Civil War.

47. Circe Sturm, "Blood Politics, Racial Classification, and Cherokee National Identity:
The Trials and Tribulations of the Cherokee Freedmen," in *Confounding the Color Line,* 240.

48. May, *African Americans and Native Americans,* 176–78, 197–98, 257 (quote). May
defines Creek "black Indians" as "African Americans with or without Creek ancestry who
had resided among the Creeks longer than two decades and whose parents were born among
the Creeks" (172). Cherokee "black Indians" are defined similarly.

49. Harry H. Rogers to U.S. Indian Agent, Muskogee, February 23, 1906, and Grant
Bruner to Kelsey, February 27, 1906, Docs. 39518-L and 39518-M, Smn. 2-7, sec. X, file 2,
Indian Archives, Oklahoma Historical Society.

50. Mary E. Diament to Secretary of the Indian Department, February 8, 1899, Dawes
Commission, Seminole 1897–1905, 497–99.

51. Chart 1 is based on information contained in the Seminole Indian, Seminole freed-

man, Creek Indian, and Creek freedman census cards, M1186, rolls 77–93; *Campbell's Abstract of Creek Freedman Census Cards and Index; Campbell's Abstract of Seminole Indian Census Cards and Index;* and *Moore's Seminole Roll and Land Guide.* Because the Dawes Commission arbitrarily allotted Newborn Seminole Indians and Newborn Seminole freedmen forty acres each, their landholdings were not representative of Indian and maroon settlement patterns and have not been included.

52. Information on the Noble family is contained in Seminole Indian census cards 231, 232, 253, 284, 288, 313, 354; Newborn Seminole Indian census cards 79, 94, 103, 180; Seminole freedman census cards 623, 638, 656, 657, 705, 808; Newborn Seminole freedman census cards 2, 6; and Creek freedman census card 1810, M1186, rolls 89, 92, 93.

53. Information on the Coody and Warrior families derives from Seminole Indian census cards 303, 314, 343, 354, 592; Seminole freedman census cards 625, 645, 652, 664, 737; and Creek freedman census cards 259, 1290, M1186, rolls 85, 88, 92, 93.

54. Tiya Miles, "Uncle Tom Was an Indian: Tracing the Red in Black Slavery," in *Confounding the Color Line,* 145. Miles's broader generalizations—that "the children and grandchildren of Indian and Black Families were considered Native by their Native relatives and Black by their Black relatives," that "Black Indian people were viewed as Indian by Native community members," that "the majority of Native people ignored exclusionary laws against Blacks and continued to view Black Indian relatives as kin," and that "[Black] Indians were Indians"—require closer definition and stronger evidentiary support. Ibid., 145, 147, 157–58n30, 149.

55. Miles, *Ties That Bind,* 215.

56. Saunt, *Black, White, and Indian,* quotes on 4, 11, 282n1, 195.

57. James F. Brooks, quoting from W. Jeffrey Borroughs and Paul Spickard, in his introduction to *Confounding the Color Line,* 7.

58. Quoted in *Cherokee Advocate,* January 16, 1875.

59. John Jumper to Commissioner of Indian Affairs, May 15, 1885, RG 75, LR BIA 1881–1907, 11673–85.

60. Chupco and Fos Hutchee to Baldwin, December 29, 1869, M234-804, B524-69 enc.

61. Meacham to Hayt, November 20, 1878, M234-870, frames 724–25.

62. *ARCIA 1869,* Doc. 132, Report of Baldwin, 419; *Muskogee (Creek Nation) New State Tribune,* May 17, 1906.

63. Chupco and Jumper to Chairman of Senate Committee on Indian Affairs, February 12, 1869, "A Copy of Laws of the Seminole Nation passed in General Council (Feby.) 11th, 1869 at Wewoka Seminole Nation," Chupco and Fos Hutchee to Baldwin, December 29, 1869, Baldwin to Parker, August 27, 1869, Chupco and Jumper to Parker, August 27, 1869, Chupco and Jumper to Baldwin, November 25, 1869, and Baldwin to Parker, May 4, 1870, M234-804, H107-69, B451-69, B524-69, B366-69 and enc., B484-69, B726-70; "Act of Seminole Council relative to the control of their annuity funds, passed May 12, 1871," Jumper and Factor to G. N. Ingalls, February 26, 1875, Shanks, "List of Liabilities on Seminole Nation at 3 March 1875," Wewoka, Seminole Nation, May 17, 1875, and Shanks to Smith, August 9, 1875, M234-805, B782-72 enc., I233-75, S1275-75 and enc.; *ARCIA 1872,* Doc. 19, Report of Breiner, 242.

64. David Stanley to Adjutant General, Department of Texas (hereafter cited as AGDT), May 19 (quote), May 24, June 19, 1882, 1st endorsement to Stanley to AGDT, May 24, 1882, C. C. Augur, May 25, 1882, 2nd endorsement, Philip Sheridan, June 1, 1882, 2nd endorsement to Stanley to AGDT, June 19, 1882, Sheridan, June 28, 1882, National Archives Microfilm Publications, M619, Record Group 75, Records of the Bureau of Indian Affairs,

Letters Received, file 488-70, "Papers Relating to the Return of the Kickapoo and the Seminole (Negro) Indians from Mexico to the United States, 1870–1885," 2 rolls (hereafter cited as M619), roll 800, frames 627–29, 631, 639–40, 625–26, 638.

65. Jumper to Tufts, August 2, 1882, M619-800, frames 651–52.

66. Tufts to Hiram Price, August 11, 1882, Price to Secretary of the Interior, September 9, 1882, M619-800, frames 652, 647–49; Tufts to Price, March 26, 1884, RG 48, SF, box 48, Choctaw Freedman File, 6172–84, enclosed with Teller to Commissioner of Indian Affairs, May 2, 1884, 8582–84.

67. Frederick H. French to AGDT, May 23, 1883, M619-800, frames 656–57.

68. Jumper to Tufts, September 17, 1883, M619-800, frames 695–98. Sheridan refuted Jumper's charge that the Texas maroons were "a turbulent lawless band," stating that he always had found them to be "law abiding, well disposed and worthy of consideration." Sheridan to Adjutant General, October 27, 1883, M619-800, frames 703–704.

69. Jumper to Tufts, March 1, 1884, Tufts to Price, March 26, 1884, Jumper to John F. Brown, March 31, 1884, Teller to Commissioner of Indian Affairs, May 2, 1884, and Brown to Commissioner of Indian Affairs, February 12, 1885, RG 48, SF, box 48, Choctaw Freedman File, 6172–84, enc. A with 8582–84, 6781–84 (enc. 2 with 8582–84), 8582–84, 3139–85; Price to Secretary of the Interior, April 25, 1884, E. L. Stevens to Tufts, May 17, 1884, and Price to Tufts, February 18, 1885, RG 75, LS and LB 1881–1907, Letter Book L 124, 494, Letter Book L 125, 413, Letter Book L (February 1885), 133–35; "I Want to Go to My People and Settle in a Home," in Porter, "Freedom over Me."

70. Listings of Joe Scippio (Scipio) and Caesar Bruner Bands, Seminole Census Records 1890, 64–81, 90–97, Cutlip Collection, box 4; Ledger Book documenting cash payments to Seminole Indians by bands, 1898, Seminole vol. 6, listings for Dosar Barkus and Caesar Bruner bands, 46–48, 81–90; List of Headrights paid Seminole Indians by bands, J. F. Brown and Son, Headright 1901, Seminole vol. 7, listings for Dosar Barkus and Caesar Bruner bands, 47–69, 124–35, SMN 1, Microfilm, Indian Archives, Oklahoma Historical Society; U.S. Commission to the Five Civilized Tribes, *The Final Rolls of the Citizens and Freedmen of the Five Civilized Tribes in Indian Territory; Prepared by the Commission and Commissioner to the Five Civilized Tribes, and Approved by the Secretary of the Interior on or prior to March 4, 1907* (Washington, D.C.: Government Printing Office, 1907), listings of Seminole freedmen, 627–34.

71. Stanley, May 16, 1885, 1st endorsement to C. H. Smith to AGDT, May 9, 1885, M619-800, frames 786–88; Petition of Florida Seminole Negroes, received by BIA, February 9, 1888, RG 75 LR 1881–1907, 3565–88; "I Want to Go to My People and Settle in a Home," in Porter, "Freedom over Me"; Army Discharge Papers of David Bowlegs of the Seminole Negro Indian Scouts, 1873–80, Epton (Hicks) Collection, Manuscripts Divison, Western History Collections, University of Oklahoma; Porter, "Seminole in Mexico," 167–68 and n39.

72. Jumper to Tufts, September 17, 1883, M619-800, frames 695–98; Jumper to Tufts, March 1, 1884, and Jumper to Brown, March 31, 1884, RG 48, SF, box 48, Choctaw Freedman File, 6172–84 enc. A, 6781–84, both enclosed with 8582–84.

73. Historians Donald Grinde and Quintard Taylor estimated that between ca. 1870 and 1890, freedman immigrants to the Indian Territory from neighboring states tripled the area's African American population. Moreover, they suggest, "some blacks, especially in the Creek and Seminole nations, advanced claims of citizenship through dubious Indian ancestry, while others married Indian or ex-slave women in order to remain." Donald A. Grinde, Jr., and Quintard Taylor, "Red vs. Black: Conflict and Accommodation in the Post Civil War Indian Territory, 1865–1907," *American Indian Quarterly* 8 (1984): 218.

74. J. Tyler Powell to N. G. Taylor, March 7, 1868, M574, roll 11, file 87, frame 44; Memorandum to Hayt, November 20, 1878, M234-870, frames 724–25; *ARCIA 1882,* Report of Tufts, 87; U.S. Census Office, *Five Civilized Tribes in Indian Territory,* 7, 20, 69; *Indian Journal,* March 27, 1896; *Muskogee (Creek Nation) New State Tribune,* May 17, 1906.

75. Antoinette C. Snow Constant, "Seminoles: Earliest Missionaries, Missions and Schools among the Seminole Indians," 27 pp. holographic ms., Antoinette C. Snow Constant Papers, sec. X, Indian Archives, Oklahoma Historical Society (hereafter cited as Constant Papers), 12; U.S. Census Office, *Five Civilized Tribes in Indian Territory,* 69–70; Coe, *Red Patriots,* 188; Norman A. Graebner, "The Public Land Policy of the Five Civilized Tribes," *Chronicles of Oklahoma* 23 (1945): 108; Julian Ralph, "The Unique Plight of the Five Nations," *Harper's Weekly* 40 (January 4, 1896): 12, 14.

76. U.S. Census Office, *Five Civilized Tribes in Indian Territory,* 69–70; C. Guy Cutlip, "History of Seminole County," 23 pp. typescript, Cutlip Collection, miscellaneous manuscripts, 12–14; *Daily Oklahoman,* January 22, 1922; *Holdenville (Creek Nation) Tribune,* April 20, 1905; Indian Pioneer Papers, vol. 9, interview 5281, A. P. Shaw, 244–45, vol. 17, interview 6768, F. D. Brown, 9, vol. 20, interview 9416, Henry Cotton, 514–15, vol. 37, interview 6249, J. P. Montgomery, 20–22, vol. 77, Louis C. Brown, 311–12, and vol. 104, interview 13827, E. H. Burnett; William F. Jones, *The Experiences of a Deputy U.S. Marshal of the Indian Territory* (n.p., 1937, 40 pp.), 13; Newsom, *Wild and Modern Indian,* 118–20; *Seminole (Seminole Nation) Capital,* December 20, 1906.

77. *ARCIA 1871,* Doc. 114, Report of Breiner, 582; Meacham to Hayt, November 20, 1878, M234-870, frames 724–25; Jenkins to Secretary of the Interior, September 26, 1902, National Archives Record Group 48, Records of the Department of the Interior, Indian Division, Letters Received, 6043-02; U.S. Census Office, *Five Civilized Tribes in Indian Territory,* 69–70; Chaney, "Seminole Indians," 85–88; Coe, *Red Patriots,* 186; W. D. Crawford, "Oklahoma and the Indian Territory," *New England Magazine* 15 (1890): 456; Henry King, "The Indian Country," *Century Magazine* 30 (1885): 602; Seminole Laws 1903.

78. D. F. Littlefield, *Seminole Burning,* 19.

79. Sattler, "Siminoli Italwa," 346. Sattler offers explanations for the strength and resilience of Seminole conservatism on 354 et seq.

80. *ARCIA 1871,* Doc. 144, Report of Breiner, 582; Crockett, "Health Conditions," 31–33.

81. Perhaps the best example of that is provided by Union agent Tufts's inability to eject from the Seminole Nation the maroon immigrants from west Texas, although Seminole leaders requested and his superiors in Washington ordered him to do so.

82. American Baptist Home Mission Society, *Baptist Home Missions in America, Including a Full Report of the Proceedings and Addresses of the Jubilee Meeting and a Historical Sketch of the Baptist Home Mission Society, Historical Tables, etc., 1832–1882* (New York: Baptist Home Mission Rooms, 1883), 573–74; *ARCIA 1869,* Report C3, W. Morris Grimes to Vincent Colyer, March 9 and 10, 1869, 79; *Atoka (Choctaw Nation) Vindicator,* March 27 and April 3, 1875; "Baptist Prominence in the Indian Territory," *Baptist Home Mission Monthly,* January 1892; Belt, "Baptist Missions to the Indians," 130–32; Carleton, *Not Yours,* 64; Chaney, "Seminole Indians," appendix A; C. T. Foreman, "John Jumper," 146–51; Hamilton, *Gospel among the Red Men,* 81, 99–100; Adoniram J. Holt, "How the Gospel Was First Introduced in Oklahoma," and miscellaneous letters sent by Israel G. Vore, Indian Territory, ca. February 1879, in "Seminoles-Vore Letters, 1870s," Foreman Gilcrease, box 16, vol. 2, 5, 7, 61; Holt, *Pioneering in the Southwest,* 104–23; Indian Pioneer Papers, vol. 77, Louis C. Brown, 311–12; John J. Methvin, "Reminiscences of Life among the Indians," *Chronicles of Oklahoma* 5 (1927):

169; Newsom, *Wild and Modern Indian,* 122–23; *Proceedings of Indian Territory Baptist Convention, 1887–1889* (Ottawa, Kans.: J. B. Kassler, n.d.), 9, 11, 15; Rister, *Baptist Missions,* 102; Routh, *Oklahoma Baptists,* 53–54, 66; *McAlester (Choctaw Nation) Star Vindicator,* August 31, 1878; Charles L. White, *A Century of Faith* (Philadelphia: Judson, 1932), 91.

83. *ARCIA 1869,* Report C3, Grimes to Colyer, March 9 and 10, 1869, 79; Presbyterian Church in the USA, *Historical Sketches,* 27.

84. Ramsay, "Autobiography," 75–76.

85. S. H. Doyle, *Presbyterian Home Missions* (Philadelphia: Presbyterian Board of Publication, 1902), 85.

86. Alexander Spoehr, "Kinship System of the Seminole," *Publications of the Field Museum of Natural History, Anthropological Series* 33, no. 2 (1942): 44.

87. *ARCIA 1876,* Statistics, 213; *ARCIA 1884,* Statistics, 290–91.

88. Antoinette C. Snow Constant, "Story of Modern Witchcraft," 11 pp. holographic manuscript (incomplete), Constant Papers.

89. "Statistics of Indian Tribes in Union Agency, Indian Territory," November 8, 1877, M234-868, Union Agency 1877, frame 922; E. J. Brown to Commissioner of Indian Affairs, August 20, 1881, RG 75 LR BIA 1881–1907, 15166–81.

90. Seminole census card 8, enrollee 24, M1186-92. See also *Daily Oklahoman,* May 1, 1949; Duke Collection, vol. 45, interview T-211, Dave McIntosh, 27.

91. *ARCIA 1888,* 132; *ARCIA 1889,* 204–205, 211.

92. Diament to Secretary of Indian Department, February 8, 1899, Dawes Commission, Seminole 1897–1905, 497–99; W. A. Jones to Secretary of the Interior, January 11 and February 6, 1901, and Thomas Ryan to Jones, January 16, February 20, and April 2, 1901, Records of the Commission to the Five Civilized Tribes, Letters Received, Letters Sent, Report Books, Revenue, Citizenship Cases, Instructions and Miscellaneous, 243 vols., Indian Archives, Oklahoma Historical Society (hereafter cited as Dawes Commission, Letters Received and Miscellaneous), vol. 230, nos. 31–34 and enc., 71–78, 101–102.

93. Seminole census card 8, enrollee 25, and census card 553, enrollee 1771, M1186, roll 92.

94. Conclusions drawn from analysis of the Seminole Indian, Seminole freedman, Creek Indian, and Creek freedman census cards, M1186, rolls 77–93. See also *Kansas City Star,* "Report on the Five Civilized Tribes, 1897, by the Kansas City *Star,* 7 February 1897," *Chronicles of Oklahoma* 48 (1970): 426. The initial roll enumerated 1,899 Seminole Indians. That number was adjusted to 1,890 on the Final Rolls.

95. *ARCIA 1876,* Statistics, 212–13. On the paucity of whites in the Seminole Nation during this period, see, for example, U.S. Census Office, *Five Civilized Tribes in Indian Territory,* 4, 69; Constant, "Seminoles: Earliest Missionaries," 8; Bruce G. Carter, "A History of Seminole County, Oklahoma," M.A. thesis, University of Oklahoma, 1932, 93; Indian Pioneer Papers, vol. 71, interview 12701, Moses Chapone, 455–56, and vol. 112, interview 13428, H. M. Thornton, 213; and Ralph, "Unique Plight," 14.

96. "Statistics of Indian Tribes in Union Agency, Indian Territory," November 8, 1877, M234-868, frame 927.

97. In 1889, fewer than 60 whites were reported to be on the Seminole reservation, and in 1890 just 96. *ARCIA 1889,* 202; *ARCIA 1890,* 541–43. The number of whites among the Chickasaws is included in Debo, *And Still the Waters Run,* 13.

98. Baum, "Agriculture," 84.

99. *ARCIA 1888,* 132.

100. *ARCIA 1895,* Report of D. M. Wisdom, 157.

101. Thomas W. Alford, *Civilization, as Told to Florence Drake* (Norman: University of Oklahoma Press, 1936), 164; Indian Pioneer Papers, vol. 98, interview 9610, Grover Rutherford, 471–72, and vol. 103, interview 13923, W. M. Clark, 27; *Muskogee (Creek Nation) Evening Times,* January 12, 1898; unpublished manuscript material relating to the Mont Ballard case in Foreman OHS box 17, Seminole Indians. By far the best account of the Mont Ballard case is D. F. Littlefield, *Seminole Burning.* See also Geraldine M. Smith, "Violence on the Oklahoma Territory–Seminole Nation Border: The Mont Ballard Case," M.A. thesis, University of Oklahoma, 1957.

102. Indian Pioneer Papers, vol. 81, interview 10443, J. L. Minton, 43.

103. Interviews with Mr. A. Seran, who settled in the Seminole Nation in 1894, conducted by Louise Welch of Seminole, Oklahoma, July 2 and August 23, 1955, 4 pp. typescript notes. Copy provided by Welch.

104. Debo, *Road to Disappearance,* 275–76; John B. Meserve, "Chief Isparhecher," *Chronicles of Oklahoma* 10 (1932): 53–69; Orpha B. Russell, "William G. Bruner, Member of the House of Kings, Creek Nation," *Chronicles of Oklahoma* 30 (1952): 397.

105. Population statistics for Indians and freedmen in the Seminole Nation from Reconstruction to Oklahoma statehood are included in M574, roll 11, file 87; Seminole Annuity Roll 1870, RG 75, BIA, Seminole Annuity Rolls; Loyal Seminole Roll, as Prepared by James E. Jenkins, Special Indian Agent, March 8, 1901, and "Voucher No. 2, Abstract E, 2nd Quarter 1875, Per Capita Roll of Seminole Nation," Foreman Gilcrease, box 49, R14, R12; "Statistics of Indian Tribes in Union Agency, Indian Territory," November 8, 1877, M234-868, frame 922; "Ledger" showing family groupings and band affiliations in 1890 and 1892, Cutlip Collection, box 4; "Headright" Payment Rolls 1895, 1896, 1897, National Archives Records Group 75, Bureau of Indian Affairs, Records of the Commissioner to the Five Civilized Tribes Relative to Enrollment, Tribal Rolls—Seminole, 1868–97, Docs. 100594, A-5-20-7 1895–96, 100595, A-5-20-7 1895–97, and 100592, A-5-20-7 1897, National Archives, Southwest Region, Fort Worth, Tex.; Seminole Indian, Seminole freedman, Newborn Seminole Indian, and Newborn Seminole freedman census cards, M1186, rolls 92, 93; National Archives Microfilm Publications, T529, National Archives Record Group 48, Indian Division Office of the Secretary of the Interior, Final Rolls of Citizens and Freedmen of the Five Civilized Tribes in Indian Territory, 1907, 1914, 3 rolls, roll 3, Creek and Seminole rolls.

106. Sattler, "Siminoli Italwa," 336.

107. I am grateful to Dick Sattler for pointing this out to me.

108. These conclusions are based on information contained in the Seminole Indian, Newborn Seminole Indian, Seminole freedman, Newborn Seminole freedman, Creek Indian, Newborn Creek Indian, Creek freedman, and Newborn Creek freedman census cards, M1186, rolls 77–93.

9. LANGUAGE, SOCIETY, AND CULTURE

1. Tyler Powell to Taylor, March 7, 1868, M574, roll 11, file 87, frame 53.

2. Bateman, "Naming Patterns," 238–45; Rebecca Bateman, pers. comm., June 6, 2004.

3. Family genealogies can be traced through the Seminole freedman census cards and *Campbell's Abstract,* and residence patterns through *Moore's Seminole Roll and Land Guide.* Chart 3, showing freedman band distribution, is based on those sources. As with chart 1, Newborn freedman allotments have not been included, as they are not indicative of settlement patterns. See also Gallaher, "Seminole Freedmen," 22–24. Gallaher stated that Noble

Town and Scipio shared a cemetery, but Bateman, citing Otis Hume in Indian Pioneer Papers, vol. 113, no. 6672, and her own fieldwork in 1986, suggests that each had its own. Rebecca Bateman, pers. comm., April 4, 2006.

4. Deposition of Caesar Bruner, May 4, 1911, RG 75, LR BIA 1907–39, 50266-11, enc. with 14334-11, file 816.21.

5. Tyler Powell to Taylor, March 7, 1868, M574, roll 11, file 87, frame 53.

6. M574, roll 11, file 87; Seminole Annuity Roll 1870, RG 75, BIA, Seminole Annuity Rolls.

7. Gallaher, "Seminole Freedmen," 111.

8. Seminole Annuity Roll 1879, RG 75, BIA, Seminole Annuity Rolls; "Ledger" showing 1890 and 1892 Seminole Indian and freedman band membership, Cutlip Collection, box 4; Warrant Vouchers, Seminole Nation, Seminole Officers Payment for Quarters beginning April 1, 1906, July 1, 1906, and October 1, 1906, Dawes Commission, Seminole 1906–13. On changes in Seminole band organization during this period, see Sattler, "Siminoli Italwa," 310–15.

9. Rogers to U.S. Indian Agent, Muskogee, February 23, 1906, and Grant T. Bruner to Kelsey, February 27, 1906, Docs. 39518-L, 39518-M, Smn. 2-7, sec. X, file 2, Indian Archives, Oklahoma Historical Society; Mary Walker, "Caesar Bruner," 6 pp. unpublished typescript, 1956, based on interviews and correspondence with individuals who knew Bruner, copy provided by Louise Welch; Chaney, "Seminole Indians," 89; Olatunde Bayo Lawuyi, "Seminole Freedmen's Identity in Plural Setting," Ph.D. thesis, University of Illinois at Urbana–Champaign, 1985, 74; Seminole census card 453, enrollee 1528, Newborn Seminole census card 23, enrollee 34, Seminole freedman census cards 694, 698, 704, 718, 740, 777, enrollees 2203, 2216, 2260, 2297, 2337, and 2493, M1186 rolls 92, 93. Caesar Bruner's great-grandson told the author that Caesar eventually fathered nineteen children. Interview with "Pompey" Bruner Fixico, November 11, 2005.

10. Old Abraham, leader of the maroon community at Pilaklikaha prior to Removal, was said to be a medicine man in the freedman community after the Civil War. He apparently died in the early 1880s. *Indian Journal,* March 27, 1884.

11. Seminole Annuity Roll 1870, RG 75, BIA, Seminole Annuity Rolls.

12. Rebecca Bateman, pers. comm., May 4, 2002; Bateman, "Africans and Indians," 13–18; Gallaher, "Seminole Freedmen," 63–64, 111–113.

13. Bateman, "Africans and Indians," 13–18; Bateman, "We're Still Here," 23–27, 35–37nn2–3, 144–61.

14. Mary Helms, "Black Carib Domestic Organization in Historical Perspective: Traditional Origins of Contemporary Patterns," *Ethnology* 20 (1981): 82–83; Price, *Maroon Societies,* 19, 241, 346–47, 354.

15. Bateman, "We're Still Here," 292–93; *Daily Oklahoman,* January 1, 1922; Foster, *Negro-Indian Relationships,* 52; Gallaher, "Seminole Freedmen," 4.

16. Sattler, "Siminoli Italwa," 336.

17. Bateman, pers. comm., May 4, 2002.

18. *ARCIA 1871,* Statistics, 627; Baum, "Agriculture," 105; Chaney, "Seminole Indians," 87–88; Duke Collection, vol. 43, T-280, Primus Dean, 22–23; Ben Randall, "Early Occupational Life of the Negro," 2 pp. typescript, Grant Foreman Collection, Library Resources, Oklahoma Historical Society, Oral History and Ex-Slave Narratives, 1 box.

19. Newsom, *Wild and Modern Indian,* 63–64.

20. Duke Collection, vol. 45, T-210, Dave McIntosh, 17; Gallaher, "Seminole Freedmen," 19–25; Alexander Spoehr, "Oklahoma Seminole Towns," *Chronicles of Oklahoma* 19 (December 1941): 378–79.

21. *ARCIA 1869,* Statistics, 471; *ARCIA 1872,* Doc. 19, Report of Breiner, 240, and Statistics, 403; Bateman, "We're Still Here," 67; Baum, "Agriculture," 107–108; Duke Collection, vol. 43, T-280, Primus Dean, 6–8, 22–23, and vol. 45, T-210, Dave McIntosh, 2–3, 11, and T-211, Dave McIntosh, 18–22; Indian Pioneer Papers, vol. 95, interview 13122, Eliza Washington, 369; Randall, "Life of the Negro."

22. Duke Collection, vol. 43, T-210, Dave McIntosh, 20.

23. Baum, "Agriculture," 110; Duke Collection, vol. 43, T-280, Primus Dean, 15–16, and vol. 45, T-211, Dave McIntosh, 21–22; Indian Pioneer Papers, vol. 95, interview 13122, Eliza Washington, 369–70.

24. Carter, "Seminole County," 31; Duke Collection, vol. 43, T-280, Primus Dean, 9–10, and vol. 45, T-211, Dave McIntosh, 12; Indian Pioneer Papers, vol. 6, interview 47, Charley Lena, 211; Ralph, "Unique Plight," 14.

25. Duke Collection, vol. 45, interview T-210, Dave McIntosh, 8–9; Indian Pioneer Papers, vol. 93, interview 13642, Carrie Marshall Pitman, 348–49.

26. S. W. Harman, *Hell on the Border: A History of the Great United States Criminal Court at Fort Smith and of Crimes and Criminals in the Indian Territory and the Trials and Punishment Thereof before His Honor, United States Judge Isaac C. Parker* (Fort Smith, Ark.: Hell on the Border, 1953 [1898]), 140–41.

27. Indian Pioneer Papers, vol. 93, interview 13642, Carrie Marshall Pitman, 347–48.

28. Burton, *Black, Red, and Deadly,* 40–82.

29. Harman, *Hell on the Border,* 97–99.

30. Alexander Crain to Kelsey, June 3, 1911, Thomas Bruner, Affidavit, J. L. McDonell to J. G. Wright, February 26, 1913, and John Collier to A. M. Landman, July 9, 1934, RG 75, LR BIA 1907–39, Seminole 31733-34 and encs., file 053; Seminole freedman census card 612, enrollee 1910, M1186 roll 92.

31. Indian Pioneer Papers, vol. 21, interview 6674, Carrie Cyrus, 399, and vol. 93, interview 13642, Carrie Marshall Pitman, 347–49.

32. "The Battle of 'Violent' (Violet) Springs," as told by Isaac Bottley, 6 pp. unpublished typescript, Cutlip Collection, box 2; Teall, *Black History in Oklahoma,* 105.

33. Duke Collection, vol. 45, T-210, Dave McIntosh, 10.

34. Marshall Town, in the Creek Nation, had a similar reputation for harboring desperadoes. See Debo, *Road to Disappearance,* 253; Carolyn T. Foreman, "Marshalltown, Creek Nation," *Chronicles of Oklahoma* 32 (1954): 52–57.

35. Newsom, *Wild and Modern Indian,* 63–64.

36. *Daily Oklahoman,* February 15, 1914. See also Indian Pioneer Papers, vol. 26, interview 7013, Bud Gordon, 190–91.

37. Outsiders viewed the Little River community as isolated, inhospitable, and dangerous. Its reputation for producing or harboring violent criminals added to that image, increasing the likelihood that the maroons would be left alone. Richard Price has suggested that founding settlements in inaccessible and easily defensible locations is a feature of maroon community development throughout the hemisphere. Because of that, maroon societies proved attractive to pirates, renegades, deserters, illicit traffickers, and other criminals. See Price, *Maroon Societies,* 5–15 et seq. Bateman has suggested that the Little River maroons escalated their violent behavior after Oklahoma statehood and that it continued well into the 1920s. Bateman, "We're Still Here," 139–44, 164n2, 171–74, 229–30. She notes that the Little River maroons had been making the world precarious for white people for a long time and that perhaps their "criminal" activities should be viewed more as a continuation of their resistance than as lawlessness. Rebecca B. Bateman, pers. comm., July 10, 2003.

38. Gallaher, "Seminole Freedmen," 100–104.

39. Ramsay, "Autobiography," 72.

40. *ARCIA 1868,* no. 86, Report of Ramsay, 286.

41. Ibid.

42. Ibid.; Report of Employees in the Seminole Agency for the Year 1869, T. A. Baldwin, Agent, M234-804, B376-69.

43. *ARCIA 1870,* no. 112, H. C. Shook to Baldwin, May 27, 1870, 304.

44. Breiner to Clum, November 16, 1871, M234-798, Schools 1871, frame 45. Maggie Lilley had married Henry E. A. Washbourne, the brother of Josiah Washbourne, in March 1857. Michael Welsh, "The Missionary Spirit: Protestantism among the Oklahoma Seminoles, 1842–1885," *Chronicles of Oklahoma* 61 (1983): 46–47n10.

45. *ARCIA 1872,* Doc. 19, Report of Breiner, 242 (quote); Letter from Breiner, Seminole Agency, October 1, 1872, *ARBIC 1872,* 157–58.

46. *ARCIA 1872,* Doc. 19, Report of Breiner, 242.

47. Ibid.

48. Antoinette C. Snow Constant, "A Sketch of Mr. Constant's Work among the Seminoles," 2 pp. holographic manuscript, Constant Papers, 1; Duke Collection, vol. 45, T-210, Dave McIntosh, 1–2, and T-211, Dave McIntosh, 2; Israel Vore to Hayt, August 12, 1878, M234-870, frames 1260–64; Ramsay, "Autobiography," 95.

49. Thomas J. Bruner to Secretary of the Interior, n.d. but received February 17, 1911, and file of accompanying papers and correspondence, RG 75, LR BIA 1907–39, 14334-11, file 816-21.

50. Statistics of Indian tribes in Union Agency, Indian Territory, November 8, 1877, M234-868, frame 927. This referred to the reopening of the Ramsay mission school in Wewoka.

51. U.S. Census Office, *Five Civilized Tribes in Indian Territory,* 16.

52. Constant, "Seminoles: Earliest Missionaries," 14.

53 Indian Pioneer Papers, vol. 71, interview 12701, Moses Chapone, 455.

54. Constant, "Seminoles: Earliest Missionaries," 15–17; Indian Pioneer Papers, vol. 93, interview 13642, Carrie Marshall Pitman, 350.

55. Constant, "Modern Witchcraft," 10–11; Constant, "Seminoles; Earliest Missionaries," 16–17.

56. Constant, "Seminoles; Earliest Missionaries," 18, 25.

57. Constant, "Modern Witchcraft," 10–11.

58. Ibid., 1–11; Constant, "Seminoles: Earliest Missionaries," 27.

59. Constant, "Modern Witchcraft," 10–11 (quotes); Seminole freedman census card 718, enrollee 2297, M1186 roll 93. For a study of the Hampton Institute the Seminole freedman students experienced, see Donal F. Lindsey, *Indians at Hampton Institute, 1877–1923* (Urbana: University of Illinois Press, 1995), esp. 205–208, 238n29. According to her census card, Louisa Bruner was formerly a slave of George Cloud. Her mother was Mariah Foster. Louisa Bruner died in her mid-forties in December 1904.

60. "Benjamin F. Bruner Obituary"; Seminole freedman census card 828, enrollee 2705, M1186 roll 93. Benjamin F. Bruner's parents were John Bruner and Grace Bruner (née Bowlegs). His census card suggests that he also was known as Ben Johnson (i.e., son of John). See Seminole freedman census card 708 and Creek freedman census card 923, M1186, rolls 93, 87.

61. Ramsay, "Autobiography," 89. Ramsay had married Eliza Chupco, a relative of John Chupco, in July 1856. Eliza Chupco and Maggie Lilley (married name Washburn or

Washbourne), later a teacher at the Noble Town school, had attended the Steubenville Academy in Ohio together from June 1852 to the summer of 1855. Welsh, "Missionary Spirit," 33, 35.

62. Ramsay, "Autobiography," 76, 93, 95, 99; Chaney, "Seminole Indians," 80; Indian Pioneer Papers, vol. 113, interview 7733, Leister Reed, 290.

63. Chaney, "Seminole Indians," appendix C.

64. Duke Collection, vol. 43, T-280, Primus Dean, 12–14, vol. 45, T-210, Dave McIntosh, 28–29, and vol. 51, T-44, Lizzie Johnson Kernell, 2; Robert E. Trevathan, "School Days at Emahaka Academy," *Chronicles of Oklahoma* 38 (1960): 265.

65. Duke Collection, vol. 52, T-48, Billy Spencer, 6.

66. Ibid., vol. 43, T-280, Primus Dean, 11, 13, 19; J. D. Benedict to Commissioner of Indian Affairs, January 6, 1908, and copy of *The Western World: Creek-Seminole College News,* Boley, Okla., with accompanying correspondence, RG 75, LR BIA 1907–39, 98785-07, 92801-07, file 811.

67. Duke Collection, vol. 52, T-48, Billy Spencer, 7.

68. Ibid., vol. 43, T-280, Primus Dean, 13.

69. Superintendent of Schools in Indian Territory to Commissioner of Indian Affairs, September 12, 1906 (twice), C. F. Larrabee to Superintendent of Indian Schools in Indian Territory, November 9, 1906, and Quarterly Report of Red Day Seminole Freedman School, First Quarter 1911, Dawes Commission, Seminole 1906–13; *ARCIA 1905,* part 1, 115–16, 749, part 2, 222; U.S. Inspector for Indian Territory, *Annual Report of the Inspector for Indian Territory* (hereafter cited as *ARIIT*) *1906,* 735, 761; Chaney, "Seminole Indians," 100.

70. Melinda Beth Micco, "Freedmen and Seminoles: Forging a Seminole Nation," Ph.D. dissertation, University of California, Berkeley, 1995, 149; interview with Ben Warrior, Wewoka, Okla., January 24, 1979; interview with Ben Warrior, Sasakwa, Okla., March 1, 1983 (quote).

71. Thomas J. Bruner to Secretary of the Interior, n.d. but received February 17, 1911, and accompanying papers and correspondence, RG 75, LR BIA 1907–39, 14334-11, file 816-21.

72. Indian Pioneer Papers, vol. 28, interview 5338, Rina Henderson, 410.

73. Interview with Ben Warrior, March 1, 1983.

74. Gallaher, "Seminole Freedmen," 70–75; Indian Pioneer Papers, vol. 18, interview 6671, George Butner, 29–30.

75. Indian Pioneer Papers, vol. 104, interview 13738, Viola Chandler, 273–74.

76. *ARBIC 1883,* 47; *ARCIA 1887,* Statistics, 355; *ARCIA 1888,* 123.

77. Quoted in Wyeth, *Poor Lo,* 114.

78. Gallaher, "Seminole Freedmen," 117–19 and n73.

79. "The Battle of 'Violent' (Violet) Springs."

10. RELATIONS WITH SEMINOLES IN OKLAHOMA

1. *ARCIA 1894,* Report of Wisdom, 141; *ARCIA 1895,* Report of Wisdom, 159–60; *ARCIA 1899,* part 1, 113, 197; U.S. Commissioner to the Five Civilized Tribes, *Annual Report of the Commissioner to the Five Civilized Tribes* (hereafter cited as *ARCFCT*) *1899,* part 2, 11–13; Kappler, *Indian Affairs,* vol. 1, 662–65.

2. Kappler, *Indian Affairs,* vol. 1, 662–65.

3. *ARCFCT 1899,* part 2, 11–13.

4. *ARCIA 1901,* part 1, 152.

5. A. C. Tonner to Secretary of the Interior, January 11, 1901, and three encs., RG 48, SF, box 52, no. 123.

6. Ibid., no. 124.

7. Ibid., no. 127.

8. Ibid., no. 126.

9. W. A. Jones to Secretary of the Interior, January 11 and February 5, 1901, and Sam Mahardy to Secretary of the Interior, November 15 and December 27, 1902, RG 48, SF, box 48, no. 129 enc. 1, no. 497 enc. 2, no. 7187, no. 117; Ryan to Commissioner of Indian Affairs, February 20, 1901, Dawes Commission, Letters Received and Miscellaneous, vol. 230, 79–84; Acting District Superintendent in Charge, Office of Five Civilized Tribes, to Commissioner of Indian Affairs, June 5, 1928, Charles H. Burke to Mahardy, June 13, 1928, and Mahardy to Commissioner of Indian Affairs, June 20, 1928, RG 75, LR BIA 1907–39, Seminole, file 53, 21798-28 and encs.; Seminole freedman census card 843, enrollees 2739, 2741, and 2742, M1186, roll 93. Some of the Mahardy testimonies are included in Angela Y. Walton-Raji, *Black Indian Genealogy Research: African American Ancestors among the Five Civilized Tribes* (Bowie, Md.: Heritage Books, 1993), 58–66.

10. Tams Bixby to Secretary of the Interior, January 2, 1906, RG 75, LR BIA 1880–1907, 1784-06; Bixby to Secretary of the Interior, January 21, 1907, RG 75, LR BIA 1907–39, Seminole, file 53, 10033-07.

11. Ryan to Commissioner of Indian Affairs, January 16 and February 8, 1901, and Bixby to Secretary of the Interior, January 26, 1901 enclosing Commissioner of Indian Affairs to Secretary of the Interior, RG 75, LR BIA 1880–1907, 3623-01, 8454-01, 6174-01 and enc. 1.

12. *ARCIA 1905,* part 1, 135.

13. Bixby to Secretary of the Interior, June 5, 1906 (twice with encs.), July 28, 1906, and January 11, 1907, RG 75, LR BIA 1881–1907, 49069-06, 65697-06 and encs., 65698-06, 3865-07; National Archives Record Group 75, Records of the Bureau of Indian Affairs, Applications for Enrollment from the Five Civilized Tribes, 1910–15, Chickasaw, Creek, Seminole, 1 box, cases 5, 6, 16.

14. *ARCIA 1907,* 294.

15. *ARCFCT 1900,* 28; *ARCIA 1902,* part 1, 206; *ARCFCT 1902,* part 2, 43–45.

16. See, for example, Bixby to Secretary of the Interior, March 31, 1903, RG 75, LR BIA 1907–39, Creek 313, 12831-08. This relates to Caesar Bowlegs, who claimed he held improvements on Creek land allotted to Lillie Harjo. Bowlegs requested payment for his property.

17. *ARCFCT 1902,* part 2, 49.

18. *ARIIT 1903,* 10.

19. *ARCIA 1905,* part 1, 627–28; *ARCIA 1906,* 638.

20. Commissioner to Five Civilized Tribes to Secretary of the Interior, September 18, 1909, National Archives Record Group 75, Records of the Bureau of Indian Affairs, Records of the Commissioner to the Five Civilized Tribes, Letters Sent to the Commissioner of Indian Affairs or Secretary of the Interior Relating to the Commission's Activities, September 1907–May 1911, 3 vols., National Archives, Southwest Region, Fort Worth, Tex., vol. 2, 152–53; *ARIIT 1901,* 47–48; Mel H. Bolster, *Crazy Snake and the Smoked Meat Rebellion* (Boston: Brandon Press, 1976); Mel H. Bolster, "The Smoked Meat Rebellion," *Chronicles of Oklahoma* 31 (1953): 37–55; Mace Davis, "Chitto Harjo," *Chronicles of Oklahoma* 13 (1935): 139–45; Duke Collection, vol. 43, interview T-280, Primus Dean, 20; Gideon, *Indian Territory,* 121 et seq.; Indian Pioneer Papers, vol. 6, interview 5358, Wm. Frank Jones, 34, vol. 18, interview 5340, Nettie Cain, 94, vol. 31, interview 7014, Henry Jacobs, 100–103, vol. 39, interview

12091, Dora P. Parnell, 112–14, vol. 70, interview 7306, Louis Rentie, 477, vol. 82, interview 7873, D. L. Stipes, 425, vol. 86, interview 7617, Wm. Jones, 66, and vol. 89, interview 13504, Billie Brant, 140–42; Jones, *Experiences of a Deputy,* 7–9; Daniel F. Littlefield, Jr., and Lonnie E. Underhill, "The Crazy Snake 'Uprising' of 1909: A Red, Black, or White Affair?" *Arizona and the West* 20 (1978–79): 307–24; John B. Meserve, "The Plea of Crazy Snake (Chitto Harjo)," *Chronicles of Oklahoma* 11 (1933): 899–911; Helen Starr and O. E. Hill, *Footprints in the Indian Nation* (Muskogee, Okla.: Hoffman, 1974), 30–47.

21. Indian Pioneer Papers, vol. 113, interview 7733, Leister Reed, 290.

22. Quotes from C. Guy Cutlip, "History of Seminole County," unpublished typescript, n.d., 23 pp., Cutlip Collection, box 2, 16. See also *Daily Oklahoman,* December 5, 1926, and obituary of J. Coody Johnson, *Wewoka (Okla.) Capital-Democrat,* March 3, 1927.

23. Cutlip, "Seminole County," 15. Cutlip (1881–1938) made the run into Oklahoma Territory with his family in 1889. In 1901, he became a stenographer for a lawyer in Wewoka and began his long residence there. He eventually became an attorney, a judge, and, in 1921, Wewoka's first mayor. He also was a friend and close business associate of Johnson's and was included in his will, so his statements regarding the Seminole freedman attorney should be viewed with some caution. See http://libraries.ou.edu/etc/westhist/cutlip.htm (November 13, 2003).

24. Cutlip, "Seminole County," 15–17; J. B. Shoenfelt to Commissioner of Indian Affairs, January 7, 1904, and Seminole delegation to Commissioner of Indian Affairs, January 12 and February 6, 1904, RG 75, LR BIA 1881–1907, 3772-04, 9621-04 and enc.; *Holdenville (Creek Nation) Tribune,* April 20, 1905; *South McAlester (Choctaw Nation) Capital,* December 1, 1904, and March 30, 1905.

25. Seminole Indian census card 9, enrollee 29, M1186, roll 92.

26. Indian Pioneer Papers, vol. 1, interview 52, F. G. Alex, 76. Alex was born after the Civil War. He enrolled as a fullblood Creek. Creek Indian census card 1946, enrollee 6101, M1186, roll 79.

27. Welsh, "Missionary Spirit," 40.

28. Berry, "Pioneer Doctor," 17.

29. *South McAlester (Choctaw Nation) Capital,* March 30, 1905.

30. Seminole census card 9, Creek freedman census cards 85, 966, M1186, rolls 92, 85, 87.

31. Wright to Secretary of the Interior, June 29, 1905, National Archives Record Group 75, Records of the Bureau of Indian Affairs, Records of the U.S. Inspector for the Indian Territory, Letters Sent to the Department of the Interior, June 14, 1899, to January 23, 1906, 8 vols., National Archives, Southwest Region, Fort Worth, Tex., vol. 7, 279–85; Frank L. Campbell to Secretary of the Interior, July 22, 1905, Dawes Commission, Seminole 1897–1905, 8182-05; *ARCIA 1905,* part 1, 11; *Holdenville (Creek Nation) Tribune,* April 20 and May 11, 1905; *Muskogee (Creek Nation) Democrat,* May 6, 1905; Seminole Indian census card 302, enrollee 1035, M1186, roll 92; *Sulphur (Chickasaw Nation) Post,* April 27, 1905.

32. Cutlip, "Seminole County," 16–17; Hoffman, "Oklahoma's Black Panther," 1–8; Otis Hume, "Cemeteries—Seminole; Johnson," June 21, 1937, Indian Pioneer Papers, vol. 56, 423–24; *Oklahoma State Capital,* March 27, 1907; *Seminole (Seminole Nation) Capital,* August 24, 1905; *Seminole (Okla.) Producer,* April 2, 1927; Will of J. Coody Johnson, October 11, 1923, 8 pp. holographic manuscript, Epton (Hicks) Collection (quote); obituary of J. Coody Johnson. Hoffman suggests that Johnson's "Black Panther" nickname derived from his being a member of the Creek Panther clan. Although Cutlip praised him as a "progressive, fine, upstanding citizen" whose every possession was "at the behest of his community if it needed it," there apparently was another side to Johnson. Bateman suggests that besides having many

black sharecroppers work his extensive landholdings north of Wewoka, he partnered with whites in schemes to defraud Indians and freedmen of their land: "Johnson is [remembered] by those who knew him as a man who 'grafted his own.'" Bateman, "We're Still Here," 101–102, 119–20n5 (quote on 119).

33. *ARCIA 1905,* part 1, 137, 217; *ARCFCT 1906,* 740; 35 Stat. L. 312.

34. Violet P. Crain to Secretary of the Interior, May 8, 1906, and Witty Cudjo to Secretary of the Interior, April 18, 1906, Smn. 2–7, sec. X, file 2, Indian Archives, Oklahoma Historical Society. Violet Crain was not enrolled as a Seminole citizen, but mixed-race Crains appeared on both the Seminole Indian and freedman rolls. She likely was advocating for members of her family. Rebecca Bateman, pers. comm., July 7, 2006.

35. *ARCIA 1911,* 45. By far the most thorough treatment of the injustice Seminole freedmen experienced during and after enrollment and allotment is Bateman, "We're Still Here," chaps. 3 and 4.

36. W. H. Ketcham, "Seminole Indians of Oklahoma," together with exhibits A and C, U.S. Board of Indian Commissioners, *Special Reports: Board of Indian Commissioners,* vol. 1, 1915–18, 429–38, esp. 430–31.

37. 31 Stat. L. 1447.

38. Frank A. Balyeat, "Segregation in the Public Schools of Oklahoma Territory," *Chronicles of Oklahoma* 39 (1961): 180–92; Grinde and Taylor, "Red vs. Black," 225; D. F. Littlefield, *Cherokee Freedmen,* 254; Philip Mellinger, "Discrimination and Statehood in Oklahoma," *Chronicles of Oklahoma* 49 (1971): 340–77; Teall, *Black History in Oklahoma,* 192 et seq.; Arthur L. Tolson, *The Black Oklahomans: A History, 1541–1972* (New Orleans: Edwards, 1974), 140–61; Murray R. Wickett, *Contested Territory: Whites, Native Americans, and African Americans in Oklahoma, 1865–1907* (Baton Rouge: Louisiana State University Press, 2000), chap. 7; Murray R. Wickett, "The Fear of 'Negro Domination': The Rise of Segregation and Disfranchisement in Oklahoma," *Chronicles of Oklahoma* 78 (2000): 44–65.

39. Peter Wallenstein, "Native Americans Are White, African Americans Are Not: Racial Identity, Marriage, Inheritance, and the Law in Oklahoma, 1907–1967," *Journal of the West* 39 (2000): 57.

40. Bateman, "We're Still Here," 53–56, 287; Foster, *Negro-Indian Relationships,* 66–68; Gallaher, "Seminole Freedmen," 88–91; Lawuyi, "Seminole Freedmen's Identity," 3, 142.

41. Black History Canada, http://blackhistorycanada.ca (February 22, 2006); "Black Settlers Come to Alberta," http://www.abheritage.ca/pasttopresent/settlement/black_settlers .html (February 22, 2006); Gwen Hooks, *The Keystone Legacy: Recollections of a Black Settler* (Edmonton, Alberta: Brightest Pebble, 1997 or 1998); D. Chongo Mundende, "The Undesirable Oklahomans: Black Immigration to Western Canada," *Chronicles of Oklahoma* 76 (1998): 282–97; Howard Palmer and Tamara Palmer, *Peoples of Alberta: Portraits of Cultural Diversity* (Saskatoon, Saskatchewan: Western Producer Prairie Books, 1985), 370–72; Michael Payne, "'Deemed Unsuitable': Black Pioneers in Western Canada," *Canadian Encyclopedia* (online version), http://www.thecanadianencyclopedia.com (February 22, 2006); R. Bruce Shepard, *Deemed Unsuitable: Blacks from Oklahoma Move to the Canadian Prairies in Search of Equality in the Early 20th Century Only to Find Racism in Their New Home* (Toronto: Umbrella Press, 1997), 61–126; R. Bruce Shepard, "North to the Promised Land: Black Migration to the Canadian Plains," *Chronicles of Oklahoma* 66 (1988): 318; Harold M. Troper, "The Creek-Negroes of Oklahoma and Canadian Immigration, 1909–1911," *Canadian Historical Review* 53 (1972): 272–88.

42. William E. Bittle and Gilbert L. Geis, *The Longest Way Home: Chief Alfred C. Sam's Back-to-Africa Movement* (Detroit: Wayne State University Press, 1964), 79, 81, 98.

43. Charles C. Bush, "The Green Corn Rebellion," M.A. thesis, University of Oklahoma, 1932.

44. Bateman, "We're Still Here," 53–54, chaps. 5–8; Foster, *Negro-Indian Relationships,* 66–68; Gallaher, "Seminole Freedmen," 64; Micco, "Freedmen and Seminoles," chap. 5.

45. Indian Pioneer Papers, vol. 46, interview 12475, Wesley Tanyon, 201–202.

46. Schultz, *Seminole Baptist Churches of Oklahoma,* 52.

47. Bateman, "Africans and Indians," 13–18, 20–21n11–12; Bateman, "Naming Patterns," 227–57; Bateman, "We're Still Here," 21–29, 35–37n1–2, 144–61, 292–93, 343–54; Gallaher, "Seminole Freedmen," 63–64, 77, 111–13; Lawuyi, "Seminole Freedmen's Identity," 124–25.

48. Bateman, "Slaves or Seminoles?"; Matthew Kelly, pers. comm., February 3, 2003.

49. I am grateful to Matthew Kelly for explaining to me the importance of that distinction to Seminoles. Kelly, pers. comm., February 3, 2003. Indians view the current disputes as concerning the Seminole Nation's right to determine its own membership as a sovereign entity. In effect, the Seminoles are arguing that the "tribe" should be considered the "nation." The freedmen argue that, as citizens of the nation, they should be entitled to the same benefits as Seminole Indians. The Seminoles counter that even though the freedmen became citizens of the new Seminole Nation in 1866, they were not members of the old Seminole Nation (or tribe) that preceded it. Therefore, they are not entitled to participate in benefits deriving from the award the Seminoles received from the federal government for lands lost in Florida in 1823. Nor, Seminoles argue, did freedmen become members of the "tribe" after 1866. While the BIA does not consider the freedmen to be Indian, it favors their inclusion in Seminole awards and other benefits as citizens of the Seminole Nation recognized by the United States in the treaty of 1866.

50. *Seminole Nation v. United States,* 78 Ct. Cls. 455 (1933).

51. *Seminole Nation v. United States,* 90 Ct. Cls. 151 (1940); *Seminole Nation v. United States,* 10 Ind. Cl. Com. 450 (Docket 152; August 22, 1962).

52. Interview with Charles E. Grounds, Seminole, Oklahoma, January 24, 1979; Welsh, "Road to Assimilation," 294; Charles Wisdom, "Report on the Social Condition of the Oklahoma Seminole, 1937," 28 pp. unpublished typescript, Applied Anthropology Unit Report no. 9727. A copy of Wisdom's report was provided to the author in 1980 by William Dawson of Seminole, Oklahoma. At that time, Dawson served as an attorney for the Seminole freedmen.

53. Quoted in Bateman, "We're Still Here," 242–43.

54. Wisdom, "Report on the Oklahoma Seminole," 4.

55. Ibid., quotes on 22, 26.

56. Ibid., 15–16.

57. Ibid., 18, 22; Bateman, "We're Still Here," 248–49.

58. Bateman, "We're Still Here," 262–66.

59. Quoted in ibid., 266–67.

60. Ibid., 267 (quote); interview with Rev. William C. Wantland, Oklahoma City, January 12, 1979. Wantland told the author that he was one-eighth Seminole, a citizen of the Seminole Nation, and a member of the Tuskeia Harjo band and that he spoke Creek. He was attorney general for the Seminole Nation, 1969–72, 1975–77; executive director of the Seminole Housing Authority, 1971; attorney general for the Seminole Housing Authority, 1971–77; and director of the Seminole Nation Enterprise, 1975–78. The reverend was especially helpful in providing information regarding the negotiations resulting in the Seminole Nation Constitution of 1969.

61. Interview with William Wantland. In February 2000, Wayne Thompson, a registered lobbyist and a former Black Panther, sought a compromise between the Seminoles and the freedmen by proposing that the freedmen seek federal recognition as an independent tribal nation (Ron Jackson, "Black Seminoles Sue for a Place in History," *Sunday Oklahoman,* November 7, 1999; Ron Jackson, "Black Seminoles Seek Recognition," *Daily Oklahoman,* March 27, 2000). In December 2002, I presented a paper entitled "Marronage among the Seminoles" at the fifth annual Gilder Lehrman Center International Conference, "Unshackled Spaces: Fugitives from Slavery and Maroon Communities in the Americas," at Yale University. Questions and comments from participants focused on what might happen if the freedmen were recognized as maroons and independent of the Seminoles. Seminole historian Susan Miller has argued that members of indigenous Seminole maroon communities are "Africans whose history in the Americas is as noble and glorious as any descendant could desire. But Maroons are not American Indians." Miller also reinforces the point that the freedmen "cannot have been both Maroons and American Indians" (Miller, "Seminoles and Africans," 30, 34.) The Seminole maroons could argue that they meet standard definitions of an indigenous group in their own right and therefore should be recognized as a legally distinct corporate entity. See, for example, A. T. Durning, "Supporting Indigenous Peoples," in *State of the World 1993,* Worldwatch Institute (New York: W. W. Norton, 1993), 81; and IUCN Inter-Commission Task Force on Indigenous Peoples, *Indigenous Peoples and Sustainability: Cases and Actions* (Utrecht: International Books, 1997), 27–30. The United Nations Draft Declaration on the Rights of Indigenous Peoples goes so far as to omit a definition of the term "indigenous," instead favoring the right to individual and collective self-definition. See United Nations Working Group on Indigenous Populations, *The UN Draft Declaration on the Rights of Indigenous Peoples,* UN Doc. E/CN.4/Sub.2/1993/29 (1993), Annex, Article 8. But an even more promising approach would be for the group to argue that it matches definitions of "tribal peoples," a distinct category developed by international organizations but equal in weight to "indigenous." "Tribal peoples" is used in International Labor Organization, "Indigenous and Tribal Peoples," ILO Convention 169, http://www.ilo.org/ ilolex/ cgi-lex/convde.pl?C169 (June 19, 2004), and covered under the World Bank's Operational Directive 4.20, *Indigenous Peoples* (1991), http://wbln0018.worldbank .org/Institutional/Manuals/OpManual.nsf/0/0F7D6F3F04DD70398525672C007D08ED?OpenDocument (June 19, 2004.) The Organization of American States (OAS), *Proposed Declaration on the Rights of Indigenous Peoples,* also includes other tribal peoples "whose social, cultural and economic conditions distinguish them from other sections of the national community, and whose status is regulated wholly or partially by their own customs or traditions or by special laws or regulations." See OAS, Inter-American Commission on Human Rights, *Proposed American Declaration on the Rights of Indigenous Peoples,* Approved by the Inter-American Commission on Human Rights on February 26, 1997, at its 1,333rd Sess., 95th Regular Sess., http://www.cidh.org/Indigenous.htm (June 21, 2004). Fergus MacKay, of the Forest Peoples Programme, has suggested, "Afro-American peoples, such as Suriname and Jamaican Maroons, would enjoy the same rights as Amerindian peoples under this instrument." See Fergus MacKay, "The Rights of Indigenous Peoples in International Law," in *From Concept to Design: Creating an International Environmental Ombudsperson,* a project of the Earth Council, San José, Costa Rica, March 1998, 7, and see also 3, 6; Fergus MacKay, "Indigenous People's Rights in the Commonwealth Caribbean," paper presented at Indigenous Rights in the Commonwealth Caribbean and Americas Regional Expert Meeting, Amerindian Peoples' Association, Guyana, June 2003, 2, http://www.cpsu.org.uk/downloads/Fergus_MacKay .pdf (June 4, 2004). The same could be suggested for the Seminole freedmen of Oklahoma. If

the Seminole maroons were recognized as a tribal people, some interesting possibilities might open up. Besides better ensuring their individual human rights and their corporate economic, social, political, and cultural rights, the freedmen could become eligible for targeted developmental funding as a group. In Suriname, Amerindian and maroon indigenous peoples have collaborated in pursuing issues of mutual interest and concern relating to their land rights, ecosystems, and the environment. See, for example, Forest Peoples Programme, "Indigenous Peoples and Maroons in French Guiana Demand Land Rights in Proposed National Park," September 7, 1998, http://hartford-hwp.com/archives/41/322 .html (June 1, 2004); United Nations Development Program, http://sgp.undp.org/index.cfm (June 1, 2004). Might it not be possible for Seminole Indian indigenous people and Seminole maroon tribal people to do likewise?

62. For a discussion of some of the issues attached to Indian nations' sovereign right to choose their own members, see Eva Marie Garroutte, "The Racial Formation of American Indians: Negotiating Legitimate Identities within Tribal and Federal Law," *American Indian Quarterly* 25 (2001): 224–39, and Melissa L. Meyer, "American Indian Blood Quantum Requirements: Blood Is Thicker than Family," in *Over the Edge: Remapping the American West,* Valerie J. Matsumoto and Blake Allmendinger, eds. (Berkeley: University of California Press, 1999).

63. Bateman, "We're Still Here," 268–69; Constitution of the Seminole Nation of Oklahoma, ratified April 15, 1969, copy in author's possession; interview with Richmond Tiger, principal chief of the Seminole Nation, January 25, 1979; interview with William Wantland. The Seminoles and freedmen approved the 1969 constitution by a vote of 637 to 249. Strength of indigenous practices and lack of white acculturation remained features of Seminole Indian society into the late 1960s. Ethnohistorian Melinda Micco has suggested that a remarkable 90 percent of the council could not read or write English at the time the Seminole Constitution was adopted. Micco, "Freedmen and Seminoles," 157.

64. Quoted in Micco, "Freedmen and Seminoles," 167–68.

65. In 1988, the twins traveled to West Africa, where they met other Cudjoe descendants. Both died in 1994. Jackson, "Forefather Prepared Family"; Micco, "Blood and Money," 127.

66. Beckloff, "Tribe's Freedmen Seek Share"; "Black Seminoles File Racial Discrimination Suit against Federal Government and Bureau of Indian Affairs," *National Bar Association Magazine* (January–February 1996): 24; "Black Seminoles Urged to Fight for Share of Funds," *Sunday Oklahoman,* February 19, 1995, A16; Aaron R. Brown, "Judgments: 'Brothers' Fighting over Indian Money; The Right of Seminole Freedmen to a Portion of the Indian Claims Commission Judgment Fund," *American Indian Law Review* 11 (1983): 111–12; KOCO-TV, Oklahoma City, noon news report featuring interview with Seminole principal chief Jerry Haney on blood quantum requirements and the freedmen's application for Certificate of Degree of Indian Blood (CDIB) cards, February 24, 1995, notes in author's possession; Alvin Peabody, "Black Seminoles File Lawsuit against Federal Government," *Washington (D.C.) Informer,* January 24, 1996. Legal scholar Martha Melaku suggests that the Seminole Nation could make a stronger argument for excluding the freedmen from the award by "acknowledging that the land given to the Black Seminoles by the Nation falls in the category of services provided to the tribe." She continues: "Both the land ceded to the United States and the land used by the Black Seminoles was property of the Nation. Merely because the Black Seminoles were allowed use of the land as their own does not mean they are entitled to compensation based on the Nation's cession of Florida to the United States. The Black Seminoles used the land with the knowledge and the authorization of the rightful owner, the Seminole Nation." Melaku also explores other possible legal options for the freedmen. Mar-

tha Melaku, "Seeking Acceptance: Are the Black Seminoles Native Americans? Sylvia Davis v. the United States of America," *American Indian Law Review* 27 (2002–2003): 541, 546 (quote), 548–50.

67. Melaku, "Seeking Acceptance," 548.

68. *Davis v. United States,* 192 F. 3d 951, 954, 10th Circuit 1999, U.S. App.; *Davis v. United States,* 199 F. Supp. 2d 1164-80, W. Dist. Okla. 1996, 2002, U.S. Dist. See also "Black Seminoles Urged to Fight"; Jackson, "Black Seminoles Sue"; Lydia M. Edwards, "Protecting Black Tribal Members: Is the Thirteenth Amendment the Linchpin to Securing Equal Rights within Indian Country?" May 20, 2005, ExpressO Preprint Series, Working Paper 626, 66 pp., 20–31, http://law.bepress.com/expresso/eps/626 (March 7, 2006); Stacy D. Johnson, "Seminole Freedmen Apply for Benefits, Expect Denial," unidentified press clipping from February 1995, copy in author's possession; Micco, "Freedmen and Seminoles," 178; Tiya Miles and Celia E. Naylor-Ojurongbe, "African-Americans in Indian Societies," in *Handbook: Southeast,* 759; Netsu Taylor Saito, "From Slavery and Seminoles to AIDS in South Africa: An Essay on Race and Property in International Law," *Villanova Law Review* 45 (2000): 1172–74, 1191–92.

69. Bateman, "Slaves or Seminoles?"; William Glaberson, "Who Is a Seminole and Who Gets to Decide?" *New York Times,* January 29, 2001, A1, 14; Jackson, "Black Seminoles Seek Recognition"; Keilman, "Bloodlines"; Robyn Lydick and Bob Doucette, "Rivals Both Lose Bids for Seminoles' Top Office," *Daily Oklahoman,* July 18, 2001; Michael McNutt, "Seminoles OK Government Changes," *Daily Oklahoman,* July 7, 2000; David Melmer, "Dialogue Opens on Black Indians in Indian Country," *Indian Country Today,* November 29, 2000; Miller, *Coacoochee's Bones,* 186; Stack, "Tribal Rift."

70. Seminole Nation, Dosar-Barkus and Bruner Bands of the Seminole Nation of Oklahoma, Intervenor-Plaintiffs in *Seminole Nation of Oklahoma v. Babbitt,* (D.D.C. December 20, 2000), no. 00 CV 02384 (CKK). "Babbitt" and "Norton" refer to Secretaries of the Interior Bruce Babbitt (1993–2001) and Gale Norton (2001–2006).

71. Mark H. Goldey, attorney for the Seminole freedmen, pers. comm., October 5, 2001; Kelly, "Naturalizing Seminole 'Racism,' " 5 (quote); *Seminole Nation of Oklahoma v. Norton,* 206 F.R.D. 1 (D.D.C. September 27, 2001); *Seminole Nation of Oklahoma v. Norton,* 223 F. Supp. 2d 122 (D.D.C. 2002), http://www.dcd.uscourts.gov/02-739.pdf (May 3, 2005). Kelly suggests that Seminole freedmen did participate in the 2001 election and that the reports were unfounded. Kelly, pers. comm., February 3, 2003, and July 26, 2004. See also Bateman, "Slaves or Seminoles?"; Glaberson, "Who Is a Seminole?"; Lydick and Doucette, "Rivals Both Lose Bids"; Stack, "Tribal Rift."

72. "Cherokee Chief Moves to Remove Cherokee Citizens" (quote), African–Native American Genealogy Forum, http://www.afrigeneas.com/forume/ (March 18, 2006). For background on the Cherokee freedmen citizenship issue, see Chad Previch, "Freedmen to Become Citizens," *Daily Oklahoman,* March 9, 2006. To keep abreast of the various lawsuits involving freedmen citizenship claims, see Descendants of Freedmen of the Five Civilized Tribes, http://www.freedmen5tribes.com (March 20, 2006).

73. Bentley, "Seminole Freedmen Recognized"; Melissa Beggs, "The Black and the Red," *Oklahoma Gazette,* November 6, 2003, 21–24; "Freedmen Granted Benefits," *Tulsa World,* December 26, 2003; Sam Lewin, "Black Seminoles See Case Dismissed," *Native American Times* (Tulsa), July 7, 2004; Melaku, "Seeking Acceptance," 543–46; Miller, "Seminoles and Africans," 28–29; Brian Scraper, "Oklahoma Seminoles to Refile Lawsuit," *Oklahoma Daily,* July 14, 2004.

74. James H. Howard, *Oklahoma Seminoles: Medicines, Magic, and Religion* (Norman: University of Oklahoma Press, 1984), 6–7.

75. Josephine Johnston, "Resisting a Genetic Identity: The Black Seminoles and Genetic Tests of Ancestry," *Journal of Law, Medicine, and Ethics* 31 (2003): 262–, p. 2 of 23 pp. electronic version.

76. Judy Gibbs Robinson, "Freedmen's Descendants Discover Past," *Daily Oklahoman,* June 3, 2005; Descendants of Freedmen of the Five Civilized Tribes Association, 2005 Conference Program, University of Oklahoma, http://www.freedmenconference.com/index.htm (July 8, 2005). Educator Jean West also reported, "In 1997, scientists studied the DNA of 37 Florida Seminole. They found about five percent of their mitochondrial DNA (transferred by mothers) was African." Jean M. West, "Slaves and Seminoles: Florida's Freedom Seekers," http://www.slaveryinamerica.org/history/hs_es_seminole.htm (March 4, 2006).

77. Johnston, "Resisting a Genetic Identity," 2, 12–17 (quote on 15–16), electronic version. See also Amy Harmon, "Seeking Ancestry in DNA Ties Uncovered by Tests," *New York Times,* April 12, 2006.

78. Kimberly TallBear, "DNA, Blood, and Racializing the Tribe," *Wicazo Sa Review* 18 (2003): 84, and see also 95–97.

79. Quoted in Glaberson, "Who Is a Seminole?"

80. Jackson, "Black Seminoles Sue."

81. Smithsonian Institution, http://www.si.edu/maroon (November 12, 2002), http://www.folklife.si.edu/resources/maroon/presentation.htm (December 9, 2006).

82. Guinn, *Our Land Before We Die;* Mulroy, *Freedom on the Border;* Porter, *Black Seminoles.*

83. Bateman, "We're Still Here," 293; Dillard, *Black English,* 150–55.

84. Simmons, *Notices of East Florida,* 76.

85. Gallaher, "Seminole Freedmen," 56–75, 119–25 (quote on 75).

86. Ibid., 144.

87. Frazier, "Gullah-Seminole Link" (Wickman quote); Andrew Metz, "A Nation Divided: Seminole Rift More Than a Black-and-White Issue," *Newsday,* December 22, 2003 (Haney and Warledo quotes); Miller, "Seminoles and Africans," 42 (Miller quote).

88. CBS TV, "A Nation Divided."

89. Miss Charles Emily Wilson, pers. comm., summer 1993; "The Word Maroon," *Seminole Quarterly* (Newsletter of the National Association of Black Seminoles) 1, no. 1 (Fall 1992): 3.

90. Charles Emily Wilson, "Texas Seminole Scouts," in *1992 Festival of American Folklife,* Peter Seitel, ed., program (Washington, D.C.: Smithsonian Institution, 1992), 80.

Bibliography

This is a listing of references included in the endnotes, together with some additional resources that have influenced this work.

ARCHIVAL AND MANUSCRIPT COLLECTIONS

Bell, Peter Hansborough. Governor's Papers, 1849–53. Archives, Texas State Library and Archives Commission, Austin.

Berry, Virgil (Dr.). Collection. Manuscripts Division, Western History Collections, University of Oklahoma Libraries.

Brown, John F. Governor John Brown and Wewoka Trading Company Collection. Manuscripts Division, Western History Collections, University of Oklahoma Libraries.

Casey, John C. Collection. Archives, Gilcrease Museum, Tulsa.

Chase, Charles Monroe. Collection. Manuscripts Department, Kansas State Historical Society, Topeka.

Constant, Antoinette C. Snow. Papers. Section X, Indian Archives, Oklahoma Historical Society, Oklahoma City.

Creek Nation—Civil War. File. Section X, Indian Archives, Oklahoma Historical Society, Oklahoma City.

Cutlip, C. Guy. Collection. Manuscripts Division, Western History Collections, University of Oklahoma Libraries.

Duke, Doris. Oral History Collection. 55 vols. Library Division, Western History Collections, University of Oklahoma Libraries. Vols. 43, 45, 51, 52.

Epton (Hicks). Collection. Manuscripts Division, Western History Collections, University of Oklahoma Libraries.

Foreman, Grant. Collection. Archives, Gilcrease Museum, Tulsa.

——. Collection and transcripts. Indian Archives, Oklahoma Historical Society, Oklahoma City.

——. Oral History and Ex-Slave Narratives; Seminole Indian file. Library Resources, Oklahoma Historical Society, Oklahoma City.

Indian Pioneer Papers. 116 vols. Indian Archives, Oklahoma Historical Society, Oklahoma City.

Jumper, John. Collection. Manuscripts Division, Western History Collections, University of Oklahoma Libraries.

Lilley, Mary Ann. "The Autobiography of Mary Ann Lilley." 64 pp. typescript, n.d. Section X, Indian Archives, Oklahoma Historical Society, Oklahoma City.

Loyal Seminoles. List. Section X, Indian Archives, Oklahoma Historical Society, Oklahoma City.

Micco, Hulbutta. Collection. Manuscripts Division, Western History Collections, University of Oklahoma Libraries.

Missions and Missionaries. Files. Section X, Indian Archives, Oklahoma Historical Society, Oklahoma City.

Murrow, Joseph S. (Rev.). Collection: Scrapbook. Bacone College Library, Bacone, Okla.

Porter, Kenneth Wiggins. Papers. Manuscripts, Archives, and Rare Books Division, Schomburg Center for Research in Black Culture, New York Public Library.

Presbyterian Missionaries. Letters from the American Indian Correspondence (Missions), 1841–87, in the Presbyterian Historical Society, Philadelphia. Manuscripts Division, Western History Collections, University of Oklahoma Libraries. Rolls 1, 2, 7 of 7 microfilm rolls.

Ramsay, James Ross (Rev.). "Autobiography." 100 pp. typescript (Santa Paula, Calif.: James Robinson Ramsay, 1939). Library Division, Western History Collections, University of Oklahoma Libraries. Microfilm 42-66 (1 roll, 1970).

Seminole Indians. File. Library Resources, Oklahoma Historical Society, Oklahoma City.

———. Papers: folder 2, 1821–58. Archives, Gilcrease Museum, Tulsa.

Seminole Nation. Records. Indian Archives, Oklahoma Historical Society, Oklahoma City. Microfilms SMN1 and SMN2 (2 rolls).

Seminole Nation of Oklahoma. Constitution, April 15, 1969. Copy in author's possession.

Seran, A. M. Collection. Photographic Archives Division, Western History Collections, University of Oklahoma Libraries.

Sturtevant, William C. "Seminole Maroons, Andros Island, Bahamas, 8–11 March 1977." Field notes. Copy provided by Sturtevant.

Swanton, John R. Collection. National Anthropological Archives, Smithsonian Institution, Washington, D.C.

United States. Records of the Bureau of the Census. National Archives Record Group 29. Eighth Census of the United States, 1860. National Archives Microfilm Publications, M653, roll 54, Arkansas (Slave Schedules).

United States. Records of the Bureau of Indian Affairs. National Archives Record Group 75.

Applications for Enrollment from the Five Civilized Tribes 1910–15, Chickasaw, Creek, and Seminole. National Archives, Washington, D.C.

Applications for Enrollment of the Commission to the Five Civilized Tribes, 1898–1914. National Archives Microfilm Publications, M1301, rolls 400–402.

Bureau of Indian Affairs. Letters Received, 1881–1907, 1907–39. National Archives, Washington, D.C.

———. Letters Sent. National Archives Microfilm Publications, M21, rolls 31, 32, 57, 60.

———. Letters Sent and Letter Books, 1881–1907. National Archives, Washington, D.C.

———. Report Books, 1838–85. National Archives Microfilm Publications, M348, rolls 2, 3, 10, 50–53.

Documents Relating to the Negotiation of Ratified and Unratified Treaties with Various Indian Tribes, 1801–69. National Archives Microfilm Publications, T494, roll 8.

Enrollment Cards for the Five Civilized Tribes, 1898–1914. National Archives Microfilm Publications, M1186, 93 rolls, esp. rolls 1, 77–93.

Miscellaneous Muster Rolls, 1832–36: Seminole. National Archives, Washington, D.C.

Office of Indian Affairs. Letters Received, 1824–81. National Archives Microfilm Publications, M234:

> Creek Agency, 1839–68 (rolls 226–31).
>
> Florida Superintendency, 1824–50; Florida Superintendency Emigration, 1828–53 (rolls 286–91).
>
> Schools, 1871 (roll 798).
>
> Seminole Agency, 1824–76 (rolls 800–805).
>
> Seminole Agency Emigration, 1827–59 (rolls 806–807).
>
> Southern Superintendency, 1851–71 (rolls 833–39).
>
> Texas Agency, 1847–59 (roll 858).
>
> Union Agency, 1875–80 (rolls 865–77).
>
> Western Superintendency, 1840–51; Western Superintendency Emigration, 1836–42 (rolls 923–24).

Office of the Secretary of War. Letters Received by the Secretary of War Relating to Indian Affairs, 1800–23. National Archives Microfilm Publications, M271, rolls 2 and 4.

Receipt Roll for $50,000 Payment Made to Loyal Seminoles, 1868. National Archives, Southwest Region, Fort Worth, Tex.

Records of the [Dawes] Commission to the Five Civilized Tribes:

> Letters Received, Letters Sent, Report Books, Revenue, Citizenship Cases, Instructions, and Miscellaneous. 243 vols. Indian Archives, Oklahoma Historical Society, Oklahoma City.
>
> Seminole File, 1897–1905. Indian Archives, Oklahoma Historical Society, Oklahoma City.
>
> Seminole Miscellaneous File, 1906–13. Indian Archives, Oklahoma Historical Society, Oklahoma City.

Records of the Commissioner to the Five Civilized Tribes. Letters Sent to the Commissioner of Indian Affairs or Secretary of the Interior Relating to the Commission's Activities, September 1907–May 1911. 3 vols. National Archives, Southwest Region, Fort Worth, Tex.

Records of the Commissioner to the Five Civilized Tribes Relative to Enrollment. Tribal Rolls: Seminole, 1868–97. National Archives, Southwest Region, Fort Worth, Tex.

Records of the Southern Superintendency, 1832–70; Western Superintendency, Letters Received, 1849–51. National Archives Microfilm Publications, M640, roll 7.

Records of the U.S. Inspector for the Indian Territory. Letters Sent to the Department of the Interior, June 14, 1899, to January 23, 1906. 8 vols. National Archives, Southwest Region, Fort Worth, Tex.

Records Relating to the Enrollment of the Five Civilized Tribes. Letters Received Relating to Choctaw and Other Freedmen, 1878–84. National Archives, Washington, D.C.

Records Relating to Loyal Creek Claims, 1869–70. National Archives, Washington, D.C.

Records Relating to Ratified Indian Treaties, 1722–1869. National Archives Microfilm Publications, M668, roll 14.

Seminole Annuity Rolls, 1860–98. National Archives, Washington, D.C.

Seminoles and Seminole Immigration, 1823–60. National Archives, Washington, D.C.

Special Files of the Office of Indian Affairs, 1807–94. National Archives Microfilm Publications, M574:

> "Beams Negroes, Suits for Freedom and Attorneys' Claims for Fees, 1854–1859," file 227 (roll 75).

"Claims of Loyal Seminole for Losses Suffered During the Civil War, Submitted Under Provisions of the Treaty of March 21, 1866," file 87 (roll 11).

"Seminole Claims to Certain Negroes 1841–1849," file 96 (roll 13).

United States. Records of the Department of the Interior, Indian Division. National Archives Record Group 48:

Final Rolls of Citizens and Freedmen of the Five Civilized Tribes in Indian Territory, 1907, 1914. National Archives Microfilm Publications, T529, roll 3, Creek and Seminole Rolls.

Letters Received, 1881–1907. National Archives, Washington, D.C.

Letters Sent, 1849–1903. National Archives Microfilm Publications, M606, rolls 4, 39–44.

Special Files. Indian Territory Division. Choctaw Freedmen File, boxes 48, 52. National Archives, Washington, D.C.

United States. Records of the Department of War. "Regimental Letter and Order Book; 79th (New) U.S. Colored Troops." Microfilm. National Archives, Washington, D.C.

United States. Records of the Office of the Adjutant General, 1780s–1917. National Archives Record Group 94:

General Jesup's Papers. National Archives, Washington, D.C.

Letters Received. National Archives Microfilm Publications, M619, file 488-70, "Papers Relating to the Return of the Kickapoo and the Seminole (Negro) Indians from Mexico to the United States, 1870–1885" (rolls 799–800).

United States. Records of the U.S. Army Continental Commands, 1821–1920. National Archives Record Group 393:

Fort Gibson. Letters Received, Letters Sent, and Volume "Indian Affairs." National Archives, Washington, D.C.

Second and Seventh Military Departments, Letters Received and Letters Sent. National Archives, Washington, D.C.

Van Horn, Benjamin. "Autobiography," 1909. 30 pp. typescript. Benjamin Van Horn Collection, misc. doc. 42706. Manuscripts Department, Kansas State Historical Society, Topeka.

GOVERNMENT DOCUMENTS AND PUBLICATIONS

Burke, William S. "Official Military History of Kansas Regiments: During the War for the Suppression of the Great Rebellion." In *Report of the Adjutant General of the State of Kansas 1861–1865*. 2 vols. Topeka: Kansas State Printing Co., 1896 [1867].

Capron, Louis. "The Medicine Bundles of the Florida Seminole and the Green Corn Dance." *Bureau of American Ethnology Bulletin* 151. Washington, D.C.: Government Printing Office, 1953.

Carter, Clarence E., comp. and ed. *Territorial Papers of the United States*. 28 vols. Washington, D.C.: Government Printing Office, 1934–75.

Densmore, Frances. "Seminole Music." *Bureau of American Ethnology Bulletin* 161. Washington, D.C.: Government Printing Office, 1956.

Kappler, Charles J., comp. *Indian Affairs: Laws and Treaties*. 3 vols. Washington, D.C.: Government Printing Office, 1904–13.

McCauley, Clay. "The Seminole Indians of Florida." In *United States Bureau of Ethnology, Fifth Annual Report, 1883–1884*. Washington, D.C.: Government Printing Office, 1887.

Official Opinions of the Attorneys General of the United States. 112 vols. Washington, D.C.: Farnham, 1852–70.

Preliminary Report of the Eighth Census, 1860. Washington, D.C.: Government Printing Office, 1864.

Report of the Adjutant General of the State of Kansas, 1861–1865. 2 vols. Topeka: Kansas State Printing Co., 1896 [1867].

Royce, Charles C. "The Cherokee Nation of Indians." In *United States Bureau of Ethnology, Fifth Annual Report, 1883–1884.* Washington, D.C.: Government Printing Office, 1887.

Swanton, John R. "Early History of the Creek Indians and Their Neighbours." *Bureau of American Ethnology Bulletin 73.* Washington, D.C.: Government Printing Office, 1922.

——. "Religious Beliefs and Medical Practices of the Creek Indians." In *United States Bureau of Ethnology, Forty-second Annual Report.* Washington, D.C.: Government Printing Office, 1928.

——. "Social Organization and the Social Usages of the Creek Confederacy." In *United States Bureau of Ethnology, Forty-second Annual Report.* Washington, D.C.: Government Printing Office, 1928.

U.S. Board of Indian Commissioners. *Special Reports: Board of Indian Commissioners.*

U.S. Bureau of Indian Commissioners. *Annual Report of the Bureau of Indian Commissioners, 1870–1917.*

U.S. Census Office. *The Five Civilized Tribes in Indian Territory: Extra Census Bulletin, Census Office, Department of the Interior.* Washington, D.C.: U.S. Census Printing Office, 1894.

U.S. Commission to the Five Civilized Tribes. *The Final Rolls of Citizens and Freedmen of the Five Civilized Tribes in Indian Territory; Prepared by the Commission and Commissioner to the Five Civilized Tribes, and Approved by the Secretary of the Interior on or prior to March 4, 1907.* Washington, D.C.: Government Printing Office, 1907.

U.S. Commissioner of Indian Affairs. *Annual Report of the Commissioner of Indian Affairs, 1838–1915.*

U.S. Commissioner to the Five Civilized Tribes. *Annual Report of the Commissioner to the Five Civilized Tribes, 1894–1907.*

U.S. Congress. *American State Papers.* 38 vols. Washington, D.C.: Government Printing Office, 1832–61. Vol. 6, *Foreign Affairs;* vol. 7, *Military Affairs.*

——. House. *Indians—Creek and Seminole.* 33d Cong., 2d sess., H. Exec. Doc. 15, 1854.

——. House. *Negroes, etc., Captured from Indians in Florida.* 25th Cong., 3d sess., H. Doc. 225, 1839.

——. House. *Report on the United States and Mexican Boundary Survey.* William H. Emory. 3 vols. 34th Cong. 1st sess., H. Exec. Doc. 135, 1857–59.

——. Senate. *Investigation of Condition of Indians in Indian Territory: Testimony on Industrial, Social, Moral, and Political Condition, Primarily of Five Civilized Tribes, and Condition of Freedmen in Indian Territory.* 49th Cong., 1st sess., S. Rep. 1278, part 2, 1886.

——. Senate. *Journal of the Provisional Congress of the Confederate States of America.* 7 vols. 58th Cong., 2d sess., S. Doc. 234, 1904–1905.

——. *United States Statutes at Large,* 1789–2004. 117 vols.

U.S. Inspector for Indian Territory. *Annual Report of the Inspector for Indian Territory,* 1898–1907.

U.S. War Department. *The War of the Rebellion: A Compilation of the Official Records of the Union and Confederate Armies.* 4 ser., 130 vols. Washington, D.C.: Government Printing Office, 1880–1901.

COURT CASES

Davis v. United States, 192 F. 3d 951, 954, 10th Circuit 1999, U.S. App.

Davis v. United States, 199 F. Supp. 2d 1164–80, W. Dist. Okla. 1996, 2002, U.S. Dist.

Seminole Nation of Oklahoma v. Babbitt (D.D.C. December 20, 2000), no. 00 CV 02384 (CKK).
Seminole Nation of Oklahoma v. Norton, 206 F.R.D. 1 (D.D.C. September 27, 2001).
Seminole Nation of Oklahoma v. Norton, 223 F. Supp. 2d 122 (D.D.C. 2002), http://www.dcd.us
    courts.gov/02-739.pdf (May 3, 2005).
Seminole Nation v. United States, 78 Ct. Cls. 455 (1933).
Seminole Nation v. United States, 90 Ct. Cls. 151 (1940).
Seminole Nation v. United States, 10 Ind. Cl. Com. 450 (Docket 152; August 22, 1962).

INTERVIEWS

Thomas Coker. Seminole, Okla., January 24, 1979.
"Pompey" Bruner Fixico. Los Angeles, November 11, 2005.
Charles E. Grounds. Seminole, Okla., January 24, 1979.
Robert Lee Miller. Meetings. Norman, Okla., winter 1978–79.
T. B. Miller. Wewoka, Okla., January 25, 1979.
A. Seran (Mr.). Interviews conducted by Louise Welch, Wewoka, Okla., July 2 and August
    23, 1955. 4 pp. typescript notes. Copy provided by Welch.
Richmond Tiger. Wewoka, Okla., January 25, 1979.
Rev. William C. Wantland. Oklahoma City, January 12, 1979.
Ben Warrior. Wewoka, Okla., January 24, 1979.
——. Freedman participant discussion session facilitated by Dan Reeves, Oklahoma Histor-
    ical Society, February 11, 1979. Copy of tape in author's possession.
——. Sasakwa, Okla., March 1, 1983. Conducted with Susan Miller.
William "Dub" Warrior. Brackettville, Tex., September 15, 1990.
Miss Charles Emily Wilson. Brackettville, Tex., June 19, 1990.

DISSERTATIONS AND THESES

Balyeat, Frank A. "Education in Indian Territory." Ph.D. dissertation, Stanford University,
    1927.
Bateman, Rebecca B. "We're Still Here: History, Kinship, and Group Identity among the
    Seminole Freedmen of Oklahoma." Ph.D. dissertation, Johns Hopkins University, 1990.
Baum, Laura E. "Agriculture among the Five Civilized Tribes, 1865–1906." M.A. thesis,
    University of Oklahoma, 1940.
Belt, Loren J. "Baptist Missions to the Indians of the Five Civilized Tribes of Oklahoma."
    Th.D. dissertation, Central Baptist Theological Seminary, 1955.
Berringer, Dieter G. "Mexican Attitudes towards Immigration 1821–1857." Ph.D. disserta-
    tion, University of Wisconsin, 1972.
Black, Charles H. "One Hundred and Twenty Years of Baptist Missionary Administration in
    Oklahoma." Th.D. dissertation, Central Baptist Theological Seminary, 1950.
Boyd, Thomas J. "The Use of Negro Troops by Kansas during the Civil War." M.A. thesis,
    Kansas State Teacher's College, 1950.
Brown, Walter L. "Albert Pike, 1809–1891." Ph.D. dissertation, University of Texas, 1955.
Buice, S. David. "The Civil War and the Five Civilized Tribes: A Study in Federal-Indian
    Relations." Ph.D. dissertation, University of Oklahoma, 1970.
Bush, Charles C. "The Green Corn Rebellion." M.A. thesis, University of Oklahoma, 1932.
Carter, Bruce G. "A History of Seminole County, Oklahoma." M.A. thesis, University of
    Oklahoma, 1932.

Chaney, Margaret A. "A Tribal History of the Seminole Indians." M.A. thesis, University of Oklahoma, 1928.

Dagley, A. W. "The Negroes of Oklahoma." M.A. thesis, University of Oklahoma, 1926.

Duffner, Michael Paul. "The Seminole-Black Alliance in Florida: An Example of Minority Co-operation." M.A. thesis, George Mason University, 1973.

Gallaher, Arthur, Jr. "A Survey of the Seminole Freedmen." M.A. thesis, University of Oklahoma, 1951.

Howard, Rosalyn. "The Promised is'Land: Reconstructing History and Identity among the Black Seminoles of Andros Island, Bahamas." Ph.D. dissertation, University of Florida, 1999.

Jackson, Neeley B. "Political and Economic History of the Negro in Indian Territory." M.A. thesis, University of Oklahoma, 1960.

Jeltz, Wyatt F. "A Study of the Choctaw and Chickasaw Indians as Slaveholders." M.Sc. thesis, Kansas State Teacher's College, 1945.

Jordan, H. Glenn. "Joseph Samuel Morrow: The Man and His Times." Ph.D. dissertation, University of Oklahoma, 1982.

Kiker, Ernest. "Education among the Seminoles." M.A. thesis, Oklahoma A&M College, 1939.

Krauthamer, Barbara. "Blacks on the Borders: African-Americans' Transition from Slavery to Freedom in Texas and the Indian Territory, 1836–1907." Ph.D. dissertation, Princeton University, 2000.

Landers, Jane G. "Black Society in Spanish St. Augustine, 1784–1821." Ph.D. dissertation, University of Florida, 1988.

Lawuyi, Olatunde Bayo. "Seminole Freedmen's Identity in Plural Setting." Ph.D. thesis, University of Illinois at Urbana–Champaign, 1985.

Micco, Melinda B. "Freedmen and Seminoles: Forging a Seminole Nation." Ph.D. dissertation, University of California, Berkeley, 1995.

Miles, Tiya A. "'Bone of My Bone': Stories of a Black-Cherokee Family, 1790–1866." University of Minnesota, 2000.

Moffit, James W. "A History of Early Baptist Missions among the Five Civilized Tribes." Ph.D. dissertation, University of Oklahoma, 1946.

Moore, A. N. "The Social and Economic Status of the Seminole Indians." M.S.W. thesis, University of Oklahoma, 1939.

Mulroy, Kevin. "Relations between Blacks and Seminoles after Removal." Ph.D. thesis, University of Keele (England), 1984.

Naylor-Ojurongbe, Celia E. "'More at Home with the Indians': African-American Slaves and Freedpeople in the Cherokee Nation, Indian Territory, 1838–1907." Ph.D. dissertation, Duke University, 2001.

Rampp, Lary C. "The Twilight of the Confederacy in the Indian Territory, 1863–1865." M.A. thesis, Oklahoma State University, 1968.

Riordan, Patrick. "Seminole Genesis: Native Americans, African Americans, and Colonists on the Southern Frontier from Prehistory through the Colonial Era." Ph.D. dissertation, Florida State University, 1996.

Roethler, Michael D. "Negro Slavery among the Cherokee Indians, 1540–1866." Ph.D. dissertation, Fordham University, 1964.

Sameth, Sigmund. "Creek Negroes: A Study of Race Relations." M.A. thesis, University of Oklahoma, 1940.

Sattler, Richard A. "Siminoli Italwa: Socio-political Change among the Oklahoma Seminoles between Removal and Allotment, 1836–1905." Ph.D. dissertation, University of Oklahoma, 1987.

Smith, Geraldine M. "Violence on the Oklahoma Territory–Seminole Nation Border. The Mont Ballard Case." M.A. thesis, University of Oklahoma, 1957.

Weik, Terrance M. "A Historical Archaeology of Black Seminole Maroons in Florida: Ethnogenesis and Culture Contact at Pilaklikaha." Ph.D. dissertation, University of Florida, 2002.

Welsh, Michael E. "The Road to Assimilation: The Seminoles in Oklahoma." Ph.D. dissertation, University of New Mexico, 1983.

Wilson, Raleigh A. "Negro and Indian Relations in the Five Civilized Tribes from 1865 to 1907." Ph.D. dissertation, University of Iowa, 1949.

Zellar, Gary W. " 'If I Ain't One, You Won't Find Another One Here': Race, Identity, Citizenship, and Land; The African Creek Experience in the Indian Territory and Oklahoma, 1830–1910." Ph.D. dissertation, University of Arkansas, 2003.

UNPUBLISHED PAPERS

Bateman, Rebecca B. "Slaves or Seminoles?" 12 pp. typescript, 2002. Copy provided by Bateman.

Kelly, Matthew. "Naturalizing Seminole 'Racism' and the Multicultural Self." Paper presented at the Human Rights Workshop, University of Chicago, May 25, 2004. 33 pp. http://humanrights.uchicago.edu/workshoppapers/kelly.pdf (February 8, 2006).

KOCO-TV, Oklahoma City. Noon news report featuring interview with Seminole principal chief Jerry Haney on blood quantum requirements and the freedmen's application for CDIB cards, February 24, 1995. Notes in author's possession.

Larose, Thomas. "The African Influences on Seminole Beadwork." Paper presented at the twelfth Triennial Symposium of the Arts Council of the African Studies Association, St. Thomas, U.S. Virgin Islands, April 25–29, 2001. Copy provided by Larose.

Littlefield, Daniel F., Jr. "The Seminole Nation in the Dawes Era." 22 pp. typescript, n.d. Copy provided by Littlefield.

MacKay, Fergus. "Indigenous People's Rights in the Commonwealth Caribbean." Paper delivered at the Indigenous Rights in the Commonwealth Caribbean and Americas Regional Expert Meeting, Amerindian Peoples' Association, Guyana, June 2003. http://www.cpsu.org.uk/downloads/Fergus_MacKay.pdf (June 4, 2004).

Mankiller, Wilma, moderator. "Exploring the Legacy and Future of Black/Indian Relations." Panel, 57th annual session, National Congress of American Indians, St. Paul, Minn., November 14, 2000. 25 pp. transcript. http://web.mit.edu/wjohnson/www/kiaanafh/NCAI_pdf_Transcript.pdf (July 7, 2002).

Mulroy, Kevin. "Marronage among the Seminoles." Paper delivered at the fifth annual Gilder Lehrman Center International Conference, "Unshackled Spaces: Fugitives from Slavery and Maroon Communities in the Americas," Yale University, December 6–7, 2002.

——. "Seminole Maroon Diplomacy." Paper delivered at the conference "Passages to Freedom: The Underground Railroad in American History and Legend," sponsored by the National Underground Railroad Freedom Center and the Smithsonian Institution's National Museum of American History, Washington, D.C., February 28, 2003.

Newton, Bertram A. "A History of Red Bays, Andros, Bahamas." 5 pp. typescript, 1968. Copy provided by William C. Sturtevant.

Walker, Mary. "Caesar Bruner." 6 pp. typescript, 1956. Copy provided by Louise Welch.

Wisdom, Charles. "Report on the Social Condition of the Oklahoma Seminole, 1937." Applied Anthropology Unit Report no. 9727. 28 pp. typescript. Copy provided by William Dawson.

Zellar, Gary. "Europe Speaking to America through Africa: African Creeks and the Establishment of Christianity in the Creek Nation." Indigenous and African Experiences in the Americas Seminar, Hall Center for the Humanities, University of Kansas, Fall 2005, 31 pp. http://www.hallcenter.ku.edu/seminar/Africa (October 24, 2005).

ARTICLES AND ESSAYS

Abbott, L. J. "The Race Question in the Forty-sixth State." *Independent* 6 (July 1907): 206–11.

Abel, Annie H. "The Indians in the Civil War." *American Historical Review* 15 (1910): 281–96.

Adams, Mischa B. "Naming Practices among the Black Seminole of the Texas-Mexico Border Region." *Journal of the Big Bend Studies* 11 (1999): 119–44.

Anderson, Robert L. "The End of an Idyll." *Florida Historical Quarterly* 42 (1963): 35–47.

Andrews, T. F. "Freedmen in Indian Territory: A Post–Civil War Dilemma." *Journal of the West* 4 (1965): 367–76.

Antle, H. R. "Interpretation of Seminole Clan Relationship Terms." *Chronicles of Oklahoma* 14 (1936): 343–48.

———. "The Legend of Abuska." *Chronicles of Oklahoma* 20 (1942): 255–56.

Aptheker, Herbert. "Maroons within the Present Limits of the United States." *Journal of Negro History* 24 (1939): 167–84.

Ashcraft, Allan C. "Confederate Indian Troop Conditions in August 1864." *Chronicles of Oklahoma* 41 (1963): 270–85.

———. "Confederate Indian Troop Conditions in 1864." *Chronicles of Oklahoma* 41 (1963): 442–49.

———. "Confederate Indian Troop Conditions in 1865." *Chronicles of Oklahoma* 42 (1964): 421–28.

Ballenger, R. L. "The Colored High School of the Cherokee Nation." *Chronicles of Oklahoma* 30 (1952): 454–62.

Balman, Gail. "The Creek Treaty of 1866." *Chronicles of Oklahoma* 48 (1970): 184–96.

Balyeat, Frank A. "Joseph Samuel Morrow, Apostle to the Indians." *Chronicles of Oklahoma* 35 (1957): 297–313.

———. "Segregation in the Public Schools of Oklahoma Territory." *Chronicles of Oklahoma* 39 (1961): 180–92.

Banks, Dean. "Civil War Refugees from Indian Territory in the North, 1861–1864." *Chronicles of Oklahoma* 41 (1963): 286–98.

"Baptist Prominence in the Indian Territory." *Baptist Home Mission Monthly,* January 1892.

Bateman, Rebecca B. "Africans and Indians: A Comparative Study of the Black Carib and Black Seminole." *Ethnohistory* 37 (1990): 1–24.

———. "Naming Patterns in Black Seminole Ethnogenesis." *Ethnohistory* 49 (2002): 227–57.

Bearss, Edwin C. "The Civil War Comes to Indian Territory, 1861: The Flight of Opothleyohola." *Journal of the West* 11 (1972): 9–42.

Beckloff, Lisa. "Tribe's Freedmen Seek Share." *Daily Oklahoman,* February 21, 1992.

Beggs, Melissa. "The Black and the Red." *Oklahoma Gazette,* November 6, 2003, 21–24.

Bender, Norman K. " 'We Surely Gave Them an Uplift.' " *Chronicles of Oklahoma* 61 (1983): 180–93.

"Benjamin F. Bruner Obituary, Saturday, June 10, 1939." http://seminolenation-indianterri tory.org/benjamin_f_bruner_obituary.htm (November 22, 2003).

Bennett, Lerone, Jr. "The Road Not Taken: Colonies Turn Fateful Fork by Systematically Dividing the Races." *Ebony* 25 (1970): 71–77.

Bentley, Mac. "Seminole Freedmen Recognized." *Daily Oklahoman,* October 25, 2003.

Bilby, Kenneth. "Ethnogenesis in the Guianas and Jamaica: Two Maroon Cases." In *History, Power, and Identity: Ethnogenesis in the Americas,* Jonathan D. Hill, ed. Iowa City: University of Iowa Press, 1996.

——. "Maroon Autonomy in Jamaica." *Cultural Survival* 25, no. 4 (2002): 12 pp. http://www.cs.org/publications/csq/csq-article.cfm?id=1399 (December 9, 2006).

——. "Swearing by the Past, Swearing to the Future: Sacred Oaths, Alliances, and Treaties among the Guianese and Jamaican Maroons." *Ethnohistory* 44 (1997): 655–90.

Bilby, Kenneth, and Diana Baird N'Diaye. "Creativity and Resistance: Maroon Culture in the Americas." In *1992 Festival of American Folklife,* Peter Seitel, ed. Program. Washington, D.C.: Smithsonian Institution, 1992.

Billington, Monroe. "Black Slavery in Indian Territory: The Ex-Slave Narratives." *Chronicles of Oklahoma* 60 (1982): 56–65.

"Billy Bowlegs and Suite." *Gleason's Pictorial Drawing Room Companion* 3, no. 17 (1852): 257.

"Billy Bowlegs in New Orleans." *Harper's Weekly,* June 12, 1858.

Bittle, W. E., and Gilbert L. Geis. "Racial Self-Fulfillment and the Rise of an All-Negro Community in Oklahoma." *Phylon* 18 (1957): 247–60.

"Black Seminoles File Racial Discrimination Suit against Federal Government and Bureau of Indian Affairs." *National Bar Association Magazine* (January–February 1996): 24–.

"Black Seminoles Urged to Fight for Share of Funds." *Sunday Oklahoman,* February 19, 1995.

"Black Settlers Come to Alberta." http://www.abheritage.ca/pasttopresent/settlement/bla ck_settlers.html (February 22, 2006).

Blackburn, Bob L. "From Blood Revenge to the Lighthorsemen: Evolution of Law Enforcement Institutions among the Five Civilized Tribes to 1861." *American Indian Law Review* 8 (1980): 49–63.

Bloom, Leonard. "Role of the Indian in the Race Relations Complex of the South." *Social Forces* 19 (1940): 268–73.

Blunt, James G. "General Blunt's Account of His Civil War Experiences." *Kansas Historical Quarterly* 1 (1932): 211–65.

Bolster, Mel H. "The Smoked Meat Rebellion." *Chronicles of Oklahoma* 31 (1953): 37–55.

Bolt, Christine R. "Red, Black, and White in 19th Century America." In *Minorities in History,* A. C. Hepburn, ed. London: Butler and Tanner, 1978.

Boyd, Mark F. "Asi-Yaholo, or Osceola." *Florida Historical Quarterly* 33 (1955): 249–305.

——. "Events at Prospect Bluff on the Apalachicola River, 1808–1818." *Florida Historical Quarterly* 16 (1937): 55–96.

——. "Horatio S. Dexter and Events Leading to the Treaty of Moultrie Creek with the Seminole Indians." *Florida Anthropologist* 11 (1958): 65–95.

——. "The Seminole War: Its Background and Onset." *Florida Historical Quarterly* 30 (1951): 3–115.

Braund, Kathryn E. Holland. "The Creek Indians, Blacks, and Slavery." *Journal of Southern History* 57 (1991): 601–36.

Britton, Wiley. "Some Reminiscences of the Cherokee People—Returning to Their Homes the Exiles of a Nation." *Chronicles of Oklahoma* 6 (1928): 163–77.

Brooks, James F. Introduction to *Confounding the Color Line: The Indian-Black Experience in North America,* James F. Brooks, ed. Lincoln: University of Nebraska Press, 2002.

Brown, Aaron R. "Judgments: 'Brothers' Fighting over Indian Money; The Right of Seminole Freedmen to a Portion of the Indian Claims Commission Judgment Fund." *American Indian Law Review* 11 (1983): 111–24.

Brown, Canter, Jr. "The Florida Crisis of 1826–1827 and the Second Seminole War." *Florida Historical Quarterly* 73 (1995): 419–42.

——. "The 'Sarrazota, or Runaway Negro Plantations': Tampa Bay's First Black Community, 1812–1821." *Tampa Bay History* 12 (1990): 5–19.

——. "Tales of Angola: Free Blacks, Red Stick Creeks, and International Intrigue in Spanish Southwest Florida, 1812–1821." In *Go Sound the Trumpet: Selections in Florida's African American History,* David H. Jackson, Jr., and Canter Brown, Jr., eds. Tampa: University of Tampa Press, 2005.

Brown, Loren N. "The Dawes Commission." *Chronicles of Oklahoma* 9 (1931): 71–105.

——. "The Establishment of the Dawes Commission for Indian Territory." *Chronicles of Oklahoma* 18 (1940): 171–81.

Brown, T. E. "Seminole Indian Agents, 1842–1874." *Chronicles of Oklahoma* 51 (1973): 59–83.

Bryce, J. Y. "Some Notes of Interest Concerning Early Day Operations in Indian Territory by Methodist Church South." *Chronicles of Oklahoma* 4 (1926): 233–41.

Buck, S. H. "The Settlement of Oklahoma." *Transactions of Wisconsin Academy* 15 (1907): 325–80.

Burk, J. L. "Oklahoma Seminole Indians: Origin, History, and Pan-Indianism." *Chronicles of Oklahoma* 51 (1973): 211–23.

Burton, Arthur T. "Seminole Light Horse Police." http://www.seminolenation-indianterri tory.org/lighthorse.htm (July 7, 2005).

Bushnell, Amy Turner. "Ruling 'the Republic of Indians' in Seventeenth-Century Florida." In *Powhatan's Mantle: Indians in the Colonial Southeast,* Peter H. Wood, Gregory A. Waselkov, and M. Thomas Hatley, eds. Lincoln: University of Nebraska Press, 1989.

Carrier, Toni. "Black Seminoles, Maroons, and Freedom Seekers in Florida." University of South Florida Africana Heritage Project, 2005. http://www.africanaheritage.com/blac k_seminoles_1.asp (June 25, 2005). From this URL, follow links to other parts in the series.

Carter, L. Edward. "The Seminole Nation after Leaving Florida, 1855–1860." *Chronicles of Oklahoma* 55 (1977): 433–53.

Castel, Albert. "Civil War Kansas and the Negro." *Journal of Negro History* 51 (1966): 125–38.

Chamberlain, A. F. "African and American: The Contact of Negro and Indian." *Science* 17 (1891): 85–90.

Chapman, Berlin B. "Freedmen and the Oklahoma Lands." *Southwestern Social Science Quarterly* 29 (1948): 150–59.

——. "The Pottawatomie and Absentee Shawnee Reservation." *Chronicles of Oklahoma* 24 (1946): 293–305.

Chase, Charles M. "An Editor Looks at Early-Day Kansas: The Letters of Charles Monroe Chase." Lela Barnes, ed. *Kansas Historical Quarterly* 26 (1960): 113–51.

"Cherokee Chief Moves to Remove Cherokee Citizens." African–Native American Genealogy Forum. http://www.afrigeneas.com/forume/ (March 18, 2006).

Clifford, Roy A. "The Indian Regiments in the Battle of Pea Ridge." *Chronicles of Oklahoma* 25 (1947): 314–22.

Cody, Cheryll Ann. "There Was No 'Absolom' on the Ball Plantations: Slave-Naming Practices in the South Carolina Low Country, 1720–1865." *American Historical Review* 92 (1987): 563–96.

Coe, Charles H. "The Parentage and Birthplace of Osceola." *Florida Historical Quarterly* 17 (1939): 304–11.

——. "The Parentage of Osceola." *Florida Historical Quarterly* 33 (1955): 202–205.

"Communication from the Payne County Historical Society Concerning the Site of the First Battle of the Civil War in the Indian Territory." *Chronicles of Oklahoma* 28 (1950): 210–11.

Condra, George E. "The Opening of the Indian Territory." *Bulletin of the American Geographical Society* 39 (1907): 321–40.

"Confederate Memorial Scroll to the Indian Officers in the War between the States." *Chronicles of Oklahoma* 28 (1950): 206 and facing plate.

Conlan, Czarina Colbert. "Schools of the Five Civilized Tribes: Choctaw, Chickasaw, Seminole, Cherokee, and Creek Indian Schools." *Southern Magazine* 3 (1936): 9–10, 48.

Cornish, Dudley T. "Kansas Negro Regiments in the Civil War." *Kansas Historical Quarterly* 20 (1953): 417–29.

Corwin, H. D. "Protestant Missionary Work among the Comanches and Kiowas." *Chronicles of Oklahoma* 46 (1968): 41–57.

Covington, James W. "An Episode in the Third Seminole War." *Florida Historical Quarterly* 45 (1966): 45–49.

——. "The Negro Fort." *Gulf Coast Historical Review* 5 (1990): 79–91.

Crawford, W. D. "Oklahoma and the Indian Territory." *New England Magazine* 15 (1890): 455–57.

Creel, Margaret W. "Gullah Attitudes towards Life and Death." In *Africanisms in American Culture,* Joseph E. Holloway, ed. Bloomington: Indiana University Press, 1990.

Crockett, Bernice N. "Health Conditions in Indian Territory, 1830 to the Civil War." *Chronicles of Oklahoma* 35 (1957): 80–90.

——. "Health Conditions in the Indian Territory from the Civil War to 1890." *Chronicles of Oklahoma* 36 (1958): 21–39.

Crow, Charles. "Indians and Blacks in White America." In *Red, White, and Black: Symposium on Indians in the Old South,* Charles M. Hudson, ed. Athens: University of Georgia Press, 1971.

Cubage, Annie R. "Engagement at Cabin Creek, Indian Territory, July 1 and 2, 1863." *Chronicles of Oklahoma* 10 (1932): 44–51.

Cunniff, M. G. "The New State of Oklahoma." *World's Work* 13 (1906): 7603–19.

Danziger, Edmund J. "The Office of Indian Affairs and the Problem of Civil War Refugees in Kansas." *Kansas Historical Quarterly* 35 (1969): 257–75.

Davis, J. B. "Slavery in the Cherokee Nation." *Chronicles of Oklahoma* 11 (1933): 1056–72.

Davis, Mace. "Chitto Harjo." *Chronicles of Oklahoma* 13 (1935): 139–45.

Davis, T. Frederick. "The Seminole Council, October 23–25, 1834." *Florida Historical Quarterly* 7 (1928): 330–56.

——. "United States Troops in Spanish East Florida, 1812–1813." Parts 1–5. *Florida Historical Quarterly* 9 (1930): 3–23, 96–116, 135–55, 259–78; 10 (1931): 24–34.

Debo, Angie E. "The Location of the Battle of Round Mountains." *Chronicles of Oklahoma* 41 (1963): 70–104.

——. "The Site of the Battle of Round Mountain, 1861." *Chronicles of Oklahoma* 27 (1949): 187–206.

——. "Southern Refugees of the Cherokee Nation." *Southwestern Historical Quarterly* 35 (1932): 255–66.

Demorse, Charles. "Indians for the Confederacy." *Chronicles of Oklahoma* 50 (1972): 474–78.

Densmore, Frances. "Traces of Foreign Influence in the Music of American Indians." *American Anthropologist* 46 (1944): 106–13.

De Rosier, Arthur H., Jr. "Pioneers with Conflicting Ideals: Christianity and Slavery in the Choctaw Nation." *Journal of Mississippi History* 21 (1959): 174–89.

Doran, Michael F. "Antebellum Cattle Herding in the Indian Territory." *Geographical Review* 66 (1976): 48–58.

———. "Negro Slaves of the Five Civilized Tribes." *Annals of the Association of American Geographers* 68 (1978): 335–50.

———. "Population Statistics of Nineteenth Century Indian Territory." *Chronicles of Oklahoma* 53 (1975): 492–515.

Downs, Dorothy. "Possible African Influence on the Art of the Florida Seminoles." In *African Impact on the Material Culture of the Americas,* Conference Proceedings, Diggs Gallery, Winston-Salem State University. Winston-Salem, N.C.: Winston-Salem Museum of Early Southern Decorative Arts, 1996.

Duncan, Otis D. "The Fusion of White, Negro, and Indian Cultures at the Converging of the New South and the West." *Southwestern Social Science Quarterly* 14 (1934): 357–69.

Dundes, Alan. "African Tales among the North American Indians." *Southern Folklore Quarterly* 29 (1965): 207–19.

———. "Washington Irving's Version of the Seminole Origin of Races." *Ethnohistory* 9 (1962): 257–64.

Durning, A. T. "Supporting Indigenous Peoples." In *State of the World 1993,* Worldwatch Institute. New York: W. W. Norton, 1993.

Edwards, Lydia M. "Protecting Black Tribal Members: Is the Thirteenth Amendment the Linchpin to Securing Equal Rights within Indian Country?" (May 20, 2005). ExpressO Preprint Series, Working Paper 626, 66 pp. http://law.bepress.com/expresso/eps/626 (March 7, 2006).

Faulk, Odie B. "Projected Mexican Military Colonies for the Borderlands, 1848." *Journal of Arizona History* 9 (1968): 39–47.

Fischer, Leroy H. "Honey Springs Battlefield Park." *Chronicles of Oklahoma* 47 (1969): 515–30.

———. "Introduction to Civil War Battles in the West." *Journal of the West* 19 (1980): 3–8.

Fischer, Leroy H., and Kenny A. Franks. "Confederate Victory at Chusto-Talasah." *Chronicles of Oklahoma* 49 (1971): 452–76.

Fischer, Leroy H., and J. Gill. "Confederate Indian Forces outside of Indian Territory." *Chronicles of Oklahoma* 46 (1968): 249–84.

Fischer, Leroy H., and William L. McMurry. "Confederate Refugees from Indian Territory." *Chronicles of Oklahoma* 57 (1979): 451–62.

Fite, Gilbert C. "Development of the Cotton Industry by the Five Civilized Tribes in the Indian Territory." *Journal of Southern History* 15 (1949): 342–53.

Foreman, Carolyn T. "Billy Bowlegs." *Chronicles of Oklahoma* 33 (1955): 512–32.

———. "Black Beaver." *Chronicles of Oklahoma* 29 (1951): 137–52.

———. "Dr. and Mrs. Richard Moore Crain." *Chronicles of Oklahoma* 35 (1957):72–79.

———. "Early History of Webber's Falls." *Chronicles of Oklahoma* 29 (1951): 444–83.

———. "John Jumper." *Chronicles of Oklahoma* 29 (1951): 137–52.

———. "Journal of a Tour in the Indian Territory." *Chronicles of Oklahoma* 10 (1932): 219–56.

———. "The Jumper Family of the Seminole Nation." *Chronicles of Oklahoma* 34 (1956): 272–85.

———. "The Light-Horse in Indian Territory." *Chronicles of Oklahoma* 34 (1956): 17–43.

——. "Marshalltown, Creek Nation." *Chronicles of Oklahoma* 32 (1954): 52–57.

——. "Miss Sophia Sawyer and Her School." *Chronicles of Oklahoma* 32 (1954): 395–413.

——. "North Fork Town." *Chronicles of Oklahoma* 29 (1951): 79–111.

——. "Notes on the Chickasaw Light-Horsemen." *Chronicles of Oklahoma* 34 (1956): 484–85.

——. "Organization of the Seminole Light-Horse." *Chronicles of Oklahoma* 34 (1956): 340–44.

——. "Two Notable Women of the Creek Nation." *Chronicles of Oklahoma* 35 (1957): 315–37.

Foreman, Grant. "The Centennial of Fort Gibson." *Chronicles of Oklahoma* 2 (1924): 119–28.

——, ed. "The Journal of Elijah Hicks." *Chronicles of Oklahoma* 13 (1935): 68–99.

——, ed. "Notes from the *Indian Advocate.*" *Chronicles of Oklahoma* 14 (1936): 67–83.

——. "Salt Works in Early Oklahoma." *Chronicles of Oklahoma* 10 (1932): 474–500.

Forest Peoples Programme. "Indigenous Peoples and Maroons in French Guiana Demand Land Rights in Proposed National Park." September 7, 1998. http://hartford-hwp.com/archives/41/322.html (June 1, 2004).

Franklin, Marcus. "Excavators Seeking Freedom Pioneers." *St. Petersburg (Fla.) Times,* February 7, 2005.

Franks, Kenny A. "An Analysis of the Confederate Treaties with the Five Civilized Tribes." *Chronicles of Oklahoma* 50 (1972): 458–73.

——. "The Confederate States and the Five Civilized Tribes." *Journal of the West,* Special Edition 12, no. 3 (1973).

——. "The Implementation of the Confederate Treaties with the Five Civilized Tribes." *Chronicles of Oklahoma* 51 (1973): 21–33.

——. "Operations against Opothleyohola." *Military History of Texas and the Southwest* 10 (1972): 187–96.

Frazier, Herb. "Black Seminoles Seek $100M of Retribution from Government." *Charleston (S.C.) Post and Courier,* July 6, 1999.

——. "Gullah-Seminole Link Comes to Light." *Charleston (S.C.) Post and Courier,* July 6, 1999.

——. "Seminole, Gullah Ties Traced." *Charleston (S.C.) Post and Courier,* November 14, 1998.

"Freedmen Granted Benefits." *Tulsa World,* December 26, 2003.

Freeman, Charles R. "The Battle of Honey Springs." *Chronicles of Oklahoma* 13 (1935): 154–68.

Freeman, Ethel C. "The Least Known of the Five Civilized Tribes: The Seminoles of Oklahoma." *Florida Anthropologist* 17 (1964): 139–52.

Frontier Freedman's Journal: An African American Genealogical and Historical Journal of the South, Indian Territory, and the Southwest. 1992–. Spring 2000 issue devoted to Seminole maroons.

Gage, Duane. "Oklahoma: A Resettlement Area for Indians." *Chronicles of Oklahoma* 47 (1969): 282–97.

Gammon, Tim. "Black Freedmen and the Cherokee Nation." *Journal of American Studies* 2 (1977): 357–64.

Gardner, Charles. "Lawyer Discusses Seminoles." *Dartmouth,* January 19, 2001.

Garroutte, Eva Marie. "The Racial Formation of American Indians: Negotiating Legitimate Identities within Tribal and Federal Law." *American Indian Quarterly* 25 (2001): 224–39.

Garvin, Russell. "The Free Negro in Florida before the Civil War." *Florida Historical Quarterly* 46 (1967): 1–18.

Geist, Christopher D. "Slavery among the Indians: An Overview." *Negro History Bulletin* 38 (1975): 465–67.

Glaberson, William. "Who Is a Seminole and Who Gets to Decide?" *New York Times,* January 29, 2001.

Goggin, John M. "An Anthropological Reconnaissance of Andros Island, Bahamas." *American Antiquity* 5 (1939): 21–26.

——. "The Seminole Negroes of Andros Island, Bahamas." *Florida Historical Quarterly* 24 (1946): 201–206.

Graebner, Norman A. "Cattle Ranching in Eastern Oklahoma." *Chronicles of Oklahoma* 21 (1943): 300–311.

——. "Pioneer Indian Agriculture in Oklahoma." *Chronicles of Oklahoma* 23 (1945): 232–48.

——. "Provincial Indian Society in Eastern Oklahoma." *Chronicles of Oklahoma* 23 (1945): 323–37.

——. "The Public Land Policy of the Five Civilized Tribes." *Chronicles of Oklahoma* 23 (1945): 107–18.

Graves, Gregory R. "Exodus from Indian Territory: The Evolution of Cotton Culture in Eastern Oklahoma." *Chronicles of Oklahoma* 60 (1982): 186–209.

Grinde, Donald A., Jr., and Quintard Taylor, Jr. "Red vs. Black: Conflict and Accommodation in the Post Civil War Indian Territory, 1865–1907." *American Indian Quarterly* 8 (1984): 211–29.

Halliburton, Janet. "Black Slavery in the Creek Nation." *Chronicles of Oklahoma* 56 (1978): 298–314.

Halliburton, Rudy. "Origins of Black Slavery among the Cherokees." *Chronicles of Oklahoma* 52 (1974): 483–96.

Hallowell, Irvin A. "American Indians, White and Black: The Phenomenon of Transculturalization." *Current Anthropology* 4 (1963): 519–31.

Hamilton, J. P., Sr. "Indian Refugees in Coffey County." Reprinted in the *Le Roy (Kans.) Reporter,* August 14 and 21, 1931.

Hammond, Sue. "Socioeconomic Reconstruction in the Cherokee Nation, 1865–1870." *Chronicles of Oklahoma* 56 (1978): 158–70.

Hancock, Ian F. "Maroon Societies and Creole Languages." In *1992 Festival of American Folklife,* Peter Seitel, ed. Program. Washington, D.C.: Smithsonian Institution, 1992.

——. "Texas Gullah: The Creole English of the Brackettville Afro-Seminoles." In *Perspectives on American English,* Joseph L. Dillard, ed. The Hague: Mouton, 1980.

Hancock, Marvin J. "The Second Battle of Cabin Creek." *Chronicles of Oklahoma* 39 (1961): 414–26.

Hand, Margaret B. "Necrology: Virgil Berry M.D." *Chronicles of Oklahoma* 32 (1954): 236–37.

Harger, C. M. "Oklahoma and the Indian Territory as They Are Today." *American Review of Reviews* 25 (1902): 177–81.

Harmon, Amy. "Seeking Ancestry in DNA Ties Uncovered by Tests." *New York Times,* April 12, 2006.

Harriman, Helga H. "Economic Conditions in the Creek Nation, 1865–1871." *Chronicles of Oklahoma* 51 (1973): 325–34.

Heath, G. N. "The First Federal Invasion of Indian Territory." *Chronicles of Oklahoma* 44 (1966): 409–19.

Helms, Mary. "Black Carib Domestic Organization in Historical Perspective: Traditional Origins of Contemporary Patterns." *Ethnology* 20 (1981): 77–86.

——. "Negro or Indian? The Changing Identity of a Frontier Population." In *Old Roots in New Lands: Historical and Anthropological Perspectives on Black Experiences in the Americas,* Ann M. Pescatello, ed. Westport, Conn.: Greenwood Press, 1977.

Henslick, Harry. "The Seminole Treaty of 1866." *Chronicles of Oklahoma* 48 (1970): 280–94.

Hill, Mozell C. "The All-Negro Communities of Oklahoma: The Natural History of a Social Movement." *Journal of Negro History* 31 (1946): 254–68.

——. "Basic Racial Attitudes towards Whites in an Oklahoma All-Negro Community." *American Journal of Sociology* 49 (1944): 519–23.

——. "A Comparative Analysis of the Social Organization of the All-Negro Society in Oklahoma." *Social Forces* 25 (1946): 70–77.

——. "Race Attitudes in the All-Negro Community in Oklahoma." *Phylon* 7 (1946): 260–68.

Hill, Mozell C., and Eugene S. Richards. "Demographic Trends of the Negroes in Oklahoma." *Southwestern Journal* 2 (1946): 47–63.

Hinds, Roland. "Early Creek Missions." *Chronicles of Oklahoma* 17 (1939): 48–61.

Hinton, R. J. "The Indian Territory, Its Status, Development, and Future." *American Review of Reviews* 23 (1901): 451–58.

Hoffman, Abraham. "Oklahoma's Black Panther." *War Chief of the Indian Territory Posse of Oklahoma Westerners* 6 (1972): 1–8.

Holt, Adoniram J. "Early Baptist Mission Work in the Indian Territory." *Baptist Messenger,* June 14, 1928.

Hood, Fred. "Twilight of the Confederacy in the Indian Territory." *Chronicles of Oklahoma* 41 (1963): 425–41.

" 'I'm in the Wewoka Switch': Heard in the Oil Fields over the World." *Chronicles of Oklahoma* 41 (1963): 455–58.

Inscoe, John C. "Carolina Slave Names: An Index to Acculturation." *Journal of Southern History* 49 (1983): 527–54.

"An Interim Report on the Site of the Battle of Round Mountain." *Chronicles of Oklahoma* 28 (1950): 492–95.

Irving, Washington. "The Seminoles." *Indian Historian* 2 (1969): 35–37.

Jackson, Ron. "Black Seminoles Seek Recognition." *Daily Oklahoman,* March 27, 2000.

——. "Black Seminoles Sue for a Place in History." *Sunday Oklahoman,* November 7, 1999.

——. "Forefather Prepared Family for Challenge." *Sunday Oklahoman,* November 7, 1999.

James, Parthena L. "Reconstruction in the Chickasaw Nation: The Freedman Problem." *Chronicles of Oklahoma* 45 (1967): 44–57.

Jeltz, Wyatt F. "The Relations of Negroes and Choctaw and Chickasaw Indians." *Journal of Negro History* 33 (1948): 24–37.

Johnson, Guy B. "Personality in a White-Indian-Negro Community." *American Sociology Review* 4 (1939): 516–23.

Johnson, Michael. "Runaway Slaves and the Slave Communities in South Carolina, 1799–1830." *William and Mary Quarterly* 38 (1981): 418–41.

Johnson, Stacy D. "Seminole Freedmen Apply for Benefits, Expect Denial." Unidentified press clipping, February 1995. Copy in author's possession.

Johnson, Willard B. "Tracing Trails of Blood on Ice: Commemorating 'the Great Escape' in 1861–62 of Indians and Blacks into Kansas." *Negro History Bulletin* 64 (2001): 10 pp. electronic version.

Johnston, J. H. "Documentary Evidence of the Relations of Negroes and Indians." *Journal of Negro History* 14 (1929): 21–43.

Johnston, Josephine. "Resisting a Genetic Identity: The Black Seminoles and Genetic Tests of Ancestry." *Journal of Law, Medicine, and Ethics* 31 (2003): 262–. 23 pp. electronic version.

Jones, Rhett S. "Black and Native American Relations before 1800." *Western Journal of Black Studies* 1 (1977): 151–63.

Kansas City Star. "Report on the Five Civilized Tribes, 1897, by the Kansas City *Star,* 7 February 1897." *Chronicles of Oklahoma* 48 (1970): 416–30.

Katz, William L. "Black and Indian Co-operation and Resistance to Slavery." *Freedomways* 17 (1977): 164–74.

——. "Justice and African Seminoles." *Black World Today,* March 15, 2001. http://www.tbwt .com/content/article.asp?articleid=221 (March 16, 2001).

Keen, Cathy. "Florida Researchers Launch First Excavation of Black Seminole Town." *University of Florida News,* June 14, 2001. http://news.ufl.edu/2001/06/14/black-seminole/ (December 9, 2006).

Keiff, J. W. "The Last Days of the Seminoles." *Sturm's Oklahoma Magazine* 4 (1907): 1–4.

Keilman, John. "Bloodlines Drawn over Money." *Chicago Tribune,* April 4, 2002.

Kensell, Lewis A. "Phases of Reconstruction in the Choctaw Nation." *Chronicles of Oklahoma* 47 (1969): 138–53.

Kersey, Harry A., Jr. "The Seminole Negroes of Andros Island Revisited: Some New Pieces to an Old Puzzle." *Florida Anthropologist* 34 (1981): 169–76.

King, Henry. "The Indian Country." *Century Magazine* 30 (1885): 599–606.

Klos, George. "Black Seminoles in Territorial Florida." *Southern Historian* 10 (1989): 26–42.

——. "Blacks and the Seminole Removal Debate, 1821–1835." *Florida Historical Quarterly* 68 (1989): 55–78.

Kly, Y. N. "The Gullah War, 1739–1858." In *The Legacy of Ibo Landing: Gullah Roots of African American Culture,* Marquetta L. Goodwine, ed. Atlanta: Clarity Press, 1998.

Kopytoff, Barbara K. "Colonial Treaty as Sacred Charter of the Jamaican Maroons." *Ethnohistory* 26 (1979): 45–64.

Kremer, Gary R. "For Justice and a Fee: James Milton Turner and the Cherokee Freedmen." *Chronicles of Oklahoma* 58 (1980): 377–91.

Krogman, Wilton M. "The Racial Composition of the Seminole Indians of Florida and Oklahoma." *Journal of Negro History* 19 (1934): 412–30.

——. "The Racial Type of the Seminole Indians of Florida and Oklahoma." *Florida Anthropologist* 1 (1948): 61–73.

——. "Vital Data on the Population of the Seminole Indians of Florida and Oklahoma." *Human Biology* 7 (1935): 335–49.

Landers, Jane G. "Acquisition and Loss on a Spanish Frontier: The Free Black Homesteaders of Florida, 1784–1821." In *Against the Odds: Free Blacks in the Slave Societies of the Americas,* Jane G. Landers, ed. London, and Portland, Oreg.: Frank Cass, 1996.

——. "African Presence in Early Spanish Colonization of the Caribbean and Southeastern Borderlands." In *Archaeological and Historical Perspectives on the Spanish Borderlands East.* Vol. 2 of *Columbian Consequences,* David Hurst Thomas, ed., 3 vols. Washington, D.C.: Smithsonian Institution Press, 1990.

——. "Africans and Native Americans on the Spanish Florida Frontier." In *Beyond Black and Red: African-Native Relations in Colonial Latin America,* Matthew Restall, ed. Albuquerque: University of New Mexico Press, 2005.

——. "Black Community and Culture in the Southeastern Borderlands." *Journal of the Early Republic* 18 (1998): 117–34.

——. "Black-Indian Interaction in Spanish Florida." *Colonial Latin American Historical Review* 3 (1993): 141–62.

——. "The Central African Presence in Spanish Maroon Communities." In *Central Africans and Cultural Transformations in the American Diaspora,* Linda M. Heywood, ed. Cambridge: Cambridge University Press, 2002.

——. "Cimarrón Ethnicity and Cultural Adaptation in the Spanish Domains of the Circum-Caribbean, 1503–1763." In *Identity in the Shadow of Slavery,* Paul E. Lovejoy, ed. London and New York: Continuum, 2000.

——. "Free Black Plantations and Economy in East Florida, 1784–1821." In *Colonial Plantations and Economy in Florida,* Jane G. Landers, ed. Gainesville: University Press of Florida, 2000.

——. "Gracia Real de Santa Terese de Mose: A Free Black Town in Spanish Colonial Florida." *American Historical Review* 95 (1990): 9–30.

——. Introduction to *Colonial Plantations and Economy in Florida,* Jane G. Landers, ed. Gainesville: University Press of Florida, 2000.

——. "Spanish Sanctuary: Fugitive Slaves in Florida, 1687–1790." *Florida Historical Quarterly* 62 (1984): 296–313.

——. "Traditions of African American Freedom and Community in Spanish Florida." In *The African American Heritage of Florida,* David R. Colburn and Jane G. Landers, eds. Gainesville: University Press of Florida, 1995.

Lawal, Babatunde. "Reclaiming the Past: Yoruba Elements in African American Arts." In *The Yoruba Diaspora in the Atlantic World,* Toyin Talola and Matt D. Childs, eds. Bloomington: Indiana University Press, 2004.

"A Letter from Koweta Mission, 1850." *Chronicles of Oklahoma* 46 (1968): 338–40.

Lewin, Sam. "Black Seminoles See Case Dismissed." *Native American Times* (Tulsa), July 7, 2004.

Lewitt, Robert T. "Indian Missions and Antislavery Sentiments: A Conflict of Evangelical and Humanitarian Ideals." *Mississippi Valley Historical Review* 50 (1963): 39–55.

Littlefield, Daniel F., Jr. "Black Dreams and 'Free' Homes: The Oklahoma Territory, 1891–1894." *Phylon* 34 (1973): 342–57.

Littlefield, Daniel F., Jr., and Mary Ann Littlefield. "The Beams Family: Free Blacks in Indian Territory." *Journal of Negro History* 61 (1976): 16–35.

Littlefield, Daniel F., Jr., and Lonnie E. Underhill. "The Crazy Snake 'Uprising' of 1909: A Red, Black, or White Affair?" *Arizona and the West* 20 (1978–79): 307–24.

——. "Negro Marshals in Indian Territory." *Journal of Negro History* 56 (1971): 77–87.

——. "Slave 'Revolt' in the Cherokee Nation, 1842." *American Indian Quarterly* 3 (1977): 121–31.

Lollar, Wayne B. "Seminole-U.S. Financial Relations 1823–1866." *Chronicles of Oklahoma* 50 (1972): 190–98.

"Lone Dove Hill: A Place in History, Four and One-Half Miles Northwest of Sasakwa in Seminole County." *Chronicles of Oklahoma* 45 (1967): 477–78.

"Looking for Angola." *Quest (Magazine of the University of Central Florida, College of Arts and Sciences)* (Spring 2005): 20.

Loomis, Augustus W. "Scenes in the Indian Territory, Kowetah Mission." *Chronicles of Oklahoma* 46 (1968): 64–72.

Loughlin, Patricia. "The Battle of the Historians of Round Mountain: An Examination of Muriel Wright and Angie Debo." *Heritage of the Great Plains* 31 (1998): 4–18.

Lovett, Laura L. " 'African and Cherokee by Choice': Race and Resistance under Legalized Segregation." In *Confounding the Color Line: The Indian-Black Experience in North America,* James F. Brooks, ed. Lincoln: University of Nebraska Press, 2002.

Luvall, J. A. G. "The Indian Territory, the Negroe's Friend." *The Voice* (March 1907): 135–38.

Lydick, Robyn, and Bob Doucette. "Rivals Both Lose Bids for Seminoles' Top Office." *Daily Oklahoman,* July 18, 2001.

MacKay, Fergus. "The Rights of Indigenous Peoples in International Law." In *From Concept to Design: Creating an International Environmental Ombudsperson.* San José, Costa Rica: Earth Council, 1998.

——. "The Rights of Maroons in International Human Rights Law." *Cultural Survival* 25, no. 4 (2002): 10 pp. http://www.cs.org/publications/csq/csq-article.cfm?id=1395 (December 9, 2006).

Mackey, Alice H. "Father Murrow: Civil War Period." *Chronicles of Oklahoma* 12 (1934): 55–65.

Macmillan, E. A. "Indian Standard Lowered by Seminole Negroes Sent to Oklahoma." *Daily Oklahoman,* February 15, 1914.

McAdam, Rezin W. "An Indian Commonwealth." *Harper's New Monthly Magazine* 87 (1893): 884–97.

McAuliffe, Denny. "African American Indians." http://www.reznetnews.org (September 17, 2003).

McCabe, Scott. "Searching for Peliklakaha, Land of the Forgotten Seminoles." *Palm Beach (Fla.) Post,* August 20, 2001.

McLoughlin, William G. "The Choctaw Slave Burning: A Crisis in Mission Work among the Indians." *Journal of the West* 13 (1974): 113–27.

——. "Indian Slaveholders and Presbyterian Missionaries 1837–1861." *Church History* 42 (1973): 535–51.

——. "Red Indians, Black Slavery, and White Racism: America's Slaveholding Indians." *American Quarterly* 26 (1974): 367–85.

——. " Red, White, and Black in the Antebellum South." *Baptist History and Heritage* 7 (1972): 69–75.

McLoughlin, William G., and Walter H. Conser, Jr. "The Cherokees in Transition: A Statistical Analysis of the Federal Cherokee Census of 1835." *Journal of American History* 65 (1977): 678–704.

McNeil, Kenneth. "Confederate Treaties with the Tribes of the Indian Territories." *Chronicles of Oklahoma* 42 (1964): 408–20.

McNutt, Michael. "Seminoles OK Government Changes." *Daily Oklahoman,* July 7, 2000.

Megehee, Mark K. "Creek Nativism since 1865." *Chronicles of Oklahoma* 56 (1978): 282–97.

Melaku, Martha. "Seeking Acceptance: Are the Black Seminoles Native Americans? Sylvia Davis v. the United States of America." *American Indian Law Review* 27 (2002–2003): 539–52.

Mellinger, Philip. "Discrimination and Statehood in Oklahoma." *Chronicles of Oklahoma* 49 (1971): 340–78.

Melmer, David. "Dialogue Opens on Black Indians in Indian Country." *Indian Country Today,* November 29, 2000.

Meserve, John B. " Chief Isparhecher." *Chronicles of Oklahoma* 10 (1932): 52–76.

——. "Chief Opothleyohola." *Chronicles of Oklahoma* 9 (1931): 439–53.

——. "The MacIntoshes." *Chronicles of Oklahoma* 10 (1932): 310–25.

——. "The Plea of Crazy Snake (Chitto Harjo)." *Chronicles of Oklahoma* 11 (1933): 899–911.

Methvin, John J. "Reminiscences of Life among the Indians." *Chronicles of Oklahoma* 5 (1927): 166–179.

Metz, Andrew. "A Nation Divided: Seminole Rift More Than a Black-and-White Issue." *Newsday,* December 22, 2003.

Meyer, Melissa L. "American Indian Blood Quantum Requirements: Blood Is Thicker than Family." In *Over the Edge: Remapping the American West,* Valerie J. Matsumoto and Blake Allmendinger, eds. Berkeley: University of California Press, 1999.

Micco, Melinda B. " 'Blood and Money': The Case of the Seminole Freedmen and Seminole Indians in Oklahoma." In *Crossing Waters, Crossing Worlds: The African Diaspora in Indian Country,* Tiya Miles and Sharon P. Holland, eds. Durham, N.C., and London: Duke University Press, 2006.

Miles, Tiya. "Uncle Tom Was an Indian: Tracing the Red in Black Slavery." In *Confounding the Color Line: The Indian-Black Experience in North America,* James F. Brooks, ed. Lincoln: University of Nebraska Press, 2002.

Miles, Tiya, and Celia E. Naylor-Ojurongbe. "African-Americans in Indian Societies." In *Handbook of North American Indians,* vol. 14, *Southeast,* Raymond D. Fogelson, ed. Washington, D.C.: Smithsonian Institution Press, 2004.

Miley, Cora. "Life among the Seminoles." *Harlow's Weekly* 21 (December 23, 1922): 6–7.

Miller, Susan A. "Seminoles and Africans under Seminole Law: Sources and Discourses of Tribal Sovereignty and 'Black Indian' Entitlement." *Wicazo Sa Review* 20 (2005): 23–47.

Milligan, John D. "Slave Rebelliousness and the Florida Maroon." *Prologue* 6 (1974): 4–18.

Minges, Patrick N. "Beneath the Underdog: Race, Religion, and the Trail of Tears." *American Indian Quarterly* 25 (2001): 453–79.

Moore, Jessie R. "The Five Great Indian Nations: The Part They Played on Behalf of the Confederacy in the War between the States." *Chronicles of Oklahoma* 29 (1951): 324–36.

Moore, John H. "The Mvskoke National Question in Oklahoma." *Science and Society* 52 (1988): 163–90.

Morrison, James D. "Notes on Abolitionism in the Choctaw Nation." *Chronicles of Oklahoma* 38 (1960): 78–84.

Morton, Ohland. "Confederate Government Relations with the Five Civilized Tribes." Parts 1 and 2. *Chronicles of Oklahoma* 31 (1953): 189–204; 299–322.

——. "Reconstruction in the Creek Nation." *Chronicles of Oklahoma* 9 (1931): 171–79.

Mulroy, Kevin. "Ethnogenesis and Ethnohistory of the Seminole Maroons." *Journal of World History* 4 (1993): 287–305.

——. "John Horse." In *American National Biography Online.* Oxford and London: American Council of Learned Societies; Oxford University Press, 1999. http://www.anb.org/arti cles/20/20-01870.html, December 2003 update (January 20, 2004).

——. "Seminole Maroons." In *Handbook of North American Indians,* vol. 14, *Southeast,* Raymond D. Fogelson, ed. Washington, D.C.: Smithsonian Institution Press, 2004.

Mundende, D. Chongo. "The Undesirable Oklahomans: Black Immigration to Western Canada." *Chronicles of Oklahoma* 76 (1998): 282–97.

Murrow, Joseph S. "Biographical Sketch of John Jumper." *Home Mission Monthly* 14 (1892): 35–36.

Nash, Gary B. "The Hidden History of Mestizo America." *Journal of American History* 82 (1995): 941–62.

Naylor-Ojurongbe, Celia E. " 'Born and Raised among These People, I Don't Want to Know Any Other': Slaves' Acculturation in Nineteenth-Century Indian Territory." In *Confounding the Color Line: The Indian-Black Experience in North America,* James F. Brooks, ed. Lincoln: University of Nebraska Press, 2002.

Nelson, John C. "An Alliance Asunder: The Dissolution of the Seminole-Black Partnership." *Michigan Journal of History* (Fall 2004): http://www.umich.edu/historyj/papers/fall2004/ nelson.htm (November 1, 2005).

"Notes and Documents: Fort Gibson in Early Days." *Chronicles of Oklahoma* 23 (1945): 291–93.

Ogunleye, Tolagbe. "The Self-Emancipated Africans of Florida: Pan-African Nationalists in the 'New World.' " *Journal of Black Studies* 27 (1996): 24–38.

"Oklahoma and Statehood." *Outlook* 85 (March 30, 1907): 727–28.

"Oklahoma's Racial Constitution." *Outlook* 87 (October 5, 1907): 229.

Parker, Susan R. "The Cattle Trade in East Florida, 1784–1821." In *Colonial Plantations and Economy in Florida,* Jane G. Landers, ed. Gainesville: University Press of Florida, 2000.

——. "Success through Diversification: Francis Philip Fatio's New Switzerland Plantation." In *Colonial Plantations and Economy in Florida,* Jane G. Landers, ed. Gainesville: University Press of Florida, 2000.

Paschal, Andrew G. "History Shows Indians and Blacks Natural Allies in Battle against American Treachery." *Muhammad Speaks* 8 (November 22, 1968): 27, 30, 32.

Pascoe, Peggy. "Race, Gender, and Intercultural Relatives: The Case of Interracial Marriage." In *Writing the Range: Race, Class, and Culture in the Women's West,* Elizabeth Jameson and Susan Armitage, eds. Norman: University of Oklahoma Press, 1997.

Payne, John Howard. "The Green Corn Dance." *Chronicles of Oklahoma* 10 (1932): 170–95.

Payne, Michael. " 'Deemed Unsuitable': Black Pioneers in Western Canada." Canadian Encyclopedia (online version). http://www.thecanadianencyclopedia.com (February 22, 2006).

Peabody, Alvin. "Black Seminoles File Lawsuit against Federal Government." *Washington (D.C.) Informer,* January 24, 1996.

Peck, Solomon. "History of the Missions of the Baptist General Convention." In *History of the American Missions to the Heathen.* Worcester, Mass.: Spooner and Howland, 1840.

Perdue, Theda. "Cherokee Planters: The Development of Plantation Slavery before Removal." In *The Cherokee Nation: A Troubled History,* Duane H. King, ed. Knoxville: University of Tennessee Press, 1979.

——. "Cherokee Planters, Black Slaves, and African Colonization." *Chronicles of Oklahoma* 60 (1982): 322–31.

——. "Race and Culture: Writing the Ethnohistory of the Early South." *Ethnohistory* 51 (2004): 701–33.

——. "A Reply to Saunt et al." *Ethnohistory* 53 (2006): 407.

Peterson, Jacqueline, and Jennifer S. H. Brown. Introduction to *The New Peoples: Being and Becoming Métis in North America,* Jacqueline Peterson and Jennifer S. H. Brown, eds. Lincoln: University of Nebraska Press, 1985.

Phillips, W. B. "Jim Noble: Oklahoma's Negro Governor." *Phylon* 20 (1959): 90–92.

Pierpoint, Mary. "Jim Crow Legacy Still Disrupts Oklahoma Seminoles." *Indian Country Today,* March 5, 2002.

Porter, Kenneth W. "Billy Bowlegs (Holata Micco) in the Seminole Wars." Part 1. *Florida Historical Quarterly* 45 (1967): 210–43.

——. "Billy Bowlegs (Holata Micco) in the Civil War." Part 2. *Florida Historical Quarterly* 45 (1967): 391–401; 46 (1967): 148.

——. "The Cowkeeper Dynasty of the Seminole Nation." *Florida Historical Quarterly* 30 (1952): 341–49.

——. "Davy Crockett and John Horse: A Possible Origin of the Coonskin Story." *American Literature* 15 (1943): 10–15.

——. "The Early Life of Louis Pachecho, Né Fatio." *Negro History Bulletin* 7 (1943): 52–53, 67–70.

——. "The Episode of Osceola's Wife—Fact or Fiction?" *Florida Historical Quarterly* 26 (1947): 92–98.

——. "Farewell to John Horse: An Episode of Seminole Negro Folk History." *Phylon* 8 (1947): 265–73.

——. "The Founder of the Seminole Nation: Secoffee or Cowkeeper?" *Florida Historical Quarterly* 27 (1949): 362–84.

——. "Lament for Wild Cat." *Phylon* 4 (1943): 39–48.

——. "Louis Pachecho: The Man and the Myth." *Journal of Negro History* 28 (1943): 65–72.

——. "Negro Guides and Interpreters in the Early Stages of the Seminole War, 28 December 1835–6 March 1837." *Journal of Negro History* 35 (1950): 174–182.

——. "Negroes and Indians on the Texas Frontier, 1831–1876: A Study in Race and Culture." *Journal of Negro History* 41 (1956): 185–214.

——. "Negroes and Indians on the Texas Frontier, 1834–1874." *Southwestern Historical Quarterly* 53 (1949): 151–63.

——. "Notes on the Seminole Negroes in the Bahamas." *Florida Historical Quarterly* 24 (1945): 56–60.

——. "Origins of the St. John's River Seminoles: Were They Mikasuki?" *Florida Anthropologist* 4 (1951): 39–45.

——. "Osceola and the Negroes." *Florida Historical Quarterly* 33 (1955): 235–39.

——. "Relations between Negroes and Indians within the Present Limits of the United States." *Journal of Negro History* 17 (1932): 287–367.

——. Review of *Africans and Seminoles: From Removal to Emancipation,* by Daniel F. Littlefield, Jr. *Pacific Historical Review* 48 (1979): 423–24.

——. "Seminole Flight from Fort Marion." *Florida Historical Quarterly* 22 (1944): 112–33.

——. "Seminole in Mexico, 1850–1861." *Chronicles of Oklahoma* 29 (1951): 153–68.

——. "Thlonoto-sassa: A Note on an Obscure Seminole Village of the Early 1820s," *Florida Anthropologist* 13 (1960): 115–19.

——. "Three Fighters for Freedom." *Journal of Negro History* 28 (1943): 51–72.

——. "Tiger Tail." *Florida Historical Quarterly* 24 (1946): 261–71.

Pratt, Carla D. "Tribes and Tribulations: Beyond Sovereign Immunity and toward Reparation and Reconciliation for the Estelusti." *Washington and Lee Race Ethnic Ancestry Law Journal* 11 (2005): 61–132.

Previch, Chad. "Freedmen to Become Citizens." *Daily Oklahoman,* March 9, 2006.

Price, Edward T. "A Geographic Analysis of White-Negro-Indian Racial Mixtures in the Eastern United States." *Annals of the Association of American Geographers* 43 (1953): 138–55.

Price, Richard. Introduction to *Maroon Societies: Rebel Slave Communities in the Americas,* Richard Price, ed. Rev. ed. Baltimore: Johns Hopkins University Press, 1979.

——. "Maroons: Rebel Slaves in the Americas." In *1992 Festival of American Folklife,* Peter Seitel, ed. Program. Washington, D.C.: Smithsonian Institution, 1992.

——. "Maroons in the Americas: Heroic Pasts, Ambiguous Presents, Uncertain Futures." *Cultural Survival* 25, no. 4 (2002): 3 pp. http://www.cs.org/publications/csq/csq-article.cfm?id=1394 (December 9, 2006).

Ralph, Julian. "The Unique Plight of the Five Nations." *Harper's Weekly* 40 (January 4, 1896): 10–15.

Rampp, Lary C. "Confederate Sinking of the *J. R. Williams.*" *Journal of the West* 11 (1972): 43–50.

——. "Negro Troop Activity in Indian Territory, 1863–1865." *Chronicles of Oklahoma* 47 (1969): 531–59.

Reed, Ora E. "The Passing of the Seminoles." *Sturm's Oklahoma Magazine* 3 (September 1906): 11–12.

Richards, Eugene S. "Trends of Negro Life in Oklahoma as Reflected by Census Reports." *Journal of Negro History* 33 (1948): 38–52.

Richards, Eugene S., and Mozell C. Hill. "The Negroes in Oklahoma: A Demographic Study." In *Report of the Third Conference of Negro Land Grant Colleges for Coordinating a Program of Co-operative Social Studies.* Washington, D.C.: Howard University Press, 1946.

Richards, Ira D. "The Battle of Poison Spring." *Arkansas Historical Quarterly* 18 (1959): 338–49.

Riordan, Patrick. "Finding Freedom in Florida: Native Peoples, African Americans, and Colonists, 1670–1816." *Florida Historical Quarterly* 75 (1996): 24–43.

Rivers, Larry E. "A Troublesome Property: Master-Slave Relations in Florida, 1821–1865." In *The African American Heritage of Florida,* David R. Colburn and Jane G. Landers, eds. Gainesville: University Press of Florida, 1995.

Robinson, Judy Gibbs. "Freedmen's Descendants Discover Past." *Daily Oklahoman,* June 3, 2005.

Routh, Eugene C. "Henry Frieland Buckner." *Chronicles of Oklahoma* 14 (1936): 455–66.

Russell, Orpha B. "Ekvn-hv-Iwuce, Site of Oklahoma's First Civil War Battle." *Chronicles of Oklahoma* 29 (1951): 401–407.

——. "William G. Bruner, Member of the House of Kings, Creek Nation." *Chronicles of Oklahoma* 30 (1952): 397–407.

Saito, Netsu Taylor. "From Slavery and Seminoles to AIDS in South Africa: An Essay on Race and Property in International Law." *Villanova Law Review* 45 (2000): 1135–94.

Sattler, Richard A. "Cowboys and Indians: Creek and Seminole Stock Raising, 1700–1900." *American Indian Culture and Research Journal* 22 (1998): 79–99.

——. "Remnants, Renegades, and Runaways: Seminole Ethnogenesis Reconsidered." In *History, Power, and Identity: Ethnogenesis in the Americas,* Jonathan D. Hill, ed. Iowa City: University of Iowa Press, 1996.

——. "Seminole in the West." In *Handbook of North American Indians,* vol. 14, *Southeast,* Raymond D. Fogelson, ed. Washington, D.C.: Smithsonian Institution Press, 2004.

——. "Women's Status among the Muskogee and Cherokee." In *Women and Power in Native North America,* Laura F. Klein and Lillian A. Ackerman, eds. Norman: University of Oklahoma Press, 1995.

Saunt, Claudio. " 'The English Has Now a Mind to Make Slaves of Them All': Creeks, Seminoles, and the Problem of Slavery." *American Indian Quarterly* 22 (1998): 157–80.

——. "The Paradox of Freedom: Tribal Sovereignty and Emancipation during the Reconstruction of Indian Territory." *Journal of Southern History* 70 (2004): 63–94.

——. "Taking Account of Property: Stratification among the Creek Indians in the Early Nineteenth-Century." *William and Mary Quarterly* 57 (2000): 733–60.

Saunt, Claudio, et al. "Rethinking Race and Culture in the Early South." *Ethnohistory* 53 (2006): 399–405.

Savage, William S. "The Negro in the Western Movement." *Journal of Negro History* 25 (1940): 531–39.

——. "The Role of Negro Soldiers in Protecting the Indian Territory from Intruders." *Journal of Negro History* 36 (1951): 25–34.

Schafer, Daniel L. "A Class of People Neither Freemen nor Slaves: From Spanish to American Race Relations in Florida, 1821 to 1861." *Journal of Social History* 26 (1993): 587–610.

——. "St. Augustine's British Years." Special issue, *El Escribano: The St. Augustine Journal of History* 38 (2001).

——. " 'Yellow Silk Ferret Tied round Their Wrists': African Americans in British East Florida, 1763–1784." In *The African American Heritage of Florida,* David R. Colburn and Jane G. Landers, eds. Gainesville: University Press of Florida, 1995.

——. "Zephaniah Kingsley's Laurel Grove Plantation, 1803–1813." In *Colonial Plantations and Economy in Florida,* Jane G. Landers, ed. Gainesville: University Press of Florida, 2000.

Scraper, Brian. "Oklahoma Seminoles to Refile Lawsuit." *Oklahoma Daily,* July 14, 2004.

Searcy, Martha C. "The Introduction of African Slavery into the Creek Nation." *Georgia Historical Quarterly* 66 (1981): 21–32.

Sefton, James E. "Black Slaves, Red Masters, White Middlemen: A Congressional Debate of 1852." *Florida Historical Quarterly* 51 (1972): 113–28.

"The Seminoles, or History Corrected." *Indian Journal,* April 12, 1877.

Shepard, R. Bruce. "North to the Promised Land: Black Migration to the Canadian Plains." *Chronicles of Oklahoma* 66 (1988): 306–27.

Shirk, G. H. "The Place of Indian Territory in the Command Structure of the Civil War." *Chronicles of Oklahoma* 45 (1967): 464–71.

Shoemaker, Arthur. "The Battle of Chustenahlah." *Chronicles of Oklahoma* 38 (1960): 180–84.

Shoemaker, Nancy. "How Indians Got to Be Red." *American Historical Review* 102 (1997): 625–44.

"Slavery among the Indians." *Southern Literary Messenger* 28 (1859): 333–35.

Smith, Julia F. "Slavetrading in Antebellum Florida." *Florida Historical Quarterly* 50 (1972): 252–61.

Smith, Rhea M. "Racial Strains in Florida." *Florida Historical Quarterly* 11 (1932): 118–30.

Southall, Eugene P. "Negroes in Florida Prior to the Civil War." *Journal of Negro History* 19 (1934): 16–86.

Speck, Frank G. "Negroes and the Creek Nation." *Southern Workman* 37 (1908): 106–10.

Spoehr, Alexander. "Camp, Clan, and Kin among the Cow Creek Seminole of Florida." *Publications of the Field Museum of Natural History, Chicago, Anthropological Series* 33, no. 1 (1941): 1–27.

——. "Changing Kinship Systems: A Study in the Acculturation of the Creek, Cherokee, and Choctaw." *Publications of the Field Museum of Natural History, Chicago, Anthropological Series* 33, no. 4 (1947): 159–235.

——. "The Florida Seminole Camp." *Publications of the Field Museum of Natural History, Chicago, Anthropological Series* 33, no. 3 (1944): 115–50.

——. "'Friends' among the Seminoles." *Chronicles of Oklahoma* 19 (1941): 252.

——. "Kinship System of the Seminole." *Publications of the Field Museum of Natural History, Chicago, Anthropological Series* 33, no. 2 (1942): 29–113.

——. "Oklahoma Seminole Towns." *Chronicles of Oklahoma* 19 (1941): 377–80.

Springer, Debi. "Dig Planned at Likely Site of Slave Haven." *Herald Tribune* (Southwest Fla.), October 24, 2004.

Stack, Megan K. "Tribal Rift Is a Matter of Blood." *Los Angeles Times,* May 16, 2002.

Staples, Brent. "The Black Seminole Indians Keep Fighting for Equality in the American West." *New York Times,* November 18, 2003.

——. "The Seminole Tribe, Running from History." Editorial Observer, *New York Times,* April 21, 2002.

——. "When Racial Discrimination Is Not Just Black and White." *New York Times,* September 12, 2003.

Stowell, Daniel W. Introduction to *Balancing Evils Judiciously: The Proslavery Writings of Zephaniah Kingsley,* Daniel W. Stowell, ed. Gainesville: University Press of Florida, 2000.

Strickland, A. E. "Toward the Promised Land: The Exodus to Kansas and Afterward." *Missouri Historical Review* 69 (1975): 376–412.

Sturm, Circe. "Blood Politics, Racial Classification, and Cherokee National Identity: The

Trials and Tribulations of the Cherokee Freedmen." In *Confounding the Color Line: The Indian-Black Experience in North America,* James F. Brooks, ed. Lincoln: University of Nebraska Press, 2002.

Sturtevant, William C. "Creek into Seminole." In *North American Indians in Historical Perspective,* Eleanor Burke Leacock and Nancy Oestreich Lurie, eds. New York: Random House, 1971.

——. "The Medicine Bundles and Busks of the Florida Seminoles." *Florida Anthropologist* 7 (1954): 31–70.

——. Review of *Africans and Seminoles: From Removal to Emancipation,* by Daniel F. Littlefield, Jr. *American Anthropologist* 81 (1979): 916–17.

——. "Seminole Myths of the Origin of Races." *Ethnohistory* 10 (1963): 80–85.

Sturtevant, William C., and Jessica R. Cattelino, "Florida Seminole and Miccosukee." In *Handbook of North American Indians,* vol. 14, *Southeast,* Raymond D. Fogelson, ed. Washington, D.C.: Smithsonian Institution Press, 2004.

Sutton, Martin. "A Civil War Experience of Some Arkansas Women in Indian Territory." Leroy H. Fischer, ed. and annotator. *Chronicles of Oklahoma* 57 (1979): 137–63.

TallBear, Kimberly. "DNA, Blood, and Racializing the Tribe." *Wicazo Sa Review* 18 (2003): 81–107.

TePaske, John J. "The Fugitive Slave: Intercolonial Rivalry and Spanish Slave Policy, 1687–1764." In *Eighteenth-Century Florida and Its Borderlands,* Samuel Proctor, ed. Gainesville: University of Florida Press, 1975.

Thomas, Robert K. Afterword to *The New Peoples: Being and Becoming Métis in North America,* Jacqueline Peterson and Jennifer S. H. Brown, eds. Lincoln: University of Nebraska Press, 1985.

Thornton, John M. "The Seminole Nation: A Model Indian Government." *Indian Journal,* March 27, 1896.

Thybony, Scott. "Against All Odds, Black Seminole Won Their Freedom." *Smithsonian* 22 (1991): 90–101.

Tolson, Arthur L. "Black Towns of Oklahoma." *Black Scholar* 1 (1970): 18–23.

Trees, May. "Socioeconomic Reconstruction in the Seminole Nation, 1865–1870." *Journal of the West* 12 (1973): 490–98.

Trevathan, Robert E. "School Days at Emahaka Academy." *Chronicles of Oklahoma* 38 (1960): 265–73.

"Tribute to Alice Brown Davis: Delivered by Mrs. William S. Key." *Chronicles of Oklahoma* 42 (1965): 96–101.

Trickett, Dean. "The Civil War in the Indian Territory, 1861." *Chronicles of Oklahoma* 17 (1939): 315–27, 401–12; 18 (1940): 142–53, 266–80.

——. "The Civil War in the Indian Territory, 1862." *Chronicles of Oklahoma* 19 (1941): 55–69, 381–96.

Troper, Harold M. "The Creek-Negroes of Oklahoma and Canadian Immigration, 1909–1911." *Canadian Historical Review* 53 (1972): 272–88.

Turner, C. W. "Events among the Muskogees during Sixty Years." *Chronicles of Oklahoma* 10 (1932): 21–34.

Waldowski, Paula. "Alice Brown Davis: A Leader of Her People." *Chronicles of Oklahoma* 58 (1980): 455–63.

Walker, Willard B. "Creek Confederacy before Removal." In *Handbook of North American Indians,* vol. 14, *Southeast,* Raymond D. Fogelson, ed. Washington, D.C.: Smithsonian Institution Press, 2004.

Wallenstein, Peter. "Native Americans Are White, African Americans Are Not: Racial Identity, Marriage, Inheritance, and the Law in Oklahoma, 1907–1967." *Journal of the West* 39 (2000): 55–63.

Warde, Mary Jane. "Now the Wolf Has Come: The Civilian Civil War in the Indian Territory." *Chronicles of Oklahoma* 71 (1993): 64–87.

Warren, Hanna R. "Reconstruction in the Cherokee Nation." *Chronicles of Oklahoma* 45 (1967): 180–89.

Washington, Booker T. "Boley, a Negro Town in the West." *Outlook* 88 (1908): 28–31.

Watts, Jill. " 'We Do Not Live for Ourselves Only': Seminole Black Perceptions and the Second Seminole War." *UCLA Historical Journal* 7 (1986): 5–28.

Webb, Alex S. "Campaigning in Florida in 1855." *Journal of the Military Service Institution* 45 (1909): 397–429.

Weik, Terrance M. "The Archaeology of Maroon Societies in the Americas: Resistance, Cultural Continuity, and Transformation in the African Diaspora." *Historical Archaeology* 31 (1997): 81–92.

Weisman, Brent R. "The Plantation System of the Florida Seminole Indians and Black Seminoles during the Colonial Era." In *Colonial Plantations and Economy in Florida*, Jane G. Landers, ed. Gainesville: University Press of Florida, 2000.

Welburn, Ron. "A Most Secret Identity: Native American Assimilation and Identity Resistance in African America." In *Confounding the Color Line: The Indian-Black Experience in North America*, James F. Brooks, ed. Lincoln: University of Nebraska Press, 2002.

Welch, Louise. "Seminole Colonization in Oklahoma." *Chronicles of Oklahoma* 54 (1976): 77–103.

Welsh, Michael. "The Missionary Spirit: Protestantism among the Oklahoma Seminoles, 1842–1885." *Chronicles of Oklahoma* 61 (1983): 28–47.

West, Jean M. "Slaves and Seminoles: Florida's Freedom Seekers." http://www.slaveryiname rica.org/history/hs_es_seminole.htm (March 4, 2006).

Wichs, H. S. "The Opening of Oklahoma." *Chronicles of Oklahoma* 4 (1926): 128–42.

Wickett, Murray R. "The Fear of 'Negro Domination': The Rise of Segregation and Disfranchisement in Oklahoma." *Chronicles of Oklahoma* 78 (2000): 44–65.

Wilkins, David. "Red, Black, and Bruised." http://www.alternet.org/rights/17111/ (November 4, 2003).

Willey, William J. "The Second Federal Invasion of the Indian Territory." *Chronicles of Oklahoma* 44 (1966): 420–30.

Williams, Nudie E. "Black Men Who Wore the 'Star.' " *Chronicles of Oklahoma* 59 (1981): 83–90.

Willis, William S., Jr. "Divide and Rule: Red, White, and Black in the South East." In *Red, White, and Black: Symposium on Indians in the Old South*, Charles M. Hudson, ed. Athens: University of Georgia Press, 1971.

Willson, Walt. "Freedmen in Indian Territory during Reconstruction." *Chronicles of Oklahoma* 49 (1971): 230–44.

Wilson, Charles Emily. "Texas Seminole Scouts." In *1992 Festival of American Folklife*, Peter Seitel, ed. Program. Washington, D.C.: Smithsonian Institution, 1992.

Wittner, Marcilene. "African Influences on Florida Indian Patchwork." *Southeastern College Art Conference (SECAC) Review* 11 (1989): 269–75.

Woodhull, Frost. "The Seminole Indian Scouts on the Border." *Frontier Times* 15 (1937): 118–27.

"The Word Maroon." *Seminole Quarterly* (Newsletter of the National Association of Black Seminoles) 1, no. 1 (Fall 1992): 3.

Wright, Irene. "Dispatches of Spanish Officials Bearing on the Free Negro Settlement of Gracia Real de Santa Terese de Mose, Florida." *Journal of Negro History* 9 (1924): 144–95.

Wright, James Leitch, Jr. "Blacks in British East Florida." *Florida Historical Quarterly* 54 (1976): 425–42.

——. "A Note on the First Seminole War as Seen by the Indians, Negroes, and Their British Advisers." *Journal of Southern History* 34 (1968): 565–75.

Wright, Muriel H. "Colonel Cooper's Civil War Report on the Battle of Round Mountain." *Chronicles of Oklahoma* 39 (1961): 352–97.

——. "General Douglas H. Cooper, C.S.A." *Chronicles of Oklahoma* 32 (1953): 142–84.

——. "Seal of the Seminole Nation." *Chronicles of Oklahoma* 34 (1956): 262–71.

——. "Seals of the Five Civilized Tribes." *Chronicles of Oklahoma* 40 (1962): 214–18.

Wright, Muriel H., and Leroy H. Fischer. "Oklahoma Civil War Sites." *Chronicles of Oklahoma* 44 (1966): 158–215.

Wrone, David R., ed. "The Cherokee Act of Emancipation." *Journal of Ethnic Studies* 1 (1973): 87–90.

Yelvington, Kevin A. Foreword to *True-Born Maroons,* by Kenneth M. Bilby. Gainesville: University Press of Florida, 2005.

Zellar, Gary. "First to Fight for Freedom: African Creek Soldiers Enter the Civil War." *Journal of the Indian Wars* 1 (2000): 1–20.

——. "Occupying the Middle Ground: African Creeks in the First Indian Home Guards, 1862–1865." *Chronicles of Oklahoma* 76 (1998): 48–71.

NEWSPAPERS AND PERIODICALS

Most newspaper and periodical articles are listed by author or title in "Articles and Essays." This section includes newspaper and periodical runs, together with references for individual articles cited without a main entry.

Alva (Oklahoma Territory) Review, 1901

Arkansas Intelligencer, 1844–46, 1849, 1855

Army and Navy Chronicle, 1835–37

Atoka (Choctaw Nation) Vindicator, 1875

Baptist Home Mission Monthly, 1892

Baptist Messenger, 1932

Baptist Missionary Magazine, 1843

Baptist Weekly Journal, 1833

Cherokee Advocate, 1845–50, 1875

Daily Oklahoman, 1921–23, 1926, 1932, 1938–39, 1949

El Reno (Oklahoma Territory) News, 1901

Fort Gibson (Okla.) Post, 1909

Fort Smith (Ark.) Herald, 1850

Holdenville (Creek Nation) Times, 1906

Holdenville (Creek Nation) Tribune, 1905

Indian Advocate, 1849, 1854

Indian Journal, 1884

Indian Republican, 1905

Le Roy (Kans.) Reporter, 1931

McAlester (Choctaw Nation) Star Vindicator, 1878

Muskogee (Creek Nation) Democrat, 1905
Muskogee (Creek Nation) Evening Times, 1898
Muskogee (Creek Nation) New State Tribune, 1906
Muskogee (Creek Nation; Okla.) Phoenix, 1894, 1910
New York Herald, 1858
Niles Weekly Register, 1838
Oklahoma City Weekly Times Journal, 1907
Oklahoma State Capital, 1907
Portland (Maine) Daily Advertiser, 1836
Purcell (Choctaw Nation) Register, 1894
San Antonio Western Texas, 1850–52
Seminole (Seminole Nation) Capital, 1905, 1906
Seminole (Okla.) Producer, 1927
South McAlester (Choctaw Nation) Capital, 1904, 1905
Southern Literary Messenger, 1859
Sulphur (Chickasaw Nation) Post, 1905
Tulsa Democrat, 1905
Twin Territories: The Indian Magazine, 1898–1904
Vinita (Cherokee Nation) Weekly Chieftain, 1904
Wewoka (Okla.) Capital-Democrat, 1927
Wewoka (Okla.) Daily Times, 1966

BOOKS

Abel, Annie H. *The American Indian as Participant in the Civil War.* Cleveland: Arthur H. Clark, 1919.

———. *The American Indian as Slaveholder and Secessionist: An Omitted Chapter in the Diplomatic History of the Southern Confederacy.* Cleveland: Arthur H. Clark, 1915.

———. *The American Indian under Reconstruction.* Cleveland: Arthur H. Clark, 1925.

Agnew, Brad. *Fort Gibson, Terminal on the Trail of Tears.* Norman: University of Oklahoma Press, 1980.

Alford, Thomas W. *Civilization, as Told to Florence Drake.* Norman: University of Oklahoma Press, 1936.

American Baptist Home Mission Society. *Baptist Home Missions in America, Including a Full Report of the Proceedings and Addresses of the Jubilee Meeting and a Historical Sketch of the American Baptist Home Mission Society, Historical Tables, etc., 1832–1882.* New York: Baptist Home Mission Rooms, 1883.

Aptheker, Herbert. *American Negro Slave Revolts.* New York: Columbia University Press, 1943.

Bailey, M. Thomas. *Reconstruction in Indian Territory: A Story of Avarice, Discrimination, and Opportunism.* Port Washington, N.Y.: Kennikat Press, 1972.

Baker, T. Lindsay, and Julie Baker, eds. *The WPA Oklahoma Slave Narratives.* Norman: University of Oklahoma Press, 1996.

Barber, John W., and Henry Howe. *Our Whole Country, or the Past and Present of the United States, Historical and Descriptive.* 2 vols. Cincinnati: Henry Howe, 1861.

Barr, J. *A Correct and Authentic Narrative of the Indian War in Florida.* New York: J. Narine Printer, 1836.

Bartram, William. *Travels through North & South Carolina, Georgia, East & West Florida, the*

Cherokee Country, the Extensive Territories of the Muscogulges, or Creek Confederacy, and the Country of the Choctaws. 2nd ed. London: Reprinted for J. Johnson, 1794. (1st ed., Philadelphia: James and Johnson, 1791.)

Beadle, J. H. *The Undeveloped West, or Five Years in the Territories.* Philadelphia: National Publishing, 1873.

——. *Western Wilds and the Men Who Redeem Them.* San Francisco: A. L. Bancroft, 1880.

Bemrose, John. *Reminiscences of the Second Seminole War.* John K. Mahon, ed. Gainesville: University of Florida Press, 1966.

Benson, Henry C. *Life among the Choctaw Indians and Sketches of the Southwest.* Cincinnati: L. Swormstedt and A. Poe, 1860.

Berry, Brewton. *Almost White.* New York: Macmillan, 1963.

——. *Race and Ethnic Relations.* 3rd ed. Boston: Houghton Mifflin, 1965.

Bilby, Kenneth M. *True-Born Maroons.* Gainesville: University Press of Florida, 2005.

Billington, Monroe Lee, and Roger D. Hardaway, eds. *African Americans on the Western Frontier.* Niwot: University Press of Colorado, 1998.

Bittle, William E., and Gilbert L. Geis. *The Longest Way Home: Chief Alfred C. Sam's Back-to-Africa Movement.* Detroit: Wayne State University Press, 1964.

Blair, Margaret Berry, with R. Palmer Howard. *Scalpel in a Saddlebag: The Story of a Physician in Indian Territory; Virgil Berry M.D.* Oklahoma City: Oklahoma Western Heritage Books, 1979.

Board of Missions of the Protestant Episcopal Church in the Indian Territory. New York: Daniel Dana, Jr., 1844.

Boggess, Francis C. M. *A Veteran of Four Wars: The Autobiography of Francis Calvin Morgan Boggess; A Record of Pioneer Life and Adventure, and Heretofore Unwritten History of the Florida Seminole Indian Wars.* Arcadia, Fla.: Printed at the Champion Job Rooms, 1900.

Bolster, Mel H. *Crazy Snake and the Smoked Meat Rebellion.* Boston: Brandon Press, 1976.

Braund, Kathryn E. Holland. *Deerskins and Duffels: The Creek Indian Trade with Anglo-America, 1685–1815.* Lincoln: University of Nebraska Press, 1993.

Britton, Wiley. *The Civil War on the Border.* 2 vols. New York: G. P. Putnam's Sons, 1890–1904.

——. *Memoirs of the Rebellion on the Border, 1863.* Chicago: Cushing Thomas, 1882.

——. *The Union Indian Brigade in the Civil War.* Kansas City: Franklin Hudson, 1922.

Brooks, James F. *Captives and Cousins: Slavery, Kinship, and Community in the Southwest Borderlands.* Chapel Hill: University of North Carolina Press, 2002.

——, ed. *Confounding the Color Line: The Indian-Black Experience in North America.* Lincoln: University of Nebraska Press, 2002.

Brown, Canter, Jr. *African Americans on the Tampa Bay Frontier.* Tampa: Tampa Bay History Center, 1997.

——. *Florida's Peace River Frontier.* Orlando: University of Central Florida Press, 1991.

Burton, Arthur T. *Black, Buckskin, and Blue: African-American Scouts and Soldiers on the Western Frontier.* Austin, Tex.: Eakin Press, 1999.

——. *Black, Red, and Deadly: Black and Indian Gunfighters of the Indian Territories.* Austin, Tex.: Eakin Press, 1991.

Burton, Jeffrey. *Indian Territory and the United States, 1866–1906: Courts, Government, and the Movement for Oklahoma Statehood.* Norman: University of Oklahoma Press, 1995.

Campbell, J. B. *Campbell's Abstract of Creek Freedman Census Cards and Index.* Muskogee, Okla.: Phoenix Job Printing, 1915.

——. *Campbell's Abstract of Seminole Indian Census Cards and Index.* Muskogee, Okla.: Oklahoma Printing, 1925.

Carleton, William A. *Not Yours, but You*. Berkeley, Calif.: William A. Carleton, 1954.

Carter, Clarence E., comp. and ed. *Territorial Papers of the United States: The Territory of Florida, 1821–1824*. New York: AMS Press, 1956.

Castel, Albert. *A Frontier State at War: Kansas, 1861–1865*. Ithaca, N.Y.: Cornell University Press, 1958.

Catlin, George. *The North American Indians: Being Letters and Notes on Their Manners, Customs and Conditions, Written during Eight Years' Travel amongst the Wildest Tribes of Indians in North America, 1832–1839*. London: Tesswill and Myers, 1841.

Chan, Sucheng, Douglas Henry Daniels, Mario T. Garcia, and Terry P. Wilson, eds. *Peoples of Color in the American West*. Lexington, Mass.: D. C. Heath and Co., 1994.

Chatelain, Verne Elmo. *The Defenses of Spanish Florida, 1565 to 1763*. Carnegie Institute of Washington Publication 511. Washington, D.C., 1941.

Clark, Ransom. *Narrative of Ransom Clark, the Only Survivor of Major Dade's Command in Florida: Containing Brief Descriptions of What Befel Him from His Enlistment in 1833, till His Discharge, in 1836; With an Account of the Inhuman Massacre, by the Indians and Negroes, of Major Dade's Detachment*. Binghamton, N.Y.: Printed by Johnson and Marble, 1839.

Cline, Howard F. *Notes on Colonial Indians and Communities in Florida, 1700–1821; Notes on the Treaty of Coweta*. Vol. 1 of *Florida Indians*, 3 vols. *American Indian Ethnohistory: Southern and Southeast Indians*, David A. Horr, comp. and ed. New York: Garland, 1974.

——. *Provisional Historical Gazeteer, with Locational Notes on Florida Colonial Communities, 1700–1823*. Vol. 2 of *Florida Indians*, 3 vols. *American Indian Ethnohistory: Southern and Southeast Indians*, David A. Horr, comp. and ed. New York: Garland, 1974.

Coe, Charles H. *Red Patriots: The Story of the Seminoles*. Cincinnati: Editor Publishing Co., 1898.

Cohen, Myer M. *Notices of Florida and the Campaigns, by an Officer of the Left Wing*. Charleston, S.C.: Burges and Honour; New York: B. B. Hussey, 1836.

Coker, William S., and Thomas D. Watson. *Indian Traders of the Southeastern Spanish Borderlands: Panton, Leslie and Company, and John Forbes and Company, 1783–1847*. Pensacola: University of West Florida Press, 1986.

Colburn, David R., and Jane G. Landers, eds. *The African American Heritage of Florida*. Gainesville: University Press of Florida, 1995.

Corden, Seth K., and W. B. Richards, comps. *The Oklahoma Red Book*. 2 vols. Oklahoma City: Democrat Printing, 1912.

Cornish, Dudley T. *The Sable Arm: Negro Troops in the Union Army 1861–1865*. New York: Longmans, Green, 1956.

Cotterill, R. S. *The Southern Indians: The Story of the Civilized Tribes before Removal*. Norman: University of Oklahoma Press, 1954.

Covington, James W. *The Billy Bowlegs War, 1855–1858: The Final Stand of the Seminoles against the Whites*. Chuluota, Fla.: Mickler House, 1982.

——. *The Seminoles of Florida*. Gainesville: University Press of Florida, 1993.

Creel, Margaret W. *"A Peculiar People": Slave Religion and Community Culture among the Gullahs*. New York: New York University Press, 1988.

Cunningham, Frank. *General Stand Watie's Confederate Indians*. San Antonio, Tex.: Naylor Co., 1959.

Cusick, James G. *The Other War of 1812: The Patriot War and the American Invasion of Spanish East Florida*. Gainesville: University Press of Florida, 2003.

Dawson, J. E. *The Five Civilized Tribes*. Washington, D.C.: Office of Indian Affairs, 1931.

Debo, Angie E. *And Still the Waters Run: The Betrayal of the Five Civilized Tribes*. Princeton, N.J.: Princeton University Press, 1940.

——. *The Rise and Fall of the Choctaw Republic*. Norman: University of Oklahoma Press, 1941.

——. *The Road to Disappearance: A History of the Creek Indians*. Norman: University of Oklahoma Press, 1941.

——. *Tulsa: From Creek Town to Oil Capital*. Norman: University of Oklahoma Press, 1943.

Descendants of Freedmen of the Five Civilized Tribes Association. 2005 Conference Program, University of Oklahoma. http://www.freedmenconference.com/index.htm (July 8, 2005).

Dillard, Joseph L. *Black English: Its History and Usage in the United States*. New York: Random House, 1972.

——, ed. *Perspectives on Black English*. The Hague: Mouton, 1975.

Downey, Fairfax. *Indian-Fighting Army*. New York: Charles Scribner's Sons, 1941.

Downs, Dorothy. *Art of the Florida Seminoles and Miccosukee Indians*. Gainesville: University Press of Florida, 1995.

Doyle, S. H. *Presbyterian Home Missions*. Philadelphia: Presbyterian Board of Publication, 1902.

Drake, Samuel S. *Indians of North America*. New York: Hurst and Co., 1880.

Epple, Jess C. *Honey Springs Depot, Elk Creek, Creek Nation, Indian Territory*. Muskogee, Okla.: Hoffman Printing, 1964.

Eyma, Louis X. *La vie dans le Nouveau-Monde*. Paris: Poulet-Malassis, 1862.

Fairbanks, Charles H. *Ethnohistorical Report on the Florida Indians, Commission Findings by Indian Claims Commission*. Vol. 3 of *Florida Indians,* 3 vols. *American Indian Ethnohistory: Southern and Southeast Indians,* David A. Horr, comp. and ed. New York: Garland, 1974.

Fischer, LeRoy H., ed. *The Civil War Era in Indian Territory*. Los Angeles: Lorrin L. Morrison, 1974. Articles reprinted from *Journal of the West* 12 (1973).

Fitzpatrick, Kirby. *Fitzpatrick's Indian Title Chart with a Digest of the Laws on Alienation of the Lands of the Five Civilized Tribes*. Oklahoma City: Harlow, 1917.

Fogelson, Raymond D., ed. *Handbook of North American Indians*, vol. 14, *Southeast*. Washington, D.C.: Smithsonian Institution Press, 2004.

Forbes, Jack D. *Africans and Native Americans: The Language of Race and the Evolution of Red-Black Peoples*. Urbana: University of Illinois Press, 1993.

Forbes, James G. *Sketches, Historical and Topographical, of the Floridas, More Particularly of East Florida*. Gainesville: University of Florida Press, 1964 [1821].

Foreman, Carolyn T. *North Fork Town*. Muskogee, Okla.: Hoffman, 1963.

Foreman, Grant. *Advancing the Frontier*. Norman: University of Oklahoma Press, 1933.

——, ed. *Adventure on Red River: Report on the Exploration of the Red River by Captain Randolph B. Marcy and Captain G. B. McClellan*. Norman: University of Oklahoma Press, 1937.

——. *Beginnings of Protestant Christian Work in Indian Territory*. Muskogee, Okla.: Star Printery, 1933.

——. *The Five Civilized Tribes*. Norman: University of Oklahoma Press, 1934.

——. *Fort Gibson: A Brief History*. Norman: University of Oklahoma Press, 1936.

——. *Indian Removal*. Norman: University of Oklahoma Press, 1932.

——. *The Last Trek of the Indians*. Chicago: University of Chicago Press, 1946.

——. *Marcy and the Gold Seekers: The Journal of Captain R. B. Marcy, with an Account of the Gold Rush over the South Route*. Norman: University of Oklahoma Press, 1939.

——, ed. *A Traveller in Indian Territory: The Journal of Ethan Allen Hitchcock, Late Major-General in the United States Army.* Cedar Rapids, Iowa: Torch Press, 1930.

Foster, Laurence. *Negro-Indian Relationships in the Southeast.* Philadelphia: published by the author, 1935.

Fox, William F. *Regimental Losses in the American Civil War, 1861–1865.* Albany, N.Y.: Albany Publishing Co., 1889.

Gaskin, J. M. *Baptist Milestones in Oklahoma.* Oklahoma City: Baptist General Convention of Oklahoma, 1966.

——. *Trail Blazers of Sooner Baptists.* Shawnee: Oklahoma Baptist University Press, 1953.

Gibson, Arrell M. *The Chickasaws.* Norman: University of Oklahoma Press, 1971.

Giddings, Joshua R. *The Exiles of Florida; or, The Crimes Committed by Our Government against the Maroons, Who Fled from South Carolina, and Other Slave States, Seeking Protection under Spanish Laws.* Columbus, Ohio: Follett, Foster, and Co., 1858.

Gideon, D. C. *Indian Territory: Descriptive, Biographical, and Genealogical, Including the Landed Estates, Country Seats, etc., with a General History of the Territory.* New York and Chicago: Lewis, 1901.

Gifford, John C., ed. *Billy Bowlegs and the Seminole War, with Notes and Comments by John C. Gifford.* Coconut Grove, Fla.: Triangle, 1925.

Gittinger, Roy. *The Formation of the State of Oklahoma 1803–1906.* Norman: University of Oklahoma Press, 1939.

Glisan, Rodney. *Journal of Army Life.* San Francisco: A. L. Bancroft and Co., 1874.

González, Nancie L. Solien. *Sojourners of the Caribbean: Ethnogenesis and Ethnohistory of the Garífuna.* Urbana: University of Illinois Press, 1988.

Goode, William H. *Outposts of Zion, with Limnings of Mission Life.* Cincinnati: Poe and Hitchcock, 1864.

Green, Michael D. *The Politics of Indian Removal: Creek Government and Society in Crisis.* Lincoln: University of Nebraska Press, 1982.

Gregg, Josiah. *Commerce of the Prairies.* 2 vols. New York: H. G. Langley, 1844.

Guinn, Jeff. *Our Land Before We Die: The Proud Story of the Seminole Negro.* New York: Jeremy P. Tarcher/Putnam, 2002.

Halatsz, Nicholas. *The Rattling Chains: Slave Unrest and Revolt in the Antebellum South.* New York: McKay, Van Rees, 1966.

Halliburton, Rudy, Jr. *Red over Black: Black Slavery among the Cherokee Indians.* Westport, Conn.: Greenwood Press, 1976.

Hamilton, Robert. *The Gospel among the Red Men.* Nashville: Sunday School Board of the Southern Baptist Convention, 1944.

Hancock, Ian F. *Creole Features in the Afro-Seminole Speech of Brackettville, Texas.* Society for Caribbean Linguistics Occasional Paper no. 3. Mona, Jamaica: University of the West Indies, 1975.

——. *Further Observations on Afro-Seminole Creole.* Society for Caribbean Linguistics Occasional Paper no. 7. Mona, Jamaica: University of the West Indies, 1977.

——. *The Texas Seminoles and Their Language.* African and Afro-American Studies and Research Center, ser. 2, no. 1. Austin: University of Texas, 1980.

Harman, Samuel W. *Hell on the Border: A History of the Great United States Criminal Court at Fort Smith and of Crimes and Criminals in the Indian Territory and the Trials and Punishment Thereof before His Honor, United States Judge Isaac C. Parker.* Fort Smith, Ark.: Hell on the Border, 1953 [1898].

Harper, Francis, ed. *The Travels of William Bartram: Naturalist's Edition*. Athens: University of Georgia Press, 1998 [1791].

Harrington, Fred Harvey. *Hanging Judge*. Norman: University of Oklahoma Press, 1996 [1952].

Harris, N. Sayer. *Journal of a Tour in the "Indian Country."* New York: Daniel Dana, 1844.

Hastain, E. *Township Plots of the Seminole Nation*. Muskogee, Okla.: Model, 1913.

Hauptman, Laurence M. *Between Two Fires: American Indians in the Civil War*. New York: Free Press, 1995.

Heard, J. Norman. *The Black Frontiersmen: Adventures of Negroes among American Indians 1528–1918*. New York: John Day, 1969.

Hitchcock, Ethan Allen. *Fifty Years in Camp and Field: Diary of Major General Ethan Allen Hitchcock*. W. A. Croffut, ed. New York: G. P. Putnam's Sons, 1909.

Hodge, Frederick W. *Handbook of American Indians, North of Mexico*. 2 vols. Washington, D.C.: Government Printing Office, 1910.

Holloway, Joseph E., ed. *Africanisms in American Culture*. Bloomington: Indiana University Press, 1990.

Holt, Adoniram J. *Pioneering in the South West*. Nashville: Sunday School Board of the Southern Baptist Convention, 1923.

Hooks, Gwen. *The Keystone Legacy: Recollections of a Black Settler*. Edmonton, Alberta: Brightest Pebble, 1997 or 1998.

Howard, James H., and Willie Lena. *Oklahoma Seminoles: Medicines, Magic, and Religion*. Norman: University of Oklahoma Press, 1984.

Howard, Oliver O. *My Life and Experiences among Our Hostile Indians: A Record of Personal Observations, Adventures, and Campaigns among the Indians of the Great West, with Some Account of Their Life, Habits, Traits, Religion, Ceremonies, Dress, Savage Instincts, and Customs in Peace and War*. Hartford, Conn.: A. D. Worthington, 1907.

Howard, Rosalyn. *Black Seminoles in the Bahamas*. Gainesville: University Press of Florida, 2002.

Hudson, Charles M., ed. *Red, White, and Black: Symposium on Indians in the Old South*. Southern Anthropological Society Publication. Athens: University of Georgia Press, 1971.

———. *The Southeastern Indians*. Nashville: University of Tennessee Press, 1976.

Ingersoll, Thomas N. *To Intermix with Our White Brothers: Indian Mixed Bloods in the United States from the Earliest Times to the Indian Removals*. Albuquerque: University of New Mexico Press, 2005.

IUCN Inter-Commission Task Force on Indigenous Peoples. *Indigenous Peoples and Sustainability: Cases and Actions*. Utrecht: International Books, 1997.

Jones, William F. *The Experiences of a Deputy U.S. Marshal of the Indian Territory*. N.p., 1937. 40 pp.

Joyner, Charles. *Down by the Riverside: A South Carolina Slave Community*. Urbana: University of Illinois Press, 1984.

Jumper, Betty Mae Tiger, and Patsy West. *A Seminole Legend: The Life of Betty Mae Tiger Jumper*. Gainesville: University Press of Florida, 2001.

Jumper, John. *Speech Delivered by Col. John Jumper to the Creeks and Seminoles Comprising the First Seminole Regiment, July 6th, 1864*. Fort Towson, Choctaw Nation, Indian Territory: Choctaw Government Printing Office, 1864.

Katz, William L. *Black Indians: A Hidden Heritage*. New York: Atheneum, 1986.

——. *The Black West: A Documentary and Pictorial History.* Garden City, N.Y.: Doubleday, 1971. 3rd rev. ed., Seattle: Open Hand, 1987.

Kennedy, Joseph. *Population of the United States in 1860, Compiled from the Original Returns of the Eighth Census under the Direction of the Secretary of the Interior.* Washington, D.C.: Government Printing Office, 1864.

Kieffer, Chester L. *Maligned General: A Biography of Thomas S. Jesup.* San Rafael, Calif.: Presidio Press, 1979.

Krogman, Wilton M. *The Physical Anthropology of the Seminole Indians of Oklahoma.* Rome: Failli, 1935.

Landers, Jane G. *Black Society in Spanish Florida.* Urbana: University of Illinois Press, 1999.

——, ed. *Colonial Plantations and Economy in Florida.* Gainesville: University Press of Florida, 2000.

Lanman, Charles. *Adventures in the Wilds of the United States and British American Provinces.* 2 vols. Philadelphia: J. W. Moore, 1856.

Lauber, Almon W. *Indian Slavery in Colonial Times within the Present Limits of the United States.* New York: Columbia University Studies, 1913.

Laumer, Frank, ed. *Amidst a Storm of Bullets: The Diary of Lt. Henry Prince in Florida, 1836–1842.* Tampa: University of Tampa Press, 1998.

——. *Dade's Last Command.* Gainesville: University Presses of Florida, 1995.

——. *Massacre!* Gainesville: University of Florida Press, 1968.

Leaming, Hugo Prosper. *Hidden Americans: Maroons of Virginia and the Carolinas.* New York: Garland, 1995.

Lindsey, Donal F. *Indians at Hampton Institute, 1877–1923.* Urbana: University of Illinois Press, 1995.

Littlefield, Daniel C. *Rice and Slaves: Ethnicity and the Slave Trade in Colonial South Carolina.* Baton Rouge: Louisiana State University Press, 1981.

Littlefield, Daniel F., Jr. *Africans and Creeks: From the Colonial Period to the Civil War.* Westport, Conn.: Greenwood Press, 1979.

——. *Africans and Seminoles: From Removal to Emancipation.* Jackson: University Press of Mississippi, Banner Books, 2001. 1st paperback ed. (Orig., Westport, Conn.: Greenwood Press, 1977.)

——. *The Cherokee Freedmen: From Emancipation to American Citizenship.* Westport, Conn.: Greenwood Press, 1978.

——. *The Chickasaw Freedmen: A People without a Country.* Westport, Conn.: Greenwood Press, 1980.

——. *Seminole Burning: A Story of Racial Vengeance.* Jackson: University Press of Mississippi, 1996.

Loomis, Augustus W. *Scenes in the Indian Country.* Philadelphia: Presbyterian Board of Publication, 1859.

Loughridge, Robert M., and David M. Hodge. *English and Muskokee Dictionary: Collected from Various Sources and Revised; Dictionary of the Muskokee or Creek Language in Creek and English.* Okmulgee, Okla.: Baptist Home Mission Board, 1964 [1890].

Lowrie, John C. *A Manual of Missions, or Sketches of the Foreign Missions of the Presbyterian Church: With Maps, Showing the Stations and Statistics of Protestant Missions among Unevangelized Nations.* New York: A. D. F. Randolph, 1854.

Mahon, John K. *History of the Second Seminole War, 1835–1842.* Rev. ed. Gainesville: University of Florida Press, 1985 [1967].

Marcy, Randolph B. *Thirty Years of Army Life on the Border.* New York: Harper and Bros., 1866.

Marcy, Randolph B., and G. B. McClellan. *Exploration of the Red River of Louisiana in the Year 1852*. Washington, D.C.: R. Armstrong, Public Printer, 1853.

May, Katja. *African Americans and Native Americans in the Creek and Cherokee Nations, 1830s to 1920s: Collision and Collusion*. New York and London: Garland, 1996.

Maza, Francisco F. de la. *Código de colonización y terrenos baldíos de la República Mexicana 1451–1892*. Mexico City: Secretaría de Fomento, 1893.

McAfee, George F. *Presbyterian Missionaries to the Indians of the United States*. New York: A. D. F. Randolph, 1893.

McCall, George A. *Letters from the Frontiers: Written during a Period of Thirty Years' Service in the Army of the United States*. Philadelphia: J. B. Lippincott, 1868.

McCoy, Isaac. *History of Baptist Indian Missions*. William M. Morrison, ed. New York: H. and S. Raynor, 1840.

———. *Periodical Account of Baptist Missions within the Indian Territory for the Year Ending December 31, 1836*. Shawnee Baptist Mission House, Indian Territory: Isaac McCoy, 1837.

McDonogh, Gary W., ed. *The Florida Negro: A Federal Writer's Project Legacy*. Jackson: University Press of Mississippi, 1992.

McKenney, Thomas L., and James Hall. *The Indian Tribes of North America*. New ed. 3 vols. Frederick W. Hodge and David I. Bushnell, eds. Edinburgh: John Grant, 1933–34.

McLoughlin, William G. *After the Trail of Tears: The Cherokees' Struggle for Sovereignty, 1839–1880*. Chapel Hill: University of North Carolina Press, 1993.

McReynolds, Edwin C. *Oklahoma: A History of the Sooner State*. Norman: University of Oklahoma Press, 1954.

———. *The Seminoles*. Norman: University of Oklahoma Press, 1957.

Miles, Tiya. *Ties That Bind: The Story of an Afro-Cherokee Family in Slavery and Freedom*. Berkeley: University of California Press, 2005.

Miles, Tiya, and Sharon P. Holland, eds. *Crossing Waters, Crossing Worlds: The African Diaspora in Indian Country*. Durham, N.C., and London: Duke University Press, 2006.

Miller, Susan A. *Coacoochee's Bones: A Seminole Saga*. Lawrence: University Press of Kansas, 2003.

Mills, Lawrence. *The Lands of the Five Civilized Tribes*. St. Louis: F. H. Thomas Law Book Co., 1919.

Miner, H. Craig. *The Corporation and the Indian: Tribal Sovereignty and Industrial Civilization in Indian Territory 1865–1907*. Columbia: University of Missouri Press, 1976.

Minges, Patrick N., ed. *Black Indian Slave Narratives*. Winston-Salem, N.C.: John F. Blair, 2004.

———. *Slavery in the Cherokee Nation: The Keetowah Society and the Defining of a People, 1855–1867*. New York: Routledge, 2003.

Mooney, Charles W. *Localized History of Pottawatomie County, Oklahoma, to 1907*. Midwest City, Okla.: Lithographics Printers, 1971.

Moore, J. Read. *Moore's Seminole Roll and Land Guide*. Wewoka, Okla.: Lasiter, 1915.

Morris, John W., Charles R. Goins, and Edwin C. McReynolds. *Historical Atlas of Oklahoma*. Norman: University of Oklahoma Press, 1976 [1965].

Morrison, Michael A. *Slavery and the American West: The Eclipse of Manifest Destiny and the Coming of the Civil War*. Chapel Hill: University of North Carolina Press, 1997.

Morse, Jedidiah. *A Report to the Secretary of War of the United States on Indian Affairs: Comprising a Narrative of a Tour Performed in the Summer of 1820, under a Commission from the President of the United States, for the Purpose of Ascertaining, for the Use of the Government, the Actual State of the Indian Tribes in Our Country*. New Haven, Conn.: Southern Converse, 1822.

Motte, Jacob R. *Journey into Wilderness: An Army Surgeon's Account of Life in Camp and Field during the Creek and Seminole Wars, 1836–1838.* James F. Sunderman, ed. Gainesville: University of Florida Press, 1953.

Mulroy, Kevin. *Freedom on the Border: The Seminole Maroons in Florida, the Indian Territory, Coahuila, and Texas.* Lubbock: Texas Tech University Press, 1993.

Nash, Gary B. *Red, White, and Black: The Peoples of Early America.* Englewood Cliffs, N.J.: Prentice-Hall, 1974.

Nash, Roy. *Survey of the Seminole Indians of Florida.* Washington, D.C.: Public Office of Indian Affairs, 1932.

Newcomb, James P. *History of Secession Times in Texas and Journal of Travel from Texas through Mexico to California, and a History of the "Box Colony."* San Francisco: n.p., 1863.

Newsom, J. A. *The Life and Practice of the Wild and Modern Indian: The Early Days of Oklahoma; Some Thrilling Experiences.* Oklahoma City: Harlow, 1922.

Nye, Wilbur S. *Carbine and Lance: The Story of Old Fort Sill.* Norman: University of Oklahoma Press, 1937.

O'Beirne, Harry F., and E. S. O'Beirne, comps. *The Indian Territory: Its Chiefs, Legislators, and Leading Men.* St. Louis: C. B. Woodward, 1892.

Olmsted, Frederick L. *A Journey through Texas: A Saddle-Trip on the Southwestern Frontier.* J. Howard, ed. Austin: Von-Boeckman–Jones, 1962 [1857].

Organization of American States (OAS), Inter-American Commission on Human Rights. *Proposed American Declaration on the Rights of Indigenous Peoples.* Approved by the Inter-American Commission on Human Rights on February 26, 1997, at its 1,333rd Sess., 95th Regular Sess. http://www.cidh.org/Indigenous.htm (June 21, 2004).

Palmer, Howard, and Tamara Palmer. *Peoples of Alberta: Portraits of Cultural Diversity.* Saskatoon, Saskatchewan: Western Producer Prairie Books, 1985.

Parker, David, and Miri Song, eds. *Rethinking Mixed Race.* London: Pluto Press, 2001.

Patrick, Rembert W. *Florida Fiasco: Rampant Rebels on the Georgia-Florida Frontier, 1810–1815.* Athens: University of Georgia Press, 1954.

Perdue, Theda. *Cherokee Women: Gender and Culture Change, 1700–1835.* Lincoln: University of Nebraska Press, 1998.

——. *"Mixed Blood" Indians: Racial Construction in the Early South.* Athens: University of Georgia Press, 2003.

——. *Nations Remembered: An Oral History of the Five Civilized Tribes.* Westport, Conn.: Greenwood Press, 1980.

——. *Slavery and the Evolution of Cherokee Society, 1540–1866.* Knoxville: University of Tennessee Press, 1979.

Peterson, Jacqueline, and Jennifer S. H. Brown, eds. *The New Peoples: Being and Becoming Métis in North America.* Lincoln: University of Nebraska Press, 1985.

Piker, Joshua. *Okfuskee: A Creek Indian Town in Colonial America.* Cambridge, Mass.: Harvard University Press, 2004.

Porter, Kenneth W. *The Black Seminoles: History of a Freedom-Seeking People.* Alcione M. Amos and Thomas P. Senter, eds. Gainesville: University Press of Florida, 1996.

——. *The Negro on the American Frontier.* New York: New York Times, Arno Press, 1971.

Potter, Woodburne. *The War in Florida: Being an Exposition of Its Causes and an Accurate History of the Campaigns of Generals Clinch, Gaines, and Scott, by a Late Staff Officer.* Baltimore: Lewis and Coleman, 1836.

Pratt, Julius W. *Expansionists of 1812.* New York: Macmillan, 1925.

Presbyterian Church in the USA. *Historical Sketches of the Missions under the Care of the Board of*

Foreign Missions of the Presbyterian Church. Philadelphia: Woman's Foreign Missionary Society of the Presbyterian Church, 1886.

Price, Richard, ed. *Maroon Societies: Rebel Slave Communities in the Americas.* Rev. ed. Baltimore: Johns Hopkins University Press, 1979.

Proceedings of Indian Territory Baptist Convention, 1887–1889. Ottawa, Kans.: J. B. Kassler, n.d.

Rader, Brian F. *The Political Outsiders: Blacks and Indians in a Rural Oklahoma County.* San Francisco: R and E Associates, 1978.

Rampp, Lary C., and Donald L. Rampp. *The Civil War in Indian Territory.* Austin, Tex.: Presidial Press, 1975.

Rawick, George P., comp. and ed. *The American Slave: A Composite Autobiography.* 41 vols. Westport, Conn.: Greenwood Press, 1972–79. Oklahoma Narratives, vol. 7 (1st ser.), vol. 12 (1st suppl. ser.), vol. 1 (2nd suppl. ser.).

Remini, Robert. *Andrew Jackson and His Indian Wars.* New York: Viking, 2001.

Richardson, Albert D. *Beyond the Mississippi.* Hartford, Conn.: American, 1867.

Richardson, Rupert N. *The Comanche Barrier to South Plains Settlement: A Century and a Half of Savage Resistance to the Advancing White Frontier.* Glendale, Calif.: Arthur H. Clark, 1933.

Rister, Carl Coke. *Baptist Missions among the American Indians.* Atlanta: Home Mission Board, 1944.

———. *The Southwestern Frontier, 1865–1881.* Cleveland: Arthur H. Clark, 1928.

Rivers, Larry E. *Slavery in Florida: Territorial Days to Emancipation.* Gainesville: University Press of Florida, 2000.

Rodenbough, Theodore F., and William L. Haskin. *The Army of the United States: Historical Sketches of Staff and Line with Portraits of Generals-in-Chief.* New York: Maynard, Merrill, 1896.

Routh, Eugene C. *The Story of Oklahoma Baptists.* Oklahoma City: Baptist General Convention of Oklahoma, 1932.

Satz, Ronald L. *American Indian Policy in the Jacksonian Era.* Norman: University of Oklahoma Press, 2002.

Saunt, Claudio. *Black, White, and Indian: Race and the Unmaking of an American Family.* New York: Oxford University Press, 2005.

———. *A New Order of Things: Property, Power, and the Transformation of the Creek Indians, 1733–1816.* Cambridge: Cambridge University Press, 1999.

Schoolcraft, Henry R. *Historical and Statistical Information Respecting the History, Condition and Prospects of the Indian Tribes of the United States: Collected and Prepared under the Direction of the Bureau of Indian Affairs per Act of Congress of March 3, 1847.* 6 vols. Philadelphia: Lippincott, Grambo, 1851–57.

Schultz, Jack M. *The Seminole Baptist Churches of Oklahoma: Maintaining a Traditional Community.* Norman: University of Oklahoma Press, 1999.

Seitel, Peter, ed. *1992 Festival of American Folklife.* Program. Washington, D.C.: Smithsonian Institution, 1992.

Shepard, R. Bruce. *Deemed Unsuitable: Blacks from Oklahoma Move to the Canadian Prairies in Search of Equality in the Early 20th Century Only to Find Racism in Their New Home.* Toronto: Umbrella Press, 1997.

Simmons, William H. *Notices of East Florida, with an Account of the Seminole Nation of Indians.* Gainesville: University of Florida Press, 1973 [1822].

Spickard, Paul R. *Mixed Blood: Intermarriage and Ethnic Identity in Twentieth-Century America.* Madison: University of Wisconsin Press, 1989.

Sprague, John T. *The Origin, Progress, and Conclusion of the Florida War.* New York: D. Appleton and Co.; Philadelphia: G. S. Appleton, 1848.

Starr, Helen, and O. E. Hill. *Footprints in the Indian Nation.* Muskogee, Okla.: Hoffman, 1974.

Sturm, Circe. *Blood Politics: Race, Culture, and Identity in the Cherokee Nation of Oklahoma.* Berkeley: University of California Press, 2002.

Sturtevant, William C., ed. *A Seminole Sourcebook.* New York: Garland, 1987.

Taylor, Quintard, Jr. *In Search of the Racial Frontier: African Americans in the American West, 1528–1990.* New York: Norton, 1998.

Teall, Kaye M. *Black History in Oklahoma: A Resource Book.* Oklahoma City: Oklahoma City Public Schools—Title III, ESEA, 1971.

Thoburn, Joseph B., and Muriel H. Wright. *Oklahoma: A History of the State and Its People.* 4 vols. New York: Lewis Historical, 1929.

Thompson, Alvin O. *Flight to Freedom: African Runaways and Maroons in the Americas.* Kingston, Jamaica: University of West Indies Press, 2006.

Tindle, Lela J. McBride Brockway. *Opothleyohola and the Loyal Muskogee: Their Flight to Kansas in the Civil War.* Jefferson, N.C.: McFarland, 2000.

Tolson, Arthur L. *The Black Oklahomans: A History, 1541–1972.* New Orleans: Edwards, 1974.

Tuller, Roger. *"Let No Guilty Man Escape": A Judicial Biography of Isaac C. Parker.* Norman: University of Oklahoma Press, 2001.

United Nations Working Group on Indigenous Populations. *The UN Draft Declaration on the Rights of Indigenous Peoples.* UN Document E/CN.4/Sub.2/1993/29. 1993.

Walton-Raji, Angela Y. *Black Indian Genealogy Research: African American Ancestors among the Five Civilized Tribes.* Bowie, Md.: Heritage Books, 1993.

Wardell, Morris L. *A Political History of the Cherokee Nation, 1838–1907.* Norman: University of Oklahoma Press, 1938.

Waring, Antonio J., ed. *Laws of the Creek Nation.* University of Georgia Libraries Miscellaneous Publications no. 1. Athens: University of Georgia Press, 1960.

Washington, Nathaniel J. *Historical Development of the Negro in Oklahoma.* Tulsa: Dexter, 1948.

Webb, Walter Prescott. *The Texas Rangers: A Century of Frontier Defense.* Boston: Houghton-Mifflin, 1935.

Weisman, Brent R. *Like Beads on a String: A Culture History of the Seminole Indians in North Peninsular Florida.* Tuscaloosa: University of Alabama Press, 1989.

Whipple, Charles K. *Relation of the American Board of Commissioners for Foreign Missions to Slavery.* Boston: R. F. Wallcut, 1861.

White, Charles L. *A Century of Faith.* Philadelphia: Judson, 1932.

White, Christine Schultz, and Benton R. White. *Now the Wolf Has Come: The Creek Nation in the Civil War.* College Station: Texas A&M University Press, 1996.

Wickett, Murray R. *Contested Territory: Whites, Native Americans, and African Americans in Oklahoma, 1865–1907.* Baton Rouge: Louisiana State University Press, 2000.

Williams, George W. *A History of the Negro Troops in the War of the Rebellion, 1861–1865.* New York: Harper and Bros., 1888.

Williams, John L. *The Territory of Florida.* Gainesville: University of Florida Press, 1962 [1837].

Willson, Minnie Moore. *The Seminoles of Florida.* New York: Moffat Yard and Co., 1920 [1896].

Wilson, Joseph T. *The Black Phalanx: A History of the Negro Soldiers of the United States in the Wars of 1775–1812, 1816–1865.* Hartford, Conn.: American, 1888.

Winks, Robin W. *The Blacks in Canada: A History.* New Haven, Conn.: Yale University Press, 1971.

Wood, Peter. *Black Majority: Negroes in Colonial South Carolina from 1670 through the Stono Rebellion*. New York: Knopf, 1974.

Wright, James Leitch, Jr. *Creeks and Seminoles: The Destruction and Regeneration of the Muskogulge People* (Lincoln: University of Nebraska Press, 1986).

——. *The Only Land They Knew: The Tragic Story of the American Indians in the Old South*. New York: Free Press, 1981.

Wright, Muriel H. *A Guide to the Indian Tribes of Oklahoma*. Norman: University of Oklahoma Press, 1951.

Wyeth, Walter N. *Poor Lo: Early Indian Missions; A Memorial*. Philadelphia: Walter N. Wyeth, 1896.

DOCUMENTARY FILMS

Black Indians: An American Story. Steven R. Heape, executive producer. Riche-Heape Films, 2000.

Black Warriors of the Seminole. Denise Mathews, producer and writer. WUFT-TV, Channel 5 production. Gainesville, Fla., 1989.

WEB SITES

African–Native American History and Genealogy. Created and maintained by Angela Y. Walton-Raji. http://www.african-nativeamerican.com (September 14, 2005).

AfriGeneas: African Ancestored Genealogy from Africa to the Americas. http://www.afrigeneas.com (February 6, 2006).

Black History Canada. Historica. http://blackhistorycanada.ca (February 22, 2006).

CBS TV. "A Nation Divided." *60 Minutes II* story. http://www.cbsnews.com/stories/2002/07/01/60II (July 12, 2002).

Descendants of Freedmen of the Five Civilized Tribes. http://www.freedmen5tribes.com (March 20, 2006).

International Labor Organization. (Indigenous and tribal peoples.) ILO Convention 169. http://www.ilo.org/ilolex/cgi-lex/convde.pl?C169 (June 19, 2004).

Seminole Nation, Indian Territory. http://www.seminolenation-indianterritory.org (November 17, 2006).

Seminole Nation of Oklahoma. http://www.seminolenation.com (April 7, 2006).

Smithsonian Institution. (Maroons.) http://www.si.edu/maroon (November 12, 2002), http://www.folklife.si.edu/resources/maroon/presentation.htm (December 9, 2006).

United Nations Development Program. (Indigenous and tribal peoples.) http://www.undp.org (June 1, 2004).

University of Florida. Florida Archaeology Collection, Florida Museum of Natural History. (Seminole and maroon archaeological discoveries in Florida.) http://www.flmnh.ufl.edu/flarch/collections.htm (June 14, 2005).

University of Oklahoma. Western History Collections. (C. Guy Cutlip biography and collection description). http://libraries.ou.edu/etc/westhist/cutlip.htm (November 13, 2003).

World Bank. (Indigenous and tribal peoples.) http://wbln0018.worldbank.org/Institutional/Manuals/OpManual.nsf/0/0F7D6F3F04DD70398525672C007D08ED?OpenDocument (June 19, 2004).

Index

References to illustrations are in italic type.

A Halleck Hadjo, 101
Abayaca, 44
Abbott, L. J., 230
Abel, Annie Heloise, 136
Abraham, 32, 36, 43, 47–48, 131, 133–34, 234, 272, 382n10
Abraham, Washington, 131, 134, 272–73
Abraham's town. *See* Pilaklikaha
Acculturation acceptance, Cherokees, Chickasaws, Choctaws, Creeks, 56, 86, 93–94, 225–26, 262, 340n5, 376n46
Acculturation resistance, Seminole, 86–89, 93–94, 340n5, 347n20; Christianity, 89–91, 141, 347n20, 358n117; and Civil War sympathies, 161, 165; Crazy Snake Rebellion, 300–301; as incorporation success factor, 256–64; in Florida, 6, 40–41; in leadership rivalries, 159–60; political structures, 92–93; schooling, 91–92
Adoption practices, 30–31, 32, 206, 228, 260–61
Africa relocation proposals, 68, 308
African heritage, 14–15, 30, 31, 39, 139–40, 333nn38–39
Africans and Seminoles (Littlefield), 330n23
Afro-Seminole Creole language, 32, 139, 274, 309
Alachua bands/towns: maroon community association, 10, 11–12, 13, 33, 36, 38; Removal, 54, 56; Seminole Wars, 16, 17, 45; subsistence lifestyle, 23–24, 28

Alex, F. G., 303
Allen, Joe, 284
Allen, Ned, 284
Alligator (mikko). *See* Hulbutta Harjo
Allotment/enrollment processes, 279, 294–300, 304–305, 310, 349–50n63
Andrews, Rebecca, 240
Angola plantation, Florida, 17
Annexation, and slavery practices, 19, 39–40
Annuity payments: bandleader responsibilities, 279, 281; Marcellus Duval's involvement, 78, 82; and enrollment process, 295, 297, 299; and intermarriage theory, 136; lighthorse protection, 207; Reconstruction period, 203, 221–22, 225, 227, 231, 253, 257, 260, 277
Apalachee bands/towns, 3, 11, 23–24, 43, 53–54
Apalachicola bands/towns, 5, 38, 43, 53–54
Apilchapcoche, 19, 36
Apilchopko, 36
Arbuckle, Matthew: Africa relocation proposal, 68; Fort Gibson maroons, 60–61, 67, 70, 73, 74; Hardridge's slaving activities, 64; Love's slave claim, 107; maroon transfer activities, 77, 78–79
Arkansas Colored Town, 301
Arkansas River, 167–69, 175, 190
Armstrong, Chapman, 286, 287
Armstrong, William, 56, 57, 61–62, 117–18
Ash Creek Church, 91, 92
Asi Hacho, 43
Asin Yahola, 26, 36, *37,* 44, 48, 233–34, 374n34

433

Aspberry, Daniel Boone, 106, 110–11, 112–14
August (as a name), 140
August (maroon leader), 36

Babbit, Seminole Nation of Oklahoma v., 319
Bagby, Joseph, 252
Bahamas, maroon communities, 20
Baldwin, T. A., 206
Ballard, Mont, 263
Bandoleers, 30
Bands: freedman, 138, 219–21, 268–72, 274,
    280–81, 309, 324; Seminole, 6, 30–32, 53–54,
    92–93, 219–21
Baptist missionaries / churches, 90, 91, 92, 142–
    44, 258–59, 290–92. *See also* Brown, John F.;
    Factor, James; Heniha Mikko; Murrow, Joseph
    Samuel; Talomas Mikko
Barber, John, 94
Barkus, Dosar, 269, 273
Barkus, Joe, 278
Barkus, Jonas, 288
Barkus, Joseph, 273
Barkus, Willie, 288
Barnet, Tony, 68, 131, 134
Barnett, Timmy, 190
Bartram, William, 6–7, 24
Bateman, Rebecca, 237, 274, 308, 354n15, 381–
    82n3, 383n37, 387–88n32
Baxter Springs camp, 175, 177
Bayou Bernard, Battle of, 174
Beadwork, 30
Beams family, 134
Beck (slave of Hothli Hopoya), 111–12
Belknap, William, 73–74, 77, 81
Bell, John, 33
Bemo, John. *See* Talomas Mikko
Ben Bruner band, 120, 220, 272–73
Bennett, Leo, 228
Berry, Virgil, 210–11, 212, 303
Big Jim, 146–47
Bilby, Kenneth, 14, 333n38
Black Indians (as a term), 329–30n20
Blake, William, 288
Blood quantum requirement, 314, 315, 318–19,
    321
Blount, John. *See* Yawohli
Blunt, James, 180
Bob Dosar gang, 278
Boggy Island settlement, 26–28, 35, 36
Boley, Sauree, 290
Bottley, Isaac, 219, *242,* 288
Boudinot, Elias, 165
Bowlegs, Amy, 209

Bowlegs, August, 209
Bowlegs, Bess, 296–97
Bowlegs, Billy. *See* Holata Mikko; Sonaki Mikko
Bowlegs, Billy (son of George Bowlegs), 209
Bowlegs, Bob, 241
Bowlegs, Bud, 209
Bowlegs, Caesar, 207–12, 291, 386n16
Bowlegs, Charley, 278–79
Bowlegs, Cyrus, 165, 178
Bowlegs, David, 251–52, 253, 345–46n95
Bowlegs, Dolly, 165, 209
Bowlegs, Eliza, 12, 99, 102, 103, 207, 209, 296,
    349n57
Bowlegs, Friday, 345–46n95
Bowlegs, George, 178, 209
Bowlegs, Grace. See Bruner, Grace (née
    Bowlegs)
Bowlegs, Hager, 165
Bowlegs, Harriet, 12, 99, 101, 104, 112, 130,
    131, 349n57
Bowlegs, Henry, 296–97
Bowlegs, Jack, 80, 209, 345–46n95
Bowlegs, Jim, 80, 81, 122–23, 126, 166, 174,
    175, 345–46n95, 354n26
Bowlegs, Jimmie, 209
Bowlegs, John, 296–97, 298
Bowlegs, Johnie, 209
Bowlegs, Johnson, 175
Bowlegs, Lydia, 273
Bowlegs, Matt, 273
Bowlegs, Mollie, 175
Bowlegs, Pin, 103
Bowlegs, Polly, 241
Bowlegs, Robert, 178
Bowlegs, Scipio, 20
Bowlegs, Sharper, 207
Bowlegs, Stella, 209
Bowlegs, Swamp William, 122, 123
Bowlegs, Tony, 175
Bowlegs, William, 175
Bowlegs families, 12, 104, 268, 273, 349n57
Bowlegs (mikko). *See* Hothli Hopoya
Bowles, John, 180
Bowles, William Augustus, 10
Bradley (mixed-race leader), 35
Braund, Kathryn E. Holland, 332n22, 337n36
Breiner, Henry, 206, 210, 258, 282–83
Britain, in Florida, 3, 5, 7–8, 9, 10, 12–13
Britton, Wiley, 174, 176, 179, 181–82
Brown, Alice. *See* Davis, Alice Brown
Brown, Andrew J., 257, 258–59
Brown, Canter, 34
Brown, Charley, 114

Brown, Elijah, 206, 207, 260
Brown, Isaac, 132
Brown, Jim, 296, 297
Brown, John, 268–69
Brown, John F., *255*; as Christian minister, 258–59; Civil War period, 182, 189; Reconstruction-era leadership, 251, 254, 257, 301–302, 303–304; Reconstruction treaty negotiations, 196, 197, 199, 200, 203–204
Brown, Levin, 132
Brown, Lige, 214
Brown, Lucy, 261
Bruce, Dick, 290
Bruner, Affy, 120
Bruner, August, 290
Bruner, Ben, *158*; band leadership, 267, 269, 272; Civil War period, 188–89; compensation claim, 120, 121, 122; emancipation, 130; as interpreter, 134, 157, 159
Bruner, Benjamin F., 188, 285, 287
Bruner, Caesar: band leadership, 120, 219, 269, 271; Civil War period, 175, 188; compensation claim, 122; home, *275*; minister role, 290; photo, *272*; in Reconstruction treaty negotiations, 195; Turkey Creek (town), 267, 268
Bruner, Cumsey, 214, 215
Bruner, George Washington, 271
Bruner, Grace (née Bowlegs), 188, 384n60
Bruner, Grant, 214, 238, 239, 271
Bruner, John, 120, 188, 384n60
Bruner, Louisa, 271, 283, 285, *286*, 287, 384n59
Bruner, Perry, 188
Bruner, Rachel, 272
Bruner, Sancho, 120
Bruner, Thomas, 214
Bruner, Ucum, 269, 271, 290
Bruner, Will, 188
Bruner families, generally, 188, 222–23, 268
Bruner Town, 267, 268, 269, 280, 282, 290
Buckner, Henry, 143, 144
Buckra Woman's town, 13, 33–34
Buffalo soldiers, 217, 219
Bureau of Indian Affairs, U.S., 189, 209, 252, 306, 314, 318–20
Bureau of Indian Affairs (Confederate), 163
Burial practices, 291
Burke, William, 179
Butler, Pierce, 58–59

Caballo, Juan. *See* Horse, John
Cabin Creek, Battles of, 178–79, 183–84
Caesar, John, 35, 36, 44
Caesar Bruner band, 120, 244, 269–71

Call, Richard, 44
Campbell's Abstract, 369–70n63
Camp Dade agreement, 46–48, 49
Camp Jumper, 191
Canada, Oklahoma freedman immigration, 308
Canadian River settlements, 54, *63*, 65, 74-75
Canby, E. R. S., 58
Carballo, Julian, 11
Carruth, E. H., 163
Carter, Bob, 241
Carter, Jim, 240, 241, *242*
Carter, Rachael, 240
Cattelino, Jessica, 6
Cattle ranching, 12, 13, 222–23, 268, 276
Cavallo, Charles, 35, 58
Cavallo's town, 35
CDIB cards, 318, 320
Census cards, Seminole and freedman, 375–76n40
Chandler, Viola, 291
Chapone, Moses, 284–85, 303
Charles, Hattie, 165
Charles, Lou, 209
Charles, Mike, 209
Charlotte Harbor, 20, 36
Chase, Charles Monroe, 185
Checote, 209
Cherokee Bill. *See* Goldsby, Crawford
Cherokee Indians: acculturation, 86, 93–94, 225–26, 262; allotment approach, 294–95; black intermarriage, 237–38, 244–45, 377n54; Civil War period, 161, 163–65, 174, 176, 179, 191, 226; kidnapping practices, 119–20; nation/tribal membership debate, 320; Reconstruction era, 225–27; Reconstruction treaty negotiations, 194–95, 198–99, 201, 224; slaveholding practices, 88, 103, 192, 347n16
Chiaha, 11
Chickasaw Indians: acculturation, 86, 93–94, 225–26, 262, 376n46; allotment/enrollment processes, 294–95, 297; black intermarriage, 237-38; Civil War period, 161, 162, 164, 170, 179, 226; Reconstruction era, 225–29; Reconstruction treaty negotiations, 194–95, 198–99, 201, 224; slaveholding practices, 88, 103, 192
Chitto Harjo, 69, 131, 300–301
Chocochatti, 19
Choctaw Indian Brigade, 181
Choctaw Indians: acculturation, 86, 93–94, 225–26, 262, 376n46; allotment approach, 294–95; black intermarriage, 237–38; Civil War period, 161, 162, 164, 179, 181, 191, 226; Reconstruction era, 225–28; Reconstruction

Choctaw Indians (*continued*)
    treaty negotiations, 194–95, 198–99, 201, 224;
    slaveholding practices, 88, 103, 347n16; War of
    1812, 16
Chosto, 207
Christianity, 89–91, 141–44, 146–54, 159, 258–
    59, 282–83, 289–92, 347n20, 358n117
Chupco, Eliza, 288, 384–85n61
Chupco, John, *222, 249*; Civil War period, 163,
    165, 172, 182; on compensation claims,
    353n10; leadership role, 157, 186;
    Reconstruction-era leadership, 195, 199, 206–
    207, 248, 250–51; slaves of, 102
Chupco, Nancy, 126, 166
Churches. *See* Christianity
Chustenahlah, Battle of, 169
Chusto-Talasah, Battle of, 182
Chutcote Harjo, 195, 199
Citizenship, U.S., 306–307
Civil rights movement, and intermarriage theory,
    235
Civil War period: alliance negotiations, 161–64;
    battles/enlistments, 167, 169, 172–75, 176–
    85, 190; as incorporation success factor, 247–
    48; journeys/camps, 165–71, 175–77, 185–
    88, 191–92; surrenders, 192; tribal divisions,
    163, 164–65
Clans, Indian, 30–32, 92, 99, 137–38, 256–57
Clark, Ransom, 45, 339n71
Clary's family, 119–20
Cloud, George, 182, 196, 384n59
Cloud, Thomas, 182, 251
Coacoochee. *See* Kowakochi
Coe, Charles, 231
Coffin, William, 186
Cohen, Myer, 13
Coi Harjo, 48, 56
Coker, Charles, 301
Coleman, Henry, 252
Colerain treaty (1796), 9–10
Collamore, George, 171
Collins, Juan Bautista, 13
Comanche Indians, 81–82, 83
Communal lands, 6–7, 26, 35, 65, 123–24, 222–
    23, 336n19
Compensation claims: Civil War damages, 88,
    120–23, 125–26, 203, 221–22, 353nn9–10; in
    Confederacy alliance treaty, 164; Florida land
    losses, 315–16, 391–92n66; in Reconstruction
    treaty negotiations, 195; Second Seminole War
    damages, 133, 164
Confederacy idea, Indian and maroon, 72, 76,
    79–81

Confederate Seminoles: camps, 191–93; Recon-
    struction era, 248–51; in Reconstruction
    treaty negotiations, 194–201, 367n1; recruit-
    ment/negotiations, 161–64, 226; slavery prac-
    tices, 188; surrender, 192; tribal divisions, 164–
    72
Conservatives, tribal recognition movement,
    311–12
Constant, Antoinette Snow, 284–87
Constant, David, 283, 285
Constitutions, 307, 314–15, 391n63
Coody, Adoca, 122
Coody, Amey, 243
Coody, Bill, 243
Coody, Bob, 243, 244
Coody, Daniel, 243
Coody, Dosar, 243, 244
Coody, Joseph, 243, 244
Coody, Nellie, 243
Coody, Sarah, 243, 244
Coody, Tom, 243
Cooley, Dennis, 195, 199, 204–205, 229, 367n1
Cooper, Douglas, 167–70, 192
Corn crops, 23–24, 122
Cotton farming, 276
Court cases, 309–10, 314, 316, 318–20, 389n49,
    391–92n66
Cowkeeper (mikko), 3, 5
Cox, John, 174, 186
Crain, Alexander, 260
Crain, Violet, 305–306, 388n34
Crawford, T. Hartley, 54
Crazy Snake. *See* Chitto Harjo
Crazy Snake Rebellion, 300–301
Creation story, 40–42
Creek Council, 92, 95, 115–16
Creek House of Warriors, 301
Creek Indians: acculturation, 86, 93–94; allot-
    ment approach, 294–95; black intermarriage,
    237–38, 245, 337n36; Christianity, 142, 143;
    Civil War period, 161, 162, 164–65, 167–70,
    172–75, 176, 191; clan system, 31; emancipa-
    tion revocation aftermath, 78–79, 81; in Flor-
    ida, 3–6, 10–11; kidnapping practices, 111,
    112, 119–20; Kowakochi's Mexican colony,
    82–83; languages, 3, 5, 271, 274; Reconstruc-
    tion treaty negotiations, 194–95, 198–201,
    203–204, 224–25; Red Sticks, 5, 16, 19, 56;
    Removal period, 43, 54; runaway slave epi-
    sode, 127, 128–29; Seminole unification con-
    flicts, 56, 61–62, 64–65, 68, 69, 71–72, 76,
    95–96; slaveholding practices, 88, 103, 129;
    tribute system, 6–7; War of 1812, 16

Creek-Seminole College, 289
Creole language. *See* Afro-Seminole Creole
    language
Criminal activity, 235, 277–81, 301, 308,
    374n68, 383n37. *See also* Kidnapping threats/
    campaigns; Law enforcement; Lighthorsemen
Crocket, Bud, 325
Cuba, 9, 20
Cudgomicco, 11
Cudjo, Florence, 299
Cudjo, Josephine, 299
Cudjo, King, 288
Cudjo, Ned, 123, 278
Cudjo, Sam, 165, 178, 214
Cudjo, Stephus, 277–78
Cudjo, Witty, 306
Cudjo (maroon leader), 33, 43, 134, 140
Cudjoe, Lance, 140, 316, *317*
Cudjoe, Lawrence, 140, 316, *317*
Cudjoe, Sarah, 244
Cuffee, Fred, 272–73
Cuffy, 85, 140
Cully, Marcy, 314
Cultural practices, 138–47, 152, 223, 257–59,
    323–24
Curtis Act (1898), 295, 296, 297
Cuskowilla, 5
Cutlip, C. Guy, 302–303, 304, 387n23, 387n32
Cyrus, Carrie, 213, 279–80, 285
Cyrus, Dennis, 213, 214, *215,* 280
Cyrus, Harry, 284
Cyrus, Paldo, 209
Cyrus, Peter, 209

Dade Massacre, 44–45
Dalton gang, 279, 280
Daniel (son of Sarah Factor), 132
Davies, Bob, 175
Davis, Affie, 244
Davis, Alice Brown, 261, 288
Davis, "Big Sarah," 190, 206
Davis, Bob, 290
Davis, Buss Luckey, 278
Davis, Charlotte, 296
Davis, Daily, 121
Davis, Donnell E., 318, *319,* 322
Davis, Jacob, 165
Davis, Joe. *See* Scipio, Joe
Davis, Mattea, 244
Davis, Pompey, 214
Davis, Robert, 240
Davis, Scipio, 267, 273
Davis, Sylvia, 318, *319,* 322

Davis v. United States, 318, 320
Dawes Commission, 101–103, 227, 294–300,
    316, 349–50n63, 375–76n40
Dean, Charles, 105–106, 108–109, 118–19
Dean, Ezra, 288
Dean, Primus, 119, 289
Debo, Angie, 306
Deep Fork settlements, 54, 56, 58, *63,* 65, 74–75,
    98, 117–18, 142
Denis (free black), 131
Dennis, John, 214
Densmore, Frances, 30
Dexter, Horatio, 19–20, 22, 24, 26, 28, 29, 35–36
Dillard, Joseph, 139, 323
Dilley, Davy, 121
Dinah (Seminole freedwoman), 240
Dindy, Caesar, 280
Dindy, Sam, 299
Disease: Civil War period, 170–71, 172, 176–77,
    185–86, 187, 192–93; population impact, 85;
    Reconstruction era, 211
Distribution Act (1990), 316
DNA testing, 320–21
Dole, William, 162, 172
Dolly (sister of David Bowlegs), 252
Dolly (wife of Pompey), 11
Dora (wife of Jack Bowlegs), 209
Dosar, Bob, 278
Dosar Barkus band, 138, 141, 209, 269–71, 279
Doser, March, 240
Drennen, John, 77
Drew, Thomas, 113
Drew, William, 133, 149
Duncan, Otis, 232
Durant, Monday, 142, 143
Duval, Marcellus: Florida Seminoles, 79–80; and
    Kowakochi's Mexican colony, 82, 94–95; ma-
    roon transfer period, 76, 77, 81; and Mikko
    Mucasa, 72, 131, 319n56; on Seminole accul-
    turation resistance, 91, 92; on Seminole econ-
    omy, 87
Duval, William J., 73, 78, 108
DuVal, William P., 44

Echo Hadjo (or Hadjochee), 101, 349n59
Echo Harjo, 54, 143, 349n59
Echoille band, 243
Economic activity: Florida, 6–7, 12–13, 14, 19,
    20, 26–28, 58; Indian Territory, 67–68, 87,
    134; Reconstruction era, 219, 222–23, 257,
    262, 268, 276. *See also* Tribute system
Edwards, Lucinda, 244
Eighty-third U.S. Colored Infantry, 183–84

Eleck, Jenetta, 298

Eleck, Philip, 240, 298

Eleck, Rinah (née Noble), 240, 298

Eliot, Davy. *See* Asi Hacho

Emahaka Academy, 260, 288

Emancipations: Jesup's proclamation, 48–49, 51, 62, 64, 65, 67, 70, 74, 349n59; revocation and aftermath, 70–71, 73–74, 76–78, 81; Seminole practices, 58, 111–12, 129–31, 132, 133

Emathla, Charley, 43, 101, 349n59

Emathla (and town), 13, 35, 36

Emigration. *See* migrations

Enrollment/allotment processes, 279, 294–300, 304–305, 310, 349–50n63

Ensel (guide), 26

Essex, James, 90–91

Etheridge, Florence, 232

Ethnicity, in early maroon community formation, 15, 333n39

Eustis, Abraham, 45

Factor, August, 64

Factor, Black, 132, 332n22

Factor, Dembo, 59, 62, 79, 80, 85

Factor, Hardy, 62, 64, 85

Factor, James: as Christian minister, 258–59; Civil War period, 182, 188; conversion to Christianity, 89–90, 143, 144; marriage, 261; Reconstruction-era leadership, 196, 207, 248, 254

Factor, John, 215, 243–44

Factor, Nancy, 132, 133

Factor, Nelly, 62, 69, 99, 101, 106, 132

Factor, Rose Sena, 11, 132–33, 234, 332n22

Factor, Sally, 59, 106

Factor, Sam, 11, 132, 234, 332n22

Factor, Sarah, 132

Factor, Thomas, 80

Factor, William Sena (Billy), 132–33, 332n22

Family units, freedman annuity roll listings, 272–74

Farming: and Civil War compensation claims, 120–23; Florida, 6–7, 19, 23–26, 354n15; as subsistence lifestyle, 87, 118, 123–25, 276–77

Festival of American Folklife, 322, 325–26

First Kansas Colored Infantry, 177, 178–82, 269

First Seminole Battalion, 167, 182

First Seminole War, 17, 39–40, 247

Five Civilized Tribes, commonalities and differences, 86–89, 161-65, 194, 198–99, 224–29, 294, 295. *See also* Cherokee Indians; Chickasaw Indians; Choctaw Indians; Creek Indians; Seminole *entries*

Flat Rock Fort, 183

Flint, F. F., 73, 77, 127

Florida: annexation effects, 39–42; economic activity, 6–7, 12–13; maroon communities generally, 19–23, 25–26, 30–35, 38–39; migrations into, 3–6, 7, 9; Seminole slavery practices, 7–8, 9–15, 19–20, 28–30, 331n6. *See also* Removal period

Floyd, John, 15–16

Fohutshe, 195

Foreman, Grant, 61

Fort Arbuckle, 133–34, 163, 167

Fort Cobb, 163

Fort Gibson, antebellum period: commissary construction, 65, 342n37; as maroon refuge, 56, 57, 64, 65, 67, 68–69; removal of maroons, 70–71, 73–74, 75–76

Fort Gibson: Civil War period, 176–77, 178–79, 183, 186, 187; Reconstruction period, 206

Fort Gibson treaty (1833), 43–44, 53, 315–16

Fort Mose, 8–9

Fort Roe, 170

Fort Scott, 178, 183

Fort Smith, 64, 181

Fort Smith Council, 194–97, 367n1

Fort Washita, 163, 191

Fos Harjo, 125, 165, 172, 195, 199

Fos Hatchee Cochuehue, 182, 196

Foster, A. (slave owner), 147, 151, 152

Foster, Adeline, 278

Foster, Mariah, 384n59

Foster, Robert. *See* Johnson, Robert

Foster, Robin. *See* Johnson, Robert

Franklin, John Hope, 327n2

Free blacks: Florida, 8–9, 13, 36, 38, 130, 132; Indian Territory, 64, 70–71, 74, 111–12, 130, 131, 134-35. *See also* Horse, John

Freedman-Seminole relations. *See specific topics, e.g.,* Incorporation success factors; Intermarriage practices; Maroon communities; Seminole Nation/tribal membership; Separation custom; Slavery *entries;* Towns

Fushachi Hacho, 155

Gaines, Edmund, 25

Gallaher, Art, 269, 324, 381–82n3

Gardiner, Esau, 279

Gender roles, 26, 33, 276–77

Genetic testing, 320–21

Georgia, 8, 9–10, 11, 15–16, 19

Gibbons, John, 112

Gibbs, Waddy, 312, 314

Giddings, Joshua, 33, 46

Gideon, D. C., 231
Gillis, John, 303
Glass, Dick, 280
Glass, Osceola, 299
Glisan, Rodney, 83
Goat, John, 288
Goldsby, Crawford, 278
Goodin, James, 177–78
Gopher John. *See* Horse, John
Gouge, Scipio, 177–78
Grand Council (1845), 72
Grand River settlement, 57
Gray family, 107
Grayson, E. B., 204
Grayson, Joe, 213
Grayson family, 245
Green Corn Rebellion, 308
Greenwood, W. Barton, 314
Grierson, Robert, 245
Grinde, Donald, 378n73
Grounds, Charles, 310
Guardianship system, Seminole, 100, 105–106, 114, 116
Gun and horse ownership, maroon, 119, 122, 123, 124, 125, 126

Hadjo, Toney, 43
Halleck Tastanaki, 79–80, 113–14, 165, 169, 172
Hamilton, Robert, 143, 347n20
Hampton Institute, 287
Hancock, Ian, 139
Handbook of American Indians (Hodge), 231–32
Haney, Jerry, 324
Hannah (runaway), 127, 128
Hannah (Seminole freedwoman), 244
Hardridge, Elias, 177–78
Hardridge, Nero, 177–78
Hardridge, Siah, 59, 62, 64, 79, 81, 106
Harjo, Anna Nulcup, 285
Harjo, Lillie, 386n16
Harlan, James, 194
Harney, William, 367n1
Harper's Weekly, 157
Harred, Dicey, 244
Harris, N. Sayer, 84, 118
Harrison, Jacob, 303
Harrison, Jefferson, 303
Harrison, Sampson, 303
Hausa people, 39
Hawkins, Elizabeth. *See* Johnson, Elizabeth
Heliswa, 271
Henderson, Rina, 290
Heniha Emathla, 40–41

Heniha Mikko: Christian beliefs, 90, 144, 258–59; Civil War period, 146, 162, 163, 167, 169, 182–83, 188–90, 192; leadership, 95, 159–61, 196, 207, 248, 250–54, 256; and Mahkahtist-chee's slaves, 113; and Mikko Mucasa, 343n56; and Robert Johnson, 153; slaves of, 102, 103, 105, 188, 298
Herrod, Thomas, 177–78
Hester, 244
Hicks, John. *See* Tacosa Emathla
Hitchcock, Ethan, 57, 88
Hitchiti language, 3, 5, 274
Hodge, Frederick, 231–32
Holata Mikko: death, 160, 360n18; leadership rivalry, 159–60; lineage, 34, 337n42, 349n57; Removal resistance/agreement, 79–80, 155–57; slaves of, 12, 81, 99, 101, 102, 103, 296, 298, 359n5
Holatoochee, 56, 101, 130
Holiday celebrations, 292
Holt, Adoniram, 143
Honey Springs, Battle of, 178, 179–81
Hopothli Yahola, 54, 165, *166,* 225, 361n41
Horse, John: Christianity, 142–43; compensation claims, 65; conflicts with Seminoles, 60–61, 64, 67, 69; early Indian Territory years, 57–58; economic success, 58, 60; emancipation, 130; in Florida, 35, 36, 46, 48, 50, 338n49; freedom concerns, 69–71, 76; as interpreter, 58–60, 134; leaves for Mexico, 80; purchase of step-nephew, 131; Washington, D.C., trips, 59, 65, 67; Wewoka Creek settlement, 75, 76
Horse, Susan, 68, 69
Hothli Emathla, 130, 343n56
Hothli Hopoya, 12, 13, 34, 103, 111–12, 130, 233
Household goods, 122–23, 124, 125, 148, 275–76
Houses, 30, 89, 274–76
Howard, James, 320
Howe, Henry, 94
Hubbard, David, 163
Hulbutta Harjo, 46, 50, 57, 58, 59
Hulbutta Harjochee, 243
Hulbutta Mikko, 205, 251, 301–303
Humphreys, Gad, 22–23, 119
Hunting, 6, 87–88, 277

Ikonchatta Mikko, 40, 43
Incorporation success factors, Reconstruction period, 245–64, 300–304
Independence treaty, Seminole-Creek (1856), 96–97

Indian Claims Commission, 315
Indian Home Guard. See Union Indian Brigade
Indian Removal Act (1830), 42
Indian Reorganization Act (1934), 310
Ingersoll, Thomas, 374n38
Inheritance practices, 12, 19–20, 34, 39, 99–100, 309
Intermarriage practices: and acculturation, 86–87, 260–61, 340n5, 376n46; and allotment/enrollment processes, 296, 300; census evidence, 236–38, 240–45, 375–76n40, 376n41; Florida, 7, 32, 337n36; misinterpretation, 136–37, 229–36, 374n31, 374n39
Interpreters, 28, 60, 134, 139, 303
Iron Bridge, Battle of, 183
Island, Harry, 199, 203
Islands, Joseph, 142
Isparhecher, 225

Jackson, Andrew, 17, 19, 39
Jacobs, Newman, 288
Jamaican Maroons, 14, 274
Jennie (Seminole), 243
Jesup, Thomas, 45–50, 51, 59, 60, 65, 67, 69, 70, 131, 234
Jim Crow laws, 307
Jim Lane band, 120, 207, 268–69
Joe Scipio band, 209
John Brown band, 268–69
John Chupco band, 209
Johnson, Elizabeth, 150–51, 189–90, 206, 273
Johnson, Grant, 217
Johnson, James Coody, 302; birth, 190; characterized, 387–88n32; and C. Guy Cutlip, 302–303, 387n23; enrollment status, 206; leadership, 147, 206, 283, 301–304; schooling, 283, 285, 286, 288
Johnson, Kitty, 150
Johnson, Nancy, 150
Johnson, Robert: background, 147–48; band membership, 268, 273; burial location, 358n105; children/marriage, 150–51; Civil War compensation claim, 123; Civil War period, 123, 189–90; as interpreter, 146–47, 148–53, 174, 190–91, 206–207; Luke's travel pass episode, 127, 128, 354n34; Reconstruction era leadership, 205–207, 248; in Reconstruction treaty negotiations, 195, 199, 203
Johnson, Willard B., 361n41
Johnston, Josephine, 321
Jones, George, 312, 313
Juan (interpreter), 28
Judge, Thomas, 64, 146

July, Sampson, 80
July (as a name), 140
July (maroon leader), 36
Jumper (Seminole leader). See Hothli Emathla
Jumper, Betty Mae Tiger, 31
Jumper, Jim. See Mikko Mucasa
Jumper, John. See Heniha Mikko
Junkin, Dr. & Mrs., 283

Kanard, Jack, 10
Kapichee Mikko, 11, 12, 35, 106, 114
Katz, William Loren, 232, 328n3, 329–30n20
Kawita Mikko, 199
Kawita people, 19, 39
Kellum, Charles, 142
Kelly, Matthew, 320, 327–28n2, 389n49
Kennard, Moty, 128, 163, 167
Kibbetts, John, 32, 85, 141, 150
Kibbetts, Nancy. See Johnson, Nancy
Kidnapping threats/campaigns, 57, 58, 59, 62, 67, 68, 79, 110–12, 119–20, 131–34
King, Jim, 209
King, Rina, 209
King Phillip. See Emathla
Kingsley, Zephaniah, 14, 24, 333n38
Kinhijah. See Kapichee Mikko
Kinkehee, 211
Kinship slavery, defined, 109, 119
Kinship systems, generally, 30–32, 273–74. See also matrilineal descent system
Kittles, Rick, 321
Klee Harjo, 365n127
Kotchoche, 199
Kowakochi, 48, 57, 59, 61–62, 70–72, 78–80, 82–83, 123
Krogman, Wilton, 374n39

Landers, Jane, 12, 333n39
Land ownership, Florida, 6–7, 35, 315–16, 391–92n66
Land ownership, Indian Territory: allotment process, 239, 294–95, 299–300, 304–305; cessions, 96, 201, 204; communal approach, 65, 123–24, 222–23; fraud problems, 305–306; Reconstruction treaty negotiations, 201–203, 221–22, 227–28
Lane, James, 177, 186–87, 268–69
Langston, Oklahoma Territory, 201
Languages, 3, 28, 32, 89, 139, 274, 281, 309, 323
Larney, Este, 284
Larney, Millie, 284
Larney, Robert, 284
Larose, Thomas, 30

Laurel Grove Plantation, 14, 24, 333n38
Lawal, Babatunde, 30
Law enforcement, 209–10, 212–19, 221, 257, 278–79, 280–81, 292
Lawuyi, Olatunde Bayo, 308
Lee, Robert E., 192
Lighthorsemen, 82–83, 111, 209–10, 212–17, 222
Lilley, J. L., 282
Lilley, John, 90, 92, 142–43, 146–48, 189–90
Lilley, Mary Ann, 111, 135, 147, 152, 189–90
Lilley, Mary M., 281
Lincoln, Eliza, 279
Lincoln, Nancy, 271
Lincoln, Philip, 279
Lindquist, G. E. E., 232
Literacy rates, 260, 391n63
Littlefield, Daniel F., Jr., 86, 174, 258, 330n23, 364n107
Little River area, 54, 62, 90–92, 98, 143, 267, 268, 280, 290, 336n19, 383n37
Little River (town). See Thomas Town
Livestock: Civil War compensation claims, 120–23; Florida, 6, 11–12, 13, 19, 28; Reconstruction period, 222–23, 268, 276; in subsistence lifestyle, 124–25
Locust Grove, Battle of, 174
Loomis, Augustus, 148, 150
Loomis, Gustavus, 68–69
Lottie, Eliza, 298
Loughridge, Robert, 89, 90, 149, 354n29
Lousianna (Seminole), 240
Love, Hugh, 107
Love, John, 107–108
Love, W. E., 108
Lowrie, Walter, 149
Loyal Seminoles: compensation claims, 120–23, 125–26, 221–22, 353nn9–10; as incorporation success factor, 248–56; journeys/camps, 165–72, 175–77, 185–87, 361n41; oppose Confederacy alliance treaty, 163; in Reconstruction treaty negotiations, 194–201, 203–204, 367n1; Union enlistments/battles, 172–75, 176–85
Lucy (Seminole), 243
Luke (runaway), 127–28
Lynn, C. P., 210

MacKay, Fergus, 390–91n61
Macmillan, E. A., 280
Mahardy, Betsy, 297
Mahardy, Lyman, 297
Mahardy, Sam, 297–98

Mahkahtistchee, 99, 101, 106–10, 113–14, 115, 351n79
Mahpahyistchee, 99, 106, 107, 108, 110–11
Manumission practices. See emancipations
Maroon communities, generally. See specific topics, e.g., African heritage; Civil War period; Incorporation success factors; Separation custom; Slavery entries; Towns
Maroon communities, illustrated, 4, 18, 27, 46, 63, 66, 202
Maroons (as a term), 336–37n34
Marriage. See Intermarriage practices; Polygyny practices
Marshall, Dan, 219, 279–80
Marshall, Polly, 252
Mason, John T., 65, 342n32
Mason, John Y., 70, 342n32
Mason, Richard, 60, 342n32
Matrilineal descent system: and enrollment process, 238, 240; Florida, 6; freedman band membership, 274; and inclusion in Seminole or maroon society, 137, 238, 240-45, 375n40; indigenous society as incorporation success factor, 257–58; as intermarriage barrier, 32, 238; and slave ownership, 99–101
May, Katja, 225, 237–38
McAdam, Rezin, 229
McCabe, Edwin P., 201
McCall, George, 23, 28
McCauley, Clay, 359n4
McCulloch, Benjamin, 163
McGeisey, Thomas, 288
McGillrey, Joseph, 219
McHardy, Wyatt, 297
McIntosh, Chilly, 132
McIntosh, Dave, 119, 219, 277, 284
McIntosh, James, 169–70
McIntosh, Mary, 288
McIntosh, Roley, 56, 78, 81, 82, 119
McIntosh, William, 19
McKee, John, 58
McLoughlin, William, 331n6
McNeil, John, 181
McQueen, Peter, 19
Medical care, 210–12
Medicine men, 213–14
Mekasukey Academy, 260, 288–89
Melaku, Martha, 391–92n66
Melinda (wife of Pompey), 11
Membership. See Seminole Nation/tribal membership
Methodist missionaries/churches, 90–91, 92, 291

Mexico, maroon and Seminole communities, 72, 79–83, 84, 85, 94–95, 97–98, 150, 303

Micanopy. *See* Mikkoanapa

Micco, Melinda, 391n63

Middle Boggy, Battle of, 182

Middle Creek Church, 290

Migrations: after Oklahoma statehood, 308; into Florida, 3–6, 7, 9; Reconstruction period, 251–54, 256, 378n73. *See also* Bahamas; Canada; Cuba; Mexico; Removal period

Mikasuki people, 11, 12, 38, 40, 155, 316

Mikkoanapa, 12, 46, 54–56, 59, 60, 62, 72, 100, 101, 103, 107–108

Mikko Mucasa, 72, 75, 78, 95, 106, 108, 131, 343n56

Mikkopotokee, 101, 106

Mikkos in Florida: emancipation declarations, 58; slaveholding practices, 7, 10, 11–12, 13–14, 29–30, 56–57; tribute system, 6–7, 14, 22–26

Mikkos in Indian Territory: and band power, 92–93; emancipation practices, 131; and Fort Gibson maroons, 70–71, 73–74, 76; as slaveholders, 97, 98–103, 113–16; tribute system, 86, 88, 98

Milam, James, 315–16

Miles, Tiya, 244–45, 377n54

Military service, Florida, 8, 16–17, 28, 43–47, 60. *See also* Civil War period

Miller, Betsy, 165, 169

Miller, Susan, 31, 42, 137, 165, 324, 374n31, 390–91n61

Miller, William, 132

Mills, Andrew, 69

Mills, James, 278

Mills, Juana, 64, 80

Mills, Linus, 64

Mills, Sam, 64

Mills, Sarah, 64

Mills, Susie, 240–41

Minatti village, 19

Miscegenation. *See* Intermarriage practices

Missionaries, 89–92, 142, 258–59, 284–85. *See also* Christianity

"Mixed bloods." See Intermarriage practices

Mixed-race families. See Intermarriage practices

Montiano, Manuel de, 8

Moore, John Willis, 299

Motte, Jacob, 28

Moultrie, John, 9

Moultrie Creek treaty (1823), 39, 42, 315–16

Mount Zion Baptist Church, 284, 290

Mulatto Girl's town, 33–34

Mulatto King. *See* Waka Puchasi

Murrow, Clara, 92

Murrow, Joseph Samuel: on church numbers, 291; Civil War period, 146, 162, 170, 189; congregation division, 144, 159; interpreters, 153; mission establishment, 91

Naming practices, 34, 139–41, 238, 274, 323

Nash, Gary, 373–74n29

Neamathla. See Heniha Emathla

Necksucky, 113

Negro Fort, 16–17

Nelson, John, 331n6

Neosho River Valley, 170–72, 175, 185–87, 206

Newborn rolls, Dawes Commission, 298–99

Newman, Daniel, 16

Newsom, J. A., 229, 275–76, 280

New York treaty (1790), 9–10

Nicholls, Edward, 16

Noble, Albert, 240

Noble, Dora, 209

Noble, George, 111–12, 134, 253

Noble, John, 284

Noble, Leah, 240, 241

Noble, Logan, 240

Noble, Nero, 240

Noble, Rinah, 240, 298

Noble, Sam, 178

Noble, Scipio, *241*

Noble, Simon (Civil War casualty), 178

Noble, Simon (Creek freedman), 209

Noble, Tom, 175, 219, 238, 241–42

Noble, Whistler, 284

Noble, William, 240, 267, 269, 273, 290

Noble families, generally, 268

Noble Town, 267, 269, 281–82, 283–84, 285, 290, 381–82n3

Noble–Wasutke marriage, progeny, 240–43

Nocosilla Thlocco, 244

Nogusa Emathla, 165

Nokos Alochee, 180

Nokos Harjo, 157

North Fork Town, 142

Norton, Seminole Nation of Oklahoma v., 319

Oak Ridge Mission (and school), 90, 92, 142–43

Ogunleye, Tolagbe, 31, 336–37n34

Oil boom, 308

Oil Springs camp, 191

Okchar Harjo, *302*

Okfusky's band, 220

Okihamki, 33

Oklahoma Indian Welfare Act (1936), 310

Oklahoma statehood, 307–309

Oklawaha settlement, 35, 36
Okoni band, 3, 5, 155–57
Oktarharsars Harjo, 199
Oktiarche band, 240, 241
Oponay's plantation, 19
Opothleyohola. *See* Hopothli Yahola
Origin of races. *See* Creation story
Osceola. *See* Asin Yahola
Outlaws. *See* Criminal activity; Law enforcement;
   Lighthorsemen

Pacheco, Louis, 44–45
Page, Francis, 75
Paladore (son of Sarah Factor), 132
Papy, Miguel, 132
Parker, Ely, 367n1
Parker, Isaac, 278, 301
Pascofar, 88, 165, 185, 186, 195, 197–98
Passes, travel, 127–28, 129
Passock Yohola, 114, 196
Patrilineal descent, and naming practices, 274
Payne, Abram, 122
Payne, Angeline, 299
Payne, Caesar, 214–15, 278
Payne, Calina, 122, 175
Payne, Cathrine, 122
Payne, Gibson, 273
Payne, Pompey, 267
Payne, Rebecca, 121, 122
Payne, Thomas, 214, 267, 273
Payne (mikko), 10, 11–12, 13, 34, 102, 103
Payne families, 268
Payne's Landing treaty (1832), 42–43
Peace motives, incorporation success factor, 247–
   48
Pea Ridge, Battle of, 182
Pease Creek settlements, 19, 36
Perdue, Theda, 41–42, 340n5
Philatouche, 11
Physicians, 210–12
Pike, Albert, 163
Pilaklikaha, 12–13, 22–24, 26, 28, 33, 35–36,
   45, *46*, 335n3
Plains Indians, and Kowakochi's confederacy, 72,
   76, 79–81
Poison Spring, Battle of, 181–82
Political institutions, Seminole: Indian Territory,
   92–93; indigenous tradition, 256–57; maroon
   participation, 136, 205–206, 219–21, 225,
   312; twentieth-century changes, 310–12, 314–
   16, 318–20
Polk, James, 70
Polly (daughter of Leah Noble), 241

Polly (wife of Hothli Hopoya), 130, 131, 233
Polygyny practices, 32, 271, 273–74, 309
Pompey, 11, 35, 244
Pompey Payne band, 268, 269
Pompey's town (Florida), 36
Pompey Town (Indian Territory), 267
Population statistics, 5, 11, 35–36, 74, 84–85,
   220, 260, 264–65
Porter, Kenneth W., 10, 25, 174, 232, 253,
   330n23, 360n18, 374n34
Porter, Pleasant, 374n38
Potter, Woodburne, 23, 29
Prairie Bill, 240
Prairie Grove, Battle of, 176
Prairie Mission, 90, 147
Pratt, Carla, 233
Presbyterian missionaries/churches, 89, 90, 92,
   142–43, 144, 146–47, 258–59, 291. *See also*
   Lilley, John; Lilley, Mary Ann; Ramsay, James
   Ross; Talomas Mikko
Price, Richard, 383n37
Prince, Henry, 26, 28, 35
Progressives, tribal recognition movement, 311–
   12
Property ownership. *See* Compensation claims;
   Land *entries;* Slavery practices, Seminole
Prospect Hill school, 91
Pryor, Cornelius, 111, 112–15, 131
Pulepucka, 19
Pulmusky, 215–16

Quapaws, Civil War period, 170, 174

Racism: at Oklahoma statehood, 307–309; and
   Seminole Nation/tribal membership conflicts,
   309–12, 314
Ramsay, James Ross: arrival in Seminole country,
   90; on Baptist converts, 144, 146; departure for
   Prairie Mission, 146–47; Luke's travel pass epi-
   sode, 127–28, 354n34; marriage, 384–85n61;
   Reconstruction era, 259, 260; and Robert
   Johnson, 149–50, 151–53; schools, 281–82;
   on Wewoka settlement, 135
Ramsay, Maggie, 288
Ramsay mission school, 287–88, 384n50
Read, John, 153
Reconstruction treaty negotiations, 120, 194–
   204, 221–22, 224–27, 309–10, 367n1
Rector, Elias, 136, 160, 163
Rector, Henry, 161
Reed, Ora Eddleman, 231
Reeves, Bass, 217, *218*
Refugee camps, Civil War, 185–87

Religion. *See* Christianity
Removal period: departures/arrivals, 43, 53–54; resistance and conflicts, 43–53, 56–57, 59–60, 155–56; treaties/agreements, 42–43, 46–52, 156–57;
Rentie, Ellen, 287
Rentie, Lessie, 209
Reservations, Florida, 40, 42, 50
Revolutionary period, U.S., 9–10
Reynolds, George, 187, 197, 199, 204, 205, 206
Reynolds, John, 107
Rice farming, 24, 69, 121, 276, 354n15
Richardson, Albert, 347n16
Rivers, Larry, 34
Roberts, Louvina, 244
Robertson, Ezekiel, 132
Ross, John, 161, 165
Round Mountain, Battle of, 167, 169, 182
Rufus-Buck gang, 278
Runaway slaves: Florida, 7–8, 9–10, 16, 39–40, 48; Indian Territory, 127–29, 354n29. *See also* Bahamas; Mexico
Rutherford, Samuel, 162, 163, 188–89

Sac and Fox Agency, 170–71, 185–86
Saint Augustine, 7, 8
Salt Creek Church, 290
Sam, Alfred "Chief," 308
Sanborn, John, 197–98
Sancho (interpreter), 153
Sanco, Aaron, 181
Sango, July, 290
Sasakwa Female Academy, 288
Sasakwa, 91, 257
Sattler, Richard, 23, 36, 38–39, 87, 176, 237, 258, 274
Saunt, Claudio, 10–11, 12, 31, 42, 109, 233, 244, 245, 340n5, 374n31
Saxton, Rufus, 155
Sayers, Philip, 122
Sayers, Polly, 175
Schafer, Daniel, 14, 333n38
Schools, 40–41, 91–92, 258, 259–60, 281–89, 304, 384n50
Schultz, Christine, 361n41
Schultz, Jack, 308–309
Scipio, Joe, 269
Scipio, Renty, 279
Scipio Church, 291
Scipio (town), 267–68, 381–82n3
Second Kansas Colored Infantry, 181, 183, 364n107
Second Seminole War, 36, 44–50, 54, 58, 247

Selden, Francis, 65
Sells, Elijah, 193, 197, 204, 367n1
Seminole, name origins, 5
Seminole Constitution (1969), 315
Seminole Council, 92–93, 161, 219–21, *222*, 314, 318
Seminole Female Academy, 260
Seminole-freedman relations. *See* freedman-Seminole relations
Seminole maroons. *See specific topics, e.g.*, African heritage; Civil War period; Incorporation success factors; Maroon communities, illustrated; Separation custom; Slavery *entries;* Towns
Seminole Nation, lands, *63*, 96, 201, 202. *See also* Allotment/enrollment processes; Dawes Commission
Seminole Nation, treaties. *See* Treaties; *specific treaties, e.g.* Fort Gibson treaty (1833); Payne's Landing treaty (1823)
Seminole Nation of Oklahoma v. Babbit (Norton), 319
Seminole Nation v. United States, 309–10
Seminole Nation/tribal membership: overview, 136–38; adoption practices, 30–31, 32, 206, 228, 260–61; constitution provisions, 314–15, 318–19; court cases, 309–10, 314, 389n49; genetic testing proposals, 320–21; nation-tribe distinction, 200, 309-10, 389n49; Reconstruction treaty aftermath, 225, 226–28, 292–93; and Reconstruction treaty negotiations, 195, 196, 197–200, 204–205; and white intermarriage, 86-87, 260–61
Seminole Wars, 17, 36, 39–40, 44–50, 54, 58, 155–56, 247
Separation custom, 264–66, 322–26. *See also specific topics, e.g.,* Incorporation success factors; Intermarriage practices; Maroon communities; Seminole Nation/tribal membership; Slavery practices *entries*; Towns
Seventy-ninth U.S. Colored Infantry, 183–84
Shanks, John, 207
Shields, Jeanetta, 287
Shoeboots family, 244–45
Shook, Cora, 282
Short Billy, 146–47
Short Bird's band, 220
Shortman, Jack, 121, 165
Simency, 13
Simmons, William Hayne, 22, 25, 26, 28–29, 31, 35
Simon, Caesar, 219
Sinnugee, 245
Sitarkey, 12, 19, 34–35

Slavery practices: among Cherokees, Chickasaws, Choctaws, Creeks, 56–57, 86–89, 226, 347n16; Mexican prohibition, 79

Slavery practices, Seminole: and acculturation process, 88–89, 93–94; Civil War period, 161, 164, 188–91, 192, 366n140; and freedmen's compensation claims, 120–26; emancipation options, 58, 111–12, 129–31; and emancipation revocation, 70, 73–74, 76; Florida, 7–8, 9–15, 19–20, 28–30, 38–40, 331n6; historical consistency, 103–104, 117–19; inheritance customs, 99–101, 113, 114; and kidnapping conflicts, 110–12, 131–34; and Kowakochi's Mexican confederacy, 134–35; and leadership rivalries, 159–60; ownership statistics, 101–103; as incorporation success factor, 246–49; and Removal agreements, 47–50, 51–52, 59–60, 70; sales circumstances, 104–10, 112–16; travel customs, 126–27, 129; and unification treaty, 61–62, 64–65. See also Tributary allies; Tribute system

Smallpox, 185–86, 187, 193, 211. See also Disease

Smedley, Joseph, 91, 142

Smith, E. P., 207

Smith, Kirby, 192

Smith, Thomas, 16

Smithson, Bryan, 95, 112

Smoked Meat Rebellion. See Crazy Snake Rebellion

Snake Doctor, 213–14

Snow, George, 170, 172, 175–76, 185–86

Solano, Matteo, 132

Sonaki Mikko, 160–61, 163, 165, 171–72, 180, 186, 360n18

Sonuck Harjo, 169, 360n18

Southern Literary Messenger, 94

Spain, in Florida, 3, 5, 7–9, 10, 12–13, 19

Spencer, Billy, 289

Spoehr, Alexander, 259

Spring Creek Baptist Church, 290

Stanley, David, 253

Staples, Brent, 327n2

Stepney, Fred, 290

Stepney, John, 290

Stewart, Ed, 296, 297

Stewart, Reynolds, 277–78

Stiggins, George, 31

And Still the Waters Run (Debo), 306

Stone, Wallace, 278

Sturm, Circe, 237

Subsistence lifestyle. See farming

Suwannee River settlements, 17–19, 24

Swanton, John, 337

Syms, Hagar, 290

Tacosa Emathla, 39–40

TallBear, Kimberly, 321

Talley, C. O., 314

Talomas Mikko, 90, 91, 111, 144, 145, 146, 147, 153, 190

Tarthloga, 243, 244

Taxes. See Tribute system

Taylor, Quintard, 378n73

Taylor, Zachary, 131

Tecumseh, Ransom, 273

Teller, Henry, 253

Templeton, William, 90

Terminology for group identification, 329–30n20, 336–37n34

Texas, 43, 251–54, 256

Third Seminole War, 155–56, 247

Thoburn, Joseph, 232

Thomas, Harry, 278

Thomas Town, 267, 268, 280, 290, 383n37

Thompson, New, 88

Thompson, Wayne, 390–91n61

Thompson, Wiley, 23, 25, 28, 29, 44, 132

Thompson (son-in-law of Joseph Bagby), 252

Thornton, John, 231

Tiger, Tatekke, 192–93

Timon, Ann, 290

Timucua people, 3

Tina (wife of Nocosilla Thlocco), 244

Tohopikalika, 13–14, 35, 36

Tolokchopco, 36

Towns, Florida, 4, 6–7

Towns, freedman, 202, 267–68, 271–72, 273; churches, 289–92; criminal activity, 278–81; daily life, 276–78; schools, 281–89

Travel rules for slaves, Creek and Seminole differences, 126–29

Treaties: Civil War alliances, 163–65; in Florida, 9–10, 19, 39–40, 42–43; Creek-Seminole unification (1845), 61–62, 64; of Paris (1763), 9; Reconstruction (1866), 120, 194–203, 221–22, 224–27, 309–10, 367n1; Removal, 43–44, 46–48, 53–54, 315–16; Seminole independence (1856), 96–97

Tribal membership. See Seminole Nation/tribal membership

Tribal recognition movements, 310–12, 314–15, 390–91n61

Tributary allies, 29–30, 38–39

Tribute system: Florida, 6–7, 9, 13–14, 22–26, 38–39, 335n3; Indian Territory, 75, 98, 104

Tuckabatchee band, Creek, 54
Tufts, John, 251–52, 253
Tulwa Harjo, 279
Turkey Creek (town), 267, 268, 269, 284, 290
Tuskeneehau, 106

Uncle Fay (interpreter), 147
Unification conflicts, Indian Territory, 56, 61–62, 64–65, 68, 69, 71–72, 76, 95–97
Unification treaty, Creek-Seminole (1845), 61-62, 64
Union Indian Brigade, 172–75, 178–81, 182, 190
Usage Plan (1991), 316, 318

Van Horn, Benjamin, 171, 177–78
Vann, Marilyn, 320
Velie, Jon, 327n2

Waka Puchasi, 40, 43, 233
Waka Puchasi band, 11
Walker, Ben, 312
Walker, John, 43
Walker, Tandy, 181
Walking Joe, 76
Wantland, William, 389n60
Ward, John, 141
Warledo, Jackie, 324
War of 1812, 16
Warrior, Amos, 244, 278
Warrior, Ben, 141, 290
Warrior, Jack, 141, 243–44
Warrior, Levi, 244
Warrior, Stella, 244
Warrior, William "Dub," 141
Warrior (as a name), 141
Washbourne, Henry, 384n44
Washbourne, Josiah, 95, 133–34, 162
Washbourne, Maggie (Washburn), 282, 384n44, 385–86n61
Washington, Booker T., 304
Wasutke, 240, 241
Watie, Stand, 165, 169–70, 176, 178, 179, 183

Wealth distribution, among Seminoles and maroons, 87–88, 125-26
Weer, William, 175
Weik, Terrance, 13
Weisman, Brent, 24–25, 335n13
Welch, George, 163
Wewoka Creek settlements, 65, 75, 81, 135, 209–10, 257, 281–82, 284–88
Whipple, Charles, 347n16
White, Benton R., 361n41
White intermarriage, among Seminoles, 86-87, 260–61
Whitfield, Luther, 299
Wickman, Patricia, 324
Wild Cat. See Kowakochi
Wildcat Creek settlements, 62, 65
Wiley, Dickey, 296
Wilkins, William, 60–61
William Noble band, 220, 273
Williams, John Lee, 25–26, 29
Willis (interpreter), 147
Wilson, Miss Charles Emily, 326
Windham, John, 278
Winslett, John, 20
Winters, Iza, 290
Wisdom, Charles, 311–12
Wisey, 243
Wisner, Jeanetta, 288
Wister, Thomas, 367n1
Woodbine, George, 17
Worth, William, 50
Wright, Muriel, 232

Yamasee people, 3, 5, 7
Yawohli, 40, 43
Yellow Camp, 191, 192–93
Yonge, Philip, 13
Yoruba influences, 30
Younger gang, 279–80

Zellar, Gary, 172, 176
Zuniga y Cerda, José de, 8